Handbook of Research on Digital Information Technologies:
Innovations, Methods, and Ethical Issues

Thomas Hansson
University of Southern Denmark / Blekinge Institute of Technology, Sweden

INFORMATION SCIENCE REFERENCE

Hershey · New York

Acquisitions Editor:	Kristin Klinger
Development Editor:	Kristin Roth
Senior Managing Editor:	Jennifer Neidig
Managing Editor:	Jamie Snavely
Assistant Managing Editor:	Carole Coulson
Copy Editor:	April Schmidt and Brenda Leach
Typesetter:	Amanda Appicello
Cover Design:	Lisa Tosheff
Printed at:	Yurchak Printing Inc.

Published in the United States of America by
Information Science Reference (an imprint of IGI Global)
701 E. Chocolate Avenue, Suite 200
Hershey PA 17033
Tel: 717-533-8845
Fax: 717-533-8661
E-mail: cust@igi-global.com
Web site: http://www.igi-global.com

and in the United Kingdom by
Information Science Reference (an imprint of IGI Global)
3 Henrietta Street
Covent Garden
London WC2E 8LU
Tel: 44 20 7240 0856
Fax: 44 20 7379 0609
Web site: http://www.eurospanbookstore.com

Library of Congress Cataloging-in-Publication Data

Handbook of research on digital information technologies : innovations, methods, and ethical issues / Thomas Hansson, editor.

    p. cm.

  Summary: "This book provides a collection of successful designs, defined as communicative relation-building solutions, for individuals and collectives of interlocutors. It includes a longitudinal perspective of past mistakes, current trends and future opportunities, and is a must-have for beginners in the field as well as qualified professionals exploring the full potential of human interactions"--Provided by publisher.

  ISBN-13: 978-1-59904-970-0 (hbk.)

  ISBN-13: 978-1-59904-971-7 (e-book)

  1. Communication and technology. 2. Educational technology. 3. Information technology. I. Hansson, Thomas.

  P96.T42H364 2008

  303.48'33--dc22

2007043952

British Cataloguing in Publication Data
A Cataloguing in Publication record for this book is available from the British Library.

Editorial Advisory Board

List of Contributors

Table of Contents

Section I
Innovations

Section II
Methods

Section III
Ethical Issues

Detailed Table of Contents

Section I
Innovations

Abdul K. M. Azad, Northern Illinois University, USA

This chapter describes a software facility being remotely controlled over the Internet and thus enabling the students to get access to full laboratory equipment any time from any location. The students utilize the facility extensively and learn efficiently. The laboratory allows an administrator to monitor the use of the facility.

Carl Bagley, University Durham, UK

This chapter presents an experimental design for involving audiences in multimedia happenings. The chapter describes an innovative design for producing qualitative data. The results emerge from a UK government project on social exclusion. The text explores the (re)telling of a tale through the lens of bounded and unbounded (re)presentational forms. Critically-informed debate around the legitimacy of inter-textual multimedia forms is a productive way of representing and re-evaluating what and how people learn.

Mads Bo-Kristensen, Resource Centre for Integration–Vejle, Denmark
Bente Meyer, School of Education, Univeristy of Aarhus, Denmark

This chapter provides a historical perspective on how digital technologies have helped develop a number of solutions for intensive foreign language learning. Principles of computer assisted language learning (CALL) plus remediation rather than technological control, ensures the emergence of dialogical relationships, a crucial contributor to language learning. The technology allows intelligent language labs to be established in private contexts as well as in public spaces.

Chapter IV

Leena Hiltunen, University of Jyväskylä, Finland
Tommi Kärkkäinen, University of Jyväskylä, Finland

This chapter describes a content-based development method for designing and implementing online web courses. Instructors, students of computer science, teacher education, and university educators from different educational fields have participated in an experimental design. The result is a Web course repository with re-usable learning objects plus pedagogical and technical solutions readily available for the next university course.

Chapter V

Hamish Holewa, International Program of Psycho-Social Health Research,
Central Queensland University, Australia

This chapter contains a description of challenges associated with the management of an international research program. A Web-based collaborative management tool is built around the idea of a centralized resource for distribution and access of information. The integration of responsive IT processes has increased automation in information search and the quality of research efficiency. Responsive IT processes have removed redundancies and increased automation and research efficiency.

Chapter VI

Göran Karlsson, IT University of Gothenburg, Sweden
Jonas Ivarsson, University of Gothenburg, Sweden

This chapter outlines animations in science education, displaying complex carbon cycle processes. They have created a learning environment in which 3-D computer animations depict processes in the biochemical cycle. The students' reasoning runs the risk of focusing the attention on misleading aspects, isolated reasoning, or varying understandings of what resources to use in performing a task. Interactivity is suggested as a valid way of safeguarding against willful conceptualizations.

Chapter VII

Andrew Kitchenham, University of Northern British Columbia, Canada

This chapter focuses on transformative learning elements in situations where learners use their own computers. Laptop technology and 1:1 computing are related to issues of infusion that transforms teachers and their worldviews. An increasing number of students use laptops and we acknowledge that the technology is here to stay. Different kinds of reflection and transformative learning form the theoretical body of this chapter.

This chapter introduces a computer-aided system for teaching undergraduate science courses and providing an adequate laboratory experience. The system contains learning management system: computerized course curriculum adjustment; virtual labs, and animated illustrations; a threaded discussion board; computerized test; student feedback, summarization and analysis. A checklist for the science teacher is included.

Chapter IX

This chapter presents the foundations of an intercultural project by portraying a local learning community based on an interactive, constructive, and collaborative Fifth Dimension model. Through dialogical exchanges, local ICT learning communities generate neo-cultures in which citizens, students, researchers, and technologists grow. Participation in shared activities gave rise to a network of meanings that crystallize into a common micro-culture.

Chapter X

This chapter compares digital storytelling with traditions in the oral and written mode. Digital storytelling is a productive activity as it facilitates learning, personal growth, and societal development. Digital storytelling promotes critical thinking and carries a potential to support the students development of new thoughts, ideas, and knowledge about the world.

Chapter XI

This chapter gives an account of how such collective settings carries a potential to reach all levels of teachers and students in an appealing way. Collaborative educational games challenge beginning teacher reactions to using them for middle school students. The authors provide some faculty perspectives about these newer forms of educational technology.

Section II
Methods

This chapter proposes a method for applying social software in informal learning environments as a way of creating collective learning networks, that is, situated adult learning contexts where online communication and information exchanges empower the learners. The chapter provides pathways for facilitating informal learning strategies. Examples illustrate areas where educators need to be aware of inhibitors and facilitators of learning.

This chapter illustrates a method for providing authentic e-learning in a virtual scientific conference. The authors present an e-learning scenario designed to promote learning in a distance university course. In this online course, a simulation of a scientific conference is used as the main pedagogical strategy. The chapter describes the learning scenario, depicts the learning environment and the students' feedback. The main characteristics of this e-learning situation are based on literature pertaining to the design of authentic learning environments.

This chapter explores ways of moving toward theory and technique for online focus groups. The authors display results of research where face to face discussion groups are compared to online focus groups negotiating health-related topics like HIV/AIDS, smoking, and drinking. The fact that the research setting influences the findings is taken as a basis for forming a theory of online focus group techniques suited to the study of specific aims and topics.

This chapter demonstrates ways of dealing with online pedagogical effectiveness in adult contexts. In a longitudinal study the authors investigate pedagogical effectiveness. They consider a framework that integrates the current pedagogies of online, learner-centered environments. Their model re-defines the roles of teachers, learners, designers, peers, and colleagues. The authors suggest a focus on collaborative interchangeable roles and collaborative meta-cognitive support.

This chapter clarifies the significance of a reflective e-learning pedagogy. The authors discuss the roles of the instructor and student in e-learning. They describe the key pedagogical approaches that increase the students' commitment. The authors stress the importance of reflection. Constructivist and student-centered pedagogical approaches are suggested as a means to increase students' ownership and responsibility of the quality of their learning.

This chapter indicates that the quality of interaction between adults and students is important. Interaction between pedagogues and students has an impact on learning outcomes. Teachers should negotiate the intention and the topic of an assignment with their students. Information literacy is a core competence in education as it covers an ability to use different strategies and sources of information in various media.

This chapter claims that literacy is a socially and culturally situated practice framed in digitally-mediated, globalized societies. New technologies enable for people to create innovative text genres, thus opening up new literacies and demanding new pedagogies. The author discusses a Canadian program of collaborative school-university action research in an urban elementary school.

This chapter demonstrates ways of improving online readability and information literacy. The author surveys current online readability programs, stressing the need for foreign language teachers and students to access such sites. The stakeholders need to be able to assess the reading level of any text or Web site and appropriate graded materials, teleconferencing, assessment tools, Web-dictionaries, multimedia assistance, hypertext environments, and glossing engines. The chapter shows new ways to improve accessibility, comprehensibility, and readability of online texts.

This chapter covers a description of a course designed around a real life work-based problem. It is carried out in authentic steps with a final learning object that is usable in the workplace. A specific course for Shell EP shows that conceptual ideas related to formal and informal learning can be successfully realized in practice. Also included is an account of the distributed and situated nature of thinking, reasoning, knowledge and experience.

This chapter stresses the need for integration of methodological and technological approaches. Examples of globally competitive environments in Australia and the United Kingdom suggest that a strategically planned, systematically integrated, and institutionally comprehensive student support infrastructure provides a model for sustainable distance education.

This chapter presents education research with electronic focus groups, a field of research that needs exploring. The need is accentuated by the emergence of electronic and synchronous focus groups on the one hand and online asynchronous focus groups on the other. The authors say that modern software has the capacity to scaffold complex thinking and foster collective sense making, thus enabling incorporation of group interview strategies and generative social processes that are suitable for robust qualitative research data collection.

Chapter XXIII

Staffan Selander, Stockholm Institute of Education, Sweden
Anna Åkerfeldt, Stockholm Institute of Education, Sweden

This chapter increases access to information and new patterns of communication challenges the traditional forms of interaction which operate through curricular contents and pedagogy. Today the teachers play the role of individual coaches, and the students form their own learning paths and strategies. The authors' perspective on designs for learning captures these attitudinal changes in education.

Section III
Ethical Issues

Chapter XXIV

Thomas Hansson, Blekinge Institute of Technology, Sweden

This chapter suggests a categorization of collective, relational and communicating systems. Concepts like cybernetic control, systems thinking, contingency, dialogism, autopoietics, didactics, and feedback demonstrate how control, instruction, and technology contribute to cooperative learning. The argument is that if ICT users only practiced systems thinking they would become pro active learners who deliberately plan for, design, try out, modify, and apply new knowledge.

Chapter XXV

Agnes Kukulska-Hulme, The Open University, UK

This chapter describes the workings of human factors and innovation with mobile devices, arguing for a human-centered perspective on mobile technologies. Informal learning goes well with the use of mobile devices for inter-human communication. Technology-led development is a fact of life, but it is important that human factors are placed at the center of innovation if the full potential of mobile devices is to be realized. Usability issues must be taken as a starting point, extending to less predictable and evolving outcomes of self-controlled human interactions.

Chapter XXVI

Irit Kupferberg, Levinsky College of Education, Israel

This chapter explores a discursive-interactive theme on self-construction in computer mediated discourse. The chapter presents a theoretical and methodological framework of a discourse-analytic approach to the study of self-construction through interaction. The author argues that computer mediated discourse (CMD) is a suitable approach for studying how the major traces of Self are imprinted in discoursed language. The approach foregrounds the process of discursive positioning, showing how micro- and macro-levels of analysis are integrated in the exploration of self-construction.

This chapter examines how the design of an ICT system supports strategic knowledge-sharing between plant growers. The evolving industry-based virtual community functions well only if a sense of trust is established between the users. Therefore, the system must support decision making processes by trust-enabling functions like digital evidence and system managed credentials.

This chapter investigate what might happen when things go wrong. The authors explore the intersections between pedagogy, ethics, and technology. Their model gives an insight into issues raised by the introduction of ICT to the learning and teaching environment. Combined social and technical systems at times have unintended consequences of ethical relevance. Their case is far from unique and the authors suggest that research into e-teaching and e-learning should apply the suggested model to additional case studies in order to illuminate issues raised by the overlap between pedagogy, ethics, and technology.

This chapter discusses the ethical implications associated with veracity, identity, and ownership. They also cover the impact of the mentioned ethical dimensions on human behaviour in digital technologies. The authors conclude that identity is by far the most important dimension, arguing that without identity, people are unable to prove ownership of an intellectual idea. Without identity people would be unable to trust that a Web site or electronic work is what it seems to be.

This chapter provides an in-depth investigation of the philosophy of Web-based mediation. The concept of mediation is studied from a phenomenological perspective. This is a classical philosophy approach to modern media and mediational ethics. Quantification, modeling, and regulation of communications describe aspects of mediation. On the one hand mediation of meaning through technical devices makes it possible to develop new kinds of learning environments. On the other hand, virtual applications form a challenge for university teachers and for library users.

This chapter employs video data together with screen captures for presenting cases where the students try to match questions to search expressions, make decisions about whether they are allowed to visit a certain site, and examine how the students make decisions about relevance and credibility. Information always appears to be unstructured to the students and restructuring of information poses a socio-technical dilemma involving appreciation of an ideological and ethical nature.

This chapter uses learning theory for exploring democracy related to the development of e-learning. The importance of an ethical perspective on online education is exemplified with Lévinas theory and the concept of the Other. With an ethical perspective and the responsibility for the Other, the implications of democracy is extended towards a view in which the Other becomes a partner for negotiating value disputes. Democracy and ICT are less of a question of access and skills and more of a move beneath the surface, appearing as a de-contextualized trace of the Other.

This chapter focuses on interaction between people transformed by mobile devices. The technology poses a significant challenge as ethical issues appear in novel situations. We need to devise procedures and protocols that are ethically acceptable in a wider cultural, social, and competitive society permeated by mobile and wireless technologies. This chapter brings together the practical aspects of ethical challenges and identifies practical problems and solutions to the ethics of evaluating mobile learning linked to wider social changes.

Foreword

It is with great honor and pleasure that I compose a foreword for this publication. It has been my ambition that the scope and contents of the handbook should provide commercial, educational, and public enterprises with the necessary and sufficient tools for designing, implementing, managing, and evaluating information and communication technologies (ICT). Geographically this ambition has been met as the contributors reside in Asia, Australia, Europe, and North America. The included chapters describe a global perspective on technical-software and social-human cases associated with a variety of approaches to learning management systems, language labs, children's drawings and business applications. The integrative cross-curricular and cross-disciplinary quality of the handbook is welcome and useful. Taken together the chapters form a comprehensive whole suited to a number of settings.

Digital information technologies play a vital role in assisting communities of practice with the complex control required to design, manage, and maintain virtual and situated exchanges. The new technology harbors important elements for collective and individual learning, human resource management, systems thinking, and change processes. The technology also supports routines for dealing with communicative dynamics and structural stability. Therefore the authors' approaches underpin continuous development of educational, social services, and business strategies.

In my role as editor of this publication, I have had the fortune of first hand contact with academics and practitioners. Today people seek professional guidance on the implementation of digital information technologies. I believe that for a number of reasons many categories of people will value the extensive analysis of requirements, application of designs, pieces of advice, and evaluation of results.

The handbook integrates a special kind of academic and practitioner knowledge, assisting individuals and organizations in their attempts at gaining benefits from theoretical and empirical perspectives. The handbook offers the reader useful knowledge derived from the implementation of a variety of technologies and contexts. It contains a display of wide-ranging project management and extensive academic research performed by authors of many disciplines, businesses, and cultures.

This book will help theorists and practitioners equally to separate between *technics* and *techniques* in modern media. The former approach signifies the actual tool for producing artifacts or artificial items like computer machines, software, or screwdrivers. The latter approach signifies human knowledge and skills about the methods for sharing knowledge about how to produce artifacts. It is a natural thing that in a society where technological innovation has contributed to so much progress, people should adopt a socio-technical way of thinking. We tend to confuse physical-technics with socio-technical manipulation, and we believe that such a way of thinking would be void of ethics, compassion, empathy, or brotherhood.

This handbook, however, suggests that new forms of reasoning, sense-making, and spiritual life form a trademark of the technology. New sources of inspiration and cultural values will emerge. But it is hardly possible to hold a view about how a new moral of life could build on a discussion of the conditions for human co-existence and fulfillment of individual ambitions. Such aspects emerge regardless of how the socio-technical perspective of man-machine interactions develops. Historically, however, philosophers have defined an ethics independent of technology. Therefore, it is reasonable to believe that before a new ICT-ethics can develop, people will form their own view of values, upbringing, goals, and attitudes.

It is my ambition that the handbook will play the role of a vital primer for organizations that wish to embark on the implementation of digital information technologies related to for example conflict resolution, digital competence, epistemologies, storytelling, e-learning effectiveness, ethical issues, internet simulations, language labs, learning management systems, mobile learning devices, multimedia, multi-user virtual learning environments, social software, online focus groups, readability, technology enhanced corporate learning, reflective learning, systems thinking, self-construction, philosophy, Web-based mediation, socio-technical dilemmas, teacher education, trust enabling functions, virtual scientific conferences, networks, Web-course designs, and science teaching. These approaches will help individuals and organizations to plan, implement, and manage the next generation of virtual systems.

I am pleased to recommend this book, regardless if the readers are looking for strategies, management procedures, software materials, information management clues, Web content or learning management systems. I wish you all the best success with the planning, implementation, and management of your social and technical systems.

Thomas Hansson
University of Southern Denmark / Blekinge Institute of Technology, Sweden
December 2007

Preface

CONCEPTUALIZING INNOVATIONS, METHODS, AND ETHICAL ISSUES

It is reasonable to assume that modern media have an impact on societal structures. A variety of technologies penetrates individual spheres of life and affect collaborative processes between people. A typical phenomenon stemming from the spread of Web-based media is a shift in people's modes of communication. As a result, the use of digital information and communication technologies (ICT) has become prominent in business, in education, and in administration. However, it is far from obvious that the technology will change the way organizations teach and individuals learn. The reason is that politicians, employees, management, and students are confined to rather closed environments, limiting interfaces and narrow patterns of communication.

INTRODUCTION

The once over-enthusiastic vision of whole populations communicating via expert systems has failed to materialize. For quite some time now, this failure to meet early expectations on ICT has overshadowed the prospects of wide and flexible access to innovation, methodology and ethics that the current e-learning community is developing. Many organisations, schools, and enterprises are bringing digital information technologies into the mainstream of their information systems, thus forming an integral part of an on- and offline contents oriented coursework. The early enthusiasm originally embodied an idea of growth through the media. This ideal still prevails, but how do people value new socio-technical systems, and how do they apply different solutions?

Communication, interaction, and mediation of meaning form a multi-faceted process that is hard to analyse in simple terms. It is a fact of life that people, interaction, and mediation are related to societal development. Continuous development of physical, visual, and linguistic resources forms a most effective tool for cultural growth. If applied to social systems they contribute to the sustainability of emerging, developing, and shared knowledge and skills. It is worth noticing, however, that in spite of the emerging technology, face-to-face interaction still makes up the most crucial mechanism for mediation of information, intentions, and aspirations. Any conversation between any people at any time is enabled by mediation. Through higher mental functions like memory, reflection, and speech, people provide endless resources for shared communication. An oral description of an event, an e-mail question, a sympathetic nod of the head or wink of the eye mediates descriptions, ideas, opinions, and aspirations so exclusively that the oral mode facilitates for the interlocutor to learn about Self, Other and the world in one and the same process. One interlocutor's way of thinking, negotiating, and reasoning can easily be adopted, copied, acquired, or appropriated by another interlocutor. For example, when a computer reacts differently than expected, a helpful colleague may intervene and suggest some appropriate measures. Furthermore, mediation is brought about in many kinds of virtual and situated communities of practice, primarily through adapted application of language games, verbal procedures, and technical instrumentation.

Hence, digital information technologies presuppose the existence of a mediating artifact that facilitates our understanding of the world. As such, mediating artifacts like languages, teambuilding interactions, or computing machines verify to the contention that mediation is a precondition for the development of higher psychological functions in the human race. The very same mediating function reappears when modern man operates a screwdriver, a car, or a digital information system. The functions that first appear in a child's unique and lifelong perspective are a carbon copy of what happens when adults interact with the help of pre-designed technologies and social systems. Mediation of meaning(s) is an old phenomenon for human growth, but a lot remains before we can say that the full potential of mediating artifacts has been reached. This book indicates one way to approach the ongoing evolution of instrumentally and socially mediated human exchanges.

HOLISTIC UNITY VS. FRAGMENTED ATOMISM

The focus of this handbook is on communication in the widest sense of the word. Thus it includes ways and results of reasoning, thinking, and learning. In this perspective, it is necessary to take into account the contexts in which human communications appear. But it is also necessary to outline the actual operations and the final outcomes of such communications. Of course there are many ways of approaching communicative functions and results. This framework allows authors to explore, construct, evaluate, and criticize ICT-related phenomena.

There is a need to learn about methods for applying a growing number of hard- and software "systems" to the users. The authors of this handbook are familiar with this line of thinking about actionable knowledge. They refrain from merely introducing the products as fragmented inspirations. Instead, they try out and present their findings on the most effective methods for using the products. They avoid management by objectives in the classical conditioning (behaviorism) tradition. On the contrary, they account for management by cognitive problem solving. And most importantly, they emphasize relation building between interlocutors. Taken together, this ability in the authors of the handbook to synthesize innovative products, emerging methods, and ethical issues builds on a shared perspective, that is, a holistic view building on a (Dewey, 1910; Mead, 1934) inter-subjective symbolic interactionism perspective and a (Vygotsky, 1978; Leontev, 1981) socio-cultural/cultural-historical perspective.

This shared perspective is an achievement because today it is a trick of the trade for experts, development leaders, and consultants to define a number of more or less elaborate, intelligent, and innovative systems. As a consequence, almost anything is labeled a system, that is, the universe, the human brain, a refrigerator, or a community of practice. However, it is far from obvious what the experts imply by the notion of a system. It is hard to tell if they refer to a big-influential, a social-live, a new-emerging, or a dynamic-flexible unit of analysis. It is a minimal requirement that those who take on the role of systems identifiers should clarify the organizing principle for their definitions, delimitations, and applications. As this is rarely the case, the authors of this handbook provide such a structuring principle.

Clearly, a (sub-) system like a chapter in a handbook or an individual in a crowd is a wholeness separated by (semi-)permeable borders often related to the main system. The credo of holism (*holo*, gr.

meaning *whole*) also says that the scope-size-power-impact-influence of a unit defined as a system is bigger than the sum of its parts. However, it is difficult to clarify the specific implications of this motto. And more seriously, the motto only applies to some systems. In fact, the above definition of holism is valid only for so called non-additive systems. In clarifying different systems we have to account for the fact that the way that the functioning of a holistic (non-additive) system is organized cannot be grasped by understanding how the individual elements are internally organized and related. On the contrary, we must identify the organizing principle that decides how the elements are internally related. More specifically, if you know the particular purpose that the unit of analysis (system) serves, you understand why the individual elements operate the way they do. If, on the other hand, your understanding of a system is based on the individual elements that constitute the (sub) system, wholeness is understood as something emerging from the quality, functioning and impact of the individual elements within the system. In such an atomistic view of additive systems, it is natural to adopt a mechanistic-deterministic view of people and the world. Needless to say the authors of this handbook have adopted a non-additive view of human activity systems.

Innovation vs. Tradition

Some old concepts still hold true for analysis of the information society. "Mediation" and "artifacts" are part and parcel of a dialectic relation between man and machine, that is, 21st century interlocutors and computers. First of all, mediation is a relational man-to-man term. But it would be a mistake to define the concept as something that merely supports communication, understanding, and learning. People use many mediating instruments today. Unfortunately, ICT is an implied rather than explicit mediating instrument, especially for those who merely observe the phenomenon from the outside. It is hard for them to discern any kind of structural order in the chaotic mix of instruments, situations, procedures, people, and outcomes. Therefore, it takes a lot of experience and professional experimentation to understand the functioning of certain texts, music through notes, or Web-based research. Luckily, face to face mediation outscores text-based mediation of multi-faceted and factually complex themes. By engaging in direct contact the interlocutors adapt to each other, provide feedback and co-ordinates processes for reaching a shared understanding.

The chapters of this handbook deal with artifacts. Engeström (1987, p. 60-61) develops the concept as a way of understanding human use of tools, instruments, and 'dead' physical objects. Another understanding covers processes of verbal communication and a third understanding is the contextualised setting where a purposeful activity takes place. Wartofsky (1979, p. 202, 208) says: "*Primary artefacts* are those directly used in production; *secondary artefacts* are representations of such modes of action." The tertiary level of artefacts "can come to constitute a relatively 'autonomous world' in which the rules, conventions and outcomes no longer appear directly practical, or which, indeed, seem to constitute an arena of non-practical, or 'free' play or game activity." To the above, Cole (1999, p. 91) remarks that tertiary instruments or possible worlds—like for example virtual communities or Web-based universes—"can come to color the way we see the existing world, acting as tools for changing current praxis." Some authors describe and explore computer machines, software, and similar innovations as primary artefacts. Other authors present procedures and routines as social practices, providing the optimal methods for information exchange. But the majority of the authors of this publication explore computers and ICT-routines as a practical method for developing collective knowledge through developmental functions like human thinking, reflecting, negotiating, and learning.

As we can see from the above, there are many buzz words around. "Web 2.0" and "learning objects," for example, cover characteristics, processes, relations, and outcomes of many applications. The concept of Web 2.0 refers to an improved form of the World Wide Web, the latest generation of Internet hypes based on new applications or services. These innovations let ordinary Internet users create contents, cooperate, and share information in ways that used to be impossible. The concept of learning objects also represents a communicative environment that supports growth for the interlocutor, as a public knowledge-constructor and as a responsible person. As a matter of fact, the handbook represents a non-digital entity learning object, that may be used for learning, education, or training. It is also a resource that can be reused to support learning in different contexts. Some chapters describe Web-based interactive chunks of e-learning designed to explain stand-alone learning objectives. Other chapters describe digitized entities which can be used or referenced during technology supported learning. However, the variety of definitions of the buzz words offers little help in the concrete cases. Therefore, the main idea of the handbook is to break the contents down into chunks that can be reused in various communicative environments, to form new ways of thinking about textual and actionable contents, and to communicate independent and self-contained units of learning that can be applied to multiple contexts for multiple purposes.

Producing and Analyzing Data

The intensity of situated research in the field of digital information technology has by far exceeded many other fields of science, and the sheer impact of discoveries has become the driving force of emerging technologies and applications. The field of digital information technology contains a collection of many disciplines that researchers have explored. This methodological development has been accomplished through innovative research methods producing results that clarify people's understanding of the potentials, problems, and challenges of old methodological approaches and disciplines.

During the 1970s, computer technology was mainly deployed for numerical data processing. In the 1980s, the new technology had a focus on dissemination of information. The advent of PC's in the 1990's and the ability of users to communicate regardless of location directed information technology into the lives of the whole society. During the past decades, www-technologies have allowed people to exchange information on a global basis. Today the technology allows readily available communication for everybody, thus utilizing its full potential. Many chapters in this handbook center on the idea of field research. Situated approaches to researching, understanding and describing ICT-applications build on the researcher's emphasis on studying local customs rather than theories about general practices (Friedman, 2001). The authors' methodological approaches to research and development is based on a shared problem solving procedure. Their common goal is to find a solution, expand an activity, satisfy personal curiosity, and generate new knowledge. Such research presupposes committed participation from the practitioners of a researched context because they supply actionable knowledge based on a local theory about situated activities and they assess the likelihood of success for a specific initiative for change. Thus understood, committed research help change people's attitudes to for example work, stability and change, helping them become the cultural carriers of Web-based values. The handbook chapters illustrate approaches that favor an attractive democratic strategy for collecting and analyzing data. But even more important, the methodological approaches and strategies will survive as situated practices, change projects or organizational development. Actors, activities and (sub) cultures will have a realistic chance of spread, renewal and spin-off.

ETHICAL ISSUES

The marriage between values and computers by way of communication indicates a method for examining and understanding moral issues pertaining to computing and information technology. Initially, people referred to "ICT ethics" as "computer ethics." In doing so they understood analysis of the social impact of computer technology. Eventually, and due to the proliferation of the Internet the term "Internet ethics" came into existence. However, today the term "cyberethics" or "netiquette" is becoming popular. Cyberethics is a relatively young discipline, relating to moral issues of privacy, accuracy, ownership, and accessibility of data on the Internet. The rise of a combination of techniques and ethics as a self-sufficient discipline reflects the attempts of the industry to deal with social issues in general. People who display ethically correct behavior refrain from harassment, fraud, or crimes, and their moral behavior is concerned with how they as employees and/or citizens consider the effects of their Internet activities on other people and their communities.

Some 20 years ago, Victor and Cullen (1987) proposed a model for understanding ethical issues related to ICT. Their model contains personal, informal, and formal categories. The first component refers to an individual's private code of ethics regarding communication and computer technology. The second component includes peer influence such as expectations and accepted behaviour. The third component covers production logics, company interest, codes of practice plus business rules and regulations. So, ethically correct interactions, attitudes and behaviours contribute to a work climate of either caring, instrumental or rule-oriented interactions. In general terms, it is reasonable to argue that an ethically correct ICT-related workplace climate is useful for profitable business. And an ethical environment supported by an explicit constitution is one way of managing the risk of unethical behaviour.

There is bound to be some development of morals, values, and ethical behaviour when novice interlocutors are invited, introduced, and eventually accepted as members of virtual communities of practice. Lave and Wenger (1991) describe morally acceptable participation in social systems. More specifically, they outline how beginners become legitimate members of communities of practice. Newcomers become full members by practising basic but yet productive verbal exchanges. Through such interactions, they become acquainted with the tasks, the vocabulary, the goals, and the organizing principles of the community. Gradually they get more engaged, adopt culturally valid behaviours, and carry the culture of their community forward as expert communicators. This process of gaining acceptance, influence, and authority implies an ability in the beginner to negotiate a morally acceptable personality. The new-born expert's identity incorporates the past and the future of the beginner plus his/her experiences and participation in the shared culture. Lave and Wenger (1991) argue that legitimate peripheral participation is something other than an elaborate pedagogical strategy or teaching technique. It is a way of understanding learning as situated and as a function of the activity and culture in which it occurs. This appreciation stands in sharp contrast to most classroom learning situations, which are operated, changed, and analysed as being abstract and out of context. Therefore educators should strive to always apply the basic principles of situated cognition into their practices by way of morally just arrangements. They should present learning in an authentic context, and encourage social interaction and collaboration. Such pre-defined and rich contexts for interactive teaching and learning reflect the students' interpretation of the real world and help improve their transfer of knowledge and their ethically correct behaviour to/in a variety of situations.

SUMMARY

In launching a handbook project, it is necessary to cover a wide scope of inventions, applications, and values related to people's technology mediated communications. Researchers from all over the world have assisted in providing a number of approaches to the development of digital information technologies. One major objective has been to mirror the variety of research related to global and local environments, academic disciplines, and national cultures, thus providing a comprehensive list of references related to innovations, methods and ethics.

In order to provide a balanced coverage of issues related to ICT, some 70 researchers were asked to submit thematic proposals describing their potential contribution to a handbook. Their contributions were carefully reviewed, their records of similar work with the proposed topics were scrutinized, and the best 33 chapters were selected. The goal was to assemble the broadest possible coverage for publication in a handbook of digital information technologies. Upon the receipt of full chapter proposals, each submission was forwarded to two expert reviewers in a double-blind peer review process. The finally included chapters are written by knowledgeable, dedicated, and distinguished scholars. Consequently, this handbook covers a comprehensive set of relevant findings, methods, concepts, issues, and emerging technologies.

The contents of the handbook will expand knowledge in this field because the coverage of the chapters provides a source of reference for trans-disciplinary approaches to digital information technologies. Practitioners, scholars, and decision makers will find a rich source for understanding concepts, issues, problems, trends, challenges, and opportunities related to ICT. This publication and its comprehensive pieces of information will assist practitioners, research, students, and decision makers in their work. I hope that the handbook will inspire readers to take on new approaches to ICT, thus contributing to the growing body of discoveries in this field.

Thomas Hansson
Editor, University of Southern Denmark / Blekinge Institute of Technology, Sweden
December 2007

REFERENCES

Cole, M. (2003). *Cultural psychology: Some general principles and a concrete example.*

Dewey, J. (1910). *How we think.* New York: Prometheus Books.

Engeström, Y., Miettinen, R., & Punamäki, R. L. (Eds.) (n.d.). *Perspectives on activity theory.* Cambridge: Cambridge University Press.

Friedman, V. (2001). Action science: Creating communities. Inquiry in communities of practice. In P. Reason & H. Bradbury (Eds.), *Handbook of action research.* London: Sage.

Lave, J., & Wenger, E. (1991). *Situated learning: Legitimate peripheral participation.* Cambridge: Cambridge University Press.

Leontev, A.N. (1981). *Problems in the development of the mind.* Moscow: Progress.

Mead, G.H. (1934). *Mind, self and society.* Chicago: Chicago University Press.

Victor, B., & Cullen, J. B. (1988). The organizational basis of ethical work climates. *Administrative Science Quarterly*, (33), 101-125.

Vygotsky, L.S. (1978). *Mind in society.* In M. Cole, V. John-Steiner, S. Scribner, & E. Souberman (Eds.). Cambridge, MA: Harvard University Press.

Wartofsky, M. (1979). *Models: Representation and scientific understanding.* Dordrecht: Reidel.

Acknowledgment

I would like to acknowledge the help of all involved in the collation and double blind review process of the handbook, without whose support this project could not have been successfully completed. Deep appreciation is due to the Department of Management (MAM) at Blekinge Institute of Technology, particularly Anders Nilsson, and also Institute of Philosophy, Pedagogy and Religious studies (IPFR) at University of Southern Denmark for ongoing sponsorship in terms of allocation of on- and offline Internet resources plus other editorial support services necessary for coordinating a longitudinal project.

Some of the authors of the chapters in the handbook also served as referees for chapters composed by their peers. Thanks for your constructive and comprehensive reviews. Your work helped improve the quality of the handbook. Some additional efforts need to be mentioned as they set an international benchmark. They include Steve McRobb of De Montfort University, Agnes Kukulska-Hulme of The Open University and Bob McClelland of Liverpool John Moores University. Support of the department of information technology at the above universities is acknowledged for archival server space in the virtual online review process.

Finally, I wish to extend special thanks to the publishing team at IGI Global. Their contributions have been invaluable. In particular many thanks go to Deborah Yahnke, Kristin Roth, and Julia Bonner. They urged me on via e-mail for keeping the project on schedule. Also, I express my gratitude to Dr. Mehdi Khosrow-Pour, whose enthusiasm motivated me to initially accept an invitation to take on this project. Most of all, however, I wish to thank the authors for their contributions to this handbook.

Thomas Hansson
University of Southern Denmark / Blekinge Institute of Technology, Sweden
December 2007

Section I
Innovations

Chapter I
The Modular Design of an Internet–Based Laboratory

Abul K. M. Azad
Northern Illinois University, USA

ABSTRACT

This chapter presents the development of a modular Internet-based laboratory facility using cutting edge technologies along with its implementation for offering a laboratory course. The modules are developed using commercial products and are adaptable with a variety of laboratory experiments with little effort or maintenance cost. The developed facility has in-built capability to collect systems' operational data that are used to evaluate the effectiveness of the system and assess the students learning behavior. Provision was also made to assess the level of learning while using the facility. An Internet-based laboratory facility involves real laboratory equipment controlled remotely over the Internet that enables students to get access to laboratory equipment any time from any location, where most laboratory equipment is idle for a major part of its working life. Having these advantages, there is very little effort or interest within the academic community to implement the Internet-based laboratories for course offerings due to the complexity of operation, complicated design, extensive maintenance effort, higher implementation cost, lack of human interactions, and ethical issues. To address these problems, the author has developed this modular Internet-based laboratory facility and studied its performance through a laboratory course.

INTRODUCTION

Traditional Laboratory Facility: Traditional laboratory classes are scheduled only for a limited time period. Considering the mixed ability level of students, the allocated time is often not enough for all students to complete their tasks satisfactorily and also gain sufficient experience through the process (Boyle, Bryon, & Paul, 1997; Grose, 2003). Sometimes students also want or feel a need to perform additional experiments beyond their assigned tasks. It is difficult to accommodate such extra experimentation because universities often lack resources to keep their laboratories open (Bengu & Swart, 1996). Additionally, laboratory facilities are usually inaccessible to the students of other departments within the same institution because of their geographical location. Ironically, too much laboratory equipment lies idle during most of its usable lifetime (Palais & Javurek, 1996). An Internet-based laboratory facility would address these problems by providing unlimited access to an experiment and hence maximize the use of available resources.

Limitations of Internet-based education in terms of laboratory facility: One of the major limitations of existing Internet-based distance-learning courses is their failure to deliver the laboratory-related courses (Swearengen, Barnes, Coe, Reinhardt, & Subramanian, 2002; Vohra, 2002). While simulation and multimedia provide a good learning experience for effective and complete learning, especially in applied engineering and technology programs, a mixture of theoretical and practical sessions is needed. Currently, students have to visit a campus to perform the laboratory sessions for these kinds of courses, or there has to be an arrangement of mobile laboratories stationed at a few predetermined locations for a given period of time (Henson, Fridley, Pollock, & Brahler, 2002). With such arrangements, students get access to the hands-on facility for only a short period of time, which is usually insufficient to allow them to complete their learning process. Making the laboratory experiments accessible through the Internet would address this need.

Benefits of Internet-based laboratory facility: In addition to being a part of a distance-learning program, the Internet-based laboratory facility can also be used to complement the traditional laboratory classes. The Internet has already proven to be effective in preparing rural and inner-city high school students where there is no provision of advanced placement courses. It enables them to compete with other students in top colleges and move toward bridging the digital divide (Hagg & Palais, 2002). An Internet-based laboratory would allow them to perform laboratory experiments to enhance their theoretical knowledge and better prepare them for college. The Internet-based laboratory facility may allow students to familiarize themselves with experiments before proceeding to actual laboratory sessions. This kind of facility, either as replacement or supplement of traditional laboratories, has valuable benefits by allowing a more efficient management of the laboratories as well as facilitating distance-learning programs.

Moreover, this will allow for interlaboratory collaboration among universities and research centers by providing research and student groups access to a wide collection of experimental resources at geographically distant locations. An added benefit is the reduced costs incurred when different educational departments and institutions share facilities, since automated, remotely accessible systems are more cost effective than scheduled laboratory sessions conducted by salaried assistants and technicians, not to mention the cost and effort needed to maintain the laboratories.

Current status of Internet-based laboratory facility: A number of attempts have been made to provide students and researchers with practical exercises or experimentation experience over the Internet. In this light, some of the initiatives toward the development of laboratory experiment are discussed. In two cases, researchers have developed experimental demonstrations in which robots can perform a few simple manipulations from a distant location over the Internet (Fletcher, 2004; Kamrani & Salhieh, 2000). Implementing these demonstrations required the development of a complex system. Iowa State University, meanwhile, has developed an experimental facility to train K–12 teachers (Chumbley, Hargrave, Constant, Hand, Andre, & Thompson, 2002). This facility provides hands-on experimental experience with a scanning electron microscopy (SEM). Considering the cost of an SEM, it would be impossible to provide this training without the Internet-based experiment facility. However, implementation of this experiment was quite costly. Some researchers meanwhile implemented Internet-based laboratory experiments for a communication course (Safaric, Calkin, Parkin, & Czarnecki, 1998), while in another effort, a civil engineering structure was made accessible for remote operation over the Internet (Ko, Chen, Hu, Ramakrishnan, Cheng, Zhuang, & Chen, 2001). All of these were implemented to perform only one experiment while the data are not available to the clients' PC. Chao and Mohr (2001) also developed a mechanism for performing experiments via the Internet. Their system, although cost effective, could not address the problem of accessing multiple experiments without human intervention. In addition, the data cannot be made available to the clients' PCs. Some recent initiatives have attempted to provide a couple of experiments on a dynamic systems laboratory and a basic electronics laboratory over the Internet (Esche, 2001; Manasseh, Kausel, & Amaratunga, 2004). All these initiatives suffer restrictions in data accessibility from clients' PCs and of being capable of operating only one experiment at a time.

This chapter begins with discussing the necessity of Internet-based laboratory facilities along with their anticipated impact on students' learning. This will be followed by reporting the current status of the development of Internet-

based laboratories. To do this, the author will illustrate various reported research works in this area along with highlighting their contributions and weaknesses. As the main body of the chapter, a description has been provided for the use of a modular Internet-based laboratory facility to offer a digital electronics laboratory course as a part of an undergraduate program. This includes a description of the system, course delivery strategy, and the evaluation outcome. This is followed by future trends in this area and conclusions.

INTERNET-BASED LABORATORY FACILITY

This section presents the Internet-based laboratory facility that has been developed by the project investigator for delivering an undergraduate level digital electronics laboratory course as a part of an electrical engineering technology program. This facility allowed the students to perform experiments over the Internet with unlimited access time. The system was developed through a grant from the National Science Foundation (Course, Curriculum, and Laboratory Improvement program) (NSF, 2007). All the laboratory experiments are located in a teaching laboratory

Figure 1. Modular system structure of the Internet-based laboratory facility

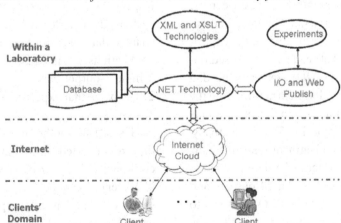

within the Technology Department of Northern Illinois University (NIU). The uniqueness of the developed facility is its modularity in design, use of commercially available hardware and software technologies, and in-built assessment, evaluation, and monitoring facility.

Adopting a modular approach to the problem of designing an Internet-based laboratory facility promises to dramatically improve the adaptability to a range of experiments that entails a wide range of uncertainties (Azad & Nadakuditi, 2006). The idea is to decouple design decisions that are likely to change, so the decisions can be changed independently with minimum effects on the system as a whole (Gershenson & Prasad, 1997; Sullivan, Griswold, & Hallen, 2001). By adopting this strategy, one can develop modular hardware and software blocks that can be easily adaptable with a range of experiments.

Figure 1 shows a block diagram of the designed facility. The modules are (a) experiments, (b) input/output (I/O) and Web publish, (c) XML and XSLT technologies, (d) SQL server, (e) Visual Studio .NET, (f) Internet cloud, and (g) Clients (Azad, 2007).

INTERFACING HARDWARE AND SOFTWARE

The first step toward the Internet-based laboratory facility is to establish an interfacing between the computer and the experiments. The computer will be the gateway to the Internet, while the experiments are the facility that needs to be accessed/operated over the Internet. All the experiments that need to be accessed are digital in nature. Both the inputs and outputs to-and-from the experiments are logic 0 (0V) and logic 1 (+5V), respectively. A digital I/O card from National Instruments is employed as the interfacing hardware. This is a PCI-6528 with 24 inputs and 24 outputs and is enough to provide sufficient I/O channels to drive a number of experiments at the same time

(MathWorks, 2004; National Instruments, 2004; Special Issue, 2000).

The software part of the interfacing process was implemented by using LabVIEW, which is also from National Instruments. The LabVIEW software has much more flexibility for data acquisition and control over the Internet. This can also be used along with other third party software, making it more attractive for development applications such as this one. Apart from these, the other reason for choosing LabVIEW is for its inbuilt server facility that can be utilized to publish a GUI for Internet access to the experiments (Essick, 1999; Travis, 2000).

GRAPHICAL USER INTERFACE AND WEB PRESENTATION

One of the main components of the Internet-based laboratory facility is the GUI. This is serving as the media between the experiments and the students. It is important to provide a user-friendly and effective GUI to attract students, while performing experiments that are usually provided during a traditional laboratory class without any physical supervision and assistance. LabVIEW provides a facility to develop a GUI called virtual instrument (VI) that can serve both of the mentioned purposes (Kariya, 2003).

The concept of VI is to create more powerful, flexible, and cost-effective instrumentation systems using a PC. A VI can easily export and share its data and information with other software applications. An image of a GUI developed for a 3-input 1-output experiment is shown in Figure 2. The particular experiment is Laboratory 3 and Task #1.

The left side of the GUI shows all the 3-inputs that are generated within LabVIEW. These inputs could switch between two levels, logic 1 and logic 0. A user can change the time period between the switching. The state of an input can be monitored, either through an LED or on a graph window.

Figure 2. A GUI for 3-input 1-output system (©2007, Dr Abul K. M. Azad. Used with permission)

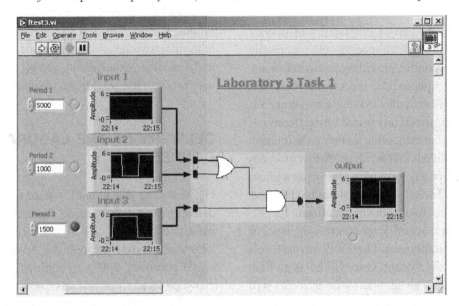

The graph windows are labeled as input 1, input 2, and input 3. The state of output can also be monitored through a graph window as well as through an LED, which is shown on the right side of the GUI. The logic diagram between the two sets of graphs is the hardware system that has been used for the specific experiment. The GUI passed the inputs to the experiment and receives corresponding output through appropriate ports of the I/O card.

For the target course, inputs and outputs are digital in nature. This allows grouping the experiments in terms of the number of inputs and outputs and develops a single GUI for each group. A GUI for one group can be used for all the experiments of that group, only with minor modifications. For the specific course, there are a total of 10 reusable GUIs that will handle all 37 tasks for 12 laboratory sessions. The 10 GUIs are 1input-1output; 2input-1output; 2input-2output; 2input-3output; 3input-1output; 3input-2output; 4input-1output; and 4input-2output.

Presenting a GUI over the Internet involves publishing the GUI as a dynamic Web page. The published GUI is stored within the server at a particular location, and a Web application can point the location and file name for access to the GUI. LabVIEW allows multiple numbers of GUIs to be published at the same time, thus allowing the system to handle multiple experiments simultaneously.

A Web server is hosting the Web site for the facility, including all the applications and interfacing hardware and software. In terms of hardware, the Web server has a 3.6 GHz processor, 2 GB of RAM, 80 GB of HD, and National Instrument's I/O card. For the software part, it has Windows 2003 Server (OS), LabVIEW, Internet information services (IIS) server, .NET, XML (EXtensible Markup Language), XSLT (EXtensible Stylesheet Language Transformations), and SQL server 2000.

INTERNET DELIVERY

Internet delivery part of this facility involves a number of issues: system access levels, user profile and password control, providing documentations, performing experiments, weekly surveys, and administrative activities. All these issues are addressed within the facility to make it as effective as possible. Similar to the other modules, the Internet delivery module is independent of other modules and can accept any form of experiments without any change. The only thing that has to change is the experiment related documentations.

The system access level controls the level of access by a facility user. There will be two levels of access to the system. One will be as a client and the other as an administrator. Students will be allowed with client level access. With this status, one can perform or view an experiment, change password and demographic details, and complete the weekly survey questionnaire. An administrator level of access will allow management of experiments and monitor and gather access profile and survey data. Apart from the home page, the client level of access allows the users to have three areas to browse: Documentations, UserProfile, and Experiments. With the administrative level of access, one can activate and deactivate experiments and get access to the user profiles and weekly survey data.

DELIVERY OF THE LABORATORY COURSE

NIU uses the Blackboard system for its course delivery, and it has some features that were identified as beneficial for the delivery of the laboratory course through the developed facility (Blackboard, 2007). In addition, Blackboard provided an additional level of network security. With this understanding, Blackboard was used as a gateway for the laboratory course offering. The students performing experiments through remote laboratory were enrolled in a Blackboard course. A block diagram presenting the weekly cycle of actions is shown in Figure 3.

The start block shows the starting point for the process and demonstrates the weekly cycle of

Figure 3. Internet-based laboratory protocol for the delivered course (©2007, Dr Abul K. M. Azad. Used with permission)

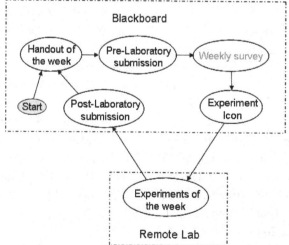

the delivery. A handout of the week was posted on Blackboard and students needed to perform some prelaboratory tasks. After completing the prelaboratory tasks, the handout was submitted through the course drop box (within Blackboard). At the end of each week, students needed to complete a survey considering last week's experience about the whole remote laboratory facility. This survey allowed the facilitator to update the system for better performance and also gather students' perceptions about the facility. The facility was set up with an arrangement that one cannot have access to the following week's laboratory until completion of the previous week's survey. Once inside the remote laboratory facility, one could perform all the tasks that are posted for the given week.

A flowchart showing the access levels to an experiment is shown in Figure 4. An experiment could be performed by a single user at any point in time, while other users could only view the experiment without any control over it. Depending on the availability of an experiment, a client could get access either as a performer or as a viewer. Only a performer is able to manipulate/control an experiment.

ADMINISTRATIVE ACTIVITIES

The administrative level of access to the facility allows a user to have additional capabilities, such as maintenance of available experiments, gathering user activity data, and results of weekly surveys. These application features allow an administrative user to activate or deactivate a given laboratory session or a specific task within a session at the Internet level. Activation of any experiment should be followed by loading of appropriate GUI and connecting the hardware experiment with the facility. All these need to be synchronized to make a specific experiment available through this facility.

Considering this is a 24/7 facility, the system can be accessed any time from anywhere. To

Figure 4. Level of access to the experiments (©2007, Dr Abul K. M. Azad. Used with permission)

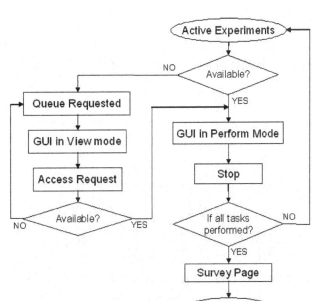

understand the user access profile, the system is provided with a provision to gather user activity data in terms of client login time, logout time, and performance duration for each client for a given experiment. With this application, the administrator gathers data using various filters. The filters are UserID, Access Type, Lab Number, and Task Number. These data can be exported to Excel for further analysis. Similar to the activity data, the weekly survey data can also be gathered by an administrative user and exported to Excel for analysis. Considering the academic use of this facility, these data will allow the course administrator to use this information (in addition to other course data) toward assessment and also to study the students' learning behavior using this facility. These will also enable the administrator to assess the usefulness of the developed facility and adjustments/changes to make the system more efficient and effective.

EVALUATION

The evaluation process is divided into four parts: (a) assess the achieving learning outcomes; (b) assess students' learning behavior in terms of the access time and duration of use (in terms of the use of the facility); (c) assess the effectiveness of the facility and students' perception about the facility; and (d) assess ethical issues. The first two were achieved through quantitative analysis, while the last two were performed through both quantitative and qualitative analysis. Professor Herbert J. Walberg, Research Professor of Education and Psychology at the University of Illinois at Chicago and Visiting Professor at Stanford University, acted as the external evaluator for the project. He is a world renowned scholar and researcher in teaching psychology and evaluation. Dr. Walberg advised on questionnaire design, evaluation of the pedagogical effects of the system, data analysis, and interpretation.

Assess the achieving learning outcomes: To assess the level of student learning, the class was divided into a control group and a test group. The control group took the course using an existing traditional laboratory, while the test group performed the experiments developed through the Internet-based laboratory facility. The test group was composed of male and female students with diverse ethnicity and mixed educational abili-

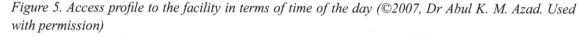

Figure 5. Access profile to the facility in terms of time of the day (©2007, Dr Abul K. M. Azad. Used with permission)

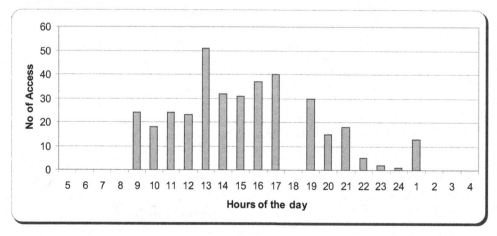

ties. Both the groups were tested with pre- and post-tests, and the results were compared for any difference. It has been observed that there were statistically significant differences between pre- and post-tests for both the test and the control groups with the mean of post-test scores significantly higher than the mean pre-test scores with paired, one-tail t-tests. It has also been observed that these differences for the test group and the control group were not statistically different based on two-tail and nonpaired t-tests. This can be interpreted that both test group and control group learned effectively and the difference between the two groups are not significant.

Assess students' learning behavior: To assess students' learning behavior in terms of the access time and duration of use, the developed facility has in-built capacity to collect students' login and logout times along with the time taken to perform each experiment. These data allow the facilitator to know the level and timing of use of the facility and hence provide a broader understanding of the students' behavior in terms of use of the facility. The details of the user activities data collection are provided in the section on administrative activities.

These data allow comparing the leaning efficiency of control group and test group and also the students' behavior in terms of the use of the facility. It has been found that there are statistically significant differences between the test and the control groups in their time spent on the laboratory tasks with the test group spending 67% less time than the control group on the average. It can be interpreted that the test group learned more efficiently than the control group. In terms of access time to the facility, it has been found that the time of the day when students in the test group perform their laboratory tasks ranged between 9:00 a.m. and 1:00 a.m., which is a duration of 17 hours, indicating great flexibility and convenience for students that are otherwise impossible because of the cost and administrative limitations under a traditional laboratory configuration (Figure 5).

Assess the students' perception about the facility: The third evaluation issue was to assess the effectiveness of the facility and students' perception about the facility. This has been done through a weekly survey, along with a descriptive statement from the test group students at the end of the semester. The Internet-based laboratory course is a new concept, and evaluation of the facility for its usefulness will provide an understanding in terms of students' point of view. Toward this, a weekly survey was incorporated within the facility that students needed to complete at the end each laboratory session. The questions were designed in such a way that these allowed the facilitator to get an understanding about the facility's performance in terms of accessibility, user friendliness, logical arrangement of the information provided, and level of attraction with the Web presentation. Students were queried regarding their interest level in the material, adequacy of background preparation, usefulness of the handouts, effectiveness of the tutorials, knowledge acquired from each topic, relevance of course materials, ease of access to the Internet facility, and suggestions for improvement. The collected data have both short term and long term use. As a short term use, the responses were reviewed by the facilitator on a weekly basis and will be modified, upgraded, or altered through improvement/updating of the teaching materials, experimental facility, and delivery approach. The long term use involves the quantitative analysis of the collected data for a complete semester to identify the aspects of the facility that can be enhanced for future developments.

The survey results show that in general students liked the environment and found the arrangement to be useful. However, in terms of learning, they found that the remote laboratory is almost the same as the traditional lab arrangement. Students also found the system was easy enough to operate. For quantitative data, each test group student wrote a descriptive statement on personal view towards remote laboratory, benefits of remote laboratory, and what can be done better for the future. The main benefit that was pointed out by almost all the students is the anywhere, any time feature of the remote laboratory facility. This allowed them to perform experiments at the times of their own choice that fit with their busy work schedule. Some students raised the point that the remote laboratory does not provide any hands-on experience. This is true, but much research shows that, other things being equal, hands-on laboratory experience does not add knowledge and understanding beyond nonlaboratory instruction. Mastering particular apparatus in a laboratory, moreover, may not be applicable to other apparatus and circumstances. Few mentioned the tight schedule for pre- and postlaboratory submission. Considering a junior level undergraduate course (where all of the labs and coursework are closely supervised), remote laboratory was a major responsibility, and most of them were not totally comfortable to deal with this.

Assess ethical issues: The last and most difficult issue for the Internet-based laboratory facility is the ethical issue. With this arrangement, students performed the experiments on their own, without any direct supervision and also needed to manage other lab related activities in a timely manner. Along with the laboratory course, students also needed to take a teaching course to cover the theoretical part of the topics. So the faculty had an opportunity to meet the students on a weekly basis and address any issues related to the Internet-based laboratory. One of the problems was to ensure whether a student really performed all the experiments or not. At the beginning, a few students submitted the final report without performing all the experiments in a timely manner. The developed facility is equipped with recording of all the laboratory activity timings. With this, the faculty identified the violating students and discussed the matter with the whole class to avoid any repetition of such practice.

FUTURE OF REMOTE LABORATORIES

Performing laboratory experiments over the Internet is a relatively new concept. As discussed earlier, researchers are pursuing this problem in an abrupt manner and have not yet come up with a sustainable solution. Any development in this area requires expertise from computer interfacing, data acquisition and control, computer networking, Web security, and real-time control. For the developed facility as reported in this chapter, the author has developed a modular system, which is cost effective, expandable, and sustainable to some degree. In comparison to other reported systems, the uniqueness of the proposed system is its ease in implementation, modularity in design, Web security, and student evaluation facility. The modularity in system design will enable it to integrate with a large variety of laboratory experiments with very little cost and effort.

In its current form, the developed facility is implemented only with single laboratory course with a small number of students. The outcome of the study is quite encouraging. However, more study needs to be done to explore various aspect of learning outcomes and system effectiveness. The author is now working towards implementing this facility for additional laboratory courses along with the evaluation schemes.

Internet-based laboratory systems are still in their infancy. There are different kinds of experiments in terms of their input(s) and output(s), speed of operation, data collection restrictions, and data presentation. Considering these, a number of issues need to be addressed to develop an effective, versatile, cost effective, and sustainable system to make this concept acceptable and feasible for general use. The issues are identification of modules, standardization for module input(s) and output(s), and collaboration between academia and industry. The technologies that are used for remote laboratory systems (electronics and computer science) are developed extensively; however, these need to be further customized and even to develop new products to maximize the benefit.

CONCLUSION

The use of an Internet-based laboratory facility for offering a digital electronics laboratory course along with an integrated evaluation process has been presented through this chapter. The system is developed using a modular approach, so that the system can be implemented for other experiments without much effort in terms of time and resources. Considering the ease of use, flexibility, and Internet adaptability, NI hardware and software are used to provide the interfacing between the experiment and a PC. Internet access is provided by using an IIS Web server, ASP, ActiveX, MS Access, Windows media player, and Windows media encoder. Some of these software are part of the Windows XP operating system, while the others are available as freeware.

A series of Web pages have been developed for implementing the client access and for monitoring the system's use. The authorized clients will be allocated userIDs and passwords and this will protect the experiments from any mishandling. To obtain a meaningful outcome from an experimental run, only one authorized client can have control over an experiment for any particular period of time.

The provision of the administrator page allows the system administrator to assess the level of use of the system along with the students' learning behavior in terms of their access time. The developed facility can be used as a stand-alone laboratory course within a distance-learning program and also to complement a traditional laboratory course. It could also be used at the high-school level to provide an affordable laboratory experience that would better prepare students for college level courses.

The evaluation outcome highlights that students like the provision of 24/7 access to the facil-

ity and have utilized to access the experiments over an extended period of time. Although there is no difference in learning for the test group and control group, it has been found that there are statistically significant differences between the test and the control groups in their time spent on the laboratory tasks with the test group spending 67% less time than the control group on the average. It can be interpreted that the test group learned more efficiently than the control group. The facility is also equipped with an in-built data collection facility that allows an administrator to monitor the proper use of the facility as required by the students.

ACKNOWLEDGMENT

Part of the work reported through this chapter is based on the project titled "Design and Development of Internet-based Physical Laboratory Facility for an Undergraduate Course" and is funded by the National Science Foundation (USA) under NSF Award Number DUE-0442374.

REFERENCES

Azad, A. K. M., & Nadakuditi, P. (2006). Internet-based facility for physical laboratory experiments. *Advanced Technology for Learning*, *3*(1), 29-35.

Azad, A. K. M. (2007). Delivering a remote laboratory course within an undergraduate program. *International Journal of Online Engineering*, *3*(4), 27-33.

Bengu, G., & Swart, W. (1996). A computer-aided total quality approach to manufacturing education in engineering. *IEEE Transactions on Education*, *39*(3), 415-422.

Blackboard. (2007). Retrieved March 15, 2008, from http://www.blackboard.com/us/index

Boyle, A. P., Bryon, D. N., & Paul, C. R. C. (1997). Computer-based learning and assessment: A palaeontological case study with outcomes and implications. *Computers and Geosciences, 23*(5), 573-580.

Chao, N., & Mohr, B. (2001, June 25). *Real hand-on laboratory experiments, anytime, anywhere.* Paper presented at the ASEE National Conference, Albuquerque, NM.

Chumbley, L. S., Hargrave, C. P., Constant, K., Hand, B., Andre, T., & Thompson, E. A. (2002). Project ExCEL: Web-based scanning electron microscopy for K-12 education. *Journal of Engineering Education, 91*(2), 203-210.

Esche, S. K. (2001, September 15-18). *Remote experimentation: One building block in online engineering education.* Invited presentation at the 2001 ASEE/SEFI/TUB International Colloquium on Global Changes in Engineering Education, Berlin, Germany.

Essick, J. (1999). *Advanced LabVIEW Labs.* New York: Prentice Hall.

Fletcher, G. H. (2004, May). Editorial. *Technical Horizons in Education*, pp. 6-8.

Gershenson, J. K., & Prasad, G. J. (1997, August). Modularity in product design for manufacturability. *International Journal of Agile Manufacturing, 1*(1).

Grose, T. K. (2003, April). Can distance education be unlocked? *PRISM,* pp. 19-23.

Hagg, S., & Palais, J. C. (2002). Engineering online: Assessing innovative education. *Journal of Engineering Education, 91*(3), 285-289.

Henson, A. B., Fridley, K. J., Pollock, D. B., & Brahler, C. J., (2002). Efficacy of interactive Internet-based education in structural timber design. *Journal of Engineering Education, 91*(4), 371-387.

Kamrani, A. K., & Salhieh, S. M. (2000). *Product design for modularity.* Boston: Kluwer Academic Publishers.

Kariya, S. (2003, May). Online education expands and evolves. *IEEE Spectrum*, pp. 49-51.

Ko, C. C., Chen, B. M., Hu, S., Ramakrishnan, V., Cheng, C. D., Zhuang, Y., & Chen, J. (2001). A Web-based virtual laboratory on a frequency modulation experiment. *IEEE Transaction on Systems, Man, and Cybernetics: Part-C, Applications and Reviews, 31*(3), 295-303.

Manasseh, M., Kausel, E., & Amaratunga, K. (2004, June 20-23). A Web-accessible shaking table experiment for the remote monitoring of seismic effects in structures. In *Proceedings of the 2004 American Society of Engineering Education Annual Conference and Exposition,* Salt Lake City, UT.

MathWorks. (2007). *Developers of MATLAB and Simulink for technical computing.* Retrieved March 15, 2008, from http://www.mathworks.com/

National Instruments. (2007). Measurement and automation. Retrieved March 15, 2008, from http://www.ni.com/

National Science Foundation. (2007, May 10). US NSF- National Science Foundation. Retrieved March 15, 2008, from http://www.nsf.gov/

Palais, J., & Javurek, C. G. (1996). The Arizona State University electrical engineering undergraduate open laboratory. *IEEE Transactions on Education, 39*(2), 257-264.

Safaric, R., Calkin, D. W., Parkin, R. M., & Czarnecki, C. A. (1998, September 9-11). Control of a robot system via Internet. In *Proceedings of the 6th UK Mechatronics Forum International Conference,* Skovde, Sweden (pp. 829-833).

Special Issue: LabVIEW applications in engineering education. (2000). *The International Journal of Engineering Education, 16*(3).

Sullivan, K. J., Griswold, W. G., & Hallen, Y. C. B. (2001, September). The structure and value of modularity in software design. In *Proceedings of the Joint International Conference on Software Engineering and ACM SIGSOFT Symposium on the Foundation of Software Engineering,* Vienna, Italy.

Swearengen, J. C., Barnes, S., Coe, S., Reinhardt, C., & Subramanian, K. (2002). Globalization and the undergraduate manufacturing engineering curriculum. *Journal of Engineering Education, 94*(2), 255-261.

Travis, J. (2000). *Internet applications in Lab-VIEW.* New York: Prentice Hall.

Vohra, P. (2002, April 12). Communication technologies: Are we jumping in too fast? In *Proceedings of the ASEE IL-IN Sectional Conference,* Illinois Institute of Technology, Chicago, IL.

KEY TERMS

Client: User of the Internet-based laboratory facility.

Control Group: The group of student who has not used the Internet-based laboratory facility.

Graphical User Interface: A graphical screen that is used between an user and underlying process so that the user can manipulate the process without much knowledge about the process itself.

Input/Output Card: An electronic board that constitutes the hardware part of interfacing.

Interfacing: A provision (combination of hardware and software) that needs to be provided to connect a computer/computing system with any other system for data transfer.

Internet-Based Laboratory: A facility where laboratory experiments can be performed over the Internet.

Modular-Based System: A system that has been designed by using independent modules, where any of these modules can be changed or updated without affecting other modules connected with it.

Test Group: The group of students who have used the Internet-based laboratory facility.

Web Publication: The process of posting of GUI within a Web server for user access.

Web Server: A special type of computer that is mainly used to host a Web site.

Chapter II
Exploring Multimedia Performance in Educational Research

Carl Bagley
University of Durham, UK

ABSTRACT

This chapter draws on the analysis and (re)presentation of qualitative research undertaken on a UK government project known as Sure Start, an initiative based on the principle of bottom up community-based engagement dealing with social exclusion. The data from interviews, observation, and documentation arise from ethnographic immersion by the author in a local working class community over a period of two years. Based on these data the chapter explores the (re)telling of the same research tale through the lens of bounded and unbounded (re)presentational forms, and in so doing, envisions some of the challenges and opportunities for multimedia performance as a methodological approach within the academy.

THE RESEARCH CONTEXT

In theoretical and conceptual terms, I would like to place this chapter within the parameters of the postmodern project as elucidated by Constas (1999, pp. 36-37) providing a typology that aims to distinguish postmodern educational research and its representation from other forms of inquiry. Constas does this by offering a "three-dimensional model" that elucidates the key aspects and "unify-ing elements" which signify "the discourses of educational inquiry as it moves towards a post modern perspective." The three primary dimensions of the postmodern perspective are labeled political, methodological, and representational.

The *political* Constas (1999, p. 38) identifies as relating to the way in which power is treated in the research process. In particular, the move away from a "taken for granted view on the nature of power in education" to one in which power relations are problematized, and "de-centered," for example, in relation to gender or ethnicity.

In terms of the *methodological*, it relates to the ways in which data are collected and theorized with a movement away from normative approaches and concerns with prescribed guidelines and issues such as validity and reliability to more idiosyncratic approaches which place emphasis on more individualized and stylized features and preferences, emphasizing the uniqueness of each research project, and the significance of the researcher's relationship to the study and other individuals within it. The *representational* in Constas' (1999, pp. 38-39) dimension concerns the forms and ways in which data are reported and presented and a move way from "depersonalized, distanced and objective" writing styles often in the third person which he refers to as discursively "highly bounded" and exclusive to alternative "unbounded" representational styles such as performance.

In the same way, Constas' (1999) framework delineates educational research according to political, methodological, and representational variants, so qualitative investigations like Atkinson (1990, 1992) and Wolcott (1990) are concerned with both a research process and product. The process relating to the conducting of fieldwork and the analysis of the data, the product concerned with the way in which the data resulting from the process is (re)presented. Over the last 20 years, qualitative researchers like Atkinson and Coffey (1995) and Marcus and Fischer (1986) have, in relation to the "product" of qualitative research, become increasingly concerned with how to (re)present the cultural and social worlds under their analytical gaze. The search is for greater utilization of genres to (re)present findings which provide a closer alignment between the phenomena we study and the way we portray those phenomena, and which create disruptive spaces to celebrate the subjectivity, diversity, and difference in the readings, viewings, and interpretations they afford.

In essence, this chapter explores how as researchers we communicate information about the social world we research and the ways in which the form we choose to convey our findings impacts upon the meanings and influences attributed to it (Eisner, 1991; Finley, 1998). In recent years, qualitative researchers (see Eisner & Barone, 2006) have begun to look beyond traditional printed textual modes to embrace more artistic print and nonprint forms of representation. In literary form, these include the use of short story (Kilbourne, 1998), creative nonfiction (Angrosino, 1998), and musical lyric (Jenoure, 2002). For example, Richardson (1992, 2000) uses poetry to (re)present sociological research. She transposes the life worlds of those she has interviewed and incorporating evocative poetic devices such as rhymes, meters, and pauses, sensitively and meaningfully portrays her data as verse or ethnopoetics.

Researchers like Becker, McCall, Morris, and Meshejian (1989); Bluebond-Langer (1980); Ellis and Bochner (1992); Goldstein (2001, 2002); McCall (2000); Mienczakowski (2001); Paget (1990); and Richardson and Lockridge (1991) have chosen to use drama and theatre to present ethnographic data as a way to immerse performers and audience in the range of meanings, emotions, and feelings associated with a research. Mienczakowski's (2001) ethnodramatic work encompasses a notion of praxis in which the data in dramatic form are staged in front of an audience comprised of policy makers and practitioners from the field depicted. In exposing the thoughts, experiences, and feelings of the people with whom policy makers and practitioners work, it is hoped that the research will have an impact on policy and practice.

Equally, Minh-ha (1991) uses visual textual forms through the medium of film to deprivilege the single analytical (male) voice and enable the participating viewer to engage with and reveal the multiple layered experiences of women's lives. Also, in relation to life histories and educational research, Finley (2002) (re)presented data on faculty socialization and teacher education using the art forms of screenplay and painting/collage. The use by researchers of other nonlinguistic art forms includes music (Rasberry, 2002), photography (Knowles & Thomas, 2002), and dance (Bagley & Cancienne, 2001) to (re)tell their educational stories. Interestingly, Skjulstad, Morrison, and Aaberge (2002, pp. 212-213) explore in an aptly entitled educational research project called Balectro, a multimedia fusion of dance and digital media, discussing ways of conducting, and understanding research as and through performance.

Undoubtedly, while an increasing number of researchers are experimenting with the use of artistic textual forms to (re)present research, particularly in the U.S., the task of breaking away from conventional (re)presentational forms nevertheless remains at the cutting edge of methodological endeavors certainly within European educational research. The need remains for the exploration and development of artistic forms of interpretation and (re)presentation, especially those which are less prevalent and which encompass and incorporate the visual and multimedia performing arts. According to Stern and Henderson (1993) cited in Denzin (2003a, p. 546), this is a way of: "drawing for its materials not only upon the live bodies of performers but upon media images, television monitors, projected images, visual images, film, poetry, autobiographic material, dance, architecture and music." In (re)telling a qualitative tale, the following thoughts come to mind.

I am viewing multimedia performance art as a multilayering, interplaying, and interconnecting set of textual forms incorporating, music, visual art, dramatic performance, dance, and movement, and as such, the work presented may be viewed as intertextual (Bagley & Cancienne, 2002). For those committed to an unbounded open methodological approach, I take the notion of intertextuality to be a discursively more accurate and useful description of the work presented here than the more commonly used notion in Eisner (1997) of alternative forms of representation. The concept

"alternative" implies and reinforces bounded notions of (re)presentation in which text as the written word is able to maintain its mainstream position at the center of the academy and other artistic textual forms are located and confined to the periphery. The intention is neither to claim that all data have to be represented intertextually or artistically nor to devalue or underestimate the historical significance and power of the written word. Rather, the intention is to facilitate a conversation between equal partners about the strengths and weaknesses of using different textual forms to (re)present data.

In terms of the intertextual multimedia work presented here, I wish to start by placing the research topic in context and provide an outline of the focus of the research from which the data were derived. I will then turn to issues related to the interpretation and (re)presentation of data and, mediated through the lens of data generated from the study, offer (in the form of two extracts) examples of ways in which the *same* data were presented at two conferences. The examples used here relate not simply to the same overall data, but speak to the same subdata set. In effect, the chapter offers the same issue/point presented through two representational lenses.

The first telling is in a standard traditional form associated with conference paper presentations. The second or (re)telling of the same qualitative tale is in a performative (re)presentational intertextual multimedia form that was experimental in its approach and incorporated a range of different artistic forms like digital media and sound, dance, drama, picture, and spoken and printed text. As Skjulstad et al. (2002, p. 217) note:

In contrast to computer games, which by definition must be played on screen, or online, many performance pieces which use digital media do so by shifting between different types of screens, projections and media types; together these are part of an emerging live event in which plot, movement, music and scenography may all be in flux. The intention of the artist is thus often that of mediating this flux to an audience.

Clearly, any attempt to (re)present what was performed will lose something in a translation to the more bounded form of print-based text used in its (re)presentation in this chapter. I am however happy to live within this paradox and engage with print-based text in order to bring some essence of the undertaking to a wider audience. Nevertheless, in returning to a more bounded form of data representation, the question remains extremely pertinent regarding the extent to which the reader needed to see the performance to gather its real impact and significance. An edited DVD version of the performance I made, and which in its own right constitutes a (re)reading and (re)presentation of the data, makes up an opportunity of at least a form of (re)showing. In the final two sections of the chapter, I draw on my own thoughts and feelings plus those of the audience to reflect critically on these bounded and unbounded tellings and the opportunities and challenges arising from the use of arts-based multimedia performance to (re)present data.

THE SURE START DATA AND ITS (RE)PRESENTATION

In 2001 and 2002, the School of Education at the University of Durham secured the funding bids to conduct evaluations of four community-based health and education related programs known as Sure Start. It was one of the UK Labour Government's major initiatives in the prevention of social exclusion and its remit was to improve the life chances of young children through better access to early education and play, family support and advice on nurturing, and health services specifically aimed at children. The program was targeted explicitly at children under four and their families who reside in areas of need and disadvantage and was delivered locally at the point of need by a self-contained, interdisciplinary, multiagency team of professionals working in partnership with voluntary agencies and community groups.

In terms of Constas' (1999) frame, the research undertaken can be conceived as politically decentered, as it recognized the power relationships between working class parents and the state. The approach was methodologically normative (Constas, 1999) as the data were generated through a traditional ethnographic method utilizing documentation relating to the program, attendance and observation at meetings, and semistructured interviews conducted with local parents, volunteers, and employees associated with the program. The interviews were subsequently recorded, transcribed, and analyzed using open coding from grounded theorizing (Glaser & Strauss, 1967). In (re)presentational terms the research was both bounded and unbounded. For example, at the bounded level, the data have formed the basis for two traditional conference papers presented at the British Educational Research Association Annual Conference 2003 and the European Educational Research Association Annual Conference in 2004. These conference papers were subsequently published in the *Journal of Education Policy* (see Bagley & Ackerley, 2006; Bagley, Ackerley, & Rattray, 2004).

At the unbounded level, the data from the same project in the form of transcripts and tapes were given to a group of performing artists to interpret and stage. The performance (re)presented as a part of a keynote address I was invited to give at the UK's inaugural (2005) conference on arts-based educational research at Queens University in Belfast (see Bagley, 2008). In this context, the performance constituted both the conference paper and its presentation. Extracts from these bounded and unbounded (re)presentational forms are offered in the following, starting with the bounded form.

THE BOUNDED TRADITIONAL (RE)PRESENTATIONAL FORM

The scene is as follows. The text "'Much More Than Just a Mum': Social Capital, Empowerment and Sure Start" is scheduled to be presented at the 11–12 a.m. parallel session of the Ethnography and Education Network. The researcher/presenter turns up to the relatively small seminar room on the Campus of the University of Crete at 10:45 a.m. By 11 a.m., the room is filled with approximately 14 conference delegates, all seated in rows facing the front of the classroom. The facilities for the delivery of the presentation are limited to an overhead projector facing a white classroom wall. I have been time-tabled to talk for approximately 15 minutes.

Researcher (facing audience with OHP at his side): "The neighbourhood in which the parents lived was very working class, with high levels of unemployed, a deteriorating housing stock with a large number of one parent families and teenage pregnancies. There was however pre-dating the Sure Start programme a sense of community amongst residents with some local self-help initiatives already in place. Building on this sense of community one of the most positive preliminary findings from the study was the way in which the inter-agency team working with local parents had seemingly managed to engender a sense of empowerment. The Cornell Group define empowerment in the following terms" (OHP slide):

An intentional ongoing process centred in the local community, involving mutual respect, critical reflection, caring and group participation, through which people lacking an equal share of valued resources gain greater access to and control over those resources. (Cornell Empowerment Group, 1998, p. 3)

Researcher: "Our research indicated that parents did feel that a sense of partnership had been engendered between themselves and the inter-agency team of professionals working with them and that this had resulted in life changes and feelings of inclusiveness and empowerment. Several of the parents put it in the following terms: (OHP slide displays the parents' words):

"We're all at the same level, it's brilliant, because you don't feel any different, yes you're a parent and yes they're a member of staff but it's a team effort from all areas. ...you've got a sense of belonging, there is that sense of community within the team and parents are included in that team.

"It has definitely helped me. ...I feel that I am much more than just a mum."

"It was there, it was available and it was in my community and it has changed my life completely. I thought yes I like this and I can help people, I have got something to give and if I can help people and give something back to the community then I will. I have lived in this community all my life and now I can do something to help that community."

The session ends and the majority of the audience remains seated (although two people stand up and leave without making eye contact with the presenter, heads bowed as they make for the door). About five minutes has been allocated to the audience for comment and questions.

Silence (5 seconds).   Silence (10 seconds).   Silence (15 seconds)

Chairperson: Are there no questions or comments?

Silence (10 seconds)

Chairperson: Okay, if there are no questions I would like to thank Carl for his very enlightening—and positive—presentation.

Audience claps (5 seconds)

Researcher: (Slightly embarrassed by lack of questions and feeling a sense of irony in what he is about to say): I do have some copies of the text with me if anyone is interested and would like one.

Session ends with audience pushing past each other to obtain a copy of the text!

THE UNBOUNDED INTERTEXTUAL MULTIMEDIA (RE)PRESENTATIONAL FORM

The scene is as follows. An audience of 100 conference delegates enters a dimly lit corridor of a theatre. They enter five or so people at a time. They sense the smell of burning toast emanating from a toaster at the far end of the corridor in the direction in which they are walking fills the air getting stronger and more pungent as they move towards it. On the floor of the corridor, they walk pass discarded items of children's clothing and nappies. They turn the corner at the end of the corridor and enter the wide open space of the equally dimly lit auditorium. All the seats have been removed, and the audience find themselves on stage, adjusting awkwardly and tentatively to their unfamiliar and unexpected surroundings. On the stage are pieces of household furniture, a table with a lighted birthday cake, a washing machine, an ironing board, a pair of men's slippers, and a tabloid newspaper. One of the female performers stands washing dishes at a sink while a man sits at a table with a kettle about to make a cup of tea. In the air is the noise of digitally generated whispering voices, interspersed with a variety of low key musical notes.

On one of the walls is a large white bed sheet acting as a screen with computer generated images showing at first a washing machine followed by that of a Playstation console, a toothbrush, a bottle of ketchup, each flashed on to the sheet for a few seconds. On the floor in one corner is marked out a starting line with running lanes. The audience

Figure 1. Illustration of performance

explores the space, viewing, touching, hearing, smelling, and feeling their environment. The digitally generated sound stops. There is silence.

Performer (1) from amongst the audience says "Take your positions please" as other performers emerge from the audience and take their position at the starting line marked on the floor in the corner of the auditorium. A very low pitched digitally generated sound is audible as background noise.

Performer (1) as if starting a race says "On your marks (noise builds slightly), get set (noise increases) hold" (see Figure 1). A false (un)sure start. The performers stand up and walk away.

The actual context, actors, and activity is described by a photo in Figure 1.

The words "More Than Just a Mum" are flashed on the white back cloth accompanied by a sound of a deep pitched noise; the audience attention is grabbed as they look towards the cloth. As they gaze upwards, two performers intermingle unnoticed with the audience.

Performer 2 (a woman) walks in a snake like pattern in between different audience members, stops and says: "You know I feel I am much more than just a mum"

Performer 3 (a man) walking between and up to members of the audience) says: "Ministers have defined the problem and set the framework; local people are designing and delivering the solutions."

Performer 2 We have already applied for funding outside government.

Performer 3 Ministers have defined the problem and set the framework; local people are designing and delivering the solutions.

Performer 2 You know I feel I am much more than just a mum.

Performer 3 The real premise and the key to success is getting the participation of the parents.

Performer 2 Yes, you're a parent and they are a member of staff, but it's a team effort from all areas. It's brilliant.

Performer 3 Ministers have defined the problem and set the framework; local people are designing and delivering the solutions.

Performer 2 When I first used to go I never said a word, now they can't shut me up. It was there, it was available and it was in my community. I thought I like this and I can help people. I feel I am much more than just a mum.

After a period of around 15 minutes, the performance finishes with the performers reprising the earlier call to start a race, and this time it is a successful or "sure start." The audience and performers leave the auditorium and go into a rehearsal room to discuss the performance. (It is perhaps interesting to note that while the whole audience discussion—or absence of it—of the bounded representational form was presented earlier, only an extract of the discussion following the unbounded discussion is included.) One of the performers opens the discussion.

Performer We hoped you enjoyed the performance. The promenade staging of the performance and the breaking down of the barriers between you as audience and us as performers was very important, which is why we asked you to walk in and through the performance. We also wanted to provide a basic structure to frame the piece, hence the repeated "ready steady go" segments but also make it sensuous and challenging with the performed pieces and a range of sights sounds and smells.

Audience memb (1) It made me feel quite literally immersed in the data.

Audience memb (2) I found this extremely powerful. No talk or text could touch me in the way this performance did. The experience will stay with me for a long time.

Audience memb (3) It was … evocative for all of us who experienced it, it touched on all the senses, we walked in we got smell, we got sight, we got sound … we walked through the findings we were very much part of it and the performance touched and moved me.

Audience memb (4) It was the combination of things that struck me sound, sight, smell, leading me, drawing me in, creating an uncertain but inclusive atmosphere, making me wary but wanting to know more.

Audience memb (5) I did feel emotional. …I could feel these people's lives and the struggles to get off that starting line.

After approximately 30 minutes, the discussion ends.

CRITICAL REFLECTIONS

In reflecting critically on the (re)telling of the qualitative tale, I would situate the intertexual multimedia piece highlighted here, in the context of Eisner's (1997) conceptual thinking around the value of what is termed arts-based educational research (Barone & Eisner, 2006). First, Eisner (1997, p. 8) believes it can assist researchers to engender "a sense of empathy for the lives of the people they wish to know." Human feeling in the form of empathy is seen as important for providing access and understanding of the lives of others and the situations they face.

In contrast to traditional presentations, more artistically crafted narratives are perceived as having the evocative power to engage and capture "in the reader what the reader needs to experience to know the person someone portrays." While Eisner (1997, p. 8) is speaking to literary crafted narratives, I would extend this to encompass those viewing/reading a multimedia performance art piece such as the one (re)presented here. Whereas in the first bounded (re)presentational extract, seated delegates listened to a researcher reporting

secondhand on the findings of an ethnographic study, so in the unbounded (re)presentational piece, the audience found themselves immersed metaphorically and literally in the data. Arguably, in the same way in which ethnographic researchers (Skjulstad et al., 2002, p. 213) endeavor to "become part of the fabric of the context they are researching" so on walking into the piece the audience were "in the field," sensuously and empathetically wrapped in its richness, diversity, and complexity, something not possible in the traditional qualitative reading.

Second, intertextual multimedia pieces provide a sense of "particularity and dimension" (Eisner, 1997, p. 8). Namely, when produced and directed well, readers and viewers of artistic work are able to see the situation and know and feel the characterizations as they take on their own distinctive qualities. In effect, "particularity and dimension" introduce a sense of authenticity to the (re)presentation, conferring a "sense of what is being portrayed is real" (Eisner, 1997, p. 8). Intertexual multimedia forms may in the current academic climate be perceived somehow as less authoritative in the sense that they do not conform to audience expectations of qualitative data delivery, while nevertheless actually providing a more authentic representation of the social worlds they describe.

In the traditional reading, it was possible to capture and present the voices of the parents as text in an overhead on a screen. But this relatively limited audience access to experiential ethnographic narrative needs to be viewed and situated alongside the sensuous access facilitated by the performance. In the performance piece, the smell of toast, the visual physical presence of the discarded nappies, the live performer/actor washing at the sink, and another about to make a cup of tea, all sensuously resonate with the everyday lived experience of the audience.

Moreover, the performers/actors in character speaking the actual words of the interviewees and addressing the audience directly brought the bounded data (as (re)presented by the researcher in the first extract) to unbounded dramatic life. The audience was able to (re)visualize the actors as parents and, in so doing, engage with and convey the feelings and meanings of the words spoken to the audience in a way in which I as researcher in the traditional reading could not hope achieve.

Third and related to the previous comment, whereas conventional social science aims to "reduce ambiguity and increase certainty by seeking to offer explanations, rival hypotheses or personal judgement" (Eisner, 1997, p. 8). Intertextual multimedia forms of data representation can provide what Eisner (1997, p. 8) terms "productive ambiguity" where data are evocative rather than denotative. In contrast to more conventional accounts which are in the main constructed from a single authorial or "monovocal perspective," the researcher is positioned as sole narrator claiming authority while writing/presenting from a dominant perspective (as in the first extract). The evocation of intertextual multimedia data disrupt such monovocal narrative and propagate a discernment of multiple meanings, interpretations, and voices which provide a multivocal fragmented text to engage and decanter the viewer.

The unbounded interactive use of performance art and the space it created made the data (re)presentable to the audience in a way that was not achievable in the more bounded representational form. In particular and importantly, its visual and visceral qualities created an opportunity to feel and know the seen and unseen, the said and unsaid. The performative reading and (re)presentation of the research findings bringing into relief the social and cultural context of the interviewees in which their empowerment had been engendered, in effect, providing an experiential tableau of the everyday which the bounded textual form could never hope to achieve or depict.

Fourth, as intertextual multimedia forms increase and are developed, their use as genres for research will produce "new ways of seeking" (Eisner, 1997, p. 8). Their use will identify new

research questions and raise new issues to be addressed and resolved. Thus, in reflecting on the ways in which we might (re)present data, we are required to consider the experiences, voices, meanings, and understandings in the data. In this respect, the process and product of qualitative research, as arguably associated with the first reading, might, according to Coffey and Atkinson (1996, p. 13), "escape from analytical perspectives that have become stereotypical and stale."

One might further speculate that it was the staleness and sameness in terms of bounded traditional telling that intellectually numbed the audience to the point were they had no desire to engage with the session in terms of commentary or questions. It might equally however have related to a number of other factors such as the make up of the audience, the topic, the time of day, the skills of the presenter, the nature of the environment, and so forth.

CONCLUDING THOUGHTS

This is an analysis and a (re)presentation of ethnographic research data. In highlighting the methodological potential, and notwithstanding the notable work of Denzin (2003b) in sociology and Barone and Eisner (2006) in education, one of the potential dangers in advocating and using forms of intertextual multimedia data (re)presentation remains the possible backlash within the wider academic community which at best might find the work difficult to contextualize, comprehend, and judge and, at worst, unacceptable and ridiculous (Eisner, 1997).

In safeguarding against overcritical and negative responses, it is necessary, says Eisner (1997, p. 9), to describe the interpretative context in which data are to be presented, and for self-reflexive practice which ensures that "novelty and cleverness" in the use of intertextual (re)presentational form does not replace substance. As Coffey and Atkinson (1996, p. 109) stipulate, "there is no merit in the mindless pursuit of the avant-garde anymore than there is the unthinking adoption of tried and tested approaches."

The problem however even for self-reflexive practitioners with an appropriate interpretative context is that whereas the "tried and tested" by definition remain safe and acceptable, so the use of nontraditional unbounded forms can be perceived as highly risky and unacceptable, especially in the present academic climate with the need to establish a published research record and to share and disseminate data. Consequently, the practical and logistical constraints on the use of nonprint-based intertextual multimedia forms remain quite significant. The limited opportunity to find a performance space within academic research-based conferences is itself testimony to the difficulties still to be faced.

Significantly, technological advances accompanying the increased use of online journals might make a cross-fertilization of (re)presentational genres encompassing combinations of text as print, image, voice, and movement increasingly possible and more widely accessible. As the then editor-in-chief of the online *American Communication Journal* (Schrag cited in Rich, Johnson, & Olsen 2003, p. 8) eloquently observes:

For decades ... centuries ... we have attempted to share our insights regarding a dynamic process, communication, in a static environment—print. I am truly intrigued by what we might discover when the medium through which we distribute our findings shares the characteristics of the phenomena we study.

Undoubtedly, any such advances—whether opportunities provided technically through developments in ICT or practically by more physical performance spaces at conferences—will all need to be matched by a change in the culture of the social science academy to afford much greater scholarly recognition to academics working in intertextual multimedia forms. A signifier of the cultural academic emphasis still placed on the traditional text-based paper is perhaps shown in the desire—even from an audience who appeared from their verbal unresponsiveness to be relatively uninterested in the topic—to obtain a copy of the written paper associated with the bounded presentation. Nevertheless, whatever the methodological, professional, and institutional challenges to be faced, I would contend that critically informed debate around the legitimacy of intertextual multimedia forms—of how researchers most appropriately (re)present what they have learned—can help to re-evaluate the meaning of research, the ways in which it should be conducted, and its epistemological value.

REFERENCES

Angrosino, M. (1998). *Opportunity house*. London: Altamira Press.

Atkinson, P. (1990). *The ethnographic imagination: Textual constructions of reality*. London; Routledge.

Atkinson, P. (1992). *Understanding ethnographic texts*. London: Sage.

Atkinson, P., & Coffey, A. (1995). Realism and its discontent: On the crisis of cultural representation in ethnographic texts. In B. Adams & S. Allan (Eds.), *Theorizing culture: An Interdisciplinary Critique after Postmodernism*. London: UCL Press.

Bagley, C. (2008). Educational ethnography as performance art: Toward a sensuous knowing and feeling. *Qualitative Research*, *18*(1), 53-72.

Bagley, C., & Ackerley, C. (2006). "More than just a mum": Social capital, empowerment and Sure Start. *Journal of Education Policy, 26*(6), 717-734.

Bagley, C., Ackerley, C. L., & Rattray, J. (2004). Social exclusion, sure start and organizational social capital: Evaluating inter-disciplinary multi-agency working in an education and health work programme. *Journal of Education Policy, 19*(5), 595-607.

Bagley, C., & Cancienne, M. B. (2001). Educational research and intertextual forms of (re)presentation: The case for dancing the data. *Qualitative Inquiry, 7*(2), 221-237.

Bagley, C., & Cancienne, M. B. (Eds.). (2002). *Dancing the data*. New York: Peter Lang.

Barone, T., & Eisner, E. (2006). Arts-based educational research. In J. Green, G. Camilli., & P. Elmore (Eds.), *Complementary methods in research in education*. Washington, DC: American Educational Research Association.

Becker, H. S., McCall, M. M., Morris, L. V., & Meshejian, P. (1989). Theatres and communities: Three stories. *Social Problems, 36*(2), 93-98.

Bluebond-Langer, M. (1980). *The private worlds of dying children*. Princeton: Princeton University Press.

Coffey, A., & Atkinson, P. (1996). *Making sense of qualitative data: Complimentary research strategies*. London: Sage.

Constas, M. A. (1999). Deciphering postmodern educational research. *Educational Researcher, 27*(9), 36-41.

Cornell Empowerment Group. (1998). Empowerment and family support. *Networking Bulletin, 1*, 1-23.

Denzin, N. K. (2003a). Reading and writing performance. *Qualitative Research, 3*(2), 243-268.

Denzin, N. K. (2003b). *Performance ethnography: Critical pedagogy and the politics of culture*. Thousand Oaks: Sage.

Eisner, E. (1991). *The enlightened eye*. New York: Macmillan.

Eisner, E. (1997). The promise and perils of alternative forms of data representation. *Educational Researcher, 26*(6), 4-10.

Ellis, C., & Bochner, A. P. (1992). Telling and performing stories: The constraints of choice in abortion. In C. Ellis & M. G. Flaherty (Eds.), *Investigating subjectivity: Research on lived experience*. Los Angeles: Sage.

Finley, S. (1998, April). *Alternative modes of data (re)presentation: Exploiting the power of form to inform*. Paper presented at the Annual Meeting of the American Educational Research Association, San Diego, CA.

Finley, S. (2002). Women myths: Teacher self-images and socialization to feminine stereotypes. In C. Bagley & M. B. Cancienne (Eds.), *Dancing the data*. New York: Peter Lang.

Glaser, B., & Strauss, A. (1967). *The discovery of grounded theory*. New York: Aldine.

Goldstein, T. (2001). Hong Kong, Canada. *Qualitative Inquiry, 7*(3), 279-303.

Goldstein, T. (2002). Performed ethnography for representing other people's children in critical educational research. *Applied Theatre Researcher, 3*(5), 1-12.

Jenoure, T. (2002). Sweeping the temple: A performance collage. In C. Bagley & M. B. Cancienne (Eds.), *Dancing the data*. New York: Peter Lang.

Kilbourne, B. (1998). *For the love of teaching*. London: Althouse Press.

Knowles, J. G., & Thomas, S. M. (2002). Artistry, inquiry, and sense of place. In C. Bagley & M. B. Cancienne (Eds.), *Dancing the data*. New York: Peter Lang.

Marcus, J., & Fischer, M. (Eds.). (1986). *Anthropology as cultural critique*. Chicago: University of Chicago Press.

McCall, M. (2000). Performance ethnography. In N. Denzin & Y. Lincoln (Eds.), *Handbook of qualitative research* (2nd ed.). London: Sage.

Mienczakowski, J. (2001). Ethnodrama. In P. Atkinson, A. Coffey, S. Delamont, J. Lofland, & L. Lofland. (Eds.), *Handbook of ethnography*. London: Sage.

Minh-ha, T. (1991). *When the moon waxes red.* London: Routledge.

Paget, M. (1990). Performing the text. *Journal of Contemporary Ethnography, 19*, 136-155.

Rasberry, G. W. (2002). Imagine inventing a data-dancer. In C. Bagley & M. B. Cancienne (Eds.), *Dancing the data*. New York: Peter Lang.

Rich, M. D., Johnson, J. R., & Olsen, D. S. (2003). Order, chaos and the (cyber) spaces betwixt and between: The interconnections of performance and technology. *American Communication Journal, 6*(3), 1-9.

Richardson, L. (1992). The consequences of poetic representation: Writing the other, writing the self. In C. Ellis & M. G. Flaherty (Eds.), *Investigating subjectivity: Research on lived experience*. Los Angeles: Sage.

Richardson, L. (2000). Writing: A method of inquiry. In N. K. Denzin & Y. S. Lincoln (Eds.), *Handbook of qualitative research* (2nd ed.). Thousand Oaks: Sage.

Richardson, L., & Lockridge, E. (1991). The sea monster: An ethnographic drama. *Symbolic Interaction, 13*, 22-83.

Skjulstad, S., Morrison, A., & Aaberge, A. (2002). Researching performance, performing research: Dance, multimedia and learning. In A. Morrison (Ed.), *Researching ICTs in context*. Blindern: Intermedia, University of Oslo.

Wolcott, H. (1990). *Writing up qualitative research*. London: Sage.

KEY TERMS

Arts-Based Educational Research: An inquiry process which encompasses linguistic and nonlinguistic art forms to engage with and increase understanding of education.

Intertextual: Text conceived not simply as a print-based written form but encompassing all genres of representation such as music, sound, dramatic performance, and their interrelationship.

Monovocal: The way in which traditional print based texts have been constructed and presented from one singular and alleged authoritative perspective or voice.

Multimedia: A multilayering, interplaying, and interconnecting set of audio-visual forms incorporating, music, sound, visual art, dramatic performance, dance, and movement as a means of communication.

Multivocal: The way in which multimedia (re)presentations are able to create texts which signify and convey multiple meanings and perspectives.

New Ways of Seeking: The way in which the use of arts-based genres raise new research issues to be addressed and resolved.

Particularity and Dimension: The way in which arts-based genres enable the reader/viewer to obtain a sense of authenticity of the social world (re)presented.

Performance Art: A theatrical live performance that utilizes performer(s)/artist(s) as well as imagery, film, movement, music, and poetry for creative expression.

Productive Ambiguity: The way in which arts-based genres enable research data to be presented in an evocative manner that propagates in the reader/viewer a discernment of multiple meanings and engagement with the complexity of the social world (re)presented.

Sense of Empathy: The way in which arts-based genres enable the reader/viewer to have access and understanding to the lives of others and the situations they face.

Chapter III
Transformations of the Language Laboratory

Mads Bo-Kristensen
Resource Centre for Integration–Vejle, Denmark

Bente Meyer
School of Education, Univeristy of Aarhus, Denmark

ABSTRACT

This chapter focuses on the relationship between remediation and educational innovation in information and communications technology (ICT) intensive learning environments, as exemplified by the language laboratory (language lab) and its digital descendants. Historically, the language laboratory has been affected by a number of technological and instructional changes, transforming the deadend of behavioural methodology into the current sociocollaborative paradigms of language learning. The language laboratory has thus been transformed into a learning environment that incorporates and refers to several generations of technology-based language learning. The principles of computer-assisted language learning (CALL) will serve as this chapter's theoretical framework. It will also deal with the issues of repurposing and remediation raised by Bolter and Grusin (1999). Remediation is defined as a process of transformation wherein older media are represented and refashioned in new media contexts. It will also be argued that there is a dialogical relationship between the processes of remediation inherent in the genealogy of the language laboratory and the processes of educational innovation. In addition to this, the chapter will suggest ways of rethinking and reforming the language laboratory through mobile-assisted language learning (MALL).

INTRODUCTION

The debate on the educational uses of technology has taken a number of turns, including the well-known argument that technology will eventually force practitioners to reform educational practices (Lemke, 1998; Warschauer, 1999). While this argument may still be essential in the manner in which educators see the role of technology in education, it may also be increasingly imperative to discuss the way they conceptualise technology and learning, and how these conceptualisations may affect the way technologies are integrated in education. Warschauer (2003, p. 205) argues that technology is embedded socially, including the workings of organizations, institutions, and society at large. Similarly, Bolter and Grusin (1999, p. 19) claim that new media "are not external agents that come to disrupt an unsuspecting culture. They emerge from within cultural contexts and refashion other media, which are embedded in the same or similar context. The difficulty of integrating technologies in social and institutional contexts may precisely reside in the complexity of these social and cultural relationships, including those that affect education.

This chapter will discuss how institutional conceptualisations of language teaching and learning, as exemplified through the multimedia language laboratory, interact with technological change. The language laboratory is an example of how language teaching and technologies are embedded in institutional settings, as these are technology-rich environments that have had a central role in language instruction since the 1950s. Over the years, language instruction has significantly benefited and continues to do so from technologies because they either give access to authentic communication or provide "comprehensible input." The language laboratory is embedded in the viewpoints that technology supports and interacts with language teaching and learning, the language laboratory being a learning environment that incorporates several generations of technology-based language learning, both analogue and digital.

In this chapter, the theory of remediation will be used for the purpose of tracing media implementations in analogue, digital, and Internet-based language laboratories. Bolter and Grusin (1999) have developed a general theory on how older media are represented and refashioned in digital media on the basis of what they call a *genealogy* (Foucault, 1977). This genealogy, rather than a history of mediation, is "an examination of descent [that] … permits the discovery under the unique aspect of a trait or a concept, of the myriad events through which—thanks to which, against which—they were formed" (p. 314). From the perspective of education, the process of remediation similarly involves a process of redidactisation, a process defined by Sørensen, Hubert, Risgaard, and Kirkeby (2004, p. 59, our translation):

Redidactisation can be understood as the process through which traditional ways of teaching and learning are integrated into new media and embrace the potentials of these media. In this process traditional ways of teaching and learning are transformed and changed in their representational forms.

In this chapter, we argue that the processes of remediation inherent in the genealogy of the language laboratory involve processes of redidactisation, that is, of educational change in media contexts. The dialectics of this interaction will determine how technology can reform traditional ways of teaching and learning, and how teaching and learning a language can incorporate and embrace the potentials of the media.

The chapter sets out by outlining the history of the language lab, focusing on the relationship between technology and theories of language acquisition. The concepts of *remediation, immediacy,* and *hypermediacy* are then introduced to establish a connection between the changing uses and representations of technology within the language lab's conceptual matrix. The language lab and its educational uses will then be discussed through an empirical example based on the use of language labs in a college of military education. Finally, the future of the language lab will be outlined, and recommendations will be forwarded for rethinking and reforming the lab through mobile learning.

TRANSFORMATIONS OF THE LANGUAGE LABORATORY

The language lab has had a unique—though often problematic—position in the history of mediated language education. It was originally invented in the 1950s to suit the growing needs of the language teaching profession in the early postwar period. Underwood (1984, p. 34) even referred to the situation as a crisis. The response to these needs was a technological venture characterised by large-scale investments in language laboratories as "schools everywhere rushed to buy the new machines, and a lot of money (including federal grants) was spent."

Unfortunately, it was quickly realized that the language laboratory was unable to live up to expectations: On the one hand, the pedagogical uses of the lab were generally mandated by administrators with no knowledge of language learning (Otto, 1991; Underwood, 1984). On the other hand, the most dominant method used then was the audiolingual method, which was deeply embedded in the learning theories of the postwar era. Although founded on the principle of providing classroom teaching with (semi)authentic audio material, this method was generally based on behavioural approaches popular at the time, that is, on repetitive and decontextualized drills that were supposed to enable students to internalize pattern structures and respond automatically. "Language learning during the 1950s and 1960s is frequently remembered in grim scenarios of students herded into rooms, deposited into impersonal niches and turned into parrots, yawning or doodling in boredom, ultimately incapable of producing spontaneous utterances," says Otto (1991, p. 14).

As Hayes (1968, p. 1) has suggested, the language laboratory is essentially "a classroom or other area containing electronic and mechanical equipment designed and arranged to make foreign language learning more effective than is usually possible without it." However, the

contextualisations of this matrix are historically determined because methodologies and technological innovations have shaped the configuration of the language lab, as well as its role and uses in language education.

The evolution of the language laboratory is dependent on a number of changes in the genealogy of *computer-assisted language learning* that Warschauer and Healey (1998, p. 57) have classified into phases of *behaviouristic CALL*, *communicative CALL,* and *integrative CALL*. The transformation of these phases of CALL may be described as such. The role of technology in language learning has moved away from an association with drills, grammatical explanations, and translation tests (*behaviouristic CALL*) into more communicative-based contexts (*communicative CALL*) where task-based, project-based, and content-based approaches are integrated with technologies (*integrative CALL*). Thus, this process has made language teaching considerably more complex, but also "more exciting" according to Kern and Warshauer (2000, p. 1).

In the original language laboratory (behaviouristic CALL), the audio material was presented to students through heavy audio tape machines, often placed in booths separated by glass walls. In recent times associated with communicative and integrative CALL, the language laboratory has been renamed and reinvented to suit the acquisition and learning theories of the late 20th century. The language laboratory of the 1990s and 2000s has transformed into a *multimedia centre, language media centre,* or *language resource centre* (Liddell & Garrett, 2004; Pérez-Paredes, 2002; Scinicariello, 1997). In this connection, the affiliations with the original language laboratory may no longer be obvious, as the late multimedia centres seem to be safely removed from the dread and "deadend" of behavioural methodology.

In spite of the modernisations of the lab and its supposed transcendence of methodological fallacies, however, the struggle over the role and conceptualisation of the language laboratory has

29

not yet ended. To a certain extent, the language laboratory may overcome the "post-Sputnik era" (Otto, 1991, p. 14) of the 1950s and 1960s, but the technologies of these decades and the instructional practices associated with them may well have survived into the multimedia labs of the 1990s and 2000s. This may be because systemic and mechanical understandings of technology persist in modern conceptualisations of digital tools for education and that these are generally co-constituted with the concept of language as a system of decontextualised structures to be learned in isolated units. Moreover, the lab's original technology (i.e., tape recorders, which are still metaphorically present in digital labs through remediation), enhances the conceptualisation of language learning as a process of one-way communication that relies on repetition and behavioural adaptation. While language laboratories may no longer be exclusively audio-based, they may, however, be audio conceptualised, in the sense that audio-based labs may be understood as a matrix of the language lab itself, including its digitalised versions.

If the language laboratory can be said to incorporate and refer to earlier (analogue) generations of language laboratories in a regressive rather than a progressive sense, it may also be claimed to be ideally suited to the digital era of the multimedia lab. Thus, the metaphor of the lab generally fits the era of constructivism and learner-based approaches, as the laboratory is etymologically associated with the experiential processes of learning and producing knowledge. In addition to this, the reality of the multimedia laboratory as a heterogeneous space of hypermedial presence "multiplies the signs of mediation and in this way tries to reproduce the rich *sensorum* of human experience" (Bolter & Grusin, 1999, p. 34). In this sense, the potentials of the language lab are indeed a far cry from the behavioural drills of the postwar era, which is why Pérez-Paredes (2002, p. 73) says:

We are definitely tempted to state that existing language laboratories have adapted the impact of recent communicative based language teaching and the newest socio collaborative paradigms of language teaching, readjusting the gaze and scope of the 'old lab' to a more diverse, richer learning environment which equally preserves and incorporates teaching practices.

The realities of this claim will be discussed in the following empirical examples that take their starting point in the role of language laboratories in military settings. According to Pérez-Paredes (2002. p. 64), the military has had a significant role in the history of the language lab (as in the history of technological evolution as such), as "it was prestigious for an educational institution to have a language laboratory, not only because technology was implied, but, more importantly, because the military used it and promoted it, both intensively and extensively."

IMMEDIACY AND REMEDIATION IN LANGUAGE TEACHING

If language laboratories are generally steeped in and deeply affected by the genealogy of the media laboratory in language learning, the media and learning practices associated with the former generations of labs are both transferred and transformed into newer generations through the process of remediation. Bolter and Grusin define *remediation* based on Marshall McLuhan's popular posit that "Whenever a new medium comes in, it takes its initial content from the old" (1964, p. 16). Remediation is therefore a refashioning of old media in new media forms, to erase the traces of mediation itself to reach the representational transparency of what Bolter and Grusin (1999, p. 24) term *immediacy,* which is often associated with "the need to deny the mediated character of digital technology altogether"; that is, it is a process of immersion wherein the opacity of mediation is temporarily overcome. In contrast, hypermediacy relies on the act of making representations visible by multiplying the signs of mediation, for instance, in the heterogeneous, windowed visual style of Web pages. Whereas *hypermediacy* may be dialectically associated with immediacy, or even act as its opposite number, immediacy and the desire for the real dominate in media contexts as—according to Bolter and Grusin (1999, p. 5)— "our culture wants...to erase its media in the very act of multiplying them." The significance of this process for CALL is underscored by Bax (2003, p. 23) who claims that CALL's goal is "normalisation," that is, "the stage when the technology becomes invisible, embedded in everyday practice and hence *normalised*."

Language labs are rich and complex sites for the processes of remediation: They are metaphorically and conceptually dependent on the representations and *content* of older media. As stated earlier, the metaphorical presence of tape recorders and audio materials are continually present in language labs, although these may have transformed into multimedia language labs in the digital era of the 1990s and 2000s. Similarly, video material is generally refashioned in digital labs as authentic video documents are used to enhance instruction and learning. These processes of remediation may be described as representations without irony in the sense that the older media are seemingly "poured into" the new one without the conceptual distance of one media representation to the other (Bolter & Grusin, 1999, p. 45). Therefore, if multimedia laboratories are complex sites for the processes of remediation, then they are also spaces in which struggles over the (re)conceptualisation and practical implementation of language teaching and learning take place. Remediation thus enters into a dialectical relationship with redidactisation.

THE GENEOLOGY OF THE LANGUAGE LAB

From 2005 to 2007, the Danish University of Education implemented a project at the Royal Danish Defence College (RDDC) in Copenhagen, which involved the observation and study of several digital language laboratories over a two-year period. The purpose was to assess how digital implementations of the language lab enhance and qualify language-learning vis-à-vis the educational goals of the Royal Danish Defence College. RDDC's purpose is primarily to train and educate language officers for interpretation assignments in conflict zones. The languages currently being taught are chiefly Arabic and Russian.

Language labs have been intrinsic to language teaching at RDDC since 1957, when the education in Russian for language officers was initiated. The laboratories were originally furnished with heavy tape recorders of the Tandberg type, which were later replaced in the late 1970s by lighter versions of tape recorders. In the 1980s, video machines were added to accommodate authentic video materials. In the 1990s, the labs were digitalised to facilitate usage and easy access to authentic learning material.

The lab has had a number of roles in language education at RDDC, as historical circumstances have affected the physical setup and organisation of the lab itself. Whereas both Arabic and Russian language education have generally appropriated—and to some extent integrated the approaches of modern language teaching (i.e., communicative approaches and the provision of comprehensible input)—language education at RDDC, in general, still relies on audio-lingual methodology, behavioural drills, and teacher-defined tasks. These approaches are partly justified by the fact that languages must be learned within a short timeframe (less than two years) and that almost 50 years of experience of RDDC with language labs have proved that drills and audio-based methodology work well in a language course of this kind. Warschauer and Healey (1998, p. 59) defend this view by arguing: "Drills do have a place in language learning, particularly in the first stages of vocabulary acquisition where giving the same information in multiple modes, such as visual plus aural plus textual, enhances recognition and recall."

The methodologies of the RDDC are closely associated with the processes of remediation and redidactisation based on earlier versions of the language lab as well as the representation of media forms found in the Sanako software that is used. In describing the process of learning to access and use the latest (digital) generation of the language lab, a teacher said that:

Moving from the tape recorder to a digital language lab is not necessarily a big step in the sense that one must only do something different in a technical sense, because one can do the same exercises just transferred to electronic material. (Authors' translation)

Similarly, another teacher suggested that:

The whole digital era has been one sweeping movement…without noticing it you update yourself. So I found it was quite unproblematic as home pages and mailboxes have a sort of common logic. I also think that the modern language laboratory is based on a template, you know, it's user-friendly, it draws on logic that people already have because they are used to the Internet, because they are used to using e-mail. (Authors' translation)

Finally, a student said: "Getting to know that programme (i.e., the Sanako software) is relatively easy. After a couple of weeks, we felt that we had been doing it all the time. It is a very simple technology." This comment was prompted by a direct reference to the interface of the software which shows the front of a tape recorder, including the well-known buttons "play," "rewind," and so on.

These statements suggest that, in general, the digital language lab is not seen as a new and independent configuration of the language resource centre type, but that the digital language lab is deeply immersed in the earlier generations of the language lab, and that these generations indeed belong to the same matrix or template. The language lab is thus conceptualised, as it was originally understood, that is, as a technology-rich environment suited for audio language learning through tape recorders. The significance of this legacy, and the legacies of the digital age (e.g., e-mail and the Internet) provide the users with a technology that is easily accessible, wherein earlier media forms ensure that tools are easily recognised and learned. Remediation is central to these processes of re-appropriation and repurposing, and re-didactisation is intrinsically connected to the processes of remediation.

Whereas behavioural and audio-lingual methodology are somehow consolidated by the processes of remediation, these processes are also occasionally challenged by the students at RDDC, who use the Internet to develop and support translation tasks through Web-based resources such as Google, Wikipedia, and online translation sites. In this sense, the remediation of the analogue lab co-exists with its newer versions, in this case, the virtual language lab, opening new potential for language learning in a multimedia learning context. The most recent transformations of the language lab and their potential for language learning will be discussed in the following.

THE VIRTUAL LANGUAGE LAB

We have argued that the digital language lab is metaphorically dependent on earlier (analogue) versions of the lab, and that that the processes of remediation and reappropriation may help consolidate the practices of audio-lingual and behavioural methodology. In the late 1990s, yet another version of the language lab appeared—the virtual language lab. The Internet technology has generally made it possible for significant transformations of the language lab towards educational innovation in the fields of foreign and second language education (Bo-Kristensen, 2004; White, 2006).

Just as the language lab's digital media replace the analogue media, there is a tendency to replace the classroom of the digital lab with the spatial and temporal flexibility of the Internet. This process of remediation is nourished by the idea of a break with the physical classroom and the transferral of learning to informal environments. In this context, *immediacy* is achieved through a greater flexibility in time and place. In this setting, the user determines for himself/herself how and where the use of the language lab will take place. With a computer, Internet access, and a headset with a microphone, the user may work at home, at an open learning centre, at a library, or at the workplace. Today, more and more virtual language labs are gradually surfacing, for example, http://www.esl-lab.com and http://babel.uoregon.edu/YLC-AV.

In the virtual language lab, it seems important to get much closer to the student's needs and behaviours than was possible in the digital language lab. The pedagogy of such virtual labs takes into consideration that the student is not always in a formal learning setup. He or she may need to engage in learning activities in less formal places. One may thus conjecture that an educational scenario that meets such needs comes close to total immediacy (Bolter & Grusin, 1999).

In a manner of speaking, this scenario removes the border between the formal educational settings and everyday contexts. The media become transparent through the integration of these two spaces. Finally, the Internet has made it possible to get immediate access to pictures, sound, and text associated with the target language. In a split second, one can access home pages from the coun-

try in which the foreign language is spoken. The amazing film and radio archives of the BBC and the materials produced by its educational services unit are good examples of such Web sites.

THE MOBILE LANGUAGE LAB

Today's mobile technology is so well developed that it is possible to create a so-called mobile language lab (Rybner & Bo-Kristensen, 2006). This section will discuss the potential of the mobile phone and its technology to improving the qualification of the audio pedagogy, by citing an existing mobile language lab as example. The Resource Centre for Integration in Denmark (www.vifin.dk) has developed a mobile language lab where adults are able to profit from connections between the Internet and the mobile phone, independent of time and place. The lab targets adults who are learning Danish as a second language. Apart from profiting from the technology's potential for increasing students' linguistic consciousness, a major aim of the lab is to offer students new ways of acquiring Danish through ordinary daily and workplace conversations. The lab consists of videos of exemplary conversations and a number of exercises.

The mobile language lab enables students to download and upload video and sound clips, as well as work on clips and exercises. Here, the pedagogy is based on the ethnographic method, focusing on the connection between the classroom, daily and workplace settings (Gordon, 2002). Moreover, the pedagogy uses the Internet integrated mobile phone's possibilities of recording, processing, and sharing audio and video material. As with the virtual lab, the mobile language lab is based on modern listening pedagogy. The mobile lab also seeks to develop existing concepts of this pedagogy. At the core of this kind of pedagogy lies the relevance of the listening material and the authenticity of the listening material (Mendelsohn, 1998).

The mobile language lab enables the teacher to offer students interaction with relevant and authentic language at times and places that fit into their daily lives. In the digital and virtual language labs, it was still the teacher who decided on the relevance and authenticity of the material; with the mobile language lab, it is now the student who, to a much higher degree, defines relevance and authenticity. The mobile recording and playing devices redefines these two concepts.

As opposed to the digital lab, the virtual lab explicitly supports the concept that it is the teacher who produces his/her own materials and exercises. In this manner, the teacher had moved from being a *user* of listening material, to being the *producer* of such materials. In this sense, it was possible to plan teaching that corresponded to the needs of the class and the individual students. The mobile devices take this a step further and turn the student into a producer of his or her own learning materials. The student can audio- or video-record conversations from an everyday context outside of the formal educational setting, and upload them to the virtual environment where they can be treated linguistically, discursively, pragmatically, socioculturally, and strategically. Simply put, it is the student, who, as a producer, decides on what is relevant for the learning process. Production may be done through consulting the teacher or fellow students who are natural collaborators in the student's learning process. Recorded conversations and exercises may be shared between students by way of, for example, the mobile phone's Bluetooth or as files sent or uploaded to the class' online language lab.

Authenticity also acquires a new meaning in the mobile language lab. Authenticity is not a prefabricated description or reproduction of the reality of others. The student documents his or her own reality through the mobile phone. The relevance and authenticity of the listening material acquires new meanings as a result of the technology's potentials. The virtual lab represented a remediation of the digital language laboratory, where technology served to move parts of the learning outside the classroom. The latest generation of the lab—the mobile lab—remediates the Internet-based lab in the sense that listening material now acquires an even greater relevance and authenticity.

CONCLUSION

This chapter presents the relationship between remediation and educational innovation in analogue, digital, and Internet-based language labs. The language lab's transformations as a conceptual matrix in language education provides a basis for a genealogical view on how approaches to language learning and technology have interacted in a number of settings, and how the dialectical relationships between generations of laboratories are initiated through remediation. From a genealogical perspective, the apparently successive implementations and developments of the language lab are in reality, a site of struggle, where generations of labs not only descend from each other (or break with each other) but where they exist simultaneously within a conceptual matrix that defines the use and implementation of technology in language education. The relevance and aim of these uses of technology in language education is often a desire for immediacy that will enable users to transcend the spatial and linguistic confinements of the classroom.

From a genealogical perspective, the mobile language lab is the latest remediation of the traditional language lab and represents a significant re-didactisation of the generations of the lab that succeeded the behaviouristic conceptualisation of the analogue lab. Technological development in this context seems to be moving faster than the pedagogical conceptualisations associated with its potential. This is apparent in the transformation of the virtual to the mobile lab. Even before the virtual lab has been implemented pedagogically and practically, new significant options emerge in the form of the mobile language lab. Even before the latest lab has showed its pedagogical potential, yet another lab scenario is emerging in the form of pervasive computing and learning.

Finally, we provide a word of wisdom about the future of the language lab. Technologically speaking, it is a future that is already possible. Pervasive computing has made the interaction between the mobile phone and the radio frequency identification (RFID) tags a possible new step for the language lab. With a reader, a mobile telephone or a personal digital assistant (PDA) can read RFID-tagged information (text, sound, image). These tags can be placed in relation to different artefacts in learning environments and will allow the learner to interact with these artefacts through the mobile unit. One scenario is the home of the learner, where he or she places tags on artefacts that are relevant for vocabulary training, pronunciation, and communicative content. A pervasive or intelligent language lab of this kind can be established in both very private contexts and in public spaces (at work, at the train station, in the supermarket, library, cafes, etc.). In these kinds of scenarios, the concepts of relevance and authenticity as well as immediacy and hypermediacy seem to give new and promising significance to the language lab.

REFERENCES

Bax, S. (2003). CALL: Past, present and future. *System, 31*. Elsevier Science Ltd.

Bo-Kristensen, M. (2004). *Multimediedidaktik i dansk som andetsprog for voksne: Bidrag til andetsprogsdidaktisk forankring af undervisningens multimediedidaktik*. Doctoral dissertation, Danish Educaitional University, Copenhagen.

Bolter, J., & Grusin, R. (1999). *Remediation: Understanding new media*. The MIT Press. Dunkel, P. (Ed.). (1991). *Computer-assisted language learning and testing: Research issues and practice*. Newbury House.

Foucault, M. (1977). Nietzsche, genealogy, history. In D. F. Bouchard (Ed.), *Language, counter-memory, practice: Selected essays and interviews*. Cornell University Press.

Gordon, J. (2002). *Beyond the classroom walls: Ethnographic inquiry as pedagogy*. Routledge.

Hayes, A. S. (1968). *Language laboratory facilities*. Oxford University Press.

Krashen, S. D. (2003). *Explorations in language acquisition and use: The Taipei lectures*. Heinemann.

Lemke, J. L. (1998). Metamedia literacy: Transforming meanings and media. In D. Reinking et al. (Eds.), *Handbook of literacy and technology: Transformations in a post-typographic world*. Lawrence Erlbaum Associates Publishers.

Liddell, P., & Garrett, N. (2004). The new language centers and the role of technology: New mandates, new horizons. In S. Fotos & C. M. Browne (Eds.), *New perspectives on CALL for second language classrooms*. Lawrence Erlbaum Associates.

McLuhan, M. (1964). *Understanding media: The extensions of man*. New American Library.

Mendelsohn, D. J. (1998). Teaching listening. *Annual Review of Applied Linguistics, 18*, 81-101.

Otto, S. E. K. (1991). The language laboratory in the computer age. In *Modern technology in foreign language education: Applications and projects*. National Textbook Company.

Pérez-Paredes, P. (2002). From rooms to environments: Techno-short-sightedness and language laboratories. *International Journal of English Studies, 2*(1).

Rybner, L., & Bo-Kristensen, M. (2006). Dansk på mobilen, *Sprogforum*, nr. 38. Kbh: The Danish University of Education (pp. 50-58).

Scinicariello, S. G. (1997). Uniting teachers, learners, and machines: Language laboratories and other choices. In M. D. Bush & R. M. Terry (Eds.), *Technology-enhanced language learning.* National Textbook Company.

Sørensen, B., Hubert, B., Risgaard, J., & Kirkeby, G. (2004). *Virtuel skole.* Danmarks Pædagogiske Universitets forlag. Retrieved March 15, 2008, from http://www.dpu.dk/eve-rest/tmp/040810142620/ITMF153.pdf

Underwood, J. H. (1984). The language lab analogy: Uses and misuses of technology. In Underwood (Ed.), *Linguistics, computers, and the language teacher: A communicative approach.* Newbury House Publishers.

White, C. (2006). Distance learning of foreign languages. *Language Teaching, 39,* 247-264. Cambridge University Press.

Warschauer, M. (1999). *Electronic literacies: Language, culture, and power in online education.* Lawrence Erlbaum Associates.

Warschauer, M. (2003). Technology and social inclusion: Rethinking the digital divide. The MIT Press.

Warschauer, M., & Healey, D. (1998). Computers and language learning: An overview. *Language Teaching, 31.* Cambridge University Press.

Warschauer, M., & Kern, R. (2000). *Network-based language teaching: Concepts and practice.* Cambridge University Press.

KEY TERMS

Authenticity: Authenticity is central to modern language learning theory. Authentic learning content reflects the real-life situations in which the language student is going to use and face the foreign or second language.

Behavioristic Approach: Learning approach whereby language, for example, is learned through trial-and-error leaving no room for reflection.

Communicative Approach: Learning approach whereby language, for example, is learned through communicative content and activities.

Hypermediacy: Hypermediacy relies on the act of making representations visible by multiplying the signs of mediation, for instance, in the heterogeneous, windowed visual style of Web pages.

Integrative Approach: Learning approach whereby, for example, is learned through task-based, project-based, and content-based activities.

Redidacitisation: Redidactisation can be understood as the process through which traditional ways of teaching and learning are integrated into new media and embrace the potentials of these media.

Remediation: Remediation is defined as a process of transformation wherein older media are represented and refashioned in new media contexts.

Chapter IV
A Topic–Case Driven Methodology for Web Course Design

Leena Hiltunen
University of Jyväskylä, Finland

Tommi Kärkkäinen
University of Jyväskylä, Finland

ABSTRACT

A topic-case driven methodology for a Web course design and realization process is based on software engineering metaphors for capturing the necessary steps in creating Web courses by means of a content-based development method. The methodology combines instructional issues to design phases that guide teachers and instructors to design and implement online courses. The methodology has been used by students of teacher education in computer science, as well as professional university educators from different educational fields. The results from these experiences have been reported as case studies. In this chapter, the methodology is introduced with the summarized results from three case studies.

INTRODUCTION

Even today, Web courses are often based on the idea of exporting traditional written materials to the Web without the proper planning and pedagogical design. However, we need more than just a translation of books and lectures into an electronic format along with Web delivery. We need online courses that teach and present information adequately. There should be no more page-turning or scroll-down architectures where the learner just presses the button for the next page or scrolls down the screen. Moreover, students need to be more active while they learn. By not being passive TV-viewers, the students will learn by doing, by accomplishing tasks, not by being told (for example, Bork 1986; Schank, 1998). As Twigg (2001, p. 7) points out, "we need to be more thoughtful about course design so that we include structures and activities that work well with diverse types of students."

Many online communications take place in written format without students seeing or hearing their learning mates. New knowledge is being built through communication with other learners and teachers or instructors. Learning is no longer confined to institutions such as schools, colleges, and universities. Technology provides new possibilities: easy access to information and opportunities for lifelong learning—also online. To support lifelong learning, we need more quality in online learning context; instead of using new technology to do the same old things differently, we should focus on doing new things in new ways (for example, McDonald, 2002). In many cases, while realizing a Web course, testing and evaluation are just forgotten and educators are satisfied with having something up and running. Such simplistic approaches do not support students in their individual learning styles which lead them to poor learning experiences and an unwillingness to take part in the next Web course.

The creation of digital contents is regarded as the next wave in the development of the information society (see Council of European Union, 2000, 2005; Finnish Ministry of Education, 2006). At the core of content production and independent of the purpose of the material to be produced, one should employ a content creation and development process, which supports structural and incremental development and thus also reusability of the resulting materials as suitable learning objects.

The content of a Web-based course is similar to the functionality of a computer program: they are both drivers for further development, presenting functionality and content to all users and students

to enhance usage and learning. In software engineering, Humphrey (1998) emphasizes effective planning and quality management. Both of these are also useful principles in Web course design. Thus, Web course design requires good planning and documentation as well as some development process to follow (McNaught, 2002). However, all of the existing methodologies fail to describe a development process that allows well-managed integration and incorporation of structural and multigranular digital material with pedagogical knowledge as well as, for example, communication and cognitive tools.

The key questions for Web course design is how to design learning material that benefits from using the Web and how and when to integrate such a (Web-) pedagogy into training that enhances learning. Although these are important steps towards a structured method in which to develop Web courses, we feel that these two central aspects are not clearly captured in the existing approaches. White (2000), Montilva (2000), Baloian, Fuller, and Ochoa (2001), and Anglada (2002) seem to apply mainly an organization-centric approach; that is, time and schedule drive the development of content that is immediately organized, for example, in weekly units. Here there is very little learning-centric focus on what to learn and how to learn the contents. In some models, a pedagogical design has been included, but the whole content of the Web course is supposed to fit under the same pedagogical solution. Our contribution to this quality problem in e-learning is a topic-case driven approach for Web course design. The approach utilizes metaphors from software engineering, following the unified process in Jacobson, Booch, and Rumbaugh (1999) to describe a unified way to design and realize Web courses, but those are blended together with educational issues. This approach allows incremental and iterative development of the Web course. Moreover, it can be utilized as a content development mini-project within other similar methods.

BACKGROUND

Before teachers-instructors can design usable learning environments (Horila, Nokelainen, Syvänen, & Överlund, 2002), they have to understand the basic rules of teaching and learning. Most learners and educators have a long educational history in the classroom environment and therefore it might be hard to move into the virtual learning environment. New requirements for learners have been set (Mäki-Komsi, 1999; Palloff & Pratt, 1999; Yang & Cornelious, 2005), and the recognition of individual learning styles becomes even more essential. Learners should have more internal motivation, and they need to be proactive, independent, creative, and reflective (Mäki-Komsi, 1999; Canada, 2000). Teachers are no longer physically present during the process, and most of the interaction happens through written text without people seeing, hearing, or touching those with whom they are communicating.

The role of the teacher transforms when the responsibility for learning transfers from teacher to student. Learning becomes more learner-centered, but the role of the teacher as an instructor is still essential (Yang & Cornelious, 2005). New technology opens new kinds of possibilities to utilize different educational methods. Assessment of the learning outcome is also changing; traditional final exams are much harder to execute online, so we need new, more authentic assessment methods.

These issues are essential, especially in pedagogical design. This is one of the main differences in this proposed methodology compared to other existing ones. As a baseline, some of the existing design processes and models which have been used so far in Web course design are briefly reviewed in the next subsections.

The Unified Process

Building a Web course is similar to the design and implementation of a software application. Hence, the terms related to software processes that form the basis of software development, such as a *concept phase* (feasibility study), *analysis, architecture, design and implementation, testing, iterative,* and *incremental* can also serve as a well-established conceptual framework for Web course design. This has also been the starting point of the approaches that will be reviewed in this chapter. Due to the fact that the initial stages of the presented Web course development method mimic the unified process (UP), we briefly review this approach with quotations based on Jacobson et al. (1999). The *unified software development process* is, like all other process models, a development process where a set of activities are described to transform the user's requirements into a software system. The unified process is use-case driven, architecture-centric, iterative, and incremental. The goal of the process is, according to Jacobson et al. (1999, p. 33), "to guide developers in efficiently implementing and deploying systems that meet customers' needs." We do so by following some good pieces of advice in Jacobsen et al. (1999, p. 4): first we look at user requirements, then start a software development process, and finally, design a software system.

Software systems should be designed to serve their users, so we must know what the prospective users want and need. The user could be a human or another system that interacts with our (the main) system. In response to the user's actions, the system performs a sequence of actions that leads to a response. Jacobson et al. (1999, p. 7) describes this sort of interaction as a *use-case,* "a piece of functionality that gives a user a result of the value." Moreover, "all the use-cases together make up the use-case model which describes the complete functionality of the system" by capturing all functional requirements.

The *use-case model* answers the question: What is the system supposed to do? We should think about the value of the functions to users, and not just speculate as to what functions might be desirable. With use-cases, we can find the true requirements and represent them in a suitable way for users, customers, and developers. Use-cases are not just tools to capture all the requirements of a system. They also drive its design, implementation, and test when developers create design and implementation models that realize the use-cases.

The unified process is use-case driven, but the system architecture (i.e., general structure of software) establishes the skeleton for technical design. The architecture is illustrated using different views of the system being built; it is a view of the whole design with the important characteristics made more visible by leaving details aside. This "process helps the architect to focus on the right goals, such as understandability, resilience to future changes, and reuse" (Jacobson et al., 1999, p. 6). While using the unified process model in the software development project, individuals may play different roles defined as workers. One can perform more than one role, for example, project manager, system analyst, use-case specifier, user-interface designer, architect, use-case engineer, component engineer, system integrator, test engineer, integration tester, or system tester (Jacobson et al., 1999; Scott, 2002).

According to Jacobson et al. (1999, p. 7):

In every iteration, the developers identify and specify the relevant use-cases; create a design of the chosen architecture as a guide, implement the design in components, and verify that the components satisfy the use-cases. If an iteration meets its goals...developers proceed with the next iteration. When an iteration does not meet its goals, the developers must revisit their previous decisions and try a new approach.

The ADDIE Model

The *ADDIE model*, which stands for analysis, design, development, implementation, and evaluation, represents one of the basic models of instructional design that can be used to develop Web courses (Anglada, 2002; Peterson, 2003). The ADDIE model is an iterative *instructional design process* where the results of the formative evaluation of each phase may lead the instructional designer back to any previous phase.

The process starts with an *analysis* phase where one should first define the learning goals (or needs) and objectives for the course. Second, one should consider the age of the learners, cultural backgrounds, past experiences, interests, and educational levels to understand learners and their needs. Third, the timeline and resources for the development project have to be settled. Finally, one should also determine the overall content and evaluation strategies for the course during this first phase.

The second phase, *design*, is concerned with the actual content. During this phase, one should design the user interface, determine user objectives, develop content outline, storyboard the course, make media selections, and produce any materials required for instruction on the subject matter. In some cases, it is a good idea to create a prototype for quick testing. By evaluating the prototype, designers will get precious information for further development of the course.

The actual creation of the Web course takes place in the third phase called the *development* phase. During this phase, one should construct and develop the content, script, and program functional elements, create graphics and animation sequences, and write supplement learning guides. The fourth phase is the *implementation* phase. The purpose of this phase is the effective and efficient delivery of instruction—putting the plan into action. The implementation requires identification of the elements of the learning environment and development of teaching strategies.

Implementation should be based on pedagogical theory that guides the delivery of the material—the ones used in the development of the content. The implementation phase also includes course orientation, syllabus adjustment, and scheduling of synchronous elements.

Evaluation of the experience is the last phase of the ADDIE model. It provides information that should be used during the later iterations. Evaluation can be both formative and summative. Formative evaluation impacts the process as it is happening, while the summative evaluation is being done at the completion of the process. Both forms of evaluation are helpful in this model.

Web Course Development Understood as a Process

White (2000) describes the Web course development process used at the University of Houston Clear Lake (UHCL) for creating selected courses in software engineering. The process is divided into three concurrent subprocesses: *standards and policy creation, course material creation,* and *Web-site/Web-page creation*. These subprocesses can be treated separately, but this requires an evolutionary style of development. In each subprocess, key process players and major results/documents that must be produced have been introduced. White's model reminds one of *a modified waterfall model* for software development (for example, McConnell, 1996).

White (2000) uses software engineering metaphors when she describes the major activities of the Web course development process. During some stages (Figure 1), there is more than one concurrent activity occurring during the same stage. Also, exact documentation during all stages is applied according to the general practices in software engineering processes. Next the actual activities within the development steps are briefly described. During the first stage, all risks and benefits that the online course might produce are analyzed. Next, all the needed resources (hardware, software, and

people support) are considered, once the courses to be provided are selected. In the second stage, courses are assigned content experts to develop the course materials and to form the development teams. A schedule for development of the courses is also planned. The third stage is the actual design phase and includes the creation of the course syllabus, course policy, course objectives, and content design. Content design is restricted to weekly unit overviews (topic of the week, objectives, and major assessments). The Web developer designs the top-level Web structure of the course based on design documents produced by the content expert and instructional designer. This structure contains material and communication mechanisms like chat rooms and bulletin boards as part of the initial Web-site design. During the

Figure 1. Major activities of the Web course development process by White (2000) (©2007, Leena Hiltunen. Used with permission)

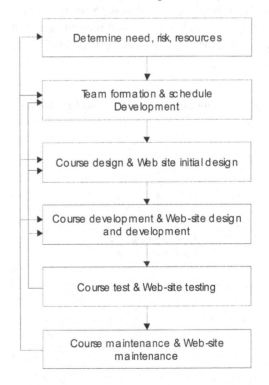

fourth stage, the actual course content is created and finalized. Fifth, a testing stage follows after the course has been fully developed and becomes available online.

A Software Engineering Approach

Montilva (2000, p. 1) describes "a method that applies object-oriented software engineering to the process of developing Web-based courses." Moreover, Montilva (2000) describes the phases, steps, activities, and techniques as follows: *analyze* and specify the technical and instructional requirements of a course; *design* the structure, interface, content, and interaction of the course; *produce* the content, user interface, and media required by the course; and *deliver* the Web-based course to its users. Montilva's phase method in Figure 2 has been employed to develop Web-based study guides for distance education. The method begins with an analysis of the Web course domain and iterates over the entire development cycle ending with its delivery. The evaluation phase including verification and validation plays a central role. This means that the evaluation of results begins in the first phase, instead of being

executed at the end. This model resembles *the star model* in Preece, Rogers, Sharp, Benyon, Holland, and Carey (1994) for human-centered software development.

According to Montilva (2000), one of the most important features of the method is its emphasis on the quality of the product. The method is specific to Web study guides, and it covers the whole life cycle. Besides, verification and validation processes are used as a continuous activity that has to be performed through all phases of the method.

COMPONENT-BASED COURSEWARE DEVELOPMENT

Baloian et al. (2001) presented a model of courseware development which is based upon a *component-based development model* (for example, Sommerville, 2004) for software. In this model, courseware learning goals are managed as if they were user requirements. The model itself is called *component-based courseware development*. The model uses both incremental and iterative development for building courseware. It is based on three

Figure 2. The phases of the method by Montilva (1998) (©2007, Leena Hiltunen. Used with permission)

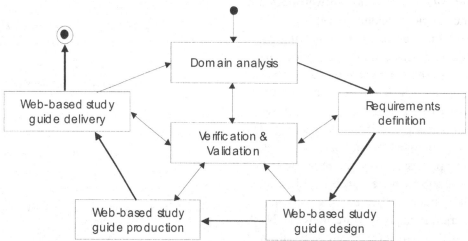

main ingredients: an evolutionary methodology, a visual modeling language, and a framework of software components. Methodology guides the development process and, during the analysis and design phases, defines a model of the courseware structure or the course curriculum with the visual modeling language. Furthermore, the framework of software components is used for creating the courseware during the implementation phase. According to Baloian et al. (2001, p. 3), "this framework supports the different kinds of learning activities that are to be carried out during the course and it also contains the computer-based learning material to be used." The component-based courseware development model follows software engineering life cycle consisting of four phases: analysis, design, implementation, and validation.

TOPIC-CASE DRIVEN DEVELOPMENT

Key questions for Web course design covers design granular learning material that benefits from using the Web and a way to integrate such (Web) pedagogy into training that enhances learning. We feel that these two central aspects are not clearly captured in the existing approaches and process models. There are some respectable models, for example, by Baloian et al. (2001) which also include pedagogical issues, but they exclude a variety of different pedagogical solutions at the beginning of the design process. Then there are also educational models, like the ADDIE model (Anglada, 2002), which are based on instructional design. These models have almost equal phases and activities, but they do not support granularity of learning materials.

The constructive ingredient of this chapter is to describe a Web course design and development process that first allows well-managed integration and incorporation of structural and multigranular digital material with pedagogical knowledge as

well as, for example, communication and cognitive tools. Second, it utilizes metaphors from software engineering, that is, the unified process. In particular, the proposed methodology naturally supports the utilization of large, possibly distributed teams of domain experts for creating the key content. Moreover, it supports structural and incremental development and reusability of the resulting materials as suitable learning objects. Finally, it also supports blended learning. The proposed topic-case driven methodology for Web course design and realization was introduced in Hiltunen and Kärkkäinen (2004). The proposed approach blends together metaphors from software engineering with educational (especially pedagogical) issues. Similarly to the use-case driven-ness and architecture-centricity of the unified process, the proposed approach is topic-case driven and content-centric. In general, the Web course design and realization process in Figure 3 contains phases of *background study*, *content design*, *pedagogical design*, *technical design*, and *realization and assessment*.

The development process starts with the Background study phase where all the issues that have an effect on the feasibility of the planned Web course are analyzed and considered:

- Why are you designing a Web course? What are the benefits compared to a traditional classroom course? (In the proposed approach, a Web course is not a must, but an option and/or a possible enhancement of the traditional classroom course.)
- How are you using the Web? What is the role of the Web? Is the course (or parts of it) going to be an output (static): self-accessed course or learning material delivery forum for classroom activities; or a process (dynamic): supportive learning activities for face-to-face teaching or totally online course (Hein, Ihanainen, & Nieminen, 2000)? How highly structured (in advance) or controlled

Figure 3. Phases of topic-case driven Web-course design and realization process (©2007, Leena Hiltunen. Used with permission)

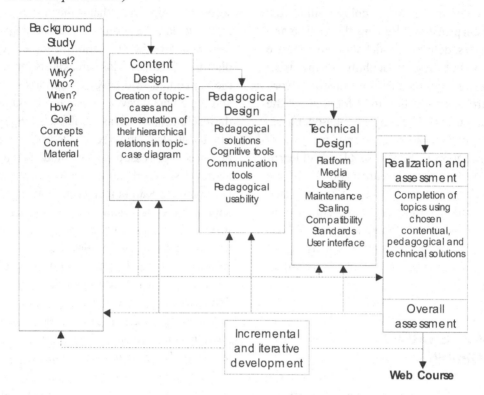

learning will be (Moore, 1983), and is there going to be dialogue or not?

• What is the target group? Who are the students? What kind of learning strategies and learning styles do they use?

• How much time and resources do we have?

• What kind of technical infrastructure do we have at our disposal?

• What are the basic ideas, focus, and learning goals of the course?

• How do you handle copyrights and agreements, for example, concerning content creation?

• Are there some organizational regulations that might affect the design process, for example, support only for certain course management systems?

As a result of the phase, one should have a project plan with a time table, resource allocation, financing plan, possible limitations, and baselines of the course. During the background study, a useful technique for creating a general view on the content of a course is concept mapping (for example, Novak, 1998).

The design process of any course usually starts from the content, because different course contents should fit together and form an extensive curriculum. Therefore, the second phase of the presented development process is content design. This phase could also be called domain modeling or conceptual modeling because the main idea in this phase is to document the content as well as the main concepts of the planned course as topic-cases, and the possible relationship between them are captured in the topic-case diagram (cf. use-case and use-case diagram in UP; Jacobson et al., 1999).

The topic-case is a short but structured description of the basic lines of the single course topic or the course itself at the beginning. Topic-cases are authenticated with numbers and names that also describe the amount of topic-cases, help to evaluate the time table of the course, and can be used for defining the presentation order of topic-cases. Naturally, the creators of topic-cases should also be documented. Materials engaged with topic-cases can be in any form, for example, books, articles, video clips, and recordings. We notice that Humphrey (1998) uses similar kinds of course descriptions in connection to software engineering courses with four attributes: objectives, prerequisites, course structure, and course support. Formally, the definition of a set of attributes defines metadata concerning a topic-case, that is, its interface (cf. component and object interfaces in software engineering). A topic-case diagram defines the basic contentual hierarchy of the Web course, serving as a more precise content map showing what knowledge is required before a certain topic-case and which knowledge would be useful to be made available, but is not compulsory for the following topic-case.

Content design can be documented as a text document or as a large concept map that also defines alternative learning paths for different kinds of learners. In case studies, teachers and Web course designers have used *CMapTools program* (http://cmap.ihmc.us/) to define the content, learning paths, and attached short topic-case descriptions to the concept in CMapTools concept map. CMapTools program is easy to use, enabling linking between different parts of the content map to define preliminary knowledge requirements.

It enables visualisation of alternative learning paths and also functions as a content map of the final Web course.

After finishing the content design, one has selected topics for the current iteration that should be augmented with advisable pedagogical activities in the pedagogical design phase to support and to describe the teaching and learning of that topic. Pedagogical problems are usually related to the roles of teachers and students, ways of teaching and learning, and actions in different learning situations, learning tasks with different characteristics, guidance and control in learning, assessment, and feedback. In addition, pedagogical design includes the extension of topic-cases with new attributes: actors, description, pedagogical solutions and relations, and the integration of communication and cognitive tools into the Web course and consideration of pedagogical usability. If one prefers to emphasize a pedagogical model like problem-based learning during the planned Web course, it is possible to convert the content-based development process to a pedagogic-based one by changing the order of the second and third phases. In this case, the pedagogical design phase would follow the background analysis phase (see Figure 4), and the content will be designed based on the selected pedagogical solutions later on during the content design phase.

The technical design phase includes technical solutions on how contents and pedagogical solutions will be realized in practice and decisions concerning technical issues, like use of a course management system, media in use, maintenance, scaling, compatibility, user interface, and so forth. During this phase, one should also keep in mind the usability issues and different standards, for example, IEEE Standard for Learning Object Metadata (LOM, 2002) and human-centered design process for interactive systems (ISO 13407, 1999). Technical decisions are not recommended here, because there are many ways to implement a Web course. There might also be limited tools and

Figure 4. Pedagogical drive in a modified topic-case design process (©2007, Leena Hiltunen. Used with permission)

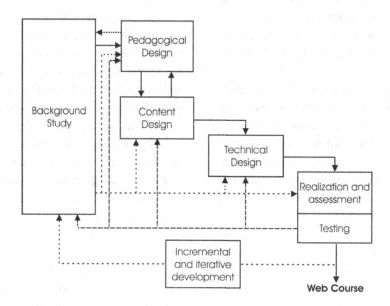

software available in different projects. So, how the Web course is actually implemented is based on available resources and knowledge in use.

In the final phase, realization and assessment, the final implementation consists of completing the individual topic-cases using the chosen pedagogical and technical solutions. This means that the content is enlarged to the final length, and teaching and learning actions are described in detail in connection to the final content and the media in use. Assessment is an activity that should be an essential part of the development process and the maintenance phase. We divide the overall assessment into reviews during the development phase; assessment of topics and content after realization; and assessment of user's required technical, pedagogical, and contents skills.

The topic-case driven development process is an iterative and incremental workflow that supports the creation of a Web course repository, where the existing topics are related to different courses, through which the overall topic-case diagram (and/or through the overall content map) are contents-wise related to each other. The topic-case driven approach can also be applied, in addition to the Web course and repository design, to the training program design. Topic-cases can be used to define an individual course, and content maps/general topic-case diagrams can be used to define relations between different courses. As a result, one is able to produce a pedagogically designed and assessed training program.

REVIEW OF THE CASE STUDIES

The proposed methodology was first tested with a group of computer science graduate students (Case

1). Then, the methodology was introduced to the staff of the local university (Case 2), and, finally, to the educators of different Finnish universities (Case 3). The goal was to find the best practices for Web course design training with case studies by testing and modifying educational methods, roles, scheduling, and grouping. The starting point was the "rooming-in" individual hand-on-hand guidance that, however, can be too time-consuming requiring a lot of guiding resources. All these case studies are introduced, and the results are briefly summarized.

Case 1: Web Course Design by Graduate Students

The presented methodology was first tested with a group of computer science graduate students in a Web Course Design and Implementation course during the autumn term 2004. There were 27 students who started the course, 14 distance students and 13 campus students.

Case Study Arrangements

Teaching activities on the course included two-hour lectures twice weekly. During some weeks, we had only four hours of exercises related to video photography, sound treatment, Web page design, graphics processing, and animating. We used the Optima course management system where all the learning materials were linked. Lectures were streamed as online videos so that students were able to watch the lectures in real time where ever they were. Lectures were also videotaped and linked to the virtual learning environment so that students were also able to see those lectures later on. Learning activities on the course were divided into six learning assignments which followed the phases of the topic-case driven approach (see Figure 3). By doing these learning assignments and by following this topic-case driven methodology, students designed and

implemented their own Web courses. A lecturer introduced each learning assignment beforehand, and the students were able to get as much guidance as needed during each assignment. Most of the guidance was given by e-mail.

Results of the First Case Study

Based on the analysis of the results, the case study was successful as a whole. According to participating students, phasing activities with learning assignments that were based on the phases of the proposed design methodology was an excellent idea; it made designing easy and even fun. The phasing and learning assignments spread the workload equally from the beginning of the course in September 2004 to the end of the course in December 2004. All the students agreed with the traditional dictum: "well designed is half done." Realization is much easier with good designs. Before taking this course, most of the students had not realized how many different aspects they need to consider during the pedagogical design, for example, different approaches, interaction, communication, guiding, tutoring, design of assignments, authenticity, and different learning styles. The course was organized for the first time, so first time enthusiasm might have had slightly positive effects on the results. Moreover, working habits of both blended and distance learning groups are strongly based on the teacher's success in organizing and activating students. Furthermore, a relatively small group size and working alone or in pairs as well as better computational skills of students leads us to the conclusion that these results cannot be straightforwardly generalized to larger design groups. Still, very encouraging results were obtained concerning the topic-case driven methodology and its utilization in the corresponding course in a bootstrap fashion. This case study and the corresponding results were presented in more detail at the EDEN 2005 Conference (Hiltunen & Kärkkäinen, 2005).

Case 2: Learning-by-Design Workshop

Most of the support that teachers and instructors at the Finnish educational institutions are initially able to get is related to technological support, for example, use of different course management systems like Optima and Moodle, video recording, and editing of lessons, Flash, and video-conferencing. Comprehensive support is not available for the design process as a whole. So-called "rooming-in" individual hands-on guidance is usually available. To help teachers at the University of Jyväskylä in their design process, we planned out several workshops with the same content for teachers. So-called *learning-by-design workshops* were organized for different multidisciplinary groups. The main educational focus was on learning-by-design. Each workshop was divided into three four-hour computer class sessions where each had its own theme. Participants worked on their own topic and design goal: to design their (in many cases, first) Web course. They received instructions, tips, and guidance during the session when needed, between sessions through e-mail or virtual learning environment where all the instructions and assignments were delivered to participants.

Background and Contents

During the first session, teachers analyzed and documented the backgrounds of their course. Next they focused on the content: domain and concept, and created a visual content map from their own course content. Content maps (cf. concept maps) were created with the CMapTools program. Content maps served as documentation of this session.

Pedagogical Design

The theme of the second computer class session was pedagogical design. During this session,

participants continued their work by designing pedagogical solutions, like models, scripts, and assignments, for their own Web course. They could follow some comprehensive model, for example, problem-based learning (PBL), anchored learning, learning through design, or collaborative learning in their Web course. Otherwise, each learning situation was designed separately by using more simple models or scripts that phases learning, for example, scripts that guide and help students to collaborate, find information, or create cognitive conflicts—whatever best suited their Web course and its content. During the pedagogical design session, the teachers also planned several assignments for the students taking the Web course to motivate them, promote learning, and support their individual learning processes. All these issues were documented for later use.

Technical Design and Follow-up

During the third and last computer class session, teachers concentrated on the technical design, how to implement the content technically with the desired pedagogical solutions. The first participants had to decide if they wanted to use some course management system or not (open Web pages). Local university supports two course management systems: Moodle (http://moodle.org/) and Optima (http://www.discendum.com/english/), so in most cases teachers wanted to use either one of these. Then teachers made some media choices: what kind of media to use to present the content and to support different kinds of learners, for example, text, pictures, graphs, videos, sounds, animations, or simulations. Other technical solutions that were considered and documented for later use during this session were design of user interface, usability, maintenance, scaling, and compatibility of the final Web course, and reusability of learning objects (content items or topic-cases). Next, based on all decisions made and previous documentation, teachers write the production manuscript for their Web course. The production manuscript contains detailed instructions for implementation or realization, how to complete individual content items (topic-cases) using the chosen pedagogical and technical solutions.

Results of the Learning-by-Design Workshop

The workshop ended at the point where teachers had their detailed plans for the implementation. Teachers were able to continue the process by themselves or to hire somebody else to realize their plans. All teachers were satisfied with the guidance they got during the workshop. Participating in the workshop helped them to find enough time to do the required planning that they would not have done in time without the workshop schedule. They also got a lot of new ideas and tips for the design process as well as encouragement that they really are able to do their own Web courses by themselves, and they are not the only ones with difficulties, but most of all, they were all very pleased to get a phased process model or checklist as someone concluded to guide in what to do and when; this kept driving them forward. The phased process model also divides a large project into smaller pieces that are easier to handle.

Case 3: Learning Network Workshop

The proposed methodology was introduced to 70 university teachers from different Finnish universities in the so-called *learning network workshop* that was a part of their *Educational Use of ICT* training. The main educational focus was on learning networks and reciprocal teaching. A workshop was held with a more compact time table; the whole design process was carried out in four hours during two consecutive days. This approach differs significantly from the first workshop: participants worked in groups (nine multidisciplinary groups) to prepare someone's single topic and the goal was to design only a skeleton of the final Web course so that the group

members were able to learn how to follow the design process by themselves later on. Furthermore, the focus was more on quality issues: how this kind of design model or process could promote quality assurance in the planned Web courses. Working in groups was structured with different roles for the participants as follows (cf. workers in UP; Jacobson et al., 1999):

- **Responsible teacher (or content master):** The owner of the content; defines the target group and sets learning goals; takes care of sizing the content and financial issues; makes final decisions, when needed; produces the content map with the help of other group members
- **Pedagogical master:** The person in charge of pedagogical solutions; documents pedagogical solutions based on group work
- **Learning material master:** The person in charge of learning materials related to content and pedagogical solutions; defines different types and use of learning materials, what has already been made and what has to be produced; documents and decisions based on group work
- **Technical master:** The person in charge of technical solutions related to content and pedagogical solutions; defines a conceivable course management system as well as learning and content creation tools and techniques together with responsible teacher; documents technical issues based on group work
- **Support master:** The person in charge of analyzing different types of support needed in different states of design and implementation process, as well as, during the learning process; defines the requirements for technical and pedagogical support; documents the requirements and methods for support based on group work
- **Quality master:** The person in charge of quality assurance; analyzes different quality

factors, sets and documents criteria and indicators for quality based on group work

All group members participated in all discussions, and workshop materials were available during face-to-face group work and also later on when discussions continued online.

Background and Contents

Role differentiation and selection of the topic was made at the beginning of the first part of the workshop based on the participants' preparations: all participants were asked to prepare their own proposal for the Web course topic of their group in advance. Some even had a lot of material about their topic with them or ready on the Web. Choices to make were up to group members. Roles were selected based on willingness, competences, or experimental (some were willing to try and learn something what they had never done before).

The next task was to define a target group for the Web course. The content master whose topic was selected played a key role here: described the target group as it should be in the real Web course. Group work continued with the background analysis and content design in a similar way as in the described local workshop. Groups had to draw basic guidelines for the content and form a basic content map with central concepts. Group members argued, rationalized, justified, and explained intensively to achieve agreement. They were very annoyed if their work was interrupted too often; groups wanted to get all the information at once and then be left alone while working intensively. Group work was supervised and help was available when needed.

Pedagogical Design

Design process continued with the second part, pedagogical design, in a rather similar way as in the local workshop: at first there was a short introduction to the topics aim, and then design groups

defined and documented pedagogical solutions as well as learning materials for their own Web course. It was astonishing how design groups kept working so intensively around a totally foreign topic for most of the group members.

Technical Design and Follow-Up

The third part of the workshop started with technical design. The goal was to define technical solutions related to the content and pedagogical solutions of the groups' own Web course: conceivable course management system (if used) as well as learning and content creation tools and techniques. Before starting the group work, there were a few short presentations to show how things are managed at the local university. These included the use of a Web publishing platform and content management system *Plone* (http://plone.org/) to maintain different kinds of content to the students, some examples of executed learning materials and Web courses, and the introduction to as course management system that covers registration, scheduling, and assessment of courses as well as self-assessment, a personal study plan, and soon also e-portfolios. At the end of this part, follow-up was introduced. This included, for example, how to implement the designed Web course, how to test and assess it, and how to expand it during the next incremental iterations.

Online Discussions

The design groups finished the workshop with documented content, pedagogical, and technical solutions. Documents were stored into an online learning environment where groups continued their discussions. Group members were also asked to write a short description from their role point of view. After this, they were asked to discuss how this kind of workshop and design process could elicit quality in the designed Web course.

RESULTS OF THE LEARNING NETWORK WORKSHOP

Participants were satisfied with receiving a new instructional way of designing Web courses, although some of them would rather have designed their own Web course during the workshop. Altogether, working in groups was considered a positive experience. During the online discussion, participants discussed the Web course design and implementation process and its effects on quality assurance. Quality requirements were easier to find when the design process was phased into smaller tasks. Actual quality indicators were much harder to define. Discussions are concluded in Table 1.

As overall conclusions, the model reminds and guides to high-quality preparation and realization of the necessary plans and artifacts for Web courses.

FUTURE TRENDS

Results from the introduced workshops were so encouraging that a third workshop, *consulting workshop*, for 50–100 participants has been planned. The difference between the other two workshops will be in individual design work; all participants will design their own Web course while still working in design groups sharing experiences. The educational focus will be on consulting, and the design process is going to be supported by technical and pedagogical experts. Moreover, for future work, pedagogical design with multiple pedagogical patterns and scripts is an interesting area as well as the development of technical tools to support the design process. This first research interest supports teachers in their design process when they try to find the best possible solutions and activities for their Web courses; during their design, they could use a Web course repository, explore it, and find suitable pedagogical solutions (reusable learning objects) into their courses or at least develop some new ideas.

The second research interest, how to support the design process with technical tools, is also essential. Before teachers are really willing to adapt new techniques, these should be easy to use and really help them in their work. A tool that follows the presented methodology and automatically guides teachers during the design process would form the documentation automatically based on a user's choices and answers. The outcome from the design process and use of such a tool would be a ready-to-use Web course. There are suitable tools and techniques available already (for example, XML, EML, LAMS, and IMS Learning Design Specification), but none of these existing tools and techniques would support the topic-case driven methodology separately. There is a need for integration and further study.

CONCLUSION

To be able to support and promote online learning, virtual learning environments have to be carefully designed and implemented. Effective planning and quality management are the key issues on the way to achieve a good learning outcome. Effective planning requires methodological support. Key questions for Web course design is how to design granular learning material that benefits from the use of the Web and how and when to integrate such a (Web-) pedagogic into training that enhances learning.

Most of the educational institutions do not use any particular design and implementation model in Web course authoring. Based on these case study experiences, teachers need more guidance and unified ways to proceed during the design process. In our case, teachers do not need to work alone while designing their own Web courses; we can utilize multidisciplinary design groups. The design process can be supported with "rooming-in" individual guidance,

Table 1. From online discussion about the quality requirements in design process

Phase	Advances
Design model as a whole	• Clarifies, facilitates, and simplifies the design process with proper instructions, decisions are documented for later use, best practices are easy to copy from documentation
	• Guides to gather feedback from the students and teachers, and redesign the Web course incrementally and iteratively if needed
Background analysis	• Helps efficient exploitation and optimization of resources and workload, realistic scheduling, and collaboration between different participants
	• Reminds to define and document learning goals and desired learning outcomes
Content design	• Helps to define domain and concepts, and size and structure explicit contents as a whole
	• Guides to diverseness and illustrates learning materials, reminds of workload and dosage of information
	• Reminds of functionality and sufficiency of information and simplicity of instructions
Pedagogical design	• Guides to implement pedagogically designed learning situations, and individual learning paths
	• Guides to design teaching acts that provoke desired learning acts
	• Guides to design assessment of learning outcomes based on learning assignments, assess absorbed knowledge and skills, and adaptation for use in real life contexts
	• Guides to evaluate attained learning goals and to create coherent assessment practices
	• Reminds to pays more attention to guiding; enough and well-timed, individually, emphasises correctness, competence, consistency, reliability, supportivity, and simplicity
	• Guides to support different learning styles and strategies
Technical design	• Reminds about importance of extensive support, both pedagogical and technical
	• Reminds about testing before using and comprehensive evaluation of whole process
	• Reminds about usability, accessibility, availability, scalability, and pedagogical usability of technical solutions

learning-by-design workshops (tailored), and learning network workshops (reciprocal and cost effective). Topic-case driven methodology effectively supports individual as well as group design, different group sizes, multidisciplinary groups, and group members with different levels of technical and pedagogical skills.

With a phased design model, Web course design and realization can be divided into smaller parts so that quality assurance becomes easier. However, while the quality of the process is rising with the support of the used methodology, quality of the Web course itself also depends on the quality of the selected content and pedagogical solutions.

The topic-case driven development process is an interactive and incremental workflow that naturally supports the creation of a Web course repository, where the existing topics are related to different courses, the overall topic-case diagram and hierarchically depicts the whole content. After designing and implementing several Web courses one has, not only a lot of reusable topic-cases, but also several solutions for pedagogical and technical issues. From these different objects and solutions, one can create a Web course repository with reusable learning objects and pedagogical and technical solutions for the next Web courses.

REFERENCES

Anglada, D. (2002). Applying a basic instructional design model: An introduction to instructional design: Utilizing a basic design model. *Cornerstone Newsletter, 1*(2). Retrieved March 16, 2008, from http://www.pace.edu/ctlt/newsletter/Volume%202%20Issue%201/articles/idm.htm

Baloian, N., Fuller, D., & Ochoa, S. (2001). A model for component-based courseware development (CBCD). In *Proceedings of the International Conference on Software Engineering and Knowledge Engineering (SEKE '01)* (pp. 363-370).

Bork, A. (1986). Advantages of computer based learning. *Journal of Structural Learning, 1*(9), 63-76.

Canada, M. (2000, Winter). Students as seekers in online courses. In R. E. Weiss, D. S. Council of European Union. (2000). *eContent Programme*. Retrieved March 16, 2008, from http://www.cordis.lu/econtent/

Council of European Union. (2005). *eContentplus Programme*. Retrieved March 16, 2008, from http://europa.eu.int/information_society/activities/econtentplus/index_en.htm

Finnish Ministry of Education. (2006). *The National Knowledge Society Strategy 2007-2015*. Retrieved March 16, 2008, from http://www.tietoyhteiskuntaohjelma.fi/esittely/en_GB/introduction/

Hein, I., Ihanainen, P., & Nieminen, J. (2000). Tunne verkko. *Opetus & Teknologia, 1*, 5-8. (In Finnish)

Hiltunen, L., & Kärkkäinen, T. (2004). Topic-case driven approach for Web course design. In *Proceedings of the 6th International Conference on New Educational Environments (ICNEE '04)* (Session 5.2/B: Web-Based Courseware).

Hiltunen, L., & Kärkkäinen, T. (2005). Case study: Web course design with the topic-case driven methodology. In *Proceedings of the EDEN 2005 Annual Conference, Lifelong E-Learning: Bringing E-Learning Close to Lifelong Learning and Working Life: A New Period of Uptake* (Session E3: Finnish e-Learning Panorama).

Horila, M., Nokelainen, P., Syvänen, A., & Överlund, J. (2002). *Pedagogisen käytettävyyden kriteerit ja kokemuksia OPIT-oppimisympäristön käytöstä Hämeenlinnan normaalikoulussa syksyllä 2001*, DL-projektin osaraportti. Hämeen ammattikorkeakoulu, Hämeenlinna. Retrieved March 18, 2008, from http://www.hamk.fi/julkaisut/julkaisu.php?id=287 (In Finnish)

Humphrey, W. S. (1998). Why don't they practice what we preach? *Annals of Software Engineering, 6*, 201-222.

ISO 13407. (1999). Human-centered design process for interactive systems: International Organization for Standardization (ISO). Retrieved March 16, 2008, from http://www.iso.org/

Jacobson, I., Booch, G., & Rumbaugh, J. (1999). *The unified software development process*. Massachusetts: Addison-Wesley.

LOM. (2002). *IEEE standard for learning object metadata* (IEEE Std. 1484.12.1-2002). Retrieved March 16, 2008, from http://ltsc.ieee.org/wg12/

Mäki-Komsi, S. (1999). *Opettamisen ja oppimisen muodot muuttuvat, muuttuuko oppimis- ja opettamiskulttuuri - heijastuksia opetuksen kehittämisprojekti OpinNetista*. (In Finnish).

McConnell, S. (1996). *Rapid development*. Redmond: Microsoft Press.

McDonald, J. (2002). Is "as good as face-to-face" as good as it gets? *Journal of Asynchronous Learning Networks, 2*(6), 10-23.

McNaught, C. (2002). What, why, who and how of designing for effective online learning. In

Proceedings of the 15th Annual NACCQ (pp. 63-71). Retrieved March 16, 2008, from http://site.tekotago.ac.nz/staticdata/papers02/papers/mcnaught73.pdf

Montilva, C. J. A. (1998). Designing Web-based study guides for distance education courses. In *Proceedings of the IASTED International Conference on Computer Advanced Technologies in Education (CATE'98)* (pp. 83-90).

Montilva, C. J. A. (2000, March 24). *Development of Web-based courses: A software engineering approach*. Paper presented at the Symposium on 21st Century Teaching Technologies: A Continuing Series of Explorations.

Moore, M. (1983). On a theory of independent study. In D. Seward, D. Keegan, & B. Holmberg (Eds.), *Distance education: International perspectives* (pp. 68-94). London: Croom Helm.

Novak, J. D. (1998). *Learning, creating, and using knowledge: Concept maps as facilitative tools in schools and corporations*. Lawrence Erlbaum Associates.

Palloff, R. M., & Pratt, K. (1999). *Building learning communities in cyberspace*. San Francisco: Jossey-Bass.

Peterson, C. (2003). Bringing ADDIE to life: Instructional design at its best. *Journal of Educational Multimedia and Hypermedia, 3*(12), 227-241.

Preece, J., Rogers, Y., Sharp, H., Benyon, D., Holland, S., & Carey, T. (1994). *Human-computer interaction*. Harlow: Addison-Wesley.

Schank, R. C. (1998). Horses for courses. *Communications of the ACM, 5*(41), 23-25.

Scott, K. (2002). *The unified process explained*. Boston: Addison-Wesley.

Sommerville, I. (2004). *Software engineering* (7th ed., Chap. 19: Component-based software engineering, pp. 439-461). Addison-Wesley Pearson.

Twigg, C. A. (2001). *Innovations in online learning: Moving beyond no significant difference*. New York: The Pew Learning and Technology Program 2001, Center for Academic Transformation, Rensselaer Polytechnic Institute.

White, S. A. (2000). Experience with a process for software engineering Web-course development. In *Proceedings of the 30th ASEE/IEEE Frontiers in Education Conference* (T1C, pp.13-18).

Yang, Y., & Cornelious, L. F. (2005). Preparing instructions for quality online instruction. *Online Journal of Distance Learning Administration, 1*(8). Retrieved March 16, 2008, from http://www.westga.edu/~distance/ojdla/spring81/yang81.htm

KEY TERMS

Background Study: A phase in topic-case driven methodology that includes analysis of, for example, functional, user, content, and system requirements and learning goals for Web course design.

Content Design: A phase in topic-case driven methodology that includes design of relevant and effective Web courses contents with domain (or conceptual) modeling and content manuscript. Actual contents are developed later on during the design process.

Pedagogical Design: A phase in topic-case driven methodology that includes design of learning situations (learning activities, teaching or tutoring activities, and learning assignments) based on learning goals; design of steps that are required to be taken to achieve settled learning goals.

Realization and Assessment: A phase in topic-case driven methodology that includes both completions of individual topic-cases using the chosen pedagogical and technical solutions, and assessment of the design process and final Web course.

Technical Design: A phase in topic-case driven methodology that includes design of technical solutions on how contents and pedagogical solutions made earlier during the design process will be realized in practice.

Topic-Case: A short but structured description of basic lines of the single course topic.

Topic-Case Diagram: A display that defines the basic contentual hierarchy of the Web course, serving as a more precise content map showing what knowledge is required before certain topics (topic-cases) and which knowledge would be useful to be available, but is not compulsory for the following topics (topic-cases).

Topic-Case Driven Methodology: A Web course design and implementation model that is based on software engineering metaphors for capturing the necessary steps for creating Web courses using a content-based development method.

Web Course: An instructional or training course delivered via Web pages and sites accessible via the Internet or some course management system, for example, Blackboard or Moodle. Web course is a synonym for online course.

Web Course Design: Design and implementation of a Web course that has some content and pedagogical ground. Web course design is a synonym for authoring.

Chapter V
New Paradigms:
A Collaborative Web-Based Research Tool

Hamish Holewa
International Program of Psycho-Social Health Research,
Central Queensland University, Australia

ABSTRACT

The chapter aims to document the challenges associated with the management of an international research program and to look at innovative, information technology (IT) based ways of tackling these. Through the medium of a case study, insights gained from practical experience developing and implementing an original Web based collaborative research management tool are discussed. This tool is based on a centralised model of information distribution and access. It was designed following a reductionist analysis of existing research processes and procedures. The ways in which the integration of responsive IT processes into the management of a large international research program have removed redundancies and increased automation and research efficiency are also discussed.

INTRODUCTION

This chapter presents, through the medium of a case study, insights gained from practical experience developing and implementing an original Web based collaborative research tool to assist and enhance the management of an existing, qualitative research program. The case example used is that of the International Program of Psycho-Social Health Research (IPP-SHR). This case study provides the reader with insights into the ways in which information technology (IT) processes can be used to overcome problems associated with the postmodern research environment. Within this context, the major challenges are to address the fragmented nature of research locations, staff, and project administration within a global setting.

Technological advances have paved the way for global research, enabling it to transcend physical, geographical, and cultural boundaries. However, there are still great challenges to be overcome in conducting a truly international research program.

The chapter aims to document the challenges associated with the process and management of a large international research program and to look at innovative, IT based ways of tackling these.

The International Program of Psycho-Social Health Research provides international leadership through research, publication, education, media, newsletters, and podcasting activities in the area of psycho-social health research. This program explores a broad range of psycho-social health issues including: the lived experience of serious and terminal illness; haematology and oncology; palliative care; indigenous health; rural and remote health; mental health; obstetrics; bio-ethics; and the interface between patients and the health care system. The core aim of IPP-SHR is to make a difference by informing policy and service delivery in the real world of health care.

This program utilises a qualitative, or naturalistic, research methodology, which seeks to document the voice of research participants from their own worldview (Streubert & Carpenter, 1995). Such methodologies are underpinned by a philosophical perspective that listens to, rather than imposes on, the experience of others and has a sensitivity to the disempowered and marginalised (Latimer et al., 2003). The large and diverse amount of the data gained from using such methodologies, coupled with diverse and geographical isolated data collection sites of an international program, necessitated the design and construction of a central based management system.

After extensive literature searches in major databases, consultation with software and project management vendors, and collaboration and discussion with international leaders in qualitative methodologies, it was evident that no such program existed to meet the specific requirements of IPP-SHR or collaborative multisite qualitative research projects. As such, to meet the challenges and technical difficulties associated with IPP-SHR's methodology and operation, an Internet based research tool was designed. Server side technologies were utilised to achieve a central research portal for IPP-SHR practitioners to use and collaborate through, independent of their physical location. The maturing of server side and Internet connectivity and speed are major contributors to the success of such a system. The system uses a central Web site, where users with appropriate security credentials like correct user name, password, and encryption key can deposit files related to the research processes; implement automatic workflow processes for dictation, transcription, and coding processes; view work and project flows and progress; and schedule appointments and stipulate task for other users or team members. The system improves research efficiency and lowers research costs. This is achieved through a streamlined Web site portal offering best practice security, enhanced ethics compliance, limited or reduced redundancy between processes and team members, and accurate information on the process and state of each particular research project. The software also provides team building and mentoring activities through the use of project reporting, a bulletin board, discussion forums, and team feedback.

BACKGROUND AND CHALLENGES

The research paradigm and context within which IPP-SHR operates presents unique challenges. Although the program has developed gradually over the last decade, it has only recently evolved to the level of national and international research data collection and collaboration. As a qualitative research program with a focus on the human interface of health care, the challenge is collecting and managing the magnitude and complexity of data gained from naturalistic methodologies over extensive geographical areas. This section details the challenges and problems associated with running a decentralised, location unspecific international research program. It also introduces the equity and ethical considerations associated with research.

IPP-SHR operates in an environment, characterised by the fragmentation of location, staff skills and expertise, participant groups, disciplinary focus, and broad topic interests. Translated to the practicalities of research activities, this means data collection and analysis occurs in many geographical locations and time zones and focuses on a multiplicity of research topics. Additionally, staff management needs to address a multiplicity of duties and responsibilities, and access and control of project information, some of which is confidential. Also posing challenges are the practical necessities of enabling simultaneous access by multiple team members to a broad range of specific documents, and creating processes for multisite data entry and analysis.

As a core component of IPP-SHR's philosophy is to 'make a difference' and to 'document the human experience of human illness,' IPP-SHR's qualitative methodology focuses on a phenomenological perspective using exploratory, iterative, and open-ended interviews. A phenomenological perspective is used with data analysis and process as its inherent aim is to document and record the particular phenomena or appearance of things as a lived experience (Streubert & Carpenter, 1995). Data gathered during the interviewing process is then transcribed verbatim and analysed from the view point of the participiant (McGrath & Holewa, 2006). Such analyses and exploration are undertaken without imposing specific theoretical or conceptual frameworks on the interview or data analyses to ensure that the individual experience is recorded (Polit & Hungler, 1995). As such, it is methodologically important for the data management system to not only store data correctly and without corruption but to ensure that research staff can engage in a rigorous data analysis process. IPP-SHR has a particular pride and a documented history of ensuring a rigorous

data analysis process by which the findings are driven by a meticulous coding of all statements by participants.

Due to the rigour of IPP-SHR's application of qualitative methodologies, even relatively small research projects produce large amounts of data. For example, a small project in which 10 participants are interviewed will on average produce over 200 pages of language texts, excluding supplementary data such as descriptive statistics. The sheer quantity of data produced by IPP-SHR's qualitative methodologies necessitates that the discrete processes of qualitative research (i.e., verbatim recording and transcription of interviews, managing coding processes) be streamlined.

Although the data gained in IPP-SHR projects are usually qualitative, occasionally descriptive data are also included. Thus, any system that is to facilitate and streamline IPP-SHR's research processes also needs to be scalable and flexible so as not to disadvantage collaboration and research efficiency if projects required support for different methodologies. Additionally, each project has differing qualitative methodological requirements, which vary according to project size, participant numbers, interviews per participant, and time frames. As such, any software implementation needs to support IPP-SHR's diverse projects which requires flexibility, scalability, and durability, plus continuity of access over extended periods of time.

Additional requirements and challenges posed to the development of a software system are stipulated by the regulatory and policy frameworks within which IPP-SHR operates. Human Research Ethic Councils (HRECs) stipulate privacy, informed consent, confidentiality, and audit requirements for research approval involving humans (AIATS, 2004; Australian Federal Government, 1988; NHMRC, 2003). Additionally, audit requirements necessitate that data be stored in a confidential and secure location for a period of time from five to seven years. The challenges imposed by such policy and regulatory frameworks require IPP-SHR to store and be legally liable for any information which is gathered throughout the research process. This is particularly important within IPP-SHR's operating paradigm due to the decentralized composition of IPP-SHR research projects and staff. Document control, ethical requirements, and privacy issues represent a major concern and challenge for the research process and for any software system designed to support such research.

IPP-SHR research practitioners have not previously been exposed to a high level of IT involvement and were reticent based on lack of familiarity. Consequently, an additional challenge for incorporation and implementation of the system was the development of comprehensive and supported training packages. The case study highlights the need for mutual understanding from both academic and IT disciplines in developing the system and the positive outcomes that can be gained from incorporating such diverse professional viewpoints. This case study profiles the importance of IT leadership and innovation in meeting the outlined challenges.

DESIGN AND IMPLEMENTATION

Design and implementation of the technological interface created for the research program required a detailed understanding and high level analysis of the challenges, backgrounds, procedures, needs, and desires of proposed users of the system. This required both research practitioners and IT consultants to have a high level of cooperation and effective discourse focused on the needs and wishes of the research practitioners. Although research practitioners bring to their work an understanding of the role and function of IT, this was insufficient for translating their work into an innovative and original incorporated

system. What became evident in this experience was the need to provide IT leadership, collaboration, and experience in translating the research work components and wishes into a sustainable and usable system.

Design and implementation of the system needed to be in a bottom-up fashion. Effective translation, education, and implementation assisted in establishing a self-perpetuating and learning experience for users. Users are able to see advances that technology can make and can suggest, modify, and drive new innovations and uses. Understanding this user determined innovation variable allows users and IT designers to implement user friendly software with practical outcomes which correctly and efficiently operationalise research processes. That is, by a process of continual feedback and discussion between research practitioners and IT consultants, both parties were able to understand and learn the constraints, practicalities, and possibilities of automating the research process. Development and specification of the software requirements was partly informed by the Institute of Electrical and Electronics Engineers (IEEE, 1998) document referring to recommended practice for software requirement specifications.

Such in-depth discourse between the two professional groups and the development of a thorough understanding of the research processes allowed for extra innovative features to be created and other unnecessary ones to be omitted. This assisted in producing an effective program with an efficient design. For example, features such as user control and public and private files were not proposed in the original design; however; after extensive consultation, this feature was warranted as crucial. This was in particular reference to identifiable participant data which, in line with HREC agreements, only authorised persons should be able to view. Without consultation and ongoing discussion between both professional groups, this feature would have been omitted from the final product. Additionally, features proposed by the IT professionals were omitted as they did not add value and could potentially complicate use of the final software interface.

All parties agreed on final software specifications before commencement of programming and software construction. The use of specification allowed for accurate budgeting and time frame projections. It also allowed for a medium in which users from both professional groups could suggest and implement changes before programming. This is particularly important in relation to the ethical imperative of efficient and effective use of resources, as changes made to the system once programmed are costly and expensive compared to alterations made in the preprogramming stage (Diaz & King, 2002).

This considered, laborious, and collaborative consultative period before manufacture of the software began is an essential step for any project which bridges two disparate disciplines. Continual communication between research practitioners and IT consultants, coupled with referable specification documents, allowed for greater flexibility, increased innovation, and design features, producing a software package that is of direct use and benefit to its intended users.

WORKFLOW ANALYSIS, PROGRAM SPECIFICATIONS, AND IMPLEMENTATION

Extensive research and market searches indicated that no suitable, scalable, and location-independent software was available to serve the unique demands and constraints faced by the research group. Although there are numerous research software packages specifically designed for qualitative methodologies (e.g., NUD*IST or Atlas/ti) (Barry, 1998), there was an absence of project management software which incorporated qualitative methodologies and associated workloads.

In order to fill this gap, a software program was designed to handle such programmatic demands and incorporate data analysed within the major qualitative data analyses programs. A full working commercial version of this program can be found at www.quadrant-pm.com

A reductionist analysis of the workflow and procedures that IPP-SHR uses to operationalise its research was critical for successful design and implementation of the software program. This process involved detailing and referencing every activity conducted by researchers. All components produced by the research process were discretely assigned a unique identifier. Components were then tracked in order to ascertain a step by step understanding of the research process. For example, the interviewing of a participant produced a component, "audio voice file." This file was then forwarded to the transcriber, who by transcribing the audio voice file produced another component, "text document of interview verbatim." The flow and process of information creation (arrangement of participant interview) to research output (publishing and dissemination of information) was tracked and compiled into a flow diagram (see Figure 1).

After construction of the flow diagram, each process was analysed to identify redundant processes and avenues through which automation and efficiency could be increased. For example, a redundant process found was the duplication of communication occurring between team members in the activity of scheduling an interview. Although in its simplest form scheduling can be achieved through one person (enrols the participant, schedules and conducts the interview, compiles and stores documents relating to the interview, and transcribes the interview), this is a rarity due to the aforementioned operating challenges of the research program. It is IPP-SHR's experience that there can be up to four people involved in the process of arranging, conducting, and transcribing an interview. Similar issues of

Figure 1. Procedural, sequential information creation and flow (©2007, Hamish Holewa. Used with permission)

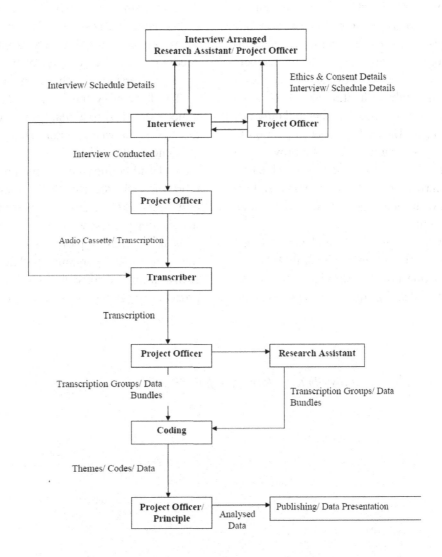

redundancy and repetition of tasks were found within the interface between transcription, coding, and record keeping.

Analysis of data flow and information creation in Figure 1 suggested that many tasks undertaken within a project only need to be completed once if every member involved had access to such information. As such, a centralised distribution model of information storage, provision, and access was developed to enable this streamlining to occur. Using the centralised model, users of the system with appropriate rights and security credentials have access to each component of information that is relevant to the specific needs of their task. This enables users to maintain up-to-date information and accurate data repositories, which assists in smooth and efficient running of research processes. Furthermore, duplication, redundancy, and errors are reduced as only one record exists per each research instance per project. Instead, for example, of four team members keeping individual records of each particular research instance and coordinating changes between each other, only one record is kept and only one change is made. Using the model in relation to interviewing, scheduling would be provided to the centralised data source (such as a Web based calendar) and information given to other members associated with such interview will be provided from such source.

As shown in Figure 2, research staff interact individually with the central dynamic Web site and information flow occurs via a centralised, distributed model. This distinctly contrasts with the processes formerly used, whereby information flow was procedural, sequential, and task oriented. Once information has been created, research team members with appropriate security credentials can access the most up-to-date source of information through a Web site portal without needing to ask other team members for the status and latest version of such information.

The depicted system in Figure 2 also removes unnecessary and redundant tasks with the motivation of increasing automation and realising efficiencies through the process. Once implemented and configured, simple procedural and reporting tasks are completed automatically. In previous workflow, the researchers were involved in a six-step process which included: (1) research assistant (RA) enrols participant; (2) schedules an interview time; (3) organises HREC compliance such as informed consent and project description procedures; (4) the interviewer (INT) completes

Figure 2. Centralised and distributed information flow (©2007, Leena Hiltunen. Used with permission)

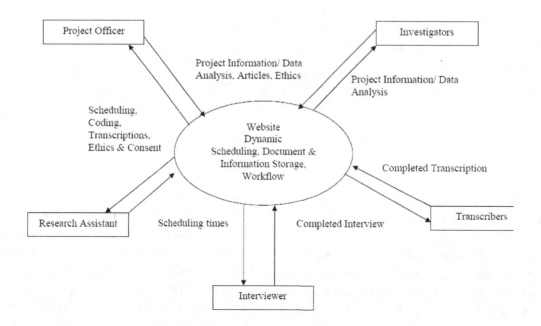

the interview and produces a digital recording; (5) the recording is sent to the transcriber (TRS) who completes transcription processes; and (6) send completed transcription to RA or project officer (PO), who initiates coding and qualitative analysis. At any point in the process, each member is reliant on another member to complete her scheduled task, record appropriate details, and ensure HREC and other policy guidelines are complied with. Furthermore, the PO or investigator may have to contact up to four people to receive an accurate report on the progress of the research project.

A major advance has been achieved on the automation and reduction of the described processes. This is done through the automatic storage and referencing of documents and information (participant details, consent forms, digital interview files, transcriptions) which is completed at each stage and by each individual person responsible for such tasks. Once each task is completed by the assigned research team member, the team member interfaces with the Web site portal and flags its completion and uploads the accompanied file or information. The Web site will then contact the next research team member within the process. For example, once an interviewer has completed the interview, this is flagged within the system and the corresponding sound file is uploaded to the Web site portal. Once uploaded, the Web site sends an alert to the transcriber of the need for an interview to be transcribed. This process reduces record keeping times and ensures an up-to-date report on progress.

The distributed, centralised model of project workflow implementation has been realised through the use of four discrete online modules operating within the project management portal: calendar and scheduling; project workflow and progress; document and version control; and administration. Included are different levels of user access and control and differing levels of information categories, ranging from public to private. Access to the Web site portal occurs

through a computer with Internet connectivity and browser support. The Web site server runs on a combination of client and server side code attached to a centralised database. Most computation and processing is completed on the remote server and, apart from Internet connectivity, there is little computational demand on client computers.

SELF-DIRECTED LEARNING COMMUNITIES

The development of a community centred upon online collaborative applications is a well regarded method for increasing the use and accessibility of a system and for encouraging users to engage in self directed interaction and learning (Neus, 2007). The implementation and use of community based initiatives has been successful within this case study. The provision of a message board, collaborative document sharing applications, version control, and work processes has encouraged community building and increased collaboration and use of the service. It has also facilitated self directed learning and enquiry and has supported a forum for public discussion.

Evidence associated with the development of an online community and self directed learning stemmed from online dialogue evident within the bulletin board feature and the minimum formal training needed for new users. Through anecdotal records and conversions with users of the system, it was noted that software training and learning was largely conducted within the system. Although software training was required for initial users of the system, the historical dialogue between such users provided a self directed learning environment for new users, and assisted in development of an environment conducive to posting public comments and asking questions to the group of users. However, it should be noted that the development of such a community of self-directed learning may be further successful due to the separate and disparate physical location of the users. It is unclear whether such development of a bulletin board and self directed learning would have developed if the user were located in the same physical space, for example, in the same office.

The central place assumed by the software within the research program creates a responsive medium through which staff concerns, ideas, and issues can be raised. This enables research staff to pose research-related questions and comments and provide direct feedback on the program's usability. The facilitation of such open communication allowed for quick development of ideas and creative problem solving. It also helped to foster team culture and shared identity while acting as an effective training tool.

The software program's ability to dynamically provide users with up-to-date project information has encouraged individual and team ownership of the research projects. As the program allows for instant viewing of research project status and progress, research members are also able to identify any aspects of the research process hindering overall progress. Additionally, staff training and supervision, early identification of potential problems, and feedback were facilitated by the availability and ease of gauging project progress.

FUTURE ADVANCES AND ETHICAL IMPLICATIONS

It is anticipated that further development of the system will occur through a user driven, evolutionary response. Increased and synchronised communication avenues are predicted with a decreasing need of physical presence. This is particularly evident with the advent of increased access and data throughput as a result of increasing bandwidths and the emergence of new and maturing technologies (Choudrie & Dwivedi, 2007). It is envisaged that access to the research collaboration tool will occur through more diverse means,

and not be limited to a computer with Internet connectivity. This has strong positive implications for the processes of qualitative research, as many research activities are conducted in the setting of the participant and away from traditional computing equipment. There is potential to limit the redundant activities presently associated with scheduling, interviewing, and recording by allowing handheld or portable devices access to the software.

Additionally, the immediacy of information access between research staff and the potential for real-time communication is an important avenue for future advances. Instant messaging and voice-over-Internet-protocol advances have the potential to contribute to stronger group collaboration, communication, and a sense of community. The use of such technologies also has the potential to lower communication costs and provide greater access to research opportunities for marginalised or disadvantaged groups. The adoption and inclusion of such technologies has the opportunity to lower research costs, providing greater potential outputs from fewer resources.

Increased security represents another domain in which future advancements may occur. This aligns with the ethical imperative of maintaining rigorous privacy and confidentiality protocols within the research process, particularly when using centralised models of information storage collaboration and project management work. The transfer, storage, and processing of information within the aforementioned system is governed by strict HREC and other policy requirements. Effective system security and regulating access and use are paramount to fulfilling the ethical and policy requirements of privacy, confidentiality, and cost effective use of research resources. Although the system currently uses best practice security practices, such as encryption, user access and password, security certificates, and user training, the advent of increased processor and computational capabilities and increased Internet users and connectivity means that security issues are a priority area for ongoing future advancement.

The software program has the potential to increase user engagement between researchers, health professionals, and stakeholders in qualitative research processes, especially for groups whose lack of access to traditional research institutions may have formerly acted as a barrier to participation. This use of IT solutions within qualitative research has the potential to bridge geographical and social communication gaps, opening up the potential for increased collaboration and information sharing between researchers worldwide. From IPP-SHR's experience implementing and using such a program, it is evident that the integration of IT management structures into a qualitative research program can be instrumental in bridging geographical constraints and fostering global research collaboration. The potential of this new technology is clearly evidenced by the way in which it has enabled IPP-SHR to effectively engage in research collaboration that spans national boundaries and multiple time zones.

CONCLUSION

This chapter has presented, through the medium of a case study, insights gained from the practical experience of developing and implementing an original Web based collaborative research tool to assist and enhance the management of an existing qualitative research program. This tool is based on a centralised model of information distribution and access and was designed following a reductionist analysis of existing research processes and procedures. The ways in which the integration of responsive IT processes into the management of a large international research program have removed redundancies and increased automation, and research efficiency has also been discussed. The program opens up avenues for increased research participation and

collaboration and makes an important contribution to overcoming the challenges that a fragmented, globalised environment poses.

REFERENCES

AIATS. (2000). *Ethical guidelines for research.* Australian Institute of Aboriginal and Torres Strait Islander Research. Retrieved March 16, 2008, from http://aiatsis.gov.au/research_program/gratns/gratns_assests/ ethics_guidelines.pdf

Australian Federal Government. (1988). *Privacy Act 1988 Australia Privacy Policy.*

Australian Federal Government. Retrieved March 16, 2008, from http://www.comlaw.gov.au/comlaw/management.nsf/lookupindexpagesbyid/

Barry, C. A. (1998). Choosing qualitative data analysis software: Atlas/ti and Nudist compared. *Sociological Research Online, 3*(3). Retrieved March 16, 2008, from http://www.socresonline.org.uk/socresonline/3/3/4.html

Choudrie, J., & Dwivedi, Y. K. (2007). Broadband impact on households consumers: Online habits and time allocation patterns on daily life activities. *International Journal of Mobile Communications, 5*(2), 225-241.

Diaz, M., & King, J. (2002). How CMM impacts quality, productivity, rework and the bottom line. *CrossTalk, 15*(3), 9-16.

IEEE (Software Engineering Standards Committee of the IEEE Computer Society). (1998). *IEEE recommended practice for software requirements specifications.* Author.

Latimer, J., et al. (Eds.). (2003). *Advanced qualitative research for nursing.* Malden, MA: Blackwell Publishing.

McGrath, P., & Holewa, H. (2006). Missed opportunities: Nursing insights on end-of-life care for haematology patients. *International Journal of Nursing Practice, 12*(5), 295-301.

Neus, A. (2007). Managing information quality in virtual communities of practice: Lessons learned for a decade's experience with exploding Internet communication. In *Proceedings of the 6th International Conference on Information.*

NHMRC. (2003). *Values & ethics: Guidelines for ethical conduct in aboriginal and Torres Strait Islander health research.* National Health and Medical Research Council. Retrieved March 16, 2008, http://www.nhmrc.gov.au/publications/synopses/e52syn.htm

Quality at MIT. Retrieved March 16, 2008, from http://opensource.mit.edu/papers/neus.pdf

Polit, D., & Hungler, B. (1995). *Nursing research: Principles and methods* (5th ed.). Philadelphia: Lippincott.

Streubert, K., & Carpenter, D. (1995). *Qualitative research in nursing: Advancing the humanistic imperative.* Philadelphia: Lippincott.

KEY TERMS

Information Technology (IT): As defined by the Information Technology Association of America, IT is "the study, design, development, implementation, support or management of computer-based information systems, particularly software applications and computer hardware."

Phenomenology: A method of inquiry based around the exploration, description, and analysis of a particular phenomenon, untainted by presupposed theories, beliefs, and assumptions.

Psycho-Social Research: Research processes which aim to explore and document social and psychological aspects of the human experience.

Qualitative Research: A non-numerical research methodology which aims to describe and understand, rather than explain, human behaviors and experiences.

Redundant Processes: Unnecessary processes or tasks that through analyses of such process can be removed without affect the output of such tasks.

Server Side Technology: A form of Web server technology in which users' requests are fulfilled by running a script directly on the Web server to generate dynamic HTML pages. It is used to provide interactive Web sites capable of interfacing with databases and other data stores.

Chapter VI
Animations in Science Education

Göran Karlsson
IT University of Gothenburg, Sweden

Jonas Ivarsson
University of Gothenburg, Sweden

ABSTRACT

The overall aim of this chapter is to explore some of the pedagogical potentials, as well as limitations, of animations displaying complex biochemical processes. As the first part of our larger research project, a learning environment was developed where visualisations by means of 3-D animations depicted some of the processes in the carbon cycle. In the analysis, we describe how three groups of students made use of and reasoned about the computer animations. In relation to the aim, three salient themes are discernible in the video material of the students' reasoning; the risk of focusing the attention on misleading aspects of the animation, the possible occurrence of a form of isolated reasoning, and the students' varying understandings of what resources they are expected to use when performing a given task.

INTRODUCTION

One of the grand themes of educational research in general and science education in particular is the notion of misconceptions. Students' misconceptions of various scientific principles are recurrent topics in numerous studies, for instance, in physics (Brown, 1992; Jones, 1991), biology (Brown, 1990; Odom, 1995), and chemistry (Goh, 1993; Nicoll, 2001; Sanger & Greenbowe, 1999). The means to meet the educational challenges spelled out by educators and educational researchers has obviously varied, but throughout the 20th century, the use of technological innovations has been an increasingly frequent strategy (Petraglia, 1998a, 1998b).

For higher biology and medical education, several digital applications have been developed.

Camp, Cameron, and Robb (1998) created virtual 3-D simulations enabling medical students to examine anatomic models, and Karr and Brady (2000) describe interactive 3-D technologies for teaching biology. Virtual learning environments for primary school (Mikropouls, Katsikis, Niko-lou, & Tsakalis, 2003) and high school (Kameas, Mikropoulos, Katsikis, & Pintelas, 2000) have been developed and, in some respect, been tested out and evaluated.

Given all the time and effort invested in these matters, however, positive and stable results from the use of educational technologies are remarkably few. To underscore this observation, we would like to point to a claim by Euler and Müller (1999) who hold that, within the area of physics education, the technology known as *probeware* is the *only* computer-based learning environment that has a proven general positive learning effect. Adding to the picture that the area of physics education is intensely studied renders Euler and Müller's remark even more conspicuous. Thus, as a general pattern, students seem to be invariably immune to any simple technological treatments; despite whatever new technologies we introduce into our educational systems, *learning* continues to be a struggle for educators and students alike.

In spite of this rather gloomy outlook, ever-new items are added to the list of possible remedies of educational dilemmas and student difficulties. One item on this list and the topic of the current chapter is the use of *animations* as educational resources. Our specific field of investigation concerns secondary school science education, and the aim is to analyse the reasoning students perform when working with animated sequences of the carbon cycle.

THE CARBON CYCLE AS A TOPIC FOR EDUCATION

One of the main topics in curricula for primary and secondary schools for education of natural

science is the carbon cycle and its vital importance for conditions concerning life on earth. Studies of the two main processes in the carbon cycle, *photosynthesis* (Barak, Sheva, & Gorodetsky, 1999; Cañal, 1999; Eisen & Stavy, 1993) and *respiration* (Sanders, 1993; Seymour & Longden, 1991; Songer & Mintzes, 1994) report that students' knowledge of these gaseous processes is poorly understood and that misconceptions are frequent. In consideration of the utilisation of fossil fuel and the ensuing global warming, combustion is another process in the carbon cycle deemed increasingly important. This process is chemically equal to the respiration with the exception that it is not a cellular process.

A major problem with the conceptualisation of the processes in the carbon cycle is that they involve gaseous forms that are not directly observable and therefore have to be grasped through some representational system. The traditional textbooks most often illustrate the carbon cycle in pictures furnished with arrows describing the course of the circulating material. Given an educational framing, one could conclude that there should be potential gains from developing educational material that builds on more dynamic forms of representations, for example, computer animations. From a research perspective, however, this still remains an open question. Before turning to the specific but still problematic question concerning the animation of the carbon cycle, we will briefly discuss recent work done on the use of different animations in education.

COMPUTER ANIMATIONS IN EDUCATION

The scientific results emanating from research exploring the educational value of animated graphics, as compared to the use of its static counterparts, are hitherto inconsistent. The research results so far display a complex and confusing array of outcomes in different educational settings. From an initial euphoria over the vast educational possibilities associated with multimedia technologies, a more composed picture is now emerging. However, the expectations of multimedia in educational settings, although somewhat moderated, still exist and they call for further research in the area.

Based on a series of studies, Mayer (1997) argues to have found consistent support for a generative theory of multimedia learning, and offers the explanation that coordinated presentation of explanatory words and pictures is effective because it helps guide students' cognitive processes. In addition, he demonstrates what he calls a contiguity effect when visual and verbal information is presented closely together. For the prospects of computer-based learning, he concludes: 'In computer-based multimedia learning environments students have the opportunity to work easily with both visual and verbal representations of complex systems, but in order to fruitfully develop these potential educational opportunities, research is needed in how people learn with multimedia' (p. 17). Most investigations comparing the learning outcomes of students' work with animated vs. static pictures, however, have not been able to show any enhanced learning efficacy brought by the animations. The results rather indicate the contrary. In a comprehensive research review, Tversky, Morrison, and Betrancourt (2002) could not find evidence supporting the view that animations are superior to the use of static graphics in education. Lowe (1999, 2003) suggests that merely providing an accurate animated depiction of the to-be-learned material may not in itself be sufficient to produce the desired outcome. In his studies of how meteorological novices worked with animated weather maps, the extraction of information appeared to be largely driven by perceptual characteristics of the display. Students unfamiliar with the depicted subject matter tended to extract information about components of the animation with characteristics such as structural coherence, distinctive appearance, and dynamic change more readily than they extracted information about components lacking these qualities. Retention also seemed more likely for those aspects of the dynamic graphics that were relatively easy to extract. This extraction and retention of the most perceptual salient characteristics of animations, irrespective of their relevance with regard to the intended subject matter, is something one has to take into account when designing educational animations. Lowe (2003) also concludes that the problem appeared to stem from lack of explicit information about the relative importance of various aspects of the animation, and he conjectures that students could be helped by providing the learning environment with specific visual and temporal guidance. Consequently, he proposes that further research is needed to determine if these findings can be generalised and how the animations might be manipulated in order to modulate the way in which students' attention is distributed between features that differ in their intrinsic perceptibility.

Mayer, Hegarty, Mayer, and Campbell (2005) made four experiments comparing the learning outcomes of the use of computer-based animations and narration versus paper-based static diagrams and text. Based on these experiments, the authors argue that static presentations containing illustrations and printed text can be superior to dynamic presentations containing narrated animation. Their reasoning is further given a theoretical framing, from within which static media is seen as having the advantage of engaging people in less extraneous cognitive processing. By that line of reasoning, one is therefore able to engage in deeper cognitive processing when learning from static illustrations and text, as compared to dynamic animations and commentaries. On the other hand, Mayer et al. (2005) remark that their study should not be interpreted as if animations are ineffective in all situations. For example, animations are said to improve understanding for learners with limitations in spatial ability or when they are used to visualise processes that are not visible in the real world.

When comparing individual and collaborative learning with interactive animated pictures vs. static ones, Schnotz, Böckheler, and Grzondziel (1999) found that animated pictures could result in better learning about dynamic subjects for individual learners but lead to lower learning results in collaborative learning. They attribute their results to the effect that collaborative learners have to devote a substantial proportion of their cognitive processing capacity to both operating the visual presentation and coordinating their learning activity with those of their partner. In accordance with this view, learners working collaboratively would have less cognitive resources available for processing the learning content. However, conflicting results are presented by Rebetez, Sangin, Bétrancourt, and Dillenbourg (2005) who demonstrate a positive effect of animated graphics over static ones for students learning in pairs compared to individual learners. These authors interpret their results by the *underwhelming effect* described by Lowe (2003): participants working on their own were less active because they simply had to attend to the animation and not to build a shared representation of the animation with a partner leading to the illusion of comprehension. In summary, both the referred studies explored computer animations and compared students working individually to students working in pairs, but they come to contradicting conclusions. One possible explanation is that the learning conditions were quite different in the two studies. For example, Schnotz et al. (1999) used interactive animated pictures while the participants in the study by Rebetez et al. (2005) had no control over the presentation. In relation to this, we hold that there is a need to consider the educational setting, in which animations are used for understanding the learning outcome.

Under the auspices of cognitive load theory, another factor thought influencing the learning outcome when using animations is the students' learning prerequisites. Animated pictures are regarded as having a facilitating function insofar as they allow an external simulation process that makes an alleged corresponding mental simulation less demanding (Schnotz & Rasch, 2005). Accordingly, this is seen as beneficial for learners who would not be able to perform this operation without external support but, on the other hand, as harmful to learners who could perform the mental simulation on their own. In the latter case, the authors argue that the animation reduces the cognitive load but also reduces germane load that is necessary for learning. Schnotz and Rasch conclude that, 'The use of animation in multimedia learning environments seems to be beneficial only under some circumstances, whereas it can have negative effects under other circumstances' (p. 57).

What advantages can an interactive computer animation entail in comparison with, for example, viewing a film illustrating the same process? By breaking down an animated presentation into short segments, Mayer (2001) showed that students who were able to control the presentation pace—by clicking on a button to receive each of the segments—performed better on transfer tests than did students who viewed the entire presentation as a continuous unit. Thus, it seems as if this form of interactivity can help overcome some of the difficulties of perception and comprehension associated with animations. As argued by Tversky et al. (2002), simply enabling the starting, stopping, and replaying of an animation will allow for re-inspection and facilitates the user to focus on specific parts and events.

The interest for computer games is considerable among the youth today, and many students are therefore familiar with virtual environments of this kind. Among educators, there have been recurring attempts to buy one's way into the success of the gaming industry by adopting part of its format. One example is the Viten project which has its roots in WISE (developed by the WISE-project at the University of California, Berkeley and available at http://wise.berkeley.edu). Like WISE, the Viten project is free and open software (available at http://viten.no), enabling science teachers to use Web-based science curriculum materials. It presents programs combining text, simulations, and animations in topics of science and mathematics. In the most popular Viten program, Radioactivity, the interactive animations and other features are described to contribute to student learning by making the 'invisible' visible (Mork, 2005). When summarising students' positive comments, Mork (2005) identifies a number of categories which are thought to provide some general insights about what is appreciated in a teaching sequence, that is: using computers, variation, informative materials, working together, and student control. On the one hand, these are key words to have in mind when planning any teaching sequence or when developing new learning materials. On the other hand, they are also very general descriptions, too abstract in order to provide any substantial insights, and every such term must therefore be disambiguated and given a specific content on every new occasion and in every new educational design (Lindwall & Ivarsson, 2004, in press).

AIM OF THE STUDY

So far, studies of the educational use of animations have mainly been concentrating on the learning outcomes in quantitative terms. In this study, we analyse the reasoning and interaction taking place when groups of students collaborate in connection to a set of animations. Interaction analyses of knowledge building in small groups is an emerging and important methodology in the area of computer supported collaborative learning (CSCL) (Stahl, 2006). Arguably, the better we understand the students' collaborative reasoning on a given topic, the better we can design specialist computer support and the surrounding learning environment in which this support is intended to serve. Evaluating new educational setups also raises the problem of how technology interacts with the students' emerging conceptualisations. By analysing the students' interaction and talk, we aspire to gain insights into their interpretations of the depicted phenomena. The overall aim of this study is to explore some of the pedagogical potentials, as well as limitations, of animations displaying complex biochemical processes. As the first part of our larger research project, a learning environment was developed where visualisations by means of animations depicted some of the processes in the carbon cycle.

APPLICATION DESIGN

The background and motive of developing a sequence of computer animations can be found in the educational situation of the specific subject matter: the carbon cycle. As already alluded to, the teaching of this topic could, as seen from the science teacher point of view, potentially benefit from having an educational material that builds on dynamic forms of representations.

The intention in forming the design was to make the illustrations in the graphics as concrete as possible and to concentrate on just one event in every sequence. Software for the production of 3-D animations was used for the development of the pedagogical application (available at http://www.ituniv.se/~gorkar/). The index page in Figure 1 contains a text describing the main outlines of the carbon atom cycle. To the left, there is a menu with links to the different pages in the application. At the bottom, there is a row of clickable miniatures that links to the different animations. The pages describe the different processes of photosynthesis, breathing, combustion, and mouldering. Each page has an explanatory text which was kept as concise as possible so as not to be considered too tiresome to be read by the students. Underneath the captions, there is a miniature image linking to the animations. The program allows for some limited interactivity as the students can start and stop the animated sequences.

Figure 1. The index page from where you navigate among the animations of the processes in the carbon atom cycle

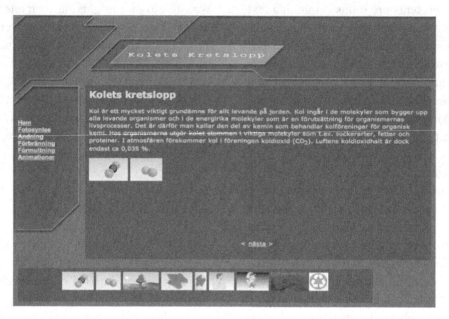

Photosynthesis is illustrated in three animated sequences. The three sequences in various ways illustrate carbon dioxide molecules diffusing into the leaves of a tree, the building up of the foliage, and oxygen molecules emitting from the leaves. *Breathing* is illustrated by the human lungs in section. The animation shows how oxygen, which is taken in through the respiratory passages, is exchanged for carbon dioxide that is exhaled. Since the breathing is an active process, the animation gives a reasonably correct picture of the actual process. However, the cellular respiratory process and gas transportation with the blood are not shown in the animation. Furthermore, the animation displays the inhalation air by means of only oxygen molecules, and similarly, only the carbon dioxides are represented in the exhalation air. In reality, there is a mix of gases in both the inhalation and exhalation air where oxygen and carbon dioxide constitute a minor part and where only the proportion of these gases differs. Thus, the animation constitutes a considerable simplification of the real events.

Mouldering and *combustion* are illustrated by a mouldering log and a log fire, respectively. The wood is used for making the connection easier between the photosynthesising tree and the mouldering or burning tree. In the animation of both mouldering and combustion, one will see oxygen molecules coming in from the side and carbon dioxide molecules leaving the log and the log fire respectively in an upward direction. Again, this is a simplified and schematic illustration of indiscernible and passive gas exchanges, and it does not show the actual processes occurring inside the wood.

In conclusion, common to all animations is that they focus on the movements of the gaseous molecules oxygen (O_2) and carbon dioxide (CO_2) in the different depicted processes. It should be noted that, as the animations are designed to emphasise these relations, this form of highlighting (Goodwin, 1994) simultaneously runs the risk of concealing other important molecular reactions. The relation between possible advantages and drawbacks connected to the use of this form of representation constitutes a major part of the empirical study, and it is this issue that we will address in the analysis.

RESEARCH DESIGN

A total of 40 students attending a science course in a Swedish secondary school took part in the study. The 16 girls and 24 boys were grouped into dyads or triads, totalling 19 groups, thus allowing peer discussions and engaging the students in reflection and comparing their different views with each other. The study was conducted during a one and a half hour study session for each group.

Before starting their exploration of the animations, the students were given a short instruction about how to manage and navigate within the learning environment. There was no tutorial introduction of the topic, but the students had the opportunity to consult their teacher during the learning session. The students also got an explanation of what a model of a phenomenon means. It was stressed that when using simulations as models for real phenomena, the students must not mistake a simulation for the actual phenomena (cf. Flick & Bell, 2000). For about 20 minutes, the students worked with the animations. During this time, they were given the task of writing down what they saw happening in the different sequences. After that, while still having access to the animations, they were assigned to discuss and jointly give answers to two problems concerning the carbon cycle.

To gain an understanding of how the students interpreted their tasks and reasoned about the animations, three groups were randomly selected and videotaped during the entire session. The

analysis builds on the work of these three groups. This analysis of the students' interaction with each other and with the technology draws on an analytic tradition which Jordan and Henderson (1995) summarise under the label *interaction analysis*. Like the authors, we find this interdisciplinary method for the empirical investigation of human activity particularly helpful in complex, multi-actor, technology-mediated work settings and learning environments. Through the detailed analysis of videotaped material, this method tries to describe the ways participants orchestrate both communicative and material resources when performing any given task (Ivarsson, 2004).

RESULTS

In relation to the aim of understanding the pedagogical workings of the specific animations displaying complex biochemical processes, three salient themes are discernible in the video material of the students reasoning. The first concerns the risk of focusing the attention on misleading aspects of the animation, a problem in some respect related to the design of the technology. A second problem observed is the possible occurrence of a form of isolated reasoning, seemingly connected to the simplified nature of the representations. The last observed problem is the students' varying understanding of what resources they are expected to use when performing a given task.

Misguided Attention

As the animations are mere models of unobservable molecular processes, the interpretations of these representations can result in several misleading inferences. One example of such a misleading feature of the animation, not really belonging to the model, is observable in an excerpt where three students are watching the animation of gaseous exchange by a photosynthesising tree.

Veronica:	now you see what is happening, what happens
Henric:	ok, carbon dioxide molecule gets stuck, in the tree
Veronica:	in the tree and oxygen, oxygen
Henric:	oxygen carb-eh-molecule
Veronica	came out
Henric	blows away

Veronica is asking Henric what happens in the animation. Henric explains what he observes with a mix between scientific designations and every day expressions like 'gets stuck, in the tree' and 'blows away.' These specific wordings are later adopted by Veronica, as shown in the next excerpt.

Veronica:	there we shall write the first picture shows that oxy carbon dioxide or what- ever it's called gets stuck in the tree and oxy blah-blah, blows away as he said
Henric:	ok, the tree catches oxygen molecules through blowing or something like that it stays so the oxygen keeps on blowing

Veronica remarks that carbon dioxide 'gets stuck' and oxygen 'blows away,' thereby referring to Henric's earlier utterance. Henric makes no distinction between the two kinds of molecules and does not comment on the assimilation of carbon dioxide. His remark about 'blowing or something like that' could indicate an uncertainty about the blowing as the driving force for the molecules. However, when subsequently asked by the teacher what is shown in the animation, he reiterates and reinforces the narrative about the 'blowing' that makes 'the tree catches oxygen molecules.'

Teacher:	yes what is happening here?
Henric:	yes we only saw oxygen molecules and by means of blowing it gets stuck

Veronica:	((*clicks at the icon showing the photo synthesis*)) look there- what's coming
Teacher:	yes look what's coming here, what is it that gets stuck

Henric responds to the teacher's question by focusing on the perceptual salient feature of the oxygen molecules as moving in one direction. In his words, this 'blowing' is the cause that makes the molecules 'get stuck' in the leaf. Veronica refers to the carbon dioxide molecules as something that is 'coming.' This particular way of talking about the depicted processes is not corrected by the teacher, not in this excerpt nor in the subsequent discussion with the group. Instead the teacher repeats the somewhat misleading characteristics of molecules as 'coming' and 'getting stuck' and tries to focus the student's attention on the actual molecules.

Isolated Reasoning

The animations show only limited parts of the complex biochemical processes occurring inside organic material. This is an inevitable feature of any model. But, the interesting question is whether the limit of scope functions differently with an animation as compared to a static picture. The observations in the next two excerpts do indicate something in that direction.

Said:	((*reads from the questionnaire*)) the following questions you can discuss with a peer and write down which conclusion you have reached, one- we breathe in oxygen and breathe out carbon dioxide, from where do the carbon atoms in the carbon dioxide that we breathe out come from (3 s) uhm yeah we breathe in oxygen and like from where do the carbon atoms in carbon dioxide that we breath out come from
Kevin:	yeah that's you know from pollution
Said:	carb- carb- the carbon atoms

Kevin: isn't it from pollution from the car and things

Said: no I don't know

Kevin: 'cause we don't breathe in 100% oxygen

Said: then from where come the carbon atoms in the carbon dioxide that we breathe out hmm (6 s) yea then isn't it so that when we breathe in then we like take when we breathe out then it becomes carbon dioxide it means that (2 s) it has to come from our lungs then

Kevin: yes

Said: where they sort of are cleaned or some cycle in our lungs like

Kevin: from where do they come, are they from, we don't breathe in 100 % oxygen do you understand what I mean?

Said: yes ((*watching the animation showing breathing*))

Kevin: then (2 s) they probably come from (3 s) exhaust pipes from cars and such

Said: I think so too

The animated sequence that the students have recently watched is making visible the processes of inhalation and exhalation and thereby focuses on the two different gases (oxygen and carbon dioxide). Similarly, the dialogue between the two boys takes its starting point from the assumption that the carbon atoms originate from an airborne external source and reach our lungs through the inhalation air. In their discussion, they stick to this rationale and endeavour to conceive of a source emitting carbon atoms into the air. As we can observe, their discussion is completely concentrated on a circulation of the carbon atoms inside the lungs. In one sense, this is an adequate way of reasoning, since the animation of the breathing is only visualising the gas exchange in the lungs. Presumably, they did not read the caption explaining the metabolism, thereby restricting the external input of their reasoning to the limited view that was given by the animation. The reading of the text was not expressed in their task, and this group did follow the instruction, which was

to discuss with a peer what they could observe and thereafter write down their conclusion. In this case, this obviously led them to an erroneous conclusion, which could possibly have been avoided if they had been encouraged to read the text captioning the breathing animation.

Another example of this somewhat isolated reasoning, and misleading inferences due to limitations of the animation, is demonstrated in the excerpt. Here, two girls are watching and discussing what happens in the animation illustrating the combustion by a burning log fire.

Gloria: oxygen comes in

Petra: and out,

Gloria: comes carbon dioxide

Petra: so oxygen is necessary for the fire to burn and out then just like in the human body when the oxygen is consumed carbon dioxide comes out

Gloria: carbon dioxide comes out

Petra: does that sound probable?

Gloria: that sounds very sensible in some way

Petra: you know from you were playing with candles when you were little when you put a glass over it takes a while before it goes out

Gloria: yeah
(7 s)

Petra: but to make something burn you have to have some material that can burn

Petra: but that's what you- that would be the oxygen then

Gloria: yes. in principle

In the beginning of this discussion, Petra displays a very knowledgeable reasoning about the requirement for oxygen in the combustion, referring to the experience of putting a glass over a candle. She then remarks on the necessity of having some burning material. Gloria suggests that this would be oxygen, whereupon Petra agrees with her. Coming to the erroneous conclusion that oxygen is the burning material can be a quite understandable consequence if only watching the animation. Here the oxygen molecules can be seen moving into the log fire and the carbon dioxide molecules leaving, whereas the firewood remains unaltered. Consequently, the animation offers no way of discerning the chemical process actually taking place during combustion.

The animations, as mentioned, focus on specific relations in the biochemical processes, and they thereby necessarily downplay, or hide, other potentially relevant aspects. Here we have two examples where this seems to become a pedagogical problem. The fact that something very specific is highlighted by the animation could also imply that one has a harder time breaking out of that offered frame. In this way, the learning environment invites to way of reasoning that, at times, becomes isolated in relation to the overall topic (for a similar discussion, see Ivarsson, 2003).

Conflicting Perspectives

The students' first task was to describe what they could observe in the animations. When analysing the reasoning of the students, this seemingly easy instruction opens into a complex task that holds two conflicting perspectives. In the excerpt, Petra and Gloria are discussing the animation of breathing.

	((*Petra clicks on Breathing in the menu and both girls read the text about breathing,* 29 sec))
Petra:	are we ready?
Gloria:	Yeah
Petra:	Oxygen
Gloria:	oxygen you breathe in so you breathe out carbon dioxide
Petra:	carbon dioxide they transform there
Gloria:	they transform in the lungs
Petra:	it must be
Petra:	yes
	((*Petra makes notes,* 28 sec))
Gloria:	but really it's not like that, that they come in and become carbon dioxide when you breathe out but it's about oxygen coming in, and going out into the cells

Petra:	Ah
Gloria:	and then they take it up
Petra:	but what you see in the animation
Gloria:	in the <u>animation</u> it is that then you see that oxygen comes into the lungs and carbon dioxide comes out
Petra:	(*reads aloud the text from the questionnaire*) it says explain in your own words what you consid- what you see happening in the different animations
Gloria:	all right then it's what you <u>see</u> sort of ((*make notes,* 9 sec))
Petra:	I wrote used up slash transforms

Here two conflicting perspectives become apparent. This is about how to explain the breathing process both described in the caption and visualised in the animation. The two girls at first conclude that there is a transformation in the lungs, but then Gloria points out that it actually is a more complex process involving the gas exchange occurring inside the cells. Petra, on the other hand, refers to the written task where they explicitly have to explain what they 'see happening' in the animation. Gloria admits that it is what they can observe that they have to report in their notes.

These conflicting perspectives between the task (as referred to by the students) and the visualisations are also visible in the excerpt from the triad group. Here Martina, sounding somewhat annoyed over her companions reading of the text, stresses that they have to write down what they 'see.' Later on in this group's discussion, the same tension arises over what their assignment really is about.

Henric:	are we going to explain what photosynthesis is?
Martina:	<u>we have to write down what we see</u>
Veronica:	photosynthesis
Henric:	yea wait there it says ((*reads the text about the photosynthesis on the screen*)) the plants absorb
Martina:	<u>in your own words or</u>

Henric: what do we have to write down (.)
             what's happening?

Martina: <u>yea that's it</u>

Henric shows that he is in a quandary over what their assignment is about. Martina emphasises three times the explicit wordings in the questionnaire, specifically what their task is about. When Henric is trying to read the text accompanying the animation, Martina interrupts him and stresses that it should be 'in your own words.' For Martina, reading the text obviously implies that they will not be able to describe what they see with their own words. Thus, she clearly regards the use of what is mentioned in the captions to be in conflict with their task.

DISCUSSION

The analysis shows how students watching the animations use expressions from their every day life to talk about what is displayed on the screen. As they, in their capacity of being students, lack knowledge of the subject matter, they have to impose an interpretation of their own, and they do this by drawing on a variety of resources. In their efforts to make the events in the animation meaningful, the students incorporate every day language in their descriptions of the depicted processes. At times, this leads them to make unintended interpretations of the scientific model. However, such use of every day language and even bodily experiences when attempting to grasp abstract phenomena, is not solely done by students, but also by professional scientists in their ordinary work (Ochs, Gonzales, & Jacoby, 1996). Consequently, we regard this as a pedagogical problem of a more general nature, and not specifically tied to the use of animations.

The earlier documented problem, that students tend to focus on perceptually salient features of the animation, could also be observed in our material. In relation to these features, Lowe (2003) found a predisposition by novices to impose simple every day cause–effect relations on the interpretations of the animations. Examples of this kind, in the excerpts, are the interpretations of molecules as 'blowing' into and away from the tree and oxygen being 'consumed.' The analyses also show how easily such inferred notions are accepted and taken up by the coparticipants and, more problematically in our case, even by the teacher. So, what kind of guidance would be necessary to overcome this problem then? An instructional text accompanying the animation could be one way of redeeming these issues, but this method offers no guarantee that the text will actually be attended to. Another suggested way of supporting animations has been narration coordinated with the animation (Mayer, 1997). Although Mayer et al. (2005) found no support for the superiority of computer based narrated animations over paper based annotated illustrations, they conclude that their study 'should not be taken to controvert the value of animation as an instructional aid to learning. Instead, this research suggests that when computer-based animations are used in instruction, learners may need some assistance in how to process these animations' (p. 246). Obviously, teacher supervision could also provide students with the guidance needed for construing animations in an adequate way. This, however, being the panacea to all educational dilemmas adds nothing new to our further understanding of the use of animations for specific learning purposes.

Another theme, worthy of further scrutiny and briefly touched upon in the analysis is the topically isolated reasoning that can be observed in connection to the animations' superficial depiction of the biochemical processes. In biological terms, respiration takes place inside the cells and the gases are transported to and from the lungs with the blood. In the animation of breathing, however, the gaseous exchange was only illustrated within the lungs, showing oxygen being inhaled and carbon dioxide leaving the lungs. This delimitation of the illustration in some cases leads to erroneous inferences like carbon dioxide being formed in the lungs or originating from an outside airborne source. In the students' effort to answer the question about the origin of carbon atoms in the exhalation air, they had to turn to resources external to the actual animation. To make the judgement of when to go outside the provided material and when to stick with it is not a trivial task, however. By using the written information in the caption, most students were able to get the correct information. But without this source, they were restricted to either their previous knowledge or to observing the animations. Given this latter scenario, a conclusion such as 'carbon dioxide reaching the lungs from an external source' is fully understandable.

In addition, we would like to comment on the distinctive situation of solving educational problems. As a general observation, students are often oriented towards the short-term goal of fulfilling a given task by the production of an answer to a specific question. When solving such a task, the students can use varying resources like earlier experiences, texts, instructional graphics, and so on. Here, the conflict over *what* kind of resources they are expected to use, and *how* to use them, can be discerned in the students' argumentation. It is in this process that an explicit formulation of how to perform a given task can be interpreted as excluding other forms of resources. The formulation in the current assignment, 'explain in your own words what you can *see* happening in the different animations,' did in this case lead some students to the conclusion that they, in their written answer, had to disregard their previous knowledge or what they could read in the text captioning the animations. Even though the intention with the question was to make the students draw their own conclusions from the animation and not only copy the text, this formulation in fact created an increased uncertainty of how to proceed. Considering this, it seems very important to pay great attention to the formulation of the

assignments that students are going to perform in their work with animations.

FINAL REMARKS

Any graphical illustration of the complex biochemical processes involved in the carbon cycle will entail simplifications of the real courses of events. As suggested by the observations, perhaps animations, more so than static images, could help create the illusion that a complete process is being illustrated. Regardless of how sophisticated the animation becomes, there will always be grounds for misinterpretations. Prescribed ways of overcoming these drawbacks have been through increased interactivity (Tversky et al., 2002) or activities that generate explanations or answering questions during learning (Mayer et al., 2005). Other ways could be through instructional guidance, either written or narrative. When text and animation are simultaneously presented, the observers' visual attention has to be split between the animation and the text. In our study, the image *presenting* the animation was captioned, but as the sequence was started, the text disappeared. Hence, the students had to change between two pages when they wanted access to the written information vs. the animations, something that should be reconsidered given a future redesign. Still, an important issue for the observed students was which of these two media, the animation or the text, were of superior significance when fulfilling their task. Here the formulations of their task sometimes led to the exclusion of the written information and even of their previous understanding of the subject matter at hand. To make the students integrate visual and verbal information, the task has to be formulated in a way that supports the utilisation of all available resources.

Finally, the observations of our study merely point out a field of investigation that needs further attention. In our view, animations provide an interesting educational offering, with some pedagogical potential. They do not, however, come without costs. What is suggested by our observations is that in a worst case scenario, the animation will operate as a counteracting force that, instead of supporting knowledge building and working against faulty interpretations, will do the exact opposite and take the role of an antagonist of conceptual development.

ACKNOWLEDGMENT

The work reported here has been financed by the Swedish Research Council through a grant to the project 'Representation in imaginative practice' and was supported by the Linnaeus Centre for Research on Learning, Interaction, and Mediated Communication in Contemporary Society (LinCS).

REFERENCES

Barak, J., Sheva, B., & Gorodetsky, M. (1999). As 'process' as it can get: Students' understanding of biological processes. *International Journal of Science Education, 21*(12), 1281-1292.

Brown, C. R. (1990). Some misconceptions in meiosis shown by students responding to an advanced level practical examination question in biology. *Journal of Biological Education, 24*(3), 182-186.

Brown, D. E. (1992). Using examples and analogies to remediate misconceptions in physics: Factors influencing conceptual change. *Journal Articles: Reports-Research, 29*(1), 17-34.

Camp, J. J., Cameron, B. M., D., B., & Robb, R. A. (1998). Virtual reality in medicine and biology. *Future Generation Computer Systems, 14*, 91-108.

Cañal, P. (1999). Photosynthesis and 'inverse respiration' in plants: An inevitable misconception? *International Journal of Science Education, 21*(4), 363-371.

Eisen, B., & Stavy, R. (1993). How to make learning of photosynthesis more relevant. *International Journal of Science Education, 15*(2), 117-125.

Euler, M., & Müller, A. (1999). *Physics learning and the computer: A review, with a taste of meta-analysis.* Paper presented at the 2nd International Conference of the European Science Education Research Association.

Flick, L., & Bell, R. (2000). Preparing tomorrow's science teachers to use technology: Guidelines for science educators. *Contemporary Issues in Technology and Teacher Education, 1*, 39-60.

Goh, N.-K. (1993). Some misconceptions in chemistry: A cross-cultural comparison, and implications for teaching. *Australian Science Teachers Journal, 39*(3), 65-68.

Goodwin, C. (1994). Professional vision. *American Anthropologist, 96*(3), 606-633.

Ivarsson, J. (2003). Kids in zen: Computer-supported learning environments and illusory intersubjectivity. *Education, Communication & Information, 3*(3), 383-402.

Ivarsson, J. (2004). *Renderings & reasoning: Studying artifacts in human knowing.* Göteborg: Acta Universitatis Gothoburgensis.

Jones, D. G. C. (1991). Teaching modern physics: Misconceptions of the photon that can damage understanding. *Physics Education, 26*(2), 93-98.

Jordan, B., & Henderson, A. (1995). Interaction analysis: Foundations and practice. *The Journal of the Learning Science, 4*(1), 39-103.

Kameas, A., Mikropoulos, T. A., Katsikis, A., Emvalotis, A., & Pintelas, P. (2000). EIKON: Teaching a high-school technology course with the aid of virtual reality. *Education and Information Technologies, 5*, 305-315.

Karr, T. L., & Brady, R. (2000). Virtual biology in CAVE. *Trends in Genetics, 16*, 231-232.

Lindwall, O., & Ivarsson, J. (2004). What makes the subject matter matter? Contrasting probeware with graphs & tracks. In J. Ivarsson (Ed.), *Renderings & reasoning: Studying artifacts in human knowing* (pp. 115-143). Göteborg: Acta Universitatis Gothoburgensis.

Lindwall, O., & Ivarsson, J. (in press). Differences that make a difference: Contrasting the local enactment of two technologies in a kinematics lab. In S. Ludvigsen, A. Lund, I. Rasmussen, & R. Säljö (Eds.), *Learning across sites: New tools, infrastructures and practices.* Amsterdam: Elsevier.

Lowe, R. K. (1999). Extracting information from an animation during complex visual learning. *European Journal of Psychology of Education, 14*, 225-244.

Lowe, R. K. (2003). Animation and learning: Selective processing of information in dynamic graphics. *Learning and Instruction, 13*, 157-176.

Mayer, R. E. (1997). Multimedia learning: Are we asking the right questions? *Educational Psychologist, 32*, 1-19.

Mayer, R. E. (2001). *Multimedia learning.* Cambridge: Cambridge University Press.

Mayer, R. E., Hegarty, M., Mayer, S., & Campbell, J. (2005). When static media promote active learning: Annotated illustrations versus narrated animations in multimedia instruction. *Journal of Experimental Psychology: Applied, 11*(4), 256-265.

Mikropouls, T. A., Katsikis, A., Nikolou, E., & Tsakalis, P. (2003). Virtual environments in biology teaching. *Journal of Biological Education, 37*, 176-181.

Mork, S. (2005). *ICT in science education: Exploring the digital learning materials at viten.no.* University of Oslo.

Nicoll, G. (2001). A report of undergraduates' bonding misconceptions. *International Journal of Science Education, 23*(7), 707-730.

Ochs, E., Gonzales, P., & Jacoby, S. (1996). When I come down I'm in the domain state: Grammar and graphic representation in the interpretive activity of physics. In E. Ochs & E. A. Schegloff (Eds.), *Grammar and interaction* (pp. 328-369). Cambridge University Press.

Odom, A. L. (1995). Secondary & college biology students' misconceptions about diffusion & osmosis. *American Biology Teacher, 57*(7), 409-415.

Petraglia, J. (1998a). *Reality by design: The rhetoric and technology of authenticity in education.* Manwah, NJ: Lawrence Erlbaum.

Petraglia, J. (1998b). The real world on a short leash: The (mis)application of constructivism to the design of educational technology. *Educational Technology Research and Development, 46*(3), 53-65.

Rebetez, C., Sangin, M., Bétrancourt, M., & Dillenbourg, P. (2005). Learning from animations is

enabled by collaboration. *Manuscript in preparation.*

Sanders, M. (1993). Erroneous ideas about respiration: The teacher factor. *Journal of Research in Science Teaching, 30*(8), 919-934.

Sanger, M. J., & Greenbowe, T. J. (1999). An analysis of college chemistry textbooks as sources of misconceptions and errors in electrochemistry. *Journal of Chemical Education, 76*(6), 853-860.

Schnotz, W., Böckheler, J., & Grzondziel, H. (1999). Individual and co-operativ learning with interactive animated pictures. *European Journal of Psychology of Education, 14,* 245-265.

Schnotz, W., & Rasch, T. (2005). Enabling, facilitating, and inhibiting effects of animation in multimedia learning: Why reduction of cognitive load can have negative results on learning. *Educational Technology Research and Development, 53*(3), 47-58.

Seymour, J., & Longden, B. (1991). Respiration: That's breathing isn't it? *Journal of Biological Education, 25*(3), 177-183.

Songer, C., & Mintzes, J. (1994). Understanding cellular respiration: An analysis of conceptual change in collage biology. *Journal of Research in Science Teaching, 31,* 621-637.

Stahl, G. (2006). *Group cognition: Computer support for collaborative knowledge building.* Cambridge: MIT Press.

Tversky, B., Morrison, J. B., & Betrancourt, M. (2002). Animation: Can it facilitate? *International Journal of Human-Computer Studies, 57,* 247-262.

KEY TERMS

Computer Animation: The art of creating moving images via the use of computers.

Computer Supported Collaborative Learning (CSCL): Research area in supporting collaborative learning with assistance of computer artifacts.

Conceptualization: Creating an idea or explanation and formulating it mentally.

Interactive: Refers to computer software which responds to input from humans.

Misconception: A false conception or abstract idea that is held by a person.

Simulation: An imitation of some real process.

Visualization: A technique for creating images or animations to communicate a message.

Chapter VII
One–to–One Computing and Teacher Transformation

Andrew Kitchenham
University of Northern British Columbia, Canada

ABSTRACT

This chapter outlines a recent study on 1:1 computing and teacher transformation. It begins with an introduction to the theoretical framework of transformative learning and an overview of the professional literature dealing with 1:1 computing and teacher transformation. The study is then outlined, including the sampling procedures, participant background, and methodologies used. The remainder of the chapter presents the findings and conclusions related to the central theme of whether 1:1 computing transforms teachers. The chapter concludes with implications for the future.

INTRODUCTION

There has been a great deal of debate in the professional literature on the benefits of 1:1 computing for elementary school children. For instance, 1:1 computing increases student achievement especially in writing, analysis, and research (Bebell, 2005; Fadel & Lemke, 2006; Livingstone, 2006; Russell, Bebell, & Higgins, 2004); improves student attendance and school enrolment (Barrios, 2004), motivates students to become self-directed learners (Livingstone, 2006) and become engaged (Cromwell, 1999; MEPRI, 2003); decreases dis-

ciplinary problems (Baldwin, 1999); leads to an increase in standardized test scores (Stevenson, 1999); and lays the foundation for constructivist learning (Bransford, Brown, & Cocking, 2000; Light, McDermott, & Honey, 2002). There has, however, been little discussion on the effect teaching with technology has on the children's teachers. My goal in this chapter is to present findings from a recent study on teachers transformed through technology in British Columbia, Canada, in particular, teachers in 1:1 classrooms; that is, I define 1:1 computing classrooms as places where every child in the class has a laptop computer with wireless Internet and printer capabilities for at least 50% of the day.

TRANSFORMATIVE LEARNING

The central theoretical framework adopted in this study was Mezirow's (1991) transformative learning theory. This theory involves a learning process of examining, questioning, validating, and revising perceptions (Cranton, 1994), which is based on constructivist assumptions of adult learning. According to Mezirow (2003, p. 58), it "is learning that transforms problematic frames of reference—sets of fixed assumptions and expectations (habits of mind, meaning perspectives, mindsets)—to make them more inclusive, discriminating, open, reflective, and emotionally able to change." The theory itself has been debated in the literature for nearly 30 years, and it has been integrated into education, psychology, philosophy, sociology, nursing, and religious studies, to name a few disciplines. It has also spawned an international journal dedicated to the theory's application in myriad studies. In his original 1975 study with 83 women in 12 different re-entry college programs, Mezirow (1978) proposed 10 phases to transformative learning. The two distinct elements of these 10 phases could be characterized as the disorienting dilemma (Phase 1) and critical self-reflection (Phases 2 to 10). Mezirow (1991, p. 94) says the disorienting dilemma "begins when we encounter experiences, often in an emotionally charged situation, that fail to fit our expectations and consequently lack meaning for us, or we encounter an anomaly that cannot be given coherence either by learning within existing schemes or by [rote] learning new schemes."

The second element, critical self-reflection, involves a close examination of the factors (Phases 2–10) which cause a change in a person's worldview. According to Mezirow (1991), it is imperative that the person consider these contributing factors

to the change so that a demonstrable transformation can occur in that phase.

In a book chapter on adult learning theory, Mezirow (1995) emphasized the importance of critical reflection in transformative learning theory. Straightforward reflection is the act of "intentional assessment" (p. 44) of one's actions whereas critical reflection not only involves the nature and consequence of one's actions but also includes the related circumstances of their origin. He presented three types of reflection and their roles in transforming meaning schemes and perspectives: content reflection, process reflection, and premise reflection. In the process of reflection, teachers ask themselves critical questions (Cranton, 1994), but they also engage in critical discourse with their peers. According to Mezirow (1991, p. 78), under optimal conditions, participation in this discourse would have:

accurate and complete information, be free from coercion and distorting self-perception, be able to weigh evidence and assess arguments objectively, be open to alternative perspectives, be able to reflect critically on presuppositions and their consequences, have equal opportunity to participate (including the chance to challenge, question, refute, and reflect, and to hear others do the same), and be able to accept an informed, objective, and rational consensus as a legitimate test of validity.

The application of distortions in epistemic, sociolinguistic, and psychological meaning perspectives and the use of critical discourse with others are clearly applicable to learning educational technology, in general, and to 1:1 computing, in particular. Teachers would need to re-evaluate what they believed they knew and what they actually knew (epistemic), what specific language was used in educational technology settings (sociolinguistic), and what they perceived about their own ways of learning (psychological) through critical discourse with other learners or mentors.

Figure 1 portrays the relationship between and among the principal elements of transformative learning. A *perspective transformation* occurs when adult learners, through critical reflection, come to the realization that new meaning structures need to be created and action needs to be taken in order to break away from constraining psychocultural assumptions (Mezirow, 1981). The perspective transformation begins with a *disorienting dilemma,* which may be positive or negative, so this element is presented first. A person might also experience *a change in meaning scheme or perspective,* which may manifest in different ways; therefore, the second deals with altered meaning schemes and meaning perspectives. A *revised frame of reference* is part of a perspective transformation, and on the basis of the findings of a previous study (Kitchenham, 2006), three

Figure 1. Summary of the transformative learning elements (©2007, Andrew Kitchenham. Used with permission)

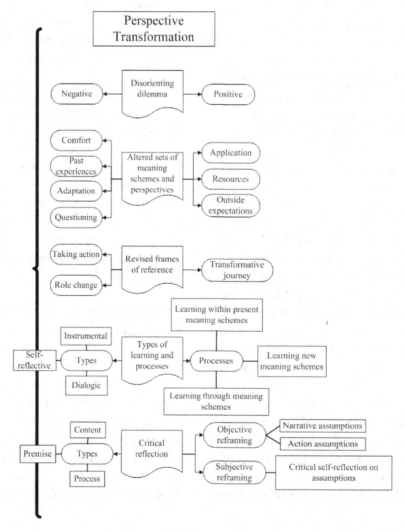

forms of this element are listed. A person might experience a *perspective transformation* through different learning types and/or learning processes, so this element relates to people's comments as they asked how, what, with whom, when, and why they were learning. Last, the crucial element of transformative learning is *critical reflection;* the different types of critical reflection, as well as *critical reflection on assumptions* and *critical self-reflection on assumptions,* are presented here. These elements will be further explored in the data analysis section of this chapter.

THE CONCEPT OF 1:1 COMPUTING

Here I discuss the studies that have been conducted on 1:1 computing schools and districts. In adherence to the brevity of this chapter, the discussion will be limited to the findings related to teacher change and teacher transformation. Bebell (2005) conducted a large-scale investigation of six 1:1 computing classrooms in New Hampshire during the first nine months of a project. In total, his sample included 35 teachers and 400 seventh grade teachers. He used teacher and student pre- and postsurveys to request information on a variety of areas and provided myriad data on the benefits of 1:1 computing. Germane to the present study on teacher transformation, he examined computer use, demographic information, teachers' attitudes towards technology, and teachers' comfort levels with technology. His findings indicated that 100% of the teachers reported that their computer skills had improved, over 70% believed that their roles in the classroom had changed, and approximately 85% of the teachers felt that their beliefs about teaching and learning had changed since teaching in a 1:1 computing classroom. In particular, he presented that "many teachers report that their participation in the program led them to change their understanding of how people learn and to reflect on education as a whole" (p. 33) which is a clear indication of transformation.

Russell et al. (2004) conducted a comparative study between two types of classrooms that included 209 students across nine classrooms. The first set of classrooms (n = 5) had access to a cart of laptops which was used for a one-week period every five weeks. In the other set of classrooms (n = 4), each student had his or her own laptop. They utilized observational checklists, recorded narrative accounts, semistructured interviews, student surveys, and a writing prompt to have students draw a picture of themselves writing in school. As with Bebell (2005), many data were generated from these rich sources of data; however, related to the present study, they reported several interesting findings. First, the 1:1 laptop teachers applied technology in their classrooms seven times more frequently than the shared laptop teachers (technology index for application=33.67 vs. 4.85 in the shared classrooms). Second, the actual classroom structure was different in the two types of classrooms as the laptop classrooms reflected a higher occurrence of laptops as peer conferencing and group presentation tools and the students tended to work independently much more often than the shared laptop classrooms. Third, as an overall conclusion, the researchers argued that technology use for a variety of educational purposes increases dramatically in either classroom environment but more significantly in the 1:1 classrooms.

Based on her survey of the professional literature, Livingstone (2006) concluded that 1:1 computing can assist teachers in planning, teaching, and communicating. She argued further that 1:1 programs lead teachers to a vast array of curricular resources that, in turn, can lead to richer lessons for the students. Last, 1:1 computing improves communication with the educator stakeholders such as students, parents, and colleagues.

Jeroski (2005, 2006) found that teachers in British Columbia changed their practices based on their 1:1 computing experiences. In particular, the teachers reported increased use of assessment practices in relation to the promising practice of informing the students of the assessment criteria in advance, using the student results to modify instruction, and utilizing the BC Performance Standards, a series of documents that describe and model authentic assessment methods, to assess the students more effectively. These results constitute a change rather than a transformation; however, a deeper examination of her description does reveal some degree of transformation. To wit, the teachers re-examined their roles in the classroom as sages on the stages to become guides on the sides. She also reports that the change in practice was difficult for the teachers, a tell-tale sign of a perspective transformation (Mezirow, 1991) and that critical discourse (Mezirow, 2003) played a major role in their changes in practice (Jeroski, 2005).

In sum, 1:1 computing leads to stronger and more confident teachers. These teachers tend to think through their lessons more carefully and become more aware of their roles as educators because of the laptop environments. They also tend to critically reflect more often on their choices and critically self-reflect on how they see themselves and others in relation to their individual life worlds. Last, laptop teachers view the teaching and learning process in a different manner than they did prior to using laptops in their classrooms. In short, 1:1 technology transforms teachers.

BACKGROUND TO THE STUDY

According to Ungerleider (2003, p. 118), the promise that "with computers teaching would be transformed" has not been realized as the changes in teaching "have not been radical or 'transformative' as implied by the rhetoric," but are due to the fact that people will only "adapt easily to new practices that they regard as equivalent alternatives to existing practices." It should be noted that he does not supply any evidence for these claims but relies on his own rhetoric to prove the point. On a practical level, this study investigated the very point he attempts to make by answering the question as to whether 1:1 computing teachers experience a perspective transformation when working with technology.

I became intrigued by the effects of educational technology on teachers after reading Cuban's (2001) scathing, but very limited, book on computers in the classroom. I went back to university to complete a second doctorate which examined the transformation of teachers through educational technology (Kitchenham, 2006). Using Mezirow's model of transformative learning, I demonstrated that the teachers in my study were transformed, not changed, through their use, integration, and teaching of technology. I made the distinction that "change" usually means altering some form of teaching strategy whereas "transformation" means a marked difference in the way that the teacher views his or her role as an educator as well as his or her view of the teaching process.

In 2005, the BC Ministry of Education invested $2.1 million across 12 school districts in order to investigate the benefits of 1:1 computing in the classroom. Their primary area of research was in student achievement following their success in the Peace River North school district. Focused in Fort St. John, the school district found significant improvement in the school children's achievement, particularly in the areas of writing and reading. As well, the province invested an additional $1.5 million to provide Webcasting capabilities to every rural secondary school and approximately half of the urban secondary schools in the province.

From the ministry-funded 12 school districts, I chose three school districts that represented three distinct 1:1 computing representations. To contextualize the study, a brief background on each school district will be presented here. In selecting the three school districts, it was important to me that I choose one school district that was at the beginning stage of their 1:1 computing so that I could examine the teachers' initial transformative stages, one school district that had been using 1:1 computing for several years to ascertain the perspective transformations of more experienced teachers, and one school district that was using 1:1 computing in an alternative manner so that I could investigate whether the format might affect the transformations.

The first school district, Cowichan Valley, became involved in 1:1 computing in 2005 as part of the BC Ministry of Education's initiative to fund laptop schools. In the year of this study, five schools were identified as pilot schools which included one or two grade 5 teachers in each school. There were 250 Apple iBooks distributed to the students and teachers. Four months before the students received their individual computers, the teachers received professional development training on the use of the computers and on effective writing strategies. As well, there were eight informationa and communication technology (ICT) teachers to assist the classroom teachers in any difficulties that might have occurred throughout the year. One teacher from each of the five schools was identified and contacted to request participation in the study. Four teachers from four of the five schools agreed to take part and completed the informed consent form. They also completed the online questionnaire and participated in the semistructured interviews at their respective school sites.

Nisga'a School District had been using 1:1 computing for three years. Of particular interest was the fact that every teacher and student in grades 4–12 had a laptop. There are 45 teachers and 440 students in the district and 120 adult learner students with approximately five instructional technology support personnel. In 2003, four grade 6 classes were chosen to pilot 1:1 computing, and each year an additional grade was added until 2006, when all classroom teachers became 1:1 computing teachers. The first few years were district funded, but the BC Ministry of Education provided funding in 2005 to assist in 1:1 computing. All schools in the district are members of the Network of Performance-Based Schools.

For the purposes of this study, four of the five schools in the district were chosen for site visits. The district principal identified 12 teachers who used the laptops in their daily teaching, and these 12 teachers were contacted for a participation request and were e-mailed an informed consent form. All 12 teachers completed the online questionnaire and were interviewed during my site visits.

The last school district, Prince George, used an alternate form of 1:1 computing in the form of a mobile lab at one school. The school included grades 6–8 with an overall population of 700 students and 200 computers. There are three stationary computer labs and one mobile lab with 30 laptops with a dedicated server, data projector, and laser printer. Every teacher in the school received a tablet computer this year with the expectation that they would use and integrate, but not necessarily teach, technology in their respective disciplines. The seven mobile lab teachers are expected to not only use and integrate technology but also to teach technology as appropriate. The vice principal of the school acts as the educational technology coordinator so that the teachers are given pedagogical as well as technical support. Any problems that extend beyond the expertise of the vice principal are referred to an on-site analyst who is shared across six schools. The mobile lab teachers sign out the lab through a log book so all teachers know who has the lab and for how long. As well, any problems with the computers are recorded in the log book, and it is reviewed at the end of each day. In this school, seven teachers were identified by the vice principal as frequent users of the mobile lab. The seven teachers were contacted for a face-to-face meeting at which the study was outlined to them and they received the informed consent forms. The results from four of the seven teachers are included in this study; the remaining three have been unable to commit to the required timelines. They will, however, be included in future results as the time constraints become less pressing.

Each participant in the study completed an informed consent form which had been approved by the respective university and school district ethics committees. Teachers were told that they could withdraw at any time for whatever reason. They chose their own pseudonyms but were also assigned alternates should their choice not be conducive for research reporting. For instance, one teacher chose "Mickey Mouse," so for the purposes of reporting her results, the alternative was used.

RESEARCH METHODS

Using an adapted model of my previous research paradigm (Kitchenham, 2006), I conducted the study in the three school districts with the 1:1 computing teachers. I used three research tools: an online questionnaire, a semistructured interview, and researcher field notes. The teacher questionnaire informed the semistructured interview, and my field notes filled in gaps among the other data instruments. That is, each data source added to and expanded on the other data sources so that the pooled data revealed significant results in relation to the degree of perspective transformation.

I asked the teachers to complete an online survey that requested their ranking of specific statements dealing with transformative learning (see Figure 2).

In particular, they dealt with their perceptions of 1:1 computing in relation to alternative understandings of a new problem, contexts of problems, critical reflection and critical self-reflection, testing new beliefs, coping with anxiety, taking action, and engaging in critical discourse. To ensure a clear distinction in the degree of perspective transformation, the teachers rated their responses on a 10-point agreement scale; a choice of "1" (Strongly Disagree) meant a low degree compared to "10" (Strongly Agree) indicated a high degree of perspective transformation. The teachers were given three weeks to complete the

survey and, as part of the response, indicated when they were available for an interview.

As well, each participant was interviewed based on his or her responses to the questionnaire. For example, if a teacher responded on the questionnaire that she critically self-reflected on her 1:1 computing evidenced by a response of 8, 9, or 10, that teacher, in the interview, was asked to provide concrete examples of the reflection in relation to 1:1 computing. Each interview lasted 30 to 90 minutes and was transcribed. The transcriptions were returned to each teacher for any clarifications and were returned to me within one week of e-mailing the documents.

The researcher field notes augmented the other sources and provided me the opportunity to record my own reflections on the teachers' perspective transformations and other related information. For instance, after teaching a mobile lab lesson to her Math 9 students, Gladys indicated that she saw her role changing from one who stood at the front of the class to one who never stayed in one place for more than a minute or two. That comment was recorded in my field notes as it clearly related to a change in frame of reference, a necessary part of a perspective transformation.

A mixed-methodology approach (Tashakkori & Teddlie, 1998, 2003), combining qualitative and quantitative research methods, was appropriate for this study. The qualitative method allowed for the coding and categorization of the rich responses from the 18 participants. The quantitative method allowed for the inclusion of frequency counts to describe the degree of perspective transformation.

RESULTS

In the analysis of the data, only comments related to teacher transformation were extracted for further examination so that any comments dealing with other influences from 1:1 computing were ignored. For instance, some discussion occurred

Figure 2. Technology Transformation Online Questionnaire (©2007, Andrew Kitchenham. Used with permission)

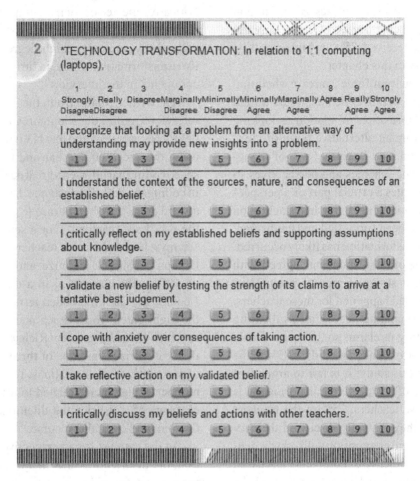

about student achievement but, unless they dealt with teacher transformation, they were not subjected to further analysis.

There were 4 male and 16 females in this study. 50% of the teachers had been at the school for three to five years; however, 35% had been teaching for 16 or more years. Before the respective projects began, 32% of the participants rated themselves as "developed" in technology, but 68% ranked themselves the same category at the time of the study. In short, the use of 1:1 computing

transformed these teachers to the extent that they perceived themselves as being more competent than previously. As well, age does not appear to be a variable for transformation as the majority of teachers had been teaching for over half of their lifetimes.

The data from the online questionnaire were analyzed for the degree of perspective transformation that had occurred. It was decided that a teacher experienced a high degree of perspective transformation if he or she chose an 8, 9, or 10 on the 10-point rating scale. Table 1 summarizes the results of the transformation section of the online questionnaire. For the purposes of discussion and to factor in some degree of error, only the statements that received 75% or higher will be elaborated upon in this chapter.

As can be seen from Table 1, an overwhelming number of teachers (95%) demonstrated a high degree of transformation in relation to looking at a problem from an alternative point of view. This examination is an important part of changing one's meaning schemes and perspectives so this datum indicates a crucial part of a perspective transformation. If someone takes action on beliefs that have been supported and confirmed, a perspective transformation has likely occurred. Given that 90% of the respondents agreed with this statement, a strong degree of perspective transformation had happened for these teachers. Adopting 1:1 computing necessitates validating beliefs and testing its claims so that a reasonable resolution can be obtained as it did for 85% of the participants in this study; it is fair to argue that a strong degree of perspective transformation is present for these teachers. 75% of the teachers indicated that they critically discussed their respective beliefs and assumption with other teachers which was predictive of comments discussed during the semistructured interviews. As well, the

same proportion of respondents indicated that they understood the origin of their beliefs and that the critically reflected on their assumptions related to their established beliefs. These data, considered collectively, indicate a high degree of perspective transformation which, in turn, supported the comments in the interviews.

All written data, from the semistructured interviews, online questionnaires, and researcher field notes, were entered into NVivo and analyzed using the speed coding bar and the coder. The speed coding bar allowed a great deal of flexibility in coding the data. For instance, I could highlight a word (e.g., "role"), a phrase (e.g., "a change in the way I see teaching"), or a sentence (e.g., "I see myself as a different teacher because of the laptops because I organize and even position myself [in the classroom] in a different way"). I could then assign a coded term, or a node, to the highlighted words. Each node, or a concept to which I wished to refer (Richards, 1999), was then categorized into one of three key elements of perspective transformations. Table 2 shows the number of statements related to the three broad elements of a disorienting dilemma, critical reflection, and critical discourse.

As the catalyst for a perspective transformation, the disorienting dilemma theme contained the least amount of comments (28, or 6.5%), but

Table 1. Online questionnaire and the corresponding percentage of responses 8, 9, 10

Statement	Percentage
I recognize that looking at a problem from an alterative way of understanding may provide new insights into a problem.	95
	•
I take reflective action on my validated belief.	90
I validate a new belief by testing the strength of its claims to arrive at a tentative best judgement.	85
I critically discuss my beliefs and actions with other teachers.	75
I understand the context of the sources, nature, and consequences of an established belief.	75
I critically reflect on my established beliefs and supporting assumptions about knowledge.	75
I cope with anxiety over consequences of taking action.	70

it represented comments from all 20 participants which indicate each person experienced this element. The overwhelming majority of comments (302, or 70.0%) were attributed to the theme of critical reflection which supports the claim that it is the critical element of perspective transformation. As well, critical discourse (101 comments, or 23.4%) which is also a major element in perspective transformations was well represented in the data.

DISORIENTING DILEMMA

According to Mezirow (1991, p. 94), the catalyst for a perspective transformation to occur is the disorienting dilemma that: "begins when we encounter experiences, often in an emotionally charged situation, that fail to fit our expectations and consequently lack meaning for us, or when we encounter an anomaly that cannot be given coherence either by learning within existing schemes or by learning new schemes." Without a disorienting dilemma, perspective transformation does not occur. In this study, the teachers identified perceived mismatches between what they believed and what they were practicing in relation to educational technology. There were many (28) instances of the teachers describing changes that caused them to question how they usually acted. Two stand out. One interviewee, clearly frustrated with the erroneous image of the school as a technologically progressive school, reported that such "hypocrisy" had changed the way she (Bea) used

to act, which was to agree with the public image of the school as a to the public as a "poster child" for what technology could do:

I would say that this school says a lot more about laptops than it's ever done. I used to agree with the party line and the district really wants to show that the money and time is worth it. I cannot agree with that idea anymore…which is making me dysfunctional, schizophrenic, and more determined to meet the perception.

She perceived this contradiction between what the principal said the teachers did technologically and what they actually did as a catalyst to change. She ensured that she learned the effective writing and technology strategies to meet the reputation of the school. This distance between the administrators and the teachers, as represented by Bea's comments, also reinforces (Hargreaves, 2003) the contention that her school culture was one of permissive individualism.

The second exemplar expressed her view on age and technology: "I initially believed that being [over 50 years old] would hamper me [but] once I evaluated my own ability to learn, the idea of using the mobile lab appealed to me. I am its strongest component but do get frustrated at my own inabilities and the pace with which the students move" (Pam). By reflecting on previously held beliefs and experiences, she saw the potential for some useful technology integration and teaching but only after she had evaluated her own learning ability.

Table 2. Transformative learning themes and the corresponding number of comments

Theme	TOTAL
Disorienting dilemma	28
Critical reflection	302
Critical discourse	101
TOTAL	431

In short, the 20 teachers, as exemplified by these examples, were experiencing their respective disorienting dilemmas as a precursor to perspective transformations (King, 2002; Mezirow, 2000). These disorienting dilemmas were clearly the catalyst for the perspective transformation as the teachers entered the "Fear and Uncertainty" phase of transformative learning (King, 2002). That is, at this stage, they were starting the process of change which involved changing their meaning schemes and perspectives at a time in their development that often involved difficult decisions and self-evaluation (Mezirow, 1978).

CRITICAL REFLECTION

The most dominant theme that evidenced in the participant responses was critical reflection and critical self-reflection (302 comments) which according to Cranton and Carusetta (2004, p. 289): "need not be linear, but is a rational process of coming to question habits of mind that become too narrow and too limiting." This section explores how the participants' comments evidenced Mezirow's (1995) critical reflection, content reflection, premise reflection, and process reflection (see Figure 1). Thinking back to past experiences is a critical element of *content reflection* (Mezirow, 1995). Sixteen participants described their prior experiences. Six cases are described in this chapter.

One teacher was direct in his content reflection as he informed me, "Years ago, I never thought that I would be a technology user. In fact, I was a little intimidated and certainly never saw myself using [the laptops] all the time. ...Years later, I thought that the computers would be abused [but] the students actually take incredible care of them" (Anthony). He thought back to when he had begun his teaching career and realized that he was, in fact, now a technology innovator because he had made the conscious decision to learn more about educational technology so he took the action of acquiring technology skills by participating in the 1:1 computing program.

Another teacher shared her beliefs on alternate ways of coming to a defensible conclusion in relation to the iBooks in her Grade 5 classroom: "Sometimes I thought that there would be one way to do something but upon reflection, I realized that there were many different and just as effective ways of working with technology" (Bea). Based on her past experiences, she recognized not only that she was single minded but also that the 1:1 computing program opened up possibilities that she would not have realized without the program.

Her colleague concurred in relation to her prior teaching as she indicated, "I thought about how we had done government before and torqued it with the laptops. The students researched on the Internet, created picture files, edited movies, and produced a movie on government using iMovie. ...It blew me away!" (Diane). Like Bea, this teacher perceived the need to take action as soon as possible after reflecting on the educational technology skills and strategies needed and to critically examine the usefulness of those skills and strategies as evidenced by the students' work.

Three additional comments demonstrate this sort of action, involving thinking back to what previously occurred: "I try to reflect right away after every lesson involving the laptops" (Tina); "I tried the reading strategies that [the Ministry of Education researcher] modelled and I didn't find them to be that useful upon reflection" (Douglas); and "After trying out the strategies, I came to the conclusion that the more I used them, the more successful I was [but] the key was to keep thinking back to what the original intention was" (Gale). In other words, these three teachers described the process of content reflection as they thought back on action that was done in the past to transform their present meaning schemes.

These six teachers had experienced the crucial element of the perspective transformation, critical self-reflection. That is, by examining their deep-seeded feelings that accompanied their original meaning scheme or perspective in the form of content reflection (Mezirow, 1991, 1994), they came to a new understanding of their learning. Without thinking back to what they had done in the past, content reflection, this perspective transformation would not have been possible. *Process reflection* was also evident as the participants considered the etiology of their actions and whether there were other factors yet to be unveiled (Mezirow, 1995). Although all participants offered comments related to this form of critical reflection, three will be highlighted here.

One specific interview comment stands out as an exemplar due to its thoroughness in describing process reflection in relation to the role of technology with special needs children: "I had a child who would do nothing for any teacher … Now because of this [1:1 computing program], he created a PowerPoint that blew us away… I had my doubts but after this experience and other numerous examples, I am absolutely convinced of [the program's] effectiveness [and] am glad that I didn't become that type of teacher that believes special needs kids can't learn" (Carol). It is quite clear that this teacher is critically self reflective as she considered her original actions and related factors ("I had my doubts"). Additionally, she had accumulated or concatenated transformations within set meaning schemes (Mezirow, 1985) ("but after this experience and other numerous examples, I am absolutely convinced of [the program's] effectiveness"). She also eschewed any "bandwagon" mentality or peer pressure to arrive at her own belief system (Mezirow, 1994) ("am glad that I didn't become that type of teacher that believes special needs kids can't learn"). Cranton and Roy (2003, p. 91, emphasis in original) characterized this intensity as individuation, or "the *process* by which we become aware of who we are as different from others," as compared to one's uniqueness and one's ability to concentrate on oneself. This critical self-reflection is a crucial

element of transformative learning as explained in Mezirow (1991).

Another teacher commented on the importance of examining the evidence for an established belief as she stated, "I believe that technology integration definitely improves writing achievement because I did the research from Fort St. John and Maine before I even volunteered to part of this project. There are many more hiccoughs that arrive each day but I can trace many of them to what others have experienced with the laptops" (Bea). She believed that if she were to enter the 1:1 computing program, she would need to conduct some background reading in studies related to its effectiveness with students. She did so but also acknowledged that there would be factors that could arrive, some which were predictable but some of which would be unknown. A third teacher, Mona, demonstrated the intensity of realizing the origins of one's actions, or process reflection:

I was at the point that I just wanted to get out of this place and started saying, "Who really gives a damn?," and I started to do the minimal of work. I saw my job as one of gatekeeper in the classroom. As I have started getting into the [1:1 computing], I realize that the students are turned on. ...they produce great papers and are not behaviour problems. [Now] I see my job as motivator and, yes, sometimes, as follower of the students. This wasn't me and I resented the change. Now I am fired up to get going every day!

Mona considered the origins of how she was acting and now what she was prepared to do in the future in the form of an intense reaction. She also characterized a role change as she moved from a Gatekeeper to a Motivator and Follower (Mezirow, 1995).

The previous examples also demonstrate that my research supports Mezirow's (1985, 1995) learning process within a learning function. In their process reflection, the teachers are operating self-reflectively by acquiring new meaning schemes that are compatible with their existing schemes within their respective meaning perspectives. The first teacher, Carol, examined her belief system of how a teacher should deal with special needs children and revised the notion to include her new belief system. The second, Bea, came to the conclusion that the 1:1 computing program was grounded in the research and was more than a philosophy. The last teacher (Mona) reflected on her previous work ethic, considered the factors related to that past, and revised her present work ethic. All three teachers needed to consider the origins of their actions and the related factors in order to adopt their new meaning schemes.

Premise reflection was evident in 18 participants' responses. Rather than thinking back to past experiences (content reflection) or considering the origin of their actions and whether there were still other factors to be unveiled (process reflection), the participants examined the broader implications of their perspective transformations (Mezirow, 1995). Three participants' comments, one from each school district, will be offered as examples. Like the previous teacher, (Carol), another teacher (Diane) reported her ideas about the role of technology with special needs children but was more particular in how her role had changed:

I now see the power of the iBooks with special needs kids. I would never have believed that these kids could produce anything, let alone the quality of what they produce. ...My established belief was that they don't need technology and they do. I know clearly see the bigger picture of this [1:1 computing] project. ...More importantly, I saw my job change from some who was a babysitter and a gloried TA (Teaching Assistant) to a person who knows some effective strategies for these special needs children.

Diane acknowledged that the laptops assisted the special needs students in completing

projects but perceived her role as a teacher has changed from "a glorified TA" to a special needs teacher.

A teacher in another school district, Pam, summed up her feelings by saying, "I am so far behind all the students and behind most of my peers. I am a failure in terms of this project but I should also say that (a) the school district has provided no training to me and (b) considering how far I have come, I am not a complete failure, I guess" (Pam). For this teacher, the broader implications of her perspective transformation were to consider herself to be a failure. The third interviewee (Lucy) who exemplified premise reflection described the process she goes through when making decisions about technology integration and teaching in her classroom:

I love the laptop program. I accept that they can be easy targets for abuse and overuse but I think carefully about every task that I give my students. So I will always be looking to see what I can do and every year I do add something new. And I adapt what I have to make it work better. Each month or so, I introduce a new program or challenge. ...For instance, this month we are looking at Chris van Allsburg books and how they can relate to the [area where we live]. I have tried Kidspiration at home for brainstorming and it looks like it will work well with these students. ...If I find that a program or task doesn't work, I look at why but I don't flog a dead horse. I do change and adapt my role as a teacher, though, so I do not become stagnant.

In other words, this teacher reflected critically on the larger view of what is operating in her value system and ensured that critical reflection was always part of her decision-making process. These three teachers were questioning their roles as teachers in a broader context and, in the process, were feeling the pressure to change their meaning schemes and perspectives. At this stage, they appear to be dialogic and critically self reflective in their approaches as they closely examine the specific context for learning to take place, and the reasoning behind learning the information. Specifically, Diane has begun to question whether schools are places where special needs students can be neglected and whether technology can be an equalizer of sorts. Pam sees her role in this project as one of slow or difficult learner and appears to be despondent as her lack of training and success with the students but is conscious of the progress she has made. Lucy critically examines what she does with the 1:1 computing and appears to be confident but is aware of being "stagnant" in her teaching without that critical reflection.

As well, these teachers are, in essence, describing what King (2002, p. 199) characterized as: "one of [the] fundamental transformations of perspectives, ways of understanding, and empowerment that goes beyond technology (the innovation) itself and is best explained through transformational learning theory." They are critically self reflective as they consider carefully the requisite information for success, the time allotted, the resources available, and the end result. When these three participants critically reflected on the broader implications of their perspective transformations, they became aware of their technology development. This awareness led to a more conscious understanding of their social roles (Diane and Pam) or to a critical examination of technology use (Diane and Lucy).

CRITICAL DISCOURSE

Mezirow (2000, pp. 10-11) defined critical discourse as: "that specialized use of dialogue devoted to searching for a common understanding and assessment of the justification of an interpretation or belief." Participating in critical discourse requires an open mind, listening emphatically, reserving judgement, seeking a common ground, and portraying emotional intelligence attributes such as self-awareness and impulse control

(Mezirow, 2003). These characteristics are often exhibited in extraverted thinkers (Cranton, 2006). Critical discourse is actualized in the form of (1) objective reframing of narrative assumptions, (2) objective reframing of action assumptions, and (3) subjective reframing of critical self-reflection on assumptions (see Figure 1). In this study, there were 101 comments related to critical discourse.

All 20 of these teachers section exemplified critical self-reflection on assumptions as they applied *narrative* critical reflection on assumptions to themselves (Mezirow, 1998) and saw the benefits of collegiality and collaboration in acquiring educational technology skills. In other words, they used insight from a narrative, such as a discussion with a colleague and expressed the need to participate in critical discourse with colleagues to make informed decisions about the benefits of educational technology within the lived experiences of their respective classrooms. Comments by one participant serves as evidence of objective reframing of narrative assumptions as the teacher offered specific evidence of her critical examination. All the participants expressed frustration at the inconsistency of the professional development offered to them regardless of the district in which they taught. One teacher (Nancy) offered pointed comments:

After the initial workshops, I critically reflected on what the presenters were saying we should do and I realized that much of what they said is defensible (but) we did get lots of information on best practice in reading but very little on how to use the laptops to get to those best practices. ...Also, only people who got in the first year got good in-services [those teachers] who weren't here then, got virtually nothing.

Nancy acknowledged that the information given to her was acceptable in theory, but she did not feel that the connection between reading achievement and the use of 1:1 computing was evident nor that the professional development was consistently presented to all project participants. Other discussants echoed the frustration of little connectedness between reading and laptop strategies and of the lack of in-services for all teachers. Interestingly, not one of the 20 participants could articulate a specific reading-laptop strategy they had learned from the workshops. All 20 participants critically examined something that was being communicated to her. Their critical reflection of assumptions, in the form of objective reframing of narrative assumptions, was an important part of their transformative journeys and technology developments. The process of critically reflecting on information being communicated to them allowed them the opportunity to see the benefits of technology infusion. When attention is shifted from (narrative) assumptions arising from statements made by others to assumptions evident in the process of an individual or group solving problems, objective reframing of *action* assumptions is evidenced. All 20 participants offered responses that exemplified objective reframing in the form of critical reflections of action assumptions. In other words, they considered their own assumptions within the context of a problem-solving situation (Mezirow, 1998). Given that all but four teachers used Apple laptops, the issue of iTunes was frequently discussed and debated. One teacher (Roxanne) explained the issue quite well:

The staff has had heated arguments about the use of iTunes or even just listening to music. I pointed out that I let my students listen as long as I know what the music is [but] it was my own children that convinced me. I watched them and talked with them about and it and they were, like, come on, just because you can't do it doesn't mean that we shouldn't. ...I challenged the teachers here to give it a try and as one teacher pointed out, the students actually write better when they listen to music. [The other teachers] have said that they found similar results. ...The discussion we had as a staff was critical to coming to a reasonable conclusion that we could all live with.

This teacher was demonstrating critical reflection of action assumptions which required her examining something that was communicated to her by her own children, critically discussing the suggestion with her colleagues, applying an empirical test, and arriving at a satisfactory conclusion based on that critical discourse.

Mezirow (1998, p. 197) argued that "learning to think for oneself involves becoming critically reflective of assumptions and participating in discourse to validate beliefs, intentions, values and feelings." Critical reflection on assumptions was evident in the subjective reframing of four types of assumptions: narrative, systemic, therapeutic, and epistemic (Mezirow, 1998), as evidenced in the responses from the 20 participants. In the interest of brevity, one example from each assumption type will be presented here.

The first type of subjective reframing of critical self-reflection on assumptions occurred as the participants applied *narrative* critical reflection on assumptions to themselves (Mezirow, 1998). That is, participants carried over insight gained from a narrative into their own experiences (Mezirow, 1989). One teacher (Bill) responded,

I found that I needed to be in control of my own learning and didn't find that I was learning a great deal beyond the surface meaning presented by [the Apple representation] at workshops. ...Discussing the ideas, the successes, and the failures was important for all of us. ...We all sighed relief when we started chatting and found that we shared the same concerns. For me, taking away that feeling of not being alone with this [1:1 computing] project gave me renewed energy. That energy came through in my teaching and in my students' learning.

In other words, the idea of applying previous conversations to their present lived experiences through critical self-reflection was an important element for this teacher and, in essence, for all 20 teachers' perspective transformations.

The second type of subjective reframing, critical self-reflection on *systemic* assumptions, was evidenced in the participant comments. One teacher questioned his role as someone who was expected to maintain contact and records with the district personnel using three media (writing, telephone, and e-mail) describing the concept of "paper pusher" rather than teacher: "So instead of having one way of communicating with [the district personnel], you have three and you're expected to check all three everyday. I know that other teachers complain about this craziness." This teacher (Douglas) discussed *systemic* critical self-reflection on assumptions (see Figure 1). That is, he self-reflected on the taken-for-granted cultural influences within his organization, the school, and questioned the utility of using three media to maintain contact with the parents (Mezirow, 1998).

The third type of subjective reframing, critical self-reflection on *therapeutic* assumptions, was typified in the respondents' comments. One teacher felt incredibly passionate about her lack of technology development as she (Helen) responded:

I feel guilty about not using the laptops more in my class. I see what [Sally] does with her students and I am mortified. I mean, we teach the same students so it can't be them. I feel left behind by them and by some other teachers. ...I have come a long way with the laptops and the [1:1 computing] project has changed how I look at my own teaching and my own development as a teacher. I just feel so inadequate with my technology skills thus far.

This teacher was discussing her *therapeutic* critical self-reflection on assumptions as she examined her problematic feelings and their related consequences (Mezirow, 1998). Her response typifies what Mezirow (1985, p. 24) characterized as an "epochal [and] painful" transformation of her sets of meaning schemes as her revised concepts, beliefs, judgments, and feelings have shaped this specific interpretation of the traditional expectation of teachers using technology (Mezirow, 1994). This expectation was in conflict with her understanding of what she believed she should be doing in comparison to her students and her colleagues.

The fourth type of subjective reframing, critical self-reflection on *epistemic* assumptions, was reflected in the teachers' comments. One teacher, Pam, in her thirtieth year as a teacher, expressed her views on age and technology adoption:

I haven't always used computers in the classroom but I adopted them in my classroom very quickly. Yes, I was critical at first as all reflective practitioners should be, but I saw the need for the students. Well before the [1:1 computing] program was implemented here, I was a strong advocate for computers in the classroom. I have been teaching 30 years this September and I know that people are surprised that I am a frequent user of the laptops but, I guess, I have always been an innovator but I wouldn't have called myself that at the time. Still don't. ...A pioneer, a risk taker. ...it's all part of my personality as a teacher.

This teacher represented *epistemic* critical self-reflection on assumptions as she investigated not only the assumptions but also the causes, the nature, and the consequences of her respective frame of reference to surmise why she was predisposed to act in a certain manner. The comments from the 20 teachers in this study reinforced the theme of a critical reflection of assumptions and critical self-reflection on assumptions as they described situations in which they were faced with a problem and had to rely on a community of learners to arrive at a reasonable solution. In other words, they posited many answers to a series of educational technology questions but agreed on set solutions by discussing the possibilities with their peers, when feasible, and adjusting their respective habits of mind (Mezirow, 1985, 1991, 2000). Given the fact that teachers are often reticent about using educational technology and the fact that the teachers in this study became more confident in their technology use as they engaged in critical discourse, critical reflection, and critical self-reflection in relation to 1:1 computing, there appears to be a sound argument for teachers using these three transformative learning elements when learning educational technology.

CONCLUSION

The first 1:1 laptop program was implemented in 1989 in Australia (Johnstone, 2003). In that brief time period, these programs thrive across North America, Europe, Australia, and South America. The benefits to the students have been well documented to the extent that the professional literature is virtually united in its finding that 1:1 programs increase student achievement, motivate students to come to school and to learn while they are in classrooms, decrease disciplinary problems, and contribute to a marked increase in student and teacher use of computers.

Mezirow's model of transformative learning contains key elements of technology adoption and infusion that have been discussed extensively as there is a clear emphasis on worldviews and frames of references being altered when teachers work with laptops. There are many instances when teachers are engaged in various types of learning and processes specific to 1:1 computing, and there are distinct times when teachers engage in critical reflection, critical self-reflection, and critical discourse as they struggle with the challenges of using the laptops in the classroom.

Technology, in general, and 1:1 computing, in particular, and all the issues related to technology infusion transform teachers as their worldviews are altered. The trend is that more and more teachers are accepting the notion of all learners having laptops in front of them for all or part of the school day. They acknowledge that technology is here to stay and that it is as natural as breathing for their students. Many teachers embrace the innovation but see that the students naturally expect to use computers for all of the school careers as they do at home.

The youth of today intuitively adapt to new technology at a rate faster than any we have seen in centuries. Across the world, researchers are presenting their findings that show how quickly we must move merely to keep pace; few of us lead the way anymore as this volume has shown. This study has proven that technology and its related issues transform the teachers but equally, it has shown that the students of today were transformed long ago and their teachers are merely catching up to them.

REFERENCES

Baldwin. (1999). Taking the laptop home. *Appalachia, 32*(1), 10-15.

Barrios. (2004). *Laptops for learning: Final report and recommendations of the Laptops for Learning Task Force.* Retrieved March 16, 2008, from the University of South Florida Web site: www.etc. usf.edu/L4L/Cover.pdf

BC Ministry of Education. (2005). *$2.1 million for computer pilot projects in schools.* Retrieved March 16, 2008, from http://www.bced.gov. bc.ca/onetoone/

Bebell, D. (2005). *Technology promoting student excellence: An investigation of the first year of 1:1 computing in New Hampshire Middle Schools.* Boston: Boston College, Technology and Assessment Study Collaborative.

Bransford, J., Brown, A., & Cocking, R. (Eds.). (2000). *How people learn: Brain, mind, experience, and school.* Washington, DC: National Academy Press.

Cranton, P. (1994). *Understanding and promoting transformative learning: A guide for educators of adults*. San Francisco: Jossey Bass.

Cranton, P. (2006). *Understanding and promoting transformative learning: A guide for educators of adults* (2nd ed.). San Francisco: Jossey Bass.

Cranton, P., & Carusetta, E. (2004). Developing authenticity as a transformative process. *Journal of Transformative Education, 2*(4), 276-293.

Cranton, P., & Roy, M. (2003). When the bottom falls out of the bucket: Toward a holistic perspective on transformative learning. *Journal of Transformative Education, 1*(2), 86-98.

Cromwell, S. (1999). Laptops change curriculum and students. *Education World*. Retrieved March 16, 2008, from http://www.education-world.com/a_curr/curr178.shtml

Cuban, L. (2001). *Oversold & underused: Computers in the classroom*. Cambridge, MA: Harvard University Press.

Fadel, C., & Lemke, C. (2006). *Technology in schools: What the research says*. Culver City, CA: Metiri Groups's Technology Solutions that Work/Cisco Systems.

Hargreaves, A. (2003). *Teaching in the knowledge society: Education in the age of insecurity*. New York: Teachers College Press.

Jeroski, S. (2005). *Research report: The wireless writing program 2004-2005*. Vancouver: Horizon Research & Development Inc.

Jeroski, S. (2006). *Research report: The wireless writing program 2004-2006*. Vancouver: Horizon Research & Development Inc.

Johnstone, B. (2003). *Never mind the laptops: Kids, computers, and the transformation of learning*. New York: iUniverse Inc.

King, K. P. (1998). *A guide to perspective transformation and learning activities: The learning activities survey*. Philadelphia: Research for Better Schools.

King, K. P. (2002). *Keeping pace with technology: Educational technology that transforms* (Volume One: The challenge and promise for K–12 educators). Cresskill, NJ: Hampton Press.

Kitchenham, A. D. (2006). Teachers and technology: A transformative journey. *Journal of Transformation Education, 4*(3), 202-225.

Light, D., McDermott, M., & Honey, M. (2002). *Project Hiller: The impact of ubiquitous portable technology on an urban school*. Retrieved March 16, 2008, from the Center for Children and Technology Web site: http://www2.edc.org/CCT/publications_report_summary.asp?numPubId=129

Livingstone, P. (2006). *1:1 learning: Laptop programs that work*. Washington, DC: ISTE Publications.

Maine Education Policy Research Institute. (2003). *The Maine Learning Technology Initiative: Teacher, student, and school perspectives mid-year evaluation*. Retrieved March 16, 2008, from http://www.cepare.usm.maine.edu_

Mezirow, J. (1978). *Education for perspective transformation: Women's re-entry programs in community colleges*. New York: Teacher's College, Columbia University.

Mezirow, J. (1991). *Transformative dimensions in adult learning*. San Francisco: Jossey-Bass.

Mezirow, J. (1994). Understanding transformation theory. *Adult Education Quarterly, 44*(4), 222-232.

Mezirow, J. (1995). Transformation theory of adult learning. In M. R. Welton (Ed.), *In defense of the lifeworld* (pp. 39-70). New York: SUNY Press.

Mezirow, J. (2000). *Learning as transformation: Critical perspectives on a theory in progress*. San Francisco: Jossey Bass.

Mezirow, J. (2003). Transformative learning as discourse. *Journal of Transformative Education, 1*(1), 58-63.

Mezirow, J., et al. (1990). *Fostering critical reflection in adulthood.* San Francisco: Jossey-Bass.

Richards, L. (1999). *Using NVivo in qualitative research* (1st ed.). Victoria, Australia: Qualitative Solutions and Research Pty. Ltd.

Russell, M., Bebell, D., & Higgins, J. (2004). *Laptop learning: A comparison of teaching and learning in upper elementary classrooms equipped with shared carts of laptops and permanent laptops.* Boston: Boston College, Technology and Assessment Study Collaborative.

Stevenson, K. R. (1999). *Evaluation report: Year 3, middle school laptop program.* Retrieved March 16, 2008, from http://www.beaufort.k12.sc.us/district/evalreport3.htm

Tapscott, D. (1998). *Growing up digital: The rise of the next generation.* Toronto: McGraw-Hill.

Tashakkori, A., & Teddlie, C. (1998). *Mixed methodology: Combining qualitative and quantitative approaches.* Thousand Oaks, CA: Sage.

Tashakkori, A., & Teddlie, C. (Eds.). (2003). *Handbook of mixed methods in the social and behavioural sciences.* Thousand Oaks, CA: Sage.

Ungerleider, C. (2003). *Failing our kids: How we are ruining our public schools.* Toronto: McClelland & Stewart.

Ungerleider, C. S., & Burns, T. C. (2002). *Information and communications technologies in elementary and secondary education: A state of the art review.* A research report prepared for 2002 Pan-Canadian Education Research Agenda Symposium, Montreal, Quebec.

KEY TERMS

1:1 Computing Classrooms: Places where every child in the class has a laptop computer with wireless Internet and printer capabilities for at least 50% of the day. Ideally, every child would have a laptop 24/7, but the reality is that the learners may have access to mobile labs with a class set of laptops and a printer within a wireless environment for half of the learning day or might have access to the laptops during school hours only.

Critical Reflection: Questioning previously held beliefs and assumptions, resulting in the acquisition of a new perspective based on that action.

Disorienting Dilemma: Within a perspective transformation, a disorienting dilemma is the catalyst for perspective transformation. Dilemmas usually occur when people have experiences that do not fit their expectations or make sense to them and they cannot resolve the situations without some change in their views of the world.

Frame of Reference: A frame of reference comprises a set of meaning schemes that encompass a habit of mind, a mindset, and a way of understanding and interpreting one's knowledge system. It is the problematic frames of reference that are transformed when one experiences a perspective transformation.

Meaning Perspective: "The structure of cultural and psychological assumptions within which our past experience assimilates and transforms new experience" (Mezirow, 1985, p. 21).

Meaning Scheme: "The constellation of concept, belief, judgment, and feeling which shapes a particular interpretation" (Mezirow, 1994b, p. 223). These beliefs, attitudes, and emotional reactions might change upon critical reflection by the adult learner.

Perspective Transformation: Occurs when adult learners, through critical reflection, come to the realization that new meaning structures need to be created and action needs to be taken in order to break away from constraining psychocultural assumptions.

Transformative Learning: A process of examining, questioning, validating, and revising perceptions which is based on constructivist assumptions of adult learning. According to Mezirow (2003, p. 58) it "is learning that transforms problematic frames of reference—sets of fixed assumptions and expectations (habits of mind, meaning perspectives, mindsets)—to make them more inclusive, discriminating, open, reflective, and emotionally able to change."

Chapter VIII
Web–Enhanced vs. Traditional Approach for a Science Course

Gennadiy Kuleshov
TUI University, USA

ABSTRACT

The use of Web enhanced curriculum to teach and reinforce science concepts based on specific learning objectives has been a positive experience for faculty and students. This chapter provides a review of the rapid development of Web enhanced science courses as a teaching-with-technology alternative to the traditional approach. The main theme of the article is a step by step introduction to the design, implementation, and usage of a computer-aided system in teaching undergraduate science (physics, mathematics, electronics, and chemistry) courses with an adequate laboratory experience. These steps are (i) the learning management system evaluation and selection; (ii) computerized course curriculum adjustment to a Web-based format; (iii) the simulations (virtual labs) and animated illustrations, either selection or development, if needed; (iv) the establishment of threaded discussion board where each student is expected to participate in discussions moderated by a professor; (v) computerized test set ups; and (vi) student feedback summarization and analysis.

INTRODUCTION

Thousands of educators across the globe are involved in activities exploring the opportunities and innovations of education in the XXI century. The Internet is now extensively used for commercial, personal, and educational purposes. One of the most popular tendencies in contemporary education is the development of either Internet based (online) or Internet enhanced or just computerized courses (Azad & Nadakuditi, 2006; Herskowitz & Kuleshov, 2004; Swearengen, Barnes, Coe, Reinhardt, & Subramanian, 2002). Various companies offer learning management systems, which provide integrated assessment tools. Among these are Blackboard, Web Course in a Box (WCB),

Web Course Tools (WebCT), CourseNet, Class-Fronter, and many others. What is the difference between these learning–teaching environments, and which one should educators select? This is the first question that appears in front of the prospective instructor. One challenge to faculty who design and implement Web enhanced courses is the development of good teaching material in an online format (Hansson & van Heugten, 2006). Simply putting the same material that was used in an on-campus class on a Web site and expecting the online students to learn at the same level as their on-campus counterparts is not logical (Encheva & Tumin, 2006). A new style of learning requires a new pedagogy and alternative teaching tools to enable the learner to grasp material without the benefit of an instructor's lecture. This is the second point to be discussed here. One of the major limitations of Internet-based courses is their failure to deliver laboratory-related courses (Azad & Nadakuditi, 2006). First of all, the lab assignments should be reconsidered and most of them should be rewritten in order to allow the users access to the simulation of an experiment not using the actual lab device. This relates to the safety aspect of college/university lab usage (Standler, 2005), a subject not considered here. This simulation interface in turn should be available to download either from the Internet or a local server. Analysis of a number of attempts that have been made to provide students and instructors with practical exercises over the Internet is the third subject to be briefly discussed here. The next topic of interest is the development of science experiment simulations. With the availability of modern programming and prototyping tools, many useful simulations and Web-based applications have been added to the regular teaching techniques (Hill, Ray, Blair, & Carver, 2003). For example, there is a lot of physics simulation freeware available on the Internet. However, some chapters of the course are not supplied with appropriate simulation software. Some easy examples of simulation application are discussed. One more topic that

deserves to be discussed is the availability of Internet tutorials and interactive tests. The article describes the set of ready to use simulation software that can be utilized for both the lesson illustrations and the virtual lab assignments. The interactive simulations allow students to explore a topic by comparing and contrasting different scenarios. Users may get a deeper exposure to the subject matter either by modifying parts of existing simulation or by building a new simulation from scratch. Another advantage for the users is the ability of simulation illustration to be paused and restarted for reflection and note taking. The last part of the article describes a set of originally developed computerized tests. They are applications of three hierarchical levels of difficulty which provide random access to the question data bank (Herskowitz, Khaitov, & Kuleshov, 2004; Kuleshov, 2006). These Web-compatible interactive tests might be used either as self-tests by online students or as local tests within a traditional class environment by on-campus students.

LEARNING MANAGEMENT SYSTEM

None of the three most popular e-learning environments (WebCT, Blackboard, and CourseNet) allow courses to be easily switched from traditional teaching style to the Web enhanced one. They are rather the frames containing more or less similar features to support either distance or Web enhanced education. Being most acquainted with the two last management systems, I will compare the Blackboard and CourseNet as two representing different tasks on which they are focused. Blackboard is a well structured and convenient tool for developing the course itself, whereas CourseNet is basically oriented on instructor–student communication including a semi-automated grading process. Three screen shots represent the hierarchical structure of the Blackboard management system branch which is related to the course itself. Course assignments scheduled weekly (see illustration) represent the components of the student activities; they are notes, Internet tutorials, virtual labs, and homework. The last two might be submitted either as hard or as soft copy (text file) stored within the digital drop box. Another extensively used option of the Blackboard environment is the discussion board, where each student might participate in discussions which are moderated by the professor. Another branch (control panel) allows the instructor to manually update the grade book, add or remove users, and set up the external links.

The next three screen shots represent the hierarchical structure of the CourseNet management system dealing with a group of students, a particular student, and the student's individual reports submitted and corrected, if necessary, by instructor. The main interface (see Figure 2) of CourseNet shows a current situation with the course progress: submitted reports, local grades,

and reports to be submitted and graded. The next personal interface for each enrolled student allows them to submit and store reports as well as to get the professor's feedback and grades. Although there is no restriction for students to communicate via regular e-mail, the CourseNet management system keeps all the information very well organized, automatically marked with date and time, and ready to use as reference. There is no option to manage the course contents. All the course materials are stored at a separate server; they also might be distributed as a CD, except additional external links and additional topics of the threaded discussions. The external link availability to be downloaded is the specific problem almost everyone has experienced. As the resources accumulated on the Internet grow, so too the browser's message "item not available" increasingly appears. So, the instructor should be able to provide the students with the working

Figure 1. Blackboard management system organization (from the left to right): main course interface, class assignment components, and animated demo

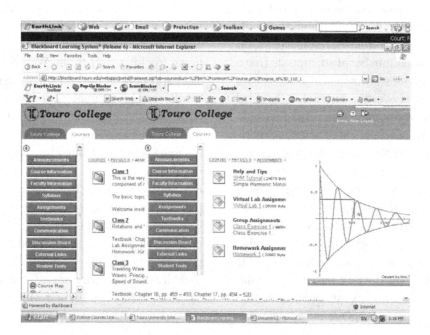

Figure 2. CourseNet management system organization: main course interface, particular student interface, and student–instructor written communication

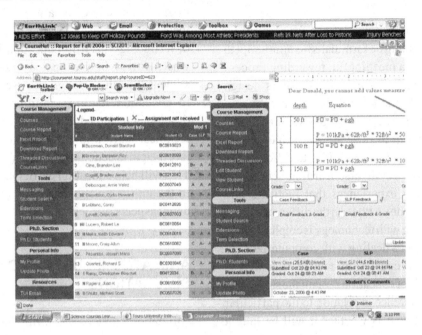

link reference immediately upon request. Such a separation of course development from running course management does not look too unnatural. Unfortunately, the Blackboard, the CourseNet, and the WebCT management systems are not oriented to support courses having laboratory as a component of the curriculum. A good example of WebCT system usage could be found at http://Webct1.northern.edu/Webct/public/home.pl with login "phystemp" and the same password.

There are a number of attempts that have been made to provide students with practical experimentation experience over the Internet. The most recent are the initiatives of the Northern Illinois University Internet-based facility for physical laboratory experiments (Azad & Nadakuditi, 2006) and of the Iowa State University to develop an experimental facility to train K–12 teachers (Chumbley, Hargrave, Constant, Hand, Andre, & Thompson, 2002). In any case, such an implementation requires the development of a complex

system in which the computer will be the gateway to the Internet, while the experimental device will be the facility that needs to be accessed via the Internet. As stated by Azad and Nadakuditi (2006), the Internet-based science laboratory systems are still in their infancy. Therefore, a number of issues need to be addressed to develop an effective, versatile, inexpensive, and sustainable system to make this approach acceptable and feasible for general use. Until there is any visible success this way, the alternatives, for example, Web applications (Ridjanovic, 2006) could be considered as an appropriate approach in developing the basis of computerized and Web enhanced learning systems. There are also other attempts at management systems development, for example, the initiative of Bradley Online University InterLabs Research Institute (2007) offering a conference style interface which is based on a combination of video, audio, and PowerPoint presentations.

COMPUTERIZED COURSE CURRICULUM

The common recommendations for curriculum development might be formulated as an attempt to make learning a meaningful, rewarding process for students and educators as educators design engaging units and lessons that align with academic standards, use research-based instructional strategies proven to raise student achievement, implement easy-to-use activities to differentiate instruction to meet diverse learning needs, and create learning experiences that motivate and engage all students. Although the difference in the style of teaching with technology is emphasized in most publications dealing with computerized (or Internet-based) courses, no matter what style is used, the goals of education remain the same. The important difference in relation to the particular course adjustment is whether it will be taught via direct or indirect communication. My own experience with teaching science courses confirms that the responsible online instructor is forced to spend even more time and apply more effort for one on one communication with his/her students than the same instructor teaching the same course traditionally. Of course, in absence of an oral lesson component of the course, it should have a well developed written background in the curriculum. It would be wrong to say that the traditional course should not have well prepared lessons.

The curriculum is a really critical problem for online courses that are supposed to include laboratory as an important part of it. The rather simple lab assignments, for example, recommended by *The Physics Teacher* journal (Shamsipour, 2006), are inappropriate for use in online classes. Meaningful online learning activities usually require a period of time for students to practice using technology tools to explore the virtual learning environment and develop a comfort level in operating in this space. To become familiar with the structure of the online (Smith-Gratto, 2006; Young, Craig, & Patten, 2005) course, students should take a quick tour of its online demo. Modification of curriculum to meet individual learner needs also might be considered as a way of course implementation (Ross, 2001). However, the inclusion of technology itself in education is only a tool; what matters is how technology is used to enhance student learning. The proper use of technology in education requires additional professional development aimed at creating instructors and technical staff who fully integrate technology into their instructional programs (Hannum, 2001). This will help education participate productively in the online revolution that is rapidly altering many aspects of society.

ANIMATED ILLUSTRATIONS AND SIMULATIONS

Animation provides a new dimension for teaching resources. The combination of movement and sound creates an effective method for learning: it is more appealing than text, photographs, or diagrams. Animated sequences can be stylized to keep them clear, simple, and easy to understand. In science, it is extremely effective, illustrating both the very fast and very slow processes at an appropriate speed of observation. Simulations of the complexities of moving molecules, or the convection currents in hot air circulating in a room are other possibilities. One of the great advantages in the use of animation and simulation in science is that the time to set up apparatus or the time elapsed for an experiment to work is removed and students can experiment with a variety of animations illustrating important scientific principles. Students can use the computer as the experimental apparatus and animations can be combined with a database and spreadsheet for further in-depth investigations (Couture, 2004; Ronen & Eliahu, 2000). There is a lot of physics and other science simulation software at relatively low cost and even freeware available on the Internet. One of the widest collections of science and other resources is the Multimedia Educational Resource for Learning and Online Teaching (MERLOT) project (Multimedia, 2007). MERLOT's strategic goal is to improve the effectiveness of teaching and learning by increasing the quantity and quality of peer reviewed online learning materials that can be easily incorporated into faculty designed courses. Since 1997, the California State University Center for Distributed Learning (CSU-CDL) has developed and provided free access to MERLOT. Another freeware resource for higher education is Open CourseWare (OCW) Consortium (Open Courseware Consortium, 2007). An OCW is a free and open digital publication of high quality educational materials, organized as courses. The consortium is a collaboration of more than 100 higher education institutions and associated organizations from around the world, creating a broad and deep body of open educational content using a shared model. The mission of the consortium is to advance education and empower people through OCW. See Figure 3.

There are also many local educational freeware collections, for example, Java Applets for Physics Education at University of Texas (University of Texas at Brownsville, 2007), HyperPhysics collection at Georgia State University (Georgia State University, 2007), Physics Academics Software at North Carolina State University (Physics Academic Software, 2007), MyPhysicsLab (Neumann, 2007), Physics Educational Technology (PhET) at Colorado State University (Colorado State University, 2007), and the commercial software collections at relatively low cost, for example, MCH Multimedia (MCH Multimedia, 2007), and many others. The common tendency in the development of physics illustration software is the conversion of schematic applications into lifelike ones. The latter versions look more attractive than the former, but it might be important rather for young high school students than for university students.

Online Tutorials

In the absence of synchronous direct communication between instructor and student, the online tutorial appears to be the most important interactive component of learning activity. Therefore, the online tutorial should follow clear step-by-step logic, stimulate student's research, compare and contrast different scenarios as well as encourage students with positive feedback. Searching the Internet for online tutoring materials may be frustrating (Serwatka, 2007). The sheer volume of Web sites is overwhelming; for example, a search for "physics tutorial" with Google returns 75,106 Web sites. There are a few attempts to create online tutorial collections, such as the University of Guelph (University of Guelph, 2007), Institute of Physics Publishing (PhysicsWeb, 2007), Open Directory Project (Open Directory Project, 2007), MERLOT project (Franco, 2003), Physics Academic Software (Risley, 2007), and others. Most ready to use online tutorial to be incorporated into particular course curriculum require the development of special assignments to adjust contents to the particular group of students. Sometimes it is even easier to develop a new tutorial to cover the specific subject of the course. In my own General Physics courses for nonphysics majors, many students experience problems with understanding, for example, concept of multiparametric functions. My students and I found that easy interactive application which allows the user to manipulate with three internal degrees of freedom (amplitude, frequency, and phase) is very helpful for exploration, visualization, and imagination of simple harmonic motion (SHM). Sets of similar tutorials have been developed for other chapters of physics, math, and principles of electronics courses. Many of these applications, by the way, have been created by my programming course students as course projects. Such a combination of programming learning and science learning activities is beneficial for both the groups of

Figure 3. Screenshots of typical interfaces for DC circuit physics lab (Colorado State University, 2007; University of Guelph, 2007)

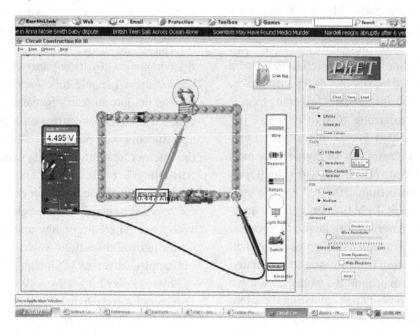

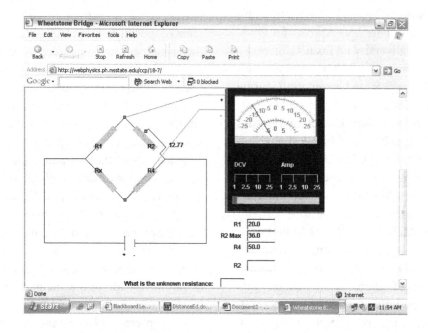

Figure 4. Interface of the Simple Harmonic Motion tutorial

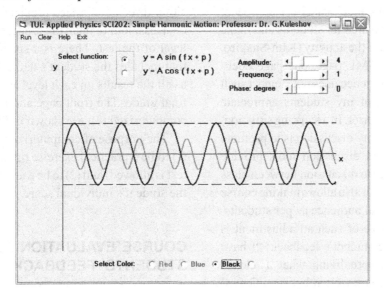

students. As an example, the interface of SHM tutorial is shown in Figure 4.

Threaded Discussions

A threaded discussion in contrast with a chat room is an online asynchronous conference. The professor can set up his/her own public or private discussion forums, and the students with a Web browser and the proper access can join in and participate in these forums. It allows forum members to view ongoing conversations, post messages to those conversations, and create new conversations. A successful online discussion has the same synergistic effect of group or in-class discussion, in which students build on one another's perspectives to gain a deeper understanding of the materials. In a threaded discussion, users have the options of responding either to the moderator (the instructor or the assigned student) or to one another directly, and then subtopics emerge as students respond to specific postings. These secondary postings are the "threads" that spin

off from the main discussion: a student responds directly to a comment made about the main topic, and another student responds to the response, and so a thread is formed. An online class discussion area can be beneficial to the learning process; at the same time, there are also drawbacks to using online discussion (Salmon, 2000). Monitoring the class discussion will help the instructor identify topics that need clarification or that have captured the interest of students, and the instructor can use the insights he or she gain to structure class contents. For some students, participating in an online discussion is less threatening than speaking in front of peers. An overloaded discussion area reported by Kortemeyer (2006) covers about a thousand discussion contributions for an enrollment of about 200 students. The sheer volume can add hours of reading to the regular course load, or distract students from other equally or more important coursework. All the learning management systems provide some form of Web-based communication. Interactive features such as online discussion or chat are likely to be built into the software. Some online instructors recommend the so called hands-off approach: create the discussion area for students and make no attempt to monitor the activity (Kim-Shapiro, 2007, interactive HTML page, one page document). My own experience does not support such an approach; most of my students appreciate feedback even if it is brief. In a learning situation, the primary goal of any discussion is to promote thinking. Web-based discussion tools provide many ways to increase discussion between class members and faculty. It also allows making course adjustment to the real audience as per students' requests. An example of such an adjustment is the response to the student's feedback: "I have had difficulty conceptualizing what a 'closed surface' is, and the connection between Gauss' Law and such surfaces" (Kim-Shapiro, 2007). This response was addition of the mathematical definition and theorems related to the Gauss' law to the background material as well as addition of appropriate external link references. At the same time, responses like that stimulate the Web tutorial development and implementation. Researchers have found that adding threaded discussion areas to a course increases student motivation and participation in class discussions (Jordan, 2001; Kortemeyer, 2006; Peters, 2007).

Computerized Tests

The computerized test (Herskowitz et al., 2004) is the Visual Basic application developed to check the student's ability to solve problems related to each covered chapter. The test has a hierarchical structure that includes problems of three levels of difficulty. On the first level, students are supposed to know just definitions. They need to answer correctly either three randomized questions in succession or at least four questions out of five to get access to the next advanced level. In the case of two incorrect answers provided on this introductory level, the student will find himself out of the test. When the student reaches the

second level, he or she will need to solve again either three randomized problems in succession or at least four of them to get access to the highest level of the test. There is a special report form that includes the student's name and ID as well as all the results on each level and the entire test final grade. The front page and flowchart of the computerized test are shown in Figure 5.

The purpose of computerized test is twofold: (1) to be a practical exercise (multi-access to the test is allowed) and (2) to be a test itself providing the student's individual score.

COURSE EVALUATION AND STUDENTS' FEEDBACK

Most publications dealing with Web enhanced education are focused on its advantages in comparison with traditional approach. As a proof of that, some authors have used "objective" mathematical tools like the Venn diagrams (Smith-Gratto, 2006) and statistically meaningful characteristics (Finkelstein, Adams, Keller, Perkins, & Wieman, 2006). I would like to emphasize that computerized technology usage (and the Internet as its delivery system) still does not guarantee a better educational process. Switching from the regular on-campus style to a remote one is not as easy as turning on the light in the classroom; in physics terms, it asks for compatible components and appropriate speed of a process (Pearce, 2007). Three teams are supposed to work consistently; they are (i) faculties, (ii) technology support and technical staff, and (iii) students. As the volume of an object in three dimensional space is proportional to the product of these three dimensions, the effectiveness of Web based education strongly depends on the relative value of each of the three factors. According to the multiplication law, if any of these factors approaches zero, the entire product is about zero as well. During the last seven years, I have had many occasions to observe such a situation at an institution where

Figure 5. Interface and flowchart of the hierarchical computerized test

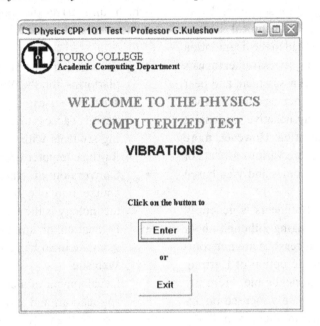

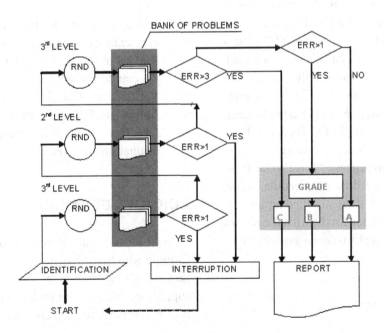

I used to work. If an aspiration to this contemporary style of teaching is not supported by an adequately prepared faculty, technical support staff, and students, it will lead to the degradation of the teaching and learning process rather than its improvement. Professional assessment and peer review of Web enhanced courses could be good tools for prevention of any negative tendencies in the computerized education. However, more studies are needed to explore various aspects of learning and teaching outcomes and Web based systems effectiveness.

Feedback from online students is generally positive and quite encouraging although about 20% of them for different reasons are not completely satisfied with online option of learning and this proportion is not negligible. From my experience, students are mainly focused on access time and timeline flexibilities, friendliness of both the instructions and interfaces, and the ability to repeat exercises if needed. Let us take a look at a students' feedback example: "I'm really amazed at how well I like Touro's approach to teaching in general. The blending of the case assignment, product reviews in the SLP's [Session Long Projects] and threaded discussion work perfectly. It's ideal for me personally since I live so far from anything and have a difficult schedule" wrote Larry Goodnite, a Summer 2006 student. There is a lot of such subjective feedback from students taking online science courses. The keywords in the citation suggest: "I live so far from everything and have a difficult schedule." Most of my online students are distributed around the world, and the only option for them to take classes is to do it in the virtual space via asynchronous communication.

CONCLUSION

Taking in account that this chapter is published in a handbook of digital information technologies, I would like to provide the reader who is going to become an online science teacher with a checklist which summarizes the common and the specific subjects of such an activity.

- Selection of the hardware and software platforms for the Web enhanced (online) science courses.
- Set up of access to the Demo course providing students with minimum requirements for the computer literacy.
- Conversion of traditional (on-campus) course into one in which teaching with technology is the focus of the curriculum.
- Evaluation of animated illustrations and simulations to be incorporated into course Web site.
- Development of a collection of virtual lab applications and assignments.
- Development of a collection of notes, homework, computerized tests, and examinations.
- Development of threaded discussions topics.
- Setting up access to the electronic version of a textbook if it is available.
- Review of the course by an expert in both the course content and online teaching.
- Verification of all the external link accessibility just before the start date.
- Development of the concepts of course evaluation and further implementation.

ACKNOWLEDGMENT

I would like to thank Professor Joyce Elizabeth Carbine who helped me to prepare this publication and all my students whose enthusiasm and support encouraged me to develop and to teach both the online and Web enhanced courses.

REFERENCES

Azad, A.K.M., & Nadakuditi, P. (2006). Internet-based facility for physical laboratory experiments. *Advanced Technology for Learning, 3*, 29-35.

Bradley Online University InterLabs Research Institute. (2007). The systems development environment. Retrieved March 16, 2008, from http://www.interlabs.bradley.edu/bradley-online/courses/cs403/default.htm

Chumbley, L.S., Hargrave, C.P., Constant, K., Hand, B., Andre, T., & Thompson, E.A. (2002, April). Project ExCEL: Web-based scanning electron microscopy for K-12 education. *Journal of Engineering Education, 91*, 203-210.

Colorado State University Physics Education Technology (PhET). (2007). Retrieved March 16, 2008, from http://phet.colorado.edu/Web-pages/index.html

Couture, M. (2004). Realism in the design process and credibility of a simulation-based virtual laboratory. *Journal of Computer Assisted Learning, 20*(1), 40-49.

Encheva, S., & Tumin, S. (2006). Web-based assessment system for teaching mathematics on undergraduate level. *Advanced Technology for Learning, 3*, 9-14.

Finkelstein, N., Adams, W., Keller, C., Perkins, K., & Wieman, C. (2006). High-tech tools for teaching physics: The Physics Education Technology Project. *MERLOT Journal of Online Learning and Teaching, 2.* Retrieved March 16, 2008, from http://jolt.merlot.org/vol2no3/finkelstein.htm

Franco A. (2003). Angel Franco's Online Physics Tutorial (MERLOT). Retrieved March 16, 2008, from http://www.merlot.org/merlot/viewMaterial.htm?id=90403

Georgia State University Department of Physics and Astronomy. (2007). HyperPhysics. Retrieved March 16, 2008, from http://hyperphysics.phy-astr.gsu.edu/hbase/hframe.html

Hannum, W. (2001, September-October). *Professional development for teaching online.* The Technology Source Archives at the University of North Carolina.

Hansson, T., & van Heugten, L. (2006). Collaborative writing in a software game: Re-enhancing a Vygotskian design. *Advanced Technology for Learning, 3*, 22-28.

Herskowitz, I., Khaitov, V., & Kuleshov, G. (2004, April). The general physics hierarchical computerized test. In *American Physical Society and American Association of Physics Teachers: Joint New York State Section Meeting and Spring 2004 Symposium*, Buffalo State College, Buffalo, New York.

Herskowitz, I., & Kuleshov, G. (2004). Distance education in the USA. *Energy, 6*, 27-33.

Герсковитц, А., & Кулешов, Г. (2004). Дистанционное образование в США (Опыт среднестатистического калледжа). *Энергия, 6*, 27-33.

Hill, J.M.D., Ray, C.K., Blair, J.R.S., & Carver, C.A., Jr. (2003, February). Puzzles and games: Addressing different learning styles in teaching operating systems concepts. In *Proceedings of SIGSE'03*, Reno, Nevada (pp. 182-186).

Jordan, D. (2001, March). The use of threaded discussions in the "online classroom." Los Angeles Mission College. Retrieved March 16, 2008, from http://lamission.org/hypernews/

Kim-Shapiro, D. (2007). Warm-up (sample). Department of Physics, Wake Forest University, Winston-Salem, North Carolina. Retrieved March 16, 2008, from http://www.wfu.edu/~shapiro/physics114/warmsam.html

Kortemeyer, G. (2006, June). An analysis of asynchronous online homework discussions in introductory physics courses. *American Journal of Physics, 74*, 526-536.

Kuleshov, G.G. (2006, December 4-14). The Web enhanced general physics course. In *Proceedings of the International Joint Conferences on Computer, Information, and Systems Sciences, and Engineering (CISSE'06)*, Institute of Electrical & Electronics Engineers (IEEE), University of Bridgeport, CT.

MCH Multimedia. (2007). Developers of interactive educational software. Retrieved March 16, 2008, from http://www.mchmultimedia.com/

Multimedia Educational Resource for Learning and Online Teaching (MERLOT). (2007). Retrieved March 16, 2008, from http://www.merlot.org/merlot/index.htm

Neumann, E. (2007). MyPhysicsLab, Physics Simulations with Java. Retrieved March 16, 2008, from http://www.myphysicslab.com/

Open Courseware Consortium. (2007). Universities working together. Retrieved March 16, 2008, from http://www.ocwconsortium.org/

Open Directory Project (dmoz). (2007). Science: Physics. Retrieved March 16, 2008, from http://dmoz.org/Science/Physics/

Pearce, H. (2007). Learning in a "Physics for Engineers" course. University of Cape Town, Department of Mechanical Engineering. Retrieved March 16, 2008, from http://www.aspect.uct.ac.za/documents/learn_phy.htm

Peters, K.M. (2007). Creative use of threaded discussion areas. WebCT community resources. Retrieved March 16, 2008, from http://www.Webct.com/OTL/ViewContent?contentID=898084

Physics Academic Software Publishing Organization. (2007). Retrieved March 16, 2008, from http://www.Webassign.net/pasnew/

PhysicsWeb. (2007). A community Web site from Institute of Physics Publishing. Retrieved March 16, 2008, from http://physicsWeb.org/resources//Education/Interactive_experiments/General_physics/

Ridjanovic, D. (2006, December 4-14). Rapid development of Web applications with Web components. In *Proceedings of the International Joint Conferences on Computer, Information, and Systems Sciences, and Engineering (CISSE'06)*, Institute of Electrical & Electronics Engineers (IEEE), University of Bridgeport, CT.

Risley, J. (Ed.). (2007). Physics Academic Software (PAS). Retrieved March 16, 2008, from http://www.Webassign.net/pasnew/

Ronen, M., & Eliahu, M. (2000). Simulation: A bridge between theory and reality: The case of electric circuits. *Journal of Computer Assisted Learning, 16*(1), 14-26.

Ross, V. (2001). Offline to online curriculum: A case-study of one music course. *Online Journal of Distance Learning Administration, 4*. Retrieved March 16, 2008, from http://www.westga.edu/~distance/ojdla/winter44/ross44.html

Salmon, G. (2000). *E-moderating: The key to teaching and learning online*. London: Kogan Page.

Serwatka, J.A. (2007, December 4-14). E-learning in technology: Using Project Merlot as a resource. In *Proceedings of the International Joint Conferences on Computer, Information, and Systems Sciences, and Engineering (CISSE'06)*, Institute of Electrical & Electronics Engineers (IEEE), University of Bridgeport, CT.

Shamsipour, G. (2006). Simple experiments for teaching air pressure. *The Physics Teacher, 44*, 576-577.

Smith-Gratto, K. (2006). Communication: The getaway to online instructional environments. *International Journal of Instructional Technology & Distance Learning, 3*. Retrieved March 16, 2008, from http://www.itdl.org/Journal/Dec_06/article05.htm

Standler, R.B. (2005). Injuries in school/college laboratories in USA. Retrieved March 16, 2008, from http://www.rbs2.com/labinj.htm

Swearengen, J.C., Barnes, S., Coe, S., Reinhardt C., & Subramanian, K. (2002). Globalization and the undergraduate manufacturing engineering curriculum. *Journal of Engineering Education, 91*, 255-261.

University of Guelph, Department of Physics. (2007). Physics tutorials. Retrieved March 16, 2008, from http://www.physics.uoguelph.ca/tutorials/tutorials.html

University of Texas at Brownsville, Department of Physics and Astronomy. (2007). Java applets for physics education. Retrieved March 16, 2008, from http://pdukes.phys.utb.edu/PhysApplets/appmenu.htm

Young, B.N., Craig, D.V., & Patten, K.B. (2005). Curriculum adaptations within the online environment. *International Journal of Instructional Technology & Distance Learning, 2*. Retrieved March 16, 2008, from http://www.itdl.org/Journal/Oct_05/article03.htm

KEY TERMS

Application Sharing: An element of remote access, falling under the collaborative software umbrella that enables two or more users to access a shared application or document from their respective computers simultaneously in real time. Generally, the shared application or document will be running on a host computer, and remote access to the shared content will be provided to other users by the host user.

Computerized Test: A method of administering tests in which the responses are electronically recorded, assessed, or both. As the name implies, computer-based testing makes use of a computer or an equivalent electronic device. Computer-based testing system enables educators and trainers to author, schedule, deliver, and report on surveys, quizzes, tests, and exams. It may be a stand-alone system or a part of a virtual learning environment, accessed via Internet.

Distance Education: Education that focuses on the pedagogy, technology, and instructional systems design that are effectively incorporated in delivering education via Internet to students who are not physically "on site" to receive their education. Instead, teachers and students may communicate asynchronously (at times of their own choosing) by exchanging printed or electronic media, or through technology that allows them to communicate in real time (synchronously).

Interactive Tutorial: A document, software, or other media on the Internet created for the purpose of instruction for any of a wide variety of tasks. Interactive tutorials usually have the following characteristics: a presentation of content, a method of review where user follows on-screen instructions (and in some cases watch short instruction movies), whereupon user does the tutorial exercises and gets feedback depending on his actions, and transition to additional modules or sections.

Learning Style: The method of learning particular to an individual that is presumed to allow that individual to learn best. Over 80 learning style models have been proposed, each consisting of at least two different styles (visual, auditory, reading/writing, verbal, logical, kinesthetic, and so on). It has been assumed that teachers should assess the learning styles of their students and adapt their classroom methods to best fit each student's learning style.

Virtual Lab: A Web site or software for interactive learning based on simulation of real phenomena. It allows students to explore a topic by comparing and contrasting different scenarios, to pause and restart application for reflection and note taking, to get practical experimentation experience over the Internet.

Web-Based Assessment: A method that enables educators and trainers to author, schedule, deliver, and report on surveys, quizzes, tests, and exams. It is well suited for both Internet and intranet environments and replaces the old pencil-and-paper testing systems and simplifies the entire exam cycle, including generation, execution, evaluation, presentation, and archiving.

Chapter IX
Microcultures, Local Communities, and Virtual Networks

José Luis Lalueza
Universitat Autònoma de Barcelona, Spain

Isabel Crespo
Universitat Autònoma de Barcelona, Spain

Marc Bria
Universitat Autònoma de Barcelona, Spain

ABSTRACT

Through a case study, we will exemplify how information communication technology (ICT) can be used in a collaborative way to constitute the foundations of intercultural projects in local and global communities. First, we present a local learning community based on the fifth dimension model where, adopting a collaborative model, each of its activities departed from the traditional teaching–learning form based on transmission. Collaboration mediated by ICT in local computer-supported learning communities, understood to be borderer zones that are not the exclusive property of any one specific cultural group, has the potential to generate genuine neocultures in which participants can share meanings and appropriate artefacts. Second, the same approach is adopted to analyse the dialogue established between educational researchers and technologists. Setting out with different goals, both groups engaged in a borderer activity involving the development of educational artefacts that could be accessed via the Internet. Common participation in those activities gave rise to a set of shared beliefs, knowledge, behaviours, and customs, that is, a network of meanings that crystallised into a common microculture.

INTERCULTURALITY THROUGH TRANSMISSION

In an earlier study (Crespo & Lalueza, 2003), we analysed a group of schools in Barcelona where all of the pupils belong to minority groups (gypsies and immigrants) in social contexts involving the risk of exclusion. Analysis of school practices allowed us to identify two main obstacles for the inclusion of pupils: The implicit representation of cultural differences as deficits which undervalues pupils in their role as legitimate interlocutors; The use of an educational model based on transmission which impoverishes the role of pupils as agents. The first impediment can be found in the teachers' discourses, where children's difficulties are represented as an individual handicap whose origin would reside in a deficient family context. Children and families are thus defined as lacking, for example, knowledge, so that the school is presented as the supplier of knowledge in a monopolistic regime, without recognising the role of the family as a generator of useful knowledge, and lacking habits and norms of behaviour, so that the school needs to discipline both the pupils and the parents, in such a way that controlling their behaviour is the principal objective, and making recourse to the authorities when the school cannot cope.

Furthermore, the consideration of cultures as essential traits leads to the negation of the joint construction of meanings. Differences are interpreted as the distance they must cover to change or adapt to our setting. Therefore, the responsibility lies only with them. This perception of cultural differences leads us to a fundamental issue: the failure to recognise the other as a legitimate interlocutor. In this way, the relations maintained with the children and their families occur in absence of dialogue and collaboration. For these children, school seems a hostile environment that is imposed upon them. Without sharing goals, it is more difficult to construct shared meanings and, therefore, meaningful learning.

The second of the obstacles consists of the predominance of an instructional model based on a theory of transmission (Rogoff, Matusov, & White, 1996), in which schoolchildren learn information and show that it has been codified and retained through certain evaluation tests that reproduce what was learned "piece by piece." The transmission model is based on a series of implicit beliefs. It is supposed that there are a number of prior agreements between the teacher and the pupils. These are never made explicit as they are considered obvious. On top of this supposedly intersubjective basis, new knowledge is deposited. Actually, a whole series of implicit negotiations occur, which are mediated by the teacher's authority. As the explicit goal is the correct codification of knowledge, whether teachers and pupils share meanings or not is of secondary importance. Indeed the meanings originating from the behaviour of the community of schoolchildren count for nothing, and are even considered a disturbance if they contradict or hinder the reception of formal knowledge. Pupils are not considered interlocutors, and in the absence of active participation; the appropriation of tools and contents becomes an arduous task.

To conclude, the combination of an ethnocentric representation in which differences are considered deficit and the transmission model of learning leaves no place for interculturality, beyond folkloric and noncontextualized actions. In the following section, we are going to describe a practical experience with an alternative model, mediated using ICT tools, and a collaborative approach that recognises the existence of a range of sociohistorical contexts that provide different sets of meanings. As opposed to the transmission model, this model is based on participation, in which the process of teaching and learning involves the creation of a new context, or a *microculture*, in which each new meaning has to be explicitly negotiated.

LOCAL COMMUNITIES FOR INTERCULTURAL EDUCATION

The Fifth Dimension Model

The assumption that minority children are at risk of being involved in nonmeaningful learning through school practices is based on the fifth dimension (5D), a model of activity developed by the Laboratory of Compared Human Cognition at the University of California, San Diego under the leadership of Michael Cole (1996). The foundation of the 5D approach is the creation of a reciprocal exchange relation between universities on the one hand, and community institutions and schools on the other. Activities mix play, learning, and involvement with university students (older peers) using a set of activities based on computers, video games, digital video, a variety of software and virtual communications including chat, e-mail and publication in blogs and photo galleries. It includes a system of rules and divisions of labour designed to facilitate the development in local communities of practices that emphasize written and oral communication in an environment saturated with different forms of culturally valued knowledge.

The 5D model responds to the need to match the objectives and methods of learning systems with the characteristics and needs of the sociocultural context. The theoretical foundations of the 5D model are based on the research findings of Michael Cole and Sylvia Scribner at the Laboratory of Comparative Human Cognition (1983). They indicate the failure of educational models that pay little attention to the role of the cultural environment in the construction of meaning. In common with other authors whose lines of research have been developed within the framework of a sociocultural paradigm (Lave, 1988; Rogoff, 1990; Wertsch, 1985), they argue that, above all, learning cannot be considered in isolation of the setting in which it takes place, given that it is a situated process.

Every 5D site is developed as a cultural microsystem that arises from the appropriation of certain artefacts by members of a learning community. Subjects participating collectively in practices organised by material and symbolic artefacts generate a *microculture*, that is, "a system of knowledge, beliefs, behaviours, and customs shared by the members of an interacting group to which the members can refer and which serves as the foundations for new interactions. Members recognise that they share experiences and that these can be alluded with the expectation that they will be understood by the other members, using them in this way to construct a reality for the participants" (Fine, quoted by Cole, 1996).

The 5D, therefore, seeks to generate *microcultures* or systems of activity whose use, based on a set of artefacts, is flexibly adapted to their local sociocultural situation and context, as well as to the needs of the community, understood here not only as the local context, but also as a complex reality in which there must be objects that are readily identifiable both by the adult members and the children in the local community, as well as by the educators and the researchers involved. In this *borderer activity*, the use of artefacts provides shared meanings, while at the same time these artefacts are modified in accordance with the goals and interests of the members of the learning community. This is possible because the 5D presents a *low level of institutionalisation* which allows this system of activity to be appropriated by very different communities, generating systems of meaning that come to form part of the network constituted by the local culture.

A LOCAL CASE

This *low level of institutionalisation* hinders the abstract description of what a 5D site is exactly. We describe one such site, set up by our team, in detail. There are 5D sites in USA, Mexico, Brazil, Sweden, Denmark, Finland, Spain, and

Australia. Our team has developed eight after-school and inner-school sites in the Barcelona Area. The oldest is "la Casa de Shere Rom" (CSR), an after-school learning community where we test new instructional uses of information and communication technologies. It is located on the premises of a Gypsy Association, in the Metropolitan Area of Barcelona, where a high percentage of the inhabitants are gypsies. Each week an average of 40 children, aged between 5 and 14, take part. In general, this group remains stable throughout the school year. Since 1998, more than 200 children have participated. Students of psychology and psychopedagogy are also involved and attend once a week for a whole semester. In total, more than 300 students have taken part to date. Finally, 18 research workers have become involved in the project for periods of more than a year, while a similar number have been involved for shorter periods.

The CSR was gradually designed through a process of negotiation between agents with different objectives, including members of the community, researchers, and educators (Crespo, Lalueza, & Pallí, 2002). The need for an educational project of this type was supported by statistics: 9.4% of the population was illiterate, to which should be added the fact that 28.7% had not completed primary education and only 3.1% had completed the higher levels of secondary education. Against this background, various interests were at stake: An association of gypsies whose members believed that the children in their community were the recipients of a poor formal education, a research team interested in accounting for the worrying rate of school drop-outs in this ethnic group, a large number of children loitering in the streets that were ready to try anything that promised to provide some fun, an equally high number of university students keen to gain some practical experience of dealing with real world problems. So, a *borderer activity* was set up, that is, a set of practices for groups of participants with different objectives, an intersection where various actors might seek to attain different goals with a certain degree of collaboration (Crespo, Lalueza, Portell, & Sanchez, 2005).

The CSR space is equipped with computers and peripherals connected to the Internet, in which tasks are undertaken collaboratively. These activities are presented in the form of a labyrinth with various rooms containing tasks (a computer game, a suggestion for collaborative writing, recording, and editing of a digital story, writing an article for a local newspaper, the chance to talk with children from other countries via the Internet, etc.). A set of task cards organises each task into different levels, and once a level has been successfully completed, the child can enter other rooms. Each child has the support of a university student, who brings his or her knowledge of the real world and formal language. Both interchange roles in order to cooperate and reach certain targets that have been negotiated beforehand. To do this, they challenge, provoke, and guide each other; they ask questions, respond, and make suggestions, sometimes getting it right and sometimes making mistakes. In short, they collaborate to reach their shared targets.

The most remarkable aspects of this activity are that: Attendance is voluntary and the atmosphere is like that of a playground; The path to be followed from one task to another is entirely flexible so the subject can choose between different rooms and taking different paths; Various forms of collaboration are encouraged. Here we can find several examples: Directly between the children themselves or by using e-mail and chat rooms; students helping the children; children helping the students; children and students asking a fictitious figure for help by e-mail or in a chat room; children in delayed time, via the clues that they leave on completing a game; and so on.

Nine years later, the management of the activity, in the beginning responsibility of the university, is now in the hands of the gypsy community, who maintain the students' participation. And we can see that children whose schools have traditionally considered them to be lacking in motivation, and largely inefficient and ill-disciplined pupils that are unlikely to succeed, continue to voluntarily attend a learning activity that requires them to reach targets in order to progress. In other words, they show discipline and use appropriate cognitive skills.

How can this be explained? We consider the CSR to have created a private universe of shared meanings between the various participants which has risen from a *borderer activity* (a space in which actors with different objectives converge) to a *microculture* (a space of shared meanings). That is to say that a learning space has been created that is centred around reading and writing activities using computers, a space that is considerably more flexible than the school and less dependent on the scripts laid down by the dominant culture. But it is by no means only a space for gypsy culture. On the contrary, it is a *microculture* which, starting out as a meeting point between actors (children, students, adult members of the gypsy community, and researchers) with very different goals, has gradually established the foundations for a private universe of meanings, shared by the participants.

An essential element in this process is that all actors are considered valid interlocutors, which is manifest in the constant explicit negotiation (from finding one's way around the labyrinth to the discussion of new games and activities) and in the collaborative set up of the activities. To belong to the same community drawn from various origins implies a mutual commitment and responsibility as regards the common undertaking, so much so that all parties are considered interlocutors. This issue takes us onto the role of intersubjectivity covered by the next section.

In the last three years, we have adapted this model of activity to other sites including six elementary schools considered to be at risk of becoming ghettos, with all pupils belonging to minority groups. In those schools, teachers collaborate with university researchers, students, and children in a set of tasks based on digital media, in the same way experienced at the CSR, but here as part of their in-school activity. Results show that children are increasingly motivated to do literacy tasks and use ICT. The main transformation resides in the fact that the introduction of 5D artefacts to schools supposes a strong adaptation of curricula considering the wide diversity of participants with different goals and motives. In this kind of *borderer activity*, teachers, students, and pupils are apprentices that collaborate and negotiate the meanings of the new practices, leading to the appropriation of these new artefacts. The role of artefacts in transforming the activity and *transforming subjects through their appropriation*, is the second issue to be examined.

Having reached this point, we can explain why 5D is a model for an inclusive intercultural education. We will discuss two basic assumptions. First, a meaningful activity requires intersubjective agreement, and participants need to see each other as valid interlocutors. Second, active participation supposes the creation of a local *microculture*, where participants appropriate the artefacts by mediating actions.

LEARNING AS INTERSUBJECTIVE AGREEMENT

It is interesting to note that authors who analyse the origins of intersubjectivity from markedly different perspectives emphasise this recognition of the role of interlocutor (i.e., the consideration of the other as a participant) as being fundamental to the establishment of intersubjectivity. Thus, for Rommetveit (quoted by Valsiner, 2003, p. 191), "we need to believe that the other understands us in order to construct this level of understanding in reality." In other words, only by considering (even foolishly) the other to be an interlocutor, can we achieve a shared understanding. Similarly, for Trevarthen (1982) before we can achieve a shared understanding, we must recognise one another as interlocutors. He speaks of the establishment of a primary intersubjectivity between the baby and those who take care of it, involving the construction of a communication channel, a state of joint attention, emotional in origin, which is manifest through protodialogues, or turns of intervention. Thus, it is a prerequisite of intersubjectivity to consider the other an interlocutor, recognising their capacity to take on this role and acting as if they were in this role. However, once the other is seen to be an interlocutor, the question is how we go about achieving intersubjective agreements.

Each culture represents a particular way of establishing its reality. This process is initiated by the family, and the other institutions of the culture are coherent with this basic objectification (Berger & Luckmann, 1966). Thus, when the child starts school, he or she encounters a universe in which they share the essential elements of this objectified world, in which there are no major contradictions, and where, therefore, it is possible to establish intersubjective agreements. The schooling of a child from a middle class, autochthonous environment is experienced by their family as an act that is performed within the community. The choice of school is generally related to the fact that the child belongs to a particular social group organised around ideological, religious, or class values. These families are part of a community in which various scripts organise their day-to-day experiences in a largely similar way. As a result, these people share a certain way of understanding the world. Belonging to the same cultural community means the possibility of sharing implicit beliefs, that is, ways of categorising reality that do not have to be explained, as they are taken for granted. The school is a piece of this universe. Its structure and the way in which it works are known, and what is more, these aspects are internalised and form part of the cultural framework. What the school seeks to impart, what a child should be, when their behaviour is appropriate, and so forth, are all questions on which there is implicit agreement.

Shweder (1986) refers to these as "constitutive suppositions," preconceived ideas that do not have to be debated or made explicit, and which each cultural community establishes as the basis for understanding. Moghadam (2003) coins the term interobjectivity to refer to the set of objectifications of reality that are common to the members of a given culture. Only by sharing this interobjectivity (or knowing and granting legitimacy to the different interobjectivities in a multicultural space) is intersubjectivity possible. For Moghadam, this connection between the objective world and intersubjectivity is simple to understand in isolated societies such as that of the Tasmanians before they were exterminated, the Yanomami whose Amazon home has yet to be devastated or the Amish communities in the USA, who shun all contact with the outside world. But the problem is more complex when we look at multicultural societies, in which different power relations exist between majority and minority groups. When the members of these minorities and majorities do not share the same interobjectivity, and especially when diametrically opposed objectivities are constructed in each community, intersubjectivity is extremely difficult to achieve.

The objectivities of a multicultural society are not static, since they are subject to processes of acculturation (Berry, 2001) and also, though operating in the opposite direction, to the generation of new differences (Ogbu, 1994). Thus, the way in which a minority group objectifies the world may gradually become more similar to, or more distinct from, the "objectivity" shared by the majority, according to the dynamics of the power relations. Clearly, this dynamic operates in the school in such a way that when dealing with the difficulties of the inclusion of a cultural group, we need to examine the barriers that stand in the way of the establishment of intersubjective agreements. When the members of a minority ethnic group with little power attend a school, they find themselves in a world in which the rules, language, relationships, and objectives of the activity are far removed from their own or they might even find that the former contradict the rules, the norms of language use, the types of relationship and objectives, established with varying degrees of explicitness, of their own family and cultural group.

The key question in education lies in how the school, here understood as an institution which shares the interobjectivity of the dominant culture, can create spaces of intersubjectivity with members of minority groups who hold different, if not diametrically opposed, objectifications of the world. The 5D model is addressed at generating shared objects that are meaningful for all participants by means of the collaborative use of ICT tools. Through playing games, editing a video, or developing a blog, participants must discuss goals and strategies at every stage. By collaborating, adults and children develop a common language referring to meanings that make full sense in the storm of the activity. So, the community is not predefined, but rather is "under construction," and each participant contributes to the design through the appropriation, that is, interiorisation and mastering of activity artefacts.

APPROPRIATION OF ARTEFACTS

Cole (1996) defines culture as a medium in which human life unfolds, and which comprises a set of interrelated instruments, shared by the members of the group and passed down from one generation to another. These artefacts include physical and symbolic instruments, the behaviours associated with the latter, knowledge, beliefs, and forms of social organisation. Taking his lead from Leont'ev, Cole presents activity as the indivisible element in the study of human behaviour. We can understand activity as being the system of complex relations between the subject, objects, and artefacts that mediate between one and the other, in a specific context of social relations. These artefacts or mechanisms of cultural mediation (tools or signs)

are supplied by the culture in the contexts of a specific activity, and the subject takes up (appropriates) these cultural media, reconstructing them in the process of the activity.

In this way, activity defines the objects and identity of subjects. The objects to be transformed are defined by the tools used, but the subject is transformed in accordance with the goals the latter sets him or herself and the artefacts he or she uses to achieve them. This is well illustrated by the classic example of the poacher who on becoming a farmer transforms his way of thinking, his way of life, and his social organisation, thanks to his new goals and tools. Learning and development can be understood to mean the appropriation of the artefacts that mediate the activity. As the "external" artefacts become internalised, the internal representations become externalised in the discourse, gestures, writing, and manipulation of the material in the environment (Engeström, 1999). That is, every activity involves a process of teaching and learning.

Formal education is a particular type of activity, where this process of appropriation constitutes the object in its own right, the main goal, albeit that the set of artefacts to be handled is decidedly complex. It should be stressed that it is not only a matter of physical tools and symbols which Cole calls primary artefacts, but also secondary artefacts or scripts that are pre-established by beliefs, ways of categorising, mental schema, and forms of social relationships. In general, the latter are understood to have been acquired by the time a child starts school, or it is supposed that they will be acquired in parallel, in other contexts of activity, such as those provided by the family. Thus, for example, the acquisition of the correct language for school is not possible if it is not articulated with extremely clear representations of its contexts of use, its appropriateness, its goals, and so forth. The same is true of reading and writing, and of mathematics, which only become meaningful in relation to a network of artefacts operating on different levels and which are supplied in various institutional settings like school or family that maintain a minimum degree of coherence between each other. So, the school is not only an institution adapted to a specific culture, but also its history has deposited within it a set of artefacts that are only meaningful in a similar culture.

The challenge facing an intercultural, inclusive education system, involves the real appropriation of its artefacts by all participating groups. In other words, an activity system whose particular culture or microculture is based in the shared construction of rules, goals, scripts, procedures for using tools, and every mediating artefact. So, the intersubjectivity and appropriation of artefacts are the two sides of the way the construction of a *microculture* share meanings through participation. The 5D model provides this kind of activity system by means of three main properties:

First, the educational institution is considered to be something that can be transformed. It is not only the children that should change, but also the educational institution. New artefacts change practices and new practices provide new identities to participants. The introduction of ICT tools is not only about primary artefacts, but also about new scripts, rituals, and narratives. Computers, digital cameras, blogs, and so forh, are mediating new forms of relationships between teachers and pupils and between pupils.

Second, participation leads to transformations in the dynamics of the institution. Negotiation is now explicit. This is a challenge for the high level of institutionalisation of the classic school, because daily practices must be constructed anew, so that activity can be redesigned starting from the actual participants. Fifth dimension activity involves very little institutionalisation, and new practices could be negotiated to introduce new and explicit goals and rules.

Third, the flexibility of roles as regards teaching/learning is legitimated, and the participants are recognised as actors. All participants play the role of learning about new artefacts, and all

personal, formal, and community knowledge is legitimated. Development of a transmission model, characteristic of the classical school, a new definition of roles, led to a collaborative model as explained in Rogoff et al. (1996).

LOOKING FOR A MODEL OF VIRTUAL ARTEFACTS

Network Construction

Teams involved in the development of 5D sites in Ronneby (SE), Copenhagen (DK), and Barcelona (ES) tackled the project of constructing tools that could create a sustainable international network of researchers, educators, students, and children. We sought to design a technological artefact that could provide a new channel of communication and collaboration between plural groups, but which at the same time could be a useful tool in the day-to-day activities of local groups, since without such a tool it would be difficult to guarantee success. Intercultural issues was a fundamental feature as it meant bringing together groups from the north and south of Europe, and both sides of the Atlantic. The intercultural nature of the 5D therefore provided us with the basis for the development of a virtual model.

The consolidation of this network had been shown in the past to be a significant factor for the sustainability and support of local activities, but now this new virtual tool could be a resource centre in which to store and share field notes, stories, articles, and so forth, concerning the whole basis of the 5D method: artefacts like the labyrinth, its magician, games, task guides, clues, logbooks, and rules. In other words, we sought to pass on artefacts and thereby facilitate the collective memory and recycling of experiences. But such a tool would have to satisfy even greater demands: It would have to be useful for those familiar with the 5D method, while allowing those without this knowledge to quickly acquire a minimum understanding so as to participate and enrich the whole group through its impartial perspective.

Therefore, it was a question of designing an artefact that could operate in a virtual environment, enabling the creation of a *microculture* which, while respecting the essential characteristics of the 5D flexibility, adaptability, intersubjectivity, laboratory for practical experiences, would provide insights into the educational model as in traditional unidirectional Webs. But above all, it should allow bidirectionality between the visitor and the Web site in a nonhierarchical environment so as to facilitate communication, collaboration, appropriation, and the recycling of experiences. In short, we sought to take the 5D community onto the network. With these aims in mind and in an effort to avoid reinventing the wheel, we sought out similar projects. We found educational Web sites, news groups, mailing lists, directories of links, resource centres, chat rooms, and so on, that had some of these characteristics, but none of these projects met all the requisites of the artefact we wished to create.

It was at this juncture, thanks to the suggestions of the technicians in our research team, that we discovered a line of well-developed research that struck us as being similar to the methods of the 5D. This line of research went by the name of the somewhat cryptic, recursive acronym of GNU. The GNU project, set up by Richard Stallman in the early 1980s and developed by the Free Software Foundation, sought the cooperative development of technological artefacts and rejected the then incipient tendency to privatise the source code of the computer programs. Stallman defended the creation of software in the community, in a similar way to that adopted in the world of gastronomy, where recipes are shared and even sometimes created in collaboration. Stallman argues in favour of the defence of the basic liberties of any software user (Cornec, 1999; Stallman, 1996) and over the last two decades he has provided an ideological umbrella that has allowed hundreds of thousands of programmers, translators, testers, and users to

organise themselves in a virtual space, drawing on the diversity of its members and creating networks of shared meaning, in short, constructing *microcultures* for the development of an almost interminable stream of technological artefacts. By sharing and adapting the same rights between equals and cooperating in the creation of artefacts, the affinity was undoubtedly, in this case, clear. To all intents and purposes, it appeared to be the reference point we had been seeking in order to build our virtual learning community (portal 5D.ORG), and so we decided to continue our search by concentrating on the work of these collectives.

APPROPRIATING ARTEFACTS

Here we present several examples of GNU projects that have similar characteristics to those that we were seeking for the 5D.ORG educational portal. Nearly all the projects we examined respected, to a greater or lesser degree, these attributes, but for the sake of maximum clarity, we shall comment in each case on the project that best exemplifies the properties we wish to highlight. One of our first discoveries was the GNU project directories such as Free Software Foundation–Savannah site (2004), SourceForge.net site (2004), and Open Source Technology Group (2004) where thousands of working groups, SourceForge boasts 80,000 projects and 800,000 users adhere to Stallman's philosophy.

Most of the GNU initiatives, and these projects are no exception, were built to meet their members' day-to-day needs by participative design, in groups in which the roles become blurred. The creator is in turn a user of the artefact that is built and the apprentice is for short periods the expert in a similar way to that experienced in the 5D. Particularly interesting was the way in which the technological tools that made up these network directories (discussion groups, loading and downloading tools for the storage of projects, tools for collaboration, Web browsers, personalisation of the portal, etc.) facilitated communication between the members, but also the accumulation and subsequent recycling of artefacts, in a very similar way to the resource-knowledge centre we wished to create. What were particularly common in these directories are key developments, where new creators adapt existing projects to their particular needs. Thus, the passing on, refining and appropriation of the artefacts that we so much wanted to achieve was also possible in the virtual world, and even it was made more simple thanks to the digital character, and hence greater flexibility, of the artefacts being used.

If we accept that knowledge should be accessible to all and free of charge, access to these communities and the use of the artefacts that are stored in them should be and was free of charge, allowing new members an unrestricted access to the portal. With just one exception, the creation of new project spaces (new communities) was filtered to guarantee responsibility for the contents. Collaboration in groups seemed to establish itself as a borderer activity, where individuals from distant settings and cultures, sharing very few objectives, found a comfortable space for virtual collaboration to satisfy their local needs, all of this in an atmosphere that we perceive as being fun and carefree, similar in many respects to that of a game. These communities were, without doubt, *the* model for the development of our 5D.ORG tool. But in our desire to eradicate all hierarchies, we continued to seek collectives in which collaboration was indeed between equals and in which no veto could be imposed, at least in terms of the tool, thereby allowing the community to organise itself as it felt fit mediated by the artefact, in order to construct a *microculture* with its own social order.

It was at this juncture that we became aware of the Wikis (The Wiki Community, 2002), another GNU project centred around the collaborative creation of Web page content that allows anybody, without any need to register or without imposing

restrictions of any kind, to edit texts that are then published at the site. The Wikis had constructed, among other artefacts, an encyclopaedia with more than 1,700,000 entries, a dictionary with more than 300,000 terms and a library with 3,500 volumes in a collaborative space par excellence that broke with all hierarchies, and surprising as it might seem it was not subject to constant acts of vandalism. The texts were written in the form of brief contributions by anyone who could provide information about the subject and they were revised in the same way, guaranteeing the continuity of the project against possible attacks by making a simple security copy. It was the best example of collaboration between peers to be found on the Web.

What remained for us to do was to translate to the virtual world an important element of the 5D: the activity as a laboratory for conducting tests. While we had seen how in various GNU project directories developments were subject to constant scrutiny, such practices were never as explicit as in the HackLabs. These laboratories, set up by the faithful disciples of hacker ethics (Himanen, Torvalds, & Castells, 2001), can be defined as uncontrolled virtual learning communities that seek to break with the traditional hierarchies of learning in order to share knowledge and resources in a space for collaboration and experimentation. All these sources of tried and tested experimentation were taken into consideration when constructing our virtual educational community (5D.ORG) as a new *microculture* on the network. Furthermore, if the results were what we hoped for, 5D.ORG might come to form a network of *microcultures* that could lend support to both local and global groups.

THE DESIGN OF A VIRTUAL COMMUNITY

Due to its particular, and often highly technical nature, we shall not detain the reader with a lengthy description of the portal design process, although we would like to briefly outline some ideas and situations that derive, as expected, from what we have said up to this point. When designing the tool, we were convinced that the projects we had studied had provided us with valuable insights, and for this reason, we chose to develop an educational portal in three blocks. We took into consideration the possibility of providing: (i) information about the 5D model using the traditional tools provided on the Web, but we knew we needed to pay special attention to the Web tools that facilitated (ii) collaboration and (iii) online training.

The block providing information needed to be dynamic, since the contents were to be subject to frequent modifications. We therefore opted to use a content management system: a technical development which would allow content experts with little technological expertise to maintain in as straightforward a fashion as possible, that is, editing directly in the Web site itself without the need of complex publishing tools, all the texts, links, and images that we wished to present there.

Based on our own experience, and as in the examined GNU projects, we considered it essential to make our artefact bidirectional. Therefore, in addition to the forums which are essential for guaranteeing the off-line communication of our future users and the field notes, narratives, and articles that we considered of great use for researchers, students, and educators, we also created a tool that would allow the user to add, make comments about, download, and eliminate, and in short automate the administration of a repository of 5D artefacts. Our study of the GNU projects showed us that in this way it would be possible to ensure the exchange of traditional 5D artefacts, which could then be tested in the many local activities-laboratories, as well as improved or adapted by any user who should wish to do so.

Convinced of the importance of local groups for the success of global collaboration, we designed another tool (My5DCommunities) in order to coordinate local activities from the virtual dimension. This tool enabled us to establish free and automated private forums, and to create picture galleries (particularly useful in the case of activities for children), activity calendars, and a local selection of traditional 5D artefacts. The tool can also be used simply as a showcase for the activity carried out.

Finally, in order to make interaction with the portal as straightforward as possible for the many different collectives visiting the site, we designed a tool that would ensure the creation of dynamic, mutable, and nonconstrictive profiles, but which in turn might offer contents and links adapted to the roles of researcher, educator, student, and child, at the same time allowing the visitor to change role, in line with the basics of the 5D principles.

When we wrote this text, 5D.ORG was no more than a recently constructed educational portal on the network in need of a number of modifications. It seeks to be a frontier space that can attract a wide range of different subjects. As it becomes more widely used, it will become possible to begin weaving a Web of meanings that are shared by the members of a large, interacting group. If this occurs, we will have developed a *microculture* that is shared by subjects from many different backgrounds, in which new knowledge can be created and interactions can take place in relation to the subjects of teaching and learning.

CONCLUSION

The collaboration established between researchers in the fields of education and technologies is characteristic of an intercultural dialogue. Setting out with different goals, both groups were engaged in a *borderer activity* involving the development of educational artefacts that could be accessed via Internet. As long as they recognised each other as valid interlocutors in spite of each group's obvious lack of competence in the other's field, the dialogue, understood as a process of constant negotiations, was developed. The assumption of shared goals, in turn, gave rise to a set of shared beliefs, knowledge, behaviours, and customs, that is, to a network of meanings that crystallised into a common *microculture*. In achieving this, no collective should renounce its respective professional cultures, even though the result was not something that belonged specifically to either. Rather, the result was a new hybrid product, in the same way as the identities involved and the objectives that were generated were new.

The shared identity between the process of creating knowledge in local 5D sites and the process for designing new artefacts on the Internet resides in the facilities for developing a particular microculture founded in participation, a low level of institutionalisation and the legitimisation of different kinds of knowledge. Both processes are examples that collaborative learning is possible as long as active participation is encouraged without calling into question the identity of any of the participants. The collaboration between legitimate interlocutors in this process has been shown to be an excellent platform for the appropriation of new artefacts by apprentices. And in a setting that shows few signs of being institutionalised and in which the roles adopted are flexible, all participants take on the role of apprentices. In these new microcultures, no one culture or group is dominant, but rather what we find is a universe of meanings accessible to the participants, who enter into explicit negotiations to collaborate in attaining their shared goals.

REFERENCES

Berger, P.L., & Luckmann, T. (1966). *The social construction of reality.* New York: Doubleday & Company.

Berry, J. W. (2001). A psychology of immigration. *Journal of Social Issues, 57*(3), 615-631.

Cole, M. (1996). *Cultural psychology: A once and future discipline.* Mambridge, MA: Harvard University Press.

Cornec, B. (1999, July 25). *HP HOWTO: Utilization and configuration guide of HP products under Linux* (Chapter 2: Presentation of Linux and Free Software, Rev. 0.8). Retrieved March 16, 2008, from http://www.linuxdocs.org/HOWTOs/HP-HOWTO/concepts.html

Crespo, I., Lalueza, J. L., & Pallí, C. (2002). Moving communities: A process of negotiation with a gypsy minority for empowerment. *Community, Work and Family, 5*(1), 49-66.

Crespo, I., & Lalueza, J. L. (2003). Culutas minoritarias, educación, y communidad.. In M. A> Essomba (Ed.) *Educación e inclusión social de immigrados y minorias* (pp. 293-3140. Tejer redes de sentido compartido. Barcelona: PRAXIS.

Crespo, I., Lalueza, J. L., Portell, M., & Sánchez, S. (2005). Communities for intercultural education: Interweaving microcultures. In M. Nilson & H. Nocon (Eds.), *School of tomorrow: Developing expansive learning environments.* Bern: Peter Lang.

Engeström, Y. (1999). Innovative learning in work teams: Analysing cycles of knowledge creation in practice. In Y. Engeström, R. Miettinen, & R.-L. Punamäki (Eds.), *Perspectives on activity theory* (pp. 377-404). Cambridge: Cambridge University Press.

Free Software Foundation. (2004, August 23). *Welcome [Savannah]* (Rev. 1.51). Retrieved March 16, 2008, from http://savannah.nongnu.org/

Himanen, P., Torvalds, L., & Castells, M. (2001). *The hacker ethic and the spirit of the information age.* London: Secker & Warburg.

Laboratory of Comparative Human Cognition. (1983). Culture and intelligence. In R. J. Sternberg (Ed.), *Handbook of human intelligence.* Cambridge: Cambridge University Press.

Lave, (1988). *Cognition in practice.* Cambridge. Cambridge University Press.

Moghadam, S. M. (2003). Interobjectivity and culture. *Culture and Psychology, 9*(3), 221-232.

Ogbu, J. U. (1994). From cultural differences to differences in cultural frame of reference. In P. M. Greenfield & Cocking (Eds.), *Cross-cultural roots of minority child development* (pp. 365-391). Hillsdale: LEA.

OSTG Open Source Technology Group. (2004). *freshmeat.net: About* (Rev. 2.6.0-pre1). Retrieved March 16, 2008, from http://freshmeat.net/about/

Rogoff, B. (1990). *Apprenticeship in thinking: Cognitive development in social context.* New York: Oxford University Press.

Rogoff, B., Matusov, E., & White, C. (1996). Models of teaching and learning: Participation in a community of learners. In D. Olson & N. Torrance (Eds.), *The handbook of education and human development* (pp. 388-414). Cambridge, MA: Blackwell.

Rommetveit, R. (1998). On human beings, computers and representational-computational vs. hermeneutic-dialogical approaches to human cognition and communication. *Culture and Psychology, 4*(2), 213-233.

Shweder, R. A. (1986). Anthropology's romantic rebellion against the enlightenment, or there's more to thinking than reason and evidence. In R. A. Shweder & R. A. Le Vine (Eds.), *Culture theory: Essays on mind, self and emotion.* Cambridge University Press.

SourceForge.net Site Documentation. (2004). *Document A01: What is SourceForge.net?* Retrieved March 16, 2008, from http://sourceforge.net/docman/display_doc.php?docid=6025&group_id=1

Stallman, R. (1996). *The Free Software Definition* (Rev. 2004/08/04 21:16:41). Retrieved March 16, 2008, from http://www.gnu.org/philosophy/free-sw.html

Trevarthen, C. (1982). The primary motives for cooperative understanding. In G. Butterworth & P. Light (Eds.), *Social cognition.* London: Harvester Press.

Valsiner, J. (2003). Editorial introduction: Beyond intersubjectivity. *Culture & Psychology, 9*(3), 187-192.

Wertsch, J. (1985). *Vygotsky and the social formation of mind.* Cambridge: Harvard University Press.

Wiki Community, The. (2002, June 27). *What is Wiki?* Retrieved March 16, 2008, from http://www.wiki.org/wiki.cgi?WhatIsWiki

KEY TERMS

Activity: Psychological analysis unit in the frame of the cultural–historical activity theory. It is an indivisible set of situated practices where we could identify subject actions oriented to goals and mediated by artifacts. All activities are articulated in a cultural framework of meanings. The perspectives introduce rules, community bonds, and division of labor as elements that must also be identified in activity analysis. Activity theory helps explain how social artifacts and social organization mediate social action.

Artifacts: Tools and symbols that, mediating the actions between subject and object, transform both. An artifact is an aspect of the material world that has changed during the history of its incorporation into human action aimed at targets. They are the basic constituent of a culture and are the constituents of its "possible" worlds and realities.

Borderer Activity: Spaces where exchange and dialogue is possible between cultures. In such

129

activities, each participant arrives with his or her particular goals and motives, but different actors and institutions can negotiate and try to construct common goals.

Collaborative Learning: Methodologies and environments in which learners engage in a common task in which each individual depends on and is accountable to each other. Groups of students work together in searching for understanding, meaning, or solutions or in creating an artifact of their learning, such as a product.

Copyleft: The Free Software Foundation and some other associations created this concept to label a set of licenses that defend different kinds of freedom in cultural creations. Those licenses are the legal base that allows the construction of a common repository of knowledge free to reach and adapt by everybody interested. Wikipedia (2007) says: "Copyleft is a form of licensing and may be used to modify copyrights for works such as computer software, documents, music, and art. In general, copyright law allows an author to prohibit others from reproducing, adapting, or distributing copies of the author's work. In contrast, an author may, through a copyleft licensing scheme, give every person who receives a copy of a work permission to reproduce, adapt or distribute the work as long as any resulting copies or adaptations are also bound by the same copyleft licensing scheme."

Content Management System (CMS): When organizations realized that a Webmaster could be a "bottleneck" for their presence in the net, new applications were developed thought to make easier to publish digital creations (texts, images, video, audio, documents, etc.) in Web pages. Those systems that define user's roles, assist during the publication workflows, and introduce a lot of automatisms to administrate content, allow authors to publish their content directly without the need of any intermediary.

Intersubjectivity: Shared meanings constructed by people in their interactions with each other and used as an every day resource to interpret the meaning of elements of social and cultural life. Intersubjectivity allows people to share a definition of the situation and is the basis for a meaningful collaboration.

Microculture: Here in the sense of ideoculture, or a system of knowledge, beliefs, behaviors, and customs shared by the members of an interacting group to which the members can refer and which serves as the foundations for new interactions. Members recognize that they share experiences and that these can be alluded to with the expectation that they will be understood by the other members, thus using them to construct a reality for the participants.

Wiki: A classical wiki is a subtype of CMS without any publication workflow (creations are directly published, without any revision), without any role (every user of the system get the same rights), and with a strong version system (that guarantee that any data will be lost). Those kind of systems that allow a kind of collaboration where every user is equal to others (so modifications could be done in a fast and easy way) become popular with "wikipedia" that is also a good example of a wiki.

Chapter X
Digital Storytelling as a Tool in Education

Monica E. Nilsson
Blekinge Institute of Technology, Sweden

ABSTRACT

The aim of this chapter is to discuss digital storytelling in the context of education. Two questions guide the study: What is a digital story? What is the motivation for making a digital story? I have examined short multimodal personally told digital stories published on the Internet. As a theoretical framework for the discussion, I have compared digital storytelling with storytelling traditions in the oral and the written culture. The result implies that the definition of a digital story depends on what is considered a narrative. By transcending what has traditionally been considered narrative and by defining narrative in a broader sense, digital storytelling is an innovative tool and serves as a promising activity facilitating learning and development in the postmodern society.

INTRODUCTION

Digital storytelling has become popular in the educational community (Davis, 2006; Farmer, 2004; Hull & Nelson, 2005; Hull & Zacher, 2004; Kajder, 2004; Marcuss, 2003; Ohler, 2005; Salpeter, 2007; Ware & Warschauer, 2006; Weis, Benmayer, O'Leary, & Eynon, 2002). It has been argued that digital storytelling mediates learning and development. Ohler (2005), for example, claims that digital storytelling facilitates criti-

cal thinking. Davis (2006) discusses the role of digital storytelling in students' identity formation. Several authors take a literacy perspective and claim that digital storytelling enables students to become competent and creative authors (Kajder, 2007; Weis et al., 2002). Others stress that digital storytelling gives rise to multimodal ways of making meaning (Hull & Nelson, 2005; Hull & Zacher, 2004; Ware & Warschauer, 2006).

I am interested in exploring the nature of digital storytelling: what needs it serves and how it might facilitate learning and development. The aim is to understand and discuss digital storytelling in the context of education. The following questions have guided this line of research: What is a (good) digital story? What is the motivation for making a digital story?

The kind of digital storytelling discussed in this chapter originated at the Center for Digital Storytelling in San Francisco (http://www.storycenter.org/index1.html) (Lambert, 2002). In this tradition, a digital story is a 1–3 minute multimodal personally told story intended to be published on the Internet. This tradition of making digital stories will be described in detail later on in the chapter.

I will start by exploring the nature of narrative—well aware of its complexity, immensity, and thus intricacy. My position is pedagogical and the aim is to obtain a useful definition for the purpose of this study. I will do this by asking: what is narrative and what is it for? I continue the chapter with a comparison of narrative in what Ong (1967) calls the *oral-aural culture*, the *alphabet* and *print culture*, and the *electronics* and *sensorium culture* of communications media. The comparison provides a theoretical framework for discussing what constitutes a (good) digital story and what motivates a digital story. As a basis for the discussion I have, in a qualitative exploratory study, grouped digital stories by using a framework called the "seven elements" for making a digital story. I discuss how we can understand digital storytelling, and finally, I consider the implications of digital storytelling for education.

DEFINING NARRATIVE

It was in the transition from mimetic communication to oral language that the coherent narrative developed as a means of understanding the world (Donald, in Nelson, 1996). Language made storytelling possible, and as a consequence, narratives facilitated explanations and the sense-making of experiences. Thus, narration is a fundamental and universal way of human communication (Ong, 1982/2002). Consequently, it is an essential way of knowing (Bruner, 1985, 1986).

Narrative, understood as communication, stands in contrast to the view of narrative as a literary endeavor, that is, as an artform (Abbott, 2002). In the "narrative turn" (Bruner, 2002), however, the boundary between every day narration (cf. Ochs & Capps, 1996, 2001) and literary narration is vanishing. Narrative is no longer perceived of as pieces of art and objects which are created and experienced individually within a cultural/artistic context. For example, Gee (1991, p. 13) states, "narrative is fundamentally a perspective that human beings take on the way in which certain themes fall into a satisfying pattern, a perspective stemming from their social identity and the resources their social group(s) make available to them." Gislén (2003) suggests that narrative should be understood as a process through which individuals and groups confirm, repeat, negotiate, and change their common reality in terms of what is and what can be possible to think and do. In that regard, narrative returns to its origins as a fundamental way of communicating.

What then is a narrative and what distinguishes narrative discourse from other forms of discourse? To define narrative unequivocally would of course be impossible. Johansson (2005) asserts that within the humanities, the discussion continues to be alive and intense. But in the social sciences, narrative theory and method is still in its infancy. As a representative from the former discipline, Abbott (2002, p. 12) suggests that narrative is "the representation of an event or a series of events." The implication (p. 16) is that "narrative is the representation of events, consisting of story and narrative discourse, story is an *event* or sequence of events (the action), and narrative discourse is those events as represented." Abbott (2002, p. 12) asserts that without an event or an action you may have "a 'description', an 'exposition', an 'argument' a 'lyric' some combination of these, or something else altogether, but you won't have a narrative." According to Chatman (1993), a narrative asks and answers the question: "What happened?," whereas an argument asks and answers: "Why do I need to do X?"; and a description answers "How is X?" Moreover, Chatman argues that there are three fundamental elements in a story: frame of action, characters and settings, and a theme. The narrative answers the question "What happened then?" which is carried out through the plot. The plot is structured by five stages: introduction, increased action or complication, climax or conflict, dissolution, and conclusion (Johansson, 2005).

An example from the social sciences and hence an alternative to Abbott's and Chatman's perspectives is Gislén's (2003) suggestion that what can be understood as a narrative is situated—it has to do with context, relevance, and viewpoint. Instead of defining narrative according to some internal structure, narrative can be defined by its function in human conversation; it deals with what is problematic. Narrative, according to Gislén, creates actual and possible human action (Ochs & Capps, 1996, 2001). Also Gee (1991) critiques the traditional way of depicting narratives as focusing on the causal and temporal structures resulting in the closed plot of the narrative. He claims that this way of thinking is a product of the modern institutionalized way of defining narrative which differs distinctively from the oral tradition of narration that can still be found in diverse ethnic communities (cf. McCabe, 1997). Instead, he wants to pay attention to the rhythmic, and poetic, together with thematic elements and qualities in narration often encountered in myths and epic narration.

In line with Abbott's (2002) and Chatman's (1993) way of categorizing texts, Bruner (1986) distinctinguishes between the narrative and the paradigmatic way of thought or forms of knowledge. In the paradigmatic or logical way of thought, the argument is in focus and concepts such as evidence, truth, and causal connections are crucial. In this mode, we ask what something *is*. In the narrative mode of thought, on the other hand, the unique case is the focal point, and we ask what things *mean* and what interpretations might be valid. Whereas in the paradigmatic mode of thought, we mean what we say, in the narrative mode of thought we mean more than we say; otherwise, the story becomes flat. The implication is that in order for a story to make sense, it needs to be interpreted; the meaning has to be constructed by the reader or viewer. In this regard, a narrative is a co-construction between the author and the reader. Bruner's (1986) approach shows both the narrator and the reader as creative and productive and as someone involved in an active process of communication, interpretation, and imagination.

Summarizing, we could say that one way to perceive narrative is through the artistic perspective. This focus is used in the literary sciences and the humanities. A different way is to perceive narrative in its role in human activity. Here the focus is on communication and meaning-making. This focus is used in the social sciences. How would this distinction make sense if we consider narrative from a historical perspective? I will sketch a background of the storytelling tradition, from the oral over the written to the digital. The outcome of this exercise will form the theoretical framework for interpreting and discussing how we can understand digital storytelling.

FROM ORAL TO DIGITAL STORYTELLING

Ong (1967) divides culture into three successive stages in terms of communications media. I will draw on this framework. His first stage is the unrecorded word in an oral or oral-aural culture. The second stage is the denatured word of alphabet and print, and the third stage is the electronics and sensorium. I will consider storytelling from a historical perspective, that is, from oral to digital storytelling. Storytelling here is interchangeable with narrative. To summarize Ong (1967), one could say that oral culture is characterized as situated, empathic, participative, additive, polemic, and redundant. On the other hand, written culture is characterized by analytical, abstract, objective, and distanced ways of thinking and articulating. In the culture of electronics and sensorium, we return to the features of the oral-aural culture. Ong (1967, p. 88) asserts, "the new age into which we have entered has stepped up the oral and aural."

In the *oral-aural culture,* storytelling had a significant role: to store, organize, and transmit information and knowledge. In a primarily oral culture, it is not possible to organize knowledge into abstract scientific categories as we do today in our written cultures. Instead, detailed stories about human actions served as containers of the culture's knowledge and perceptions (Ong, 1982/2002, p. 137). With no means to record words, narrative became the device to keep knowledge alive.

Characteristic of oral storytelling is the episodic structure, which could link a great deal of lore in relatively substantial, lengthy, and fairly durable forms that lent themselves to repetition (Ong, 1982/2002, p. 138). The epics were performed as rhythmic poems, songs, dances, rhymes, proverbs, and so forth, since these forms facilitated memorization. Thus, the poet in the oral culture was not, as Ong points out, only an entertainer, but a recaller and a repeater. Moreover, epic narrative was and is interactive. The narrative was never performed in the same way. Instead, the narratives were performed and changed depending on the situation and the interactions with the audience. Ong asserts "The oral song (or other narrative) is the result of interaction between the singer, the present audience, and the singer's memories of songs sung" (1982/2002, p. 143).

A good epic poet was a skilled and often dazzling performer. His talent, however, was not due to creativity in the sense of managing new effects. Instead, his talent was due to the extreme skill with which he performed with the given tools of his craft. As Ong asserts (1967, p. 31), "all epic poets used set formulas, but a good epic poet could spin his formulas much better than a poor one."

In contrast to this seemingly educational and cognitive role of narration, Ong (1967, p. 30) argues that verbalized learning normally took place in an atmosphere of celebration or play in oral culture. He states, "As events, words are more celebrations and less tools than in literate cultures." Words as tools might be precisely how we think of the *alphabet and print* culture to which we now turn in order to explore narrative traditions influenced by script and print. Some 6000 years ago, the oral storytelling tradition was challenged by the introduction of the writing in script. The way of telling a story by means of written text and later on, print changed the narrative. Narrative became conscious and well-conceived compared to the situated and epic form of narration in the oral tradition (Ong, 1982/2002).

In the writing of a text, the author learns and develops a feeling for how to use expressions and organize the text. This process differs from the way an oral narrator organizes and performs the narrative. The writer realizes that his words can be revised until the piece is completed. The text is given a beginning, middle, and an end (Aristotle, 1997). Thus, it turns into a completed and closed whole. Due to this increased conscious control, the plot becomes rigorous and the climactic plot replaces the oral epic plot which has no chronological order. The climactic plot of the written narrative, on the other hand, is an aggravated and linear plot which Ong calls the "Freytags pyramid" with an uphill slope followed by a downhill track. The increased course of events builds up a tension, reaches a climax, which brings about a *peripeteia* or sudden change in the plot that eventually leads to a resolution. Ong (1982/2002) asserts that if we take the linear climax plot as the paradigm for all plots, then the epic has no plot. The strict plot structure characteristic of longer narratives emerged because of the art of writing.

The climactic form reaches its culmination in the detective fiction that developed in the era of the printing press. But the climactic plot structure got its start in antique Greek drama. This drama was the first western art that was formed by script. Thus, it was the first literary genre that had the typical Freytag-pyramid structure. Moreover, it is with the Greek drama that the narrator begins to vanish. Typically, the performance of a drama lacks a narrator. The narrator is buried in the text itself and is hidden behind the characters' voices. According to Ong, the narrator was eliminated because one wanted to eliminate the episodic patterning in the plot. The episodic structure was the natural way of performing a long narrative orally. This might be because the experiences in people's lives resemble a chain of episodes rather than a Freytag pyramid. Careful selection in written narrative produces the tight pyramidal plot, and this selection is implemented as never before by the distance which writing creates between expression and real life. In sum, the use of print created the work of fiction, causing the definitive break from the epic structure.

With script and print, greater creativity and reflectivity became possible. The process of writing is slow, individual, and solitary compared to the oral performance. An author of a detective story is more conscious and reflective than an epic narrator, according to Ong (1982/2002, p. 147).

Writing…is essentially a consciousness-raising activity. The tightly organized, classically plotted story both results from and encourages heightened consciousness, and this fact expresses itself symbolically when, with the arrival of the perfectly pyramidal plot in the detective story, the action is seen to be focused within the consciousness of the protagonist—the detective.

The oral narrator's protagonist, distinguished typically by his external exploits, has been replaced by the interior consciousness of the typographic protagonist. The controlled and tight plot

distinctive of the typographical culture is in the culture of *electronics and sensorium* losing its good name, according to Ong (1982/2002). This kind of narrative is now considered too simple, that is, too controlled by consciousness. The emerging avant-gard literature eliminated the plots. However, the plot-impoverished narratives in the electronic age are not episodic narratives, according to Ong (1982/2002). They are impressionistic and image-rich variations of the plotted stories that preceded them. According to Ong (1982/2002), the narrative plot will forever be impacted by writing and typography.

Despite the claim that the art of script and print will forever have an impact on storytelling, Ong (1982/2002) discusses the culture of electronics as a "secondary orality," that is, the orality of telephones, radio, and television which depend on writing and print for their existence. The implication is that features found in the oral culture that have been suppressed by and erased from the written culture are re-emerging. Ong (1967) asserts that though the second orality is both like and unlike the primary orality, *simultaneity* is a mark of both early oral culture and the electronic culture. He states (pp. 133-134), "this new orality has striking resemblances to the old in its participatory mystique, its fostering of a communal sense, its concentration on the present moment, and even its use of formulas." In the next section, we will take a look at this culture focusing on narrative in digital media.

NARRATIVE IN DIGITAL MEDIA

What we speak of today as digital storytelling has a variety of expressions such as hypertext, computer games, interactive milieus, art, and so forth (Miller, 2004). One significant aspect of narrative in digital media is the calling into question of the coherent and traditional narrative. This is triggered chiefly by the hypertext movement (c.f Gislén, 2003; Gripsrud, 2002;). A basic assumption among the hypertext theoreticians is that what they call the "linear narrative" is an expression of and legitimizes authority. For example, Manovich (2001, p. 255) claims:

As a cultural form, the database represents the world as a list of items, and it refuses to order this list. In contrast, a narrative creates a cause-and-effect trajectory of seemingly unordered items (events). Therefore, database and narrative are natural enemies. Competing for the same territory of human culture, each claims an exclusive right to make meaning out of the world.

Neither Gripsrud nor Gislén believe that the narrative is dead but rather that it is up for redefinition. Murray (1999), for example, shows how narratives will become more floating and multimodal on the Internet. Moreover, Murray claims that we can expect a more formulaic nature of narration in digital media, as seen in oral storytelling. By formulaic Murray implies more or less stable narrative elements temporarily tacked together. The multimodal feature which Murray points out, that is, employment and combination of written and oral language, image, sound, and movement (c.f. Hull & Nelson, 2005; Kress, 2003; Kress & van Leeuwen, 2001; Ware & Warschauer, 2006) is another significant aspect of narrative in digital media. Each semiotic modality has its own unique meaning-making affordances (Gibson, 1979). Pictures, for example, do not convey meaning in the same way that language does, and as Kress (2003, pp. 1-4) notes, "the world narrated is a different world than the world displayed." Words are empty of meaning but the text requires that one read it in a linear manner and in a specific order. Images are filled with meaning, they inform better than text, but they can be read in any order. Order is free; the order is up to the author to design. In speech and writing, it is impossible to avoid notions of causality because of temporality and sequence. On the other hand, due to their simultaneity, images do not convey

notions of causality. However, the combination of modes demands interpretations even more so than only text. As Kress claims in a conference presentation (May 30-31, 2003) at the Institute of Design, IIT Chicago, Illinois: "new complexity comes on the scene because now you have to read it together, now you have to make sense of representations, image and words and that is the new task."

From a narrative perspective, this implies that new ways are developing for people to tell their stories. The written language is losing its dominance and new multimodal tools, that also have more similarities with the oral culture, are becoming available. I consider digital storytelling in the San Francisco tradition as one such tool. Before I describe and discuss that tradition, I will summarize the discussion about narrative as I have framed it by Ong's cultures of media communication.

THEORETICAL AND ANALYTICAL FRAMEWORK PLUS DATA

What emerges from this historical description of storytelling, and how could it possibly be connected to the notion of narrative as an art form or as a form of human activity and communication? The *function* of knowledge-transmission has been stressed in the discussion of storytelling in the oral culture. The context was social and collective and thus the narrator was a messenger of a collective body of knowledge. Oral storytelling was framed by space rather than time; that is, oral storytelling was immediate and compressed in time causing a "here and now" consciousness. The stories were transient due to their aural nature of language. The form was epic and oral narratives were accessible to the many.

In written cultures, the *form* has been stressed due to the technologizing of the word. The introduction of script and print resulted in the linear climax plot. Written storytelling is linear and causal framed by time. It promotes a consciousness where we make sense of the present by reflecting on the past and future. We have the ability to be creative, constructing possible worlds (Bruner, 1986). Writing is an individual enterprise and so is reading. The narrator in the written culture is the author of his or her story, and written narratives are accessible to the few.

From a historical perspective, the dichotomy between narrative as an art form vs. narrative as communication makes sense, while at the same time, it is problematic. The division makes sense because narrative as activity corresponds to the *function* of storytelling in the oral culture. It also makes sense because it corresponds to the *form* of a narrative stressed in the written culture. However, this division is problematic since it obscures viewing art and creative writing as communication. But as Bakhtin asserts in Holquist (2002), being an author is about entering into a dialogue with the world. We borrow and respond to each other's words and interpretations while we author our lives and stories (Holquist, 2002). Also Bruner's (1986) perspective on narrative as a form of thought and knowledge calls into question this dichotomy between narrative as an art form and narrative as communication.

An alternative to the dichotomy between narrative as art form vs. communication is the notion of *narrative* and *narrative activity* (Ricoeur, 1984) or narrative as *product* and *process* (Engel, 2003). Narrative activity is for Ricoeur a creative force which transforms experiences to palpable reality. What we have experienced can be summarized in a lucid form—that of narrative or narration. Thus, narrative as a product is the result of narrative as a process. This approach is useful, for example, when focusing on narrative related to identity formation and problem solving (Engel, 2003) as well as to health and therapy (Skott, 2004). However, this approach emphasizes the individual's developmental process. Thus, rather than use this approach to bridge and hence transcend the two approaches discussed so far, we have to add narrative activity or narrative process to the list.

Thus, to get a comprehensive understanding of narrative serving the purpose of a pedagogical interest, I will propose and frame the discussion by the following perspectives: Narrative as communication in collective human activities, as art, and as process. Based on this framework, what can we say about the particular form of digital storytelling that I am concerned with here? Next I will turn to what I call the San Francisco tradition and explain the approach in detail.

THE SAN FRANCISCO TRADITION OF DIGITAL STORYTELLING

The particular practice of digital storytelling that I am concerned with in this chapter derives from a tradition that started in the San Francisco area by the digital artist Dana Achley and his group (Lambert, 2002). In this tradition, digital storytelling is a short (1–3 minute) personally told story based on, for example, a memory or a significant person, place, or object. In digital storytelling, a variety of modes, such as text, image, speech, and sound, can be combined in an editing program on a computer. The program is preferably software freely available on the Internet or part of the computer's tool kit supplied by the manufacturer.

Digital storytelling is taught in two to three day workshops focusing on the seven elements. There are discrete elements or steps: a point (of view); a dramatic question; emotional content; the gift of your voice; the power of the soundtrack; economy; and pacing. (See http://www.story-center.org/memvoice/pages/tutorial_1.html and http://t3.k12.hi.us/t302-03/tutorials/digstory/elements.htm.)

The story takes its point of departure from a personal memory or experience which is recorded into the editing software. As such, it builds on the oral tradition of storytelling. The seven elements also include and stress aspects of storytelling recognized in the written culture. Such aspects are plot and conflict. The use of sound and image in combination with words are features of the electronic culture. However, the model is flexible enough not to force the author into a given structure, though it should enable good storytelling. Digital storytelling is often carried out in a community. The stories are published on the Internet by the local community and thus reach a wide audience.

METHODOLOGICAL APPROACH AND DATA

There are several media sites on the Internet hosting and displaying digital stories based on the San Francisco tradition and framework. One such site can be found at http://www.bbc.co.uk/wales/capturewales/. Other sites would be http://www.bbc.co.uk/tellinglives/ and http://oaklanddusty.org/videos.php. Yet another site is the Swedish site "Rum för berättande," in English "Room for Storytelling." This site is run by Swedish public radio and TV channel UR (Radio of Education). There were over 300 stories in February 2007 stored on the site for public display. The administrator of the site decides which stories are displayed. Thus, the site is not completely open to anyone as, for example, YouTube (http://www.youtube.com/) or Bubblare (http://bubblare.se/), a Swedish equivalent to YouTube. Most of the stories displayed are produced in workshops held by UR, but individuals can also apply to have their digital story displayed. The administrator of the site has organized the Internet stories in categories of Work, Love, Children, Learning, Computers, Power/powerlessness, Animals, Food, Commitments, Media, English, Failure, Family, Courage/fear, Party, Meeting, Future, Nature, Freedom, Travel, Leisure time, Self-confidence, Prejudice, School, Change, Sports, Happiness/sorrow, Language, History, Stress, Humor, Tolerance, Health, Faith, Identity, Young/old, Anger,

Appearance, Equality, Friendship/loneliness, and Art/music.

I present a qualitative exploratory study based on the categories in Table 1. My intention is to open up the field to investigation rather than to make strong claims. The aim of the study is to establish the big picture, which will provide the basis for more detailed studies in the future. In order to get the big picture, I have watched essentially all the stories on the UR site. I scrutinized them through the lens of the seven elements. I have chosen to take this approach because the seven elements constitute the framework for production; that is, they facilitate as well as constrain the creation of a digital story. This approach leads me to ask what kinds of stories are created with the seven elements as guidelines. Thus, I have subjected the stories to inquiries such as: what is the point?, does it engage emotionally?, is it dramatic?, and other questions concern the pace and use of sound, image, and voice. The outcome of this process is a grouping of the stories. By studying many digital stories during a limited period of time, I could discern patterns based on characteristic features. Eventually, saturation emerged, and it took a quick glimpse to categorize an individual story. In the next section, I describe the outcome of the exercise.

KINDS OF DIGITAL STORIES

In the body of digital stories that I have scrutinized, I have discerned four major groups: descriptive, argumentative, dramatic, and poetic/rhythmic. They are not clear-cut in the sense that they are unambiguous. On the contrary, each group contains features from the others. What constitutes a group is what I consider its dominating feature. For example, a story (I have used the term *story* here in order to remain faithful to the term digital storytelling used in the San Francisco tradition) in the descriptive story group might have an implicit argument, or a story in the argumentative story group might be expressed as a plot. As Abbot (2002, pp. 28-31) asserts, there are grey areas in the field of narrative; for example, whether or not a text is narrative depends on the overall effect rather than on the level of its parts or, put differently, whether story predominates or not.

We first consider the descriptive story group. The majority of the stories belong to this group. They are often about a trip, a friend, a pet, or a place. Though they include events in terms of actions (Abbott, 2002), these stories are based on experiences of every day life. Thus, they are epic and descriptive rather than climactic. Even though there is a point, it is not stressed or conspicuous. The same is true for conflicts or problems. They can be distinguished but they are most often implicit and might even be unconscious. Images in terms of personal still photos dominate in these stories, but there are occasionally drawings and video clips. The images illustrate what is said in the voiceover, but occasionally they constitute a "voice of their own." When images are given a voice, the story becomes more complex. Sometimes the images are symbols or icons. There might be a sound or music preferably at the beginning and the end. This might be due to a limitation of the editing software.

The second group of stories I consider is the *argumentative stories*. Here there is an explicit message made through a statement. One common way of telling this kind of story is by establishing a question in the beginning that gets answered in the end. Thus, Chatman's question "Why do I need to do X?" is both asked and answered. But there are also events or actions.

The third group of stories is clearly influenced by the climactic structure. Thus, I call these *dramatic stories*. They are rare. The tension or conflict and its resolution are central. As in the argumentative stories, sometimes the dramatic trick is to pose something at the beginning which is resolved at the very end. Images and music often are creatively combined with the voiceover.

Finally, I have called the fourth group *poetic* or *rhythmic stories*. Here the story is told in a poetic or/and melodious way. These stories are characterized by a "flow" of thoughts and feelings in a melodious mode. Alliteration and repetition of images and words contribute to this feeling. As with dramatic stories, images and music are often creatively combined with the voiceover. I next give some examples of each of the four groups. The first one is accessed from "Rum för berättande" at http://www.ur.se/rfb/index.php?t=1&tid=34. Find examples from each of the four groups.

Case 1: A Descriptive Story (The Birthday)

Viktor's story is about a young boy who travels with his family to Chile where they celebrate Christmas. It is Viktor's birthday and everybody is there except his father who stays in Sweden. Viktor gets presents, but he says most of them are "fairly bad." One particular gift is ok, however. It is a drawing-book and it is a good one because it is in English and it has got funny pictures. The story at the portal "Rum för berättande" (Room for Learning, http://www.ur.se/rfb/index. php?t=1&mid=159) is told in a descriptive way, though there is a drama in the conflict between being happy because of the birthday and being sad because of his father's absence. There is no music, the images are a mix of stills and drawings, and they illustrate what is told in the story.

Case 2: An Argumentative Story (Open Doors?)

Rebecka and her friends are partying at a friend's place in preparation for heading out on the town. Rebecka is nervous that they will not let her in to the bars since she is not old enough, though her friends are. But no problem, she is welcomed in by the doorman in several of the places they visit. She is puzzled and wonders if it might be due to her wheels (in the end of the story, we can see that she is in a wheel chair). The Web-based story at "Rum för berättande" (http://www.ur.se/rfb/index.php?t=1&mid=257&PHPSESSID=a472409afd285fa7b55ae11b3a9535a0#) starts with heavy music which ends when the voiceover starts. Most images are stills illustrating what is narrated. Titles are also used. The music emerges again at the close of the story.

Case 3: A Dramatic Story (A Morning)

An older woman, Signe, wakes up and everything goes wrong. She cannot find her one slipper. When rinsing her face, the water pours along and inside her pajama sleeves. Looking in the mirror, she concludes, "this is not me." She goes out to pick up the newspaper and slips on the snowy pathway. The newspaper is ruined, and while coming inside, she pours her hot coffee over the two sandwiches just made before going out for the paper. At this point, she decides to throw the tray with her breakfast in the sink. She returns to the bed contemplating the idea of starting all over again or just staying in bed for the rest of the day. The story has a pulse, and it is moving forward with small things happening one after the other until the main conflict happens (the coffee spilling all over the tray and she throwing the whole tray into the sink). It has a feeling of a thriller. There is no music, just a stable voice telling what is happening. The images are excellent drawings, made by Siri, perhaps a relative of Signe.

Case 4: A Lyrical/Rhythmic Story (Hope, Doubt, and Aroma of Vanilla)

Isabella tells about a pen pal who she does not write to anymore. She also tells about her sister, and while doing it, she asks philosophical questions about what you can know, what to trust, whether there are good things in the world, and so forth. She uses a lot of adjectives which evoke sensations such as aromas, flavors, and feelings of joy

as well as sadness. Isabella has a very sensitive and engaging voice. There is no music, and most of the images are imaginative close up stills and one drawing.

WHAT IS DIGITAL STORYTELLING?

At the beginning of this chapter, I asked: what is a (good) digital story and what is the motivation for making a digital story? I have developed a framework of three perspectives of narrative which will be used in the discussion. These are narrative as communication in collective human activities, narrative as art form, and narrative as process.

Based on this categorization of narrative, the answer to the question "what constitutes a (good) digital story?" is of course complicated. A good story is a story that mediates communication. It conforms to certain standards of what good art is in the field of narrative. Finally, a good story serves the purpose of facilitating problem solving and developmental processes such as identity formation. Among the stories that I have analyzed, all would be considered stories if applying the *communication* perspective, since they all communicate something. They make the viewer react in different ways. When we encounter the stories we interpret, we disagree or agree, reflect, argue, feel, and think. We could therefore say that whether they are good or not depends on the degree to which they engage us. Viktor's story communicates disappointments. Rebecka has concerns and questions about adults' reactions to her being in a wheelchair. Isabell communicates philosophical and relational issues, and in Signe's story, we smile with recognition and admire the skilled drawings.

Not many, though, would be considered good stories when applying the *artistic* perspective. If we would take the linear climax plot as the paradigm for all plots and thus for the way a narrative should be structured, then most of the stories would not even be considered stories. McCabe (1997) discusses what a good story is, and her position is that of not wanting to document defining features of stories in general and good stories in particular. McCabe takes a cultural perspective on storytelling and argues that there should not be only one cultural tradition of telling stories as the model for what a story is or a good story might be. This would imply that we should not judge stories from an artistic perspective if we are not aware or knowledgeable about cultural narrative traditions. But we could also say that what makes a good story is subjective. Subjectivity in turn is situated and depends on many things such as culture, class, gender, age, and so forth (Bourdieu, 1986).

In the data, there are unique stories which seem carefully prepared and designed, not necessarily built on the linear climax plot structure. For example, I would consider both Isabell's and Signe's stories as well-crafted pieces of art. Why? Because they are complex and as such they engage me, make me think and feel about new "possible worlds"; that is, they encourage me to become an author and a creator (Bruner, 2002).

Applying the *process* perspective of narrative, the digital stories that I have analyzed are stories because they have done their job as vehicles in a problem-solving or identity-formation process. From this perspective, a good story would be a story that has helped the author to push the boundaries or developed a zone of proximal development (Vygotsky, 1978). In line with this understanding, Engel (2003, p. 48) argues that story as text reveals certain aspects of a child's narrative ability and that story as process shows which narrative "problems" a child is exploring. For example, Engel describes a young boy telling a story that at times is incomprehensible and moreover is a mix of different genres and styles, "what he is imagining and feeling as he tells the story is more salient to him than his ongoing sense of what his audience is hearing or understanding." Engels leaves the child to process whatever he or

she needs to process. On the other hand, Davis (2006) gives examples of how adults can facilitate young people in their identity-formation process by discussing their stories with them.

At first glance, many of the digital stories in the descriptive category seem empty and flat. However, beneath the surface, they often deal with problematic issues. For example, in his story, Viktor reveals that he is very upset that his father did not participate in his birthday party. He has a conflict in that he is happy about the birthday party but sad that his father is absent. He says "the gifts were kind of bad." He seems to be processing this conflict and difficulty in his life.

Before turning to the issue of motive, I suggest that the definition of a (good) digital story depends on what is considered a narrative. A (good) digital story might be one which communicates significant issues well, or one that has particular qualities based on certain standards, as for example, a dramatic plot which evokes engagement and "possible worlds." Finally, a (good) digital story is a story which is or has been a tool for its creator in his or her personal development.

Now, why are people making digital stories? My approach here is to understand the motivation by studying the product. Thus, I have not interviewed people and in that way tried to find out their motives. Instead, I reason that product and motive are reciprocal in that the narrative process concludes in a product which therefore gives shape to the motive.

Most of the stories deal with every day life concerns. Both the descriptive and the dramatic stories describe a mundane event, often a loved person, pet, or place. They often have an implicit message dealing with, for example, self confidence, loneliness, appearance, need for love, and so forth. The argumentative stories deal with similar issues though in a more direct way. The author is explicit about what he or she wants to address, either by making a statement or asking a question. Rebecca's story, for example, ends with a question mark, though it is clear that she wants to make a statement. She is provocative and challenges the adult world with her question. The poetic/rhythmic stories are ambiguous in their points. To a high degree, they presume and involve the observer's own interpretation about what it is about. As with the dramatic stories, the poetic/rhythmic stories express a creative and artistic ambition. One can therefore conclude that there are many motives for making a digital story. One motivation might be to express oneself artistically and creatively, another to communicate an idea, point of view, thought, or feeling. Or perhaps the motivation might be to resolve a problem or conflict.

Summarizing digital storytelling in this way reveals that features from the oral culture are reappearing (Ong, 1967, 1982/2002). For example, the stories are rhythmic, poetic, and thematic (Gee, 1991), and the narratives are spoken rather that written. There is a narrator, but in comparison to the (male) oral singer, the contemporary narrator is "anybody"; he or she is not a professional but a layperson. Many voices are heard because of display on the Internet. Thus, the voices are public, and in this regard, the individual voices become a collective chorus.

But the heritage from the written culture is present. Words are used as tools and digital stories are vehicles for creativity and reflection. Digital storytelling also presents novelty. Images, sound, and music are combined with oral and written words, and thus new ways to make meaning are present (Hull & Nelson, 2005; Kress, 2003; Kress & van Leeuwen; Ware & Warschauer, 2006).

Moreover, the boundaries between discourses such as narrative, argument, and description seem to blur. People use the intellectual and semiotic means they have access to in order to express themselves. It is expressing oneself that seems to be important rather than adhering to standards or genres. This in turn raises the question about the existence of narrative and the need for redefining narrative (Gislén, 2003; Gripsrud, 2002). Thus, it is not only hypertext and information technology in a more instrumental sense which

changes what we mean by narrative, but the fact that public storytelling is becoming everybody's property, not only the professionals. One might argue that this has an effect on the quality, but from a democratic perspective, it is welcomed (Meadows, 2003). What are the implications of this study for education? This will be the final discussion.

IMPLICATIONS FOR EDUCATION

Working with digital storytelling in educational settings, either in schools or more informal learning contexts, we should consider digital storytelling from multiple perspectives. In this chapter, I have discussed digital storytelling from the communicative, artistic, and process perspectives. Applying different perspectives to digital storytelling enables us to make it a multidimensional tool in education.

For example, if we consider students' digital stories as invitations to communication, we have the opportunity to enter into a dialogue about important issues in their lives. Perceiving digital storytelling as process, we have the opportunity to understand where they are in their developmental processes but also where they are heading. This is a way to understand what problems students struggle with and thus how we can facilitate them in their problem solving and identity formation.

Taking an artistic and creative perspective on digital storytelling is an entrance to many aspects of learning and development. Narrative not only promotes academic competencies such as critical thinking and theory building (Ochs, Taylor, Rudolph, & Smith, 1992; Ohler, 2005; Weis et al., 2002) but has the potential to be a means for students to be creative in the development of new thoughts, ideas, and knowledge, that is, creation of "possible worlds" (Bruner, 2002; Vygotsky, 1967/2004). This last aspect of digital storytelling needs to be explored further, that is, how digital storytelling can facilitate students being creative learners and authors rather than reproducers of given knowledge. One aspect of this is the potential, yet unexplored and unexploited, which multimodality might offer. In my view, education should be about formation of subjectivity. Thus, the main duty of digital storytelling should not be an instrument to enhance "schooling," that is, to teach school subjects more efficiently, but as a tool and activity promoting and facilitating creativity, learning, and development.

REFERENCES

Abbott, H. P. (2002). *The Cambridge introduction to narrative*. Cambridge: Cambridge University Press.

Aristotle. (1997). *Poetics*. Penguin Classics.

Bourdieu, P. (1986). *Distinction: A social critique of the judgment of taste*. London: Taylor & Francis Ltd.

Bruner, J. (1985). Narrative and paradigmatic modes of thought. In E. Eisner (Ed.), *Learning and teaching the ways of knowing: Eighty-fourth year-book of National Society for the Study of Education* (pp. 97-115). Chicago: University of Chicago Press.

Bruner, J. (1986). *Actual minds, possible worlds*. Harvard University Press.

Bruner, J. (2002). *Making stories: Law, literature, life*. Harvard University Press.

Chatman, S. B. (1993). *Reading narrative fiction*. New York: MacMillan.

Davis, A. (2006) *Co-authoring identity: Digital storytelling in an urban middle school*. Retrieved March 16, 2008, from http://thejournal.org/feature/61/

Engel, S. L. (2003). My harmless inside heart turned green: Children's narratives and their inner lives. In B. Van Oers (Ed.), *Children's narrative development* (pp. 39-50). University of Netherlands Press.

Farmer, L. (2004). Using technology for storytelling: Tools for children. *New Review of Children's Literature and Librarianship, 10*(2), 155-168.

Gee, P. (1991). Memory and myth: A perspective on narrative. In A. McCabe & C. Peterson (Eds.), *Developing narrative structure*. Hillsdale, NJ: Lawrence Erlbaum.

Gislén, Y. (2003). *Rum för handling: Kollaborativt berättande i digitala medier* (Dissertation Series No. 2003:04). Unpublished doctoral dissertation, Blekinge Tekniska Högskola, Institutionen för arbetsvetenskap, medieteknik och humaniora, Sweden.

Gripsrud, J. (2002). *Mediekultur, mediesamhälle*. Göteborg: Daidalos.

Holquist, M. (2002). *Dialogism: The philosophy of M. Bakhtin*. New York: Routledge.

Hull, G., & Nelson, M. E. (2005). Locating the semiotic power of multimodality. *Written Communication, 22*(2), 224-261.

Hull , G., & Zacher, J. (2004). What is an afterschool worth? Developing literacy and identity in school. *Voices in Urban Education, 3*. Retrieved March 16, 2008, from http://www.annenberginstitute.org/VUE/spring04/Hull.html

Johansson, A. (2005). *Narrativ teori och metod*. Lund: Studentlitteratur.

Kajder, S. B. (2004). Enter here: Personal narrative and digital storytelling in popular culture. *English Journal, 93*(3), 64-68.

Kress, G. (2003). *Literacy in the media age*. New York: Routledge.

Kress, G., & van Leeuwen, T. (2001). *Multimodal discourse: The modes and media of contemporary communication*. London: Arnold.

Lambert, J. (2002). *Digital storytelling.* Digital Diner Press.

Manovich, L. (2001). *The language of new media.* Cambridge: MIT Press.

Retrieved March 16, 2008, from http://transcriptions.english.ucsb.edu/archive/courses/warner/english197/Schedule_files/Manovich/Database_as_symbolic_form.htm

Marcuss, M. (2003). The new community anthology: Digital storytelling as a community development strategy. *Communities and Banking, 14*(3), 9-13.

McCabe, A. (1997). Cultural background and storytelling: A review and implications for schooling. *Elementary School Journal, 97*(5), 453-473.

Meadows, D. (2003). Digital storytelling: Research-based practice in new media. *Visual Communication, 2*(2), 189-193.

Miller, C. H. (2004). *Digital storytelling: A creator's guide to interactive entertainment.* Burlington, MA: Focal Press.

Murray, J. (1999). *Hamlet on the holodeck: The future of narrative in cyberspace.* Cambridge, MA: MIT Press.

Nelson, K. (1996). *Language in cognitive development: The emergence of the mediated mind.* Cambridge, UK: Cambridge University Press.

Ochs, E., & Capps, L. (1996). Narrating the self. *American Review of Anthropology, 25*, 19-43.

Ochs, E., & Capps, L. (2001). *Living narrative: Creating lives in everyday storytelling.* Harvard University Press.

Ochs, E., Taylor, C., Rudolph, D., & Smith, R. (1992). Storytelling as a theory-building activity. *Discourse Processes, 15*(1), 37-72.

Ohler, J. (2005/2006). The world of digital storytelling. *Educational Leadership*, pp. 44-47.

Ong, W. (1967). *Presence of the word: Some prolegomena for cultural and religious history.* Yale University Press.

Ong, W. (2002). *Orality and literacy: The technologizing of the word.* Routledge. (Original published 1982)

Ricoeur, P. (1984). *Time and narrative.* University of Chicago Press.

Salpeter, J. (2007). Telling tales with technology. *TechLearning.* Retrieved March 16, 2008, from http://www.techlearning.com/story/showArticle.php?articleID=60300276

Skott, C. (2004). *Berättelsens praktik och teori: narrativ forskning i ett hermeneutiskt perspektiv.* Lund: Studentlitteratur AB.

Vygotsky, L. (1978). *Mind in society.* Cambridge: Harvard University Press.

Vygotsky, L. S. (2004). Imagination and creativity in childhood. *Soviet Psychology, 28*(1), 84-96. (Original published 1967)

Ware, P., & Warschauer, M. (2006). Hybrid literacy texts and practices in technology-intensive environments. *International Journal of Educational Research, 43*, 432-445.

Weis, T., Benmayer, R., O'Leary, C., & Eynon, B. (2002). Digital technologies and pedagogies. *Social Justice, 29*(4), 153-167.

KEY TERMS

Argumentative Digital Stories: Make an explicit message through a statement. A common way to tell an argumentative digital story is to establish a question at the beginning and to answer the question at the end.

Descriptive Digital Stories: Digital stories often about a trip, friend, pet, or place. They include events in terms of actions but are based on experiences taken from every day life. Descriptive digital stories are epic and descriptive rather than climactic. The point of view is neither stressed nor conspicuous. Images serve to illustrate the spoken word.

Digital Story: In the San Francisco tradition is a short (1-3 minute) personally told story based on, for example, a memory or a significant person, place, or object. In digital storytelling, a variety of modes such as text, image, speech, and sound are combined in an editing program on a computer.

Dramatic Digital Stories: Influenced by the climactic structure. In dramatic digital stories, the tension or conflict and its resolution are central. Images and music are often creatively combined with the voiceover.

Narrative as Art: Narrative framed within the humanistic sciences. Narrative in this context is well defined and expressed through literary compositions such as prose and poetry.

Narrative as Communication: Collective human activities are narrative framed within the social sciences, focusing on narrative as action and communication in everyday life.

Narrative as Process: Narrative framed within the social sciences focusing on individual change and development such as identity formation, health, and healing.

Poetic/Rhythmic Digital Stories: Characterized by a "flow" of thoughts and feelings in a melodious mode. Alliteration and repletion of both images and words contribute to this feeling. Images and music are often creatively combined with the voiceover.

Chapter XI
Multi–User Virtual Learning Environments in Education

Nancy Sardone
Seton Hall University, USA

Roberta Devlin-Scherer
Seton Hall University, USA

ABSTRACT

Today's middle school students represent a generation growing up where digital tools abound and where using them for home and school is the norm. Virtual learning environments to include multi-user virtual environments (MUVEs) are fairly new to formal educational settings as teaching and learning tools but are growing in popularity. These learning environments have an ability to reach all levels of students in ways that are both familiar and appealing. This chapter reviews interest and trends in educational games and describes beginning teacher reactions to using one of these critical thinking tools designed for middle school students. Recommendations for future implementation in classrooms are made. Faculty perspectives about these newer forms of educational technology are explored.

INTRODUCTION

The first game, *Pong*, introduced 35 years ago, kicked-off a multibillion dollar worldwide industry. Yet, the growth of this industry has not been without controversy. For some time, parents, educators, child advocates, medical professionals, and policymakers have voiced concerns over the content, purposes, and influences of interactive and immersive entertainment games. And frankly, who can blame them? A meta-analysis of 35 research studies on videogames concluded that concern is indeed warranted (Anderson & Bushman, 2001). Four patterns emerged: exposure to violent games increased physiological arousal, as well as aggressive thoughts, emotions, and actions. With a mounting level of violence, blood, and antisocial behavior found in some games, the video and computer gaming industry now self-monitors and provides outside packaging with both suggested player age and level of violent content. Despite continued concerns regarding game content, over 40% of American homes currently have a game system available (Rajagopalan & Schwartz, 2005).

However, a new genre of interactive immersive games, multi-user virtual environments (MUVEs), are used for classroom teaching and learning opportunities. Complete with embedded curriculum content standards, they are growing in popularity due to promising initial findings. They are a distant cousin to the videogames of yesterday, with a framework that supports the learning content contained within, in an age appropriate manner. A quick contrast illuminates a major difference between videogames and MUVES: in a videogame, the other characters are often enemies that are fought; in a MUVE, they help a seeker learn new information (Olsen, 2006).

Significant findings in MUVE-related studies indicated increased motivation to learn and decreased racial and gender differences as factors in student success. Games have been shown to help convince students of their academic potential with the greatest impact on the bottom third of students (Dede, Ketelhut, & Nelson, 2004; O'Hanlon, 2007). Students also develop social and technology skills and grow in scientific literacy. In addition, stemming from reformed child-rearing practices that have evolved over the last several generations, this equitable pedagogy follows the current movement's ideal of fostering student dignity in educational settings (Fuller, 2006).

MUVEs, also called augmented reality simulation games, are a natural outgrowth of this kind of reform. They represent values of learning through trial and error, collaborative, and personalized learning. They respect thinking and empower students to learn in ways meaningful to their digital culture. "A core feature underlying augmented reality simulation games is that they give students the experience of being competent, independently thinking problem solvers, enabling them to develop identities in relationship to an established community of practice" (Squire, 2006, p. 26).

As one example of alternative active learning that fosters critical thinking in which there is increasing interest, videogames are a tool teacher educators need to share. Teacher candidate understanding of effective implementation in classrooms is needed. Squire (2006, p. 19) reviews different kinds of next-generation videogames and documents the growing interest as representative of a "shift toward a culture of simulation, where digital technologies make it possible to construct, investigate, and interrogate hypothetical worlds."

Positive preliminary research in virtual leaning environments has encouraged increased funding to explore the impact of new digital media technologies on the youth culture and student learning (Anderson, 2005; eSchool News, 2006; Kirk, 2001; MacArthur, 2006; Squire, 2006). A large endeavor underway at New Media Corporation, comprised of over 250 institutions. This group is examining current technology applications. One of its main initiatives supports the study and exploration of educational gaming. In a recent conference, a session was devoted to the pervasiveness of games available on the Web and their learning potential. Discussed were browser games, alternate reality learning environments, and Web-based collaboration (NMC Conference, 2007). In addition to the study of gaming, preparing students for a future career in gaming has emerged as a trend.

Although gaming has attracted attention in academic settings, initiating a game curriculum at the university level is difficult. Games are interdisciplinary and their development requires simultaneous contributions from different fields. The field of gaming changes constantly, and few texts or teachers currently exist. Nonetheless, once outside the mainstream, the idea of game development courses have become somewhat accepted. Rajagopalan and Schwartz (2005) reported over 300 schools with courses in game development, listed on Gamasutra.com. A site, SimTeach, has been developed to support teachers of gaming, and it provides a listing of conferences, discussion opportunities, development tools, and game descriptions.

Due to these trends, this chapter reviews interest in virtual learning environments to include MUVEs. It describes teacher candidates' reactions while involved in The River City Project created at Harvard University, specifically designed to meet national middle school science content standards (Dieterle & Clarke, in press.). Recommendations for future implementation in classrooms are made. Faculty perspectives about these newer forms of educational technology are explored.

BACKGROUND

Simulation experiences in virtual environments have been a work in progress since the 1960s. Virtual environments called multi-user dungeon (MUD) games were written for the first microprocessors, circa 1970. Available in text-driven interfaces, their content was akin to the violence found in store-bought videogame cartridges. With current technology trends of reduced costs to build, manage, and store virtual environments and broadband connections more plentiful and powerful, development opportunities in this area have ensued to include 3D graphics, sound, clearer images, and content framed around curriculum standards (Panettieri, 2007).

Research on the broad context of simulations has found that they are a force that can motivate students to participate in the learning process (Meyers & Jones, 1993; Naps, Rößling, Almstrum, Dann, Fleischer, Hundhausen, et al., 2002) and appeal to a wide audience (Bransford, Brown, & Cocking, 2000; Foyle, 1995; Meyers & Jones, 1993). They have the ability to reach students in

ways that are both familiar and appealing with features that allow for the manipulation of variables to help solve presented problems (Ketelhut, 2006). In part, their appeal may be due to the placement of learners in a cognitively complex and artificially constructed, yet sufficiently realistic context for learning to occur as the situations presented emulate real-world problems (Bransford et al., 2000; Foyle, 1993; Meyers & Jones, 1993; Smith & Escott, 2004; Stasko, 1997). These tools provide students' opportunities to assume roles, examine problems, and pose solutions. According to Kirriemuir and McFarlane (2004) experience with gameplay seems to affect children's expectations of learning, in the sense that they prefer tasks that are fast, active, and exploratory. Traditional instructional methods tend not to meet such preferences particularly well.

EARLY SUCCESS IN EDUCATIONAL GAMING: ADVENTURE AND MOVEMENT

The Oregon Trail, created in 1971 by student teachers who created a computer program for a history class. It became an instant success as a way to make social studies more interactive and personal. The game was designed to teach students about the realities of 19th century pioneer life on the trail. The player assumes the role of a 1848 wagon leader guiding his party of settlers from Independence, Missouri to Oregon's Willamette Valley. The goal is to successfully traverse the trail and reach the final destination. Learning outcomes are critical thinking and problem-solving skills.

Another educational gaming success aimed at young children, ages 3–8, is a series of adventure games with an animated car, *Putt-Putt* at the helm. This series was developed and published in 1996 by Humongous Entertainment, still available for purchase on CD-ROM. One popular game in the series was *Putt-Putt Saves the Zoo.* The main focus of this adventure game is to reunite the missing baby animals with their parents. During the search for the baby animals, players can explore the three areas of the zoo, grasslands, arctic, and the jungle, and come to associate specific animals with their habitats and diet. Similar to *The Oregon Trail*, learning outcomes include the ability to critically think and problem-solve in a sequential manner. These games spawned the development of many more such as Humongous Entertainment's biggest seller, *Backyard Baseball,* which spurred an entire series of games, *Backyard Sports.* In these games, players are able to pick their own team and learn their abilities as they progress from sand lots and parking lots to the biggest stadiums.

Kinetic ability and overall fitness are current goals of some educators. One popular videogame most often found in arcades surrounded by a crowd of kids is *Dance, Dance, Revolution* (*DDR*). *DDR* is the focus of current research to measure its effectiveness on combating childhood obesity and is being piloted in select U.S. physical education classes (O'Hanlon, 2007). *DDR* comes with a video screen, sounds, lights, and a dance mat containing nine tiles. The object is to step on the tiles as they light up, while watching for clues in the form of arrows indicating where the next light will be. Initial results report better arterial response to blood flow, increase in aerobic capacity, and no weight gain. Participants were also more willing to try new activities and invite friends over to play, and demonstrated more confidence in physical education class participation.

MULTI-USER VIRTUAL ENVIRONMENT (MUVE)

The next generation of learning games that meshes educationally appropriate content and curriculum standards with the power of the Internet has surfaced. A MUVE is analogous to the first developed virtual worlds, MUDs. They are an interactive computer simulation of a geographical area, where features of the environment such as buildings, waterways, and people are represented by computer graphics. Players use a mouse to lead their chosen avatar around the area to discover, communicate with other avatars, and collect information with the goal to learn (Blaisdell, 2006). "The idea is that you 'step through' a computer screen and move into a virtual space. You control an avatar. You're participating and collaborating with other people. And you're communicating with peers" (Dieterle, as cited in Panettieri, 2006). This specific form of constructivist learning, called scientific discovery learning, evolves from an iterative cycle of planning, executing, and evaluating (Tan, 2006).

Theories of learning and enculturation in next generation learning tools, specifically multi-user virtual environments, have begun to mature and to cross over into academic disciplines in ways that help to better explain taught concepts (Brandt, Borchert, Addicott, Cosmano, Hawley, Hokanson, et al., 2005). This authentic and constructivist-based teaching strategy intends to prepare students for a world where technology is growing in influence and use as well as matching the learning styles of the digital student. Constructivist theory of learning stresses process over product (Maddux, Johnson, & Willis, 2001), and MUVEs are developed with the players in mind; their interactions, content, skill development, and process learning are the focal points rather than the capacity of the technology (DeKanter, 2005; Klopfer & Yoon, 2005). "Theoretically, games are interesting in that they are sites of naturally occurring, intrinsically motivated learning" (Squire, 2006, p. 22).

SCIENTIFIC LITERACY THROUGH MUVES

With scientific literacy a major goal for education in the 21st century, science instruction needs to become more meaningful and approachable for all students, specifically underperforming groups that include both racial minorities and female students in the middle school years (Dede et al., 2004). These groups have been at the center of much research as the long term effects of non-participation could risk further expansion of the digital divide into cognitive, attitudinal (Van Eck, 2006), and cultural separation. Middle School is a critical point as attitudinal differences can have effects beyond personal likes and dislikes. According to the American Association of University Women (2000), girls make up only 17% of computer science advanced placement test takers, 28% of computer science graduates, and 9% of engineering-related degrees.

In an online survey (n=232,781) of K–12 students, teachers, and parents from over 2,800 schools, one of many themes emerged. Regarding science and math, students state that they want to learn about these subjects through real world problem-solving, visiting places where they can see science in action, talking to professionals in those fields, and using technology in many ways (Project Tomorrow: NetDay, 2006). In an era where student interest and engagement in traditional classes is waning, novel approaches such as MUVEs might act as a catalyst for increased motivation (Ketelhut, 2007).

While Cornell University has devoted time to developing a game curriculum, both Massachusetts Institute of Technology and Harvard University have been actively developing and researching virtual environments for use in K–12 educational settings for the past few years. As a result, the effects of educational games are currently being examined in school settings. *Immune Attack*, a virtual biology learning tool, is currently the focus of pilot studies with five high schools in five U.S. states. Other scheduled pilots include two North Carolina elementary schools that are scheduled to pilot *Cool School: Where Peace Rules!,* which teaches conflict resolution (Borja, 2007), and Indiana University's *Quest Atlantis*, an environmental science learning tool, is scheduled for piloting in selected New Jersey

fourth, fifth, and sixth grade classrooms in Fall 2007 (Olsen, 2006).

Recently, the nonprofit MacArthur Foundationannounced a grant award of $1.1 million to assist in the development of a New York City public school, scheduled to open in fall 2009, aimed at teaching literacy and other skills through game design and game-inspired methods to children in grades 6–12. This grant comes as part of a larger $50 million grant scheduled for dispersion over the next five years to help examine the impact of technology on children and the ways in which they learn, both inside and outside the classroom (Dobson, 2007).

GAME CONTENT

Positive content with the purpose of teaching is already available in a variety of games at different levels. Examples representing educational games for children include *Virtual History: Ancient Egypt, Peacemaker, Hot Shot Business, Quest Atlantis, Whyville, The River City Project, Real Lives,* and *Stagecoach Island.* Some can accommodate multiple players; some are Web-based, while others are available for purchase on CD-ROM.

Virtual History: Ancient Egypt is a CD-based simulation game on culture, economics, government, and geography of ancient Egypt that lets students play the role of village leaders. *Peace-Maker* is a CD-ROM based game simulation of the Israeli-Palestinian conflict: a tool that can be used to promote a peaceful resolution among Israelis, Palestinians, and young adults worldwide. In Web-based *Hot Shot Business*, students learn financial-literacy and entrepreneurship skills as they build a virtual factory making custom skateboards and then market its products. *Quest Atlantis,* played online with multiple players was created to inspire middle school children to learn about environmental science concepts in structured ways (Olsen, 2006). *Whyville*, developed by a California-State biology professor, is designed to "teach science through interaction, rather than through books" (Olsen, 2006, p. 2). Numerous activities in this MUVE aim to stimulate questions in science and provide designed opportunities for children to learn. Organizations have sponsored centers in *Whyville*. In the NASA-sponsored center, for example, children can become certified space engineers, while engaging in and learning the laws of physics. Similarly, *The River City* Project is designed to teach science inquiry methods to middle school students in the areas of biology and ecology. Important social studies concepts are taught in *Real Lives*. It uses statistically accurate events to determine how students' virtual characters' lives will unfold by considering different cultures, political systems, economic opportunities, personal decisions, health issues, family issues, schooling, jobs, religions, geography, and whether the country in which their virtual character resides is at war or peace. In the MUVE, *Stagecoach Island,* created by Wells Fargo, players explore the island, make friends, and earn virtual money by successfully learning financial concepts.

Much like professional practice, simulation games where students learn as pilots, doctors, or architects, MUVEs allow for thinking by being in that particular world, rather than just asking students to memorize facts (Squire, 2006). The value of training in virtual worlds is faster and more effective than other channels, allowing and expecting failure in a safe environment enroute to mastery (Wagner, 2007). Well designed MUVEs aim to clarify concepts for the student through active learning. MUVEs present content knowledge using higher-ordered thinking skills and away from a controlling ideology that Fuller (2006, p. 87) frames as: "knowledge is power, and some, afraid of losing their edge, are loathe to share it."

CULTURAL AND TECHNOLOGICAL CHALLENGES

The current stress on accountability focuses teacher attention on test preparation and serves as a barrier to adoption of alternative tools like MUVEs. The emphasis on objective and short term measurement of achievement minimizes teacher ability to devote classroom time to more long range performance-based activities. Teaching in many classrooms has remained constant over the years, relying on traditional methods of instruction. In some cases, educators are reluctant about game use in classrooms as they feel that games do not represent solid pedagogy or have a preconceived notion of gaming based on the past (Cooper, as cited in Panettieri, 2006; O'Hanlon, 2007), although much development has occurred in the past 35 years in the ongoing evolution of our digital world and associated tools.

Expense and access to technology are barriers to MUVEs use as well. While some MUVEs are free and available on the Internet, others need to have software downloaded on each computer, and some require passwords and registered user names. Costs for training teachers and purchasing games are considerations for school districts. Continuous professional development for teachers is viewed as equally important as equipment (Blaisdell, 2006).

Although broadband connections have become more plentiful, access to technology at needed bandwidth and microprocessor speeds may be another limitation for potential adoption. This possible hurdle is viewed as one that will work itself out in time as the forecast is for roughly 62% of U.S. households to have broadband links by 2010, up from 29% in 2005 (Panettieri, 2007). A more pressing obstacle is one of safety, where not all parents want their children chatting online, a component available with most MUVEs. It is likely that educational MUVES will protect students by adopting the following useful limits other games have included for its participants: (1) parental approval by fax; (2) requirement for participants to pass an assessment on how to participate safely in an online environment; (3) log in on different days; and (4) deletion of unsuitable language. Other games limit participation in school and have protected passwords and user names for students. In addition, teachers check student communications for appropriateness, and communication is limited to team members (Olsen, 2006).

It is important to keep in mind, too, that all MUVEs are not created with equally valuable educational purposes. MUVEs such as *Club Penguin, Millsberry, There,* and *Habbo* appear to be designed as teen hang-outs that are not created with curriculum content standards in mind. Their design is more of a social networking appeal rather than for use in educational settings or for educational purposes.

While some educators may see games as distractions from academic work, others are starting to view them as vehicles for honing students' mathematical, problem-solving, and reading comprehension skills (Borja, 2007), strategic thinking, communication, application of numbers, and group-decision making (Kirriemuir & McFarlane, 2004). Such games have great potential to foster learning with a content-driven purpose. They enable players to explore conflicting situations (*Cool School: Where Peace Rules!, PeaceMaker*), allow insight into the world of work (*Whyville, Hot Shot Business, Stagecoach Island*), explore the world of science (*Quest Atlantis, Immune Attack, River City Project*), assume roles and experience the past (*Virtual History: Ancient Egypt, Discover Babylon*), and learn about cultural differences (*Real Lives*).

MAIN FOCUS

The main focus of this chapter is to describe the results of a research study that explored, through anonymous responses to questions,

teacher candidates' reactions to using a specific MUVE, *The River City Project*. Those who support this innovation want to engage teachers and teacher candidates in using such pedagogy, so increasing numbers of students can benefit from immersive, virtual, active learning experiences. In this context, it is important for researchers to explore teacher reactions to a MUVE experience and make recommendations about their use. As Olsen (2006, p. 2) notes, "Virtual worlds must have knowledgeable and motivated teachers driving the train."

METHOD

The River City MUVE, created at Harvard Graduate School of Education, is a virtual environment designed to teach biology and ecology concepts through a historical and social lens to the middle school age groups. The goal **is** to determine the answer to the primary question, "Why are the residents of *River City* getting sick?" Secondary teacher education students (n=24) in all academic disciplines, ages 20–25, participated in the exploration of *River City* as part of their class work in a junior level teacher education course in which they study both traditional and alternative forms of assessment.

The students explored *River City* for 60 minutes by porting back in time to the late 1800s and collecting clues that helped them resolve the primary question. Activities that helped them figure out the puzzle involved speaking to the residents, using their observations, skills, and judgments and sampling the water for level of microbes and incidence of mosquitoes. Sociological and geographical factors are considered while exploring. Where the residents live within this virtual world; their immigrant, socioeconomic, and employment status are presented as potential factors contributing to illness. Participants then responded to five open-ended questions.

The researcher recorded observed behavior and comments as students engaged in the virtual simulation. Participants were asked to respond to five questions during their experience.

DATA ANALYSIS

This study used a grounded theory approach. An open-ended questionnaire instrument was used to get at intangible constructs and, therefore, became the construct's operational definition (Krathwohl, 1998). Some of the student responses to the five open-ended questions follow:

1. *After taking a few minutes to acquaint your-self with this virtual world and learn how to navigate your avatar, please write down all the questions that you currently have about this software program.* (Can students talk to each other?; Do the townspeople answer any questions or only limited questions?; Where are some of the clues as to where to go first?)
2. *Please state what you are thinking at this moment. For example, in what capacity do you see this software being used?* (This program can be used in a math, science, or history class; I can see this program being used in many situations; A good tool for the trial and error method)
3. *What do you think middle school/high school students would learn from exposure to and engagement in this virtual world, River City?* (How to ask questions as to the outcome of the situation; Exposure to issues in various time periods of history and various socio-economic issues; Scientific method and problem-solving skills.)
4. *Do you believe virtual worlds such as River City represent a solid pedagogy designed to teach science and social studies concepts through simulations?* (It would be a very

good way to show the concept of experimentation; Yes, it is a hands-on experience; Yes, I do. I feel this would be beneficial in teaching a lesson in ecology.)

5. *What, if anything, concerns you about the use of virtual worlds in educational settings?*(Students may play more than work; There should be more possible answers from the townspeople; How much information is really being learned?)

Reported results, derived from participant survey responses and researcher observations, were examined for the emergence of themes and organized into categorical aggregations. Throughout this process, researchers tested emergent understandings by continuously returning to the data to check for alternative explanations and negative instances in order to further reduce the data and identify the central themes (Creswell, 1998).

RESULTS

In order to raise awareness about newer forms of pedagogy, an immersive virtual experience that could work in actual practice was provided. Rather than teaching through lecture, discussion, reading assignments, or anecdotes, this study enabled teaching candidates to explore a virtual environment authentically so the experience would resonate more deeply. The researcher recorded behavior and comments as students engaged in the virtual world simulation. Specific themes emerged from the survey questions and researcher observations, including: understanding the MUVEs' purpose and functions, connection to educational content, perceived learning outcomes, and concerns about facilitation and classroom management. An examination of the themes follows.

GETTING STARTED: UNDERSTANDING MUVE PURPOSE AND FUNCTION

Participants were interested yet unsure how to work the software and avatar. Their initial questions revolved around how to fly and how to navigate their avatar. Both males and females alike were engaged in trying out different roles in their avatar choices as each choice possessed a different visual personality. It appeared as if participants viewed the choice much like they did in getting themselves ready to attend a gathering, like a party.

Students had a grand time in the main room of the virtual environment after figuring out how to get their avatar to talk and make gestures, evidenced by laughing and loud chatter in the classroom. Once initial greetings were made, many students changed their avatar, re-entered the main virtual foyer, and regreeted their class-mates. The researcher observed this repetitive behavior numerous times. Once the avatar was decided upon, students began to ask other questions about how and why to teleport, ways to talk to the townspeople, and what they were supposed to do with responses.

Researcher observations noted excitement, interest, and some confusion throughout the 60-minute session. Three participants figured out why the residents of *River City* were getting ill within the first 30 minutes. Deep immersion in game tasks was noted although the majority of participants did not collect enough clues by the end of the 60-minute session to answer the primary question. Despite not reaching a solution, these participants remained highly interested in discussing the game with their peers.

Evidenced by questions directed to researcher and peers, initially positive participants remained interested throughout the game and did not experience frustration. Changed opinions about the simulation experience were found among most initially frustrated participants. After the 20-minute mark one initially frustrated respondent noted, "Once you get the hang of being in the city, it becomes like a personal time machine."

CONNECTIONS TO EDUCATIONAL CONTENT

Participants envisioned MUVE use in math, science, and history lessons using an inquiry-based model of teaching. They saw the highest potential for use in science classes because of the strong scaffold provided in learning the scientific method of inquiry. Middle and high school were selected as the most appropriate levels, while a few thought the content was within the grasp of elementary students.

Most participants saw the MUVE as engaging for middle school students as it emulates video-games most students at this level play at home. They believe it had the potential to create a sense of independence and motivation through hands-on experiences. On the other hand, while one respon-dent viewed the tool as interesting and creative, he thought it would ultimately be distracting to students because it was too "game-like."

Contrasting attitudes toward use of games in classrooms existed among participants. A few expressed concerns in line with Cooper's obser-vation of educator antagonism toward games in education (as cited in Panettieri, 2006), while the majority believed that simulation exercises have the ability to motivate students to participate in the learning process (Meyers & Jones, 1993; Naps et al., 2002).

LEARNING OUTCOMES

Development of problem-solving skills through the data collection activities is seen as the pri-mary learning outcome of this program as well as analytic thinking skills and technology skill development. One respondent stated that students

Multi-User Virtual Learning Environments in Education

would learn that education could be fun and informative at the same time. A few participants noted opportunities for social skill development, and active engagement may be successful in drawing in less interested or less involved students.

Other respondents believed students would learn that there are many factors that contribute to problems within a community, including socioeconomic and environmental hazards that can affect health. A few questioned how much information could be learned through this method of instruction since students might view it only as a game and not take it seriously. One person noted that although they did not believe the tool constituted solid pedagogy, it had the potential to be useful in teaching.

MANAGEMENT

The majority of respondents qualified their positive responses with concerns about implementation. They saw potential for task behavior and a need for constant teacher guidance and monitoring during the game. Most respondents highlighted the amount of time the game assignments would take to complete and keeping students focused on game tasks as potential problem areas. One person wondered how to assess student performance and cost of the program.

Interestingly, the perceived negative behaviors of classroom chaos that some teacher candidates fear will occur with their own students are the very behaviors that can stimulate the learning process: collaborative communication in class and online that foster sharing. Kuo and Johnson (as cited in Squire, 2006, p. 23) say: "Most gamers describe their play as a social experience, a way to connect with friends, and rare is the player who truly games alone in any meaningful sense." The social attributes associated with games demand special skills of teachers. Blaisdell (2006, p. 2) says: "To use MUVEs effectively, teachers need to be skilled in facilitating discussion—creating

and sustaining student-centered classroom inquiry—to assist students in learning to ask good questions and to collaborate in teams."

RECOMMENDATIONS

Faculty often report their beliefs that their role is to help students become independent learners through the use of collaborative and project-based activities (Yopp, 2003). Teacher education programs are a good match with the philosophy behind MUVEs if they are based on the belief that: "students are active learners who construct, interpret, and reconstruct rather than simply absorb knowledge" (Sardone & Skeele, 2003, p. 3225). In college classrooms, models of teaching more often use a traditional curriculum void of educational videogames and MUVEs.

Faculty can obtain a better understanding of the ways in which they can support classroom use of MUVEs and other interactive virtual games by asking students about their prior experience with games through a brief survey. Having the group review how they play games on their own and note how this game play may be similar and/or different in the classroom may enable a faculty member initiate gaming in a class more effectively. During the game play, if students reflect regularly on what they are learning from the game, they may attach meaning and significance to their own experience.

Preservice teacher candidates often express interest in alternative forms of teaching and assessment. However, when confronted with the complexity of implementing such reforms, even idealistic candidates who envision themselves as potential innovators express concerns about coverage and classroom management. Similar to experienced teachers, novice teacher candidates also wonder how to assess students as they construct their own learning in a game situation. Hands-on experiences with games will have deeper meaning for teacher candidates if accompanied by extended discussion to develop understanding of the advantages and applications of these tools in classrooms.

FUTURE TRENDS

Thomas Jefferson called for enlightenment of the people, meaning literacy achieved through compulsory education using existing models of instruction (Fuller, 2006). The call remains important today; however, due to rapid changes in our global society, traditional models of instruction may not be enough to reach the growing body of digital students. MUVEs have the potential to capture attention, stimulate desired interaction, and invite learning in ways that respect student dignity. They are worthy of further research and development. K–12 students have been the focus for much of the current development in the new generation of educational gaming. Educators, however, foresee MUVE development for college students to promote study of economics, criminal justice, and other curricular areas (Panettieri, 2007).

The River City Project MUVE is intended to be a lengthy curriculum unit (17 hours) and one that requires teachers to invest training time before the free program is made available. If content-driven virtual games were more intuitive and required less faculty training, they might become even more popular for classroom use. Experiences in classrooms will enable developers to work closely with teachers, and these opportunities will promote ease of use. In addition, the strengths of standard simulation games, videogames, "augmented reality" simulations, and associated pedagogy will become integrated in forthcoming games, and research on the effects on learning will continue to be conducted (Tan, 2006).

Accountability is a high priority in K–12 schools. Ways to promote active learning while effectively collecting adequate and useful assessment information on student performance is of great interest to everyone in the academic community. This exploratory study showed that future teachers need adequate guidance to employ these tools to foster student learning. Leadership of MUVES asks teachers to move from the role of providing information to an inquiry model, requiring advanced discussion and questioning skills. Future research should continue to focus on the kind and value of extended student learning that takes place during videogame play as well as the changing role of the teacher.

REFERENCES

AAUW Educational Foundation Commission on Technology, Gender, and Teacher Education. (2000). *Tech-savvy: Educating girls in the new computer age*. Washington, DC: American Association of University Women Educational Foundation. Retrieved March 17, 2008, from http://www.aauw.org/research/girls_education/techsavvy.cfm

Anderson, C. A., & Bushman, B. J. (2001). Effects of violent games on aggressive behavior, aggressive cognition, aggressive affect, physiological arousal, and prosocial behavior: A meta-analytic review of the scientific literature. *Psychological Science, 12*, 353-358.

Anderson, J. R. (2005, November-December). The relationship between student perceptions of team dynamics and simulation game outcomes: An individual-level analysis. *Journal of Education for Business, 81*(2), 11-18.

Blaisdell, M. (2006). All the right MUVEs. *The Journal, 33*(14), 28-38.

Borja, R. (2007). Video games trickle from rec rooms to classrooms. *Education Week, 26*(14), 10-11.

Brandt, L., Borchert, O., Addicott, K., Cosmano, B., Hawley, J., Hokanson, G., et al. (2005). Roles, culture, and computer supported collaborative work on planet oit. In V. Uskov (Ed.), *International Association of Science and Technology for Development (IASTED) Conference on Computers and Advanced Technology in Education* (pp. 129-140). Anaheim: ACTA Press.

Bransford, J., Brown, A., & Cocking, R. (Eds.). (2000). *How people learn: Brain, mind, experience, and school* (expanded ed.). National Research Council (U.S.) Committee on Developments in the Sciences, National Research Council (U.S.) Committee on Learning Research in Education. Washington, DC: National Academy Press.

Dede, C., Ketelhut, D., & Nelson, B. (2004). *Design-based research on gender, class, race, and ethnicity in a multi-user virtual environment.* Paper presented at the American Educational Research Association Conference, San Diego, CA.

DeKanter, N. (2005, May-June). Gaming redefines interactivity for learning. *TechTrends: Linking Research & Practice to Improve Learning, 49*(3), 26-32.

Dieterle, E., & Clarke, J. (in press). Multi-user virtual environments for teaching and learning. In M. Pagani (Ed.), *Encyclopedia of multimedia technology and networking* (2nd ed). Hershey, PA: Idea Global.

Dobson, J. (2007, June 22). New NYC school to promote gaming literacy. *CMP Media.* Retrieved March 17, 2008, from http://www.gamasutra.com/php- bin/news_index.php?story=14437

eSchool News staff and wire service reports. (2006, October 20). Scientists: Can video games save education? *eSchool News Online.* Retrieved March 17, 2008,, from http://www.eschoolnews.com/news/showstory.cfm?ArticleID=6655

Foyle, H. (Ed.). (1995). *Interactive learning in the higher education classroom.* Washington, DC: National Education Association.

Fuller, R. (2006). *All rise.* San Francisco: Berrett-Koehler Publishers, Inc.

Ketelhut, D. (2006). The impact of student self-efficacy on scientific inquiry skills: An exploratory investigation in river city, a multi-user virtual environment. *Journal of Science Inquiry and Technology.* Retrieved March 17, 2008, from http://www.springerlink.com/content/p006mh0776u28384/fulltext.html

Kirk, J. J. (2001). *An unofficial guide to Web-based instructional gaming and simulation resources.* (ERIC Document Reproduction Service No. ED472675)

Kirriemuir, J., & McFarlane, A. (2004). *Literature review in games and learning* (Report 8, Nesta Futurelab Series). Bristol: Nesta Futurelab.

Klopfer, E., & Yoon, S. (2005, May-June). Developing games and simulations for today and tomorrow's tech savvy youth. *TechTrends, 49*(3), 33-41.

Krathwohl, D. (1998). *Methods of educational and social science research: An integrated approach.* Long Grove, IL: Waveland Press.

MacArthur to invest $50M in digital learning. (2006). *eSchool News Online.* Retrieved March 17, 2008, from http://www.eschoolnews.com/news/showStoryts.cfm?ArticleID=6654

Maddux, C., Johnson, D., & Willis, J. (2001). *Educational computing: Learning with tomorrow's technologies.* Boston: Allyn & Bacon.

Meyers, C., & Jones, T. (1993). *Promoting active learning.* San Francisco: Jossey-Bass.

Naps, T., Rößling, G., Almstrum, V., Dann, W., Fleischer, R., Hundhausen, C., Korhonen, A., Malmi, L., McNally, M., Rodger, S., & Velázquez-Iturbide, J. (2002). ITiCSE working group report: Exploring the role of visualization and engagement in computer science education.

SIGCSE Bulletin, 35(2), 131-152. Association of Computing Machinery.

O'Hanlon, C. (2007). Eat breakfast, drink milk, play Xbox. *T.H.E. Journal, 34*(4), 35-39.

Olsen, S. (2006, June 12). Are virtual worlds the future of the classroom? *CNET News.com.* Retrieved March 17, 2008, from http://news.com. com/Are+virtual+worlds+the+future+of+the+cl assroom/2009-1041_3-6081870.html

Panettieri, J. (2006). Advanced teaching technologies: Brave new world. *Campus Technology.* Retrieved March 17, 2008, from http://www. campustechnology/article.aspx?aid=41718

Project Tomorrow: NetDay. (2006). National report on NetDay's 2006 Speak Up event. Retrieved March 17, 2008, from http://www.tomorrow. org/docs/Speak%20Up%202006%20National% 20Snapshot_K-12%20Students.pdf

Rajagopalan, M., & Schwartz, D. (2005, Summer). Game design and game development education. *Phi Kappa Phi Forum, 85*(2), 30-32.

Sardone, N., & Skeele, R. (2003). AT attention: Integrating accessibility awareness and computer-related assistive technologies in teacher preparation programs. *Proceedings of the Society for Information Technology & Teacher Education 14th Annual International Conference, 5,* 3222-3229.

Squire, K. (2006). From content to context: Videogames as designed experience. *Educational Researcher, 35*(8), 19-29.

Tan, J. (2006). *The use of simulations for building effective discovery learning environments.* Retrieved March 17, 2008, from http://eeecs.vuse. vanderbilt.edu/research/air/meetings/2006Fall/ Sir

Van Eck, R. (2006). Using games to promote girls' positive attitudes toward technology. *Innovate, 2*(3). Retrieved March 17, 2008, from http://www.innovateonline.info/index. php?view=article&id=209

Wagner, M. (2007, June 18). Mitch Kapor: Virtual worlds are like a drug experience. *Information Week.* Retrieved March 17, 2008, from http:// www.informationweek.com/story/showArticle. jhtml?articleID=199904918

Yopp, M. C. (2003). Current trends in business education in NBEA. *2003 NBEA Yearbook, 41,* 35-45.

KEY TERMS

Avatar: A virtual (not real) representation of a player in a game.

Digital Students: Today's students who are used to rapid communication through multiple digital devices and may have different learning styles than students in the past.

MUVE: Multi-user virtual environment refers to online opportunities accessed over the Internet, often in a game format, that allows for numerous simultaneous users to interact in a virtual world.

River City: A computer-simulated virtual environment that immerses participants in analysis of environmental and cultural issues of a certain time period, designed at the Harvard Graduate School of Education to meet national middle school science content standards.

Simulation Games: Structured activities that challenge players to use strategy, skill, and chance to participate in some aspect relating to the real world that is more about discovery learning than about winning.

Virtual World: A computer-based simulated online community intended for users to inhabit and interact via avatars, often in game or simulation format which is similar to activities that occur in the real world.

Section II
Methods

Chapter XII
Pedagogical Practice for Learning with Social Software

Anne Bartlett-Bragg
University of Technology, Sydney, Australia

ABSTRACT

This chapter proposes that social software can enable informal learning environments through collective learning networks and the fundamental social interactions embedded in those learning processes. Situated in the adult learning organisational context, the challenge for educators is how to reframe their pedagogical practices for the new technological developments and facilitate the design of online communication and information exchanges to empower the learners and create an enriched social learning landscape. The chapter presents a pedagogical framework, developed from practice and verified through doctoral research, which provides pathways through phases of development for facilitating informal learning processes and strategies that enable learners to overcome key issues that may inhibit the creation of informal learning environments. Examples from recent practice will be used to illustrate areas where educators need to be aware of both the inhibitors and their pedagogical strategies.

INTRODUCTION

In adult learning contexts, both corporate organisations and higher education institutions, the early implementations of e-learning products focused on delivery, accessibility, and distribution of content to learners anywhere, any time. While large investments of resources were spent on the technical infrastructure such as intranets, learner management systems (LMSs), and online courses with the expectation of providing improved productivity, delivery, and workplace efficiencies. Yet there is little evidence to suggest that incorporating these technologies into existing learning environments has resulted in significant change in learning processes or outcomes (Zemsky & Massy, 2004). Learners lament the loss of communication and depersonalisation of content (Sanders, 2006) and continue to attend scheduled classroom sessions even when offered alternative delivery methods, such as podcast lectures (Alexander, 2006). In these contexts, the role of the educator has become increasingly focused on dispensing, enforcing, and managing the distribution of learning through overly bureaucratic, inflexible systems that depersonalise and disconnect the learner from not only the context but also other learners within the organisation (Bartlett-Bragg, 2005).

Currently, organisations are turning their attention towards emerging technologies in an attempt to stimulate the capture of tacit knowledge from informal learning situations. Consequently, to reflect and question our underpinning pedagogical principles when creating a learning environment that fosters the development of informal learning is the potential presented by the integration of the emerging social software technologies into our teaching practices, rather than simply replicating or renovating traditional pedagogical strategies.

The aim of this chapter will be to present a pedagogical framework, developed from six years of practice and informed by doctoral research that provides pathways through phases of development for facilitating informal learning processes using social software. In particular, drawing upon specific examples from recent experiences in the organisational learning context, issues that inhibited learners when attempting to create informal learning environments with social software are identified. Also, strategies used to address these concerns will be examined.

INFORMAL LEARNING IN ORGANISATIONS

Recent organisational learning industry reports assert figures ranging from 58–80% of the learning that occurs in the workplace is informal (Chief Learning Officer, 2007; Harrison, 2006). The Chief Learning Officer Business Intelligence Industry Report (2007) claims that although informal learning is hard to measure, 20% of organisations track informal learning, while 8% have a comprehensive strategy to manage informal learning, and 47% report ad hoc strategies.

Yet how these reports define informal learning becomes a significant issue in the interpretation of the cited figures. If informal learning is considered a core notion of adult learning principles, viewed as a subset of the social learning concepts, where the recognition that learning occurs in a social context through interactions with others and subsequent learning is influenced by observing and modeling the patterns of behaviour (Cornford, 1999), then this broad definition may provide some insight into how organisations may be challenged by measurement and management.

The Chief Learning Officer Report (2007) simply explains that informal learning tends to be unplanned and unstructured, while Harrison (2006, p. 2) describes events "that take place away from the world of organized formal training" and is deep and pervasive, uncontrolled, and powerful. Nonetheless, an unambiguous definition of informal learning remains a contested issue, particularly in the organisational learning context where informal learning is generally described in contrast to formal learning or by what it is not (Colley, Hodkinson, & Malcolm, 2002). Current debates focus on the comparisons between the degree of formality and informality; the description of specific learning situations; and intentional or unintentional learning outcomes (Beckett & Hager, 2002; Billett, 2001; Hodkinson & Hodkinson, 2001). In contrast, an expanded concept of formal vs. informal learning was outlined by the European Commission (2001, pp. 32-33) into three categories:

- **Formal learning:** Provided by an educational institution, structured, leading to a qualification, and intentional by the learner.

- **Nonformal learning:** Not provided by an educational institution, structured, can result in qualification, and intentional by the learner.
- **Informal learning:** Part of daily life activities, not structured, no qualification attainable, can be intentional but generally incidental or random.

While Marsick and Volpe (1999) propose that informal learning will occur in workplaces where there is a need, motivation, and opportunities for learning and where the control of learning is primarily the responsibility of the learner. It can be depicted in the following situations in a workplace context where it is not a highly conscious activity; where it is haphazard and influenced by chance; where it is an inductive process of reflection and action; and where it is linked to learning of others through social interactions which may occur in formal learning environments.

On this basis, if we accept the contested state of defining informal learning and then refer to the conditions that can support the more unstructured approaches to learning in the organisational con-

text, these can be distinguished by the strategies that represent the formal learning processes and the current use of technologies in organisations to deliver them. Refer to Table 1.

In many instances, informal learning appears to transpire without structured interventions; however, the organisational need driven by objectives to make explicit aspects of tacit knowledge and create measurable outcomes for all learning strategies may in fact create a barrier to the effectiveness of informal learning opportunities. This chapter contends that attempting to integrate informal learning into a structured formal learning technology environment, such as the LMS, will result in constrained learning bounded by the limitations of the software. Further, to foster an informal learning environment, the introduction of social software will provide situations where interactions and knowledge sharing can occur and extend beyond the enclosed entity of the classroom, LMS, and the organisation. However, inhibitors may result in ineffective usage by learners, and without reframed pedagogical strategies to address these inhibitors, informal learning will be in jeopardy of shifting into the existing formal learning technologies and structures.

Table 1. Formal versus informal learning technologies

Formal Learning Activity	Use of Technology	Informal learning Activity	Use of Technology
• Classroom sessions: Structured Time constrained Outcome focused	• LMS: Enrolments Records attendance Tracks results Records competence Reports compliance	• Networking • Communities of Practice • Mentoring • Coaching • Learning from experts or advisors	Collaborative spaces – typically asynchronous discussion forums, email, synchronous chat or instant messaging
• Online modules: Self-paced No or little collaboration Structured Outcome focused	• LMS: Access Delivery Records progress Records completions Records competence Reports compliance	• Searching for solutions to problems	Internet (Google) Intranet email an expert
		• Information distribution	Syndication software/RSS Intranet email / listservs
		• Self-analysis or reflection	Online journals, weblogs

SOCIAL SOFTWARE IN ORGANISATIONAL LEARNING

Social software refers to the range of applications that augment group interactions and shared spaces for collaboration, social connections, and aggregates information exchanges in a Web-based environment. Social software can also be considered as the major component of the current Web 2.0 definitions and at the focal point of E-Learning 2.0, a term attributed to Stephen Downes in 2005 where he characterises the use of social software applications as "placing of the control of learning itself into the hands of the learner" (Downes, 2005, par. 12). The list of social software applications is extensive and growing rapidly; a brief overview of the more commonly used applications in organisational learning contexts is outlined.

Collaborative spaces: *Web-based collaborative publishing spaces such as Weblogs, or blogs, have been the core of the increasing popularity of social software and have developed into powerful personal spaces that allow the author to self-publish and organise information or knowledge. In addition, the interaction with authors' readers through comments or linking functions, and the ability to subscribe to updates through syndication tools has seen the Weblog technologies as the foundation to further developments in education. Commonly used applications for Weblogs include WordPress (http://wordpress.com) with free hosted services, or downloadable to organisational servers, or edublogs (http://edublogs.org) powered by WordPress specifically for educational implementations. Other Web-based shared spaces like wikis include the functionality to communicate, co-edit documents and Web pages, share calendars, view multimedia presentations, and build collaborative projects. The popularity of these applications has been attributed to the ease of use and flexibility which only requires the user to have Internet access and no HTML programming skills. Popular ex-*

amples of free wikis used in educational settings are Wikispaces (http://www.wikispaces.com), or PBWiki (http://www.pbwiki.com).

E-Portofolios: *Potentially viewed as a subset in the collaborative spaces, e-portfolios are popularly used as individual collections of artefacts—text documents such as Word or PDF files, images, and blog entries. The software typically combines functions like a blog, a social network feature, aggregator, file repository, comment functions, and categorisation of work. Applications in education are most commonly seen as a* record of that might include evidence of achievement and work records. A powerful application in this category is ELGG (http://elgg.org).

RSS–syndication and aggregation: *Really simple syndication is a method of XML-based programming that allows content to be imported into other Web pages. RSS originated in Weblog software but is now available across many other sources, like news and journal sites. RSS enables readers to subscribe to Webfeeds from sites of their choice, monitor updates, and view them in a single page from a Web-based service called an aggregator, for example, Netvibes (http://www.netvibes.com) or Bloglines (http://www.bloglines.com). The power of the aggregator for learners comes from the ability to control and manage the flow of information in a centralised manner.*

Social bookmarking or tagging with folksonomies: *Social bookmarking is a Web-based application that is similar to a favourites list in a browser, except that it allows the user to bookmark, manage, publicly publish, comment upon, and create their own tags for each URL they want to share. The objective is to publish resources for other people with similar interests. The key to the shared resource is the development of a social tagging system called folksonomies, derived from the term taxonomy, a hierarchical list, or categorisation The folksonomy focuses on a group of people cooperatively organising information into agreed categories. In addition, these tags have*

RSS feeds which can be collected into the learners' aggregator, becoming a powerful research and resource gathering tool. A prevalent example is Delicious (http://del.icio.us).

Social sharing services is similar to social bookmarking; these are applications that share other services; for example, Flickr (http://www.flickr.com) *is a Web-based photo sharing service that uses the folksonomy tagging process to collect and share photos publicly or privately across the Web. In the learning context, photos can be gathered for projects and the agreed tagging systems allow collective sharing. Digital storytelling and photo essays continue to be popular uses of Flickr which allows descriptions and comments on images to enrich the application.*

Podcasts: *Digital audio files that are downloaded from the Internet onto learners' personal audio playing devices such as iPods, where the content can be listened to at the learners' convenience. Podcasting is emerging as one of the most popular current innovations in social software with major research projects investigating the beneficial effects on learning (Impala,* http://www.impala.ac.uk), reports from educators outlining a diverse range of uses and positive feedback from learners (Alexander, 2006), and edition 10 of the *Knowledge Tree*—the Australian e-journal of flexible learning in vocational education, dedicated entirely to podcasting (http://kt.flexiblelearning.net.au/edition-10/).

Vodcasts: *A recent addition to the social software suite of applications are short video clips that are published to the Internet via sites like YouTube (*http://www.youtube.com) *where users can subscribe, download, and view on their own computers or portable devices. Early applications in learning contexts are being used for corporate communication, assessment of on the job practices, and short video essay projects.*

Reports and case studies from individual educators and several institutions incorporating social software, specifically Weblog technologies, into their practices can be found dating from early 2001

(Farmer & Bartlett-Bragg, 2005). More recently, as social software has evolved in both sophistication and ease of use, the adoptions rates have increased with a growing number of supporters claiming the social software technologies are the most significant development in online learning since the introduction of enterprise level LMS, yielding an opportunity to transform learning and rethink traditional teaching processes (Downes, 2004).

Publishing and participating online with social software creates a complex genre of communication. The social structure of the environment comprising of an infinite variety of people, both readers and writers, supporting the structure of network evolution that develops through an ecology of links and connections. The social networking and the collaborative spaces that are created by the personalising of content and sharing of information has been recognised as the basis for the human or social dimension of this phenomenon currently being observed (Blood, 2002; Bruns & Jacobs, 2006; Miles, 2005).

Although most studies in education have reported relatively positive outcomes in terms of enhanced student results and participation, there have been areas in which no significant difference or negative learning outcomes have been noted. Specifically, these educators have struggled with learner participation, getting learners to engage in the social software environment, and the challenges of renegotiating private reflective tasks into the public Internet space. Authors like Gibson (2004), Krause (2004), and MacColl, Morrison, Muhlberger, Simpson, and Viller (2005) note that educators have examined the negative issues reported and attributed them to the functionality and selection of social software options. None, however, have considered the results from a pedagogical perspective and critically evaluated their strategies.

Social software repositions the learning into an unconstrained environment that stretches beyond mere access of content to the social application of information in a constant process of re-organisation into the learners' shared context (Mejias, 2005). In my practice, social software provides opportunities for learners to personalise and manage their development of knowledge, augment potential for a deeper approach to learning through reflective writing processes and create collaborative spaces for interaction with colleagues and others beyond the formal boundaries of the classroom, thus fostering an environment where informal learning can be expected to emerge.

INHIBITORS TO INFORMAL LEARNING USING SOCIAL SOFTWARE

Many factors can inhibit the ability to learn in both formal and informal learning contexts. Informal learning may be directly influenced by availability of resources which can include time restrictions, availability of other people, and technology, motivation to learn, and capabilities of the learner that may include the level of skill or awareness to interpret, analyse, and critically reflect upon situations (Marsick & Watkins, 2001).

Similarly, the implementations of social software into learning contexts have presented my practice and research in workplace-learning contexts with the following additional inhibitors to informal learning which can be categorised into three areas: (1) organisational inhibitors; (2) individual inhibitors; and (3) pedagogical inhibitors.

Organisational Inhibitors

Organisational technology infrastructure: Educators implementing social software are confronted with the challenges of determining which applications can be accessed through organisational firewalls where limitations on social sharing sites, generally justified by fear of external se-

curity breaches through collaboration and social sharing sites; determining the speed of Internet access required, particularly if collaboration is occurring outside of workplaces where network speeds provide a superior user experience to the Internet speeds available on personal networks in the home; considering the range of software applications that are constantly changing and new entrants require educators to be frequently reviewing their choices for enhanced or additional functionality that may positively contribute to the learners experience; acknowledging limitations imposed by organisational IT departments on rich media such as graphics, photos, or videos causing pedagogical strategies to be inhibited to text only functions, potentially limiting the depth of interactions available to the learners.

All these factors can impact the educators' choices and limit the learners' ability to engage in rich social sharing environments. Furthermore, organisational culture has a strong impact and the strategic learning culture espoused or practiced by the organisation may restrict the implementation of social software and associated informal learning activities. Software applications that have collaborative functionality or rich media disabled can indirectly or directly present to the learner a culture where the sharing of tacit knowledge and experience is not actively valued. Additionally, a training culture that is structurally dependent upon competency and achievement of learning outcomes through regulatory requirements or a focus on measurable return on investment will not endorse the integration of social software and informal learning where outcomes are seen as subjective, difficult to formalise, and the development and capture of tacit knowledge, which are hard to measure.

Individual Inhibitors

Digital literacy is a term increasingly used to encompass both computer literacy and information literacy, subsequently referring to skills related to the use of computers, and additionally a person's abilities to manage, evaluate, analyse, create, and communicate in digital formats. As an inhibitor, both educators and learners are expected to understand and manage the software functionality, such as how to access, login protocols, communication processes, and the access and storage of information. Additionally, searching efficiently and evaluating the authenticity and credibility of information resources has become an expected capability for most learners. In my own practice, digital literacy is a major area of concern that has required the most attention to address through pedagogical strategies. Other educators have identified similar experiences where students are reported to be spending more time working with the technology than with the content (Sanders, 2006) and where the need for educators to develop their awareness and teaching practices are being recommended (Blackall, 2005).

In addition to the capabilities of the learner, as previously noted (Marsick & Watkins, 2001), inhibitors that have been observed to restrict the learners' ability to participate in collaborative social software environments include: the learners' dependency on the educator for direction can be related to low levels of digital literacy, pedagogical practices, and organisational culture. The learner feels an anxiety to develop an online identity, sometimes expressed as lack of self-confidence, fear of self-disclosure, invasion of privacy, and mistrust of the culture to share tacit knowledge. The learners fear of publicly publishing their thoughts can relate to the previous issues, or the learners' confidence in their writing skills to adequately represent their thoughts. There is the issue of learner control, where time management, planning, and structure are noted by the learners as issues difficult to embed into study plans or daily work patterns. Recently published papers endorse these observations (Mejias, 2006; Wijekumar, 2005).

Pedagogical Inhibitors

The educators' existing pedagogical practices developed through formal studies or influenced by organisational training structures can inhibit the development of learners towards participation within social software environments and informal learning activities. Baumgartner (2004) outlines three prototypical models for teaching that provided a valuable framework to review and reframe pedagogical strategies that enable informal learning in my doctoral research project. Refer to Table 2.

Educators intending to foster informal learning environments through the application of social software would be required to perform predominantly in a Mode 3 mindset, remaining cognisant of the need to provide some structural guidance in early phases of implementation within the Mode 2 parameters. Educators who continue to teach with social software entirely from a Mode 1 or even Mode 2 approach will cause informal learning to become structured and formalised, consequently inhibiting the learning and missing the opportunities presented by the guided strategies embedded in a Mode 3 attitude.

A FRAMEWORK TO FACILITATE INFORMAL LEARNING USING SOCIAL SOFTWARE

The pedagogical framework developed by the author has been based on six years of practice in higher education institutions and the workplace–learning context and extensive research. Informed by research into the learners' experience of using social software, the framework has evolved to encompass strategies to not only enable the learners' development, but also specifically to address inhibitors that can create barriers to the learning processes.

Table 2. Modes of teaching

Mode 1: Transfer (Directed Teaching)	Mode 2: Tutor (Facilitated Learning)	Mode 3: Coach (Informal Guide)
• Programmed instruction	• Problem solving	• Complex simulations
• To teach, to explain	• To observe, to help, to demonstrate	• To co-operate, to support
• Production of correct answers	• Selection of methods and its use	• Realization of adequate action strategies
• To know, to remember	• To do, to practice	• To cope, to master
• Transfer of knowledge	• Presentation of pre-determined problems	• Action in real situations (complex and social) (Baumgarten, 2004)

RESEARCH METHODOLOGY

The intention of the research project that tested the pedagogical framework was to investigate the adult learners' experiences of using social software with a methodology that fore-grounded the learners and focused on the group as a collective set of experiences, rather than investigating the individual's experience. A qualitative interpretive research perspective was selected, using a developmental phenomenography methodology to inform the development of research questions, gathering, and analysis of data. The interpretive perspective was underpinned by the assumption that reality is developed through social constructions such as language, consciousness, and shared meanings where the studies attempt to understand the phenomena being researched through the meanings assigned by the participants.

From this interpretive stance, the phenomenographic method for mapping the qualitative data that categorises and describes the variation in ways a group of people experience and understand various aspects of a phenomenon in their specific context was used. One of the core epistemological assumptions underpinning phenomenography is the relational view of the world from a nondualist stance. The focus of the research was not on the cognitive structures and the separation between an inner and outer world, it was the constituted internal relation between them, where Marton and Booth (1997, p. 13) say: "there is only one world, but it is a world we experience, a world in which we live, a world that is ours." Here the research object was not the phenomenon being studied, but rather the relation between the research subjects and that phenomenon (Bowden, 2005).

Theoretical perspectives that have underpinned the development of the pedagogical framework include Bandura's (1977) social learning theory; Vygotsky's (1978) theories on the development of knowledge construction through the discursive nature of Weblogs, expanded more recently by Wells (2000) to incorporate learning that is socially constructed through language and collaboration; Lave and Wenger's (1990) situated learning theory that conceptualises learning not as a separate and independent activity but as participation in a community of practice; Boud's (2001) and Schön's (1987) models of reflective writing processes; Brookfield's (1987) critical thinking process; Marton and Booth's (1997) anatomy of awareness including surface and deep approaches to learning, with critical differences in approaches identifying aspects that inform pedagogical practice; and Barabasi's (2002) models of Internet patterns of behaviour and the formation of network models that can be applied to describe patterns observed in Weblog networks.

RESEARCH PARTICIPANTS

The participants in the research project were drawn from students enrolled in two undergraduate degrees at the University of Technology Sydney in the Faculty of Education, and another group was corporate workplace trainers enrolled in a vocational qualification. 60 participants dispersed across the qualifications consented to be part of the research project. This number represents approximately two thirds of the possible total number of enrolled students. The participants' demographics vary greatly across the different subjects and the different qualifications being studied and are briefly outlined. The age group extended from 20 years (school leavers) to below 55 years (workplace organisational learning professionals). The gender distribution is predominantly female. Work experiences range from little or no experience in the organisational learning field to current organisational learning professionals with more than five years experience on average.

All studies required participants to complete learning tasks utilising social software applications for recording and managing their learning, publishing their work, and contributing to collective learning networks, regardless of the assessment requirements of the subjects or modules. There was no additional workload or time commitment for the students who participated in the research project as the process under investigation was part of the content of the subjects being completed.

THE PEDAGOGICAL FRAMEWORK

The objective of the pedagogical framework is to facilitate the development of independent learn-

ers by allowing them to become proficient in informal learning contexts using social software environments. The framework can be viewed as an enabler where the pathways through phases of development draw the focus not on the software or technology selected by the educator to create the learning environment, but on the social aspects of the learning process and strategies to support the learning experience. The progression through the pathways can occur at differing levels and allows for the learner to self-manage the processes. Although presented as a sequential process, learners may be influenced by inhibitors at any stage, on any pathway, requiring the attention of pedagogical strategies from another pathway to be foregrounded while the inhibitor can be addressed, and re-orienting the learner to the focus of the learning process. An outline of the framework and typical inhibitors will be described with examples of comments from learners to illustrate typical responses throughout the stages. Figure 1 represents the pathways and overviews the structure.

Each pathway will be outlined with a description of pedagogical strategies and examples of the inhibitors experienced during the period of the research project will be illustrated with comments from participants that have been extracted from the subgroup of learners who were completing the vocational qualification. This subgroup of participants consisted entirely of workplace organisational learning professionals completing units of competence that would be accredited towards their continuing professional development. The gender ratio was evenly mixed and their ages ranged from 25–55 years. The group was geographically dispersed across Australia and came together in a classroom environment five times over a six-month period. In-between the face-to-face sessions, social software was used to develop and support their projects. The specific locality of this subgroup is significant to demonstrate the inhibitors to informal learning in the organisational workplace–learning context

Figure 1. Pathways to develop learning networks: a pedagogical framework (©2007, Anne Bartlett-Bragg. Used with permission)

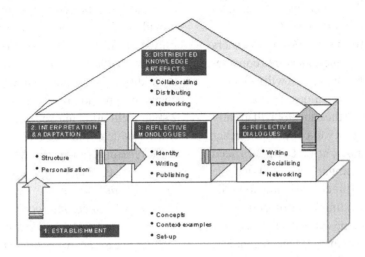

as all participation in learning events were conducted internally, within the boundaries of their organisational environment, rather than externally at the higher education institution. The groups' comments are displayed in italics to illustrate the experiences of the learners in their own words.

PATHWAY #1: ESTABLISHMENT

As the foundation of the enabling process, this pathway is continuously present at all stages of the framework. Activities completed along this pathway require the introduction and framing of the learning environment's technological and conceptual structure with examples or models for the learners to observe. In conjunction with the development of the conceptual structure, the introduction and setup of the software applications are established. Guidance and support from the educator is essential throughout this pathway, as any technological challenge or miscomprehension of concepts can dominate the learners' attention and become an impassable barrier unless addressed.

Organisational technology infrastructure: The selection of social software that can be accessed effectively within the parameters of the organisational infrastructure is exclusive to this pathway. Careful attention and testing prior to introducing learners to the technology environment is of the utmost importance.

Individual/learner inhibitors: The digital literacy levels of the learner are dominant throughout this pathway. In addition, the learners' ability to generalize and conceptualise the use of the software can have profound effects on how they manage any challenges with the technology. Learners express their challenges with demands for the educator's immediate attention: "Show me," "tell me," "do it," or "fix it for me" are common exclamations during this pathway. Frustration and insecurity relating to their abilities to complete processes require the educator to have all activities broken down into small achievable steps with examples to illustrate intended outcomes: *"The wiki is still a struggle for me at times; it never does what I want!!! I need to complete an online tutorial of how to use the wiki. At times I can be technologically challenged"* and *"Well I'm here* *after much stress and anxiety. I am beginning to think I really am a technophobe and if not, then I am definitely a little slower than most to catch on to using all the applications available to us."*

Pedagogical inhibitors: Reponses to learners at this early stage require the educator to consider and model patterns of behaviour that will influence future strategies and interventions. Typically, the patience and guidance of the educator will greatly benefit the learners' ability to cope with further technology issues that may arise. Educators need to move away from Baumgartner's (2004) Mode 1 helper/fixer styles of directed teaching towards Mode 2 questioning/guiding styles of facilitation or the longer term outcome will be learners retaining this pathway as a dominant teacher dependent position requiring high levels of attention from the educator.

PATHWAY #2: INTERPRETATION AND ADAPTATION

The core concept of this pathway is to encourage learners to start using the software and personalising the basic structure. At this stage, activities that demonstrate more software functionality and allow learners to develop personal information management are introduced, paying attention to the potential for learners to revert to pathway #1 if overwhelmed by new concepts and new technologies too quickly. Small writing activities that relate directly to topics being studied and respond to focus questions allow for practice and familiarisation with the basic publishing processes.

Individual/learner inhibitors: Digital literacy directly relating to information management can be a conceptual challenge for learners during the personalising and setup of their space. Levels of anxiety and frustration can recur and can be directed towards the educator with possible rejection and disengagement with the learning activities.

Pedagogical inhibitors: The conceptual frameworks established during Pathway #1 are the essential foundations which require the educator to provide guidance through modeling and examples. Providing answers and solutions in a Mode 1 framework does not make available to the learner the additional learning awareness skills that will enable progression through the pathways. Mode 2 style facilitation may be necessary to assist the learner to deal with the frustration and anxiety, while remaining aware that Mode 3 strategies are the objective. *"I'm struggling with my inability to compartmentalise the learning elements of this course. I'm getting lots of 'stuff' but it's not sinking in anywhere..at least not in the manner I would like to recieve it. Information Overload!. Where to start?. .. in other words FOCUS on a tested methodology instead of trying to create one.... but add your own flavour!. Draw out a structure then drill down and flesh out. The Blog, the profile, the discussion board sometimes appear to be distractions but I'll persist hoping that what bubbles to the surface will be useful."*

PATHWAY #3: REFLECTIVE MONOLOGUES

The core concept of this pathway is to further encourage the development of a personal identity. Activities at this stage include further personalising of the software applications, creating profiles, reflective writing activities generally based on guiding questions from topics being studied, and the issues of publishing publicly.

Individual/learner inhibitors: Although the learners' levels of digital literacy are still present at this stage, it has become less of a concern. The dominant issues arising are focused on creating an online identity and writing publicly.

Pedagogical inhibitors: At this stage, it is imperative the educator moves into a Mode 3 approach that supports and guides the learner, without prescribing formulas about how activities should be completed. Any Mode 1 or Mode 2 responses will undermine the learners' abilities to develop their own identity, self-confidence in writing, and personal learning management strategies. *"I know that my posts/reflections will be all over the place, much like what's going on in my head. I am quite a reflective learner who generally prefers to sit back take it all in, process and analyse at my own pace and then apply. I do this all in my head without the urge to put it into print. So I find myself in unchartered waters... pushing myself to self reflect on virtual paper."*

PATHWAY #4: REFLECTIVE DIALOGUES

The core concept of this pathway is to further develop public writing skills and to encourage socialisation and networking. By this stage, learners have developed a level of comfort with the writing, managing, and publishing activities and the focus can now facilitate the interaction with others. Activities that promote the reading and commenting of contributions, either within the cohort or beyond the constraints of the course, encourage the development of network participation.

Organisational culture: The organisation's approach to social software, collaboration, and interaction between internal learners and potentially external networks can inhibit the learners' willingness to participate and share their thoughts and ideas publicly.

Individual/learner inhibitors: Learners may exhibit a level of assurance in writing self-reflective tasks, perhaps in restricted areas of the selected software, however, when encouraged to collaborate with others, their level of self-confidence—particularly in relation to their writing capabilities—becomes a major concern and will influence how actively they seek to engage in the processes.

Pedagogical inhibitors: Ongoing Mode 3 strategies, such as participation in the development of networks, provides a model for the learners with the effect of supporting the processes, but not prescribing the method that could be interpreted as a Mode 2 or Mode 1 strategy. *"I still feel a little reserved about adding comments or updating the wiki in case the others do not like what I say and or what I say was pointless or of little value to the project. I have to learn to get my head around this and not care what others will think, to an extent."*

PATHWAY #5: DISTRIBUTED KNOWLEDGE ARTEFACTS

The core concept of this pathway is to facilitate active participation in social networking and contributions are distributed with the intention to engage in interaction with others. The learners' require limited activity direction at this stage, as they further collaborate and contribute within their networks. The writing activities can guide the learners to arrive at a collective reflection attitude which will often result in the learners becoming models for practice with other cohorts either within the organisation or externally within broader networks.

Organisational culture: The continuation and support for ongoing use of social software and collaborative networks established during a learning environment directly influence how the learners perceive their contributions to be of value to the organisation.

Individual/learner inhibitors: Digital literacy and other issues previously restricting participation have generally been addressed and are no longer dominating the learning processes. As the learners typically manage their networks with a degree of confidence, there can be a lack of engagement and commitment if they are aware that the processes will not extend beyond the timeframes of a course or qualification.

Pedagogical inhibitors: Influenced by the organisational culture, the educator may also move toward final activities within the learning environment as a completion of their role and instil a closed approach on behalf of the learners to their ongoing activities by reverting to a Mode 1 style that may link to achievement of objectives or learning outcomes. Finding an attitude that fosters continuing guidance, yet allows the learners to remain independent is both challenging and rewarding. *"While I am really looking forward to finishing the diploma, it is going to be sad because it is unlikely that we will all get together like this again, unless there is another course to attend at a later date."*

FUTURE TRENDS

It is timely to reflect upon organisational learning strategies as organisations espouse the values of informal learning in the workplace and prioritise practices of collaboration, reflection, personalisation, knowledge sharing, and networks into vision statements and strategic planning documents. Notwithstanding the importance of emergent technologies as the enabler in these processes, without reframing practice and becoming aware of the critical aspects that highlight the qualitatively different ways adult learners experience the use of social software, educators are not likely to realise the opportunity to incorporate informal learning and integrated communication networks into every day workplace activities.

Additionally, the speed of development in Web 2.0, in particular, social software applications, necessitates an open-minded approach to further enhancing informal learning practices. As the new technologies evolve, so do the opportunities presented, with more applications providing sophisticated functionality, yet remaining focused on ease of use. Accompanying these advances are new ways of accessing and distributing information, and potentially new ways of creating learning opportunities. Already, new theories of learning are being presented for review and testing (Siemens, 2006), and the face of the adult learner in the workplace is shifting as more of Generation Y enters the workforce. The consequent implications for learning constrained in the boundaries of traditional organisational practices, along with the impact of Generation Y, are recommended for future research projects.

CONCLUSION

This chapter is intended to provoke adult learning educators to reframe their pedagogical strategies to allow the creation of learning environments that facilitate informal learning through the use of social software. The framework outlined with pathways through phases of development provides opportunities for educators to enable learners to develop from a model of dependency constrained by formal learning practices to independent learners within collective learning networks and personalised, self-managed attitudes to learning. However, the barriers identified and supported by examples from practice in the workplace–learning context, require educators to be aware of the inhibitors to the informal learning spaces and prepare strategies to enable the learning processes.

If we accept the premise that social software can enable informal learning environments through collective learning networks and the fundamental social interactions embedded in those learning processes, then the challenge for adult learning educators will be how to reframe their pedagogical practices for the new technological developments and facilitate the design of online communication and information exchanges to empower the learners and create an enriched social learning landscape. Without reframing our practice and paying attention to the key inhibitors, integration of social software into existing organisational structures, as with the early implementations of other learning technologies, will be likely not to sustain the performance promises.

REFERENCES

Alexander, H. (2006, August 11). Podcast lectures a hit with conscientious university students. *Sydney Morning Herald,* Technology. Retrieved March 17, 2008, from http://www.smh.com.au/news/technology/podcast-lectures-a-hit/2006/08/10/1154803028454.html#

Bandura, A. (1977). *Social learning theory.* Prentice Hall.

Barabasi, A.-L. (2003). *Linked: How everything is connected to everything else and what it means for business, science, and everyday life.* Cambridge, MA: Plume.

Bartlett-Bragg, A. (2005). Social software: The age of connection and the connected learner. *Training and Development in Australia, 32*(5), 21-24.

Baumgartner, P. (2004). *The zen art of teaching: Communication and interactions in eEducation.* Workshop presented at ICL2004, Kassel University, Villach, Austria. Retrieved March 17, 2008, from http://www.elearningeuropa.info/extras/pdf/zenartofteaching.pdf

Beckett, D., & Hager, P., (2002). *Life, work and learning: Practice in postmodernity.* London: Routledge.

Billet, S., (2001, November). Participation and continuity at work: A critique of current workplace learning discourses. In *Joint Network/SKOPE/TLRP International Workshop on Context, Power and perspective: Confronting the Challenges to Improving Attainment in Learning at Work*, University College of Northampton, UK. Retrieved March 17, 2008, from http://www.infed.org/archives/e-texts/billet_workplaces_learning

Blackall, L. (2005). Digital literacy: How it affects teaching practices and networked learning futures: A proposal for action research. *The Knowledge Tree, 7.* Retrieved March 17, 2008, from http://knowledgetree.flexiblelearning.net.au/edition07/download/c_blackall.pdf

Blood, R. (2002). *The Weblog handbook.* Cambridge, MA: Perseus Publishing.

Boud, D. (2001). Using journal writing to enhance reflective practice. In L.M. English & M.A. Gillen (Eds.), *Promoting journal writing in adult education* (pp. 9-18, vol. 90). San Francisco: Jossey-Bass.

Brookfield, S.D. (1987). *Developing critical thinkers.* San Francisco: Jossey-Bass.

Bruns, A., & Jacobs, J. (Eds.) (2006). *Uses of blogs.* Australia: Peter Lang Publishing.

Chief Learning Officer. (2007). *Business intelligence industry report.* Retrieved March 17, 2008, from http://www.clomedia.com/biireport/BZ_2007_Summary_r2.pdf

Colley, H., Hodkinson, P., & Malcolm, J. (2002). Non-formal learning: Mapping the conceptual terrain (consultation report). *University of Leeds Lifelong Learning Institute.* Retrieved March 17, 2008, from http://www.infed.org/archives/e-texts/colley_informal_learning.htm

Cornford, I. (1999). Social learning. In J.A. Athansasou (Ed.), *Adult educational psychology* (pp. 73-97). Sydney, Australia: Social Sciences Press.

Downes, S. (2004). Educational blogging. *EDUCAUSE Review, 39*(5), 14-26. Retrieved March 17, 2008, from http://www.educause.edu/pub/er/erm04/erm0450.asp

Downes, S. (2005, October). E-learning 2.0. *eLearn Magazine.* Retrieved March 17, 2008, from http://www.elearnmag.org/subpage.cfm?section=articles&article=29-1

European Commission. (2001). Communication: Making a European area of lifelong learning a reality. Retrieved March 17, 2008, from http://www.europa.eu.int/comm/education/life/index.htm

Farmer, J., & Bartlett-Bragg, A. (2005, December). *Blogs@Anywhere: High fidelity online communication.* In Proceedings of ASCILITE2005: Balance, Fidelity, Mobility: Maintaining the Momentum?, Brisbane, Australia. Retrieved March 17, 2008, from http://www.ascilite.org.au/conferences/brisbane05/blogs/proceedings/22_Farmer.pdf

Gibson, B. (2004). A learning blogosphere. *The Community Engine.* Retrieved March 17, 2008, from http://thecommunityengine.com/home/archives/2005/03/a_learning_blog.html

Harrison, M. (2006). 13 ways of managing informal learning. *Kineo Insight.* Retrieved March 17, 2008, from http://www.kineo.co.uk/publications/informal-learning-summary.html

Hodkinson, P., & Hodkinson, H. (2001, November). Problems of measuring learning and attainment in the workplace: Complexity, reflexivity and the localised nature of understanding. In *Joint Network/SKOPE/TLRP International Workshop on Context, Power and Perspective: Confronting the Challenges to Improving Attainment in Learning at Work*, University College of Northampton, UK.

Krause, S. D. (2004). When blogging goes bad: A cautionary tale about blogs, email lists, discussion, and interaction. *Kairos 9.1.* Retrieved March 17, 2008, from http://english.ttu.edu/kairos/9.1/binder.html?praxis/krause/index.html

Lave, J., & Wenger, E. (1990). *Situated learning: Legitimate peripheral participation.* Cambridge, MA: Cambridge University Press.

MacColl, I., Morrison, A., Muhlberger, R., Simpson, M., & Viller, S. (2005, May). *Reflections on reflection: Blogging in undergraduate design studios.* BlogTalk Downunder, Sydney, Australia. Retrieved March 17, 2008, from http://incsub.org/blogtalk/?page_id=69

Marsick, J.V., & Watkins, K.E. (2001, Spring). Informal and incidental learning. *New Directions for Adult and Continuing Education, 89*, 25-34.

Marsick, V.J., & Volpe, M. (1999). The nature of and need for informal learning. In V.J. Marsick & M. Volpe (Eds.), *Informal learning on the job* (Advances in Developing Human Resources, 3). San Francisco: Berrett Koehler.

Marton, F., & Booth, S. (1997). *Learning and awareness.* Mahwah, NJ: Lawrence Erlbaum Associates.

Mejias, U. (2005). A nomad's guide to learning and social software. *The Knowledge Tree, 7.* Retrieved March 17, 2008, from http://knowledgetree.flexiblelearning.net.au/edition07/html/la_mejias.html

Miles, A. (2005, May). *Media rich versus rich media.* BlogTalk Downunder, Sydney, Australia. Retrieved March 17, 2008, from http://incsub.org/blogtalk/?page_id=74 Sanders, R. (2006). The "imponderable boom": Reconsidering the role of technology in education. *Innovate, 2*(6). Retrieved March 17, 2008, from http://www.innovateonline.info/index.php?view=article&id=232

Schön, D.A. (1987). *Educating the reflective practitioner: Towards a new design for teaching and learning.* San Francisco: Jossey-Bass.

Siemens, G. (2006). *Knowing knowledge.* Lulu.com. Retrieved March 17, 2008, from http://www.elearnspace.org/KnowingKnowledge_LowRes.pdf

Vygotsky, L. (1978). *Mind in society.* Cambridge, MA: Harvard University Press.

Wells, G. (2000). Dialogic inquiry in education: Building on the legacy of Vygotsky. In C.D. Lee & P. Smargorinsky (Eds.), *Vygotskian perspective on literacy research: Constructing meaning through collaborative inquiry.* Cambridge University Press.

Wijekumar, K. (2005). Creating effective Web-based learning environments: Relevant research and practice. *Innovate, 1*(5). Retrieved March 17, 2008, from http://www.innovateonline.info/index.php?view=article&id=26

Zemsky, R., & Massy, W.F. (2004). Thwarted innovation: What happened to e-learning and why. *The Learning Alliance.* Retrieved March 17, 2008, from http://www.thelearningalliance.info/Docs/Jun2004/ThwartedInnovation.pdf

KEY TERMS

Aggregator: A software application, often called a "feedreader," used to gather a subscriber's RSS feeds and present them in a browser page. The aggregator is automatically updated on a regular basis with new content from the RSS feeds as they are published.

Blogs (Weblogs): A Web site, generally published by a single author (although some group blogs exist), displaying dated entries in reverse chronological order. Additional features enable the author to categorize and archive each entry. Most blogs allow readers to use a comment function to provide feedback to the author.

Folksonomy: A user-generated categorizing system or taxonomy facilitated by applying popular or commonly referred to tags or labeling terms.

Podcast: A digital audio file distributed over the Internet, downloaded by subscribers for playback on computers or portable MP3 players.

RSS: Really simple syndication is a method of XML-based programming that allows content, or Web-feeds, to be imported into other Web pages by user subscription.

Social Bookmarking: A browser-based service, similar to a favorites list, that allows the user to share Internet bookmarks with others. Folksonomy tagging encourages the development of shared interest networks.

Social Software: The range of applications that augment group interactions and shared spaces for collaboration, social connections, and aggregates information exchanges in a Web-based environment. Social software is considered a major component of the current Web 2.0 applications.

Vodcast: A video podcast, or video clip distributed on the Internet and available for download through RSS subscription and aggregation for playback on computers or portable devices.

Web 2.0: A series of new generation or 2.0 release software applications available on the World Wide Web. Typically, it includes applications that have a rapid, low cost approach to development, focused on mash-ups (created by combining different sources to create a composite application). Many applications are browser-based using a programming language called Ajax, intended to make the applications behave more like desk-top based software.

Wiki: A collaborative authoring Web site application that allows users to easily write, edit, and publish to the Internet.

Chapter XIII
Authentic E-Learning in a Virtual Scientific Conference

Josianne Basque
Télé-université, Canada

Kim Chi Dao
Télé-université, Canada

Julien Contamines
Télé-université, Canada

ABSTRACT

The goal of this chapter is to illustrate how the concept of authentic learning can be implemented in a Web-based distance course. We present a collaborative e-learning scenario, inspired by socioconstructivist and situated learning theories, which encourages authentic learning. Developed as the main learning scenario of a graduate distance education course, it requires students to participate asynchronously in a simulation of an online scientific conference. We describe the learning scenario, the technological environment developed to implement this scenario, as well as some results of a course evaluation completed by students.

INTRODUCTION AND BACKGROUND

Over the last few years, online learning has become increasingly popular not only for distance education universities, but for campus-based universities as well. At the same time, all levels of the education sector have been undergoing a paradigm shift towards socioconstructivist and situated approaches to learning (Brown, Collins, & Duguid, 1989; Lave & Wenger, 1991; McLellan, 1996; Orey & Nelson, 1997). However, perhaps because of short deadlines or the absence of proper training on instructional engineering of e-learning, designers of Web-based courses often tend to reproduce traditional teaching practices used in class. They tend to use teaching strategies reflecting a view of knowledge as being something that has to be transmitted essentially by the teacher, instead of something that has to be actively constructed by the learner. Thus, instructional designers are in need of new models and ideas to help them implement socioconstructivist and situated learning principles in the design of online courses.

Authentic learning is a mainstream approach suggested by many authors to support socioconstructivist and situated learning. For example, Duffy and Jonassen (1991) propose that students should use tools to perform activities which are similar to those found in their future professional fields. Savery and Duffy (1995) also highlight the importance of creating situations which permit students to practice the competencies required by the professional environments in which they will eventually be working. Herrington and Oliver (2000) make the following recommendations for the design of authentic learning environments: (1) provide authentic context that reflects the way the knowledge will be used in real life; (2) provide authentic activities; (3) provide access to expert performances and modeling of processes; (4) provide multiple roles and perspectives; (5) support collaborative construction of knowledge; (6) promote reflection to enable abstractions to be formed; (7) promote articulation to enable tacit knowledge to be made explicit; (8) provide coaching by the teacher at critical times, and scaffolding and fading of teacher support; (9) provide for integrated assessment of learning within the task. Rule (2006) analyzed the content of 45 articles describing authentic learning in different disciplines and identified four overarching themes that repeatedly occurred: (1) real-world problems that mimic the work of professionals, with presentation of findings to audiences beyond

the classroom; (2) inquiry activities that practice thinking skills and metacognition; (3) discourse within a community of learners, that is to say, interactions and discussions with other learners, teachers; and professionals outside the learning community; and (4) student empowerment to direct their own learning in relevant project work.

Concrete examples of online authentic learning environments are still scarce (Herrington, Herrington, & Omari, 2002; Herrington, Oliver, & Reeves, 2003; Reeves, Herrington, & Oliver, 2002). This chapter describes a model for structuring all aspects of an online course at the graduate level, which, we believe, is a good illustration of how many of the authentic learning principles could be implemented in a virtual learning environment. The main idea is to have students participate in a simulated asynchronous virtual scientific conference (VSC). Few collaborative online activities reported in the literature use the scientific conference analogy to structure interactions among distant learners. Fjuk and Sorensen (1997) describe what they call "Pedagogical Online Seminars," which consist of virtual forums moderated by a professor or an expert in a given domain. Clemson (2002) describes an online course including a "virtual poster session" as a typical activity of a scientific conference. This course is conducted in a synchronous mode and implies file sharing and chatting among students. In our course, all the learners' interactions occur asynchronously and three main events guide the progression of the course: a virtual poster session, a symposium, and a plenary session.

Scientific conferences are events that graduate students, who are future high-level researchers and professionals, are likely to attend during and after their studies. Therefore, they need to familiarize themselves with the typical rules and practices of that type of event and to develop competencies in critical thinking, in formulating constructive comments, and in participating in scientific debates. Having them participate in a simulated scientific conference in the context of a course would, therefore, be a good strategy to help them develop and practice those competencies. This learning situation constitutes what Barab, Squire, and Dueber (2000) call a *practice field* or a *simulation model* of authenticity. This model is based on the assumption that a learning activity should be made as similar as possible to communities of practice outside of the learning situation. Barab, Squire, and Dueber (2000, p. 39) say:

This includes factual *authenticity, in which the environmental particulars of the task are made to be similar to those of the real world,* procedural *or* process *authenticity in which learner practices are similar to those that one would be engaged outside of schools, and* task *authenticity in which the tasks being addressed are similar to those being undertaken by communities of practice.*

This model differs from the *participation model* proposed by Lave and Wenger (1991), which implies the immersion of students into an actual scientific community, and from the *co-evolutionary model* suggested by Barab et al. (2000), which brings together students, teachers, and members of a professional community to perform a common task.

In this chapter, we describe the instructional scenario of the VSC and the technological environment developed to implement this scenario within the context of a distance education course. We then report on students' perceptions and their level of satisfaction regarding both the scenario and the environment of the virtual conference. We also discuss future trends on the issue of authentic e-learning. In conclusion, we synthesize and discuss the characteristics of the authentic learning model that we propose using the nine recommendations of Herrington and Oliver (2000) to design authentic online learning environments.

THE LEARNING SCENARIO

The VSC learning scenario was designed and tested in a 135-hour graduate course entitled *Information Technology and Cognitive Development*, which is offered entirely at a distance at the Télé-université of Québec (www.teluq.uqam.ca), a French-Canadian distance education university. The entire course is structured around the metaphor of the scientific conference. The learning scenario, which we call the "Conference Program," includes four main activities: *Preparing for the Conference*; *Participating in a Poster Session*; *Attending a Symposium*; and *Participating in the Plenary Session*.

In the first activity, students get acquainted with the conference environment and program and complete the conference registration process by introducing themselves to other participants. They also use a questionnaire to activate their prior knowledge related to the topic of the conference and are invited to begin building on this knowledge by reading some introductory documents on the subject. Finally, the participants use the virtual forum tool to discuss how those first readings have begun to change their prior knowledge of the domain.

During the second activity, students participate in a virtual poster session where they produce a poster (using Microsoft PowerPoint) which summarizes the results of two published research papers related to the conference topic. Students can find the papers by themselves or may select them from a list provided in the VSC environment. This list can easily be updated by the instructor. Each student must then write a comment or formulate a question regarding one of the posters produced. Finally, the authors of the posters must reply to these comments and questions.

In the third activity, students participate in a virtual symposium about the effects of information and communication technologies (ICTs) on learning and cognitive development. The papers presented at this symposium are, in fact, a collection of published papers which highlight various points of views by experts in the field. Thus, students attend this symposium and write a text in which they critique or defend one of the issues presented. Each participant must then comment on another's text, who, in turn, replies to the comments he or she receives.

In the fourth and final activity, learners participate in a plenary session that takes place within one of the forums of the course. The goal of this activity is to reflect upon and discuss the main ideas and conclusions they have gathered, as well as the knowledge and competencies they have developed as a result of their participation in the scientific conference.

All of the work produced throughout the conference (posters, debates, forum discussions, comments, and their replies) is used in the summative assessment of learning. Throughout the course, students are assisted by a tutor whose main tasks consist of moderating the forums, responding to questions submitted by e-mail or posted in the forums, evaluating students' productions and providing feedback to students.

THE LEARNING ENVIRONMENT

The learning environment proposed to learners has two main components: the course Web site and the collaborative environment, which is accessible from the course Web site. The interface of the course Web site replicates some aspects of a typical scientific conference Web site. For example, the main page of the learning environment (see Figure 1) presents the Conference Program (*Programme d'activités*), which identifies the four learning activities and the four main assignments of the course. Specific instructions on each activity or assignment title can be obtained by clicking on this page. Students have access to the learning resources that they need to realize the activities and assignments (documents, Web pages, or software tools) by clicking on the hyperlinks integrated in the specific instructions related to each activity or assignment. Figure 2 shows a page which presents

Figure 1. Main page of the scenario presenting the conference program (©2007, Josianne Basque. Used with permission)

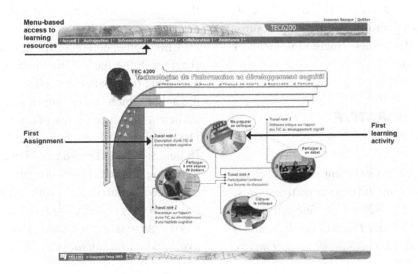

Figure 2. Instructions page for the learning activity entitled "Produce my poster" (©2007, Josianne Basque. Used with permission)

the instructions for the learning activity entitled *Produce my Poster*.

All the learning resources can also be accessed at any time from five menus located at the top of the main page of the learning scenario: *Self-management* (*Autogestion*) (personal profile, suggested schedule of the activities), *Information* (texts, bibliography, Webography), *Production* (questionnaires, text editor, PowerPoint), *Collaboration* (group profile, conference rooms, forums), and *Assistance* (methodological or technical guides).

THE COLLABORATIVE ENVIRONMENT

The collaborative environment of the VSC includes a virtual forum and two interactive spaces, which have been designed at Télé-université, called the *Poster Session Room* (*Salle des posters*) and the *Symposium Room* (*Salle des conferences*).

The virtual forum tool, an adaptation of the freeware phpBB (www.phpbb.com), is used mainly for spontaneous comments at any time during the course, for reflexive comments at the end of each activity, and for some structured interventions related mostly to the first and last learning activities. The two rooms of the VSC are used to support file sharing and discussions during the *Poster Session* activity and the *Symposium* activity, respectively.

Unlike other collaborative learning platforms (Faerber, 2001), the VSC rooms are not structured according to a spatial metaphor but a functional metaphor which, according to some authors, is sufficient to induce a sense of immersion (Daele, Deschryver, Joye, & Peraya, 2000; Jensen & Heilesen, 2004). Harrison and Dourish (1996, p. 67) argue that the critical property of computer-supported collaborative work systems "*is not rooted in the properties of space at all. Instead, it is rooted in sets of mutually held, and mutually available, cultural understandings about behav-*

iour and action. In contrast to 'space', we call this a sense of 'place'. Our principle is: 'Space is the opportunity; place is the understood reality'." The two virtual zones created for the VSC, although called rooms, have interfaces that do not represent actual, physical rooms. Indeed, these two rooms are displayed as simple electronic tables which include various posting spaces.

Basically, both rooms are organized similarly, and they offer the same functionalities. The *Poster Session Room* is illustrated in Figure 3. Both rooms allow users to post and display their papers and posters and allow for discussions about these documents. Users select an interface button to indicate the action they wish to perform; for example, they can post a file, view a posted document, ask a question, or reply with a comment.

In order to ensure that all participants have the opportunity to receive and respond to a question or comment, a first come, first serve principle was implemented in the system. The buttons are displayed dynamically: they appear gradually,

according to how the interactions unfold. This permits us to control the actions that each participant can execute at any point in the scenario. For example, as long as a posting area remains empty, a single button appears for all participants: the Speak (*Intervenir*) button. Once a participant has manifested his intention to speak in one of the posting spaces in a room, his name appears in the Contributors (*Intervenants*) column, and the Posting (*Déposer*) button appears in the column Possible Actions (*Actions possibles*) of this specific participant only. Later, once the Contributor participant has posted his or her work, the View (*Voir*) button appears automatically in the same column, inviting all participants to view the contributor's posting. When a participant posts a comment or question concerning a poster, his or her name appears in the column entitled Authors of the Questions (*Auteurs des questions*). Finally, when the contributor responds, a checkmark appears in the column Answered Questions (*Questions répondues*). By selecting the View button, a single

Figure 3. The poster session room (©2007, Josianne Basque. Used with permission)

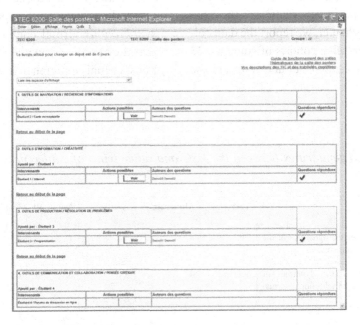

window appears where all participants can view (1) the contributor's poster or symposium paper, (2) the comment or question formulated by another participant, and (3) the contributor's reply.

Once a participant posts a file, it can be modified within a certain period of time which is set by the professor. When this time limit has expired, the system prevents users from performing any type of modification. This feature ensures that students who prepare a response to another's work do not encounter a different document at the moment they are about to post their response. The rooms have been developed in PHP-based Web applications, and data are stored in a *MySQL* database. The rooms connect the institutional instructional management system (IMS) to ensure the authentication of the students and tutor.

EVALUATION OF THE COURSE BY THE STUDENTS

At the end of the course, students are asked to volunteer their opinions by filling out a questionnaire anonymously. This questionnaire is designed as a formative assessment tool of the course in general and of its different components. It includes a section which specifically addresses the VSC questions. In this chapter, we report the data collected from the first five cohorts of students. 22 of 68 students have filled out and returned the

questionnaire by e-mail. To guarantee confidentiality, the completed questionnaires were sent to a coordinator, who transmitted them anonymously to the professor. This response rate (32%) looks low, but considering that distance students are not captive participants as they would be on campus and that they have no direct benefit like bonus marks from completing the questionnaire, a higher response rate was not expected. As a comparison, a response rate of around 30% is typical in e-mail surveys (Sheehan, 2001). We also examined the spontaneous comments regarding the VSC posted by students in the forums. The analysis of the data collected provides a portrait of the students' perceptions regarding (1) similarities between the VSC and other types of conferences, (2) technological aspects of the VSC, and (3) effect of the VSC on motivation and learning.

SIMILARITIES BETWEEN THE VSC AND OTHER TYPES OF CONFERENCES

More than half of the 22 learners who filled out the questionnaire indicated they had previously attended a live scientific conference (N=13). Eight respondents said they had previously attended a *synchronous* virtual conference, and nine said that they had participated in another asynchronous virtual conference aside from the one in

Table 1. Perceived similarities between the VSC and other types of conferences (Response frequencies)

Statements	Very	Moderately	A little	Not at all	Don't know	Total
The VSC reproduces the dynamics of the discussions in live conferences.	7	6	4	1	3	21
The VSC reproduces the dynamics of the discussions in synchronous virtual conferences.	6	4	3	0	6	19

question. These latter results are startling as the virtual conference analogy is not widely used in e-learning. We hypothesized that students probably associated this strategy to various online collaborative activities, such as discussions in forums or chat, which are only a part of what we are proposing in this paper.

Thirteen respondents felt that the dynamics of the discussions within the VSC were very or moderately similar to those occurring at live conferences (see Table 1). As one participant indicated, "it's not exactly the same as attending a live conference; however, discussions through the question-and-answer approach provide a close replica of these events." Ten respondents indicated that they encountered the same dynamics at the VSC as those typically found in synchronous virtual conferences.

In their comments, the respondents mentioned certain advantages of the VSC compared to live conferences. For example, they noted that the information is available at all times, that participants can attend according to their own schedule, and that users can research a topic before getting involved in a discussion. "In a live conference, it is difficult to gather all of the information. However, the asynchronous conference offers the possibility of consulting reference work and relevant documents," indicates a student. Others add that "the conference formula allowed me to attend the conference at my own pace" and that "this approach provides us with the opportunity to research certain topics before responding." However, some learners mentioned that the task constraints, that is, only one comment related to each production, differ significantly from the reality of live conferences. Another person noted that participants must "get into the game" to really benefit from the experience. In fact, as is the case when watching science-fiction movies, the suspension of disbelief seems to be an essential condition to engage in virtual worlds (Hand, 1994) and, more specifically, in authentic online learning environments (Herrington et al., 2003),

at least in those that adopt the practice field or simulation model of learning authenticity.

TECHNOLOGICAL ASPECTS OF THE VSC

To the statement "The organization and operation of the *Poster Session Room* are user-friendly," 13 learners indicated that they agree or that they strongly agree. However, many indicated that they had difficulty understanding how to use the *Poster Session Room,* which was the first one used in this course. Seven students indicated that they had technical problems using the VSC rooms. Two of them said they had difficulty posting their work, and some mentioned that they disliked being prevented from modifying their files after they had been in a room beyond the allotted period of time. Many of these issues were brought up during the first semester the course was offered, which resulted in a number of modifications to the operation and aspect of the rooms. Furthermore, a concise user guide to help learners navigate within the rooms was created and, if this is not enough, the tutor provides additional technical support to the participants, especially during the first activity held in the *Poster Session Room.*

PERCEIVED IMPACT ON MOTIVATION AND LEARNING

In general, students have a positive attitude towards the VSC, which is considered a motivating and stimulating tool (see Table 2). Almost all respondents (20) feel that the conference analogy is stimulating, and all (21) agree that posting their work and viewing others' work is a stimulating factor that favors learning. Most of them (17) feel that the peer discussions are very motivating, if not essential: "In my case, it favoured motivation, overachievement, collaboration and sharing expertise"; "Fantastic idea! We must act as experts, return to our assignments and reading, take a stand in front of the rest of the group..." One indicated that one advantage of the VSC is that it "allows learners to compare their knowledge with that of their peers." However, two respondents would have liked to see asynchronous activities supplemented with synchronous discussions.

All respondents enjoyed the virtual poster session (21), and most of them (19) felt similarly about the symposium. Furthermore, a majority (19) of the respondents indicated that they would recommend the use of a VSC in other e-learning courses. As for how students perceive the learning contribution of the VSC, all respondents confirmed that they had learned from participating in the VSC, whether from the virtual poster session (21) or during the symposium (18). "A wonderful synthesis!" claimed one of the respondents. When asked whether they had learned from the course overall, all respondents indicated that they had expanded their knowledge a lot (19) or moderately (2). Furthermore, the estimated mean percentage of reaching their own learning goals was 92% (SD = 2.1). Finally, 82% (18) of the respondents would recommend the course to other students.

For learners enrolled in graduate studies, it seems then that the VSC scenario would integrate many characteristics of what has been termed authentic learning (Basque, Dao, & Contamines, 2005). It seems to be an "ideal formula to favour discussions in a distance learning course," as one student commented. Compared to other types of conferences, it is even seen as an advantageous avenue, and it is considered a stimulating and motivating learning tool. Thus, it seems that most learners were satisfied with this experience and that they met their own learning objectives. However, we should be cautious with this conclusion, as our sample size was small.

FUTURE TRENDS

Based upon these results, a list of recommendations and improvements has been compiled to enhance the VSC: (1) investigate the ergonomics of the room's interface; (2) reconsider the necessity of setting a time limit in order to prevent users from modifying a posted file while considering the discussion process; (3) review the scenario to

Table 2. Impact of the VSC on motivation and learning (Response frequencies)

Statements	Strongly agree	Agree	Disagree	Strongly disagree	TOTAL
The scientific conference metaphor is stimulating for learning.	10	10	1	0	21
Having my productions accessible to others and having the possibility to view others' productions is stimulating for learning.	17	4	0	0	21
The interactions with other students in the VSC (Formulate/ Answer a question) are stimulating for learning.	11	6	2	1	20
I enjoyed the Poster Session activity.	18	3	0	0	21
I enjoyed the Symposium activity.	13	6	1	0	20
I would recommend the use of the VSC metaphor in other distance courses.	11	8	2	0	21
I have learned from the Poster Session activity.	18	3	0	0	21
I have learned from the Symposium activity.	14	4	1	1	20

allow for multiple comments on a single production; (4) prepare a more detailed description of the role of the tutor in the VSC; and (5) investigate possible adaptations of the VSC in other learning contexts.

Work on two of the five issues has begun. First, we elaborated the tutor's guide. This manual includes a description of the various tasks tutors must perform to ensure that the conference runs smoothly, tips to help students during the conference, tools to assist individual students or the entire group when problems arise, as well as various instructions to deal with difficult or delicate situations. Second, the VSC was integrated with another course at the undergraduate level. In one of the learning activities, students from different countries had to elaborate on a case study about biodiversity: each of them presented a poster of their case study in the *Poster Session Room* and posted their paper, reporting on the case study, in the *Symposium Room*. In this new scenario, students are the main speakers in the symposium, contrary to the initial design of this activity in the VSC. Moreover, each participant must comment on at least two papers or comments in each of the two rooms of the VSC, instead of only one in the initial application of the VSC.

The VSC has been designed and used as a practice field or a simulation model of learning authenticity (Barab et al., 2000) in a distance education context. A full participation model would require students to participate in a real-world scientific conference not only as attendees but as actual speakers. This would be difficult to implement because it would require all students to submit topic proposals to real scientific committees, which would then have to accept or reject them. Our students are not sufficiently advanced in their graduate studies to satisfy those requirements. They first have to learn what a scientific conference is and how one participates in this kind of event. They also have to practice their communication and debating skills in a scientific context. Also, as Achtenhagen (2003, p. 2)

demonstrated with research data on commercial apprenticeships, "real life situations do not support effective learning per se. Authenticity must be set on stage—instructional design is one means to do this efficiently."

We think the VSC is a good transition leading to a pure participation model as proposed by Lave and Wenger (1991). The VSC could even be adapted a step further toward this model. For example, actual members of the educational scientific community could post real posters or oral presentations (text, video, or audio files) in the conference rooms and could reply to the students' questions and comments. In that case, students would interact directly with members of scientific communities, yet still in a practice field.

The introduction of authentic learning principles in Web-based courses consists of an issue that should be explored further, using sound and rigorous research methodologies. We need to know more about the conditions for success of authentic learning strategies for distance education such as the one implemented in the course presented in this chapter. Additionally, it is important to evaluate the impact of these strategies on learning.

CONCLUSION AND DISCUSSION

In conclusion, we revise and discuss the main characteristics of the VSC, using the nine recommendations suggested by Herrington and Oliver (2000) to introduce authenticity in learning environments. First, it is necessary to provide an *authentic context*. According to Herrington and Oliver (2000), an authentic learning context reflects the way the knowledge will be used in real-life and preserves the complexity of the real-life setting. It must first be noted that the authentic nature of the VSC context does not touch on the targeted domain-knowledge specific to this course (learning and cognitive impacts of the use of ICTs) per se, but more on the general knowledge and competencies required to participate in real-life conferences. Next, we believe that the complexity of the setting is preserved in that numerous resources are available in the learning environment and the exchanges remain dynamic despite being at a distance. However, the learning situation had to be somewhat simplified in order to satisfy the temporal and pedagogical constraints of a distance course. For example, the limits imposed to the number of comments which can be made regarding a poster (one per poster) are a definite difference as compared to an actual live scientific conference. Additionally, to prepare their posters, the students have access to a list of specific resources available in the learning environment, while the authors of posters must find their own references in a real context.

Second, the designer should provide *authentic learning activities*. For Herrington and Oliver (2000), such activities have real-world relevance and are ill-defined. Students perform complex tasks which can be integrated across subject areas and engage them for a sustained period of time in investigation, detection of relevant vs. irrelevant information and collaboration. They can also be given the opportunity to define the tasks and subtasks required to complete the activities. As we have seen, the four learning activities of the course are entirely structured around the metaphor of the scientific conference. Students are then immersed in a complex and integrated learning situation for an extended period of time (15 weeks). Even though the theme of the conference is linked to a specific discipline, the tasks accomplished by the students (critical analysis, synthesis, etc.) are interdisciplinary. The students are called upon to consult multiple resources during the term of the course and to select the appropriate information in order to reflect upon their productions. In this sense, the VSC activities meet the criteria of an authentic learning activity. The only criterion which seems loosely met is the one which states that activities should be ill-defined. Indeed, the learning scenario and the type of productions expected are defined explicitly in the VSC: the

students do not define the goals and subgoals of the activities themselves, although they choose the specific theme of their poster and debate paper, as well as the specific students' productions on which they want to comment. However, such degrees of structure would reflect that of a real-world conference where the rules are very explicit with established deadlines, defined evaluation modalities, strict schedules, typical structure of exchanges followed by questions, editing norms for written texts, and so forth.

Third, it is necessary to provide *access to expert performance and modeling of processes*. This recommendation is being respected in certain parts of the VSC but not in others. For example, in the *Conference Room,* the students have access to texts written by expert researchers in the field. They are also invited to view some examples of posters prepared by researchers and available on the Web sites of some real-life conferences. However, in both cases, they do not have the opportunity to access expert thinking *during* the preparation of these productions, although the FSC contains video clips filmed during a real face-to-face scientific conference, which illustrate the discussions between a presenter and participants in the course of a poster session; others demonstrate an author explaining to a participant how he designed his poster and providing tips. Herrington and Oliver (2000) also suggest to provide access to learners at various levels of expertise and to have them share narratives and stories. We know students have diverse prior knowledge and competencies regarding participation in scientific conferences, as more than half of the 22 learners who filled out the questionnaire had previously attended a live scientific conference. At many points in the VSC program, students are asked to share in the virtual forums not only their thinking related to the targeted domain-dependent knowledge but also reflections of their experiences in the VSC.

Fourth, the course designer should provide *multiple roles and perspectives.* In the VSC, students are called upon to play multiple roles: creators and presenters of posters, participants at poster sessions, actors in debates, participants at a plenary session, and so forth. The information which is produced and presented in the VSC is accessible at all times: it is possible to consult the resources of the VSC whenever and as many times as desired. For the students, this was a definite advantage over a live scientific conference. Furthermore, the varied viewpoints expressed by all the students are shared within the VSC environment, allowing the expression of multiple perspectives on the topic addressed.

Fifth, it is most useful to support the *collaborative construction of knowledge*. The VSC support social knowledge construction through asynchronous interactions between students at the level of the whole group and not in small teams. We avoid describing our learning scenario as being collaborative or cooperative, which would imply, as George (2001) stated, an activity in which students grouped in small teams would follow common goals or subgoal in the former or different subgoals in the latter. It seems to us that it is more appropriate to say that our learning scenario supports the *co-construction of knowledge*, which implies that learners perform the tasks individually but share resources, negotiate meanings, and confront their viewpoints on the productions of each other. However, this learning situation is not easy to manage in a distance training context. Thus, the asynchronous conference paradigm becomes problematic for students who require a course extension for personal, professional, or health reasons. Students who complete the course beyond the regular 15-week course time frame are alienated from the group and its activities. They are no longer able to participate in the discussions related to the documents (posters and papers).

Sixth, course designers must *promote reflection to enable abstractions to be formed*. After each learning activity, the students are invited to reflect upon their learning and the difficulties encountered during the activity and then share these in the discussion forums. A list of questions is provided in order to guide their reflection. In addition, sharing their productions and their reflections on the same offers multiple occasions for students to compare their own thinking with that of others. These activities are intended to promote self-reflection and metacognitive thinking.

Seventh, it is necessary to promote *articulation in order for tacit knowledge to be turned into explicit knowledge*. The VSC responds perfectly to the recommendation to encourage explicitation of tacit knowledge. Indeed, in the VSC, the the students productions are made public to the whole group, and there is explicit encouragement for constructive criticism.

Eighth, the teacher should provide *coaching and use scaffolding and fading techniques*. During the course, the students benefit from continuous and asynchronous support from a tutor. This individual provides coaching, scaffolding, and fading depending on the emerging needs of the group. Peers can also be considered a significant source of coaching through their mutually exchanged constructive criticism. However, the role of the tutor might be more fully integrated in the metaphor of the scientific conference. For example, it would be possible to indicate that the role be more like that of a moderator in the *Conference Room* or a judge for a "Best Papers Awards."

Finally, assessment of learning should be integrated within the task. All the the students' productions (posters, debate texts, comments, replies, discussion forum participation) are used for summative evaluation of learning. Assessment is therefore perfectly integrated into the VSC activities. The evaluation criteria for each production are made explicit to students. In addition, students have the opportunity to fine-tune their productions, based on the feedback provided by the tutor, even though group management constraints limit the period of time allotted to modify these, once they have been uploaded in the VSC rooms. In fact, we had to make sure that a participant who prepared a comment on another student's production did not find a new version of the production when time came to post his or her comment.

Our analysis demonstrated that the VSC offers an authentic learning scenario and environment to higher-education students. Such an application would be quite appropriate in a virtual doctorate school. We have seen, however, that the context of the distance training restricts the use of some but few recommendations made by Herrington and Oliver (2000). It is apparently difficult, and almost undesirable, in distance learning models to apply the recommendation whereby the learning activities should be only minimally structured. The reason for this is that student autonomy is favored and the tutor is not the course designer. It is important, in this case, to carefully structure the learning scenario in order to guide the students as well as the tutor in the course environment and to describe the activities and the productions expected in a detailed manner. In a way, such a structure would enhance the authentic nature of the VSC in relation to a real face-to-face scientific conference where participants must follow explicit rules and participation modes.

Another limit to the authenticity of the VSC as a distance education environment relates to the organization and management of collective activities which, despite the fact that they are asynchronous, require the sustained participation of students during the same defined period of time for all of them. This is somewhat contradictory even to the distance education model adopted in our institution, which encourages the self-management of learning schedule at the individual level within the 15-week period of a course, the possibility to register at all times, and the possibility to delay deadlines. These restrictions are minor, however, and we believe that we should continue to find innovative ways to implement authentic learning in online courses.

REFERENCES

Achtenhagen, F. (2003). Problems of authentic instruction and learning. *Technology, Instruction, Cognition and Learning, 1*, 1-20.

Barab, S. A., Squire, K. D., & Dueber, W. (2000). A co-evolutionary model for supporting the emergence of authenticity. *Educational Technology Research & Development, 48*(2), 37-62.

Brown, J. S., Collins, A., & Duguid, P. (1989). Situated cognition and the culture of learning. *Educational Researcher, 18*(1), 32-42.

Clemson, P. (2002). Using virtual poster sessions in a distance education course. In M. Driscoll & T. C. Reeves (Eds.), *Proceedings of E-Learn 2002* (pp. 1346-1348). Norfolk, VA: Association for the Advancement of Computing in Education (AACE).

Daele, A., Deschryver, N., Joye, F., & Peraya, D. (2000). Learn-Nett: A virtual campus for supporting collaborative learning. In E. Rideling & G. Davis (Eds.), *Proceedings of the EDICT*, Vienne.

Duffy, T. M., & Jonassen, D. H. (1991). Constructivism: New implications for instructional technology? *Educational Technology, 31*(5), 7-12.

Faerber, R. (2001). Une métaphore spatiale et des outils intégrés pour des apprentissages coopératifs à distance: ACOLAD. *Actes du congrès JRES 2001* (pp. 197-204). Lyon: Ministère de l'éducation nationale et Ministère de la recherche.

Fjuk, A., & Sorensen, E. K. (1997). Drama as a metaphor for the design of situated, collaborative, distributed learning. *European Journal of Open and Distance Learning.* Retrieved March 17, 2008, from http://www.telenor.no/fou/program/nomadiske/articles/Teater.pdf

George, S. (2001). *Apprentissage collectif à distance. SPLACH: un environnement informatique support d'une pédagogie de projet.* Unpublished doctoral Thesis. Université du Maine, Le Mans, France.

Hand, C. (1994, September 14-17). Other faces of virtual reality. In *Proceedings of the East-West International Conference on Multimedia, Hypermedia and Virtual Reality*, Moscow (pp. 69-74).

Harrison, S., & Dourish, P. (1996). Re-place-ing space: The roles of place and space in collaborative systems. In *Proceedings of the 1996 ACM Conference on Computer Supported Cooperative Work* (pp. 67-76). New York: ACM Press.

Herrington, A., Herrington, J., & Omari, A. (2002). Using the Internet to provide authentic professional development for beginning teachers. In A. Williamson, C. Gunn, A. Young, & T. Clear (Eds.), *Winds of change in a sea of learning: Proceedings of the 19th Annual ASCILITE Conference* (pp. 811-814). Auckland, NZ: UNITEC Institute of Technology.

Herrington, J., & Oliver, R. (2000). An instructional design framework for authentic learning environments. *Educational Technology Research & Development, 48*(3), 23-48.

Herrington, J., Oliver, R., & Reeves, T. C. (2003). Patterns of engagement in authentic online learning environments. *Australian Journal of Educational Technology, 19*(1), 59-71.

Jensen, S. S., & Heilesen, S. B. (2004). Time, place, and identity in project work on the Net. In T. M. Roberts (Ed.), *Computer-supported collaborative in higher education* (pp. 51-69). Hershey, PA: Idea Group Publishing.

Lave, J., & Wenger, E. (1991). *Situated learning: Legitimate peripheral participation.* New York: Cambridge University Press.

McLellan, H. (1996). Situated learning: Multiple perspectives. In H. McLellan (Ed.), *Situated learning perspectives* (pp. 5-17). Englewood Cliffs, NJ: Educational Technology Publications.

Orey, M. A., & Nelson, W. A. (1997). The impact of situated cognition: Instructional design paradigms in transition. In C. R. Dills & A. J. Romiszowski (Eds.), *Instructional development paradigms* (pp. 283-296). Englewood Cliffs, NJ: Educational Technology Publications.

Reeves, T. C., Herrington, J., & Oliver, R. (2002). Authentic activities and online learning. In A. Goody, J. Herrington, & M. Northcote (Eds.), *Quality conversations: Research and Development in higher education* (vol. 25, pp. 562-567). Jamison, ACT: HERDSA.

Rule, A. C. (2006). Editorial: The components of authentic learning. *Journal of Authentic Learning, 3*(1), 1-10.

Savery, J. R., & Duffy, T. M. (1995). Problem based learning: An instructional model and its constructivist framework. *Educational Technology, 35*(5), 31-38.

Schraw, G. (1998). On the development of adult metacognition. In C. Smith & T. Pourchot (Eds.), *Adult learning and development: Perspectives from educational psychology* (pp. 89-106). Mahwah, NJ: Lawrence Erlbaum.

Sheehan, K. (2001). E-mail survey response rates: A review. *Journal of Computer Mediated Communication, 6*(2).

Wenger, E. (n.d.). *Communities of practice: A brief introduction.* Retrieved March 17, 2008, from http://www.ewenger.com/theory/communities_of_practice_intro.htm

KEY TERMS

Authentic Learning: As synthesized by Rule (2006), the concept of "authentic learning" refers generally to learning activities involving (1) real-world problems that mimic the work of professionals in the targeted knowledge domain;

(2) open-ended inquiry, thinking skills, and meta-cognition; (3) discourse among a community of learners; and/or (4) learner empowerment through choices to direct their own learning in relevant project work.

Community of Practice: "Communities of practice are formed by people who engage in a process of collective learning in a shared domain of human endeavor." They are "groups of people who share a concern or a passion for something they do and learn how to do it better as they interact regularly" (Wenger, n.d.).

Instructional Engineering: Instructional engineering refers to the whole cycle of a learning system (e.g., a course, a module, a study program, etc.), from the initial analysis of the learning problem and context to the design, development, implementation, and evaluation of the learning system. The term "instructional engineering" is somewhat equivalent to the term "instructional design," although the term "engineering" highlights more explicitly the fact that the process borrows some characters of the one used to design products or services in engineering disciplines (e.g., systematic and systemic processes, search for coherence, of efficiency and efficacy, etc.).

Metacognition: "Metacognition is a term used to describe people's knowledge and regulation of human cognition. Strictly speaking, metacogni-tion refers to cognition about one's own cognition. ...Metacognition...differs from cognition in that cognitive skills are those that help a person perform a task; metacognitive skills are those that help a person understand and regulate cognitive performance" (Schraw, 1998, p. 91).

Situated Learning: Situated learning refers to an educational paradigm which stipulates that learning occurs in a sociocultural context. Thus, the term "situated" refers not only to the immediate context of learning but to the whole culture in which the learning situation takes place and which structures the cognitive activity of the learners. Learning takes place when learners interact with others and with concrete and symbolic tools, artefacts, and social practices in use in their cultural context.

Socioconstructivist Learning Theory: Socioconstructivist learning theory emphasizes the role of interactions and collaboration between learners as well as between learners and the teacher or other members of the community in knowledge construction.

Virtual Forum: A virtual forum is a Web-based tool for asynchronous discussions among a group of participants, usually centered on specific topics.

Chapter XIV
Toward a Theory of Technique for Online Focus Groups

Albino Claudio Bosio
Universitá Cattolica del Sacro Cuore di Milan, Italy

Guendalina Graffigna
Universitá Cattolica del Sacro Cuore di Milan, Italy

Edoardo Lozza
Universitá Cattolica del Sacro Cuore di Milan, Italy

ABSTRACT

Starting from a review of current dominant points of view about online focus groups, the authors outline the results of a research project in which they compared face-to-face discussion groups with different formats of online focus groups (forum; chat; forum plus chat) in order to identify their methodological specificities. The comparison was conducted with young adults on three health-related topics with different levels of social sensitivity. Systematic analysis of the conversational and thematic characteristics of all discussion transcripts revealed interesting characteristics of the four focus group techniques considered. The results corroborate the view that the research setting influences the findings production process in qualitative research, and might be the basis for a theory of online focus group techniques that can orient the researcher in choosing the online focus group technique best suited to his or her study aims and topics.

INTRODUCTION

Qualitative research, as it is conceived today, is the result of both theoretical–methodological positions and technological developments that influence research practices (Bosio, 2000; Denzin & Lincoln, 1994; Gergen & Gergen, 2000). The importance of considering how theoretical and methodological choices frame research design and the process of data construction is widely acknowledged in qualitative research (Morse & Richards, 2001). However, less attention has been paid to how tactical choices related to data collection and findings influence the study results. From our perspective, the researcher must acknowledge the influences of all contingent choices that he or she makes in the research process (from data collection to transcription and data analysis) on his or her results not only to achieve broader researcher reflexivity (Atkinson, 1990; Hertz, 1997; Steiner, 1991) but also to make the choices that are best suited to the research process. We call this need to analyze the specific influences of all the tactical choices embedded in or alternatively supporting the findings production strategies in qualitative research a *theory of technique* (Bosio, Graffigna, & Lozza, 2006; Graffigna & Bosio, 2006).

The need for a *theory of technique* approach has become even more urgent since the introduction of multimedia technologies in the research process. Multimedia are undoubtedly useful for qualitative researchers in their work, but they are also a challenge to the researcher's flexibility and sensitivity. They change the way we do research and, thus, the meaning of "constructed data" (Brown, 2002; Coffey & Atkinson, 1996; Dicks, Mason, Coffey, & Atkinson, 2006).

In this regard, we consider the increasing use of online qualitative research as a challenging opportunity to study the influence of the situational context of data collection (i.e., the medium and the way in which it is used) on the results achieved. In particular, online focus groups are a suitable observatory for this phenomenon, not only because researchers seek to reproduce face-to-face focus groups using a different medium (the Internet) but also because the same technique (online focus groups) can be realized through different forms of computer-mediated communication: this can lead to important variations in the data-gathering process itself and can influence the knowledge construction process.

In the light of this premise, and since online focus groups can be considered a new speech context, we believe it important to reflect on how the resources and inner limitations of the Internet-mediated research setting frame the social exchange, which forms the basis of the data construction process in focus groups.

BACKGROUND

The use of online qualitative research (particularly online focus groups) has gained increasing consensus in recent years, not only in the marketing sector (Botagelj, Korenini, & Vehovar, 2002; Cheyne, 2000; Eke & Comely, 1999; Sweet, 2001) but also in the fields of health (Im & Chee, 2003, 2004; Seymour, 2001; Strickland, Moloney, Diethrich, Myerburg, Cotsonis, & Johnson, 2003) and educational research (Henson, Koinu-Rybicki, Madigan, & Muchmore, 2000; Russell & Bullock, 1999). This trend seems to be based primarily on the pragmatic advantages that the Internet brings to research design. Scholars commonly acknowledge that the decrease in time and costs of fieldwork (see Zinchiak, 2001), the possibility of bringing together people who are geographically dispersed (see Underhill & Olmstead, 2003), the speed and availability of a complete verbatim transcript of the discussion without the need for transcription (Chen & Hinton, 1999), and the anonymity guaranteed by the Internet research setting are the most appealing plus factors of online focus groups. However, these pragmatic considerations often lead to an a-critical use of online techniques and to a failure to acknowledge the impact of the Internet setting on the psychosocial and interpersonal dynamics of the discussion group.

As a result, even though the first studies to use online focus groups were carried out in the United States in the 1990s (Miller & Walkowski, 2004), the methodological and technical reflections in this field, more than 15 years later, are still limited, and little is known about the specific advantages and limitations of online focus groups. Furthermore, there is no shared definition in the literature of what an online focus group is. The duration and the characteristics of the technology used, the number and type of participants, and the moderating style of a focus group conducted in a virtual setting, for example, seem to depend not only on the research topic and objectives but, above all, on economic factors and technological resources available. For instance, a group discussion can be held on the Internet in the form of a forum, a chat, or a combination of synchronous and asynchronous communication (see Figure 1) to let participants experience different styles of discussion and to discover the one with which they are most at ease. In short, the definition of *online focus group* usually encompasses all of those techniques that share the main characteristics of text-based, computer-mediated communication (CMC, see Riva & Galimberti, 2001). Very different discussions might thus all be labeled *online focus groups*.

FORMATS OF ONLINE FOCUS GROUPS

In particular at present, the most used online focus group techniques are the following four: forum,

MEGS (mailing lists), chat, and mixed group. A forum is a virtual board where participants can interact without having to be online at the same time (asynchronous communication) as they write their messages and read others' over periods of time that can vary from four days to several months, depending on the research objectives and purposes. Mailing lists, or MEGS, are the type of group where participants communicate by e-mail messages. In some cases, they send messages directly; in others, a moderator mediates by receiving the messages, then summarizing and circulating them. In this way, a synthesis and a first elaboration of the content are negotiated among the participants. This format of online discussion is currently used less frequently than in the past, and some authors consider it a group interview rather than a focus group technique (Di Fraia, 2004). This is one of the reasons why we did not consider this technique in this study. In a chat, the participants access the Internet contemporaneously, interacting in the same way as in a face-to-face exchange (synchronous communication). Hence, some authors consider this format of discussion the closest one to a face-to-face focus group (Sweet, 2001). There is no full consensus as to the ideal number of members for this type of online focus group, although a small number is generally preferred for better management of interaction and of the conversation flow. For mixed

Figure 1. The different formats of online focus groups (©2007, A.C. Bosio, G. Graffigna, E. Lozza. Used with permission)

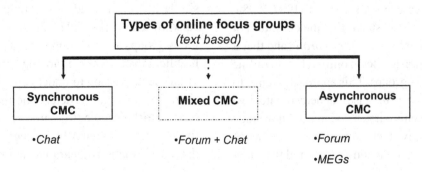

groups, there is no generally accepted definition. They consist of a combination of the two styles of communication (synchronous and asynchronous) for varied and articulate discussion and to allow richer data collection.

LACK OF METHODOLOGICAL REFLECTION ON ONLINE FOCUS GROUPS

The mentioned lack of methodological reflection seems also to be due to the widespread tendency to assimilate online focus groups with face-to-face ones. Researchers who share this assimilationist approach (Graffigna & Bosio, 2006) evaluate the credibility and trustworthiness of online focus groups (James & Busher, 2006) in terms of the equivalence of their findings to those achieved using face-to-face focus groups. From this perspective, authors often regard face-to-face focus groups as the ideal model, to which online focus groups must aspire in order to be considered a valid research tool. Thus, a researcher is required to faithfully reproduce a face-to-face focus group on the Internet, and to keep any distortions and any loss of fundamental characteristics to a minimum (Bradford, 2000; Greenbaum, 1998b; Holge-Hazelton, 2002). Besides being assimilationist, this perspective is also substitutive, as these researchers reacted to online focus groups as if they were a potential evolution of the traditional technique. As a result, sometimes this approach led to an a priori rejection of online focus groups by some traditional qualitative researchers. Greenbaum (1997, 1998a, 1998b), for instance, stated that the definition of online focus groups is an "*oxymoron*" and that it was a denigration to refer to online chats or online forums as focus groups. This approach seems, to us, open to criticism because it underestimates two potential problems. First, it does not acknowledge that all qualitative techniques have an influence on the findings production process and thus, that

qualitative findings are strictly related to the tactical choices the researcher makes in collecting his or her data. Second, this approach does not take into consideration the fact that, as we mentioned previously, the term "online focus group" is an umbrella concept covering different forms of group discussion. A discussion of the similarities and differences between face-to-face focus groups and online ones in general terms fails to acknowledge the specific characteristics of each different online focus group technique.

It would be more appropriate to consider online focus groups as new, different, and complementary tools in the qualitative researcher's toolbox (Gaiser, 1997; Im & Chee, 2004; Schneider, Kerwin, Frechtling, & Vivari, 2002; Strickland et al., 2003). In this perspective, online focus groups are a class of new techniques that may differ from traditional focus groups, and they need to be studied further and to determine their similarities and differences with each other and with respect to face-to-face focus groups (Beasley & Chapin, 1998; Coates & Frogatt, 1998; Miller & Walkowski, 2004).

To sum up, on the basis of these premises and assuming a *differential perspective*—which is opposed to the *assimilationist* one and that considers online focus groups to be a new, different, and complementary class of tools (Graffigna & Bosio, 2006)—we think that it is important to understand the specific features of online focus groups by comparing traditional face-to-face discussion groups with different formats of Internet discussion (chat, forum, and forum plus chat). We chose this approach not only to generally identify the similarities and extend the theoretical and practical knowledge achieved in the field of traditional focus groups to the online setting, but also to highlight the differences among various formats of online discussion to understand their specific characteristics and to determine the conditions relating to their choice (research questions, objectives, participants, etc.). In this regard, we believe that a systematic comparative analysis aimed at

TOWARD A THEORY OF ONLINE FOCUS GROUP TECHNIQUES

The project consisted of three studies involving face-to-face and different formats of online focus groups on three health-related topics with different levels of social sensitivity (HIV/AIDS, alcohol consumption, and smoking behaviour). We chose these research topics as the most suitable contexts in which to study the specificities of online focus groups because scholars agree that online focus groups are particularly well suited to the study of sensitive topics (Ellett, Lois, & Keffer, 2004; Haigh & Jones, 2005; Holge-Hazelton, 2002; Im & Chee, 2003, 2004). And also, these topics are particularly relevant from the perspective of preventive education.

RESEARCH PLAN AND METHODOLOGY

The research projects consisted of 24 focus groups involving 180 participants. The discussion groups were homogeneous in terms of participant numbers (6–8) and characteristics (Italian and aged 18–25), but the situational contexts in which they were conducted differed. In practice, we carried out eight discussion groups on each research topic (HIV/AIDS, alcohol, and smoking) and six discussion groups per technique (see Table 1). Six face-to-face focus groups of about two hours, led by a moderator and an observer, were conducted in the focus group laboratory of our Psychology Department. These focus groups were audio and video recorded.

- Six three-day forums, during which the participants were asked to write at least two messages a day to answer the moderator's questions and other participants' comments at a convenient time for them. The forum was conducted on a private Web site set up expressly for this research, and interviewees participated anonymously, accessing the site using a password and hiding their identity behind a personal ID assigned by the researchers. The forum Web site displayed all posted messages, so participants were able to read them at any time and to write their comments as a new message using the "post my message" button or in response to a specific message using the "reply" button.

- Six chats of about one hour, during which the online participants interacted and discussed their opinions in real time. In this setting, participants shared their opinions synchronously as in a face-to-face focus group. The chats were conducted on the same private Web site as the forum, and here, too, interviewees participated anonymously.

- Six forums plus chats each consisted of a three-day forum combined with a chat. The discussion started with a two-day forum during which participants logged into the site to write their comments at a time convenient for them (asynchronous CMC). On the evening of the second discussion day, interviewees were asked to participate in an online chat (synchronous CMC) of about one hour to continue their discussion in real time. The discussion groups ended with a final forum day to collect further comments on the topic. This discussion was also conducted on the same private Web site as previous online focus groups, and interviewees participated anonymously.

The moderating style was as non-directed as possible to allow participants to express themselves freely so that we could study how the setting influenced the content and the way the themes were explored. We chose this moderating style in order to neutralize the moderator's role in the

Table 1. Research plan (©2007, A.C. Bosio, G. Graffigna, E. Lozza. Used with permission)

	On-line			Face to face	Tot.
AIDS	2 Forums	2 Chats	2 Forums+chat	2 F-t-F	**8**
ALCOHOL	2 Forums	2 Chats	2 Forums+chat	2 F-t-F	**8**
SMOKING	2 Forums	2 Chats	2 Forums+chat	2 F-t-F	**8**
Total	**6**	**6**	**6**	**6**	**24**

discussion as much as possible and to magnify the influence of the data collection medium and the way it was used on the way the discussion developed with the different techniques. The choice of using the same low-profile moderating style for all discussion formats helped us to determine how the different discussion settings influenced the results. However, it is evident that each discussion format is best suited to a particular moderating style which should be chosen on the basis of its specific methodological features.

The semistructured guide consisted of three main interventions on the part of the moderator: (a) a starting intervention to explain the purpose of the study, in which participants were asked to express themselves freely on the discussion topic; (b) a second one after about a third of the discussion, in which participants were asked to read an information message about the topic (HIV/AIDS, smoking behaviour, alcohol consumption) and to consider it a stimulus for further discussion; and (c) a third and final one to focus the discussion on participants' personal experience concerning the topic.

DATA ANALYSIS

Verbatim notes of all online focus groups (forum, chat, forum plus chat) were available in text format, while the face-to-face focus groups were transcribed by the researchers. The entire transcripts of the 24 focus groups were analyzed by adopting a *triangulation* (Schwandt, 2001) of strategies using software-based content analysis (T-lab 5.2; Lancia, 2004), conversational analysis, and software-based computer-mediated discourse analysis (Atlas.ti). This combination of analysis strategies made it possible to compare the different focus group techniques both from a thematic and from a dynamic perspective.

Software-Based Content Analysis (T-lab 5.2)

Software-based content analysis using T-lab 5.2, in particular, allowed a quantitative analysis of how themes were explored in the different discussion formats. T-lab bases its analysis on context units (CUs) and lexical units (LUs). A corpus of text can be divided into elementary contexts (EC) and variables, which are two subsets of context units. ECs are text portions delimited by punctuation that correspond to one or more statements. Variables are the criteria that the researcher chooses when organizing and classifying the corpus of textual data, in our case, the four focus group techniques. LUs are words that are considered in the graphic forms they assume in the text or ascribed to dictionary headwords or to semantic classes (e.g., working=work; pneumonia=illness). The software produces matrices representing relations between the units of analysis (CU and LU). In the matrices, frequency numbers indicate occurrences or co-occurrences of the phenomena in question. For further information, see Lancia (2004) and http://www.t-lab.it.

Conversational Analysis

Conversational analysis (Hutchby & Wooffitt, 1998; Schegloff & Sacks, 1973) allowed us to describe the interpersonal exchange at a linguistic and at a dynamic level. At a linguistic level, we focused our analysis on lexical choices (words, adjectives, adverbs), punctuation (for written texts), grammatical structure of sentences (complex or simple), overall structure organization (phrases or sections), and conversational style of utterances (negative constructions, irony, sarcasm). At a dynamic level, we analyzed turn-taking organization (self-designation, designation of other speakers, nondesignation), silence management (lapses, gaps, pauses, silence), and sequence organization (adjacency pairs, character of preference or dispreference, repair sequences).

Software-Based Quantitative Discourse Analysis

Atlas.ti allowed a systematic analysis and comparison (Herring, 2001) of: processes of discourse construction like negotiation, cooperation, and the like; disclosure and emotional connotation of discourse like reporting of personal experience and feelings; and rhetorical strategies and interaction patterns. Although Atlas.ti was originally developed from a grounded theory perspective, it is a very flexible tool and can easily be adapted to different researcher objectives and methodological standpoints (Lonkila, 1995). In our research, we used Atlas.ti to code our texts on the basis of a heuristic classification model (Silverman, 2000), as our coding frame was designed to reflect theoretical concepts and interpretations that we judged useful for achieving our study objectives. All focus

group verbatim transcripts were coded by Atlas. ti following an ad hoc grid based on recurrent discursive and conversational patterns identified by a previous paper-based qualitative discourse analysis of first transcriptions. Our coding frame (grid) was constantly revised and updated as new data emerged during the data analysis process. The conceptualizations of some categories were extended, and some new categories were created. This continuous adaptation of the analysis grid was possible thanks to Atlas.ti's flexibility.

The coding frame was organized into four macroconceptual areas (interaction patterns, discourse co-construction, rhetorical and argumentation strategies, and disclosure of private experiences and feelings). Each macro area was exploded into categories (variables), which, in turn, were transformed into subcodes (units of analysis). Once the coding was concluded, Atlas.ti was used to count the code and thus category frequencies in each transcript. The resulting variable frequencies were then transformed into percentiles to render them comparable. The significance of variances was verified using the t-test.

MAIN FINDINGS OF THE STUDY

The focus group techniques (face-to-face focus group, forum, chat, and forum plus chat) share some common features, confirming the hypothesis of a fundamental comparability between face-to-face and online focus groups (Mann & Stewart, 2000; Underhill & Olmstead, 2003). All discussion techniques produced rich and detailed discursive materials. Some key themes were common to all discussions, although their development and weight varied according to the discussion setting. A number of main interaction and conversation patterns were present in all discussions, albeit with different characteristics depending on the discussion setting. However, each discussion format showed distinctive characteristics in terms of both conversational exchange and thematic structure of the discussion, which were ascribable not only to the general distinction between face-to-face vs. Internet-mediated focus groups but also to the different settings of online focus groups.

CONVERSATIONAL CHARACTERISTICS OF THE EXCHANGE

Each focus group technique shaped the conversational characteristics of the exchange in a way that appeared to be fairly independent of the topic under discussion and that confirmed previous studies on computer-mediated communication (Evans, Wedande, & Van't Hul, 2001; Galimberti, Ignazi, Vercesi, & Riva, 2001; Herring, 2001). It is therefore possible to summarize the main conversational characteristics of each focus group format.

The *face-to-face groups* took the shape of a *normative debate*. Since turn-taking was difficult to manage in this discussion format, leadership issues were frequent, resulting in the polarization of participants' positions. Furthermore, the physical co-presence of participants was experienced as inhibiting, and some felt uncomfortable disclosing their personal experiences and feelings about the discussion topic. As a result, discussants often adopted an impersonal and implicit rhetorical style in formulating their comments, frequently making use of impersonal constructions, such as "people think" and "they say," and courtesy formulas. This was probably an attempt to deny responsibility for what they were saying and to maintain a sort of emotional detachment from the research topic. Furthermore, this often resulted in a critical attitude, expressed in the form of accusations and negative judgments on the discussion topic or on the opinions of other participants.

"I think it's unacceptable that today, in 2003, people still don't know enough about the virus. Maybe they know how you can contract the infec-

tion...but they don't really realize the importance of safe sex....In other words: they don't see the problem in all its complexity."

"Alcohol consumption is increasing among teens...at high school people get drunk to have fun."

The *forum*, on the other hand resulted in a *"position paper"-like* discussion because of the limited interaction between discussants and the tendency among participants to argue their opinions in very long, elaborate comments. Participants often expressed their points in posts that were unrelated to the content of the other participants' messages, as if they were carrying on a sort of personal monologue. The limited interaction among participants makes it difficult to talk of conjoint discourse co-construction: In the forum, discussants mentioned other participants' comments only at the beginning of their messages and simply as a stimulus for their own reflective monologues. It follows that the discussion assumed a round table character, where each speaker delivered his or her personal statement at his or her turn regardless of the "position papers" of others. From a linguistic and rhetorical perspective, the forum comments were well thought out and carefully edited. Frequently, participants chose studied words and complex sentences to express their opinions. Modal verbs as well as conditional clauses were recurrent, as were rhetorical devices such as metaphors and paradoxes. In the end, it seems that the asynchrony of the discussion setting, in addition to keeping interaction less intense, gave participants the opportunity to write their messages unhurriedly, making revisions and corrections before sending them, and contributed to the greater reflective and intimate nature of the discussion.

"Friends might play a crucial contextual role acting as a stimulus, but in the end, fundamentally, the decision to stop smoking should be well rooted in the individual's psychology."

"I am certain that if I got HIV/AIDS tomorrow my family and friends (who were aware) would treat me dramatically different from before. I think that it would always be on my mind and their minds when in contact with one another, and it would be like having 'a big purple elephant in the room' that no one wants to talk about."

The *chat* exchange seemed more like a *brainstorming* session than a really focused discussion. Participants interacted intensely, constantly introducing new ideas and stimuli to the exchange. The interaction was chaotic but democratic, as all participants had the same time to express their opinions, taking turns to speak spontaneously without negotiating with the others. In this regard, even though the moderator of the discussion played a pivotal role in maintaining the focus of the chat discussion, and he was certainly experienced as more present than in the other group formats, he was often clearly attacked and criticized because of the greater spontaneity and democracy of relationships allowed by this research setting. As a consequence of the "inner dynamism" of the chat, participants expressed their opinions openly, without roundabout expressions or metaphors, often with very direct interventions that provoked irritation in others. This was sometimes caused by episodes of "*flaming*" (Sproull & Kiesler, 1986), in which the communicative exchange was frenzied and characterized by provocations or insults. However, the exchange appeared more direct in the chat than in other discussions, and members were more inclined to recount their experiences and emotions, thus giving rise to frequent episodes of reciprocal empathy and emotional support.

Moderator: *what do you mean? Your question isn't clear!*

Pt3: *I don't agree, at school they just gave us a leaflet saying that if you don't want to get the virus you should not have sex! It doesn't make sense!*

Pt2: *Anyway that is one way of avoiding infection!*

Pt3: *Pt2, you sound too utopian to me!*

Pt2: *What are you talking about?????*

Pt2: *Me, a utopian?? You're joking!!!*

The *forum plus chat* combined the forum-only and the chat-only conversation features. What made it different from the other online discussions was that the interaction was more organic and balanced from the beginning. Compared to the forum-only discussion, in the initial forum of the forum plus chat, participants interacted more. From the beginning, participants were aware of the other's presence, and they personally addressed messages to each other using nicknames. The initial forum allowed participants to become familiar with the discussion topic and the e-environment, and promoted a sense of group belonging that facilitated the chat debate. Thus, during the chat, participants were better able to cooperate in the discussion. Misunderstandings were less frequent despite multiple threads of content. The chat exchange in the forum plus chat was less chaotic and more developed than the chat-only, while still remaining very direct and spontaneous: Participants often commented on other's messages, addressing them by their nicknames, and they explained their opinions better. Those features of the forum plus chat suggest a progressive improvement of harmony among participants during the discussion development: In this discussion, participants interacted more and more effectively and autonomously as in a real "*working group*."

Pt1: *In order to quit...you would have to feel breathless or be sick!*

Pt 2: *Maybe showing a hardened smoker's lungs could change people's minds ... my aunt quit when her physician friend showed her a pair of such lungs!*

Pt3: *and you must be in a good period of your life*

Pt1: *or not go out with girls who smoke .... and vice versa*

Moderator: *Why don't people talk so much about HIV-AIDS?*

Pt1: *because you want to forget the risk, you prefer to minimize*

Pt2: *good post Pt1, I definitely agree!*

Pt3: *to keep one's own world peaceful!*

Pt4: *until it happens close to you, you don't feel the problem affects you!*

Pt5: *you mean, Pt4, that sometimes things go as they do in this chat: you think that the problem only concerns those who sleep around, those who see prostitutes*

Pt4: *exactly Pt5!*

COMMUNICATIVE AXES OF INTERACTION

Apart from the specific conversational characteristics that the different focus group formats presented, the interpersonal and interaction dynamics of the exchange were also framed by the discussion setting. In this regard, our software-based computer-mediated discourse analysis—performed using Atlas.ti—allowed us to analyze the main direction that the exchange assumed in the different discussions. In particular, we analyzed which interlocutors a participant designated for his or her utterances in the different discussions. We detected the following communicative axes: *subject–subject* interaction when a participant directly addressed comments to another participant; *subject–group* interaction when a participant addressed comments to the whole group as if it was an interpersonal entity; and *subject–moderator* interaction when a participant addressed comments expressly to the discussion leader.

We counted the frequency percentages of these three axes in the four discussion formats in each research case. We made 100% the total amount of addressed utterances in each discussion format.

Analysis in Figure 2 showed that the four techniques elicited specific patterns of interaction that were confirmed in all three research scenarios, albeit with a different emphasis.

In brief, we can observe that the face-to-face discussions were characterized mainly by a dyadic form of communicative interaction on the subject–subject axis. In the chats, the dyadic interaction was also frequent, although less so than in the face-to-face groups. The forums, on the other hand, were characterized mainly by subject–group interaction. Finally, in the forum plus chat discussions, the two communicative axes of subject–subject and subject–group were balanced, confirming the hypothesis of the working group feature of the forum plus chat.

It is also interesting to note that the interaction patterns in the HIV/AIDS and the smoking behaviour research scenarios are very similar. In the alcohol study, the interaction pattern is similar although less marked. We have reasons to believe that these slight differences can be explained by the thematic specificity of each issue, as will be shown in a forthcoming analysis (Bosio, Graffigna, & Lozza, in press). This is interesting evidence of the discussion setting's influence on the data construction process. Furthermore, the specific dynamic and conversational characteristics that the group exchange manifested in the different focus group techniques seem to have resulted in a distinctive exploration of the issues in each discussion format, which was fairly constant in the three cases of research and which we shall describe in the next section.

THEMATIC STRUCTURE OF THE DISCUSSIONS

In confirming that the discussion setting plays a key role in framing the data construction process, as mentioned, our computer-based content analysis, performed using T-lab 5.2, showed how the different focus group techniques frame the

Figure 2. Communicative axes in the discussion settings and three research cases (©2007, A.C. Bosio, G. Graffigna, E. Lozza. Used with permission)

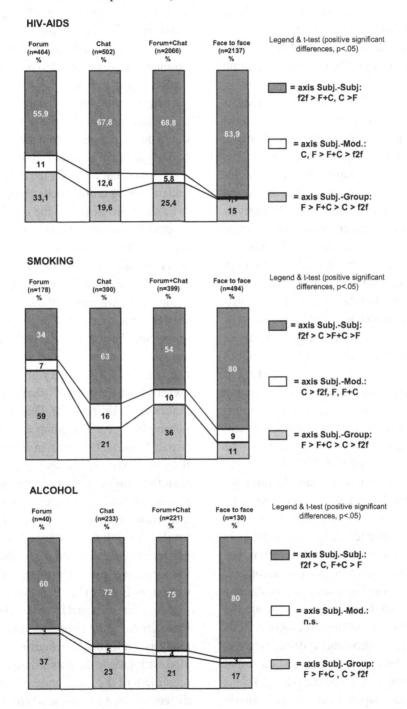

thematic structure of the discussion in specific ways. Although the thematic development of the discussion is obviously specific to each topic, it is possible to detect some recurrences. These recurrences seem to be independent of the research topic and dependent on the specific discussion setting.

As shown in Figure 3, correspondence analysis of lemmas × techniques allowed us to position the four focus group techniques on three thematic maps (one for each issue under discussion). This analysis describes the relations between semantic units (lemmas) and variables that divide the corpus (the focus group techniques). The analysis outcome consists of a matrix made up of lemmas in rows and variable levels in columns. Correspondence analysis casts light on relations between the data-gathering techniques and their specific discussion content. In other words, this analysis allows us to represent in graph form specific content (lemmas) similarities and differences among the different focus groups techniques (face-to-face; chat; forum; forum plus chat). It also detects factors that explain variance among variables. The meaning of these factors is interpreted on the basis of their constituent element threshold values, that is, the lemmas and the four levels of the considered variable. These maps highlight some distinctive thematic features for each discussion technique. Before considering the meaning of the three maps and of their constituent dimensions, we can note that the horizontal axes of the three thematic maps clearly differentiate between face-to-face and online discussion content. Furthermore, it is also interesting to note that the vertical axes of the three maps differentiate the content characteristics of the three online focus group techniques, confirming the distinctiveness of each virtual discussion format, and thus, that online focus groups should be considered a class of discussion techniques rather than a single research approach. In particular, with respect to the three horizontal axes, the face-to-face focus group content presents a more critical, ideologi-

cal, and impersonal discussion, namely on the role of Catholic Church prescriptions with regard to AIDS, the introduction of antismoking laws, the increase in alcohol consumption among high school students, and so on. Participants in the online focus groups tend to be more proactive in resolving the problems under discussion, with participants bringing their pragmatic attitudes and personal experience to the topic such as the use of condoms, personal strategies to quit smoking and not to get drunk, and so on.

The vertical axes, on the other hand, differentiate among online focus groups in a way that is linked more closely to the specific topic under discussion. In this regard, we can observe that in the cases of tobacco and alcohol, the forum is associated with a more rational, meta-analytical and thoughtful discussion, for example, what smoking means to young people, the narration of friends' experiences concerning alcohol consumption, and so on. The chat tends to elicit affective and emotional content ("what I like about smoking and what makes me angry about non-smokers," "what I do when I drink," "what I feel when alcohol makes me feel hazy," etc.). The forum plus chat, as one might expect, is mediation between the other two techniques. However, in the HIV/AIDS case, the forum plus chat tends to be somewhat more than the sum of the parts, allowing the expression of personal, intimate experiences and of real, pragmatic attitudes and behaviours toward the issue. We think that the specificity of the AIDS case could be accounted for by the sensitivity of the topic, but this is worth analysing in greater depth (see Bosio et al., in press)

Summing up, apart from the slight differences between the results observed in each study, this analysis confirms the heuristic traits associated with face-to-face and online focus groups, regardless of the issue under discussion and the differences that can occur when using each of the three online focus group techniques.

Figure 3. Correspondence analysis lemmas x techniques in the three cases of research (©2007, A.C. Bosio, G. Graffigna, E. Lozza. Used with permission)

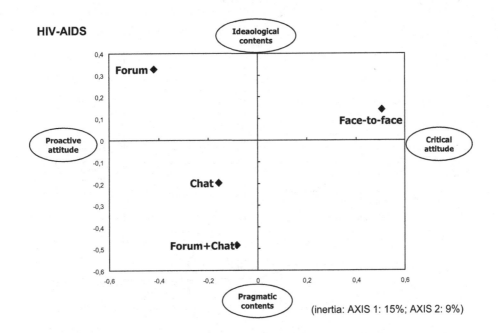

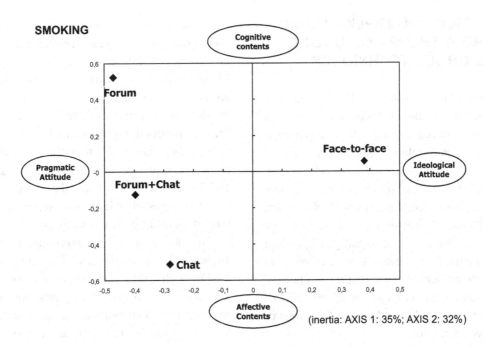

continued on following page

Figure 3. continued

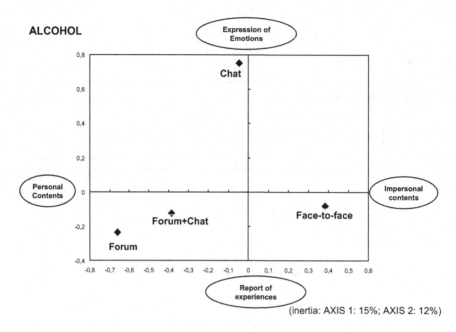

(inertia: AXIS 1: 15%; AXIS 2: 12%)

DISCUSSION AND IMPLICATIONS: TOWARD A THEORY OF ONLINE FOCUS GROUP TECHNIQUES

This study's findings confirm that the research setting, or the medium, shapes the process of data construction. More specifically, the interpersonal exchange on health-related topics is characterized by the discussion setting. This is important to the researcher in making a "situated choice" of tools and setting in relation to the research objectives. The results also confirm the importance of a *theory of technique* approach, which is partly independent from the methodological and the epistemological considerations behind the researcher's choices, to the study of the implications of data collection procedures on the production of findings in qualitative research.

In particular, our findings show that the four discussion formats have distinctive characteristics, both in terms of elicited conversational and interaction patterns and in terms of thematic structure of the exchange. These could not be ascribed solely to the general difference between face-to-face and Internet-mediated interaction. These results, thus, seem to reveal interesting differences among the forms of online focus group considered in terms of their influences on the findings production process. In the light of these results, it seems possible to outline the following preliminary typology in Figure 4 of conversational and thematic characteristics that the discussion group assumes when it involves sensitive health-related topics in different settings.

Face-to-face focus groups produce the greatest amount of discursive material. They are characterized by high levels of mainly dyadic interaction and cooperation among participants. However, the management of turn-taking is problematic, and leadership issues frequently arise. Participants tend to assume a critical attitude throughout the discussion and appear concerned about peer group norms and social desirability. Confirming previous research findings (see Duggleby, 2005;

Figure 4. Summary of online focus group choice criteria (©2007, A.C. Bosio, G. Graffigna, E. Lozza. Used with permission)

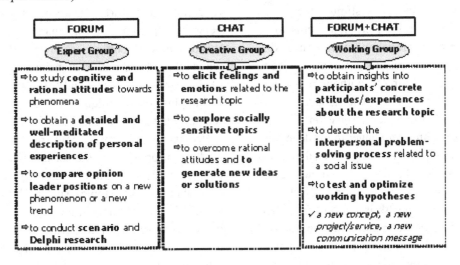

Kitzinger, 1994), the co-presence of participants tends to make the issue of social desirability particularly evident. This can prevent the disclosure of personal experiences, and participants tend to distance themselves from the topic of discussion and to assume a critical and polemical attitude. It follows that this format of discussion could be suited to the study of ideological and sociopolitical discourses related to sensitive topics and to the analysis of how individuals polarize their positions/opinions in the group exchange rather than to exploring the private dimension of the problem.

The *forum* is characterized by the lowest levels of interaction and cooperation among participants. Discussants develop their contributions in articulate monologues. Forum comments are well thought out, revealing participants' main attitudes in the form of pondered and rational observations. Moreover, participants adopt a meta-analytical approach when recounting their personal experiences and feelings, with plenty of details and analysis of the causes and consequences. Thus, participants contribute to the discussion in forums as "experts" who describe

and defend their theories in a peer group debate using rational and well thought out arguments. However, the anonymity guaranteed by the setting allows greater disclosure of personal experiences and emotions than in a face-to-face focus group. The forum might, therefore, be suitable for the study of cognitive and rational attitudes toward health risks or for obtaining a detailed and well-meditated description of personal experiences. In view of these characteristics, the forum discussion can be considered similar to a diary report written in an interpersonal setting. Participants' expert and rational attitudes, moreover, suggest that the forum discussion is potentially similar to a Delphi group. In other words, this technique could be suitable to inquiring about opinion leaders' expectations concerning future trends and social scenarios.

The *chat* is characterized by intense and sometimes chaotic interaction. Discussants participate in the debate with brief comments, and they tend to state, rather than negotiate, their opinions. The speed of interaction and the brevity of posts often cause misunderstandings and flaming phenomena. However, the rapid exchanges produce greater directness and more spontaneity in the discussion than the other techniques. Because participants continuously introduce new stimuli, ideas, and topics in the chat, this discussion seems to be more like brainstorming than a well-focused discussion group. Furthermore, participants tend to reveal their opinions directly without roundabout expressions or metaphors. The debate is more spontaneous than in other discussion formats, and participants are more eager to disclose their private experiences and feelings, even their most intimate ones. This discussion technique would, therefore, be suitable for eliciting affects and emotions related to health issues and for understanding participants' concrete strategies to avoid risks and to deal with these problems in their interpersonal relationships. Given the immediacy of participation, this setting might also be suitable for conducting a *creative discussion group*. The direct and pointed style of contributions elicited by the chat setting can be useful in overcoming rational attitudes and in generating new ideas or solutions to formulate, for instance, new prevention campaigns. However, as a consequence of the inner dynamism of the chat, participants tend to state their opinions rather than negotiate them, and this often results in the polarization of personal positions. Thus, the chat results are poorer than those obtained through the other focus group formats with respect to discussion content and themes.

The *forum plus chat* discussion format appears to be the most balanced technique. The combination of the two (chat plus forum) communication styles allows the potential of both settings to be integrated, thereby overcoming their respective limitations. In the initial forum, participants have the opportunity of becoming familiar with the e-environment and the discussion topic. This allows them to establish a rapport, which enhances cooperation in the chat. In the forum plus chat setting, the discussion is more complete and more detailed than in the other settings. This technique allows greater thematic discus-

sion and a more detailed group exchange, which can range over a variety of issues, from abstract reflections in the forum, to accounts of concrete personal experiences in the chat. It follows that this discussion technique is particularly suitable when a broad and multidimensional description of the phenomenon is sought. In our view, the forum plus chat technique is the most promising tool among the ones considered for studying the interpersonal problem-solving process related to health risk prevention and for analyzing young people's attitudes, opinions, feelings, and emotions about sensitive topics, such as those related to health. Furthermore, thanks to its *working group* character, it could also act as a new health prevention channel to assist people in proactively reflecting on their unsafe practices and negotiating strategies interpersonally to avoid risks.

CONCLUSION AND FUTURE TRENDS

The characterization of the different focus group techniques is important in situating the choice of tool in relation to research objectives and in defining more completely the technical aspects of the research project. From our perspective, these results can be considered the first step toward the formulation of a *theory of online focus group techniques* that can make the researcher conscious of the pragmatic, methodological, and theoretical implications of his or her research choices. However, this study is a preliminary foray into the controversial issue of online qualitative research. The study findings need to be further understood and confirmed by future analysis. Nevertheless, we consider the stable influence of each setting on the discussion content and interaction across different research topics extremely interesting and meaningful.

At present, we envisage at least two main directions for future research on this topic. The first one is to analyze further how the Internet is not only a vehicle of new methodological opportunities (i.e., a new data collection medium), but might also orient the development of new research questions and working hypotheses in the field of preventive health education. In other words, the Internet, being a bridge between mass and interpersonal communication (O'Sullivan, 1999), might be a privileged observatory for the study of interpersonal processes that regulate the passage from the reception to the application of preventive information in real contexts of risk. In this regard, it also seems important to understand further how different uses of the Internet specifically shape—by enhancing or inhibiting—young people's exchanges about health-related topics and how this might influence the sharing and the interpersonal co-construction of preventive practices (Bosio & Graffigna, 2006, 2007).

The second line of inquiry would be to find further support for our *online focus group theory of technique*, not only when tackling other research topics but also when dealing with other than Italian cultural contexts. In this regard, because of the global nature of the Internet and the increasing use of online focus groups in qualitative cross-country inquiries (Mann & Stewart, 2000; Miller & Walkowski, 2004; Underhill & Olmstead, 2003), we consider it important to analyze how online focus groups work across cultures. Furthermore, cross-cultural qualitative research would appear to be a good testing ground for our online focus group theory of technique. This could also help the researcher to make more culturally sensitive methodological choices that are appropriate to the sociocultural context of the inquiry (cf. Graffigna, Bosio, & Olson, 2008).

REFERENCES

Atkinson, P. A. (1990). *The ethnographic imagination: Textual constructions of reality.* London: Routledge.

Beasley, R., & Chapin, K. (1998). *Paradoxes in cyberspace: A qualitative perspective on research through the Internet.* Paper presented at the Worldwide Internet Seminar and Exhibition, Paris.

Bosio, A. C. (2000). Gli sviluppi della ricerca sociale qualitativa e le condizioni di campo dell'intervista [Qualitative social research development and the interview situation]. In G. Trentini (Ed.), *Oltre l'Intervista: il colloquio nei contesti sociali* (pp. 341-367). Torino, Italy: ISEDI.

Bosio, A. C., & Graffigna, G. (2006, May). *Conversational exchanges on AIDS in various interaction contexts: A preparatory study for an effective health campaign.* Paper presented at the 2nd International Congress of Qualitative Inquiry, University of Illinois at Urbana Campaign, Chicago.

Bosio, A. C., & Graffigna, G. (2007, February 8-9). *Preventive communication and its social reproduction in context: The role of qualitative research in analyzing the sharing of knowledge and the construction of safe practices.* Paper presented at Seminario di studio su: Metodi di analisi delle produzioni discorsive nella comunicazione di massa, AIP-Sezione Psicologia Sociale, Rome.

Bosio, A. C., Graffigna, G., & Lozza, E. (2006, July). *The influence of the setting on findings produced in face to face and online focus groups.* Paper presented at the 7th International Interdisciplinary Conference Advance in Qualitative Methods: Looking to the Future: Opportunities and Challenges for Qualitative Research, Surfers Paradise, Australia.

Bosio, A. C., Graffigna, G., & Lozza, E. (in press). Per una teoria della tecnica dei focus group on-line: quali costruzioni delle conoscenze in relazione alle opzioni strumentali [Toward a theory of online focus group technique: Which knowledge constructions according to choice of tool?]. In C. Galimberti & G. Scaratti (Eds.), *Affrontare la complessità nella ricerca psicologica.* Milan: Vita e pensiero.

Botagelj, Z., Korenini, B., & Vehovar, V. (2002, June). *The integration power of the intelligent banner advertising network and survey research.* Paper presented at the ESOMAR, Net Effects 5 Conference, Berlin, Germany.

Bradford, P. D. (2000, April). *Online focus group: Technology is virtually there.* Paper presented at the ESOMAR, Net Effects 3 Conference, Dublin, Ireland.

Brown, D. (2002). Going digital and staying qualitative: Some alternative strategies for digitizing the qualitative research process. *Qualitative Social Research, 3*(2). Retrieved March 17, 2008, from http://www.qualitative-research.net/fqs-eng.htm

Chen, P., & Hinton, S. M. (1999). Realtime interviewing using the World Wide Web. *Sociological Research Online.* Retrieved March 17, 2008, from http://eprints.unimelb.edu.au/archive/00000210/01/realtime.pdf.

Cheyne, T. (2000, April). *Research through relationships.* Paper presented at the ESOMAR, Net Effects 3 Conference, Dublin, Ireland.

Coates, D., & Frogatt, M. (1998, January). *Online qualitative research: The opportunities and limitations of conducting focus groups via the Internet.* Paper presented at the Worldwide Internet Seminar and Exhibition, Paris.

Coffey, A., & Atkinson, P. (1996). *Making sense of qualitative data analysis: Complementary strategies.* Thousand Oaks CA: Sage.

Denzin, N. K., & Lincoln, Y. S. (Eds.). (1994). *Handbook of qualitative research.* Thousand Oaks, CA: Sage.

Dicks, B., Mason, B., Coffey, A. J., & Atkinson, P. A. (2006). *Qualitative research ad hypermedia: Ethnography for the digital age.* London: Sage.

Di Fraia, G. (2004). *e-Research.* Bari, Italy: La Terza.

Duggleby, W. (2005). What about focus group interaction data? *Qualitative Health Research, 15*(6), 832-840.

Eke, V., & Comely, P. (1999, February). *Moderated email groups: Computing magazine case study.* Paper presented at the ESOMAR, Net Effects 2 Conference, Dublin. Retrieved March 17, 2008, from http://virtualsurveys.com/papers/meghtm

Ellett, C. M. L., Lois, J., & Keffer, J. (2004). Ethical and legal issues of conducting nursing research via the Internet. *Journal of Professional Nursing, 20*(1), 68-74.

Evans, M., Wedande, G., & Van't Hul, S. (2001). Consumer interaction in the virtual era: Some qualitative insights. *Qualitative Market Research: An International Journal, 4*(3), 150-159.

Gaiser, T. J. (1997). Conducting on-line focus group: A methodological discussion. *Social Science Computer Review, 15*(2), 135-144.

Galimberti, C., Ignazi, S., Vercesi, P., & Riva, G. (2001). Communication and cooperation in networked environments: An experimental analysis. *CyberPsychology and Behavior, 4*, 131-146.

Gergen, M. M., & Gergen, K. J. (2000). Qualitative inquiry: Tension and transformation. In N. K. Denzin & Y. S. Lincoln (Eds.), *Handbook of qualitative research* (2nd ed., pp. 1025-1045). Thousand Oaks, CA: Sage.

Graffigna, G., & Bosio, A. C. (2006). The influence of setting on findings produced in qualitative health research: A comparison between face-to-face and online discussion groups about HIV/AIDS. *International Journal of Qualitative Methods, 5*(3), Article 5. Retrieved March 17, 2008, from http://www.ualberta.ca/ijqm/5_3/pdf/graffigna.pdf

Graffigna, G., Bosio, A. C., & Olson, K. (2008). Face-to-face vs. online focus groups in two different countries: Do qualitative data collection strategies work the same way in different cultural contexts? In P. Liamputtong (Ed.), *Doing cross-cultural research: Ethical and methodological perspectives*. Springer.

Greenbaum, T. L. (1997). Internet focus groups: An oxymoron. *Marketing News, 31*(3), 35-36.

Greenbaum, T. L. (1998a). *The handbook for focus group research*. Thousand Oaks: Sage.

Greenbaum, T. L. (1998b). Internet focus groups are not focus groups: So don't call them that. *Quirk's Marketing*. Retrieved March 17, 2008, from http://www.quirks.com/articles/article.asp?arg_ArticleId=355

Haigh, C., & Jones, N. A. (2005). An overview of the ethics of cyber-space research and the implication for nurse educators. *Nurse Education Today, 25*, 3-8.

Henson, A., Koinu-Rybicki, V., Madigan, D., & Muchmore, J. A. (2000). Researching teaching through collaborative inquiry with outside researchers. In A. Cole & J. G. Knowles (Eds.), *Researching teaching: Exploring teacher development through reflexive inquiry* (pp. 186-197). Boston: Allyn & Bacon.

Herring, S. C. (2001). Computer mediated discourse. In D. Tannen, D. Schiffrin, & H. Hamilton (Eds.), *Handbook of discourse analysis* (pp. 612-634). Oxford. UK: Blackwell.

Hertz, R. E. (1997). *Reflexivity and voice*. London: Sage.

Holge-Hazelton, B. (2002). The Internet: A new field for qualitative inquiry. *Forum Qualitative Social Research, 3*. Retrieved March 17, 2008, from http://www.qualitative-research.net/fqs-texte/2-02/02-02holgehazelton-e.pdf

Hutchby, I., & Wooffitt, R. (1998). *Conversational analysis*. Cambridge, UK: Polity.

Im, E., & Chee, W. (2003). Feminist issues in email group discussion. *Advances in Nursing Science, 26*, 287-298.

Im, E., & Chee, W. (2004). Issues in Internet survey research among cancer patients. *Cancer Nursing, 27*(1), 34-44.

James, N., & Busher, H. (2006). Credibility, authenticity and voice: Dilemmas in online interviewing. *Qualitative Research, 6*(3), 403-429.

Kitzinger, J. (1994). The methodology of focus groups: The importance of interaction between research participants. *Sociology of Health and Illness, 16*(1), 103-121.

Lancia, F. (2004). *Strumenti per l'analisi dei testi* [Instruments for text analysis]. Milano, Italy: FrancoAngeli.

Lonkila, M. (1995). Grounded theory as an emerging paradigm for computer-assisted qualitative data analysis. In U. Kelle (Ed.), Computer-aided qualitative data analysis (pp. 41-51). London: Sage.

Mann, C., & Stewart, F. (2000). *Internet communication and qualitative research: A handbook for researching online*. London: Sage.

Miller, T. W., & Walkowski, J. (2004). Qualitative research online. Milton, WI: Research Publisher LLC.

Morse, J. M., & Richards, L. (2001). *Read-me first for a user's guide to qualitative methods*. London: Sage.

O'Sullivan, P. B. (1999). Bridging the mass-interpersonal divide. Synthesis scholarships in HCR. *Human Communication Research, 25*(4), 569-588.

Riva, G., & Galimberti, C. (2001). The mind in the Web: Psychology in the Internet age. *Cyber-Psychology and Behavior, 4*(1), 1-5.

Russell, T., & Bullock, S. (1999). Discovering our professional knowledge as teachers: Critical dialogues about learning from experience. In J. Loughran (Ed.), *Researching methodologies and practices for understanding pedagogy* (pp. 132-151). New York: Falmer.

Schegloff, E. A., & Sacks, H. (1973). Opening up closings. *Semiotica, 7,* 289-327.

Schneider, S. J., Kerwin, J., Frechtling, J., & Vivari, B. A. (2002). Characteristics of the discussion in online and face-to-face focus groups. *Social Science Computer Review, 20*(1), 31-42.

Schwandt, T. A. (2001). *Dictionary of qualitative inquiry* (2nd ed.). London: Sage.

Seymour, W. S. (2001). In the flesh or online? Exploring qualitative research methodologies. *Qualitative Research, 1*(2), 147-168.

Silverman, D. (2000). *Doing qualitative research: A practical guide.* London: Sage.

Sproull, L., & Kiesler, S. (1986). Reducing social context cues: Electronic mail in organizational communication. *Management Science, 32,* 1492-1512.

Steiner, F. (Ed.). (1991). *Research and reflexivity.* London: Sage.

Strickland, O. L., Moloney, M. F., Diethrich, A. S., Myerburg, S., Cotsonis, G. A., & Johnson, R. V. (2003). Measurement issues related to data collection on the World Wide Web. *Advances in Nursing Science, 26*(4), 246-256.

Sweet, C. (2001). Designing and conducting virtual focus group. *Qualitative Market Research: An International Journal, 4*(3), 130-135.

Underhill, C., & Olmstead, M. G. (2003). An experimental comparison of computer mediated and face-to-face focus groups. *Social Science Computer Review, 21*(4), 506-512.

Zinchiak, M. (2001). Online focus group FAQs. *Quirk's Marketing Research Review.* Retrieved March 17, 2008, from http://www.quirks.com/articles/article.asp?arg_articleid=700

KEY TERMS

Content Analysis: Qualitative data analysis strategy that is used to describe main themes and content of a textual transcript.

Conversational Analysis: Qualitative data analysis strategy that is used to describe rhetoric and argumentative strategies, turn taking management and interpersonal negotiation processes in a communicative exchange transcript.

Discourse Analysis: Qualitative data analysis strategy that is used to explain what people do in their discourses, focusing on how the discourse is structured or organized to perform different functions and achieve various effects or consequences.

Face-to-Face Focus Groups: Qualitative research technique consisting of a group interview conducted by a moderator in a face-to-face research setting, usually with 6–8 participants, and focused on a specific research topic.

Health Education: Educational and communicative strategies aimed at promoting, maintaining, or restoring safe practices related to health

Online Focus Group: Qualitative research technique consisting of a group interview conducted by a moderator in an e-environment, focused on a specific research topic.

Online Forum: This is a virtual board where participants can interact without their having to be online at the same time (asynchronous communication), as they write their messages and read others' over periods of time that can vary from 4 days to several months.

Online Chat: Online discussion whose participants access the Internet contemporaneously interacting in real time for around a couple of hours (as in a face-to-face exchange, or synchronous communication).

Online Forum Plus Chat: This is a combination of the online forum and the online chat techniques which produce a more varied and detailed discussion and allow richer data collection.

Theory of Technique: The analysis of how all the tactical choices embedded in (or supporting) findings production strategies influence the results of a research.

Chapter XV
Online Pedagogical Effectiveness in Adult Contexts

Kathryn Dixon
Curtin University of Technology, Australia

Robert Dixon
Curtin University of Technology, Australia

ABSTRACT

A longitudinal study of students in the Training and Development program at Curtin University of Technology has been undertaken in an attempt to develop a framework which describes the dimensions of pedagogical effectiveness in online teaching and learning. The research began in 2004, and data have been collected from the sample group of students in the program from 2004–2007. As a result of analysis and review of the findings, the Online Pedagogical Effectiveness Framework (OPEF) emerged incrementally. The new framework challenges the traditional importance placed on the centrality of teaching skills and the need for student interaction in online teaching and learning, which according to this study, diminished over time. This has ramifications for the interchangeability of the roles of teacher, learner, and instructional designer peers and colleagues.

INTRODUCTION

This chapter reports on a longitudinal research project into online learning practices that has been conducted in an Australian university over the past three years. The sample for the research comprised adult learners who have been enrolled in the Training and Development Program at Curtin University of Technology. Training and Development has been delivered fully online through the use of the learning management system WebCT since the late 1990s and is currently the only fully interactive online program in the Faculty of Education. The average age of the student cohort is 39 years, and they are attracted to participate in part time study as most are in full employment as educators in the public sector, industry, or private enterprise. The skills and knowledge gained through the undergraduate and postgraduate components of the course enable participants to qualify for training positions and to enhance their career prospects in their various workplace contexts.

As part of an overall evaluative approach towards the delivery and content of the Training and Development Program, the researchers decided to focus upon elements of pedagogical effectiveness and, in doing so, searched for available models and frameworks that shed light upon potential good teaching and learning practice in online environments. The study began in 2004 and used as its conceptual framework the Effective Dimensions of Interactive Learning on the Web model (Reeves & Reeves, 1997). The survey which was administered to the sample group (n=42) mapped the dimensions of philosophy, learning theory, goal orientation, task orientation, motivation, teacher role, metacognitive support, collaboration, cultural sensitivity, and flexibility on a five-point Likert scale against 15 principles of pedagogical effectiveness expressed in the Australian report authored by Brennan (2003) and funded by the National Centre for Vocational Education and Research (NCVER). These principles included the need for a learner-centred environment, constructivist approaches to teaching and learning, high quality materials design, teaching and learning strategies that develop cognitive skills, high levels of interactivity between all participants, guaranteed and reliable forms of access to the technology, engagement with online materials and learning experiences that encourage synthesis and analysis. It also incorporated the need to present opportunities for deep learning, consistent levels of feedback, and thoughtful matches between materials, learning

styles, and learning contexts. Furthermore, the report indicated a need for a model of delivery that includes thorough planning, monitoring, reviewing, and evaluating course materials and student progress and a range of navigational choices for students. Finally, it extolled the necessity for teachers who are imaginative, flexible, technologically sound, committed, responsible, and expert communicators.

The sample group contributed to three stages of the research from 2004–2007. At each stage, both quantitative and qualitative data were gathered and analysed through the administration of the instrument that was based upon the emergent Online Pedagogical Effectiveness Framework (OPEF). This new framework developed as a result of combining the work of Reeves and Reeves (1997) and the effectiveness dimensions outlined by Brennan (2003). One of the main objectives of this chapter is to describe the process that began in 2004 which has helped to illuminate various strengths and weaknesses of the online environment which is produced by the Training and Development Program. The research has helped to articulate an enhanced alignment of the units of study to improved pedagogical practice.

Currently, in Australia, the higher education sector is becoming increasingly scrutinised by both federal and state governments in terms of educational content as it relates directly to graduate outcomes. Increasingly, teaching and assessment practices in higher education have come under scrutiny as needing to be improved. Universities in Australia, and indeed in other western countries, such as the United Kingdom, the United States, and Canada, are now operating with reduced government funding (Currie, Thiele, & Harris, 2002). As a result, exploring alternative ways to boost traditional revenue sources has become imperative. International full fee-paying students have become a key source of alternative funding. Australian universities have been successful thus far in enticing overseas students onto their campuses. With university education reported to be the third highest service export industry in Australia, worth in excess of $5 billion, it is not surprising that the 'quality of university teaching and learning' is the subject of much debate in many sectors including government (Tilbrook, 2003). The stakes are indeed high if the tertiary sector is to maintain its market share, especially now that other institutions such as technical and further education (TAFE) are able to compete with universities in offering degrees. The establishment of a national body aimed at encouraging and scrutinising teaching quality in the Australian higher education sector (the Carrick Institute) and the allocation of a significant funding pool aimed at rewarding those institutions that best demonstrate excellence in learning and teaching is evidence that the government is keen to promote engagement with learning and teaching in Australian universities (DEST report, 2004).

Most universities are therefore undergoing structural and curriculum review in order to streamline course offerings and increase productivity and, by doing so, enhance funding opportunities. The study which is described in this chapter has allowed the researchers to interrogate the content and delivery of the Training and Development Program as part of the university review process that is underway and has brought about changes to the learning materials, assessment expectations, instructional design, the use of technology, and the role of both teacher and learner as they engage in the online environment.

A second main objective of this chapter is to focus upon the OPEF and the dimensions which have become more closely aligned to successful online learning over time as well as those that appear to have a diminishing influence on student engagement and learning outcomes. The OPEF was tested with students who were studying in the program in 2004, 2005, and again in early 2007 in order to map changes in attitude towards the materials and approach and patterns of interaction. It is interesting to consider the changing approaches that the students have made to their

study over time as they become more familiar with the online delivery. The research that follows in this chapter reveals a number of findings that seem to contradict the perceived value of various online pedagogical characteristics that are accepted in the literature as being important to learning such as the need for teacher skill and high levels of interactivity. As learners become more sophisticated in their use of online environments, it seems that their dependence on others such as teachers and peers diminishes in favour of direct and timely access to high quality learning systems and instructional materials. It is hoped that the study will provide a clear picture of the changing needs of adult learners in online environments over time. The longitudinal research which is reported upon in this chapter has an advantage over other investigations into online learning environments as it really does begin to search out the changing nature of the relationships which are developed between the adult learners in the sample and the environment in which they operate. As with all relationships, the terrain shifts as time moves on. A process of maturation occurs which enables the participants to interact in developing ways with each other as students, with the instructor responsible for the unit of study and with the materials themselves.

BACKGROUND

Curtin University of Technology in Western Australia has been at the forefront of innovation for flexible, online delivery of its Training and Development Program, with the course having been fully online since the late 1990s. A number of reviews and evaluations of the program have taken place since then, with changes being made in direct line with academic research, which pointed to ways of improving the quality of delivery and therefore student learning. Reeves (1997) rightly criticised a general lack of systematic evaluation of computer-based education (CBE). He indicated that CBE was being fallaciously accepted by education consumers on the basis of innovation alone, that effectiveness of CBE had been reduced to quantitative studies, which missed the complexities of implementation, motivation, and learning. Furthermore, he outlined the lack of utility of evaluations and the paucity of "useful" evaluations. Having posed the problem, he suggested that to make systematic evaluations which compare programs on an equal basis, pedagogical dimensions of CBE could serve as the appropriate conceptual framework, where pedagogical dimensions: "refer to the capabilities of CBE to initiate powerful instructional interactions, monitor student progress, empower effective teachers, accommodate individual differences, or promote co-operative learning" (p. 2). Pedagogy in an online or CBE program, according to Brennan (2003, p. 10):

covers the function, work or art of a teacher or trainer. It includes the process of teaching and instruction. It is useful to think of pedagogy as being reflected in the arrangements made to enable someone to learn something for a specific purpose...influenced by the general orientation of the teacher or trainer, the kind of knowledge to be developed, the nature of the learner and the purpose the learning is to serve.

Heiner, Matthias, Scheckenberg, Dirk, and Johannes (2001) suggested there are three dimensions in the field of online pedagogy: pedagogical principles, pedagogical functions, and pedagogical variables. These form a triangular axis of interactivity. Heiner et al. (2001) argue that the pedagogical principles reflect the shift away from teaching to learning and towards a student centred approach. This has meant that traditional instruction is replaced by the construction of learning environments, where students play an active role in learning and learning strategies, where they are expected to be self-organised, self-directed, and independent learners. Furthermore, there has been

a shift from the acquisition of knowledge towards generic competencies and learning outcomes. Interactivity and cooperative and collaborative learning have become essential. As a result of the global nature of CBE, a dimension of international and intercultural communication has been introduced. Authentic situated learning in the virtual classroom has evolved. Problem-oriented, case-oriented, and enquiry-oriented learning are favoured by the online environment.

A model for the pedagogical dimensions of Web based learning (WBL) postulated by Khan (2004) referred to teaching and learning issues by listing content, goals/objectives, design approach organisation, methods and strategies, medium, and evaluation as key components in virtual learning environments. This model acknowledges similar influences to the cited study (Heiner et al., 2001) in online environments, adding a comprehensive framework including the technological, interface design, online support, and management, resource support, ethical and institutional components in an attempt to understand design issues in flexible and distributed learning systems. However, the effective dimensions of interactive learning (Reeves & Reeves, 1997) with its basis in research, theory of instructional technology, cognitive science, and adult education remains a seminal study and provides the most appropriate model which the authors have chosen as a basis for examining the pedagogical effectiveness of the Training and Development Program. Its strength lies in the "wholeness" of its structure, the open-ended continuum of its dimensions, and the complexity of its capture of the issues relating to online teaching and learning.

THE TRAINING AND DEVELOPMENT PROGRAM

The program from which the sample has been drawn comprises both undergraduate and postgraduate components. The Bachelor of Arts and the Graduate Diploma in Training and Development are offered to educators, university lecturers and industry trainers. The main aim of the program is to improve the teaching skills of participants and other competencies associated with the establishment and management of quality learning environments for students. The participants represent the broader educational community and therefore focus upon adult education. From the total sample of 42 students, 20 were enrolled in the Bachelor of Arts program and 22 were working in the Graduate Diploma. The Bachelor of Arts program comprises 24 units of study. On a full-time basis, the program spreads over three years. The student cohorts are all engaged in the program on a part-time basis as most are in full employment and usually enrol into one or two units per semester. The first year of the program which consists of eight units is awarded to the participants upon enrolment in recognition of their prior learning. Recognition of prior learning (RPL) is a common process in place in Australian universities as higher education recognises the equivalence of workplace expertise and experience, and as a result, the components of experience gained in the workplace can be mapped against the outcomes of units of study. Years two and three of the degree each consist of eight units each. In order to graduate with the award, students must successfully complete 16 units. These units focus on effective teaching and learning strategies, program and curriculum development, and adult learning principles, including educational psychology and teaching practice. The assessment requirements for all units range across individual essays, reports, short answer applications, portfolio work, reflective journals, group work, and presentations. The Bachelor of Arts is considered a basic teaching and training qualification for those who work with adult learners in industry and technical and further education.

The Graduate Diploma in Training and Development builds upon the work completed in the undergraduate program and comprises eight units of study. As this is a higher level program with increasingly complex and more in-depth assessment requirements, students are expected to utilise skills of analysis and synthesis when navigating new materials. The aim is to locate the unit content within the context of each participant's work environment and, by doing so, comply with the principles of adult learning as espoused by Burns (2002). The program seeks to prepare students for not only effective teaching practices but also aims to equip participants with the qualities and skills required by training personnel to manage and lead educational improvement and reform in a number of settings such as public service, business, and industry. Students in this program typically engage in units which focus upon instructional design and development, effective communication skills, technologies for flexible and open learning, professional practice, organisational change, and reflective practice.

Each unit of study is constructed upon desired student outcomes. In other words, each unit needs to be clear with regard to exactly which skills and knowledge the students should be able to demonstrate as a result of having completed each unit in the program. As part of the overall Teaching and Learning Plan, Curtin University has developed a set of nine generic graduate attributes. All Australian universities have similar attributes which are stated overtly in teaching and learning documentation, and academic staff must ensure the student outcomes for their programs reflect these. The graduate attributes are clearly linked to the needs of external organisations such as potential employers and accreditation bodies. All units of study in the Training and Development Program reflect the nine attributes that the university has identified as satisfying the external environment. Table 1 displays the relationship between the overall requirements of the university and those outcomes of the Training and Development Program at both undergraduate and postgraduate level.

Table 1. University and training and development program graduate attributes

Graduate Attribute	A graduate of the Training and Development Program can:
Apply discipline knowledge, principles, and concepts	Recognise, create, and implement sound curriculum practices in their discipline area that include innovative and appropriate assessment processes, which are also current and foundational.
Think critically, creatively, and reflectively	Foster sound educational practices and effective tertiary teaching though leadership, ethical practice, and creative and innovative approaches to maximise the development of student skills and knowledge within the unique characteristics of their discipline.
Access, evaluate, and synthesise information	Research, evaluate, and synthesise scholarly and professional information relevant to tertiary teaching in a creative and professional manner.
Communicate effectively	Communicate effectively with students, as well as with peers and the wider community, by synthesising and evaluating a range of instructional and communication models appropriate to tertiary teaching and be able apply them in both face-to-face and online environments.
Use technologies appropriately	Formulate, prepare, and assemble effective and appropriate creative instructional resources that incorporate leading edge principles of visual learning and using current information and communication technology tools.
Utilise lifelong learning skills	Systematically analyse and evaluate a range of learning interactions to foster feedback and self development as a reflective practitioner and lifelong learner.
Recognise and apply international perspectives	Compare and contrast international approaches to what are considered best practices for tertiary teaching and implement appropriate standards and practices into their own discipline.
Demonstrate cultural awareness and understanding	Appreciate and value the variety and range of cultural backgrounds of tertiary students and provide considered programs and materials which are sensitive to student needs and beliefs
Apply professional skills	Demonstrate a thorough theoretical and practical knowledge of tertiary teaching and adult learning through the application of research and the presentation of this research in a scholarly manner.

MAIN FOCUS OF THE CHAPTER

The main focus of this chapter is to describe the research which has taken place at Curtin University of Technology over the past three years that has had as its major concern the evaluation of the online Training and Development Program in terms of its pedagogical effectiveness. Surveying students in the Bachelor of Arts and the Graduate Diploma in Training and Development (n=42) using Reeves and Reeves (1997) Effective Dimensions of Interactive Learning on the World Wide Web model as its starting point began in 2004.

Stage one of the research had as its first priority an evaluative function with the view to establishing a model for testing which may provide a useful framework to determine possible principles of pedagogical effectiveness in the future. The instrument consisted of the 10 dimensions of Reeves on a continuum using a five-point Likert scale. Item banks were developed for each of the dimensions, and these were designed to reflect the 15 pedagogical principles as outlined by Brennan (2003). It was agreed by the researchers that the pedagogical principles could be aligned with Reeves (1997) dimensions in order to provide a full picture of the relationships between both in the creation and maintenance of effective online learning environments. The sample (n=42) completed the survey in 2004 and also contributed to open-ended items on each of the dimensions. This approach allowed for the collection and analysis of both quantitative and qualitative data and therefore enhanced the depth of the findings. The survey data were analysed using the Statistical Package for Social Science (SPSS) in order to locate and use a descriptive statistical approach, and the open-ended responses were subjected to a content analysis in order to illuminate the emergent themes. Late in the second semester (2005), the same sample (n=42) was again involved in stage two of the research and engaged with the survey which was based upon the Online Pedagogical Effectiveness Framework. The instrument was used again in the first semester of 2007 with the same sample that had engaged in stages one and two of the research. The sample for stage three was only slightly reduced (n=38), as two students had graduated from the program and two had taken leave of absence.

The research is interpretive and focuses on a specific social setting or phenomena, which in this case is the Training and Development Program and the reaction of students in the sample towards the online delivery of learning. As noted by Erickson (1986), by Patton (1990), and by Denzin and Lincoln (2000), within the interpretive approach, there are many methods. However, they all share the same philosophical assumption, which is that reality is constructed by individuals interacting with their social worlds (Merriam, 1998). If an online environment can be considered as representing a social world, it was hoped that by combining Reeves' dimensions and Brennan's indicators into a single instrument and testing it over time with the same student sample, a picture would emerge of the changing nature of engagement with online environments and the importance of characteristics long held by educators to be essential to successful learning.

RESULTS OF THE RESEARCH

The results of stage one (2004) of the application of the survey instrument were encouraging because students placed the Training and Development Program in the area of the dimensions that indicated high level and successful design and planning. According to Reeves' (1997) application of effective dimensions model, the design enabled for the students satisfaction by, for example, facilitative teacher role, open flexibility, intrinsic motivation, and integrated metacognitive support. From an evaluative point of view, the model indicated that the program was primarily viewed as constructivist and in the cognitive domain of learning theory. The program offered a more general goal orientation, but importantly, the tasks offered were considered to be authentic and contextual rather than merely theoretical. Students perceived themselves as mostly intrinsically motivated and their tutors to be facilitative and guiding. The portfolio projects intrinsic to the program facilitated a strong sense of integrated metacognitive support, especially with regard to the reflective practice iterated in the readings and activities. Disappointingly, students rated the degree of cultural sensitivity as neutral. It may be that unit developers and facilitators in the Training and Development Program need to be more aware of and sensitive to the multicultural construction of Australian society in general and the perceptions and backgrounds of students in particular when creating learning materials. Finally, the interactive environment was considered by the sample to be flexible, open, and conducive to independent learning and the time constraints, which are typically important to adult learners.

The 15 pedagogical characteristics postulated by Brennan (2003) were used as the basis for the questionnaire items in the instrument. Students were asked to respond to these items by indicating their level of strong agreement, through to strong disagreement with regard to the Training and Development Program. The mean scores on the five-point Likert scale are summarised in Table 2.

Once again, the figures in Table 2 were encouraging for the program designers, with the notable exception of the level of interactivity between students. Initially, it appeared that the unit designers and facilitators needed to consider ways in which students could be encouraged to interact with each other in the online environment. There may also have been a need for lecturers in the program to increase their online teaching skills in order to encourage improved levels of student engagement in the communication process. The relatively high level of perception that the course was learner centred, constructivist, with a range of appropriate strategies, was satisfying. The sample indicated that the interface was easily navigated, deep learning was taking place, the quality of feedback was excellent, that accordingly materials and learning contexts matched and the quality of

the teachers was perceived as being high. Areas for improvement included a need to enhance the quality of the design of the materials, the range of learning strategies, reliability of access, and the level of engagement with online materials needed to be reconsidered. The sample also indicated that they believed there was a need for greater attention to synthesis and analysis within the structure of the units. Finally, the quality of planning, monitoring, reviewing, and evaluating needed to be improved.

Analysis of the qualitative responses to the survey instrument supported the empirical findings and offered a range of specific suggestions for inclusion in an updated and improved online learning model. As a result of the study, a potential online pedagogical effectiveness framework has emerged (Table 3).

Students in the sample group were surveyed again in the second semester of 2005. The instrument was based upon the OPEF that had emerged

Table 2. Pedagogical dimensions, Stage 2 of the training and development program

Pedagogical Characteristic	Mean	Std. Dev.
Learner centred environment	4.2	0.72
Constructivist approach to teaching/learning	4.0	0.66
Quality of material design	3.8	1.02
Range of appropriate teaching strategies	4.0	0.78
Range of appropriate learning strategies	3.4	0.67
Level of interactivity between students	2.9	0.99
Reliability of access	3.7	0.70
Ease of navigation	4.1	0.81
Level of engagement with online materials	3.9	0.98
Learning experiences that encourage synthesis and analysis	3.9	0.77
Opportunity for deep learning	4.1	0.91
Quality of feedback	4.3	0.75
Match between materials, learning styles, and learning contexts	4.1	0.80
Quality of planning, monitoring, reviewing, evaluating	3.9	0.61
Skill of teachers	4.1	0.84

earlier in 2004. In response to the results of stage one of the research, academics working in the Training and Development Program had developed a series of interventions regarding learning materials and delivery as part of the university's curriculum review process. In this way, the development of the OPEF and the investigation into its effectiveness as a way to chart student interaction with the Training and Development Program has proved to be useful to those academics whose task it was to engage in curriculum review and renewal. The research has provided a clear picture of what appeared to be working and what was problematic

for the learners. Particular attention was paid to quality of planning, monitoring, reviewing, and evaluating components of the program.

The results of stage two provided a number of interesting insights into how adult learners in the program had altered their levels and range of interactions with the online learning environment over a period of two semesters. The overall impressions of the sample towards the learner centred nature of the program held steady along with reactions to the constructivist mode of delivery. The opportunities for deep learning were seen to be available; however, the open-ended

Table 3. Potential online pedagogical effectiveness framework

Reeves Dimension	Concept	Pedagogical Effectiveness Indicator
Philosophy	Instructivist vs. Constructivist	• Learner centred environment • Constructivist approaches to teaching and learning
Learning Theory	Behavioural vs. Cognitive	• Teaching and learning strategies • Thoughtful matches between materials, learning styles, and learning contexts
Goal Orientation	Sharply Focused vs. General	Model of delivery • Planning • Monitoring • Reviewing • Evaluating
Task Orientation	Academic vs. Authentic	• Learning experiences that encourage synthesis and analysis • Opportunities for deep learning
Source Motivation	Extrinsic vs. Intrinsic	• Engagement in online materials
Teacher Role	Fixed vs. Flexible	Teachers who are: • Imaginative • Flexible technologically competent • Committed • Responsible • Expert communicators
Metacognitive Support	Unsupported vs. Integrated	Consistent levels of feedback
Collaborative Learning Strategies	Unsupported vs. Integrated	Levels of interactivity
Cultural Sensitivity	Insensitive vs. Respectful	Thoughtful matches between: • Materials • Learning styles • Learning contexts
Structural Flexibility	Fixed vs. Open	• High quality materials design • Range of navigational choices • Reliable, easy access

responses indicated that as the students became more familiar with the online format, they became far more strategic in their approach and only engaged at certain points throughout the semester as assessment requirements were initiated. The quality of learning materials saw a slight increase as staff had worked to provide increased and more effective links to source research material, and a number of the units had been updated to include more recent readings reflective of the current political and workplace environment. The learning materials were also designed in such a way as to encourage the learners to take on a more active role by selecting to engage only with those objects that were deemed authentic and could therefore be contextualised to their work worlds. In this way, the students were encouraged to become emancipated and more independent, and in doing so, they appeared to take more control over their learning journey through each unit of study. However, the level of interactivity reduced as students became more empowered with the online process. This was a surprising result as the researchers had expected group collaboration and the use of discussion boards and chat rooms to increase over time as students became more adept at navigation.

The open-ended data revealed that students believed once the initial introductory phase concluded where they were asked, for example, to describe their work environments, they believed their time was better spent concentrating on the assessment tasks instead of furthering relationships. It must be remembered that the sample represented adult learners with the average age of 39 years. Early negotiation of the online assessments suggested that these students preferred to work alone. Group work in a collaborative sense was not viewed as being attractive or effective, as 42% of the sample was situated in offshore or interstate settings thus making the alignment of time frames difficult. Of the remaining 48%, a significant number were engaged in shift work and caring for young families and again, this militated against flexible online interaction.

As expected, ease of navigation and reliability of access increased over time as the sample became more familiar with the associated protocols. The level of engagement with the online materials increased slightly, but as with the result for the pedagogical characteristic *opportunity for deep learning,* the open-ended data suggested that students had become used to accessing information quickly and only targeting sites and links that would assist in the development of assessment pieces in a strategic sense. Therefore, the sample engaged less over time as they learned to increase the speed and accuracy of their interaction.

Slight increases in the quality of the learning experiences and the perceived match between learning contexts and materials was expected as the curriculum review carried out in late 2004 and early in 2005 attempted to further place learning and assessment protocols within the reality of the students' worlds in terms of their life and work. The students indicated that the selected unit materials had more relevance to their work environments and that they had encouraged deeper analysis of the relationships between theory and practice in their own contexts. As a result, there was the suggestion that the learning experience had resulted in an ability to add value to their workplace and allowed them to implement enhanced interaction with their own students and colleagues. The quality of feedback remained important for the sample as a number of them worked and studied in extremely isolated geographic regions of Australia, and swift and effective feedback from the university via the online environment was deemed essential for these students to successfully progress through the program.

Perhaps the most interesting result was the sample's reduced need for teacher skill as identified by the framework. The open-ended responses seemed to indicate that with the progression of time and the likelihood that the materials themselves had improved in quality, relevance, and ease of access due to an ongoing cycle of curriculum review, the actual discussions with the academic in the 'teacher' role were perceived to be of lessening importance. The boundaries between 'teacher' and 'learner' had started to blur along with the traditional perceptions of the role played by each. A number of responses indicated that the 'students' saw themselves on an interchangeable footing with the 'teachers' associated with each online unit of study. As adult learners, the participants had come to trust their own skills and knowledge-building capacity and had therefore become far more independent while engaging directly with the learning environment online.

REFINEMENT OF THE ONLINE PEDAGOGICAL EFFECTIVENESS FRAMEWORK

In order to gain comprehensive longitudinal insights into the interaction employed by students in the Training and Development Program with the online environment, the sample was again accessed in semester one of 2007. At the time of the data collection, two members of the original group had taken leave of absence from their study while a further two students had graduated from the Graduate Diploma course. The 2007 sample therefore comprised 38 remaining students (n=38). Accessing the sample over time has allowed the researchers to investigate the changing nature and extent of student online interaction, study management, and navigation in terms of the OPEF as they progress through their course of study. This has provided an interesting view of the overall maturation of the relationship that the sample has developed with their online environment. The change over time may provide us with a picture of what Ulmer (2003) refers to as the 'new millennium learner.' These are the new generation of learners for whom the technology *is* the environment and for whom the process of learning means different things. The OPEF that was used in stage three of the study continued to

Table 4. Pedagogical dimensions, Stage 2 of the training and development program

Pedagogical Characteristic	Mean	Standard Deviation
Learner centred environment	4.3	0.78
Constructivist approach to teaching and learning	4.0	0.77
Quality of material design	3.9	0.92
Range of appropriate teaching strategies	4.0	0.66
Range of appropriate learning strategies	3.7	0.86
Level of interactivity between students	2.3	0.94
Reliability of access	3.9	0.88
Ease of navigation	4.2	0.75
Level of engagement with online materials	4.0	0.84
Learning experiences that encourage synthesis and analysis	4.0	1.02
Opportunity for deep learning	4.0	0.66
Quality of feedback	4.3	0.72
Match between materials, learning styles, and learning contexts	4.2	0.79
Quality of planning, monitoring, reviewing, evaluating	3.9	0.54
Skill of teachers	3.4	1.01

use as its basis the dimensions originally posited by Reeves (1997) in combination with Brennan's (2003) pedagogical effectiveness indicators. The framework was applied to further components of study in the Training and Development Program as the sample progressed through the suite of available units, defined as a period of study comprising a semester in duration and resulting in 25 credit points towards a degree or diploma. The sample (n=38) was asked to respond to items on a Likert scale as per the instrument utilised in stages one and two. They were also encouraged to respond to the open-ended items in order to provide ongoing qualitative data (see Table 5).

Stage three of the research provided a number of interesting findings, not the least of which was the continuing perceived decline of the importance of teacher skill in facilitating a successful online environment. This, coupled with the reduction in the level of interactivity between students, reflected the growing independence of the learners and the increased quality in instructional design.

The results show a decline in the need for teacher skills and peer interaction while indicating that the quality of the material design, the learner-centred environment, and the range of appropriate learning strategies had increased. The open-ended comments suggested that the sample perceived an improvement in learning materials and overall design of each unit of study, and this resulted in a feeling of having more control over their learning activities and 'space.' This is not unusual as Burns (2004) in his research into adult learning approaches has indicated that experiencing a firm locus of control over engagement with learning activities and experiences is crucial for adults who are engaging in both online and traditional learning contexts. Burns' work also suggests that adults bring a substantial context and valuable experience of their own to new learning. This has been acted upon by the instructional designers and the academics working in tandem, in that the content of each unit has been situated within the work context of the Training and Development

Table 5. Pedagogical dimensions, Stage 3 of the training and development program

Pedagogical Characteristic	Mean	Standard Deviation
Learner Centred Environment	4.4	0.61
Constructivist approach to Teaching and Learning	4.0	0.77
Quality of Material design	4.2	0.78
Range of appropriate teaching strategies	4.0	0.62
Range of appropriate learning strategies	4.0	0.61
Level of interactivity between students	2.0	0.89
Reliability of access	4.0	0.80
Ease of navigation	4.3	0.73
Level of engagement with online materials	4.3	0.92
Learning experiences that encourage synthesis and analysis	4.0	0.91
Opportunity for deep learning	4.1	0.73
Quality of feedback	4.3	0.71
Match between materials, learning styles and learning contexts	4.4	0.84
Quality of planning, monitoring, reviewing, evaluating	4.0	0.61
Skill of teachers	2.9	0.92

student cohort. Assessments have been varied, negotiated with the learners, and scaffolded in levels of difficulty to reflect reality, therefore offering the students a more authentic experience. In a number of units, self-assessment tools have been embedded, and these have met with student approval as they align themselves with a constructivist approach, which has at its core the development of fully independent learners who are key players in their own progress. Student comments indicated that their increased levels of interaction with the materials themselves was influenced by their ability to utilise new learning and assessment requirements in the workplace in a practical sense. They had begun to take control of their learning, and rather than talk to fellow online students about their progress, they were more likely to instigate a process of reflective practice with colleagues in their various workplaces. Their comments suggested that they apparently viewed this as more of a 'value-adding' process.

The sample also indicated that their opportunity for deep learning had been further enhanced. The increased use of problem solving and case-oriented learning tasks in all units seemed to impact on the students' engagement with the materials. The comments suggested that there was more of a perceived link between the quality of planning, monitoring, reviewing, and evaluating and deep learning opportunities. In other words, the materials represented a more authentic and therefore worthwhile experience. They were not seen to be merely an 'academic exercise.' Practical components such as reliability of access and ease of navigation had increased, and the open-ended comments suggested that this was due largely to the redesign of a number of units. The increased use of graphic and interactive learning materials, along with links providing easy access to reading and pictorial materials that explained difficult concepts, had resulted in the students feeling that they were not 'wasting time searching around the unit for what to do.' This increased their sense of being strategic in their approach to study; given

that as adult learners there were a multitude of other demands upon their time, not the least of which was full-time employment.

FUTURE TRENDS

Much has been written regarding the importance of interaction and collaborative learning models in both online and face-to-face contexts (Brown & Palincsar, 1989; Guzdial, Hmelo, Hubscher, Newstetter, Puntambeker, Shabo, et al., 1997; Totten, Sills, Digby, & Russ, 1991), and yet the findings, particularly from stages two and three of the research, seem to indicate a significant shift in the conceptualisation of what we understand as crucial elements of pedagogically sound online practice. It may be that Heiner et al. (2001) have been correct in their assumption that learning is the domain of the learner and that there has been a shift from teaching to learning, particularly for adult learners. The actual learning environment may have superseded the importance of collaboration with peers and teacher skill as we strive to provide authentic and situated learning opportunities for our students. As a result of stage two of this research, the Training and Development Program was reviewed and further changes and improvements were made to the overall instructional design of the units of study. Funding was sought and professional designers were employed to work alongside the academics who were teaching in the program to increase the quality of the materials, ease of navigation, and supply of reliable links to subgroup information and extension work. A number of the units have become, in a sense, 'teacher-proofed' with increasing opportunities to interact with online materials in a vivid and very real way while still adhering to the overall graduate attributes insisted upon by the university. There has been an increased use of animations, audio, and video in the majority of units to supplement traditional textual information. The results seem to indicate that while overall instructional design has become more detailed and interactive, the need for interaction with fellow students and teachers has declined.

Given the findings of this research, the question of the ongoing importance of teacher role and student interactivity in online learning environments emerges as a factor to be considered in the development of instructional materials and learning spaces in the future. As educators, we need to ask ourselves the question: what will be the emergent role of 'teachers' in online learning environments? The results of the research described in this chapter seem to indicate that a change in our perceptions of what a teacher actually *does* while engaging with online learners is no longer on the horizon but is upon us. It may be that the models for online pedagogical effectiveness such as those posited by Reeves and Reeves (1997) and Brennan (2003) and indeed others need to be revisited and tested again with cohorts of learners who are engaged in online courses of study to ascertain whether or not these two dimensions are in fact central to successful learning. This chapter therefore challenges the traditional understandings of educational thinking in that learners are dependent upon the ongoing relationships with peers and teachers in order to succeed and experience deep learning. Well-organised learning systems and student-centred instructional design that focuses upon empowerment may well take precedence over these dimensions in a reconceptualisation of the OPEF that has emerged from this study. A refined framework may need to be further developed that does not in fact include *Teacher Role* and *Collaborative Learning Strategies* as dimensions of high importance or at the very least perhaps the effectiveness indicators for both these dimensions need to redefined to reflect the new roles that learners, teachers, and designers are able to create in the new millennium. Sims and Jones (2003) have written extensively about the changing roles of designers, teachers, learners, and technicians in the educational process. They stress that we need to reassess these roles

and their relationships with online contexts. As opposed to face-to-face environments where course design can occur quite independently from actual delivery, teachers and learners can begin to blur their roles in online design and by doing so enhance the overall process. The framework that has emerged clearly requires further testing and refinement as the roles of teachers, learners, peers, and designers are interrogated to assess their interrelatedness and overall impact on learner interaction in a collaborative sense. It could be that our future understandings of the two dimensions *Teacher Role* and *Collaborative Learning Strategies* will be enhanced by combining the two as a single dimension of *Interchangeable Collaborations* where teachers, learners, designers, peers, and colleagues all interact to create optimal environments for learning. It would follow then that *Collaborative Metacognitive Support* such as consistent levels of feedback should also occur between the key players mentioned (see Table 6).

CONCLUSION

The mixed method approach to evaluating a CBE program has yielded some interesting and useful data in the ongoing pursuit of excellence in online delivery in the tertiary sector. Reeves (1997) model established a strong overview of the program within the results on his continuum. Brennan's (2003) suggestions for pedagogical indicators formed key pieces of information as to the perceptions of students undertaking the program in terms of providing valuable feedback for improvement. The combination of these notions, integrated with the data collected from open-ended questions seems to provide a balanced understanding of the needs of students in the current context of online delivery and, in particular, the changing learning approaches and needs of the adult learner engaging with an online environment over time. The Online Pedagogical

Table 6. The online pedagogical effectiveness framework

Dimension	Concept	Effectiveness Indicator
Philosophy	Instructivist vs. Constructivist	• Learner centred environment • Constructivist approaches to teaching and learning
Learning Theory	Behavioural vs. Cognitive	• Teaching and learning strategies • Thoughtful matches between materials, learning styles, and learning contexts
Goal Orientation	Sharply Focused vs. General	Model of delivery • Planning • Monitoring • Reviewing • Evaluating
Task Orientation	Academic vs. Authentic	• Learning experiences that encourage synthesis and analysis • Opportunities for deep learning
Source Motivation	Extrinsic vs. Intrinsic	• Engagement in online materials
Interchangeable Collaborations	Fixed vs. Flexible	Between: • Teachers • Learners • Peers • Designers • Colleagues
Collaborative Metacognitive Support	Unsupported vs. Integrated	Consistent feedback between: • Teachers • Learners • Peers • Designers • Colleagues
Cultural Sensitivity	Insensitive vs. Respectful	Thoughtful matches between: • Materials • Learning styles • Learning contexts
Structural Flexibility	Fixed vs. Open	• High quality materials design • Range of navigational choices • Reliable, easy access

Effectiveness Framework that emerged as a result of the three stages of research conducted in 2004, 2005, and 2007 has incorporated two enhanced dimensions and associated effectiveness indicators that more appropriately reflect the changes to online educational theory as we understand it. Dimensions of *Interchangeable Collaborations* and *Collaborative Metacognitive Support* have been developed as a result of student reactions to the importance of the 'teacher' in online learning habitats and the increasing interchanging roles played by members of an online learning initia-

tive. Supporting the work of Heiner et al. (2001) is the finding that over time the students in the sample became less reliant on teacher skill. This reflects a paradigm shift away from a teaching to a learning discourse facilitated by a student-centred design of materials.

As the students in the sample became more emancipated and empowered in their own learning and as the design of the materials improved in quality, their dependence upon the 'teacher' in the traditional sense clearly diminished. So too did their perceived need to interact with fellow students. High quality online programs which have at their core situated and authentic learning opportunities may well be creating a new generation of learners who are becoming truly independent and proactive. This indicates a shift in educational thinking where teachers and designers must accept that the learner is empowered to be in control of their learning, and as such, he/she is able to use personal preferences to contextualise experience. It may also be that online learning 'worlds' are emerging in their own right. They are no longer likely to be pale imitations of the traditional face-to-face classrooms we have been accustomed to. According to Sims (2006), independence from specific times and places is a major characteristic of the new generation of learners. This is likely to impact upon the way education is provided and also upon the interchangeable roles played by the key protagonists.

We now need to consider new models and frameworks that integrate the pedagogies of online, learner-centred environments. In some instances, we may need to unlearn tried and tested pedagogical beliefs, as these are only useful in a predictable and regular social world (McWilliam, 2005). These new models will need to redefine the roles of key participants such as teachers, learners, designers, peers, and colleagues as they collaborate in the overall learning journey. Using the refined OPEF, future research efforts will refocus on the dimensions of collaborative interchangeable roles and collaborative metacognitive support rather than the more simplistic notion of 'teacher skill' and feedback per se. The online environment is far more complex, and as such, it presents us with an opportunity to actualise its transformative potential in education in the 21ˢᵗ century.

REFERENCES

Ally, M. (2004). Foundations of educational theory for online learning. In T. Anderson & F. Elloumi (Eds.), *Theory and practice of online learning*. Athabasca, Canada: Athabasca University Press

Brennan, R. (2003). *One size doesn't fit all: Pedagogy in the online environment* (Vol. 1). Adelaide, South Australia: NCVER.

Brown, A., & Palincsar, A. (1989). Guided cooperative learning and individual knowledge acquisition. In L. Resnick (Ed), *Knowledge, learning and instruction* (pp. 307-336). Lawrence Erlbaum Associates.

Burns, R. (2002). *The adult learner at work* (2nd ed.). Allen & Unwin.

Burns, R. (2004). *The adult learner at work* (3rd ed.). Sydney, NSW: Allen and Unwin.

Currie, J., Thiele, B., & Harris, P. (2002). *Gendered universities in globalized economies*. Lexington Books.

Denzin, N., & Lincoln, Y. (1994). *Handbook of qualitative research*. Sage.

DEST. (2004). *Learning and teaching performance fund*. Australian Department of Education, Science and Training.

Erickson, F. (1986). Qualitative methods in research on teaching. In M. C. Whitrock (Ed.), *Handbook of research on teaching* (3rd ed., pp. 119-160). New York: Macmillan.

Guzdial, M., Hmelo, C., Hubscher, R., Newstetter, W., Puntambeker, S., Shabo, A., Turro, J., & Kolodner, J. (1997). Integrating and guiding collaboration: Lessons learned in computer supported collaboration learning research at Georgia Tech. In *Proceedings of Computer Support for Collaborative Learning* (CSCL '97), Toronto, Ontario (pp. 91-100).

Heiner, Matthias, Scheckenberg, Dirk, & Johannes. (2001). *Online pedagogy-innovative teaching and learning strategies in ICT environ-*

ments. Background paper of the CEVU Workshop Online Pedagogy.

Khan, B. H. (2004). The people-process-product continuum. *Educational Technology, 44*, 33-40.

McWilliam, E. (2005). Unlearning pedagogy. *Journal of Learning Design, 1*(1), 1-11. Retrieved March 17, 2008, from http://www.jld.qut.edu.au

Merriam, S. B. (1998). *Qualitative research and case study applications in education*. San Francisco: Joey-Bass.

Patton, M. (1990). *Qualitative evaluation methods* (2ⁿᵈ ed.). Sage.

Reeves, T. C. (1997). *Evaluating what really matters in computer-based education*. Education. Au. Retrieved March 17, 2008, from the World Wide Web http://www.educationau.edu.au/archives/CP reeves.htm

Reeves, T. C., & Reeves, P. M. (1997). Effective dimensions of interactive learning on the World Wide Web. In B. H. Khan (Ed.), *Web based instruction* (pp. 59-66). Educational Technology Publications.

Schlack, M. (2007). Tech Target CIO. Retrieved March 17, 2008, from http://searchcio.techtarget.com/sDefinition/0,,sid19_gci798202,00.html

Sims, R. (2006). Beyond instructional design: Making learning design a reality. *Journal of Learning Design, 1*(2), 1-7. Retrieved March 17, 2008, from http://www.jld.qut.edu.au

Sims, R., & Jones, D. (2003). Where practice informs theory: Reshaping instructional design for academic communities of practice in online teaching and learning. *Information Technology, Education and Society, 4*(1), 3-20.

Tilbrook, C. (2003). *International education: Perspectives and graduate outcomes*. The Graduates Careers Council of Australia.

Totten, S., Sills, T., Digby, A., & Russ, P. (1991). *Cooperative learning: A guide to research*. New York: Garland.

Ulmer, G. L. (2003). *Internet invention: From literacy to electracy*. New York: Longman.

KEY TERMS

Online Learning: The use of the Internet to access learning materials; to interact with the content, instructor, and other learners; and to obtain support during the learning process, in order to acquire knowledge, to construct personal meaning, and to grow from the learning experience (Ally, 2004).

Learning Management System: A learning management system (LMS) is a software application or Web-based technology used to plan, implement, and assess a specific learning process. Typically, a learning management system provides an instructor with a way to create and deliver content, monitor student participation, and assess student performance. A learning management system may also provide students with the ability to use interactive features such as threaded discussions, video conferencing, and discussion forums. (Schlack, 2007)

Training and Development Program: The program is delivered at tertiary level and comprises undergraduate and graduate components. Students are able to enroll into either the Bachelor of Arts, Graduate Certificate, and/or Graduate Diploma in Training and Development. The BA consists of 24 units of study, 8 of which are awarded in recognition of prior learning. The Graduate Certificate and the Graduate Diploma consist of four and eight units of study, respectively. The program is delivered in a fully online mode and the course content emphasizes the development of professional knowledge and skills through the practical application of theory to teaching and instruction. The program attracts educators from the broader community who are engaged in working with adult learners, and these students come from technical education, industry, and business as well as the government sector.

Unit of Study: A unit of study at Curtin University of Technology is usually considered as a 12-week program over the duration of a semester. Students are expected to contribute at least four hours a week to reading and research per unit in order to successfully complete the requirements of each unit.

Adult Learners: Adult learners are people who bring a great deal of experience to the learning environment. They expect to have a high degree of influence on what they are to be educated for, and how they are to be educated. They are active learners and participants who need to be able to see the application of new learning. Adult learners expect to have a high degree of influence on how their learning is evaluated, and they expect

responses to be acted upon when requesting feedback.

Pedagogical Characteristics: The importance of interactivity in the learning process, the changing role of the teacher from sage to guide, the need for knowledge management skills and for team working abilities, and the move towards resource-based rather than packaged learning.

Effective Pedagogical Dimensions: "'Pedagogy' covers the function, work, or art of a teacher or trainer. It includes the process of teaching and instruction. It is useful to think of pedagogy as being reflected in the arrangements made to enable someone to learn something for a specific purpose. These arrangements are influenced by: the general orientation of the teacher or trainer; the kind of knowledge to be developed; the nature of the learner; the purpose the learning is to serve" (Brennan, 2003). Effective pedagogical dimensions are those assessable characteristics or dimensions of pedagogy which illustrate effective learning outcomes.

Chapter XVI
Reflective E–Learning Pedagogy

Leah Herner-Patnode
Ohio State University, Lima, USA

Hea-Jin Lee
Ohio State University, Lima, USA

Eun-ok Baek
California State University, San Bernadino, USA

ABSTRACT

The number of learning opportunities that are technology mediated (e-learning) is increasing as institutions of higher learning discover the value of technology in reaching larger numbers of students. The challenge for those instructors who implement such technology in higher education is to correctly apply pedagogy that has been successful in student learning to these new delivery methods. In some cases, new pedagogy is being created. For successful facilitation of knowledge to take place, instructors must make students partners in the process, help them learn to reflect about their activities, and focus on course outcomes rather than the technology itself. We will share key e-learning pedagogy from different areas of specialty (mathematics education, special education, and instructional technology) in higher education.

INTRODUCTION

Dewey (1933, p. 35) says: "While we cannot learn or be taught to think, we do have to learn how to think well, especially how to acquire the general habit of reflecting." Institutions of higher education are realizing the value of the tech-mediated approach (e-learning) as a way to engage learners at a distance as well as enhance courses that meet with the instructor in the traditional setting (Edwards, 2005). While technology has made this a viable teaching alternative, the instructor has to make a concentrated effort not to let the technology overwhelm the teaching objectives of the course. Instructors must engage the learners as collaborators in the process. New e-learning pedagogy includes discussions of what to do if technology fails and how to address students' concerns about isolation from other learners. This means constructing a new way of thinking and reflecting on their own instruction, while maintaining the traditional emphasis on course objectives.

When examining e-learning through the lens of constructivism, it is important to understand the motivation of those involved, both the instructor and the students (Vygotsky, 1987). When students are asked to engage in problem solving that is relevant to their culture, true learning is constructed (Santmire, Giraud, & Grosskopf, 1999). Students in teacher education programs must examine their own culture and learn to reflect on their knowledge, skills, and dispositions. The instructor may use this reflection as a way to evaluate growth both in terms of the e-learning environment and the course content. In this chapter, we will discuss (1) roles of the instructor and the student in e-learning, (2) key pedagogical approaches to increasing students' ownership in e-learning, and (3) reflection as a means of evaluating a student's growth in e-learning.

BACKGROUND

Learning from a distance is not new. For well over 100 years, universities have offered alternatives to visiting the main campus for classes. The first of these, in the United States, was offered by Pennsylvania State University in the form of correspondence by mail courses in 1892 (Shearer, 2004). There is always a demand for access to university classes close to home. Many institutions offer distance as well as face to face instruction. In 2000–2001, 90% of public 2-year and 89% of public 4-year institutions offered distance education courses (National Center for Education Statistics, 2003). A technology-mediated (e-learning) course

is one that may incorporate a variety of technology-based educational strategies: synchronous and asynchronous collaborative communication, project/activity-based learning, and Web-based interaction and feedback (Edwards, 2005). It may take place in a wholly online environment or in a combination of online and face-to-face interactions. Technology has made e-learning an attractive option, but technology does not insure successful implementation of coursework (McVay, Snyder, & Graetz, 2005).

According to Russell (1999), there are over 200 studies on technology for distance education that report no significant difference in student learning when technology, instead of traditional classroom approaches, are used to deliver course instruction. This research shows that students achieve similar outcomes despite different uses of media. So the value of technology-mediated learning needs to lie in convenience to the students, not in trying to boost their achievement over peers receiving typical instruction.

E-learning is essentially different from traditional education in that it requires changes in pedagogical approaches (Miller & King, 2003; Moore & Kearsley, 1996). One of the most frequently pointed out concerns about e-learning is the sense of isolation and lack of human contact among its users (Baek & Barab, 2005; Baek & Schwen, 2006; Hara & Kling, 2000). When students do not fully interact with the instructor and other classmates, they do not have ample opportunity to learn content. Interaction among the class community members is vital to the success of e-learning (Moore & Kearsley, 1996; Palloff & Pratt, 2001).

A great deal of research supports constructivist and student-centered pedagogical approaches (Anderson, 2004; Baek & Barab, 2005; Baek & Schwen, 2006; Bonk, Kim, & Zeng, 2006; Carr-Chellman, Dyer, & Breman, 2000; Miller & King, 2003) as ways of increasing students' ownership and responsibility, which contribute to the improved quality of learning. One of the methods that has been successful in e-learning courses is a collaborative learning community approach (Islas, 2004; Palloff & Pratt, 2001). Specific pedagogical approaches to implement the community approach include making students partners in the learning process and helping them to engage in collaborative inquiry and to learn to reflect about their activities (Baek & Barab, 2005; Baek & Schwen, 2006; Duffy & Kirkley, 2004; Palloff & Pratt, 2001).

If instructors are expected to provide students with a learning environment that engages students in real world problem solving using their own experiences and working with others, instructors also need to experience a similar opportunity, in which they can actively search for meaning in content and apply personal experiences (Knox, 1986). Having ownership of their learning, instructors will be more likely to reflect critically on their own teaching practices and may then generate new knowledge and attitudes toward teaching and learning. Teacher education programs and practices are becoming focused on the need to help teachers become more reflective about their teaching. Reflection helps us examine questions and explore our underlying assumptions, values, and beliefs while it moves us into more uncomfortable zones to inform our practice (Al-Mahmood & McLoughlin, 2004; Brookfield, 1995). Therefore, reflection can not only help students understand underlying principles of practice (Dewey, 1933), but also assist instructors to measure students' growth.

Instructors must examine how their roles will change in the e-learning environment. They can do this by exploring new ways to approach course instruction using technology and by researching the approaches that increase student learning within this environment. The final step in the process is to evaluate the effectiveness of the course by looking at students' growth. Traditional methods of assessment can be supplemented by the instructor's and students' reflection about their growth as professionals and in the classroom.

DIVISION OF ROLES IN E-LEARNING

The techniques for working in an e-learning environment are often different from traditional face-to-face course preparation. The focus for the instructor needs to be on the overall course outcomes and objectives rather than technology issues (Bannan & Milheim, 1997; Rieber, 1993; Su, 2005). In a traditional format, the instructor assigns individual and group activities, welcomes some further communication during office hours, and receives the completed assignment in person on the assigned date. When the instructor introduces technology into the course and eliminates some or all of the face-to-face interaction, then numerous other opportunities for dialogue and feedback must be present (Su, 2005). This communication can take many forms and the knowledgeable instructor evaluates and changes her methods of communication depending on the type of course, the type of student, and the type of technology that works best for each class.

COMMUNICATING WITH THE STUDENTS

The instructor in the e-learning environment must be committed to engaging students in communicating about the course content (Su, 2005). These interactions can take a variety of forms. The instructor may be seen by the students via video conference. Verbal communication can take place between students at multiple sites. The instructor may also hold online office hours in a chat room or require chat room participation at certain times during the week. The instructor may also verbally communicate via phone. All of these are examples of real time synchronous communication, requiring everyone involved to participate at the same time. Asynchronous communication is more common in e-learning. The instructor will post assignments, questions, and announcements.

Students will respond whenever they access the computer. The instructor does need to be aware that the asynchronous nature of most online learning can create anxiety among the students because no instructor is present (Sherry, Cronje, Rauscher, & Obermeyer, 2005). This anxiety can be mitigated by a clear and organized syllabus. The instructor must also respond frequently to communications from students, and above all, the instructor must model the type of information that is expected for satisfactory information exchange (Seaton, Einon, Kear, & Williams, 2004).

When implementing an e-learning course, it is important to have a plan before the instructor starts the course, as well as contingency plans in case technology fails. Videoconferencing allows students at numerous locations to have access to the course in real time. It is helpful to have a facilitator present at each location that receives the broadcast. This person can help the instructor plan before the course starts. A facilitator can also help the instructor design the room layout and discuss the best utilization of the available equipment. The facilitator can also plan for breaks in the transmission and troubleshoot if connections fail. If no facilitator is present at the locations receiving the broadcast, then students should have a detailed class summary to follow in the event transmission is lost and they have to resort to alternative activities with their time.

ORGANIZATION AND FACILITATOR ASSISTANCE

Research from a distance learning class illustrates the need for constant communication between participating sites. Two regional campuses that are part of a large midwestern university in the United States needed a course on working with students with special needs. The administrators at both sites agreed that having the course at the same time and conducted by one instructor would be efficient and cost effective. The study sought to compare the distance learning experiences of two groups of undergraduate education students. The data was collected at the end of the course using student evaluations. The first time this course was taught, a facilitator was present at both campuses. The instructor presented one week at one campus and the next week at the other campus. The alternative campus received the course via video conference. Twice during the 10-week quarter, the connection failed. The first time it was reconnected fairly quickly, but the second time the whole class time was lost. The instructor could communicate with the class in front of her, but the facilitator at the other campus did not know what to tell the other class. He was concerned with trying to fix the connection, so he did not answer the phone when the instructor called with an alternative assignment. The second time this course was held as a distance learning course, everyone involved was more prepared. The facilitators agreed to answer the phone quickly when a connection failed, and the instructor agreed to have an agenda with alternative assignments available for each class period. The students were e-mailed the agenda prior to class each week. When the connection did briefly fail, everyone was prepared, and the students felt that the class time was not wasted. The fact that both sites had a facilitator that worked to fix the technology problems immediately also created an atmosphere of cooperation and the feeling that the students' time was valued.

The results of the student evaluations support having a facilitator who was available at both sites and a more organized approach to foreseeing and solving technology issues (see Table 1). The student evaluations were not as concerned with technology and were not as negative for the second class. The use of a knowledgeable technology facilitator was an important factor in the second course, which was perceived as more successful by the participating students. If the course is held online, the instructor can still use the support of a technology facilitator. This

Table 1. Comments related to technology in the distance learning course (©2007, Leah Herner-Patnode. Used with permission)

Quarter	Theme	Comments
Spring 2005	What aspects of the teaching or content of this course do you feel were especially good?	What changes could be made to improve the teaching or content to meet the objectives of this course?
	Notes WebCT were <u>great</u>. (2)	I really didn't like the TV-Web thing across campuses because I felt like I was distracted more and struggled with understanding the content when Dr. H was at Marion.
	WebCT was great	The technological issues were quite distracting. I think our class was the right type for good distance learning.
	Being able to reach you through email	Have two separate courses instead of sharing the same class time with another class through video conference. (2)
	Having Midterm online	We do not have the technology to facilitate class over a feed like this.
		Don't do online course. It's very distracting to the one that doesn't have the professor there. (2)
		The distance learning is a huge pain. I also never really understood what all the assignments entailed. The field word was a lot to be expected also.
		Do not do it over the Web. There were too many problems trying to get connected to Marion. (4)
		I didn't really like the distance learning. (2)
		No technology. It was horrible and distracting. (2)
		Can't think of anything but it was weird having a distance learning class.
Spring 06	Course very organized. Outstanding encouragement of student participation. (3)	Format of class made it difficult to feel engaged or interested in material.
	Liked open discussion forum and testing format.	Pretty boring, going over on-line notes not necessary.

form of technology support can be utilized for preplanning the course and deciding what aspects of available online tools will best meet the instructor's objectives. The instructor may need extra training in the use of discussion boards or chat rooms. They will also need to understand the procedures students need to follow to upload assignments. It is beneficial for the instructor to have the ability to troubleshoot some common technical issues. For example, when students upload to a Web-based course, created in a format like WebCT© or Desire2Learn©, the document will appear to upload, but if any extra characters (*, ', #) appear in the document name, it will not always successfully upload, which results in the instructor not being able to grade the document in a timely manner. The facilitator can help the instructor learn solutions for these common issues and be available as tech support when students run into more complex problems. This results in the students feeling supported throughout the course and allows them to focus more on content than the actual technology (Sherry et al., 2005).

AWARENESS OF STUDENT NEEDS

The instructor must be aware of the areas of need demonstrated by each group of students. It is beneficial to discuss the technology expectations along with course objectives (Chickering & Erhmann, 1996). One example of using Web-based course tools would be to have the syllabus state that all work is required to be posted in the Web-based course dropbox using Microsoft Word. The upload is required by the start of class on the day the assignment is due, and students are responsible for checking to make sure their work is successfully loaded. The syllabus also states that students are required to check for updates posted in the announcement section and access their student e-mail. By making these requirements a part of the official syllabus, students will view them as a natural part of the course expectations.

TECHNICAL SUPPORT

The ability to access technical support is important. Students who are new to technology may have an increased need for extra instruction. This can be accomplished by open hours in computer labs operated by course facilitators, or general university tech support, by utilizing peers, or by making appointments for face-to-face assistance with the instructor. Once the students feel confident with the technology, the student can focus on the course content. When students are frustrated about technology, they tend to persevere on that issue, and it distracts them from the course objec-

tives. Some student evaluation comments from the first time the distance learning class was taught illustrate this point. When students were asked to list changes that could be made to improve the teaching or content to meet the objectives of the course, there were a number of students who could only focus on the technology (see Table 1). Of the 44 comments from students for this quarter, 22 referred to the technology aspect of the course vs. the course content. Compare this with the Spring 2006 comments when out of 40 comments, only 6 related to the technology and 4 of the 6 were positive. When the technology issues were addressed more effectively, both in terms of planning and student support, the final course evaluations showed improvement in the rating of the instructor. The course content did not change from Spring 2005 to Spring 2006, but the final evaluations were an average of 4.2 on a 5-point scale in all categories for Spring 2006 vs. 3.7 for the previous course when the students felt more uneasy about technology. If the instructor, with the help of technical support, wants students to focus on course content, then she has to create a comfort level with technology that helps them see technology as a tool that enhances, rather than hinders, the overall course presentation. Once the instructor defines her role and the role of her students, it is important to increase the students' ownership of the course content.

PEDAGOGICAL APPROACHES AND LEARNERS' OWNERSHIP

Increasing students' ownership and responsibility will lead to quality work. A vital way in which to increase learners' ownership and responsibility is the collaborative learning community approach (Baek & Barab, 2005; Baek & Schwen, 2006; Islas, 2004; Palloff & Pratt, 2001). Most salient pedagogical approaches include making students partners in the learning process, helping them to engage in collaborative inquiry and to learn to reflect about their activities (Duffy & Kirkley, 2004; Palloff & Pratt, 2001). Let us discuss these approaches in detail with examples.

Students as Partners

In the process of inviting students as partners, it is important to consider a new power relationship and dynamics between the instructor and the students and to keep a balance between preplanned teaching activities and emergent learning activities. Even though macrolevel activities can be designed by the instructor, their realization in reality is uncertain. The instructor needs to be flexible enough to allow emergent learning agendas, which give students opportunities to negotiate meaning anew. Learning can take forms quite contrary to what the instructor intended (Baek & Barab, 2005). This implies that planned procedures and structural elements should be intertwined with students' emergent activities and needs in the design. The main considerations are providing minimal structures and allowing for opportunities in which students can contribute in defining their own learning activities. When the instructor works with adult learners such as teachers, the instructor needs to link class activities to students' interests by asking and capitalizing on learner-generated issues (Duffy & Kirkley, 2004). The structure and activities need to be flexible enough to create a learning environment that involves facilitating an intellectual curiosity utilizing students' own experiences. For example, main discussion topics and venues can be planned in advance, but this should be kept minimal, so that the culture of the class community can be filled by the day-to-day professional experiences of the students.

Collaborative Inquiry-Based Learning

Inquiry-based learning is an instructional approach that emphasizes students' active quest for meaning. It is a way of exploring the world through the process of asking questions, investigating, and making decisions to solve problems. Inquiry-based learning may take many different forms. First, as a pedagogical term, it includes various instructional models and approaches to facilitate higher-order thinking skills, using inquiry as a main conduit. Second, as a more generic term, it involves critical reflections on the learning processes on the part of learners themselves (Baek & Barab, 2005). Inquiry-based learning is established when learners take the lead in the learning process, thereby enhancing meaningful learning (Brown & Campione, 1994; Cognition & Tech. Group at Vanderbilt 1997; Collins, Brown, & Holum, 1991; Van Zee, Hammer, Bell, Roy, & Peter, 2005). Inquiry activities increase students' engagement and understanding and also teach the scientific process (Polacek 2005).

Inquiry usually takes the form of processes. Dennen (2005) suggests that different stages of discussion—initiation, facilitation, conclusion, and feedback—can be utilized in the process of inquiry. Lim (2004, p. 633) introduces the elements of the inquiry process (Figure 1): ask, plan, explore, construct, and reflect. These elements interact with share activities via discussion and collaboration. The inquiry process can be implemented by individual students or in a collaborative team and is more recursive and circular than linear as it evolves.

- **Ask:** This element presents a real-world, authentic situation, scenario, or case in which students can relate their experiences to topics in instruction. Depending on the level of the students, the level of difficulty and terminology in the scenario will be varied.

- **Plan:** This element helps students to develop investigation strategies to find information in order to answer the generated questions. In a team project, the tasks and roles need to be defined as a part of the plan.

Figure 1. Display of inquiry-based learning (©2007, Leah Herner-Patnode. Used with permission)

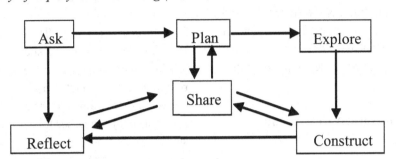

- **Explore:** The students engage in the process of investigating the problem by collecting relevant information. The process of exploration will include the use of various resources such as geographic information systems (GIS), Probeware, forensic, and educational games.
- **Construct:** The students analyze what they have found, and synthesize and build their own knowledge relative to the original question, based on the information obtained during the 'exploration.' Incorporating the concept of learning-by-design, learners will construct their knowledge via projects using podcast, wiki, and blogs.
- **Reflect:** The students have opportunities to reflect on their conclusion as well as on the entire inquiry learning process. Students' understanding on the topic/problem will be assessed.

The instructor needs to help students to create their own meaning while engaging in the collaborative learning process. Students need to be actively involved in social enterprise as members of the learning community and to have opportunities to produce objects that show their understanding from the collaborative inquiry (Wenger, 1998). In order to successfully facilitate collaborative inquiry, the instructor needs to provide a supporting structure that effectively supports the learning process, sustains student engagement, and helps students maintain focus on the performance objectives (Duffy & Kirkley, 2004).

In order to facilitate collaborative team inquiry, a number of team members will be evenly distributed among the weeks. It is important to emphasize that the main purpose of the collaborative inquiry is not to simply reduce the amount of work each individual needs to do, but to create synergy which can be difficult to achieve when working alone. Each week, for example, one of the teams serves as "hosts" of the online community; the team's responsibility is to foster communication in the online community and to facilitate students' learning. In order to foster online dialogues, the team shares the roles of initiator, supporter, and wrapper.

During the collaborative inquiry process, the instructor needs to scaffold the collaborative critical thinking to encourage challenging perspectives, and to provide a supporting environment (Duffy & Kirkley, 2004). In the inquiry process, the instructor needs to encourage students' individual and collective reflection/feedback on their participation and learning. Specific instructions and examples on good/active/responsible participation and non-examples are useful. Providing opportunities to reflect and evaluate their learning will help them increase ownership in their learning. It is useful to create rubrics for students to evaluate their own participation and learning/outcomes as well as other teams' learning/outcomes. Later, students need to explain and defend the results of their inquiry. If the instructor invites students' voices in the development of the rubrics, it will help students develop ownership in their learning.

Student Participation in Course Improvement

Along the same vein with the mentioned approaches, it is important to have students participate in course improvement. The instructor needs to structure frequent discussions about what is working with the course and what can be improved. A specific forum such as the name of a *Café, our learning community*, or *our voice*, can be dedicated to the discussion in which learners freely post their experience about the course. When the majority of community members want to modify the direction of a certain activity to better support learning, it needs to be seriously considered and possibly incorporated into the course design within the extent to which it does not cause confusion. In the next section, we will discuss a way of assessing students' learning in e-learning.

REFLECTION AS A MEANS OF EVALUATING A STUDENT'S GROWTH

"Reflection leads to self knowledge and this is fundamental to the development of our professional practice," say Kuit, Reay, and Freeman (2001, p. 139). This chapter views reflection as a means of learning and a tool for assessment. In order to understand why and how reflection demonstrates a student's learning, this section focuses on several different emphases in the study of reflection and ways of assessing reflection.

Emphases in the Study of Reflection

Reflection as process. "[Reflection] is what a teacher does when he or she looks back at the teaching and learning that has occurred, and reconstructs, reenacts, and/or recaptures the events, the emotions, and the accomplishments. It is that set of processes through which a professional learns from experience" (Shulman, 1987, p. 19). This view focuses on reflection as a reactive process, which is part of learning through teaching. Reflection as a process should be seen as a spiral procedure (Hannary, 1994; Lee, 2000), which produces informative useful knowledge for our future decisions and action (Killion & Todnen, 1991).

Reflection in practice. When teaching, instructors frequently encounter an unexpected student reaction and attempt to adjust instruction to take into account such a reaction. According to Schön (1983, 1987), reflection can be seen in two time frames: reflection-on-action, which can occur before and after an action, and reflection-in-action, which can occur during the action. Both reflection-in and reflection-on-action help reflective practitioners to develop and learn from their experience. This view supports "integration of experience with reflection and of theory with practice" (Osterman, 1990, p. 135).

Reflection in context. Schön's (1983, 1987) portrayal of reflection has been criticized, because it does not explicitly include any social processes within a learning community. The critics claim that although reflection can be individualized, it can also be enhanced by communication and dialogue with others. Therefore, instructors and students should be encouraged to consider their own practice as well as the social conditions of their practice. This idea of reflection has led to work on the issue of social practice (Solomon, 1987), which includes consideration of ethical, moral, and political principles (Colton & Sparks-Langer, 1993; Kemmis, 1987; LaBoskey, 1993; Valli, 1992; Zeichner & Liston, 1996).

Reflection in e-learning. When reflecting during the e-learning process, the focus will be on teaching and learning practices in a clearly different way and under new environmental conditions. The main difference between reflection in the e-learning environment and reflection in the general education setting is the communication mode. In the traditional setting, students reflect verbally or in writing (Lee, 2000), whereas students in the e-learning setting reflect through the written communication mode, when they are in discussion boards and chat rooms. It is clearly a new way of talking to one another. These new forms of communication and new environments for learning by using Internet technologies have the potential of collaborative reflection (Bain, 2000; Churchill, 2005).

Reflection to Measure a Student's Growth

Reflection is now seen as a general professional skill. Teacher educators and curriculum developers have been endeavoring to develop systematic criteria to assess one's reflection, as do e-learning instructors. As mentioned earlier, e-learning requires changes in pedagogical approaches (Miller & King, 2003; Moore & Kearsley, 1996) and new methods to assess student learning and performance. This section introduces reflection as an assessment tool to measure student beliefs, knowledge, and disposition. The following areas are ways to measure a student's growth by evaluating the reflection taking place in the e-learning setting.

Content of reflection. Different issues are considered by different individuals while they have experiences in the same context (Goodman, 1994; Lee, 2005; Sparks-Langer, Colton, Pasch, & Starko, 1991; Taggart, 1996; Van Manen, 1977; Valli, 1992; Zeichner & Liston, 1996). Since each individual screens a given situation using his/her own filter, there are differences in the content of reflective thinking by individuals. Reviewing con-tent of reflection provides the information about which issues should be addressed and discussed in preservice teacher education and professional development programs.

Attitudes of the reflector. Dewey (1933) claims that the necessary attitudes for reflection are open-mindedness, responsibility, and wholeheartedness. An individual who is open-minded does not attempt to hold the banner for one, and only one perspective, and does not look to other perspectives with argumentative delight (LaBoskey, 1994; Van Manen, 1991). An attitude of responsibility involves careful consideration of the consequences to which an action leads. Responsible teachers ask themselves why they are doing what they are doing and consider the ways in which it is working, why it is working, and for whom it is working (LaBoskey, 1994). Wholehearted teachers regularly examine their own assumptions and beliefs and the results of their actions and approach all situations with the attitude that they can learn something new. According to Goodman (1991), wholeheartedness enables preservice teachers to work through their fears of making mistakes, being criticized, disrupting traditions, and making changes. Thus, it provides a basis for action and growth.

Depth of reflective thinking. Lee (2005) proposed three levels of reflective thinking: recall (R1), rationalization (R2), and reflectivity (R3). R1 and R2 are considered reactive, and R3 is regarded as proactive. At the R1 level, one describes what he experienced, interprets the situation based on recalling experiences without looking for alternative explanations, and attempts to imitate ways that he has observed or was taught. At the R2 level, one is looking for relationships between pieces of experiences, interpreting the situation with rationale, searching for "why it was," and generalizing her experiences or introducing guiding principles. At the R3 level, one approaches his experiences with the intention of changing/improving in the future, analyzes his experiences from various perspectives, and is able to see the influence of his experiences/actions in other situations.

Attributes of reflective practitioners. In e-learning, students sometimes do not have opportunities to demonstrate their growth in practice, due to the lack of interaction with the instructor and other classmates. However, it is still essential to discuss best practices, such as the characteristics of an effective teacher and effective instructional approaches, through a discussion board or reflective statements. The differences between reflective teaching and teaching that is not reflective are discussed by many teacher educators (Gipe, Richards, Levitov, & Speaker, 1991; Pollard & Tann, 1994; Taggart, 1996; Zeichner & Liston, 1996). Table 2 compares the differences between technicians and reflective practitioners in approaching a situation. Teachers as technicians and teachers as reflective practitioners approach a situation in different ways. This summary provides ideas for practice that teacher educators must encourage preservice and in-service teachers to carry out (see Table 2).

The reflective practitioners described by researchers are people who make decisions; have an understanding of people; are concerned with the human, as opposed to the technical aspects of problems; and have a need for affiliation and

a capacity for warmth. They are also spontaneous, curious, adaptable, and open to new events and changes.

FUTURE TRENDS

E-learning is a rapidly growing instructional approach. Almost every institution offers some form of e-learning opportunity to its students. This will continue to grow and evolve as a viable means of instruction. To make sure e-learning is as effective as the best traditional courses, universities have to support instructors in learning about facilitating an e-learning course and the unique pedagogy involved. Continued research on best practices should be disseminated to the higher education community.

The learner-centered collaborative community approach has been considered as a viable way to increase students' ownership in e-learning. It is congruent with the result of a higher-education survey (Bonk et al., 2006) about the future prediction of pedagogical approaches for e-learning. It identified that group problem solving and collaborative tasks, and authentic cases and scenario learning will be the most widely used instructional approaches in e-learning courses. In order to

Table 2. Differences between technicians and reflective practitioners (©2007, Leah Herner-Patnode. Used with permission)

Teacher as Technician	Teacher as Reflective Practitioner
• Locates problems entirely in the students and their actions • Looks for a program or technique to fix the deviant behavior of students • Does not attempt to examine the context of the classroom • Does not seriously question the goals or values embedded in her/his chosen solution • Accepts the problems as given and tries to solve them	• Examines teacher's own motivations and the context in which the problem occurs • Looks for distinct ways to pose the problem and attempts to get a different perspective on the students and the issues involved • Questions teacher's own beliefs and orientations • Is responsive to the unique educational and emotional needs of individual students • Questions personal aims and actions • Constantly reviews instructional goals, methods, and materials

facilitate the learner-centered environment, the instructor needs to be a co-learner and partner in the practice of reflection about teaching and learning.

In the coming years, the technologies that are viable in e-learning will rapidly increase in number. Examples of such technologies will include wireless technologies, peer-to-peer collaboration tools, sharable learning/content objects, simulations and games, virtual worlds, and intelligent agents. The instructors need to be proactive in learning relevant technologies and consider appropriate pedagogical approaches that capitalize on emerging technologies for e-learning.

As mentioned earlier, reflective thinking and reflective practice are now considered general professional skills. In the context of e-learning, teacher educators should endeavor to find ways of facilitating collaborative reflection, which will strengthen a collaborative learning community and collaborative inquiry in an e-learning course. Another area to which greater attention must be paid is in developing criteria to systematically assess reflection skills. By doing so, teacher educators can not only get evidence of students' growth but also collect insightful information that will improve the quality of an e-learning course.

CONCLUSION

In this chapter, we have discussed the roles of the instructor and student in e-learning, key pedagogical approaches to increase students' ownership in e-learning, and facilitating reflection using e-learning activities. The evolution from instructor as giver of knowledge to instructor as facilitator and collaborator is a difficult route for higher education to follow. The move away from traditional course delivery often changes the role of the instructor. The instructor needs to have an organized approach with access to technology support, so that the focus can be on learner outcomes rather than technology issues (Bannan & Milheim,

1997; Rieber, 1993; Su, 2005). Communication is important in the e-learning setting and can take many forms. A good instructor gauges what works best for content delivery and utilizes the most effective form of communication with the students. An instructor who understands student needs and accommodates those who need help will provide a course that is organized and prepared for technical difficulties, and whose students will gain a good perception of the overall content. Research supports constructivist and student-centered pedagogical approaches (Anderson, 2004; Baek & Barab, 2005; Baek & Schwen, 2006; Bonk et al., 2006; Carr-Chellman et al., 2003) as a means to increase students' ownership and responsibility of the quality of their learning. If the instructor wishes to model the role of reflective practitioner, then the instructor needs to examine e-learning pedagogy carefully while constructing a course that requires critical thinking and reflection skills. It is in this way that we move towards using technology as a tool that effectively meets course objectives.

REFERENCES

Al-Mahmood, R., & McLoughlin, C. (2004, December 5-8). Re-learning through e-learning: Changing conceptions of teaching through online experience. In R. Atkinson, C. McBeath, D. Jonas-Dwyer, & R. Phillips (Eds.), *Beyond the Comfort Zone: Proceedings of the 21st ASCILITE Conference*, Perth (pp. 37-47). Retrieved March 17, 2008, from http://www.asvilite.org.au/conferences/perth04/procs/al-mahmood.html

Anderson, T. (2004). A second look at learning sciences, classrooms, and technology: Issues of implementation: Making it work in the real world. In T.M. Duffy & J.R. Kirkley (Eds.), *Learner-centered theory and practice in distance education: Cases from higher education* (pp. 209-234). Mahwah, NJ: Lawrence Erlbaum.

Baek, E., & Barab, S. (2005). A study of dynamic design dualities in a Web-supported community of practice for teachers. *Journal of Educational Technology and Society, 8*(4), 161-177.

Baek, E., & Schwen, T.M. (2006). The culture of teachers vs. a necessary culture for an online community. *Performance Improvement Quarterly, 19*(2), 51-68.

Bain, S. (2000). *LTSS guide: An introduction to learning technology.* Bristol: LTSS. Retrieved March 17, 2008, from http://www.ltss.bris.ac.kr/old-to-archive2/old-guides/ltintro/index.html - 10/10/04

Bannan, B., & Milhelm, W. (1997). Existing Web-based instruction courses and their design. In B. Khan (Ed.), *Web-based instruction* (pp. 381-387). Englewood Cliffs, NJ: Educational Technologies Publications.

Bonk, C.J., Kim, K., & Zeng, T. (2006). Future directions of blended learning in higher education and workplace learning settings. In C.J. Bonk & C.R. Graham (Eds.), *The handbook of blended learning: Global perspectives, local designs* (pp. 550-567). San Francisco: Pfeiffer.

Brookfield, S.D. (1995). *Becoming a critically reflective teacher.* San Francisco: Jossey-Bass.

Carr-Chellman, A.A., Dyer, D., & Breman, J. (2000). Burrowing through the network wires: Does distance detract from collaborative authentic learning? *Journal of Distance Education, 15*(1), 39-62.

Chickering, A., & Ehrmann, S. (1996, October). Implementing the seven principles: Technology as lever. *AAHE Bulletin*, pp. 3-6. Retrieved March 17, 2008, from http://www.tltgroup.org/programs/seven.html.

Churchill, T. (2005). E-reflections: Comparative exploration of the role of e-learning in training higher education lectures. *Turkish Online Journal of Distance Education, 6*(3). Retrieved March 17, 2008, from http://tojde.anadolu.edu.tr/tojde19/articles/churchill.htm

Colton, A.B., & Sparks-Langer, G.M. (1993). A conceptual framework to guide the development of teacher reflection and decision making. *Journal of Teacher Education, 44*(1), 45-54.

Dennen, V.P. (2005). From message posting to learning dialogues: Factors affecting learner participation in asynchronous discussion. *Distance Education, 26*(1), 127-148.

Dewey, J. (1933). *How we think: A restatement of the relation of reflective thinking to the educative process.* Boston: Heath and Company.

Duffy, T.M., & Kirkley, J.R. (2004). Learning theory and pedagogy applied in distance learning: The case of Cardean University. In T.M. Duffy & J.R. Kirkley (Eds.), *Learner-centered theory and practice in distance education: Cases from higher education* (pp. 107-141). Mahwah, NJ: Lawrence Erlbaum.

Gipe, J.P., Richards, J.C., Levitov, J., & Speaker, R. (1991). Psychological and personal dimensions of prospective teachers' reflective abilities. *Educational and Psychological Measurement, 51*, 913-922.

Goodman, J. (1984). Reflection and teacher education: A case study and theoretical analysis. *Interchange, 15*(3), 9-26.

Hannary, L.M. (1994). Strategies for facilitating reflective practice: The role of staff developers. *Journal of Staff Development, 15*(3), 22-26.

Hara, N., & Kling, R. (2003). Students' distress with a Web-based distance education course: An ethnographic study of participants' experiences. *Turkish Online Journal of Distance Education, 4*(2). Retrieved March 2nd 2007 from http://tojde.anadolu.edu.tr/tojde10/articles/hara.htm

Islas, J.R. (2004). Collaborative learning at Monterrey Tech-Virtual University. In T.M. Duffy

& J.R. Kirkley (Eds.), *Learner-centered theory and practice in distance education: Cases from higher education* (pp. 297-320). Mahwah, NJ: Lawrence Erlbaum.

Kear, K., Williams, J., Seaton, R., & Einon, G. (2004). Using information and communication technology in a modular distance learning course. *European Journal of Engineering Technology, 29*(1), 17-25. Retrieved March 17, 2008, from the Google Scholar database.

Kemmis, S. (1987). Critical reflection. In M.F. Widden & I. Andrews (Eds.), *Staff development for school improvement: A focus on the teacher* (pp. 73-90). London: The Falmer Press.

Killion, J.P., & Todnen, G.R. (1991). A process for personal theory building. *Educational Leadership, 48*(6), 14-16.

Knox, A.B. (1986). *Helping adults learn.* San Francisco: Jossey-Bass.

Kuit, J.A., Reay, G., & Freeman, R. (2001). Experiences of reflective teaching. *Active Learning in Higher Education, 2*(2), 128-142.

LaBoskey, V.K. (1993). A conceptual framework for reflection in preservice teacher education. In J. Calderhead & P. Gates (Eds.), *Conceptualizing reflection in teacher development* (pp. 23-38). London: The Falmer Press.

LaBoskey, V.K. (1994). *Development of reflective practice: A study of preservice teachers.* New York: Teachers College Press.

Lee, H.-J. (2000, April 24-28). *The nature of the changes in reflective thinking in preservice mathematics: Teachers engaged in student teaching field experience in Korea.* Paper presented at the Annual Meeting of the America Educational Research Association (AERA), New Orleans, LA.

Lee, H.-J. (2005). Understanding and assessing preservice teachers' reflective thinking. *Teaching and Teacher Education, 21*(6), 699-715.

McVay, G., Snyder, K., & Graetz, K. (2005). Evolution of a laptop university: A case study. *British Journal of Educational Technology, 36*(3), 513-524.

Miller, T.W., & King, F.B. (2003). Distance education: Pedagogy and best practices in the new millennium. *International Journal of Leadership in Education, 6*(3), 283-297.

Morre, M.G., & Kearsley, G. (1996). *Distance education: A systems view.* San Francisco: Wadworth.

National Center for Education Statistic. (2003). *Distance education at degree-granting postsecondary institutions: 2000–2001.* U.S. Department of Education.

Osterman, K.F. (1990). Reflective practice: A new agenda for education. *Education and Urban Society, 22*, 133-152.

Palloff, R.M., & Pratt, K. (2001). *Lesson from the cyberspace classroom: The realities of online teaching.* San Francisco: Jossey-Bass.

Pollard, A., & Tann, S. (1994). *Reflective teaching in the primary school: A handbook for the classroom* (2nd ed.). London: Cassell Educational limited.

Rieber, L.P. (1993). A pragmatic view of instructional technology. In K. Tobin (Ed.), *The practice of constructivism in science education* (pp. 193-212). Washington, DC: AAAS Press.

Russell, T.L. (1999). *The no significant difference phenomenon.* Chapel Hill, NC: Office of Instructional Telecommunications, North Carolina State University.

Salmon, G. (2002). Mirror, mirror, on my screen … Exploring online reflections. *British Journal of Educational Technology, 33*(4), 200.

Santmire, T., Giraud, G., & Grosskopf, K. (1999, April 19-23). *An experimental test of constructivist environments.* Paper presented at the Annual

Meeting of the American Educational Research Association. Montreal, Quebec, Canada.

Schön, D.A. (1983). *The reflective practitioner: How professionals think in action.* New York: Basic Books.

Schön, D.A. (1987). *Educating the reflective practitioner.* San Francisco: Jossey-Bass.

Shearer, R. (2004). Penn State World Campus adds live e-learning to its online curriculum. *T.H.E. Journal, 32*(3), 59-61.

Sherry, L., Cronje, J., Rauscher, W., & Obermeyer, G. (2005). *Mediated conversations and the affective domain: Two case studies. International Journal on E-Learning, 4*(2), 177-190. Norfolk, VA: AACE.

Shulman, L.S. (1987). Knowledge and teaching: Foundation of the new reform. *Harvard Educational Review, 57*(1), 1-22.

Solomon, J. (1987). New thoughts on teacher education. *Oxford Review of Education, 13*(3), 267-274.

Sparks-Langer, G.M., Colton, A.B., Pasch, M., & Starko, A. (1991). *Promoting cognitive, critical, and narrative reflection* (Report No. SP 033 326). Chicago: American Educational Research Association. (ERIC Document Reproduction Service No. ED337435)

Su, B. (2005). Examining instructional design and development of a Web-based course: A case study. *Journal of Distance Education Technologies, 3*(4), 62-76.

Taggart, G.L. (1996). *Reflective thinking: A guide for training preservice and in-service practitioners.* Unpublished doctoral dissertation, Kansas State University, Manhattan, Kansas.

Valli, L. (1992). *Reflective teacher education: Cases and critiques.* Albany, NY: State University of New York Press.

Van Manen, M. (1977). Linking ways of knowing within ways of being practical. *Curriculum Inquiry, 6*, 205-228.

Vygotsky, L. (1974). *Mind in society.* Cambridge, MA: Harvard University Press.

Vygotsky, L. (1987). Thinking in speech. In R.W. Reiber & A.S. Carton (Eds.), *The collected works of L.S. Vygotsky.* New York: Plenum Press.

Wenger, E. (1998). *Communities of practice: Learning, meaning, and identity.* New York: Cambridge University Press.

Zeichner, K.M., & Liston, D.P. (1996). *Reflective teaching: An introduction.* Lawrence Erlbaum Associates.

KEY TERMS

Asynchronous Communication: Communication between two or more parties that is not synchronized or happening in real time. The person communicating can submit her questions and statements at any time and other people in the class can see the communication when they choose to read it.

Collaborative Inquiry: The active quest for meaning. It involves a process of asking questions, investigating, and making decisions to solve them as a way of exploring the world. This may take many different forms. As a pedagogical term, it includes various instructional models and approaches to facilitate higher-order thinking skills, using collaborative inquiry as a main conduit. As a more generic term, it involves critical reflections by learners themselves on their learning.

Distance Learning: Coursework that does not take place in the traditional manner with the instructor working face-to-face with the students. Students communicate with the instructor via technology.

Learning Community: A curricular structure that consists of a group of learners. It encourages learners to actively participate and to contribute to the process of learning. The instructor typically serves as a co-learner and partners in reflective practice about teaching and learning.

Learner-Centered Approach: A pedagogical approach that respects learners' diverse needs and places learners' voices in the center of the course design. It emphasizes learners' ownership through learners' active search for meaning in content and application of personal experiences.

Reflection: Dewey (1933, p. 7) identified reflection as one of the modes of thought: "active, persistent, and careful consideration of any belief or supposed form of knowledge in light of the grounds that support it and the future conclusions to which it tends."

Technology Mediated Course: A course that may incorporate a variety of technology-based educational strategies: synchronous and asynchronous collaborative communication, project/activity-based learning, and Web-based interaction and feedback.

Chapter XVII
To Be Lost and To Be a Loser Through the Web

Louise Limberg
University of Gothenburg, Sweden

Mikael Alexandersson
University of Gothenburg, Sweden

Annika Lantz-Andersson
University of Gothenburg, Sweden

ABSTRACT

The purpose of this chapter is to present and discuss findings from a study of students' information seeking and use for a learning assignment. The overall interest is to describe the coherence between differences in the quality of students' information seeking and the quality of their learning outcomes and to relate this to issues of information literacy in the Knowledge Society. The study was framed within a sociocultural perspective of learning and adopted an ethnographic approach. Analysis of data resulted in the identification of two major categories of competences related to information seeking and knowledge formation, one of which involves serious shortcomings in meaningful learning through information seeking. There is little evidence that ICT conclusively supports the development of new knowledge in terms of seeing the world differently. Conclusions are that the school system tends to produce 'information illiterates' which may entail unwanted consequences for both individuals and for maintaining a democratic Knowledge Society.

INTRODUCTION AND AIM

The purpose of this chapter is to present and discuss findings from a study of students' informa-tion seeking and use for a learning assignment. This study is part of a larger research project in seven schools (Alexandersson & Limberg, 2003, 2005; Limberg & Alexandersson, 2003).

The overall interest is to describe the coherence between differences in the quality of students' information seeking and the quality of their learning outcomes. The discussion of findings is linked to aspects of information literacy and democracy in the Knowledge Society. The chapter opens with some considerations concerning the human competences related to information and communication technologies (ICTs) as well as consideration of problems linked to information literacy education. The next section presents the design of the study followed by a presentation of findings. The concluding section of the chapter discusses the findings by focusing on issues related to information literacy in the Knowledge Society.

BACKGROUND

It is evident that during the last decade, conditions for and ways of learning in schools have changed dramatically. These changes are partly due to the introduction and breakthrough of ICT in schools and partly to new requirements caused by the globalisation of national economies as well as migration. One characteristic of the current changes is its associated rhetoric, which is pervasive and loud. How many times have we not heard the rhetorical claims of the Knowledge Society or the new demands of the Information Society concerning the possibilities offered by ICT for our professional life as well as for our leisure time and as citizens? ICT is increasingly used as a medium to influence citizens' attitudes. In this perspective, the development of various competences, especially the ability to critically evaluate information sources, and also the ability to take an active part in the virtual debate, emerges as important requirements for the citizen. In the debate about school education and ICT, the issue of students' insufficient information competence and thereby the risk of becoming second-rate students is often raised. Will this create a new

form of class system? Without a deeper sense of information literacy, we assume that students will hardly be able to generate meaningful knowledge and to understand complex contexts. If not all students are given the chance to acquire this basic competence, the gaps between students will probably become wider.

LITERACIES AND ICT

In their annual Education Policy Analysis (EPA) the OECD (2002) treated the question of human competences in relation to economic growth as well as to private and social well-being. Competence is included in the conception of "human capital," and the OECD have suggested broadening this definition to include competences such as critical thinking, collaboration ability, self-reliance, and the ability to solve problems—and require that all of the mentioned be observed more emphatically when planning educational policies. In some countries, educational policy initiatives have been taken that recognize the importance and benefit of the development of other competences than the traditional basics: reading, writing, and arithmetic. One important competence, pointed out by the OECD (2002), is the ability to seek and use information effectively. Often this competence is referred to as "digital competence." Since the focus of this chapter is on *what* and *how* students learn through information seeking—an issue that we define with the concept *information literacy*—we want to point out similarities and differences between these two concepts. Neither concept is originally grounded in empirical research; they were developed in politically oriented educational contexts. One major difference between the concepts, however, is that the term digital competence is more oriented to issues about learning to handle digital tools and multimedia formats for various purposes, while the term information literacy implies seeking and using information for learning or other purposes, where information is not restricted to digital form but may include a range of formats such as print material, oral information, and so forth. Nevertheless, digital information and ICT tools are of central interest in the discourse concerning information literacy.

DIGITAL LITERACY: AN OPERATIONALLY ORIENTED CONCEPT

The European Union has identified eight key competences for lifelong learning considered necessary for an education system, one of which is *digital competence*. The major objective of the development of digital competence is to support students in taking part in and becoming active citizens in the Knowledge Society. Digital competence is expected to assist citizens in using electronic media both securely and critically in work and in leisure time (Commission of the European Communities 2005, p. 9). It is assumed that the basis of digital competence lies in mastering various digital technologies. This is coupled to an assumption that digital ways of communication will bring about changed learning processes and a different view of knowledge, which might deepen the quality of teaching and learning.

There are at least four aspects of digital competence that deserve mentioning, as they together form a complex whole. First, there is a technological dimension, or the ability to handle ICT as tools for teaching and learning, for administration, planning, evaluation, and different forms of communication. The claim is that if you master the technology, you can make new experiences through using it, and you can also find new possibilities for action. Second, there is a didactic dimension, or the ability to develop knowledge through ICT. The third dimension—a critical dimension—concerns developing into a critical member of society through ICT. The fourth

dimension, which is the subject of this chapter, concerns information literacy.

INFORMATION LITERACY: A CONTENT ORIENTED CONCEPT

The term *information literacy* is often used today to designate the ability to seek and use information effectively in various situations. The concept has evolved parallel to the development of ICT and has been adopted as a main concern in education and librarianship. Information literacy is seen as the generic ability of citizens in a democratic society to make well-informed choices based on the critical evaluation of a wide range of information sources. Information literacy is emphasized as a particular goal of education on a national level in many countries, as well as in local schools (Moore, 2002; Virkus, 2003).

Related to this emphasis on information literacy in education, empirical research in the field is emerging and mainly devoted to undergraduate university education (Bruce, 2003; Sundin, 2004). In an extensive literature review on information literacy, Virkus (2003) shows that in Europe the concept of information literacy is mainly used by librarians and other information specialists, while in North America and Australia information literacy is also used in public policy documents on a national level. A number of international reports and research studies (Bruce & Candy, 2000; Lupton, 2004; Moore, 2002; Virkus, 2003) confirm that information literacy education is a matter of international interest, where national goals of education are involved and where citizens' abilities as independent and critical information users are seen as crucial for democratic societies in the Information Age. In a white paper prepared for UNESCO, Moore (2002) analyses information literacy education worldwide and asserts that in order to be effective, instruction in information literacy needs to bring information problem solving and thinking to the attention of students, which rarely happens (p 8). She also claims that ICT initiatives in schools as well as teacher education seem to begin with a focus on technological awareness and then shift to a focus on enhancing learning through information literacy.

Among researchers, a considerable interest has been devoted to investigating what constitutes information literacy in various contexts such as school (Alexandersson & Limberg, 2003; Limberg, 1999; Williams & Wavell, 2006), higher education (Boon, Johnston, & Webber, 2007; Bruce, 1997; Lupton, 2004), and work life (Cheuk, 2000; Lloyd, 2006). A number of these researchers stress the link between information literacy and learning, for instance, "building a knowledge base in a new area with information" or "expanding one's knowledge using information" (Bruce, 1997). Limberg (1999) found that the quality of students' (18–19 year olds) information seeking and use during an independent learning task was closely related to the quality of their learning outcomes of that task. A recent strand in information literacy research is to investigate the relationship between theories and models of information seeking research and the practices of information literacy education, where researchers argue for closer interaction between these fields of theory and practice, for the sake of mutual benefit (Limberg & Sundin, 2006). In this chapter, we use the terms information literacy and information competence interchangeably to designate the ability to critically seek and use information for learning purposes. In the text, the term information seeking denotes the longer expression "information seeking and use," if not otherwise explicitly stated.

INFORMATIN SEEKING AS A FOUNDATION OF INFORMATION LITERACY

The changing conditions for learning imply student-centred rather than teacher-centred educa-tion. Methods of teaching and learning rely on students as active learners engaging in problem solving tasks or in in-depth inquiries related to issues concerning, for instance, science, politics, or ethics. Learning about an issue through independent information seeking puts high demands on students' abilities to identify problems, find relevant information, critically evaluate and analyse material from various sources, and construct a meaningful presentation about the matter at hand. It is worth pointing out that good reading and writing abilities are crucial in this type of work (Alexandersson & Limberg, 2003, 2005; Williams & Wavell, 2006). We identify a close connection between information seeking for learning purposes in educational contexts and students' gradual development of competence in information literacy throughout their school years.

A number of problems have been identified and described in previous research on students' information seeking connected to student centred learning, for instance, that of "text sampling" (Nilsson, 2002); that is, students cut and paste material from information sources to produce their own reports (Alexandersson & Limberg, 2003; Davis, 1994; Gordon, 1999; Large, Beheshti, Breu-leux, & Renaud, 1998). Several studies indicate that students tend to search for specific answers regardless of the media they use or whether they work with open or narrow questions (Alexandersson & Limberg, 2003; Fidel, Davis, Douglass, Holder, Hopkins, Kushner, et al., 1999). Students are often required to seek information on topics that they know very little about, which may cause considerable difficulties in the light of research results indicating that there is a close relationship between students' prior subject knowledge and the quality of their information seeking (Alexandersson & Limberg, 2003; Fidel et al., 1999; Limberg, 1999). The majority of studies in the field of ICT and education focus on information seeking and pay little or no attention to contemplating students' ways of understanding the *content* of information. In our research, this issue is central. The interest in information literacy as the ability to seek and use information for constructing or expanding one's knowledge is coherent with the conceptions of information literacy identified and described by Bruce (1997).

Our research takes its points of departure in the given problem description, and at the same time, expands the research interest in the sense that it is not restricted to students' information seeking but directs an equal interest in what students learn through information seeking, or their knowledge formation. The overall research question is: How do ICT tools contribute to students becoming information literate citizens in the Knowledge Society? More specific research questions are: What do information tools contribute to students' ways of learning and to their learning outcomes? What competences are involved and developed in students' information based learning?

DESIGN AND METHODOLOGY

The study was framed within a sociocultural perspective of learning, viewing information seeking as a social practice embedded in the practice of doing assignments in school. Knowledge is seen as constituted between people within different discursive communities, in our case, within the discursive practice of classroom teaching and learning. Learning is seen as taking place through communicative interaction between people and between people and tools. Tools, such as computers or the Internet, are not considered neutral but as mediating certain worldviews, knowledge, and values.

In this research, we concentrated on how students use information *tools*, like computers, the Internet, and *sources*, like Web sites, books, pictures, and so on, for a learning task. The study was conducted in two classes of secondary school (eighth grade, 15-year-old students). There were a total of 53 students involved, as well as two teachers and one librarian. The concrete object of study was the work carried out in the two classes on an assignment, implying students' independent information seeking and use. The goal of this task was to learn to write an academic essay, and the assignment lasted 10 weeks. The students worked individually or in pairs, and they were free to choose any topic for their essay. This resulted in a wide range of topics and subject matter being treated by the students.

The methodology used was an ethnographic approach, and data were collected through observations, field notes, and a questionnaire (48 responses). Questionnaire questions concerned what tools and sources students used for information seeking and what students meant that they learned, how they learned in collaboration with others, and who was the most significant collaborator in their learning process. Students' work process was observed from initiation to conclusion. In accordance with our theoretical frame, the focus of observation was on the communicative interaction between students and pedagogues as well as between students and tools, interpreting this interaction as shaped by and shaping the discursive practice of learning through information seeking related to a learning assignment in school. For the purpose of analysing students' use of information sources, 33 student reports were collected and analysed and compared with the sources listed in their bibliographies. This study was part of a larger research project set in 7 schools and 11 classes altogether involving 260 students (Alexandersson & Limberg, 2003; 2005; Limberg & Alexandersson, 2003).

FINDINGS

For the majority of students, information seeking was equivalent to searching the Web, despite the fact that they did not master Web-based information seeking very well. Nevertheless, the Web was seen as the natural tool and the tool to start with. Results from the questionnaire indicate that some 80% of the students viewed computers in the school library as most important for their information seeking. However, some students used various search engines smoothly while others had great problems, and observations indicated that many students were not in the habit of using computers for information seeking.

Differences in students' information seeking and learning outcomes concerned a number of aspects: (a) understandings of the goal of the task, (b) knowledge of and interest in the subject content of the essay, (c) knowledge of technological tools, (d) knowledge of information seeking and the critical evaluation and use of information sources, (e) reading and especially writing abilities, and (f) learning outcomes related to topic of essay and task. Using these aspects as parameters in our analysis of the data, we identified four categories of competences for information seeking and knowledge formation:

- Finding and copying random facts
- Elementary information seeking and compilation of facts
- Information seeking and knowledge formation
- Research-based approach including seeking, finding, and critically evaluating information for knowledge formation

For the purpose of this chapter, we selected four type cases from the two classes to illustrate differences in students' approaches to the task and to information seeking as well as differences between learning outcomes. These four cases form four "types" of approaches to information seeking embedded in learning tasks, which were characteristic of all 53 students in the particular sample and in line with the overall findings from the 260 students in the total series of studies. A comparative analysis of the four cases allows us to discuss the possibilities and problems connected to enhancing students' abilities of information seeking for learning purposes. The four cases include six students, since, in two cases, students worked in pairs. The categories of competences and the names (fictitious) of students and topics of their essays are presented in Table 1.

Find a description of categories, illustrated with extracts from the empirical data:

1. Finding and copying random facts

This category is characterised by highly limited abilities in using the technological tools as well as in overall information seeking. The girls, Sussi and Alva, chose a topic on the basis that there were many facts to be found, something that they expected would facilitate their performance

Table 1. Categories of competences of information seeking and knowledge formation and distribution of students among categories of competences

Category of competence of information seeking and knowledge formation	Case: Example of student and topic of task	Distribution among students: percentage N = 53
Finding and copying random facts	Sussi and Alva: The wreck of the Titanic	0.19
Elementary information seeking and compilation of facts	Peter and Johan: How to preserve rain forests	0.57
Information seeking and knowledge formation	Erica: Homosexuality	0.15
Research-based approach	Albin: Why am I so tall?	0.10

of the task. At the computer, they focused on finding facts to compile into their essay. These students knew little about how to search the Web. This excerpt illustrates the situation (Field notes, 2/20/2002).

Alva: I'll start searching now, do you know about any good Web page ... I'll try Titanic dot com, maybe there's ...
Sussie: Goog... something, no wait...
Sussie is now also searching the Web trying to remember the name of the search engine to help Alva. Alva is searching 'titanic.com' leading her to a page with that address.
Alva: I've found the page, I swear, look...
Alva is clicking a link to 'the ship' but gives up, since the text is in English and instead tries to search for 'titanic.se'. When this does not work she searches for 'Titanic facts' using AltaVista.
Sussie: No, wait, search on www.google.com.

The students' approach to finding facts, as discrete pieces of information, led them to browsing sources aiming at finding facts, and then to formulate questions on the basis of already found answers, as illustrated in the citation (Field notes, 2/20/2002).

Sussie: What happened to the ship, why did it sink?
Alva: Write the question; How long did it take for Titanic to sink, because I found the answer here...
Sussie: But we can't do it like that...
Alva: I've found good facts, you know, that's why I'll start to write this...
Sussie: What size was the ship? Tell me another question!

As indicated in the quote, Sussie was first reluctant to the idea of formulating questions to already found answers, but she soon accepted

the procedure as a good idea. This is similar to the findings of Fidel et al. (1998) who observed the same procedure among senior high-school students doing an assignment on plants.

A third feature of this category is the "transport and transformation of text" as a mode of utilising information. This behaviour is based in students' awareness that they must not copy from their sources but instead "write in their own words." However, it did not seem obvious to the students why they had to adopt such a practice. In order to solve the problem, students tended to copy facts from sources, paste them into their own reports, and then add or delete one or two words, in order to change the wording and make it "their own text." Thoughts, questions, and comparisons linked to the wreck of the Titanic that the girls in our study were observed discussing were not explicitly used. For instance, comparisons between the fates of the Titanic and the Estonia and possible reasons why people died were not written down and included in their final reports. The overall goal for the girls seemed to be to finish their report swiftly. The girls' experience of the task as a school assignment meant getting it done in the simplest possible way, and this became the overall structuring condition for the accomplishment of the task, thus limiting the potential of meaningful learning.

2. Elementary information seeking and compilation of facts

Elementary information seeking is characterised by a view of information seeking as Web searching coupled to certain difficulties in using Web tools. The excerpt illustrates the fumbling nature of searching via AltaVista with the aim of finding out about means of preserving rain forests. The boys, Peter and Johan, were observed entering the library and choosing a computer to explore the research questions that they had formulated prior to starting their search (Field notes, 2/22/2002).

Peter takes charge of the computer and logs on. He connects to the Internet and looks in 'favourites' but does not find any link to any search engine.

Peter: I don't know any…

Peter writes www.altavista. Nothing happens.

Peter: What a useless computer!

They wait and wait. Peter says that he often uses AltaVista for searching. Something goes wrong; the computer gives a failure message and shuts down. The boys have to start again. They wait and wait. This time Peter writes: www.altavista.nu.

Peter: Is it 'dot com'?

Johan: I don't… that's it!

A Web page opens but Peter says that he does not recognize it.

Johan: I never use AltaVista, you know…

Peter: Well I do, and it does'nt look like this.

Peter randomly clicks various links.

Johan: Something happened!

A window opens making it possible to insert search terms. Peter writes: 'rain forest'. Again they wait for a long time until a new page opens telling them that 'the page cannot be opened'. Peter goes back to clicking randomly and when nothing more happens he logs off.

Peter: Why are the school's computers so weird?

The excerpt indicates a typical feature of this approach to information seeking in terms of blaming the technology for being at fault. Students complained about the school's computers for being old, slow, and so forth, thus placing the problem outside the students' own power and reducing the difficulties to technical problems instead of identifying it as students' own deficient knowledge in information seeking. In this manner, the ways in which the qualities of the tool were experienced became a structuring condition limiting students' actions and thus their possibilities of learning.

The category of elementary information seeking competence further implies difficulties for students in using search tools in books such as indices and tables of contents. This means that they had problems selecting information, handling information overload, and assessing the relevance of various sources. This limited way of understanding becomes a structuring resource limiting students' use of retrieved sources related to their topic. In the initial phases of information seeking, students were often recommended by the teacher or the librarian to look for an overview of their topic in an encyclopedia, in order to create a background for further investigations. Quite few of the students seemed to follow this advice. Those who did had obvious difficulties searching encyclopedias, for example, identifying and finding the right volume. Second, more often than not, students experienced the language of encyclopedias as too complicated and seemingly did not understand the texts. Third, many students seemed to think that books carry "old" and therefore irrelevant knowledge for their topics. This is exemplified by the reactions of Peter and Johan to an article on rain forests they found and consulted in a large encyclopedia. Looking for the copyright year and finding 1994, the reaction was as follows (Field notes, 2/22/2002):

Johan: It's from 1994, it's ancient!

They browse the pictures absent-mindedly.

Peter: Yes, but now we know it exists.

Johan: Yes but it's useless.

In summing up the characteristic features of this category of elementary information seeking, we observed that the students managed to find quite a lot of relevant sources but they lacked the abilities to evaluate and use the sources in adequate ways for the successful execution of their task. The facts they found through information seeking were compiled in students reports, which were characterised by the transfer and limited transformation of texts from sources into the students' essays.

3. Information seeking and knowledge formation

This category of competence implies a reflective approach to the task, investigating and analysing a problem and reaching a deep understanding of both the information search process and the knowledge content of the topic of the essay. The excerpt illustrates how one student, writing about homosexuality, tried to find a source of information about a statement that she read somewhere, but did not remember where. She was aware of the fact that she should not refer to this statement without reference to a credible source. Her ambition to find this information guided and structured her way through the task (Field notes, 3/6/2002).

Erica: I read somewhere that some people thought that homosexuality was some kind of disease so I wanted to find something about that, I looked for it in Bonniers' Medical book but I didn't find anything.
Teacher: I read the other day in the paper about a new 'ombudsman' for homosexuals, somebody who would represent their issues and help them in society. He should be called Homo, search for Homo and you may find something...
Erica: I have a really old medical book at home, maybe I can look it up there... I would really like to have a good medical book.
Teacher: Write the words; homosexuality + medical then!

Erica persistently continued to search for a source to confirm her presumption that homosexuality was regarded as a disease by some people. Intent on finding an answer to this question, she spent several lessons in search for such a source. On a later occasion when Erica had finished her essay, the following conversation took place (Field notes, 4/10/2002).

Interviewer: How do you feel, are you satisfied with your essay, did you get any answers to your questions?
Erica: Yes, I found answers to most of them, the view of the Church was a bit tough, but I took some quotations from the Bible.
Interviewer: Did you manage to find the source in your search for homosexuality viewed as a disease?
Erica: Yes it went really well, I found it on the Web... under the National Swedish Board of Health and Welfare where they had a classification of diseases... and there it was viewed as a disease as late as 1979, I also found that it was considered criminal until 1944... that is, illegal.

Erica's case illustrates a straightforward problem-based approach to the task, conditioned by a topic of interest to the student, leading to intentional and conscious work toward the goal of exploring and understanding the issue. A characteristic feature of this category is that the topic of the essay was based on a specific question, formulated by the student: How is it possible that homosexuality was regarded as a disease until our days? This is an important difference from the previous categories, where students' information seeking was not guided by explicit problems or research questions. For the student, it seems that the topic overshadows the learning goal of writing an academic essay. However, strong involvement with the topic supports the student's performance and was linked both to systematic information seeking and learning about the subject matter, as well as to essay writing.

4. Research-based approach including seeking, finding, and critically evaluating information for knowledge formation

This category of competence is characterised by the student's awareness of the goal of the task as writing an academic essay, combined with an authentic research question, where there is no obvious answer. This research-based approach is not necessarily linked to expert information seeking, but as in category (3) the quality of the question guides certain aspects of information seeking, such as the assessment of relevance as well as evaluating the credibility of sources. A persistent testing of numerous different search terms, and the creative use of synonyms where there were no obvious keywords, was typical of this category. Good control of retrieved information sources was another characteristic of this category, implying an ability to keep and organise found sources.

The following excerpt illustrates the case of a boy who had chosen a topic based on genuine, personal interest, and he had an authentic question (*Why am I so tall?*). Furthermore, it was important to him to fulfil the standards of writing an academic essay since he was keen on getting a high grade. It was, however, not easy for him to know how to find useful information on the Web concerning the determination of human height. During many lessons, he tried different combinations of search terms and finally succeeded in finding a page that was both informative and comprehensible to him. The quote also indicates the student's awareness of the importance of assessing the credibility of sources. Having found a relevant source, he uses his teacher as a cognitive authority for accepting the source for use (Field notes, 4/10/2002).

Interviewer: How are things going?
Albin: It's going first-rate, I found a great page when I searched for "growth hormone + inheritance" on Google, there was this biology teacher who had written exactly about what I wanted to know... I asked my teacher and she said that it was okay to use it as a source.

Interviewer: What are you going to do now?
Albin: My teacher has just shown me the different parts that should be a part of the essay and I found out that I'd forgotten the method... so that's what I'll be doing now, and then I have the discussion to do... and after that I'll compare myself with my brother... height, that is.

In his essay and when presenting the project, Albin demonstrated that he had found various reasons for differences in human height and his ability to discuss these differences in terms of his own height as well as in terms of differences in average height between people in different parts of the world. He was also able to relate these findings to the fact that the average height of humans is increasing (Field notes, 5/24/2002).

Teacher: So the climate and sex are significant?
Albin: Yes, since we grow mostly when we are asleep and it's so dark up here in the north, so we sleep more.
Teacher: You write in your essay that 'some people mean' which makes me wonder who you mean... is it someone in your family, is it you or a researcher?
Albin: It's envious short Spanish men! (everybody laughs)
Teacher: You write and compare height between students and farmers... so you mean that work is significant?
Albin: Yes, in earlier times they worked so hard...

Summarizing the characteristics of category (4), we find features such as a genuine research question based on personal interest, conscious but not smooth information seeking, where the aspects of evaluating and organising information are more salient than formulating expert queries, combined with an awareness of the explicit goal of the task and an ambition to get high grades. This combination of features structured a qualified execution of the task resulting in expanded knowledge and a deep understanding of both academic writing and about reasons for variation in human stature.

SUMMARIZING THE FINDINGS

The description of the four categories of competences embraces great variety in students' information seeking abilities as well as in their technical skills. It is worth observing that no student seemed to demonstrate information seeking expertise (information literacy) in the way that this competence is described in the literature. The fumbling ways of seeking information, observed in our study, did not seem to be compensated by any particular abilities in digital competence, as described. However, our findings clearly indicate that important aspects of information seeking, such as the critical evaluation of sources, tended to go hand in hand with the students' involvement with the topic of the essay, and the quality of the research questions linked to this involvement. Findings further illustrate the close interaction between the quality of information seeking and learning outcomes.

Analysis of the four categories of competences indicates a main distinguishing feature between categories (1) and (2) in one group, and categories (3) and (4) in a second group. This distinguishing feature concerns the difference between two main approaches, either:

- *Random catch*, where students' information seeking and knowledge formation are shaped by the information that they happen to come across through browsing the Web or other types of sources. Research questions as well as writing a report are guided by what is found, not by what is searched for; knowledge formation tends to be poor, at least as far as it can be assessed from the students' essays which mainly consisted of

compiled facts and text transfer from the information sources used; or

- *Spearfishing*, where students systematically explore and investigate a problem or a topic, guided by a clear awareness of the meaning of their investigation. This approach is further characterised by the students' involvement with the content of the task and manifested by carefully formulated research questions. Involvement with the task and the research question support, guide, and enhance students' critical information seeking and use. The spearfishing approach coincides with qualified learning outcomes as assessed from the coherence of students' essays, where topics were treated more in-depth and from various angles.

As shown in Table 1, the proportion of students in the different categories is most uneven, with three quarters of the students in categories (1) and (2) "random catch" and only 25% with competences corresponding to "spearfishing." Now, the important question for teaching is how to increase the proportion of students who develop competences according to categories (3) and (4). The question of how to support students in changing their approaches and developing competences similar to "spearfishing" seems to be the challenge for education in order to reach the recommended goals of policy documents such as those of the OECD (2002) or the Commission of European Communities (2005). What can our findings contribute to enhancing information literacy education?

DISCUSSION OF THE FINDINGS

The identification of the various categories, implying serious shortcomings for many students as regards information seeking and knowledge formation, creates a concrete picture of ICT supported, student centred learning. The features of the different categories of competences shed light on particular difficulties for students in information based problem solving and, as a consequence, where teaching should provide particular support for improved learning outcomes.

Our findings indicate that an overall important condition for learning achievements is the quality of interaction between adults (teachers and librarian) and students. For most students, the Web was the obvious tool for seeking and finding information, while teachers and the librarian tended to promote books and other print material. The interaction between the pedagogues and the students had an important impact on the students' learning outcomes, despite the fact that teachers and students perceived the task differently. For the teachers, the task concerned writing an academic essay, but for the students, the task was about the topic of their essay. This finding indicates a necessity for teachers to negotiate the intention and the topic of a task with their students.

For the majority of students, the freedom to choose a topic was restricted by their prior understanding of the task as a school assignment to be assessed by the teacher. Many students chose a topic with the intention of getting a high grade. When a topic was chosen based on a personal interest or on a genuine wish to find answers to a specific question, students tended to be more eager to analyse concepts, develop thorough understanding, and refer to their own experiences. So, students' motivation, curiosity, and interest were relevant to the performance of the task, but the wish to achieve well in a school task emerged as important for all students.

It has been repeatedly stressed that the use of ICT has changed teaching conditions in a decisive way. In certain respects, this is confirmed in our research project. This mainly concerns access to a rich and varied amount of information sources; likewise, changing conditions affect the freedom of students to search for and select information, and how they choose to organise the

work process and their information seeking. To a certain extent, the students can choose themselves what they want to learn—either through books or through the Web. But when it is a matter of *what* the students have the possibility to learn, in other words, content in learning, we find little evidence that ICT conclusively supports the development of new knowledge in terms of seeing the world differently. On the other hand, students developed some competences in *searching* on the Web, in *finding* facts, in *transporting* texts, and in *presenting* their learning outcomes to others. A challenging issue is how such competences, often criticized as shallow and procedural (cf. Alexandersson & Limberg, 2005; Alexandersson & Runesson, 2006), can be used as a point of departure for improving information literacy education. Otherwise, there is a risk that the relation between the ways students *handle information* and what they learn about *subject matter* may be increasingly weakened.

A major conclusion of this research is that key competences for meaningful information based learning go far beyond mastering digital tools. From our perspective, *information literacy* is a core competence in education. Information literacy means, as we have pointed out, learning to use different strategies and sources in different media formats. It also means learning to understand and act in a world which is constantly changing. Seeking information is a creative process involving time, thoughts, emotions, and actions. Students around the world are expected to know how to navigate in and evaluate information in the current medial abundance. The education system is therefore expected to support students in their endeavour to create their own knowledge from large amounts of information. In this perspective, well developed literacy in information, especially the ability to critically evaluate different sources, but also the ability to take an active part in the virtual debate, becomes an important citizen competence. Our research indicates tendencies that the school system produces "information illiterates" who will stay in the shade of the Knowledge Society.

REFERENCES

Alexandersson, M., & Limberg, L. (2003). Constructing meaning through information artefacts. *The New Review of Information Behaviour Research, 4,* 17-30.

Alexandersson, M., & Limberg, L. (2005, August 23-27). *In the shade of the knowledge society and the importance of information literacy.* Paper presented at the 11th EARLI (European Association of Research on Learning and Instruction) Conference, Nicosia, Cyprus.

Alexandersson, M., & Runesson, U. (2006). The tyranny of the temporal dimension: Learning about fundamental values through the Internet. *Scandinavian Journal of Educational Research, 50*(4), 411-427.

Boon, S., Johnston, B., & Webber, S. (2007). A phenomenographic study of English faculty's conceptions of information literacy. *Journal of Documentation, 63*(2), 204-228.

Bruce, C. S. (1997). *The seven faces of information literacy.* Adelaide: Auslib Press.

Bruce, C. S. (2003) Information literacy. In Feather & Sturges (Eds.), *Routledge international encyclopedia of information and library science.* Routledge.

Bruce, C. S., & Candy, P. (Eds.). (2000). *Information literacy around the world: Advances in programs and research.* Wagga Wagga NSW: Charles Sturt University.

Cheuk, B. (2000). Exploring information literacy in the workplace: A process approach. In C. Bruce & P. Candy (Eds.), *Information literacy around the world: Advances in programs and research* (pp. 177-191). Wagga Wagga: Centre for Information Studies, Charles Sturt University.

Commission of the European Communities. (2005). *Proposal for a recommendation of the European Parliament and of the Council on Key Competences for Lifelong Learning.* Brussels: COM(2005)548 final. Retrieved March 17, 2008, from http://ec.europa.eu/education/policies/2010/doc/keyrec_en.pdf

Davis, S. J. (1994). Teaching practices that encourage or eliminate student plagiarism. *Middle School Journal, 25*(3), 55-58.

Fidel, R., Davies, R., Douglass, M., Holder, J., Hopkins, C., Kushner, E., Miyagishima, B., & Toney, C. (1999). A visit to the information mall: Web searching behaviour of high school students. *Journal of the American Society for Information Science, 50*(1), 24-37.

Gordon, C. (1999). Students as authentic researchers: A new prescription for the high school research assignment. *School Library Media Research Online, 2.* Retrieved March 17, 2008, from http://www.ala.org/ala/aasl/aaslpubsandjournals/slmrb/slmrcontents/volume21999/vol2gordon.htm

Large, A., Beheshti, J., Breuleux, A., & Renaud, A. (1998). Information seeking in a multimedia environment by primary school students. *Library and Information Science Research, 20*(4), 343-376.

Limberg, L. (1999). Three conceptions of information seeking and use. In T. D. Wilson & D. K. Allen (Eds.), *Exploring the contexts of information behaviour* (pp. 116-135). London: Taylor Graham. Retrieved March 17, 2008, from http://www.hb.se/bhs/personal/lol/ISIC98.pdf

Limberg, L., & Alexandersson, M. (2003). The school library as a space for learning. *School Libraries Worldwide, 9*(1), 1-15.

Limberg, L., & Sundin, O. (2006). Teaching information seeking. *Information Research, 12*(1).

Retrieved March 17, 2008, from http://InformationR.net/ir/12-1/paper280html

Lloyd, A. (2006). Information literacy landscapes: An emerging picture. *Journal of Documentation, 62*(5), 570-583.

Lupton, M. (2004). *The learning connection: Information literacy and the student experience.* Adelaide: Auslib Press.

Moore, P. (2002, July). *An analysis of information literacy education worldwide.* White paper prepared for UNESCO, the U.S. National Commission on Libraries and Information Science, and the National Forum on Information Literacy, for use at the Information Literacy Meeting of Experts, Prague, The Czech Republic. Retrieved March 17, 2008, from http://www.nclis.gov/lib-inter/infolitcon&meet/moore.fullpaper.pdf

Nilsson, N.-E. (2002). *Skriv med egna ord. En studie av läroprocesser när elever i grundskolans senare år skriver "forskningsrapporter"* [Write in your own words: A study of learning processes involving secondary school students writing "research reports"]. Doctoral thesis, Malmö högskola.

OECD (2002). *Education policy analysis.* Retrieved March 17, 2008, from http://www1.oecd.org/publications/e-book/9602041E.PDF

Sundin, O. (2004). Användarundervisning inför informationssökning i yrkeslivet. En kunskapsöversikt. *Human IT 7:*2 [User education for information seeking in working life]. Retrieved March 17, 2008, from http://www.hb.se/bhs/ith/2-7/os.pdf

Virkus, S. (2003). Information literacy in Europe: A literature review. *Information Research, 8*(4). Retrieved March 17, 2008, from http://informationr.net/ir/8-4/paper159.html

Williams, D., & Wavell, C. (2006). *Untangling spaghetti? The complexity of developing information literacy in secondary school students.* Aberdeen: The Robert Gordon University. Retrieved March 17, 2008, from http://www.scotland.gov.uk/Publications/2006/10/informationliteracy

KEY TERMS

Competence: Refers to a combination of knowledge, skills, and attitudes. "Key competence" defines competences necessary for all. It thus includes basic skills, but goes beyond them.

Digital Competence: Involves the confident and critical use of information society technology (IST) for work, leisure, and communication. It is underpinned by basic skills in ICT: the use of computers to retrieve, assess, store, produce, present, and exchange information, and to communicate and participate in collaborative networks via the Internet (Commission of the European Communities, 2005).

ICT: Information and communication technologies signify a range of tools and technologies for managing, storing, retrieving, and communicating information in digital form.

Information Literacy: Involves the ability to critically seek and use information effectively in various situations. In contexts of education, information literacy is seen as the ability to seek, find, critically evaluate and use information for learning of some particular knowledge content, exploring an issue or solving a problem. Information literacy is also seen more broadly as the generic ability of citizens in a democratic society to make well informed choices based on the critical evaluation of a wide range of information sources.

Information Seeking: Involves seeking and using information for learning or other purposes, where information is not restricted to digital form but may include a range of formats such as print material, oral information, and so forth. Nevertheless, digital information and ICT tools are of central interest for the research and practices of information seeking.

Knowledge Contents: Concern some subject matter or concept or aspects of a problem that form the content of a learning task.

Learning Assignment/Task: Implies a task for students to accomplish with the aim of learning particular contents, concepts, or relationships. In this text, learning assignments involve students' independent information seeking and use of a wide range of information sources.

Learning Outcomes: Involve what students learn through accomplishing a learning assignment, including intended knowledge contents as well as other contents, skills, and abilities that students may learn through an assignment.

Chapter XVIII
Digital Epistemologies and Classroom Multiliteracies

Heather Lotherington
York University, Toronto, Canada

ABSTRACT

Contemporary conceptualizations of literacy as socially and culturally situated practice must be framed in our digitally mediated, glocalized societies where networked communication technologies have created innovative texts opening up new literacies and demanding new pedagogies. This chapter discusses a Toronto-based program of collaborative school–university action research that aims to develop a pedagogy of multiliteracies in an urban elementary school. The project engaging our research collective is about guiding children to rewrite traditional children's stories as individualized digital narratives that enfold their cultural understandings and community languages. Situated within current epistemological questions about what it means to become a literate person in the 21st century, our project responds to reciprocal educational challenges: How can we facilitate the acquisition of relevant literacies for contemporary children experiencing divergent home, school, community, and societal practices? How can we redesign curricula and assessment to be socially responsive and responsible?

INTRODUCTION

Nutscracker
That's the whole point. When the helmet and the Helmholtz fuse into a single whole, you can edit the reader as well as the book, if you get my meaning. That's why we say editing technology can be external or internal. Although there's no clear boundary between them, of course. (Pelevin, 2006, p. 99)

Victor Pelevin's (2006) contemporary rewriting of *The Myth of Theseus and the Minotaur*, built around an Internet chat, introduces the epistemological terrain of the multiliteracies study discussed in this chapter. Nutscracker's description of the Helmholtz, who is a cyborg version of the Minotaur, is of a physical being fused to digital hardware who thinks through a synergetic cyber-communications processing facility. Nutscracker meets his fellow maze inmates in a chat room where they collaboratively piece together the physical world of their prison and a description of their captor. Their communications take place in digital space though they are trapped in a physical landscape that none can see from anything but a prisoner's perspective.

The research collective contributing to the study discussed in this chapter, in common with Nutscracker and his digital chat partners, uses contemporary digital technologies to extend human communication capabilities and networks and to look at learning outside the box. New language and literacy processing opportunities through digital technologies invite radically new ways of thinking about language, literacy, and texts and, in turn, require new ways of teaching literacy. Our study experiments with how digital technologies can facilitate a broader concept of literacy in the classroom that entertains children's multilingual and multicultural perspectives. In so doing, our research creates a larger picture of learning to read and write than the curricular landscape of literacy presently describes.

Contemporary digital technologies have opened up innovative communicative possibilities that create the conditions for novel literacies, requiring ways of thinking about and teaching literacy in school. Members of society engage in digital literacies without conscious notice in quotidian social life in many ways, for example, by navigating screen-based instructions to withdraw cash from an ATM (automatic teller machine); downloading an application form from an Internet site; looking up information or social contacts online; purchasing tickets, whether for a movie or a parking space, from an on-site digital dispenser; and cyber-shopping for goods, services, or even a romantic partner. People in the street, as the Helmholtz described by Nutscracker, are literally attached to hardware, such as mobile phones, palm computers, portable digital audio (MP3) players, and other pocket-sized hardware from handheld game devices to pagers, in a seamless machine–human interface that fundamentally changes the relationship between mind and communications technologies. This portrayal of social literacies is, however, at odds with educational paradigms of literacy where children in elementary schools are still learning cursive writing as primary literacy interface, and negotiating pencil and paper tests to determine their success in achieving literacy. The disjuncture between school and social literacies is widening beyond recognition as children take homework back to a home where they play computer games, engage in multiple instant messaging chats, manage profiles on social networking services such as Facebook and MySpace, and plug themselves into a variety of digital media while completing paper and pencil school assignments. Literacy in 21st century education needs to be rewritten.

At Joyce Public School (JPS) in the Greater Toronto Area (GTA), I have been working with teachers to create pedagogical models that engage children in rewriting traditional stories with a contemporary flair. Our story-rewriting project is the focus of a program of collaborative action research that aims to conceptualize and develop new possibilities for teaching contemporary literacies in the elementary classroom. Our research collective is a learning community comprising elementary school teachers and associated school staff, university faculty and student researchers, and community members who are connected locally and digitally. The mission of our project is to design a community-based pedagogy of multiliteracies, following The New London Group's (NLG, 1996) challenge to reconceptualize epistemological and pedagogical thinking about literacy education. Our project is aimed at elementary school children living in a culturally and linguistically diverse urban metropolis.

At JPS, which is typical of inner city elementary schools in the GTA, children are acquiring literacy, and, in a high percentage of cases, English as a second language (ESL) for complex digitally-mediated communication in a rapidly evolving society to which the majority of their parents are newcomers. However, across the province of Ontario, public school systems are constrained by mandatory, high stakes assessments that imagine literacy as a 20th century skill-based activity, confined to paper, sanctioned genres, and the majority languages of English and French. The restrictive notion of literacy tested in high stakes standardized tests has been widely critiqued throughout the North American context (Asselin, Early, & Filipenko, 2005; Darder, 2005; Klinger, Rogers, Anderson, Poth, & Calman, 2006; Lotherington, 2004). Our research project attempts to reposition children who are disadvantaged by the inherent Anglo-centric biases of compulsory literacy testing to engage creatively and competently with evolving multiliteracies built on traditional stories in ways designed to facilitate their learning of English and other languages, and to further their exposure to traditional literature by capturing their motivation to play with digital technologies.

Our project is realized around narrative learning and traditional stories, which are interpreted into personalized narrative forms that invite the learner to be a part of the story. Children first hear, read, and become familiar with a folk or fairy tale, myth, or fable in its canonical print form through repeated classroom exposure. Then, following the emerging multiliteracies pedagogies teachers are designing, they rewrite it through their own developing cultural and linguistic perspectives in digital forms (see Lotherington & Chow, 2006 for an example). In this way, the children become familiar with the canonical literature of social expectation, but learn to read what is otherwise exclusive literature through a process that engages them as insiders to the story: readers as writers; authors as programmers. The learner, as the helmeted Helmholtz in Pelevin's

(2006) rewritten myth, becomes fused into literacy processing in a qualitatively different way as an integral component of the narrative experience. Our exploratory study is motivated by a set of reciprocal challenges:

- How can we facilitate the acquisition of relevant literacies for contemporary children experiencing divergent home, school, community, and societal practices?
- How can we redesign curricula and assessment to be socially responsive and responsible?

As children learn to become critical and creative readers and writers, teachers are developing individual pedagogies that accommodate the contemporary social, cultural, and linguistic spaces urban children inhabit within curricular requirements (see Cummins & Sayers, 1995; Kist, 2005; Pahl & Rowsell, 2006). This chapter tells our story, highlighting current epistemological questions about what it means to become a literate person in the 21st century against our accumulating multiliteracies pedagogies.

BACKGROUND

My story as principal investigator of this project details the evolution of our current quest. I began to study multiliteracies in action several years ago, when I spent a sabbatical leave conducting an ethnographic study of emergent literacies at Joyce Public School, an inner city K-grade 5 public school in the Toronto District School Board (TDSB) located in a pocket of mixed housing juxtaposed with light industry. Most children who attend JPS live in a nearby complex of four high-rise apartments, which house an estimated 4,000 people. The school community is low income, but culturally and linguistically rich. Most parents are immigrants to Canada.

Joyce Public School has adopted a technological immersion approach to social equalization for their students who lack the cultural capital on which curricular teaching and testing are based. The school's innovative technology-infused approach to 21st century education has been internationally recognized in research (Granger, Morbey, Lotherington, Owston, & Wideman, 2002; Kozma, 2003) and in public awards. The principal has been recognized as nationally outstanding (http://www.canadasoutstandingprincipals.ca/); and many JPS teachers have won prestigious awards for their achievements, including the *Prime Minister's Award for Teaching Excellence* and the Learning Partnership's *National Technology Award.*

The teachers and the principal had much to teach me about learning and teaching in a culturally and linguistically diverse, socially underprivileged urban community. My observations of what the children had to tackle to become "literate" illuminated a critical pedagogical issue affecting the community at Joyce Public School, in common with other inner city schools in the TDSB: how to bridge the demographic reality of the school with the imagined audience of native English speakers socialized into middle class Canadian values on which the provincial curriculum and associated gate-keeping literacy assessments are based.

Research shows that children learning a second language most benefit in circumstances where the target language builds on their extant language foundation, rather than suppressing and replacing it (Cummins, 1981, 1991, 2000). This approach to language learning as additive bilingualism (Lambert, 1974) and, by extension, additive multilingualism (Cenoz & Genesee, 1998) begs a 21st century reading of Canada's 1971 multiculturalism policy, which in its current (1988) form states among its aims, to:

1. Preserve and enhance the use of languages other than English and French, while

strengthening the status and use of the official languages of Canada; and

2. Advance multiculturalism throughout Canada in harmony with the national commitment to the official languages of Canada. (Government of Canada: Canadian Heritage, 2004, section 3, Multiculturalism Policy)

The country's national multiculturalism policy thus pledges "commitment" for English and French, but, less forcefully, preservation and enhancement of the languages of all other cultural populations. However, the aim of nurturing a climate of cultural equality and preserving a pluralistic mosaic in a colonially bilingual nation requires reinterpretation in 21st century education given global push and pull factors. External pressures for the support of international languages in Canada include supranational organizations that alter language borders within our increasingly globalized world, such as the North American Free Trade Agreement (NAFTA). Internal pressures are exerted as the demographic face of the nation changes dramatically through sustained immigration, making Toronto, for example, one of the most multicultural cities on earth (http://www.toronto.ca/toronto_facts/diversity.htm). Moreover, native speakers of French are a tiny minority in the Toronto District School Board, which is home to more than 80 languages, spoken by 53% of the school population (TDSB, n.d.). A reconceptualization of language and literacy education is critical not only to facilitate educational success for the multilingual community that dominates the TDSB population, but it is timely in our glocalized society.

The term "glocalization," popularized by Robertson (1992, 1995), is explained as "a synergetic relationship between the global and the local" (Block, 2004, pp. 15-16). It describes the interplay of languages that increasingly populate our contexts of communication. In the view taken by our research collective and by other researchers (García, Skutnabb-Kangas, & Torres-Guzmán, 2006; Schecter & Cummins, 2003), second language education should capitalize on the language and cultural capital multicultural populations bring to the classroom. However, at school, children's home languages are generally suppressed rather than utilized in developing English language proficiency, which is needed to engage in formal education. English is used to assess literacy development in gate-keeping tests that are biased against diverse urban populations whose knowledge base may vary substantially from what the curriculum imagines as the expected socialization of school children. Furthermore, as paper-and-pencil tests, these provincial literacy tests are out of step with contemporary social literacies that unite children in digital play.

The effort to facilitate additive multiple language and literacy acquisition for children in diverse urban contexts is hampered in numerous ways. Opportunities for in-school support of multilingualism in urban classrooms are limited. Currently, the spaces for teaching languages other than English and French are marginalized in the public school system in Ontario, typically relegated to after school and weekend classes taught by teachers who do not necessarily have professional certification. English as a second language assistance is limited both economically and politically. Furthermore, given the crowded curriculum, and the requirement that all students study English and French in school, it is hard to imagine how teachers can create opportunities to teach and support the languages diverse children bring to the classroom, especially given the linguistic heterogeneity of most classes. This was a fundamental challenge we sought to address for both practical and ideological reasons in this project.

Following my ethnographic study of emergent literacies at JPS in 2003, I designed a longer interventionist project to rewrite traditional stories as digital narratives striving to address the mismatches in home and academic language and cultural knowledge that I saw children having to traverse. "Rewriting Goldilocks" was a forerunner of the current project which collaboratively engages teachers, learners, researchers, and community members in supporting multiple language and literacy development, developing children's individual and collective multicultural voices in inclusive resources, and creating innovative pedagogical processes by capitalizing on what the school does well: using digital technology in classroom teaching.

RECONCEPTUALIZING LITERACY

Cook-Gumperz (2006, p. 1) notes that "literacy as socially constructed is both a historically based ideology and a collection of context-bound communicative practices." Our project dynamically reconceptualizes literacy as agentive, culturally and linguistically embedded, digitally playful, and socially and academically empowering for children in elementary school. Our experimental interventions in literacy education are based on longstanding social critiques of literacy as static and determined; critiques that argue for socially embedded education nurturing agency, creativity, and empowerment.

For decades, scholars have critiqued the notion of literacy as a socially disembodied, cognitive skill, arguing for socially situated approaches to conceptualizing and teaching literacy. Freire's (1970/1998) critical approach to adult literacy queried the banking notion of transmission education towards a problem-posing model of education that articulated literacy as critical and agentive, rather than as passive and static. Heath (1983) critiqued notions of literacy as culturally neutral, and academically located, finding differential school successes in children from three geographically linked but socially and ethnically diverse communities, based on their preschool literacy socialization. Street (1984, 1995), who like Heath (1983) formulated his thoughts about literacy in anthropological research, argued that delineations of literacy as an autonomous skill were inherently ethnocentric, colonial, and developmentally simplistic in drawing a linear relationship from orality to literacy, and he posed a contrasting ideological model of literacy as socially and culturally situated. Martin-Jones and Jones (2000) took the notion of socially situated literacies to the multilingual community, engaging local languages in community interplay.

These studies understood socially situated literacies as belonging to physical cultures. Indeed, the notion of literacy is typically grounded in the physical world as Warschauer demonstrates in a description of a school principal who vetoes an after school online journalism project so teachers can concentrate on improving literacy (2006a, p. 1). However, culture is also digital (Beavis, 1997; de Castell & Jensen, 2003; Gee, 2003; Suoranta & Lehtimäki, 2004).

Negroponte (1995) is credited with first distinguishing the contrasting worlds of atoms and bits that construct different worlds of information:

The best way to appreciate the merits and consequences of being digital is to reflect on the difference between bits and atoms. While we are undoubtedly in an information age, most information is delivered to us in the form of atoms: newspapers, magazines, and books (like this one). Our economy may be moving toward an information economy, but we measure trade and we write our balance sheets with atoms in mind. (p. 11)

Since the inception of the Internet as a public space in 1991, the notion of community has been extended to the virtual world, in which new literacies and new identities are rapidly developing, challenging exclusive constructions of literacy as paper-based (see Cummins & Sayers, 1995; Gee, 2003; Hawisher & Selfe, 2000; Kress, 2003; Lankshear, Gee, Knobel, & Searle, 1997; Lankshear & Knobel, 2003; Snyder; 1997, 2002).

The complexities of contemporary literacy were articulated as *multiliteracies* by the New London Group (1996), who called for new multiliteracies pedagogies to answer to contemporary social needs.

First, we want to extend the idea and scope of literacy pedagogy to account for the context of our culturally and linguistically diverse and increasingly globalized societies, for the multifarious cultures that interrelate and the plurality of texts that circulate. Second, we argue that literacy pedagogy now must account for the burgeoning variety of text forms associated with information and multimedia technologies. This includes understanding and competent control of representational forms that are becoming increasingly significant in the overall communications environment, such as visual images and their relationship to the written word—for instance, visual design in desktop publishing or the interface of visual and linguistic meaning in multimedia. Indeed, this second point relates closely back to the first; the proliferation of communications channels and media supports and extends cultural and subcultural diversity. (¶ 2)

Early 20th century theorists foreshadowed the epistemological challenge of 21st century literacies, tying the notion of an in-the-making electronic universe to communication arenas (McLuhan, 1964; Ong, 1980, 1982). McLuhan's theorized global village projected new platforms for communication long before the digital world as we know it today: "'The medium is the message,' means, in terms of the electronic age, that a totally new environment has been created" (p. vii).

Buckingham (2003, p. 173) describes media convergence in contemporary literacies, pointing out that proliferating digital technologies do not displace older communication technologies so much as merge cultural forms and practices previously seen as distinct. Researchers including Lankshear and Knobel (2003) and Kellner (2002) have called for an epistemological reconceptualization of education that envisions the scope of 21st century literacies. To rewrite possibilities for literacy education for a cohort of elementary school children living in a culturally and linguistically diverse community in an urban landscape unified by digital pop culture was our challenge.

EXPERIMENTAL DIGITAL LITERACIES AT JOYCE PUBLIC SCHOOL

Complex modern societies involve the networking together of different social practices across different domains or fields of social life (e.g., the economy, education, family life) and across different scales of social life (global, regional, national, local). Texts are a crucial part of these networking relations. (Fairclough, 2003, p. 30)

Secondary Orality in the Digital Era: Sandra's *Goldilocks* Stories, Grade 2

The pilot project in grade 2 began with the decision to rewrite the timeless story of *Goldilocks and the Three Bears*, which was found to be very popular with children in the primary grades. However, getting to the story adaptation process was impeded by a protest that would ultimately lead us to rich understandings about the potential of digital literacies. Subsequent to approaching the principal about the idea of rewriting traditional stories from the children's cultural and linguistic vantage points utilizing the innovative technological infrastructure the school was renowned for, which she was extremely supportive of, a small group of interested teachers was presented with the preliminary idea. The ESL teacher, with whom I had worked very closely the preceding year, was concerned: for her, as an Asian immigrant to Canada, Goldilocks had been a quintessential element in her Canadian socialization. To change the characterization of the protagonist was un-

necessarily destructive. Goldilocks should remain young, blonde, and female.

Surprised by the ESL teacher's misapprehension that Goldilocks was Canadian, I decided to research the origins of the story in the Osborne Collection at the Toronto Public Library, where, with guidance, I traced a trajectory of Goldilocks' becoming from a cautionary Scottish folk tale of a fox who invades the lair of three bears and is eaten for her transgression, through interpretations of the vixen as old lady, to more youthful versions of the protagonist in the mid–late 19th century until the emergence of the little blonde girl we recognize as Goldilocks today, appearing in early American story editions around the turn of the 20th century (Lotherington, 2005). Oddly, the story did ultimately have a Canadian connection: the first known text of the story, a beautifully handwritten, watercolor-illustrated manuscript, was permanently housed in the Osborne Collection, a bequest of heirloom children's books donated to the Toronto Public library in the mid-20th century. Like so many of the children enjoying the story at Joyce Public School, Goldilocks, herself, was an immigrant.

The protagonist of *The Three Bears* had changed over time to become the Goldilocks we expect today, fossilized as a little blonde girl in 20th century print versions. But the folktale had been told long before Goldilocks was cemented into her modernist identity. With the postmodern publication opportunities of the Internet, I questioned whether we could not resuscitate the age-old storytelling tradition of individualizing the narrative to the audience at hand; we could use digital media to tailor individual versions.

Our investigations into digitally mediated storytelling recall the work of literary scholar Walter Ong, whose conceptualization of *secondary orality* (1980, 1982) challenges expectations of linearity in the relationship of orality to literacy. Ong, whose work presaged the digital era, spoke to a world of electronic media such as radio and television that creates a secondary orality distinct from the primary orality of human speech development. "Because we live in a media-conscious world, we are unable to make the contrast between oral speech and writing" (Ong, 1980, p. 204).

The concept of secondary orality provides a useful lens for looking at 21st century communication modalities, such as instant messaging chat, blogs, and interactive video games that bridge oral and written proficiencies in novel ways (Baron, 2004; Crystal, 2006; Herring, 2004; Lotherington & Xu, 2004; Warschauer, 2006b), creating new genres, interactional spaces, and identities (Hawisher & Selfe, 2000; Lankshear & Knobel, 2003). In turn, digital applications provide rich opportunities for retelling stories in a facelifted oral tradition.

The children in Sandra's grade 2 class were read the story of Goldilocks in its 20th century realization several times before hearing "twisted fairy tale" versions that subverted the story in terms of setting or time. As the children gained familiarity with the narrative, they embarked on rewriting it, first as a class story, and then as individual narratives, which were developed on HyperStudio (Lotherington & Chow, 2006). The stories were printed as booklets to be read to family members on Father's Day. Meanwhile, the teacher experimented with the digital versions of the stories the children had produced to see how they could be animated and narrated using available technologies.

The children's renderings of *Goldilocks and the Three Bears* far outstripped my expectations of grade 2 children's narrative processing and cultural retelling. Thinking in terms of superficial replacement of the character as self, I had pictured a localization of the story setting to Toronto high rise dwellings, and a protagonist with Asian or African facial features. However, as can be seen in Figure 1, children's cultural worlds are highly

Figure 1. Sugi and the three aliens (©2007, Children's school work. Used with permission)

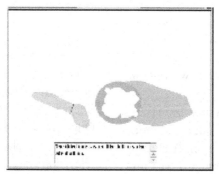

influenced by digital pop culture. Their rewriting of Goldilocks was anything but skin-deep. Instead, the children created coherent, clearly motivated protagonists who were hungry, neglected, adventurous, needy, naughty, or just plain nasty.

For example, in Figure 1, Sugi, a space explorer, enters the UFO of three space aliens who are out for a space walk, where he encounters three bowls of slime, which, in the mind of a 7-year-old boy, may well describe porridge. The bowls of food are suitably gruesome until he encounters the third, which tastes like jello, a cultural interpretation of something worth eating if you have been so bad as to illegally enter someone's house.

In Figure 2, we meet Stinky Robber, who it turns out, enters the bears' house because he is hungry. When the bears discover him, cringing in the corner of the bedroom, they invite him to eat some soup. The compassionate bears in Stinky Robber are subverted hilariously in Sharky (see Figure 3), who is a bully that invades the home of three goldfish out for a swim before returning to their fish food. Sharky eats papa's (not baby's!) food; then he breaks papa's chair and goes for a nap in papa's bed. When the goldfish return after their outing, they find Sharky lounging in papa's bed. Sharky, annoyed by being woken, simply eats the three goldfish and lives happily ever after.

Figure 2. Stinky robber and the three bears (©2007, Children's school work. Used with permission)

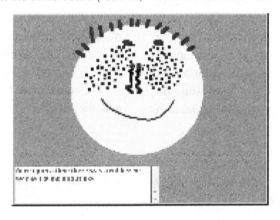

Figure 3. Sharky and the three goldfish (©2007, Children's school work. Used with permission)

 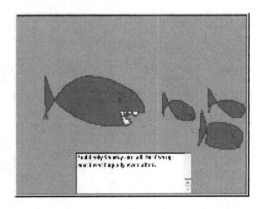

After the children had completed their Hyper-Studio stories, Sandra experimented with form, venturing into iMovie versions of these hypertext stories, which opened up new avenues for exploration in multiliteracies education.

Moving from Paper to Screen: Leon's *Chicken Little* Stories, Kindergarten

Leon's pull-out senior kindergarten group rewrote stories in the library that were inspired by *Chicken Little*, whose scenario of the sky falling speaks to children's fears of the world around them collapsing. At this age, children cannot read or write independently; additionally, these children were in the process of acquiring English as a second language. Leon is an award-winning teacher who sees the screen as the site of contemporary literacy instruction. He was interested in teaching children to link paper and screen realizations of their stories: an important pedagogical moment that traditional literacy teaching and testing do not yet seem to have pedagogically realized in meaningful ways.

Leon read the story of *Chicken Little* to the children who, when ready to tell their own "fear" stories, drew their narratives in little paper books simply created from a sheet of folded paper, using crayons. The children narrated their picture stories to Leon, who typed and printed them, then cut and pasted one or two sentences per page to describe each child's picture story (see Figure 4). Leon then showed them how, using either a digital camera or a scanner, they could move their books from paper onto screen, importing their handdrawn pictures complete with transcribed story text into a digital slide tray (see Figure 5). The children then chose their preferred software from iMovie, Kid Pix, or PowerPoint, all of which facilitate animation and narration. This simple transformation takes basic paper and pencil literacy to a programming dimension, merging writing technologies. In essence, these kindergarten children are programming before they can manage alphabetic literacy, exemplifying Prensky's (2006) notion of 21st century literacy as programming.

This movement between the world of atoms and the world of bits (Negroponte, 1995) is a

Figure 4. A captioned page from a little boy's "fear" story about a big dog (©2007, Children's school work. Used with permission)

moment in literacy instruction that is critical, yet at present poorly realized in curriculum and pedagogical practices, and unrealized in provincial literacy tests, despite being so conceptually simple that it can be successfully accomplished at the kindergarten level. In this class, Leon went on to have the children narrate their stories, so they literally retold their stories in their own voices. We began to think about how they could retell stories in multiple languages in ways that we could capture and save.

Making Spaces for Multiple Language Learning: Michelle's *The Lion and the Mouse*, Kindergarten

Primary teachers, and especially kindergarten teachers, inherently understand and teach mul-

timodal literacies: they tell stories across genres using story books, drawing and painting, songs, puppets, crafts, play-acting, and other concrete play activities. This interconnectedness between modalities of expression tends to become diminished in more advanced education as the printed page becomes the focus.

Michelle, who taught a kindergarten class at JPS, had wonderful ideas about how to involve children in the learning and creation of narratives. She used PowerPoint to document a photo-story of her children enacting the plot of *The Gingerbread Man* in a baking activity where the finished gingerbread cookies mysteriously disappeared, leaving a little trail of cookie crumbs for the children to follow. Their treasure hunt for the runaway gingerbread cookies was directed by

Figure 5. Optional digital slide trays for children's stories: iMovie, Kid Pix, PowerPoint (©2007, Children's school work. Used with permission)

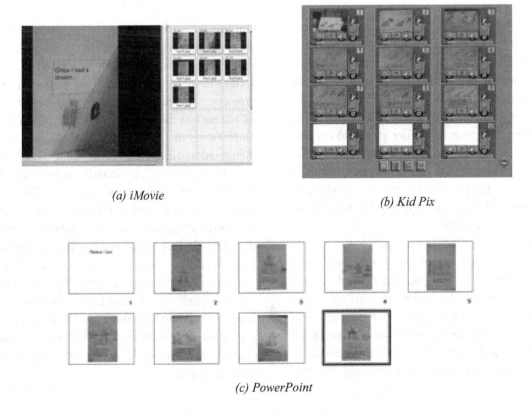

(a) iMovie

(b) Kid Pix

(c) PowerPoint

notes giving directions followed by the traditional refrain: "Run, run as fast as you can! You can't catch me, I'm the gingerbread man." Eventually, after faithfully following the trail of crumbs and notes, the children caught up with their naughty gingerbread cookies in their own classroom, scolded them for running away, and happily ate them all up.

The class's baking adventure exposed the children to the narrative of *The Gingerbread Man*. Michelle captured the children's participation in the narrative as a PowerPoint presentation, marking the story progression with captioned photos of the children. This provided a way for the children to literally enter and read the narrative as insiders to the story. This insider perspective is a characteristic of video gaming: the player functions as an integral component of the narrative (de Castell & Jensen, 2003; Gee, 2003). This perspective is charged with fostering participant engagement in literacy (Johnson, 2005; Prensky, 2006).

Last year, Michelle chose to work with Aesop's fable of *The Lion and the Mouse*, in which a lion is saved by a cagey mouse who had earlier talked her way out of the lion's capture. After Michelle had patiently familiarized the children with the traditional narrative by reading it to them several times in its canonical form, she scaffolded the children's personalized retelling first as a whole class activity, then in smaller groups to support those who were struggling with English. The children's beautiful stories were drawn using Kid Pix. When the picture stories were arranged in sequence, Michelle typed in the children's retold versions of the story.

During this time, our collective was experimenting with the use of machine translation in attempt to create multilingual versions of the children's stories (Lotherington, 2007). We soon discovered, unsurprisingly, in retrospect, that machine translation provides only gross literal translations (in common world languages), absolutely necessitating postmachine editing. This was

not helpful to our project of reproducing children's stories in multiple community languages with few expert resources in languages such as Turkish, Vietnamese, Tamil, and Guyanese Creole. This being the case, Michelle used her network of parents and educational assistants to help in the translation of children's stories, creating a number of beautiful multilingual stories using languages spoken in the community by the children and their families. Michelle's class created colorful, imaginative, linguistically tailored stories that engaged children on the cusp of being socialized into alphabetic literacy as authors of their own creative, digitally rendered stories told in different languages. These resources allow children to take stories home to relatives who can read them in the language of the home and in the language of the school.

Gaming the Traditional: Sandra's *Old Man Yu Removes the Mountain*, Grade 4

Our project work is conducted mostly at the primary grade levels (kindergarten to grade 3; 4–8 year olds), but when Sandra was given a grade 4 class to teach, we included the juniors in our project as well. Sandra's grade 4 class began with a Chinese folk tale, entitled (in English) *Old Man Yu Removes the Mountain* which children read, then discussed in terms of ethical education. What was Old Man Yu's dilemma and how did he choose to address it? With a class consensus about the moral of the story that faith and determination will move mountains, the children brainstormed their own desires and dilemmas and thought out ways of addressing them befitting of this moral. The class agreed that going to the Olympic games in Torino, Italy to watch the Canadian teams play hockey would be like moving a mountain. Having established a common aim, they developed characters and a plot describing how they would meet their goal.

In consultation with the research collective, Sandra decided that the class would try an adventurous digital genre in the rewriting task: a video game. According to Prensky, the children of today are born into a digital world, making them essentially "digital natives" (2006, p. 28). Those of us born prior to the net generation, on the other hand, he describes as "digital immigrants" (2006, p. 28). Prensky carries his socialization metaphor further, describing digital natives as being inherently capable of digital programming, at least at a basic level, such as personalizing cell phone options. He posits that "programming is the language and literacy of digital technology, and thus of the 21st century" (2006, p. 49).

The notion that video games not only provide useful literacy education, but that they presage the future of literacy is held by an increasing number of contemporary researchers, scholars, and educational advocates (Beavis, 1997, 2002; de Castell & Jenson, 2003; Gee, 2003; Johnson, 2005; Lotherington, 2004; Prensky, 2006). After learning to play video games with his son, Gee wrote a book on the benefits of video game playing for literacy learning, in which he posits 36 principles of learning that are an inherent part of good video games, tying video game playing into embodied cognition, new literacy studies and connectionism as a model of learning (2003, p. 7). Moreover, the problem-based nature of game playing engages learners in literacy and learning that might not otherwise be as motivating. As Johnson (2005) wryly notes, speaking of his gaming adventures with a 7-year-old boy:

The question is why kids are so eager to soak up that much information when it is delivered to them in game form. My nephew would be asleep in five minutes if you popped him down in an urban studies classroom, but somehow an hour of playing SimCity taught him that high taxes in industrial areas can stifle development. That's a powerful learning experience. ... Why does a seven-year-old soak up the intricacies of industrial economics in

game form, when the same subject would send him screaming for the exits in a classroom? (p. 32)

Professor Jennifer Jenson, researcher and professor in pedagogy and technology at York University, was happy to assist us in accomplishing our aims to use a game genre for the class narrative. She presented a guest workshop at the school on an evolving game shell using legomation: animated lego characters, and provided Web site access to the grade 4 class so they could program their story. Professor Jenson's educational game project was Web-based but designed to mimic a handheld device, such as the pocket video game platforms popularly played by children. This was inviting to children whose social literacies more closely match game playing than story-writing.

Sandra and the children set to work, individualizing the class narrative, and building the characters they had collectively created (Puppy and Horse). They worked closely with Professor Jenson and her research and development team. In fact, the grade 4 children's work usefully informed Professor Jenson's research project as to glitches and bugs in the game shell they were developing. Her computer programmer, who made a personal visit to the children at school for information sharing, programmed the children's customized legomation characters Horse and Puppy into the site to enable individualized versions of their class story. In this way, the children's grade 4 multiliteracies project usefully informed university level research on educational game construction. This is truly multidimensional learning.

The children wrote their stories as legomation games, programming their characters and settings into the game shell, and giving their characters voices in terms of speech bubbles and narration blocks, all highly literate activities. Sandra also took the generic class story to a colleague who translated it back into Chinese, creating a circular bilingualism that allowed the two languages to spiral into each other. This gave us ideas about alternative ways to consider how and where we could incorporate multiple languages in the story creation process.

FUTURE TRENDS

External technologies affect what we see, internal technologies affect what we think (Pelevin, 2006, p. 100).

This collaborative research project is ongoing and cumulative, each story creation exercise generating ideas about and avenues for how we can imaginatively and inexpensively support multiliteracies development using digital technologies in culturally and linguistically heterogeneous classrooms. As we move into our fourth year of experimental digital narratives with elementary school children, we meet shifting horizons in literacy development on different planes informing us about language inclusion and support in curricular teaching, digital pedagogies, collaborative learning possibilities, new multimodal narrative shapes, multicultural ideology, community-building online, and the jigsaw nature of fulfilling both social and curricular expectations of literacy.

Our small children's stories are showing us a new way to imagine pedagogy that is context sensitive, contemporary, authentically communicative, and motivating to teachers and children. The localized model we are creating is important. A perennial political critique of attempts to include the multiple languages of a cosmopolitan urban centre such as Toronto in education is the expensive unreality of systemically supporting the profusion of different languages, particularly in linguistically heterogeneous classrooms in which six or eight different languages might be spoken within a single class. The default becomes economically rationalized education based on the official languages, and geared to the social and economic lingua franca, with marginalized, tack-on classes in selected minority languages. My intention is not to doubt the importance of

teaching and learning English and French, nor minority languages in their current realization, nor canonical children's literature. What is lacking in this model, though, is sensitivity to what all children bring to the educational enterprise, and what all children can stand to benefit from the multilingual reality of their current classrooms. We need to take account of how second languages are most efficiently learned. Research indicates that second language learning is most effectively accomplished when tied to prior learning: incorporating multiple languages supports the language acquisition process (Cummins, 1981, 1991, 2000). The languages children and their families already speak are an important foundation in education; furthermore, they are a resource in our globalized economy that is, at present, going largely to waste.

The many pedagogical directions our project is leading us in terms of small story possibilities (that include soundscapes, wiki stories, and digital collaborations with paired schools) inform political models of language and literacy education on a much larger scale: they show how we can augment systemwide, selective language and literacy teaching and learning by including community-sensitive multiliteracies projects. Our project indicates that it is possible to support multiple languages and contemporary digital literacies with dedicated teachers, inspired ideas, and collaborative networks.

CONCLUSION

Our school–university collaborative research project works towards incorporating the languages, cultures, and communicative media of the contemporary student body in urban Toronto into curricular literacy education in order to facilitate their learning (and ours), and to revise literacy education for children who will inherit and define the future. We are bringing into the classroom the languages of the community, which are, at present, insufficiently and inequitably supported in curricular learning in Ontario; reformulating the realization of multiculturalism in literacy education; and creating new pedagogies that utilize contemporary communicative media. In so doing, we are creating collaborative discourses in a problem-based learning environment. Our work in this area fundamentally incorporates digital technologies; and our results contribute to an understanding of multiliteracies pedagogies and digital epistemologies. The study is epistemologically situated within current questions about what it means to become a literate person in the 21st century. Our process is pragmatic in orientation, guided by the questions:

- How can we facilitate the acquisition of relevant literacies for contemporary children experiencing divergent home, school, community, and societal practices?
- How can we redesign curricula and assessment to be socially responsive and responsible?

To answer these questions, our project encourages playing with narratives in the digital sandbox. It is a fulfilling if unfamiliar and occasionally bumpy journey. Joyce Public School is invested in digital pedagogy. This has been our mainstay in experimentally revising literacy education for children who, at present, are unfairly disadvantaged by their linguistic and cultural knowledge. But rather than intensively drilling English and Anglo-Canadian history into children whose cultural backgrounds are at odds with curricular expectations and assessments, we aim to revise literacy education to be inclusive of old and new cultural and linguistic knowledge, and old and new literacies. We are, in essence, telling old stories in new ways.

The teachers have taught me that digital technology can mean many different things. The hardware teachers are using in our project includes simple and relatively inexpensive pieces of equipment, such as digital cameras, scanners, printers, and photocopiers as well as more costly items such as digital videocameras and computers. Associated paraphernalia such as memory keys, microphones, and Webcams are relatively cheap and very useful. At the university level, hardware is typically envisaged in terms of complex and powerful networked computers.

A wide variety of software is freely downloadable to public schools in Ontario. What the teachers at Joyce Public School have done is to experiment with these programs to see how they can facilitate teaching and learning curricular material. Further to officially available software, we have utilized open source software, and Web-based programs. We also negotiated educational access to a research-based game shell, which benefited the project researchers as much as it did the teachers and children.

In these individual action research studies brought together for collective learning, the participating teachers have creatively used what is available to them in their quest for equitable learning opportunities for their students. This experimentation, which is demanded of digital pedagogies where learning is problem-based, distributed, and complementary, subverts the typical top-down model of formal education. As de Castell and Jenson (2003, p. 662) explain:

The cultural environment of schools today is, in many ways, antithetical to the immersiveness of play—it insists on timed activities (no room for "losing track" of time by being absorbed in reading a book or solving a mathematics problem); curriculum is designed mostly to "survey" a subject area, with little opportunity to study one or two subjects in depth; and goals and immediate feedback (both punishment and rewards) are often held back from students in institutionally sanctioned power struggles between students and teachers.

Our research collective's motive is to include the linguistic and cultural knowledge of the school community, as recognized physically and digitally, in curricular learning. We continue to struggle with pathways for fostering additive multilingualism in the heterogeneous classroom (on a budget), but our explorations have been cumulatively rewarding in what promises to be paradoxically a context-sensitive journey inviting participation from digitally connected communities in which there are complementary voices (see Lotherington, 2007). We have learned that digital technology facilitates human translation in useful, collaborative ways that include class exchanges where children can interact with and interpret other children's voices. Our context is local; it is global; it is glocal.

Our reconceptualizing of multiculturalism in the curriculum is in line with the national multiculturalism policy, which is inadequately realized in current formal education. The children have taught us, importantly, that multiculturalism must include the digital world. This continues to be an engaging problem, especially given the apparent influence of Disney as a cultural mediator in their understanding of traditional stories. The subtextual imperialism in Disney (and other) comics was brilliantly articulated by writer and literary theorist Ariel Dorfman (1983; Dorfman & Mattelart, 1984) long before the digital era. However, in the converging media environments experienced by today's media—saturated children, the commercial, Hollywood-mediated curriculum passively learned by children raised on television cartoons, connecting Web sites, and associated advertised commercial goods such as books, toys, and comics—is greatly amplified.

For three years, our research collective has been rewriting traditional narratives at an elementary school in response to the New London Group's (1996) call for action to design a pedagogy of multiliteracies. In our context, we have developed ways to teach young children to create dynamic narratives from traditional stories that support the development of individual voice, and foster cultural and linguistic inclusion using digital technologies. Teachers have developed simple and inexpensive ways of connecting physical and digital modalities to facilitate, clarify, and link paper and screen literacies, a process we term transliteracies, which is a moment in literacy history that is at present only poorly realized, if at all, in public education. Our exploration into new ways of telling stories using digital media revives Ong's theory of secondary orality (1980, 1982) in contemporary digital practice.

Our project has opened digital exchange avenues for exploratory language learning and maintenance across populations in our expanding digital community that stretches to Asia at present, encouraging collaborative, problem-based learning in distributed partnerships with the community, teachers, and researchers. The project is ongoing; the quest infinite. But at the end of each school year, we have the children's stories, which showcase important learning accomplishments in our journey.

ACKNOWLEDGMENT

I gratefully acknowledge the Social Sciences and Humanities Research Council of Canada for awarding standard research grant 410-2005-2080 in support of the research project: "Emergent multiliteracies in theory and practice: Multicultural literacy development at elementary school." I acknowledge with gratitude the Social Sciences and Humanities Research Council of Canada for funding the project: "Observing multiliteracies in action." I acknowledge with gratitude the Social Sciences and Humanities Research Council of Canada for funding the project: "Rewriting Goldilocks: Emergent transliteracies." My deep appreciation to Dr. Leslie McGrath, Head, Osborne Collection, Toronto Public Library, for her expert guidance. The ethical consent for this project permits the identification of the school and of participating teachers in research publications. The identity of children at the school, however, is protected. Thank you to Joyce Public School (previously identified as Main Street School in publications) and to Sandra Chow, Michelle Holland, and Leon Lenchner whose class projects are highlighted in this publication.

REFERENCES

Asselin, M., Early, M., & Filipenko, M. (2005). Accountability, assessment, and the literacies of information and communication technologies. *Canadian Journal of Education, 28*(4), 802-826.

Baron, D. (2004). *Technologies of the word: Reading and writing in the digital age.* Paper presented at the Illinois Library Association Annual Conference, Chicago, IL. Retrieved March 17, 2008, from http://www.english.uiuc.edu/-people-/faculty/debaron/essays/wordtech.htm

Beavis, C. (1997). Computer games, culture and curriculum. In I. Snyder (Ed.), *Page to screen: Taking literacy into the electronic era* (pp. 234-255). St. Leonards, NSW: Allen & Unwin.

Beavis, C. (2002). Reading, writing and role-playing computer games. In I. Snyder (Ed.), *Silicon literacies: Communication, innovation and education in the electronic age* (pp. 47-61). London: Routledge.

Block, D. (2004). Globalization, transnational communication and the Internet. *International Journal on Multicultural Societies, 6*(1), 13-28.

Buckingham, D. (2003). *Media education: Literacy, learning and contemporary culture.* Cambridge: Polity Press.

Cenoz, J., & Genessee, F. (1998). Pscholinguistic perspectives on multilingualism and multilingual education. In J. Cenoz & F. Genessee (Eds.), *Beyond bilingualism: Multilingualism and multilingual education* (pp. 16-32). Clevedon: Multilingual Matters.

Cook-Gumperz, J. (2006). The social construction of literacy. In J. Cook-Gumperz (Ed.), *The social construction of literacy* (2nd ed., pp. 1-18). Cambridge: Cambridge University Press.

Crystal, D. (2006). *Language and the Internet* (2nd ed.). Cambridge: Cambridge University Press.

Cummins, J. (1981). *Bilingualism and minority language children.* Ontario: Ontario Institute for Studies in Education.

Cummins, J. (1991). Interdependence of first- and second language proficiency. In E. Bialystok (Ed.), *Language processing in bilingual children* (pp. 70-89). Cambridge: Cambridge University Press.

Cummins, J. (2000). *Language, power and pedagogy: Bilingual children in the crossfire.* Clevedon: Multilingual Matters.

Cummins, J. (2006). Identity texts: The imaginative construction of self through multiliteracies pedagogy. In O. García, T. Skutnabb-Kangas, & M.E. Torres- Guzmán (Eds.), *Imagining multilingual schools: Languages in education and glocalization* (pp. 51-68). Clevedon: Multilingual Matters.

Cummins, J., & Sayers, D. (1995). *Brave new schools: Challenging cultural illiteracy through global learning networks.* New York: St. Martin's Press.

Darder, A. (2005). Schooling and the culture of dominion: Unmasking the ideology of standardized testing. In G.E. Fischman, P. McLaren, H. Sünker, & C. Lankshear (Eds.), *Critical theories, radical pedagogies, and global conflicts* (pp. 207-222). Lanham, MD: Rowman and Littlefield.

de Castell, S., & Jenson, J. (2003). Serious play. *Journal of Curriculum Studies, 35*(6), 649-665.

Dorfman, A. (1983). *The empire's old clothes: What the Lone Ranger, Babar, the Reader's Digest, and other false friends do to our minds.* London: Pluto.

Dorfman, A., & Mattelart, A. (1984). *How to read Donald Duck: Imperialist ideology in the Disney comic* (D. Kunzie, Trans., 2nd ed.). New York: International General.

Fairclough, N. (2003). *Analysing discourse: Textual analysis for social research.* London: Routledge.

Freire, P. (1998). *Pedagogy of the oppressed* (M.B. Ramos, Trans., 20th anniversary ed.). New York: Continuum. (Original work published 1970).

García, O., Skutnabb-Kangas, T., & Torres-Guzmán, M.E. (Eds.). (2006). *Imagining multilingual schools: Languages in education and glocalization.* Clevedon: Multilingual Matters.

Gee, J.P. (2003). *What video games have to teach us about learning and literacy.* New York: Palgrave Macmillan.

Government of Canada: Canadian Heritage. (2004). *Canadian Multiculturalism Act.* Retrieved March 17, 2008, from http://www.canadianheritage.gc.ca/progs/multi/policy/act_e.cfm

Granger, C.A., Morbey, M.L., Lotherington, H., Owston, R.D., & Wideman, H.H. (2002). Canada: Factors contributing to teachers' successful implementation of information technology. *Journal of Computer Assisted Learning, 18*(4), 480-488.

Hawisher, G.E., & Selfe, C.L. (Eds.). (2000). *Global literacies and the World-Wide Web.* London: Routledge.

Heath, S.B. (1983). *Ways with words: Language, life and work in communities and classrooms.* Cambridge: Cambridge University Press.

Herring, S.C. (2004). Computer-mediated discourse analysis: An approach to researching online behavior. In S.A. Barab, R. Kling, & J.H.

Gray (Eds.), *Designing for virtual communities in the service of learning* (pp. 338-376). New York: Cambridge University Press.

Johnson, S. (2005). *Everything bad is good for you: How today's popular culture is actually making us smarter.* New York: Riverhead.

Kellner, D.M. (2002). Technological revolution, multiple literacies, and the restructuring of education. In I. Snyder (Ed.), *Silicon literacies: Communication, innovation and education in the electronic age.* London: Routledge.

Kist, W. (2005). *New literacies in action: Teaching and learning in multiple media.* New York: Teachers College Press.

Klinger, D.A., Rogers, W.T., Anderson, J.O., Poth, C., & Calman, R. (2006). Contextual and school factors associated with achievement on a high-stakes examination. *Canadian Journal of Education, 29*(3), 771-797.

Kozma, R. (Ed.). (2003). *Technology, innovation, and change—A global phenomenon.* Eugene, OR: International Society for Technology in Education.

Kress, G. (2003). *Literacy in the new media age.* London: Routledge.

Lambert, W.E. (1974). Culture and language as factors in learning and education. In F.E. Abour & R.D. Meade (Eds.), *Cultural factors in learning and education* (pp. 91-122). Bellingham, WA: 5th Western Washington Symposium of Learning.

Lankshear, C., Gee, J.P., Knobel, M., & Searle, C. (1997). *Changing literacies.* Buckingham: Open University Press.

Lankshear, C., & Knobel, M. (2003). *New literacies: Changing knowledge and classroom learning.* Buckingham/Philadelphia: Open University Press.

Lotherington, H. (2004). Emergent metaliteracies: What the Xbox has to offer the EQAO. *Linguistics and Education, 14*(3-4), 305-319.

Lotherington, H. (2005). Writing postmodern fairy tales at Main Street School: Digital narratives and evolving transliteracies. *McGill Journal of Education, 40*(1), 109-119.

Lotherington, H. (2007). Rewriting traditional tales as multilingual narratives at elementary school: Problems and progress. *Canadian Journal of Applied Linguistics, 10*(2), 241-256.

Lotherington, H., & Chow, S. (2006). Rewriting *Goldilocks* in the urban, multicultural elementary school. *The Reading Teacher, 60*(3), 244-252.

Lotherington, H., & Xu, Y. (2004). How to chat in English and Chinese: Emerging digital language conventions. *ReCALL, 16*(2), 308-329.

Martin-Jones, M., & Jones, K. (2000). Introduction: Multilingual literacies. In M. Martin-Jones & K. Jones (Eds.), *Multilingual literacies* (pp. 1-15). Amsterdam: John Benjamins.

McLuhan, M. (1964). *Understanding media: The extensions of man.* New York: McGraw-Hill.

Negroponte. N. (1995). *Being digital.* New York: Vintage Books.

New London Group, The. (1996). A pedagogy of multiliteracies: Designing social factors. *Harvard Educational Review, 66*(1), 60-92. Retrieved March 17, 2008, from http://www.edreview.org/harvard96/1996/sp96/p96cope.htm

Ong, W. (1980). Literacy and orality in our times. *Journal of communication, 30*(1), 197-204.

Ong, W.J. (1982). *Orality and literacy: The technologizing of the word.* London: Routledge.

Pahl, K., & Rowsell, J. (Eds.). (2006). *Travel notes from the new literacy studies: Instances of practice.* Clevedon: Multilingual Matters.

Pelevin, V. (2006). *The helmet of horror: The myth of Theseus and the minotaur* (A. Bromfield, Trans.). Edinburgh: Cannongate. (Original work published 2006)

Prensky, M. (2006). *Don't bother me mom, I'm learning.* St. Paul: Paragon House.

Robertson, R. (1992). *Globalization: Social theory and global culture.* London: Sage.

Robertson, R. (1995). Glocalization: Time-space and homogeneity-heterogeneity. In M. Featherstone, S. Lash, & R. Robertson (Eds.), *Global modernities* (pp. 25-44). London: Sage.

Schecter, S.R., & Cummins, J. (Eds.). (2003). *Multilingual education in practice: Using diversity as a resource.* Portsmouth, NH: Heinemann.

Snyder, I. (Ed.). (1997). *Page to screen: Taking literacy into the electronic era.* St. Leonards, NSW: Allen & Unwin.

Snyder, I. (Ed.). (2002). *Silicon literacies: Communication, innovation and education in the electronic age.* London: Routledge.

Street, B. (1984). *Literacy in theory and practice.* Cambridge: Cambridge University Press.

Street, B. (1995). *Social literacies: Critical approaches to literacy in development, ethnography and education.* London: Longman.

Suoranta, J., & Lehtimäki, H. (2004). *Children in the information society: The case of Finland* (H. Liikala, Trans.). New York: Peter Lang.

Toronto District School Board. (n.d.). *Facts and figures.* Retrieved March 17, 2008, from http://www.tdsb.on.ca/_site/ViewItem.asp?siteid=302&menuid=3654&pageid=3049

Warschauer, M. (2006a). *Laptops and literacy: Learning in the wireless classroom.* New York: Teachers College Press.

Warschauer, M. (2006b). Literacy and technology: Bridging the divide. In D. Gibbs & K.-L. Krause (Eds.), *Cyberlines 2: Languages and cultures of the Internet* (pp. 163-174). Albert Park, Australia: James Nicholas.

KEY TERMS

Additive Bilingualism: An approach to second language teaching in which the second language is seen as an addition to the learner's first language rather than as a replacement for it. In additive bilingualism, educational support is offered for the first language in tandem with second language instruction.

Additive Multilingualism: Education in which subsequent languages are taught as additions to the learner's existing language repertoire rather than as replacements.

Glocalization: A sociological descriptor of the intersection of global and local culture.

Literacies: A critique of the notion of literacy as a monolithic, cognitive skill that describes literacy practices in a sociocultural context.

Multiliteracies: Developed by the New London Group (1996) to describe the complexities of contemporary culturally and socially situated literacy practices which engage multiple languages in multiple modalities, especially as described by digital communications media.

Secondary Orality: A term coined by Walter Ong to describe oral language use in postliterate electronic media contexts.

Transliteracies: My description of a phenomenon, sometimes described as "mode-switching": moving between paper and screen literacies.

Chapter XIX
Improving Online Readability and Information Literacy

John Paul Loucky
Seinan Jo Gakuin University, Japan

ABSTRACT

This chapter integrates important challenges of how to improve accessibility, readability, and learnability of online content. It is concerned with issues of how to create effective and enjoyable contents for online learning that is linguistically accessible, textually comprehensible, and readable for foreign language learners. Information literacy is an umbrella term encompassing computer, critical, digital, and media literacy. Yet a crucial area for research is the overlap of traditional reading literacy and new forms of online and digital library literacy. This area seems to have been largely overlooked and under-researched. This chapter elucidates how various threads can be more skillfully woven together so as to enhance online reading and language learning skills. The aim is to gain insights that enhance online learning and integrate information literacies in foreign language education.

INTRODUCTION

To handle vast volumes of data readily available online at just a click, global citizens of our multilingual electronic age need to develop information literacy skills. They include the ability to search for, recognize, and evaluate specific information in various fields, and then use it effectively for learning and life. In this chapter we aim to discuss improving electronic information literacy. We discuss the crucial importance of improving text readability in order to achieve what Valenza (2006, p.1) labels optimal integration and application of online tools and information for "problem-solving and decision-making skills in situations learners face in all their subject areas and in their lives beyond our classrooms."

Definitions of information literacy have involved five evolving concepts encompassing computer literacy, critical thinking and information skills, Information Technology (IT) literacy, learning how to learn (or lifelong learning) literacies, and library or digital media literacies. These have been well distinguished and clarified by Bruce (1997) and Hoppner (2004). While all of these are interrelated skills mutually contributing to the development of overall information literacy, the most basic literacy skill of reading, whether online or in print, seems to have been strangely overlooked in much discussion of these issues. This article is an attempt to remedy that, and to point to how an examination of reading and vocabulary skills and readability levels of readers and texts, whether in print or online, must always be considered of prime importance in any discussion of how to help improve information and language literacies.

The need for easy, quick, and reliable readability checking for English reading texts has recently become more pronounced and apparent. Whether assessing fiction or non-fiction for either Extensive or Intensive Reading (ER or IR) use, both language learners and teachers are in real need of helpful, user-friendly ways of assessing the readability levels of both kinds of text, as well as the reading levels of the learners themselves.

In particular there is a great need for those using or designing materials for online learning to understand how to better assess and improve the readability of any text for learners of limited reading and vocabulary proficiency from various language backgrounds. A quick survey of current online readability programs and research shows that a very large gap exists for work in this important field. It is crucial for teachers and language learning programs or E-Learning Web site developers to understand this field, especially if they want foreign language learners to be able to understand and access information on their sites effectively.

When we consider how to improve the readability of online text, there are four major related, but distinct constructs to consider. These are: the reading ability or level of the user; the readability

level of a text; its vocabulary level; and readability assessment tests, scales or indices. Regardless of what types of reading level tests are used, however, for those truly concerned with trying to help learners, the most important consideration is how to make online or print texts more readily accessible and therefore more comprehensible for them. Since reading tests and readability indices are a combination of vocabulary and comprehension tasks combining semantic and syntactical complexity, density and word length, one of the most important related pedagogical factors is to be able to assess this fourth factor, namely the *vocabulary level of particular texts,* in ways that will help the online users to be more effective in their teaching or learning. This article is focused on how to do that online.

This chapter discusses three types of readability, compares assessing that of print versus online materials, and gives an example of how the author designed an Online Reading Course for graduate engineering students, which assessed these issues in enough detail to provide language teachers with both principles and a model for designing online reading courses. Many reading teachers are looking for helpful services to be able to quickly assess any print or online text's readability. Thus showing how to do free, instant online readability checks as this chapter does, can contribute greatly to improving language learners' levels of comprehension and motivation, known to be closely related. Better matching of material appropriate to readers' levels is crucial in language classes, whether one is using an intensive or extensive reading approach, as well as for achieving maximum listening comprehension.

In addition, this article will provide strategic Web site links organized to help the reader do text analysis and readability checks for any text to help improve online readability. By improving accessibility to online lexical and concordancing tools, use of such recommended online programs can help to make any Web site or online text readily comprehensible input for learners from any major language background. A plethora of links to all sorts of Web dictionaries, encyclopedias and online dictionaries, and translation engines is also provided for translating between thousands of language pairs.

EVALUATION OF THE POTENTIAL FOR DEVELOPING VOCABULARY AND READING SKILLS

As Jamieson and Chapelle (2004) have helped us to clarify in theory, a proper evaluation of any computer assisted language learning (CALL) program or Web site's effectiveness should include both subjective or judgmental as well as objective or empirical measures for: language learning potential; learner fit; meaning focus; authenticity; impact; and practicality. Thus, when comparing various CALL and E-Learning Web sites for use by non-native learners, we must remember that unless they are readable to such users, regardless of how authentic they may be, they will not have an effective or enjoyable impact on either content or language learning, since they would be impractical and incomprehensible to learners of limited language proficiency. Such Web sites, if not carefully designed with the reading level of the learners and text carefully tailored to match or be adjustable to learner's needs (via instant glossing or other means of text simplification), would fail to qualify in all other essential areas despite their authenticity.

Whereas the majority of E-learning sites are in English, and much of our discussion will revolve around how to improve online English texts, reading and vocabulary development, this is by no means our sole intent. The range of application of this chapter's discussion encompasses all languages on the Internet, and will introduce some essential and innovative programs for assessing and improving the readability of texts and online newspapers in over 100 foreign languages. Since there are few studies available as yet about online readability or its improvement, the programs integrated by this writer's World CALL Virtual Language Education Encyclopedia (at www.CALL4ALL.us) fill a great need. This chapter begins to address this large gap of knowledge in the literature. What is most innovative about the approach being proposed in this chapter and demonstrated by this site is that it show-cases various online tools that are most helpful, even essential, for improving one's learning or teaching of over 100 major world languages. Thousands of Web dictionaries, glossing and translation engines, audio and visual aids, language learning links, collocation and concordancer engines, and vocabulary and readability profilers are all collected here at the same site for quick and easy use.

Various online readability programs, some commercial and others free, will be introduced. Among the online readability programs and research studies one finds are found at http://www.edu-cyberpg.com/Literacy/readability.asp. Some of the most useful programs and studies will be highlighted here. The *Educational Cyberplayground* site just mentioned focuses on Literacy Issues, such as readability tests, readability of a Web site, readability of a local HTML document, interpreting the results, Gunning-Fog Index, Flesch Reading Ease, Flesch-Kincaid grade level, Lexicool.com text analyzer and Check the Readability of a Piece of Writing.

Edward Fry, formerly of the Rutgers University Reading Center, created one of the most widely-used, and easy-to-use readability graphs for educators. Known as the Fry Formula, one of the most common readability formulas, it is found and explained at this site: http://school.discovery.com/schrockguide/fry/fry.html. By doing a search for "Literacy, Reading Test, Reading Assessment or Readability," one will find thousands of programs and studies to review, but not much research about improving the readability of Web sites themselves, which is the major purpose of this chapter. Other readability formulas thoroughly explained online at http://www.tameri.com/edit/levels.html

are the Gunning Fog Index, the Flesch Formula for Reading Ease & Grade Level, and the Power Sumner Kearl Formula.

Minimal most *essential threshold vocabulary* necessary for smooth, independent reading exist for all written languages. Of course these are the words occurring most often in a language, so learning them first gives readers maximum text coverage more quickly. For most languages these are the most high frequency whole words, but for some scripts like East Asian kanji characters, these include knowing a minimum number of kanji characters to be able to make word compounds and read most texts (Loucky, 2002) and at http://www.call4all.us///home/_all.php?fi=k), which compares learning English and Japanese threshold vocabularies). More discussion of the number of words needed to cross this minimal threshold follows.

IMPROVING ONLINE READABILITY ASSESSMENT AND ACCESSIBILITY

As Dodigovic (2005) noted in her summary of second language (L2) vocabulary learning research, to be able to understand a text in English, the reader needs to understand a high percentage of its vocabulary (Hirsh & Nation, 1992; Laufer, 1989; 1992). A reader who understands considerably less is not likely to learn much from such a text (true, whether in print or online), be it in terms of content or vocabulary. This is the case because in an environment with too much new information, the cognitive load (Yeung, Jin, & Sweller, 1997, p. 447) is deemed to be too high.

Although Dodigovic (2005, p. 448) repeats Alderson's (2000, p. 35) claim that "readers need to know 95% of the words in text to gain adequate comprehension," his claim that they can then guess unknown words from context does not apply to most second or foreign language readers. Often word recognition and comprehension minimal levels are confused. So for the record, adequate

90% or better comprehension of any print or online text requires that "Free or Independent" readers know 99% or more of the words, using original reading scoring criteria by Betts (1946), explained by Johnson and Kress (1965), and later by Ekwall (1976). Having only 95% knowledge of a text's words would be considered an "instructional level" of reading, but may result in only about a 75% comprehension rate for natives, and even less for those learning a foreign language. Any text where readers know less than 90% of the words may result in only 50% or less comprehension, and is thus aptly labeled as being at a "frustration level." How can such frustrating online reading be avoided? Clearly educational Web sites need to incorporate online support tools to ease the *cognitive load* for both teachers and students.

Laufer (1997) and Nation & Newton (1997) have both noted that the *minimum threshold level* required for fluent, independent reading is for students to know at least 3,000 word families, or about 5,000 words. In Laufer's (1997, p. 24) words, this level is the turning point at which "good L1 readers can be expected to transfer their reading strategies to L2 . . . Until they have reached this level, such transfer will be hampered by an insufficient knowledge of vocabulary." Nation (1990; 1994; 2001) has also painstakingly collated much useful research on second language vocabulary acquisition (or SLVA), and clarified formal measures to operationalize the most important concepts thereof. Among these are (Meara, 2002, p. 396): "tools for measuring the complexity and comprehensibility of text (Nation & Newton, 1997), tools for assessing the extent of learners' vocabulary, standardized word lists (Nation, 1990, Appendices Headword Level Lists and Tests), and so on." Yet it remains a daunting challenge to disambiguate the various aspects involved in L2 versus L1 vocabulary acquisition, and to provide a clear model thereof to help language teachers and students to teach and learn effectively.

Web sites aimed at foreign language learners or buyers need to be knowledgeable about which high frequency words to use, and teachers need to focus students' attention on them until they are mastered. More advanced or specialized words require online glossing. As Nation and Newton (1997, p. 239) point out, learners' attention should first be focused on the 2 000 most high frequency words, since they give about 87% coverage of most texts. Another 800 or 570 by Coxhead's (2000) estimates, academic words will help readers be able to comprehend from 90-95% of most texts.

By Laufer's (1997) estimates, however, having knowledge of 3,000 word families or 5,000 lexical items may only result in about 56% comprehension of text, with increases of 7% coming for each new 1,000 words learned. At such a rate students would need to reach a vocabulary of about 10,600 items before they could expect to comprehend 85% of most texts. Knowing words that are covered in a text does not automatically produce comprehension of course. Nation and Newton further note that knowledge of another 2,000 technical words will give another 3% coverage, up to about 98% of most texts. This figure of 4,800 total accords with Hirsh and Johnson's estimate of 5,000 words needed for readers to be familiar with 97% of the words in most texts. Of course texts vary with different genres and fields. The main point from all these vocabulary researchers is that helping language learners to focus on high frequency vocabulary and to learn most effective vocabulary learning and comprehension strategies can greatly help them in learning a target language.

Yet many EFL/ESL language learners, even at the college level, are yet below this minimum threshold level. For example, according to this writer's research over two decades at seven Japanese universities, most college students in Japan still seem to be far below this minimal level (Loucky, 1996; 1997; 2003; 2006). To help such language learners overcome this beginner's paradox (Coady, 1997), language learning sites should use controlled vocabularies, much like graded readers do. They also can give non-native readers several possible versions of text at various reading levels. A few online reading labs, such as L.E.A.R.N (www.learnintl.com), offer learners the option of reading the authentic original version, or an intermediate or beginning level version. Beyond this, such sites may provide instant access to various types of monolingual/ bilingual glossing and footnotes. Some go so far as to provide complete translations, but most language teachers believe this reduces motivation and chances to learn the target language. Finally, listening support via some text-to-speech (TTS) program should ideally always be available to assist those language learners in need of such support.

Laufer (1997) and Nation and Newton (1997) have all found that the *minimal threshold level required* for fluent, independent reading is for students to know at least 2,800-3,000 word families (2,000 most high frequency words, and 800 academic words), which together may provide the reader with close to 95% text coverage. Learning 2,000 more technical words will add another 3%, leaving only 2% low frequency words, which can be looked up as one comes across them.

Clearly the higher comprehension level one desires or expects to attain in English or any other language for that matter, the more words one needs to know. Many have echoed this call to focus learners' attention on most high-frequency vocabulary to build up the threshold vocabulary necessary for smooth, independent reading. Meara (1995) noted large numbers of words could be learned efficiently in a short time by learning L2-L1 pairs. Critchley (Online, 2/08/07) notes that students can later fine-tune meanings learned with lists, though most vocabulary researchers would advocate at least including collocations and sentence examples with initial learning, at least with older learners, since the meaning and use of words is determined by their context. Shillaw (1995) in the same year found that when he adopted a clear corpus of 3,000 most frequently used words, learners increased their interest and motivation for learning new words, checking with peers, dictionaries, and teachers. This seems to show that students do need proof of their own vocabulary gains to help motivate their learning.

First we will describe and discuss various kinds of readability scales, then show how online or scanned print texts may be assessed for both their reading as well as vocabulary levels by using online readability and text analysis engines. Then we will look at how to integrate the most versatile multi-lingual glossing engine to assist those wanting to learn to read and improve their vocabulary in over 100 languages.

To examine the most thorough online explanation of readability assessment, see Johnson's http://www.timetabler.com/reading.html, which discusses readability, and its relevance to the reading level of students and their school books, particularly science textbooks. The main sections of his article are: The effect of student interest and motivation; Legibility, including type, layout and reading conditions; Sentence structure, including readability formulae; Reading ages for school textbooks.

READABILITY ISSUES AND WEB READING NEEDS

For over 50 years readability formulas have been used to help guide students to books at their appropriate level of reading and interest. Three types of reading levels should all be considered when trying to best match texts or books to students: Readability level of a text or a book's grade level measures its difficulty by a given readability formula (Flesch Reading Ease, Flesch Kincaid Grade Level); interest and maturity level of a book or text's ideas and content (Lower, Middle and Upper Grades); and a particular learner's reading ability, meaning the reading and maturity level of each individual student.

A book or specific text's reading level may be abbreviated to BRL or text/passage reading level as TRL. The former usually is an average of three sections of the book, whereas for a shorter particular text, measurement is based on a word count and use of one of the scientific formulae mentioned that combine factors of lexical density and syntactic complexity, often shown by word and sentence length. Categorizing a book's audience appeal by its level of interest or maturity (BML=Book's Maturity Level) is usually grouped generally so that learners, parents, and teachers can quickly tell if a book is meant for elementary, junior, or senior high students and above. When students are reading online the listed sites can help quickly assess their approximate reading level to see if they are appropriate for one's learners.

In addition, ProQuest uses two ways to measure either print or online reading levels—Lexile Scores and SIRS. SIRS are editorially assigned reading levels: from Easy (Grades 1-4); Moderate (Grades 5-7); Challenging (Grades 8 and above); or General (all grade levels)—which take into account a text's subject matter, depth of coverage and its Flesch Reading Ease (http://readability. info/). Lexile Scores, on the other hand, provide formal measures to help track learners' reading progress, needed for some US funding. They overlap each other and run from 100 for grade 1 to 1,200-1,700 for grade 12 (www.lexile.com). Many Librarian's and System Administrators use these types of reading level advanced search options. Three are available to institutions: Lexile Reading Level; Reading Level (Generic) based on the Gunning Fogg Flesch-Kincaid Index; and 3) California Reading List Numbers (CRL #). According to the state of California's standard reading level measurement all students in grades 2-11 are tested for their CRL number using the Lexile test. This second generic Reading Level index provides a number on a scale of 0-21 that reflects the number of words with three syllables, number of words per sentence, and so forth.

Measuring a particular student's reading and maturity level may be done either objectively by using standardized reading tests, or more subjectively, by allowing them to read 2-3 passages of self-chosen books. While doing so, a teacher or parent notes that any texts in which students know 98-100% of running words would be considered in their appropriate Free or Independent Reading Level. This is based on findings by Hu and Nation (2000) stating that students need to know 98% of a text's words for it to be comprehended independently, or for them to be able to infer the meaning of new words based on this amount of known text coverage (Hirsh and Nation, 1992; Nation and Newton, 1997). Naturally self-reports are less reliable than objective testing, so many teachers would prefer getting an estimated reading grade level using standardized tests or headword level tests (Nation, 1990), both of which are more scientific and reliable.

Ekwall's (1976) classic reading education text, for example, listed about 50 standardized reading tests, all based on using such formulae for estimating American students' average independent reading level. A learner's independent reading level may be defined as the most difficult level of text one can comprehend alone without using a dictionary or another's help. Loucky (1996; 2003b; 2006) has used these kinds of tests to assess several thousand Japanese college students' English reading levels for almost two decades, finding consistent patterns that are useful for language teachers to know, especially those wanting to tailor the level of required or free readings to individually appropriate levels.

Once each learner's independent reading level has been determined compared to the average for particular grade levels, each student can be better guided to texts that are at his or her appropriate instructional level as well, defined as 1-2 grades above their free or independent reading level. Frustration levels beyond that were to be avoided at all costs. Today many proponents of Extensive Reading stress free-reading, rightly aiming to develop "fluent, independent reading," whereas instructional level reading may be reserved for practice of particular reading skills during In-

tensive Reading classes. But in order for any ER to be effective for vocabulary learning, students need to read massive amounts of comprehensible text, which few L2 learners seem to do. Word knowledge gained by ER is both incrementally slow and very partial, so that single encounters are usually insufficient for lasting learning to take place. Hunt and Beglar (2005) point out that many EFL learners have impoverished lexicons due to lack of productive use, despite years of formal study. They recommend adopting a systematic framework that combines both the promotion of both explicit and implicit lexical instruction and learning strategies. The former include especially learning decontextualized word lists, dictionary, and inferencing skills. The latter includes the use of integrated task sets and narrow reading, but mainly involves encouraging a greater volume and breadth of extensive reading in the target language. Finding the optimal balance between these two main approaches to reading, discussed previously by Loucky (2005), is open to much debate. While it is well to say (Hunt & Beglar, p. 1): "the most effective and efficient lexical development will occur in multifaceted curriculums that achieve a pedagogically sound balance between explicit and implicit activities for L2 learners at all levels of their development," defining just what that ideal balance is and implementing it is a far more challenging task.

PRINCIPLES DEDUCED FROM READABILITY STUDIES

Students generally show the most reading improvement if they regularly practice reading within a range of difficulty that is neither too challenging (known as frustration level) nor too easy for them (independent reading level). While all readability formulas are based on analyzing some aspects of a text or book's difficulty, they cannot tell the suitability of a particular text's content or literary merit for particular learners.

The choice to read is usually a decision best left up to educators and parents in consultation with the learners.

Accelerated Reader is a computerized learning information system designed to help teachers manage and monitor their learners' reading practice. Reading Renaissance offers a set of teaching practices online providing information on judging the suitability of books; articles on readability and how to use it in the classroom: What It Is and Why It's Useful. These suggestions include: start by explaining the levels to your students; note your students' reading level; guide your student to select a book with a readability level; guide your students to select books in the appropriate interest-level range; and monitor progress regularly. With proficient Upper-Grade readers teachers should emphasize the importance of variety in reading.

Most ER is said to be done at the free or independent reading level. However, there is a need for more careful, individualized testing of what exactly constitutes each student's free-reading level, particularly when it comes to foreign or second language readers. Readers having non-European native scripts have a great chance of becoming more challenged and frustrated than native readers would, due to having even more linguistic differences, as compared with reading their own native text. In addition, the complexities and different skills required to read online text fluently make it yet again a different species of reading, whether in L1 or L2. This being the case, the need for better assessing online as well as print texts in more uniform ways has now become more and more apparent to reading teachers world-wide.

In response to these needs the author (Loucky) has created a website with many pages that serve both as a World C.A.L.L. Directory of Computer-Assisted Language Learning sites organized at www.CALL4ALL.US), but also included in that site a group of online reading and language learning labs, word lists, and readability indices to help address these issues and make it much easier for any teacher or learner to assess the reading and vocabulary level of any online or offline scanned text simply at: http://www.call4all.us///home/_all.php?fi=r.

IMPROVING TEXT ASSESSMENT AND ACCESSIBILITY

Assessing and improving online readability requires learning how to assess both the level of print and online text, as well as that of any learner's target language vocabulary. As Johnson (Online, 2007) notes, how well an author succeeds in transmitting his information will depend on the readability of the text. In his words,

Readability is concerned with the problem of matching between reader and text. An accomplished reader is likely to be bored by simple repetitive texts. A poor reader will soon become discouraged by texts which s/he finds too difficult to read fluently. This is likely to happen when the text is: poorly printed, contains complex sentence structures, long words or too much material containing entirely new ideas. The term readability refers to all the factors that affect success in reading and understanding a text. These factors include: 1) The interest and motivation of the reader; 2) The legibility of the print (and of any illustrations); and 3) The complexity of words and sentences in relation to the reading ability of the reader.

To help remedy this obvious need for some kinds of online readability checkers to enable a match between the reader's ability and the level of an online or scanned print text, this author has found and linked two text analysis engines, two readability engines, one translation engine, and one glossing engine, and made them freely available to users from his language education encyclopedia Web site. In addition, programs and practical steps for estimating and improving learners' reading levels as well as online text readability assessment of any text or book, with over 20 free online Reading Labs (some bilingual) are given on the R-Reading page of that site at www.call4all.us///home/_all.php?fi=r. The use of all these tools will now be summarized.

MAKING E-LEARNING ACCESSIBLE, READABLE AND COMPREHENSIBLE

Next we will describe how to use various online and software programs to make E-learning sites more accessible, readable and comprehensible to foreign language learners as well as their teachers. Because one can reasonably expect that L2 learning patterns most likely parallel a learner's patterns of L1 vocabulary study, organization and use, and many such language processing skills are known to transfer, each individual learner's patterns of L1 and L2 reading and vocabulary learning should be more thoroughly studied and compared. While these are fairly simple and straightforward concepts to understand, designing more effective means of researching, teaching and testing the various important aspects of learning a foreign language's vocabulary and component reading skills has been both problematic and challenging in many ways.

Teachers need to be able to scale their vocabulary learning activities from those that require easy and simple processing for their lowest level students, to activities that require deep and complex lexical processing for more advanced language learners. This writer's Virtual Language Learning Encyclopedia aims to help teachers and students to solve these problems of assessing and improving the reading level matching of any text, in print or online, with that of the reader. In the right menu of each page of our site one finds the following seven glossing, dictionary translation, text, and readability analysis engines. The follow-

ing tools can help language teachers, students, and Web site designers to make any online text and E-learning site more accessible, readable and comprehensible to learners from over 100 language backgrounds. All these programs are most useful tools for improving online reading and readability: Altavista's Babelfish for instant rough translations in to eight major languages, for foreign language learners can comfortably get a quick look at resources in their own L1 http://babelfish.altavista.com/; www.WordChamp.com's glossing engine for 112 major languages; Text Analyzer Vocab Profiler http://www.lextutor.ca/vp/eng/; AWL Profiler, to assess which of 10 Academic Word List levels a text includes; http://www.nottingham.ac.uk/~alzsh3/acvocab/awlhighlighter.htm; Readability.info www.readability.info

Operating since March of 2004, this site is a great help to teachers or Web designers who want to more closely match the level of websites to the reading level of their students or users. As they state at this site, if one is "Curious about how complex your documents or Web pages are to read . . . You don't have to get a team of experts to generate your readability score: you can just use readability.info to analyze the characteristics of your writing and ascertain a multitude of readability scores. By comparing the readability score of different documents (or Web pages) you can hone your writing and make sure that you aren't creating overly complex sentences and paragraphs for your audience." Users can quickly assess their own prose in comparison to other Web pages and writing samples by choosing to either upload a Microsoft Word document or enter a URL. Those who want a good software program, including nine readability formulas as well as a Vocabulary Assessor program can examine StyleWriter at www.stylewriter-usa.com/readability.html. or us English.com http://www.usingenglish.com/resources/text-statistics.php

The Text Analysis Tool enables users to evaluate important linguistic data about any inputted text, including its readability level. The free analysis tool version gives these kinds of statistics about any text within seconds: word count; # unique words; # sentences; average words per sentence; lexical density index; the Gun Readability Index score. One can either type or paste in any English text up to 500 KB in size. Even more detailed statistics are available to paying members for a small fee using the Advanced Features version also gives a grammar analysis tool, a fully sortable word frequency list for any target text, and a complete breakdown of that text by word length. These functions enable teachers or language learners to focus their attention and time on words of a particular frequency or grammatical character, helping to reduce their cognitive load.

Listening support engines and links are found online at: L.E.A.R.N www.learnintl.com; Natural Voice Reader http://www.naturalreaders.com/; Speak Easy http://www.er.uqam.ca/nobel/r21270/cgi-bin/tts/English_tts.htm; Microsoft's new Vista has Test-to-Speech (TTS); There are also Dictionaries Galore! Links to over 2,500 web dictionaries for all languages online found on our D-Page http://www.call4all.us///home/_all.php?fi=d as well as ten of the most versatile and useful monolingual and multilingual online dictionaries conveniently placed in both right and left menus of all pages of www.CALL4ALL.us.

ONLINE READING COURSE

The writer's Japanese graduate school engineering students first used Altavista's Babelfish to quickly get a better idea of this instructor's Web site in Japanese, their mother tongue. Then they were shown how to use Dictionaries Galore bilingual and monolingual Web dictionaries, as well as www.WordChamp.com's glossing engine to help them with their online reading vocabulary learning. The course consisted of some online Extensive Readings using L.E.A.R.N (www.learnintl.com) website articles with listening; Technical reading articles found under Graduate Engineering Students' English for Advanced Purposes at http://www.call4all.us///home/_all.php?fi=g; Balsamo's Online Reading Lab articles and; Some articles uploaded based on the author's text, *Famous Leaders Who Influenced Japan's Internationalization* (Loucky, 1994).

The following is a sample text analysis. Table 1 shows the kind of table that was generated by the Vocab Profiler site for our sample Pearl Harbor Story, showing number of word Families, Types, and Tokens and their percentage of the target text. Much linguistic information is included in such summary charts. Other linguistic data important to note and summarize here can be edited from

Table 1. Linguistic analysis of Pearl Harbor target text

	Families	Types	Tokens	Percent
K1 Words (1 to 1000):	326	407	1260	76.78%
Function:	...	...	(766)	(46.68%)
Content:	...	...	(494)	(30.10%)
> Anglo-Sax =Not Greco-Lat/Fr Cog:	...	...	(253)	(15.42%)
K2 Words (1001 to 2000):	52	60	90	5.48%
> Anglo-Sax:	...	...	(21)	(1.28%)
AWL Words (academic):	40	41	44	2.68%
Off-List Words:	?	172	247	15.05%
	418+?	680	1641	100%

an excellent function provided by Tom Cobb's Vocab Profiler site called Edit/print-friendly table. Additionally, AWL words are also broken out into ten Academic Word Sub-lists.

It is important to note from results shown in Table 1 that while this sample story is reported to have only about 3% AWL words, 15% of the text are off-list words which must be known to comprehend the story or read it fluently with adequate understanding. Since no more than 5% running words should ideally be unknown even for native readers (Ekwall, 1976), encountering these close to 18% yet unknown AWL and Off-List Words would make even this short article incomprehensible or frustrating for a majority of Japanese college students, who possess an average of only about 2,500 words, with graduates averaging about 3,500 words known. These figures were derived in the past two years by using a free online vocabulary level checker known as V-Check, found in the right menu of the writer's website http://www.v-check.jp/index.html?PAGELANG=EN): None (total 0 tokens).

MEASURING AND IMPROVING THE READABILITY OF ONLINE VERSUS PRINTED TEXTS

There do not seem to be many rigorous online studies yet of Web reading done by non-natives, using both speed and accuracy tracking, and also eye cameras to somehow track and monitor perceptual movements, such as regressions, when reading online versus on paper. L.E.A.R.N. Web site has constructed online texts at three levels, two of which correspond roughly to the 1,000 and 2,000 levels flagged by the vocabulary profiler on Cobb's site at http://www.lextutor.ca/vp/eng/, plus an original level in unsimplified English. If such a comprehensive online readability grading system could be made publicly available, it might become a useful standard for both Web-based and paper-based ER materials. Two such free online

readability programs are available in the right menu of the writer's homepage. These are www.readability.info and http://www.usingenglish.com/resources/text-statistics.php. However, it may take some time for them to gain acceptance and use by various educational bodies.

Another alternative is to use the ADELEX ADA. The first **ADELEX ANALYSER (ADA)** is found at www.ugr.es/local/inped/ada. **ADELEX TEXT ANALYSER** tool is part of the research carried out by the members of the ADELEX team at the University of Granada in Spain. It enables the user to analyze the lexical difficulty of written texts in English on the basis of information contained in a 7,000-word frequency list drawn from the British National Corpus, Bank of English and Longman Corpus Network databases. Its two versions in English and Spanish attempt to provide a more accurate and updated way of analyzing texts, by using frequency bands of up to 7,000 words. Brilliantly rapid online analysis divides this list into 7 color-coded bands.

ASSESSING READABILITY ONLINE

In summary, one may assess the vocabulary and reading level of any electronic text in various ways, especially by using a combination of good online Vocabulary Profilers with Readability Programs. Readability Programs can give us a quick macro-measure of the level of any electronic text. Vocabulary Profilers, on the other hand, should be used as a micro-measure to get a quick lexical and linguistic assessment of any proposed reading text. To assess the vocabulary level of a text one may use either #1 below, the AWL Profiler to sort out higher academic words, or #2, the Vocab Profiler, to determine the number of words in each frequency band in any proposed text. Finally, a quick free readability assessment may be obtained for any Word text using its built-in readability checker if activated, item #3 below. All are described at www.CALL4ALL.

us, under specific topics on its R: Reading and Readability page. You can enter any text in any of these programs to find out its level by word frequency: **ADELEX Text Analyser** at www.ugr.es/local/inped/ada; AWL URL at http://www.nottingham.ac.uk/~alzsh3/acvocab/awlhighlighter.htm; Vocab Profiler URL: http://www.lextutor.ca/vp/eng/; Word Spelling/Grammar Checker when enabled in Word. And you can enter any book title and or its ISBN # to find out its grade level by using TASA's Depth of Reading Power, on a scale of 1-100 by Reading Renaissance's ATOS, by school grade levels relative to U.S. norms.

ONLINE READING TIMERS OR PACERS

Online reading seems to discourage word-for-word reading, since print readers can hold the entire document in their hands at once, whereas a Web document must be called up one page at a time, either by the action of scrolling or by using hyperlinks. Even better for discouraging single word reading, however, are reading pacers, some of which can be adjusted and set by the learner to at least three different speeds to adjust for their own comfort and ability level. This type of on-screen reading function is essential, for at least some Web reading, especially for lower level readers. It is available, for example, when using Eichousha's *Reading Skill Trainer* software, or *Rocket Reader* online. L.E.A.R.N. provides a self-timer, and Balsamo's Online Reading Lab motivates faster reading by using a 5-6 minute stopwatch that is counting down. But users can repeat and re-read.

STEPS TO IMPROVING ONLINE READING

Highlighted at the www.CALL4ALL.us portal in the right menu are links to each of these extremely useful text analysis and readability engines, as well as a link to a page highlighting these practical steps for Improving Online Text Readability at http://www.call4all.us///home/_all.php?fi=../misc/steps. In addition, the writer developed an integrated English for Advanced/Specific/Technical Purposes online course, combined with using various online Reading Labs linked from his site (on pages R and G). Its "Steps to help improve online reading" or Measuring and Improving Readability of any Online Text are outlined here in Table 2, from the top its R-Reading page.

HIGH-FREQUENCY WORD STUDY WITH THE WORDCHAMP WEB SITE

WordChamp is a free Web site offering numerous ways for language learners to study vocabulary and read websites in foreign languages. It also allows educators to create cyber classrooms where assignments can be assigned and monitored (see Figure 1).

The vocabulary drill page offers a number of activities including word translation, listening, reading, flashcards, and so forth. Users can access lists that have been created by other users, or they can create their own lists. Lists may be L1-L1 or they may be L1-L2. To access files for study which the author created on WordChamp (WC), the following steps should be followed: go to http://www.wordchamp.com; choose Browse from top menu bar; search for the user Global Stories to access my lists; choose Academic Word List 1- 4; peruse the list, noting unknown words; The first line labeled English Words is the definition or synonym; the second line, English synonyms is the single word to be studied. Surveys with students indicated that, whenever possible, students would prefer a definition to a single word synonym; Words that are well known can be deleted from list. Conversely, more words can be added to the list by any user; choose Practice Flashcards; see

Table 2. Steps for improving online readability

Step 1:	Scan or Copy Target Text from anywhere on the Web or from any data disc or print text document you have.
Step 2:	Input Target Text into Wordchamp.com at http://www.Wordchamp.com. Try to read the article, guessing appropriate meaning for newly learned words. WordChamp offers a variety of possible meanings in over 100 languages, so it is an excellent way to review new words being learned in any of them. Instead Webmasters can add WordChamp's WebReader code to enable this function.
Step 3:	As you read, click on any new words in Wordchamp.com, which will then be automatically archived. Then for Homework, make up questions about the story using these new terms. Ask partners these questions in the next class as a review activity, before proceeding to using the Vocab Profiler and making up some free Interview Questions using these target terms.
Step 4:	For more Pushed Output Productive Practice, then input the text into Vocab Profiler at http://www.lextutor.ca/vp/eng/
Step 5:	Print out Color-Coded Word Bands and focus especially on learning the Academic and Off-List words by making questions using them.
Step 6:	Ask your teacher to quickly check your grammar, then orally interview your partner using these questions.
Step 7:	Additional Listening-Enhanced Step for those having any text-recognition software: Listen to the text read to you electronically. Try to understand its meaning phrase by phrase, paragraph by paragraph in whole sense units.
Step 8:	Try to read the article again, guessing or substituting the appropriate meaning for any newly learned words.

Figure 1. WordChamp Web site performance charts

Using WordChamp, it's possible to track a wide variety of information about your students' progress (students' numbers are used to protect their privacy)

1. Homework Assignments

This graph shows your students, homework assignments, and completion of assignments over the course of the week. This graph makes it clear who is and isn't doing the work. You can also see that many students have chosen to do the assignments.

2. Performance

These graphs show information organized by month, week, day, or hour.

statistics and a list of words. See WordChamp Performance Charts in Figure 2.

Many vocabulary assessment forms created by the writer are now available online at http://www.call4all.us///home/_all.php?fi=v. Students can be shown how to open them in Word, fill in these online surveys, and return them as Email attachments to any teacher using them, to quickly assess their level and be better able to guide and monitor their vocabulary learning. At that same URL I have collected these CALL4All's Vocabulary Survey Forms—Vocabulary Knowledge Scales, Depth of Lexical Processing Scale, and Vocabulary Learning Strategies Taxonomy, as well as many other excellent vocabulary learning links. These include great word games and test preparation sites. Recently added is an entire online Semantic Field Keyword Approach course, which is an

Figure 2. WordChamp's online vocabulary course management system

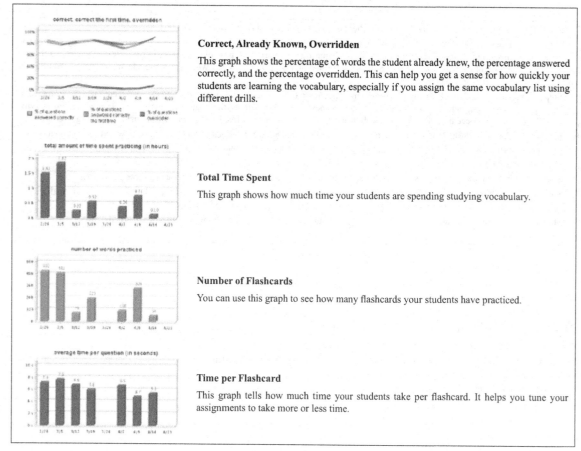

Correct, Already Known, Overridden

This graph shows the percentage of words the student already knew, the percentage answered correctly, and the percentage overridden. This can help you get a sense for how quickly your students are learning the vocabulary, especially if you assign the same vocabulary list using different drills.

Total Time Spent

This graph shows how much time your students are spending studying vocabulary.

Number of Flashcards

You can use this graph to see how many flashcards your students have practiced.

Time per Flashcard

This graph tells how much time your students take per flashcard. It helps you tune your assignments to take more or less time.

advanced vocabulary development program that helps learners to rapidly expand their English or Japanese vocabulary by learning Semantic Field Keyword groups together bilingually. It can be accessed at http://www.call4all.us///misc/sfka. php. Other language pairs can easily use the same approach, and may send their results to us to add to this rich online resource.

Among the many reading links found on this same page are both Intensive Reading skill-building links as well as "Extensive Reading World Recommended links for online ER or Web-reading." Finally there is a link to improving reading habits, and about 20 free Online Reading Labs

(http://www.call4all.us///home/_all.php?fi=r), called Electronic or Virtual Language Learning and Online Reading Labs.

WordChamp.com can be used to monitor online vocabulary learning using Student-made flashcards; Teacher/class-made flashcards; Computer-generated tests of these; A Course Management System (see Figures 1 & 2) to monitor learning in detail; or Links to related texts for contextualization and glossing. Instant online glosses into 112 languages are now provided for free through this site via its Web Reader section from http://www.wordchamp.com/lingua2/Home. do (Homepage). Its explanatory page http://www.

wordchamp.com/lingua2/HelpTeacher.do shows teachers how to track their students' Homework Assignments and Word Study Performance. For all students progress is tracked for free, including all of these aspects of development: Dictionary search of about 1.5 million words in 112 languages, over 120,000 audio clips for help with correct pronunciation, verb charts for practice, and 12 kinds of vocabulary drills.

Users must gain language skills to unlock the full potential of the Internet, which is causing globalization to spread across countries, cultures, and languages. The WordChamp® Language Toolbar is designed to assist people around the world by helping them work with any of 112 new languages, already being in use in most countries. Once activated, it allows users to see translations for difficult words and hear words pronounced by native speakers, simply by pointing at words on foreign language websites. Social networking communities will become a major market for language help technology as members begin to reach out across countries and languages to meet new friends. Global visitors reading foreign language blogs, email, or search results pages will find the WordChamp Language Toolbar indispensable.

Using the WordChamp Language Toolbar is easy, since users can simply download the toolbar for free from www.wordchamp.com and install it directly onto a Firefox or Internet Explorer browser, though other browser users must ask their Web masters to add pop up definitions and recordings of native speakers to other websites by using the WordChamp Reader API code. Once this is done, however, these great language-learning and cross-cultural communication benefits are gained: (1) The toolbar can be turned on or off as needed. (2) Users select their native language. (3) The Web site language is selected dynamically, when possible. Users can easily select the website language from a pull down menu. (4) Once turned on, users point their mouse at any word on the page and a small translation box will appear, containing translations for that word. In many cases, the user can also hear the foreign word spoken by a native speaker. (5) Users can optionally request more information on the word from Wikipedia.

The new WordChamp Language Toolbar supports the largest number of languages of any online language tool for reading foreign Web sites and texts, enabling users to quickly receive the language support they need to develop skills necessary for reading foreign Web sites. The manufacturers expect their language assistance technology in browsers to become as ubiquitous as bookmarks. People around the world will benefit from globalization and the Internet if they are able to communicate in this new world. Future releases of the WebChamp toolbar will include support for additional browsers, languages, and advanced help features, becoming an increasingly content-rich, indispensable tool to cross communication barriers between all major languages and countries.

Use of all of the mentioned online tools can greatly aid language teachers and learners by enabling them to quickly assess the level of any online text, site or story, as well as give them essential supportive functions to enhance their learning. Naturally, by making online text more readable—either by removing or glossing difficult AWL or off-list words—it becomes more readily accessible and comprehensible input for readers at any proficiency level, from any major language background for which such tools are provided. Wise and appropriate use of such online reading and vocabulary learning tools can help to break down the many complex barriers first erected at the infamous Towel of Babel.

RECOMMENDED READABILITY ASSESSMENT PROGRAMS

ReadabilityPLUS is an excellent online readability assessment program at http://www.stylewriter-usa.com/readability.html. It automates the process of determining the reading level of your materials, saving users time and money. One simply imports or pastes text into *ReadabilityPLUS*, and the program quickly analyzes a text, telling the reading level(s) of your material using up to nine of the most popular readability formulas. *ReadabilityPLUS* gives users the power of nine popular readability formulas to find the reading level and grade level of one's materials. Select as many formulas as you want at one time, and Readability Plus will find the reading and grade levels using your selected formulas, which include: the Fry Graph, Dale-Chall, Flesch Reading Ease, as well as Flesch Grade Level, FORCAST, FOG, SMOG, Powers-Somner-Kearl and Spache readability formulas. For more on the SMOG formula, see http://uuhsc.utah.edu/pated/authors/readability.html.

One other option is to use the Flesch-Kincaid Grade Level Index, which is automatically calculated in your Microsoft Word documents. When Microsoft Word completes a grammar check, one must OK Readability Statistics. The readability level of a passage using the Flesch-Kincaid Reading Formula is built into newer versions of Microsoft® Word XP. This formula is similar to the SMOG Index, and computes readability based on the average number of syllables per word and average number of words per sentence. The score in this case indicates a school grade level.

Knowing how to use a readability assessment program like *StyleWriter* also called *ReadabilityPLUS* is indispensable for being able to assess the reading level of written materials - whether by reading specialists, teachers, trainers, librarians, instructional writers, curriculum writers, policy and procedure writers, technical writers, or E-learning Web site developers. It is essential for any of these people to have an ability to quickly assess any online text for both its reading grade level and its particular type and level of vocabulary, especially in order to help language learners from various foreign cultures and linguistic backgrounds. Likewise, it is most important for these people to learn how to simplify monolingual text and also be able to add instant online bilingual glossing into the mother tongue (Ll) of each learner. This can be done at www.WordChamp.com site.

Many features make *ReadabilityPLUS* software one of the most complete and powerful programs available in today's marketplace for anyone wanting to identify all words in a document, or identify just the potentially-difficult words, and know how many times each such word occurs in the document. Whereas Readability Calculations software indicate the appropriate grade-level of text material, the Vocabulary Assessor included with this product can identify exactly which words in the text are likely to be the most troublesome for the intended readers. Vocabulary Assessor programs are frequently used with such readability calculations to help both teachers and students to focus on particular bands of essential core vocabulary, based on their word frequency, as well as on the level of the students' prior knowledge or field being studied.

ReadabilityPLUS software may be the most complete and powerful program available today for online assessment, and we found that the mentioned free programs did not always work properly for uploaded texts. This commercial program, however, includes these essential functions: Online Help, One Pass, Keyed Samples, File Samples, Scanned Text, No Size Limits, Raw Counts, Hardcopy Printout of all scores and raw data, Text Editing, User Manual and The Latest Info ReadMe file.

FUTURE TRENDS IN ONLINE READING

Many reading teachers are looking at helpful online tools and services to assess any text's readability, as well as improve access and support for learners from various language backgrounds. While there does seem to be a lack of pedagogic or theoretical models of reading online, some regional examples could be taken as models for improving all online reading. This article as noted some of them, such as Cobb's programs found at http://132.208.224.131/callwild/. The R Reader or Reading Tutor currently exists for reading Jack London's Call of the Wild online in English or French. One can read, listen to the recording, pause to click any word once for individual pronunciation, twice for examples and definition. Quick look-ups in Word-Net are also provided as well as sound.

Online readers from foreign language backgrounds can benefit most from using a program like WorldChamp for reading texts and newspapers online. E-news from 40 newspapers in 11 languages is provided at http://www.wordchamp.com/lingua2/Reader.do Since language learners need more volume of reading in their target language, using such instant glossing engines to not only read via its Web Reader, but also to save and practice new words will help learners immensely by reducing the cognitive load and high threshold barrier caused by much unknown vocabulary found on many sites students are interested in or assigned to read. Websites supported by multilingual glossing options, readability assessment, and text analysis tools in addition to text-to-speech (TTS) listening support will probably become the international norm for online E-Learning. Print texts will increasingly become scanned electronic documents to make this possible. There are many useful research opportunities in these fields for educators, linguists, scanner and imaging technicians, and Web designers to consider and contribute to.

Indeed, the reading education community seems to be a bit slow in making the transition from traditional text-based reading to online reading, which does require the teaching and learning of different perceptual approaches in both L2 text comprehension as well as in lexical acquisition and processing strategies. One online article, David Taylor's (2006) "Writing for the Web: A Comprehensive Overview," excerpted from his more well-known text The Freelance Success Book on the subject, notes some of these same factors.

Law of Unintended Consequences applies to the Internet just as it did to that other revolution in information distribution: the printing press. No one predicted that Johannes Gutenberg's little experiment in self publishing would form the foundation for the Renaissance and the Protestant Reformation...One of the ironies of the Internet is that . . . the medium that was supposed to make books obsolete has fueled a publishing bonanza and an off-line reading explosion. Glory be! The Internet is just as dependent on the written word (as other media)."

Where reading on screen differs, however, is in these areas which he further notes. First, much more skimming and scanning is used. In fact 79% of Web users were found to be using these skills rather than reading word for word. This finding has large implications for teaching skills most needed for efficient online reading. Clearly both Web writers and language teachers wanting to use online resources most effectively need to be aware of these major reading differences, as well as demonstrate sensitivity to the foreign readers for whom reading of online L2 texts is often impossible or highly frustrating. Some studies, such as that done by Sun Microsystems Science Office have claimed that "Reading from a computer screen is 25% slower than reading from paper." Once practiced and proficient at reading online, however, I would venture to guess that the opposite is true for fluent readers. Much more research comparing skills, speed and accuracy levels of online versus print text reading is needed on readers at various levels, both native and non-natives, before such general claims can be accepted. Studies are finding other differences in online reading as well.

Teachers trying to use CALL or E-learning as well as Web writers need to write in clear chunks and make text scannable at a glance, since according to eye-tracking study done by Stanford and Poynter Institute found that online readers often focus narrowly upon headlines and summaries (78% of their eye attention was here). Since online readers must use more skimming and scanning to just get the gist and locate relevant information quickly, and Web distractions can make their speed 25% slower, these principles are recommended by Taylor (2006) to improve the readability of Web copy.

We must aim to write Web materials clearly and succinctly in summary style. As Taylor (2006, Online) writes, a Web materials writer should think like a graphic artist, treating "each page like a painting that is framed by the computer on this electronic canvas are elements that you, the artist, must weave together, linearly, to form a coherent whole that can be accessed with little or no reading. . . Web writing places a premium on good organization of content and devices (navigational bars or buttons) that clarify the content's organization to the Web user." Other principles to follow include: invert the pyramid of information, using journalism's major headlines and summary first style; compress and concise is key so as to reduce word count by 50%; make one paragraph carry one major idea; make each page's text stand alone, since users can enter through hyperlinks from various places; provide needed hyperlinks, using keywords as titles/headings. In other words, make useful and relevant links to helpful resources, both within a site as well as to other sites.

Once we have a better understanding of the major differences between reading print text versus reading on-screen text, teachers and Web writers can implement better solutions for these special needs of L2 readers. Beside these clear reading differences, others have only become apparent in recent research. As Taylor (2006) noted in his online article, "In both cases, it's essential for web writers to be aware of the differences between the world of linear text flowing like a river, and the fragmented world of hypertext on a pixel screen. The most successful web writers have honed in on the key differences between writing for print and writing for the web." Finally, we must remember that the Web is rigorously democratic, in that the user is in much more control of an online, interactive learning experience, than when reading print text, or other more passive, non-responsive mass media. The Internet is a self-access mode of learning, but a majority of learners may not be self-starters, and especially foreign language learners can be quite intimidated by L2 online materials.

PEDAGOGICAL IMPLICATIONS AND INSTRUCTIONAL PLAN

In light of conclusions drawn from our examination of computerized reading and vocabulary development programs, both software and online, a specific plan was created for Improving Online Reading and Vocabulary Development. Firstly, software and Web sites that provide fully bilingualized help seem most effective and enjoyable, especially for learners with limited English proficiency (LEPs). Ideally, fully bilingualized computerized dictionaries, software, and Web sites that offer students immediate access to both L1 and L2 glossing information and explanations, along with audio and visual help, seem to promote optimal language learning and retention. Use of computerized bilingual dictionaries and programs such as *WordChamp.com's WebReader* glossing for 112 languages and *Rikai.com* glossing for four languages should be used systematically for both word learning and online text reading.

Secondly, CALL Web masters, teachers, and publishers should seek to provide language learners with more low-intermediate level reading and listening materials, both on and offline. The use of text-to-speech should be further investigated, as well as other multimedia approaches, to help enhance reading comprehension and speed, as well as learner enjoyment.

Thirdly, teachers should encourage deep and active lexical processing and use. Fourthly, teachers should encourage multiple lookups and systematic lexical processing via use of a simple, memorable framework, such as that outlined in Loucky, (2003a; 2006) which includes the most essential vocabulary, lexical processing steps, and comprehension strategies.

Finally, students need regular systematic practice in each of the essential processing areas of language acquisition, recognition, prediction, and production (Loucky, 1996). Teachers should help learners integrate development of all four communication skills, on- and offline, by prioritizing the most essential common core vocabulary, phrasal verbs, and collocations. A system for helping most learners of English to rapidly expand their TL vocabulary using a computer- assisted, bilingual Semantic Field Key Approach can be found along with many useful links to essential high frequency vocabulary lists and profilers at http://www.call4all.us///misc/sfka.php.

CONCLUSION

Having briefly surveyed current online readability programs and research, one can easily see that a very large gap exists for work in this important field. It is crucial for teachers and language learning program or E-learning Web site developers to understand this field, especially if they want foreign language learners to understand and be able to access information on their sites. Students or teachers need to be able to quickly assess the reading level of any text or website they considered reading. Those designing Web sites and E-learning materials need to have a detailed, publicly available set of level criteria for rating Web content and readability levels, which anyone producing graded materials would be able to use easily.

With such a system, it would be possible to form a community of writers all working to the same standards, making exchanges of materials more feasible and enhancing the usability of everyone's output. Using free collaborative teleconferencing tools, and new collaborative whiteboarding built into Microsoft's latest Vista OS make sharable readability standards more possible now than ever before.

The following pedagogical issues need to be considered when designing material and tasks for reading and vocabulary development online learning: Teachers employing CALL should work to ensure that the Web site's purposes and learning objectives are clear to both students and teachers using them. Teachers must consider the implications of CALL use for learners' workload, they must consider the implications for their own workloads, and finally, CALL teachers should try to ensure that end-users' online learning experiences are "of a seamless whole that incorporates all aspects of the online experience (conferencing, library, student and tutor homepage, etc.)," as stated by Shield and Kukulska-Hume (2004, p. 32), to blend these with other aspects of in-class or take-home integrated four-skills communicative language learning. In sum, the major aspects to keep in balance when designing a CALL-based reading and language program are seeking to blend and integrate: student's prior background knowledge, interest and goals with teacher's instructional goals; CALL-based programs with supportive language learning functions; reading text and vocabulary level assessment tools; and dictionary and glossing engines; multimedia, multi-sensory support, such as TTS; and printability, portability/mobility, transferability and archive-ability for either individual self-access or classroom learning environments.

Indeed all Web sites, especially those with a CALL or E-Learning purpose, should aim to improve comprehensibility of any text for learners from any cultural and linguistic background. By using collaborative techniques and communicative social networking we can help to motivate the building of language learning collaborative communities through extensive online reading, writing, speaking and listening programs. Clearly we need to provide a variety of levels (with both authentic and simplified text), entry points, and plenty of multi-media and bilingualized assistance to aid and encourage students' comprehension and language learning. Many of these factors are considered by Coll (2002); Loucky (2006), and Akbulut's (2007a & 2007b) studies of learning in hypertext environments.

In sum, this article has shown how to improve accessibility, comprehensibility, and readability of any online text by providing foreign language learners with rapid access to bilingual glossings; web dictionaries; text analysis for focused vocabulary study; text-to-speech listening support; and Readability assessment tools. By using these tools students can learn how to improve their comprehension of any text, either print or online. How to scan in any text and provide access to any of these essential reading and vocabulary level assessment tools has been explained. Lastly, we have shown that by using such innovative online tools we can help emerging readers of over 100 major world languages learn to read or translate English texts online, using various supportive electronic tools and technological functions to assist them, thus empowering their online reading.

REFERENCES

Akbulut, Y. (2007a). Variables predicting foreign language reading comprehension and vocabulary acquisition in a linear hypermedia environment. The Turkish Online *Journal of Educational Technology*, 6 (1), 53-60.

Akbulut, Y. (2007b). Effects of multimedia annotations on incidental vocabulary learning and reading comprehension of advanced learners of English as a foreign language. *Instructional Sci-*

ence. Available online at http://dx.doi.org/10.1007/s11251-007-9016-7

Bruce, C. (1997). *The seven faces of information literacy.* Adelaide: Auslib Press.

Coll, J. F. (2002). Richness of semantic encoding in a hypermedia-assisted Instructional environment for ESP: Effects on incidental vocabulary retention among learners with low ability in the target language. *ReCALL* 14 (2), 263-282.

Critchley, M. Retrieved on 2/08/07 from http://www.encounters.jp/mike/professional/publications/vocabulary.html

Dodigovic, M. (2005). Vocabulary profiling with electronic corpora: A case study in computer assisted needs analysis. *Computer Assisted Language Learning*, Vol. 18, No. 5, (Dec.). 443-455.

Ekwall, E. E. (1976). *Diagnosis and remediation of the disabled reader.* Boston: Allyn and Bacon.

Hirsh, D., & Nation, P. (1992). What vocabulary size is needed to read unsimplified texts for pleasure? *Reading in a Foreign Language,* (8), 689-696.

Hoppner, K. D. C. (2004). Information literacy for and through language learning. TEL & CL: *Zeitschrift fur Neue Lernkulturen.* 2. Quartal, April 2004, 26-31.

Hu, M., & Nation, P. (2000). Unknown vocabulary density and reading comprehension. *Reading in a Foreign Language,* 13(1), 403-430.

Hunt, A., & Beglar, D. (2005). A framework for developing EFL reading vocabulary. *Reading in a Foreign Language*, Vol. 17, No. 1 (April 2005). Retrieved on from http://nflrc.hawaii.edu/rfl/April2005/hunt/hunt.html

Johnson, K. (2007). Readability. Retrieved on from http://www.timetabler.com/reading.html

Laufer, B. (1997). The lexical plight in second language reading. In J. Coady & T. Huckin (Eds.), *Second language vocabulary acquisition* (pp. 20-34). Cambridge: Cambridge University Press.

Loucky, J. P. (1994). *Famous Leaders Who Influenced Japan's Internationalization.* Singapore: Campus Crusade.

Loucky, J. P. (1996). Developing and testing vocabulary training methods and materials for Japanese college students studying English as a foreign language. Ed. D. Dissertation on file with Pensacola Christian College, Pensacola, FL. Also available either from UMI Dissertation Services, 30 No. Zeeb Rd., PO Box 1346, Ann Arbor, MI 48106-1346; or from ERIC Center for Applied Linguistics via fax to (202) 429- 9292 or online at: <http://www.eric.ed.gov/ERICWebPortal/ Home.portal;jsessionid=FTTQv7nlnchpVWz1Z FZKQdXGgz2vwLJHYwD51QWrTq7YQYl1L2 TT!-1216994889?_nfpb=true&ERICExtSearch_ SearchValue_0=JOHN+PAUL+loucky+japanese &ERICExtSearch_SearchType_0=kw&_pageLa bel=ERICSearchResult&newSearch=true&rnd= 1171459696185&searchtype=keyword>

Loucky, J. P. (2002). When Eastern Oriental meets Western Occidental language system: Crossing the English vocabulary threshold versus breaking the Kanji Barrier. *Seinan JoGakuin Tandai Kiyo,* (48) 19-38.

Loucky, J. P. (2003a). Using CALL innovations to enhance students' English reading and vocabulary skills. In P. N. D. Lewis, C. Imai, & K. Kitao (Eds.), *Local Decisions, Global Effects: The Proceedings of JALT CALL 2002,* 121-128.

Loucky, J. P. (2003b). Testing vocabulary levels in Japan, Part II. *The Japanese Learner,* No. 29, (March), pp. 15-20. Oxford: Oxford University.

Loucky, J. P. (2005). When Eastern and Western language systems meet: Crossing the English vocabulary threshold versus breaking the kanji barrier. *GEMA Online Journal of Language Studies,* Vol. 5 (2), 2005. Retrieved on 2/14/07 from http://www.call4all.us///home/_all.php?fi=k.

Loucky, J. P. (2006). Maximizing vocabulary development by systematically using a depth of lexical processing taxonomy, CALL resources, and effective strategies. *CALICO Journal,* 23, No. 2 (January), 363-399.

Loucky, J. P. (2007). Computerized dictionaries: Integrating portable devices, translation software and web dictionaries to maximize learning. In *Major Reference Works, Encyclopedia of Computer Science and Computer Engineering.* Rawah, N. J.: John Wiley & Sons, Inc.

Meara, P. (1995). The importance of an early emphasis on L2 vocabulary. *The Language Teacher,* 19 (2), 8-10.

Meara, P. (2002). The rediscovery of vocabulary. *Second Language Research,* 18 (4), 393-407.

Nation, I.S.P. (1990). *Teaching and learning vocabulary.* New York: Newbury House.

Nation, P. (Ed.). (1994). *New ways in teaching vocabulary.* Alexandria, VA: TESOL.

Nation, I. S. P. (2001). *Learning vocabulary in another language.* Cambridge: Cambridge University Press.

Nation, P., & Newton, J. (1997). Teaching vocabulary. In J. Coady T. Huckin (Eds.), *Second language vocabulary acquisition: A rationale for pedagogy* (pp. 238-254). Cambridge: Cambridge University Press.

Shield, L., & Kukulska-Hume, A. (2004). Language learning websites: Designing for usability. *TEL & CAL: Zeitschrift fur Neue Lernkulturen.* (1. Quartal, Janner 2004), pp. 27-32.

Shillaw, J. (1995). Using a word list as a focus for vocabulary learning. *The Language Teacher,* 19 (2), 58-59.

Taylor, D. (2006). Writing for the Web: A Comprehensive Overview. Retrieved on 1/5/06, from http://www.peakwriting.com/article.php?articleid=28>

Valenza, J. (2006). Web 2.0 Meets Information Fluency: An Introduction. http://joycevalenza.edublogs.org/2006/09/17/web-20-meets-information-fluency-an-introduction/

KEY TERMS

CALL: Computer Assisted Language Learning.

Glossing: An operation that provides monolingual or bilingual meanings and examples of vocabulary.

Information Literacy: An umbrella term encompassing computer, critical, digital, and media literacy.-

Readability: A quality in online texts that includes discussion of four distinct constructs: the reading ability or level of the user; the readability level of a text; vocabulary level; and readability assessment tests, instrument scales or indices themselves.

TTS: Text-to-Speech online audio assistance.

Chapter XX
Technology–Enhanced Learning in the Corporate Context

Anoush Margaryan
Glasgow Caledonian University, UK

Betty Collis
University of Twente, The Netherlands

ABSTRACT

This chapter focuses on tools and strategies to integrate the strengths of formal and informal learning in the corporate context via the use of work-based activities within courses. The following proposition is argued: an effective course in the corporate context becomes a blend of formal and informal learning, a guided opportunity to learn from and share experiences gained through work-based activities, and to contribute one's own experiences as learning resources for others, for use in both formal and informal learning settings. Examples from practice in a multinational corporate learning context where a number of courses have been redesigned to allow integration of formal and informal learning are given. Key issues and challenges arising from this experience are discussed.

GLOBAL SOCIO-ECONOMIC CHALLENGES, ORGANISATIONS AND LEARNING FOR WORK

Workplaces are being transformed by global changes. Haughey (2000) outlines some characteristics of this transformation. Firstly, global economic integration is bringing about homogeni-sation as well as increased diversification. Secondly, advances in technology are influencing the organisation of work and traditional demarcations in the workplaces (Billett, 2001). Technological innovations are resulting in redistribution of the workforce and rise of knowledge workers (Drucker, 1999). What do these changes mean for learning in organisations?

The first implication is increased global competition, which means organisations have to be informed about potential clients and suppliers and prepared to respond to their needs in a dynamic and flexible way. They have to be able to quickly adapt in order to accommodate market changes. To do this effectively, organisations need employees who are able to solve novel complex problems for which often no previous knowledge base exists. To solve novel problems, employees must be able not only to process information, but also to generate information and create knowledge (Nonaka, 1994).

The second implication of the global transformations in the nature of work is that organisational structures change from traditional, hierarchical to task-based team models.

Thirdly, to flexibly adapt to the rapid changes, employees are required to become lifelong learners, "…actively wanting, thinking, feeling and doing beings, who will regard personal objectives as congruent with the objectives of the organisation, who will align their desires with organisational advancement, who will seek continually to adapt to its changing needs—and who therefore are sufficiently flexible and with capacity to regulate themselves" (Usher, 2000, p. 228). To develop such active and self-regulating employees, not only new models of management and organisation but also new training methods are required.

Fourthly, information and communication technology has been developing rapidly. Network technology in particular has changed the way organisations operate, at the same time creating new expectations of employees. Some of these changes include increased demand for higher levels of conceptual and symbolic knowledge; upskilling of some tasks while automating, routinising or eliminating others; re-organisation of work through electronic means; shortened and more transformational production cycles; and heightened levels of uncertainty. Billett (2001, p. 46) further argues that "these changes require workers to respond to new tasks, understand new concepts and develop new procedures."

In the context of these transformations, criteria for what constitutes effective learning are changing as well. In learning for work, employees are required to demonstrate outcomes directly relevant to organisational needs, short- and long-term goals, and the ability to solve complex workplace problems, working collaboratively in distributed, often culturally-diverse teams, building knowledge from different sources and different perspectives, and applying it in a flexible way (Jakupec & Garrick, 2000).

These new workplace demands are in sharp contrast with the traditional ways of training in organisations. The assumption that the employees will learn these highly complex skills in traditional formal learning settings divorced from workplace needs and context is no longer tenable. It is equally untenable that the knowledge and skills required for modern workplace can be picked up from experienced peers or coaches in informal, workplace learning settings alone. New learning strategies are needed that will bridge work and learning. New pedagogies are needed that will allow employees to learn while working and work while learning.

Network technology can enable such integration in unprecedented ways. It can extend learning into the workplace; provide access to resources, expert guidance, and scaffolding while learners work and learn in their own workplace; bridge prior knowledge and learning in novel situations; and support collaborative learning in distributed teams. Technology in itself, however, will not be sufficient to make the integration happen. Pedagogic methodologies premised on interdependence of work and learning are needed. A work-based learning methodology that aims to integrate formal and informal learning is proposed in this chapter. The discussion is organised around the following questions:

1. How can technology-enhanced work-based learning bridge formal and informal learning? What are characteristics of courses organised around work-based activities?
2. What are the affordances of technology for learning organised around work-based activities?
3. What are examples of learning organised around work-based activities in a specific corporate context?
4. What are key issues and challenges in bridging formal and informal learning via work-based activities?

In the next section, definitions of formal and informal learning are given, an analysis of their key strengths and weaknesses is presented, and an argument is advanced that the requirements of corporate learning may be best met by an integration of formal and informal learning within

a work-based learning approach—in ways that capitalise on their respective strengths and minimise their respective weaknesses.

FORMAL AND INFORMAL LEARNING: DEFINITIONS, STRENGTHS AND WEAKNESSES

There is a long-standing debate in the literature as to the definitions of formal and informal learning (Colley, Hodkinson, & Malcolm, 2002; Livingston, 2001; McGivney, 1999). Despite the differences in definition, formal learning is often seen as learning structured into a course, workshop or other form of learning event, delivered in classroom or at a distance, supported by an instructor or self-paced through instructional materials. In contrast, informal learning is learning that takes place in the work context and arises

Table 1. Formal and informal learning (compiled from Billett, 2001; Collis, 2001)

Strengths	Limitations
Formal learning in the corporate context	
Content is pre-selected, quality controlled, and pre-structured.	Content may become out of date or may not be relevant to particular work situations.
An instructor or tutor supports, motivates, guides, manages, and monitors the learning process.	Instructors vary in their capabilities to deal with the individual needs and differences of the participants.
Learning takes place in a specific place where distractions from ordinary work can be put aside. A tempo and discipline for learning is maintained and planned for in advance.	The times, places, and pace chosen for learning may not fit the needs of individual learners.
Learning involves social interaction and networking with fellow learners.	Social interaction may be forced or superficial and not last after the course is completed.
Informal learning	
Learning involves personally authentic experiences and is integrated within real work-based tasks.	Workplace tasks may be repetitive or non-conducive to new learning.
Learning involves the direct guidance of peers and experts: modelling, performance monitoring, collaborative learning.	The learner may learn inappropriate or limited knowledge such as shortcuts that represent unsafe working practices or work practices that encourage exclusiveness and intolerance.
Learning involves observation, listening, access to locally relevant tools and procedures; self-monitoring and self-directedness.	There may be a reluctance of experts or lack of available experts to provide guidance.
Learning is directly related to practice.	The individual may have difficulties in developing understanding in the workplace, leading to uneven conceptual development and disconnected understanding.

both from participation— doing the work—and from social interactions with peers and experts in the workplace. Typically, informal learning does not take place in a course setting. Expanding upon this, Collis (2001) noted four typical modes of formal or informal learning in the corporate context: (1) structured information with informal access; (2) structured information with organised access; (3) unstructured information with informal access; (4) unstructured information with organised access.

Category 1 involves informal learning that occurs with the support of knowledge management systems and corporate portals and databases. Classroom courses typically belong to Category 2 and represent formal learning. E-learning may fall in either of these categories depending on whether its use is formally structured or informally available. Category 3 involves the sharing of tacit knowledge within the organisation, generally accessed by making personal contacts or by spontaneous coaching or mentoring in a work context, the most frequent forms of informal learning. Category 4 relates to occasional structured events such as seminars or project meetings, where the learning that occurs may be intentional and thus formal such as in a seminar or informally acquired such as during a project meeting. Formal and informal learning each have their strengths and limitations. These are summarised in Table 1.

The challenge in terms of pedagogy is to integrate these two forms of learning in such a way that the strengths are maximised and the limitations are minimised.

A PEDAGOGY FOR INTEGRATION OF FORMAL AND INFORMAL LEARNING

In this section, a form of work-based learning is advanced as pedagogy for integration of formal and informal learning. Firstly, it is shown how this approach addresses strengths and weaknesses of formal and informal learning. Underpinning this approach are authentic work-based activities. Secondly, examples of work-based activities are described and technology affordances for work-based learning are elaborated upon.

Work-Based Activities as a Vehicle for Integration of Work and Learning

One way to integrate formal and informal learning is by blending work-based activities within formal courses. Collis (2002) defines courses oriented around work-based activities as courses which may or may not include a classroom components but will include different types of learning activities (with a focus on work-based problems), different types of learning resources (with a focus on re-use of knowledge and experience from within the company), different times and places for learning activities (with a focus on activities being carried out in the workplace), and different ways that people work and network together (with a focus on collaboration on work-based activities). Work-based learning is guided by a capable facilitator (with a focus on "teachable moments" in the course structure as well as individualised coaching in the workplace), involves regular assessment (with the focus on workplace relevance), and is integrated via a Web-based learning-support environment. Key to this learning approach are authentic work-based activities, sharing of experiences related to these activities, guidance by experienced facilitators (course instructor and a workplace coach), and a technological learning-support platform (Collis & Winnips, 2001).

By authentic work-based learning we mean activities that are anchored in everyday practice and that are focussed on developing the learners' ability to solve the problems of their everyday professional job roles. Knowledge and skills that learners acquire while carrying out the work-based activities are acquired in the situation and context in which they will be used rather than in an abstract way. In contrast to well-defined, "textbook" problems that only resemble the real-world problems, work-based problems are complex and ill-defined and need to be solved in social settings, through collaboration with other, and with scaffolding by an expert (Collins, Brown & Newman, 1989; Fox, 2002; Reeves, Herrington, & Oliver, 2002). Within this form of learning, not only work-based activities but also the submission of different types of reports and reflections based on those activities to a course Web-environment

are emphasised, which help to make the cognitive processes explicit and serve as a basis for reflection and feedback. Follow-up activities can build upon these submissions. Transfer of learning to the workplace is enhanced, since this transfer is part of the learning process. In this model, content is seen as resource for the activities, not as the initial driver of the activities. Selected learner submissions are re-used as valuable content objects for others. Classroom sessions may still occur, but with a focus on drawing together and sharing the learning that has occurred in the work-based

Table 2. Informal learning in a technology-enhanced work-based learning approach

Strengths and limitations of informal learning	How strengths and limitations are addressed in a work-based model
Strengths	
Authenticity of experiences	Emphasis on work-based activities, with content built around these
Engagement in work tasks: goal-directed activities; no separation of learning and doing	Emphasis on learners' workplace problems
Direct guidance of peers and experts—modelling, performance monitoring, collaborative learning	Facilitator/instructor to guide learning within the course; involvement of experts in the work-based activities; sharing knowledge with peers in the course, in the workplace
Indirect guidance—observation, listening, access to tools and procedures; self-monitoring and self-directedness	Building in possibilities for observation, self-monitoring into the work-based activities
Problem-solving grounded in goal-directed activity and resulting in learning	Work-based activities are problem-centred by their nature
Limitations	
Learning *inappropriate knowledge*—for example shortcuts that represent unsafe working practices	Learning takes place within a formal course, with expert facilitator guidance and feedback available
Limited access to appropriate workplace activities	Formalised work-based activities, line-manager involvement, learning agreement between learner and supervisor
Not understood goals for workplace performance	Availability of experts (line managers, coaches, mentors, etc.) to clarify workplace goals underlying the work-based activities
Reluctance of experts to provide guidance	Strategies and tools for workplace experts' involvement; availability of expert guidance from the course instructor or other subject-matter experts engaged by the instructor
Absence of expert guidance—no experts available	Experts are hired to lead the course (facilitator, peers, other external experts)
Problems in developing understanding in the workplace—uneven conceptual development, "procedures, no theory," disconnected rather than richly associated understanding	Conceptual development provided within the courses developed by designers, subject matter experts, experienced facilitators, and pedagogical experts
Reluctance to participate—because of (perceived) lack of pre-requisite skills, embarrassment with potential low performance, cultural differences, poor previous learning experiences	Participation connected with personal development planning so the instructor can provide remedial help if necessary; flexible learning activities help leverage cultural differences and address individual needs

activities. Reflections on the relations between the work-based activities and concepts to be learned in the course are stimulated and monitored by the instructor, either during face-to-face sessions or asynchronously, with submissions made electronically. Workplace supervisor and other appropriate technical subject matter experts provide coaching. In-house resources existing in knowledge management systems such as document repositories and discussion forums are used (Van Unnik, 2004). Persons throughout the company contribute their advice and share their experiences with similar problems.

Many of these characteristics are benefits of informal learning and usually do not occur in formal learning settings in organisations. However, because the work-based activities are carried out within a course context, there are also the benefits of formal learning involved. There is an instructor and perhaps a team of experts who steer and guide the linkage of theory and practice and supplement the feedback given in the workplace with their own. They also help the workplace coach in her feedback processes and extend and systematise the range of resources and contact persons available for knowledge sharing.

With respect to the particular challenges facing learning in organisations, work-based activities provide a way for courses to move quickly with new developments in the workplace, and if properly steered, can stimulate the sharing of experiences between persons in the company with experience and those just gaining the experience, regardless of their physical locations. Table 2 summarises how the issues identified in Table 1 are addressed in this approach:

Examples of Work-Based Activities

For work-based activities to be meaningful in practice, they should relate to complex, multi-step situations and thus build each of a series of steps on learning and feedback from previous steps. Table 3 gives a suggestion of a multi-step series of sub-activities that can form a work-based activity.

Technology Affordances

Technology to support work-based learning can be seen as tools for facilitating contacts, questions, discussions, finding of resources, sharing resources, archiving resources, collaboration, management, and integration, as well as the medium of learning objects themselves. Network technology in particular is a key enabler in that it can be helpful in supporting articulation (or externalisation) of reflection; sharing reflections among learners (Jaervelae, 1995); providing support for distributed groups of learners (McLoughlin, Winnips, & Oliver, 2000); and giving access to resources and expert guidance and scaffolding while learning and working in their own workplaces (Levin & Waugh, 1998). By "challenging traditional boundaries between knowledge communities and the demarcation of knowledge domains" (Bliss & Säljö, 1999, p. 9), network technologies make integration of formal and informal learning as depicted in Figure 1 possible.

While the conceptual arguments for this approach can be compelling, the approach must be carried out in practice to realise its benefits. This will require methodological changes from the classroom-based approaches, adjustments in the way that the companies organise the delivery of courses, and new uses of technology. The next section will focus on examples from a multinational company where this approach has been in realisation since 2001 and will further illustrate ways that technology can play a key role in the work-based learning model.

WORK-BASED ACTIVITIES: EXAMPLES OF IMPLEMENTATION

In this section, implementation of work-based learning in a multinational corporation will be

Table 3. Examples of work-based activities (adapted from Merrill, 2003)

Types of work-based activities	Examples
Discovery	- Search the organisation's knowledge-management resources for discussions and previous materials related to the topic - Search the Web in general to see what others (including competitors) are doing relating to the topic - Interview people with experience relevant to the topic in your own workplace
Compare/Contrast, Analyse	- Compare your own situation with that of others - Analyse your own situation in terms of key theoretical concepts.
Apply	- Describe an approach to dealing with a problem or new opportunity relating to the topic in your own setting and apply the key concepts (plan, design, predict, carry out procedures, etc.) - Interview colleagues to get insight into how they apply the concepts in their work - Get feedback from workplace peers and coaches, the course instructor, and fellow course participants on your planning or procedures
Present, reflect, leave for others to use	- Present the results of your application to relevant persons in the workplace as well as to the instructor and fellow course participants. - Compare and contrast your results with those of others in the course; what can you learn from each other's work? - Leave a reflection on your learning that can be useful for others, both in a formal course setting but also informally, such as via knowledge-management archives and discussion forums.

described. After briefly introducing the context, an overview of types of work-based learning activities that are occurring in the new form of courses is given, and a specific course is discussed as an illustration.

Shell EP and Work-Based Learning

Shell Exploration and Production (EP) is one of the five core businesses of The Royal Dutch/Shell Group of Companies and focuses on finding and producing oil. In an effort to continually improve performance among its staff of approximately 30,000 located in over 45 countries, Shell EP has to ensure that these employees acquire, share, and use new skills and knowledge. A range of learning products—training courses, workshops, and other learning events—are designed and delivered by the Shell EP Learning, Leadership and Development (LLD) unit that includes various faculties and support groups such as Design and Development, Knowledge Management, Virtual Team Working, and so on. Learning technologies are used to incorporate a new way of knowledge dissemination and restructuring learning around

the organisation's competence frameworks. The learners are petroleum engineers, geologists and other technical professionals from various Operating Units of Shell EP around the world. The work-based learning activities are integrated via a Web-based environment called TeleTOP© (Collis & Moonen, 2001). The work-based activities as the heart of learning at the Shell EPP LLD involve submission of different types of reports and reflections based on those activities to the common Web environment. Some submissions are re-used as content objects for the next cycles of the same course or other courses.

Types of Work-Based Activities at Shell EP LLD

A study by Margaryan, Collis and Cooke (2003) identified the following generic types of work-based activities:

Orientation: Activities such as the learner signing a "learning agreement" with his/her line supervisor, getting acquainted with the ground rules for the course (i.e., expectations in terms of participation in discussions, regularity of checking out the course site, completion requirements, etc.), practicing with functionalities of the course Web-site, reflecting on his/her own knowledge gaps, learning needs and expectations from the course in terms of addressing those needs, and posting some information related to his/her own background and work experience and personal details to help learners get to know each other. Some of the activities in this category are directly related to workplace and some are not. For instance, the Learning Agreement is a critical element of the course as it helps the learner and the supervisor to jointly set a workplace task that the learner will work on during the course, explicate the desired changes in performance, and make sure the course is a part of learner's competency or personal development plan (CBD or PDP), as well as agree on resources (time and place to study, computer and network access) available to the learner during the course. For courses in which some or all of the learning activities are carried out outside of a face-to-face setting, this is a particularly challenging issue, because learners are technical professionals who often work in challenging environments, such as offshore oil rigs, jungles, or desert oil fields, where finding a time, place and network access to participate in the course may be difficult to manage.

Collecting information from the workplace: Activities in this category begin with a problem related to the subject-matter of the course, and involve steps relating to analysing the information, implementing the results of the analysis (or a part of it, as is feasible given the time constraints), and sharing the findings with the course facilitator and others in the course by submitting a report to the course Web environment. To carry out this type of activity, learners can choose to contact an experienced colleague in the workplace or search in the company intranet or the specialised knowledge-sharing networks, which are special-interest discussion forums, related to various Shell EP disciplines. By integrating these

informal knowledge-sharing channels within a formal course environment, learning is expanded beyond the boundaries of the course, and learners are stimulated to make use of various existing company resources (people and technology) to solve their particular problems. Once the report on the results of the activity is submitted to the course Web environment, follow-up activities can occur. These often include the learners comparing and contrasting their problems and solutions or giving feedback to each other's submissions. The course instructor/facilitator also provides feedback and summarises the results of participants' submissions. These summaries are then used as a basis for reflection by the participants, and can also be re-used by the instructor for the following cycles of the course. This category emphasizes the social element of learning, engagement with peers in meaningful realistic tasks, collaboration, sharing of tacit knowledge, reflection, and articulation in work-based learning. This is done asynchronously, using Web-based tools, while the learners remain in their workplaces.

Product development: The third category of work-based activities relates to developing a product that can be directly used in the workplace. The products can range from development of an online-bidding project for the workplace to the development of technical models or inventories, to personal leadership-development plans. These are often multistep activities following a systematic framework (Assess-Plan-Design-Develop-Implement-Evaluate). After each step, reports summarising the results in that step are submitted to the course web environment, and the course instructor and participants can give feedback on those submissions. This category of activities sometimes involves a mid-course checkpoint with the participant's supervisor to discuss the learning progress. Such projects with direct workplace applicability make learning meaningful and relevant and support development of competences. Following a multistep systematic framework gives learners the opportunity to develop metacognitive skills for solving complex workplace problems in a systematic, process-oriented manner, and therefore increases the transferability of such skills across workplaces.

Sharing and reflecting: This category of activities relates to sharing experiences on a given topic, by posting reflective reports in the course environment. This is followed up by group (a)synchronous discussions of the submitted issues in the discussion area of the Web environment. The course instructor participates and monitors these discussions, and gives feedback or guidance when needed. These activities help learners to build a sense of a learning community, contribute to the community, activate their previous experiences, and learn from their own and others' experiences. In a corporate context, the benefit of this approach is that the tacit knowledge of the participants in a course can be articulated, submitted into a central repository (such as an appropriately configured Web-based course-management system) and re-used in other settings, increasing the productivity of experience in the organisation.

Comparing and contrasting: These activities involve comparing and contrasting each other's submissions, comparing course content with the real situation in the learner's own workplace, or comparing the learner's own experiences and ideas on the subject matter of the course with the company standards. This type of activity stimulates the participants to learn from each other, increase awareness of the situation in other workplaces throughout the company, and to reflect on their own experiences in relation to common benchmarks.

Self-analysis: These activities are mostly used in business and leadership courses that are focused on commercial rather than technical competences. Such courses relate to middle-and- top management development, development of supervision skills, networking and business skills, and skills for working and collaborating online, managing priorities and resources, creative thinking, and personal effectiveness. In these courses, learn-ers are guided through a multistep process of developing their business and leadership competence, and carry out self-analysis and reflection activities to identify their knowledge and skill gaps and development needs. Self-analysis is carried out through specialised questionnaires, guiding questions from the instructor and peers, as well as individualized coaching by a dedicated subject-matter expert and the results are applied in the workplace. Learners then share the results of the application with their peers and the instructor who provide further guidance and remedial help when needed.

Reflections: Although part of many of the other categories of activities, reflection is emphasised here as a separate category as it is often used as the final activity of the course where learners are asked to reflect on what they learned and on the results of the application of learning in their workplace. Reflection is an important part of learning which is often neglected or not possible to manage in a classroom-only setting. By taking a retrospective and critical look at their learning experience learners can understand and evaluate what they did, what they learned, how it affected their workplaces and themselves personally.

In addition to the work-based activities, more traditional learning activities also occur in the workplace portions of the Shell EP LLD courses. These include activities relating to studying the conceptual material related to the subject matter of the course that is available in the course Web site. Conceptual materials can be presented to the learners in different forms ranging from usual course handbook and PowerPoint viewgraphs to e-learning modules (text combined with video and audio), CD-ROM, intranet or internet-based material. Although content objects have a place within work-based learning model, they are seen as resources for the work-based activities, not as the initial drivers of the activities. Exercises, quizzes, case studies, and working with simulation software are also familiar types of activities carried out outside of a classroom setting via the support of the course Web environment. In the Shell EP LLD courses, exercises and quizzes are used as self-checks for the learners to assess their understanding of the conceptual material or learning how to use specialised technology or a software package. Case studies and simulations are used in courses where because of time, manageability, or safety constraints it is not possible to use real workplace situations or tasks as the main project of the course. However, such courses also use some of the described work-based types of activities to make the learning as work relevant as possible.

In Shell EP LLD courses built on work-based model, many of the activity types we have discussed are used in combination. Content materials are used in all of the courses, but as resources for, not as the drivers of, work-based activities. In the next section, a specific example of a course re-designed using the work-based approach will be discussed to illustrate this sort of combination. The course is focused on health-risk assessment and incorporates a number of the types of work-based activities described in the previous section.

A Health Risk Assessment Course: Example from the Shell EP LLD

Firstly, the health-risk assessment process at Shell EP will be explained, and then the rationale and process of re-designing the course will be elaborated upon. Finally, results from the course evaluation will be discussed.

Health-risk assessment (HRA) is a complex and critical process in Shell EP. Health risks for the employees associated with potentially dangerous tasks such as drilling or handling chemicals must be regularly monitored and prevented, and health risks associated with Shell processes for the local environments must be managed at all times with great care to prevent environment disasters. Personnel within Shell EP with job responsibilities involving health-risk assessment must be trained to identify the risks, and depending on their posi-

tion, to take preventative action or report the risks to the appropriate person.

HRA is a carefully documented process in Shell EP and hundreds of Shell professionals worldwide must be trained each year to take responsibility for the assessment process in their workplaces. The person carrying out the assessment never works in isolation, but must lead a team including the drilling foreman and superintendent, technicians, company physicians and physiotherapists, workplace team leaders, plant managers, security advisors, and general asset managers. Typically the course used to take place in a one-week classroom setting, but there were difficulties in participants not being able to travel to the classroom sessions or in the instructors being able to travel to individual regional sites. Also, the classroom sessions did not provide the opportunity to actually carry out a health-risk assessment as it occurs in the workplace and get guidance and feedback from an expert or from peer-collaborators helping one another during this process. A decision was made to re-design the course so that the activities can be carried out in participants' individual workplaces. To avoid scheduling difficulties relating to travel and location, the classroom portion of the course was omitted.

Re-Design of the Health Risk Assessment Course

The result of the main activity of the HRA course was chosen to be a complete and properly done HRA assessment of a potential health risk in the participant's own workplace in which (a) a potential health hazard is identified and a plan to minimize or eliminate the hazard is presented that is seen by the supervisor as important for the business, (b) an assessment process is carried out by the participant while staying in his or her workplace, and (c) the participant is working collaboratively with a team in his or her workplace and also with peers in the course. For the participants, the motivation is to obtain the health-risk assessor skill level without having to leave the workplace to go away to a course and in a way that generates a full HRA plan for his or her personal-competency portfolio. For the participant's workplace supervisor, the benefits are to be able to develop a team member to HRA skill level in a way that is likely to have the most direct transfer to the workplace and be the least disruptive to on-going work. For the facilitator/instructor, the time needed for continual trips away to present the one-week course can be replaced by the time, in his own workspace, that he chooses for giving feedback and guidance via the course Web environment.

The course was designed around a series of tasks leading to the generation of a full-scale health-risk assessment and a plan for the participant's own workplace. The tasks were to be carried out in a realistic manner in the workplace. They therefore require collaboration among the team that the participant needed to assemble for the health-risk appraisal process. By carrying out an actual health-risk appraisal following corporate procedures, the familiar rules and division of labour among the health-risk appraisal team still applied. However, making regular submissions relating to subtasks to the course facilitator and reflecting on the subtasks and relating to the course study resources obtained via a course Web environment calls for different roles and rules for *attending a course* than had been previously the case. For the instructor/facilitator, monitoring the assessment process as it goes on in the different workplaces of the participants, calls for new rules and procedures. For the supervisor, serving as a workplace mentor and monitor for the health-risk appraisal process may also call for changes in familiar roles and practices. Thus care needs to be taken in the course design to help all of the subjects handle these new ways of working within the course framework.

Collaborative learning among peers in the course, helping each other reflect upon and move through the different subtasks of the overall task (carrying out a HRA and producing the associated report and recommendations), was chosen as an important support instrument. Collaboration in the workplace itself through instructions for how to involve members of the health-risk appraisal team as learning supporters was also designed. In terms of resources, the PowerPoint® presentations, and previous handouts and written materials that were used at the classroom sessions were made available via the course Web environment. In addition, e-learning modules combining text, with audio and video segments as well as embedded quizzes were designed and used as a resource. Finally, in terms of electronic tools, the use of a course-management system provided a common environment for submitting, sharing, discussing, and comparing one's own progress with those of the course peers.

It was predicted that supervisor involvement in the work-based activities might be hard to stimulate, as this sort of involvement would be different from the role usually played by the supervisor in terms of a team-member's attendance in a course. Thus special attention was given to tools and strategies integrated in the course design to engage the supervisor, such as a learning agreement (Bianco & Collis, 2003), which were piloted in the course. Suggestions to the course facilitator relating to being efficient and timely in terms of responding to submissions and giving feedback were also discussed during the design process.

The result of the design process was a course that involves a number of work-based activities which progressively build upon each other to take the learner through the health-risk assessment process including preparation (identification of a competent HRA team to coach and assist the learner with the work-based assignments during the course; planning; getting permission from the manager of the assessment team to perform an HRA); identification and rating of HRA hazards; assessment of health risks to the business; application of hazard and exposure ratings identified; effective documentation for the HRA results; and reviewing the HRA and assurance process. The final HRA plans are thus available to all in the course site, as a resource for the future.

Technology Affordances for the HRA Course

An obvious role of the Web technology was to make the course possible. The participants in this were from as many locations around the world and were able to fully participate, as a learning community as well as persons carrying out work-while-learning in their workplaces, because of the Web environment. All of the study resources of the course are available via the site. All of the submissions are available, grouped by activity. Also, following many of the steps, the participants carried out a reflection or discussion activity. A chat session and a teleconference were scheduled, with instructions given in the roster and using tools available in the Web environment. Questions and answers from previous courses were available and also new questions could be entered at any time. Various tools are available for the instructor, such as the Feedback database and Administration. In the Feedback database the instructor can keep examples from previous cycles of the course and make them available as feedback or learning resources when useful. Another tool for the instructor is the Setup function, which, in the case of a course such as this, which is offered many times per year, allows simple replication of the course site, without submissions, for a new cohort. Interesting submissions from participants in each cycle are reused as learning resources, available as the instructor sees fit, such as part of the Study resources, or in the Question and Answer, or in the Feedback. All participants completed the course, as a group, even though they stayed in their own workplaces and had flexibility in timing with regard to individual submissions.

Evaluation Results

Following the pilot in July 2002 and six subsequent runs of the course until April 2003, 49 course participants were asked to reflect on their experiences with the course. Twenty-six of the course participants were Health and Safety professionals, six were engineers (including petroleum and production engineers), and 17 participants were from other job groups. Participants were from Shell EP Operating Units in Brazil, Brunei, Canada, China, Egypt, Germany, Ghana, Italy, Malaysia, Netherlands, Nigeria, Singapore, Tanzania, UK, US, and Vietnam. The majority (n=27) had 12 or more years of working experience in their discipline. The survey focused on the following aspects of the course:

- Quality of the work-based activities
- **Communication:** (1) teleconference, (2) asynchronous discussion
- **Interactions:** (1) with peers in the course; and (2) with the course instructor
- **Learning outcomes:** (1) understanding of HRA; (2) competence to perform; (3) ability to engage others in HRA; (4) awareness of resources (experts, documentation) and knowing where and who to get help from if needed.
- Application in the workplace
- **Line manager support in:** (1) participation in the course; (2) applying learning in the workplace.
- (Perceived) change in performance after the course
- Relevance of the course to the individual competence-based development (CBD) and personal development plan (PDP)
- (Perceived) business impact
- Sharing what was learned with others in the workplace
- Technology support

The results of the survey show that the learners' satisfaction with the quality of the work-based activities, interaction with the course instructor, asynchronous discussions, line manager support, was high. Particularly, learners commented that the design of the course and the work-based activities were motivating. For instance, one learner said: "Prior to taking the course, I had only a vague idea of how to go about doing an HRA. It (the course) helped me a lot to put my learning into practice in order to complete the HRA at my location."

The relevance of the course to their competence and personal development plans was perceived as very high by the majority. (Perceived) learning and increased competence, application of learning in the workplace and change in performance were also among the aspects rated as good or very good. A number of learners commented on the value of the systematic approach to HRA that they learned from taking the course. One learner commented: "It is like learning to ride a bicycle. You never forget it. Now I can use the methods and the logical approach in all other fields. There is a uniform scheme...." The learner does not only solve a problem in his/her own field, but also learns how to systematically approach similar problems, therefore, the transferability of his/her learning across workplaces increases.

Learners reported that they moved on to new job roles as a result of their increased competence, or were entrusted with new projects of high business impact either in their own OU or in other parts of the organisation, as a result of the course.

Table 4. Results of the HRA reflection survey (n= 49)

Aspect of the course	Not acceptable/None	Below average/Little	Average/Some	Good/Much	Very good / Very much
Quality of the activities	2%	0%	18%	66%	14%
Communication:					
• teleconferences	8%	6%	51%	33%	2%
• asynchronous discussion	4%	12%	33%	43%	8%
Interactions:					
• with peers in the course	6%	29%	47%	12%	6%
• with the course instructor	2%	2%	14%	55%	6%
Learning:					
• understanding of HRA	0%	2%	2%	27%	69%
• competence to perform	0%	2%	2%	33%	63%
• engaging others	0%	2%	2%	31%	65%
• awareness of resources	0%	2%	2%	20%	76%
Application in the workplace	0%	4%	18%	35%	43%
Line manager support in:					
• participation in the course	4%	8%	18%	51%	19%
• application in the workplace	8%	2%	12%	67%	11%
Change in performance	2%	2%	8%	33%	55%
Relevance to CBD and PDP	0%	0%	6%	35%	59%
Business impact	0%	4%	43%	39%	14%
Sharing knowledge	0%	2%	10%	25%	63%
Problems with technology	35%	20%	27%	14%	4%

As one learner noted, "I worked with HRA teams in Shell Egypt sister companies, Fayumgas and Natgas, and developed their level of competence (sic) and supervised their HRA, thus supporting stakeholders of Shell Egypt and adding value to the business by strengthening the relationship with other partners." The majority (43%) reported that their participation in the course was already making some business impact in their OUs, and 14% said that the impact was big. In terms of sharing what they learned with others in their team and OU, the majority (63%) said that they are already sharing a lot. This happens either by delivering training workshops to colleagues in own OU or elsewhere in the organization, raising HRA issues with the management, or guiding colleagues who are participating in the same course in carrying out their learning assignments.

As to the technology, 35% of learners did not experience any problems, but for 27% it was a minor problem, for 14% sometimes and for and 4% continuously a problem. Technology problems mostly related to lack of constant access to the course Web site, particularly for learners who work on a shift basis on offshore oil rigs, or lack of computers with Internet access in the workplace, so that the learners had to share the few available ones with colleagues. Despite reaching an agreement with the line manager on availability of resources and time to learn through the Learning Agreement, 33 % of the learners mentioned that business issues often interfered and they had to complete the activities in their own time during the weekends or stay in the office late after work.

Interaction among the learners was a relatively weak aspect of the course, with 47% of participants stating that it was only adequate and 29%—below adequate. Some reasons mentioned by learners were difficulties in participating in synchronous discussions due to difference in time zones, or pressures of daily work.

Overall, the participants' comments show that the work-based activities in this course resulted in increased competence, application of learning, sharing of knowledge in the workplace, and workplace impact. The study also indicated some key issues and challenges involved in redesigning courses for the work-based approach.

CONCLUSION

For each of the questions indicated in the introduction to this chapter, various conclusions can be drawn. The key is designing the course around a real work-based problem or process or opportunity, which is carried out in steps each done in as authentic a fashion as possible so that the final product of the activity is something that is usable and useful in the workplace. For this, the involvement of the workplace supervisor is necessary, not only to help design the task but also to provide mentoring and coaching. While there still may be a classroom component to such a course, the main aspect is the work-based activity.

An effective Web-based environment serves as an organiser, manager, gateway, communication centre, collaboration and sharing centre, and "common home" for course participants. Although in the Shell EP case, the Web environments are at the moment only being used in the workplace-based portions of the courses, in many other settings such Web environments are also valuable resources during the classroom portions of courses as well (Collis & Moonen, 2001).

A summary was given of the types of work-based activities that are emerging in practice for Shell EP and one specific course (out of more than 100) was discussed in detail. The Shell illustration shows that the conceptual ideas relating to combining formal and informal learning can be realised successfully in practice.

The Shell examples also indicate some of the key issues and challenges involved in introducing work-based learning pedagogy. Many types of changes must occur, particularly in the expectations of all involved with regard to what constitutes a "course." Work-based activities by their very nature are more difficult to manage in terms of time expectations, compared with a pre-set number of days for a classroom-only course. The new expectations for the workplace supervisor will meet with resistance, because they will be seen as new work, unless carefully supported and unless the work-based activities are directly relevant and valuable. In a shift from content delivery to activity management, instructors must learn new roles. The technology used must be simple, flexible, easy to access, and yet make sharing and communicating as transparent as possible. An integrated approach to implementation and course design is needed to manage these complex interrelated requirements. At Shell EP, such an approach has been designed and carried out (Bianco, Collis, Cooke, & Margaryan, 2002). For the approach to be mainstreamed, it must reflect corporate strategy.

With learning driven by work-based problems, tasks and situations, the boundaries between activities blur, and formal and informal learning take on new forms. A course becomes a blend of formal and informal learning, a guided opportunity to learn from and share experiences gained through work-based activities, and to contribute one's own experiences as learning resources for others, for use in both formal and informal learning settings. Such learning environments supported by network technology create opportunities for learners to collaboratively generate new ideas while working on complex learning situations in their own workplace. Collaboration and knowledge sharing occurs among the peers in the course, peers in the workplace and between teams with similar problems but different workplaces. Such learning reflects the distributed and contextualised nature of thinking, reasoning, knowledge and experience as argued by socio-cultural approaches to learning (e.g., Cole, 1966).

REFERENCES

Bianco, M., & Collis, B. (2003). Blended learning in the workplace: Tools and strategies for supervisor's involvement in the learning process. In *Proceedings of the Third International Conference of Researching Work and Learning, IV* (pp. 2-29). Tampere, Finland: University of Tampere.

Bianco, M., Collis, B., Cooke, A., & Margaryan, A. (2002). Instructor support for New learning approaches involving technology. *Staff and Educational Development International (SEDI), 6* (2), 129-148.

Billet, S. (2001). *Learning in the workplace: Strategies for effective practice.* Crows Nest: Allen & Unwin.

Bliss, J., & Säljö, R. (1999). The human-technological dialectic. In J. Bliss, R. Saeljoe, & P. Light (Eds.), *Learning sites: Social and technological resources for learning* (pp.1-11). Amsterdam: Pergamon.

Colley, H., Hodkinson, P., & Malcolm, J. (2002). *Non-formal learning: Mapping the conceptual terrain* (A consultation report). Leeds: University of Leeds, Lifelong Learning Institute. Available at http://www.infed.org/archives/e-exts/colley_informal_learning.htm

Collins, A., Brown, J.S., & Newman, S.E. (1989). Cognitive apprenticeship: Teaching the crafts of reading, writing, and mathematics. In L.B. Resnick (Ed.), *Knowing, learning and instruction* (pp.453-494). Hillsdale, NJ: Erlbaum.

Collis, B. (2001). *Linking organizational knowledge and learning.* Invited presentation at ED-MEDIA 2001 Conference, Montreal, Canada.

Collis, B. (2002). *Learning 2005: Blended learning as a key step* (Internal paper) Noordwijkerhout, Netherlands: Shell EP Learning, Leadership and Development.

Collis, B., & Moonen, J. (2001). *Flexible learning in a digital world: Experiences and expectations.* London: Kogan Page.

Collis, B., & Winnips, K. (2001). Two scenarios for productive learning environments in the workplace. *British Journal of Educational Technology, 33*(2), 133-148.

Cole, M. (1966). Cultural Psychology: A once and future discipline. Harvard: Harvard University Press.

Drucker, P. (1999). Knowledge worker productivity: The biggest challenge. *California Management Review, 41*(2), 79-95.

Fox, S. (2002). Studying networked learning: some implications from socially situated learning theory and actor network theory. In C. Steeples & C. Jones (Eds.), *Networked learning: Perspectives and issues* (pp. 77-92). London: Springer-Verlag.

Haughey, M. (2000). A global society needs flexible learning. In V. Jakupec, & J. Garrick (Eds.), *Flexible learning, human resource and organisational development: Putting theory to work* (pp. 11-29). London: Routledge.

Jakupec, V., & Garrick, J. (2000) (Eds.), *Flexible learning, human resource and organisational development: Putting theory to work.* London: Routledge.

Jaervelae, S. (1995). The cognitive apprenticeship model in a technologically reach learning environment: Interpreting the learning interaction. *Learning and Instruction, 5*, 237-259.

Levin, J., & Waugh, M. (1998). Teaching tele-apprenticeships: Frameworks for integrating technology into teacher education. *Interactive Learning Environments, 6*(1-2), 39-58.

Livingstone, D. (2001). *Adults' informal learning: Definitions, findings, gaps and future research* (NALL Working Paper No.21). Toronto: OISE/UT. Available: http://www.oise.utoronto.ca/depts/sese/csew/nall/res/21adultsifnormallearning.htm

Margaryan, A., Collis, B., & Cooke, A. (2004). Activity-based blended learning. *Human Resources Development International, 7(*2), 265-274.

McGivney, V. (1999). *Informal learning in the community: A trigger for change and development.* Leicester: NIACE.

McLoughlin, C., Winnips, J.C., & Oliver, R. (2000). Supporting constructivist learning through learner support on-line. In J. Bordeau & R. Heller (Eds.), In *Proceedings of ED-MEDIA 2000* (pp. 639-645). Charlottesville, VA: AACE.

Merrill, D. (2003). First principles of instruction. *Educational Technology Research and Development, 50*(3), 43-59.

Nonaka, I. (1994). A dynamic theory of organizational knowledge creation. *Organizational Science, 5*(1), 14-37.

Reeves, T.C., Herrington, J., & Oliver, R. (2002). *Authentic activities and online learning.* Available: http://elrond.scam.ecu.edu.au/oliver/2002/Reeves.pdf

Usher, R. (2000). Flexible learning, postmodernity and the contemporary workplace. In V. Jakupec, & J. Garrick (Eds.), *Flexible learning, human resource and organisational development: Putting theory to work* (pp. 225-238). London: Routledge.

Van Unnik, A. (2004, October). *Benefits of developing knowledge sharing communities.* Paper presented at the 11th Abu Dhabi International Petroleum Exhibition and Conference, Abu Dhabi, UAE.

KEY TERMS

Formal Learning: A wide range of definitions, but no commonly agreed one, exists in the literature. For the purposes of this chapter we define formal learning as learning structured into a course, workshop or other form of learning event, delivered in classroom or at a distance, supported by an instructor/facilitator or self-paced through instructional materials.

Informal Learning: A term for which a wide range of definitions apply, but no commonly agreed one exists in the literature. Here, informal learning is defined as learning that takes place in the work context and arises both from participation—doing the work—and from social interactions with peers and experts in the workplace.

Knowledge Worker: A term first used by Peter Drucker, signifying an employee who primarily works with knowledge and information.

Work-Based Activities: Learning activities that are anchored in everyday practice and that are focused on developing the learners' ability to solve the problems of their everyday professional job roles. In contrast to well-defined, textbook problems that only resemble the real-world problems, work-based problems are complex and ill-defined and need to be solved in social settings, involving

others for team working, and with coaching and scaffolding by an expert.

Work-Based Learning: Various models and forms of work-based learning exist both in training and education. For the purpose of this chapter, work-based learning is defined as courses oriented around work-based activities, which may or may not include a classroom components but will include different types of learning activities with a focus on work-based problems; different types of learning resources with a focus on re-use of knowledge and experience from within the company; different times and places for learning activities with a focus on activities being carried out in the workplace; and different ways that people work and network together with a focus on collaboration in the process of doing work-based activities. Work-based learning is guided by a facilitator with a focus on teachable moments in the course structure as well as individual coaching in the workplace, involving regular assessment with the focus on workplace relevance, and integrating a Web-based environment.

Chapter XXI
Using Virtual Learning Environments to Present Different Learning Blends

Robert J. McClelland
Liverpool John Moores University, UK

ABSTRACT

This work is concerned with the evolution of blended learning supports for university students in moving from early virtual learning environment (VLE) platforms and supports that were designed and facilitated by academics to those platforms designed commercially (particularly Blackboard) and developed using a mixture of commercial, collaborative, and e-learning supports. The chapter is an examination of a range of issues including production of learning resources and student learning approaches. It concludes by highlighting the importance of innovation and variety in the learning blend with increased reliance on digital collections and for learning approaches student experiences were evaluated as positive when undergoing problem-based approaches and were seen as stimulated to engage with e-learning materials based on the structure and operation of action learning sets.

INTRODUCTION

This chapter is concerned with providing a research perspective on the introduction, use and effectiveness of Virtual Learning Environments (VLEs), learning resource supports and experiences of applying these as blended learning supports for modules, and programmes in universities. Some experiences of how student feedback can inform design of the learning blend and the effects on student learning experiences in business higher education are relayed, as they have developed in this millennium.

The objectives of the chapter are:

- To communicate case outlines of developments in digital information technologies for learning in Liverpool Business School, part of one of the UK's largest universities, Liverpool John Moores University, as a means of exemplifying issues within the general sector. The target audience is digital information technologies (DIT) researchers, academics, and practitioners (designers and architects of VLEs, resource material authors, and online tutors).
- To illustrate the evolution and advances in technology commensurate with student needs over a period that has seen the transition from file servers, to Web platforms for student learning designed by academic staffs evolve to commercially designed Web platforms
- To use clear and current examples, case applications and illustrations throughout the chapter in an effort to tie the material to real world practice and thus provide interest and better understanding for the researcher and practitioner
- To provide an outline of current research and thinking to enable holistic overviews of strategy, process and blend design for researchers and practitioners who work with digital information technologies

The chapter contributes to a foundation for developing resources and implementing digital supports as they contribute to blended learning environments. It will demonstrate how academics and students behave, relate and learn in digital media and how instructors can promote blended, problem-based, and action-oriented learning. The work will outline the development of ICT-related knowledge as we have entered this millennium, to demonstrate how 'digital' learning processes and supports can be used to help academics and students meet the challenges of post-modern society characterised by norms, multi-tasking, resource developments, use of e-books, and sustainability

of the learning resource. The chapter presents a researcher with a range of currently used approaches in design, learning resource issues, and learning approaches in the practice relating to Digital Information Technologies, which will be supported with theoretical underpinnings.

BACKGROUND

Problem-based approaches to learning (PBL) have a long history of advocating experience-based education. Psychological research and theory suggests that by having students learn through the experience of solving problems, they can learn both content and thinking strategies. The process requires that the teacher acts to facilitate the learning process rather than to provide knowledge. The goals of PBL include helping students develop flexible knowledge, effective problem-solving skills, self-directed learning skills, effective collaboration skills, and intrinsic motivation. There is considerable research on the first three goals of PBL but little on the last two (Hmelo-Silver, 2004, p. 235).

Action learning approaches were originally proposed by Revans. There are various useful books, Revans (1983), but, like all powerful methods, the principle and the process are very simple and serve to direct the energy and expertise of the participants. The action learning approach is a process of disciplined small group discussion. The groups typically are no smaller than four members and no larger than seven members. Group members share a context; typically:

- They may come from the same type of organisation
- The material is always live and highly relevant to all concerned
- Action learning is learning from experience
- The group agrees to meet over a period of time

- The length of a session depends on the group size (the ideal size denoted by the project sponsors was seven and that number was used in this study)

The key aspects of the process are that each group member gets a period of strictly bounded time to discuss and present their company issues. Also the focus is on action—what he or she has done and will do—together with reflection on the action. Finally, group members, when they are not presenters, act as consultants, using the options listed above —empathy, listening, challenging, and so forth.

An excellent theoretical framework for interpreting the problem of adaptation for a changing environment, when developing learning and teaching with information and communication technologies, is presented by Kirkwood and Price (2006). They initially discuss Schön (1983), who argues that part of the reason that 'reforms' rarely reform, derives from the notion that knowledge is molecular: it can be built up from units of information that can be assembled together to form more complicated and advanced knowledge. This leads to a view that it is the business of teachers to communicate this knowledge and the business of students to receive or absorb this knowledge. This is not an outdated view (Kirkwood and Price, 2006, p. 2); also the report of Prosser et al.(1994) found that university teachers hold a variety of conceptions of learning, and that some of the less sophisticated views encapsulate a transmissive conception of their teaching role. When ICT is adopted by teachers who hold such views of learning, their ICT practices are likely to reflect transmissive approaches that do little to reform or enhance students' experiences of learning, as noted by Sept (2004, p. 49). The architects of VLEs at the Liverpool JMU certainly followed the arguments of Schön, at the end of the 1990's, before the worldwide introduction of commercial VLEs such as Blackboard and Web Course Tools (WebCT).

LEARNING RESOURCE ISSUES

Learning and Teaching at Liverpool Business School incorporates blended learning resources. Singh (2003, p.3) outlines this approach to supporting students as follows. Blended learning programs may include several forms of learning tools such as real-time virtual/collaboration software, self-paced Web-based courses, electronic performance support systems (EPSS) embedded within the job-task environment, and knowledge management systems. Blended learning mixes various event-based activities, including face-to-face classrooms, live e-learning, and self-paced learning. This often is a mix of traditional instructor-led training, synchronous online conferencing or training, asynchronous self-paced study, and structured on-the-job training from an experienced worker or mentor.

At Liverpool John Moores University (LJMU) expertise has been developed by staffs in Liverpool Business School (LBS) in the production of open learning text materials since the early 1990s, e-learning materials (2002-2004), on a regional university consortium project, and in developing e-learning supports for courses and programmes in-house (2004). The resources have formed part of the blend offered by the school to student cohorts since the early 1990s. Towards the end of the 1990's many of the resources were made available through the commercial VLE Blackboard.

COMMERCIAL VLES AND DEVELOPING LEARNING RESOURCES

Liverpool Business School within Liverpool JMU had for many years, prior to the introduction of VLEs into universities, been involved in producing open learning materials for national projects, which they had retained in electronic form. The staffs had also been involved in the Higher Education Funding Council initiatives of the mid-1990s to produce electronic resources; these were the Teaching and Learning Technology Projects (TLTPs). Wise (2005, p. 113) has said that in universities there is often clear recognition for specialist research skills and outputs, but not necessarily so for equally specialized pedagogic skills and their many outputs. There appears to be little shared view about the range of expertise and costs in the current system for producing and disseminating printed learning materials. Funding for proper economic analysis, and also transition funding to help professionals innovate and transform their learning support practices, would be helpful. Funding to create forums where academics, librarians, publishers, and technologists can all come together to ensure that their objectives are aligned for the support of e-learning would also be extremely useful in breaking down traditional professional silos.

HYBRID MODEL DEVELOPED ACROSS UNIVERSITIES

The experience and research and developments at Liverpool JMU enabled staff participation on a UK northwest university e-learning project. This consisted of a consortium management group arranging authorship of modules for an e-learning Masters in Enterprise (M.Ent.) programme to be delivered through the medium of Blackboard. The consortium commissioned approximately 25 academic authors from five regional universities (LJMU; Manchester Metropolitan; Salford; Central Lancashire and Bolton) to write e-learning materials. The aim of the programme was to support and provide e-mediated postgraduate study through flexible action learning and knowledge transfer to specifically serve employees of small to medium enterprises (SMEs) in the northwest of England. The Northwest Development Agency (NWDA) funded the project. A total of 21 masters level modules were produced each of 20 masters-level credits in size (corresponding to 200 learning

hours). Issues surrounding this hybrid model are outlined as: (1) The budget for production of electronic materials was £350,000; (2) The platform for delivery within participant universities was to be Blackboard; (3) The Action Learning model of delivery was to be used to complement learning materials. A series of aspects of development were observed. The positive aspects were collaboration between universities, peer reviewed learning materials, learning materials complemented by Web-links guides, supporting documents, e-books, and learning and teaching supports underpinned by a cross-institutional body of research. The negative aspects were the constraints of cross-institutional project management, tutor arrangements, exclusivity and intellectual property issues, and the costs of production. The blend on the modules included problem-based and/or action learning and/or traditional teaching. The following was also facilitated through the Blackboard VLE at the university:

1. Electronic/paper based course outline and recommended texts
2. A comprehensive electronic assignment guide and copies of excellent assignments
3. Staff contact details and an e-mail link
4. Ten sets of electronic learning resources, additional electronic chapters from books
5. Targeted electronic written materials all with copyright clearance
6. A list of the ten topics covered in the module with hypertext links to: resource notes— PDF; lecture presentation—in PowerPoint, containing screen dumps from any commercial packages; workshop questions— Word/PDF; revision material—Word/PDF; individual learning resources—Word; and Web links to support Web sites, articles, e-books, and on-line journals.

At Liverpool JMU equivalent supports were also provided for undergraduate modules using resources accumulated from earlier projects.

General issues for the consortium centred around robustness of each university VLE, use of cross-institutional material, copyright, and ownership issues. There were further institutional issues of staff development for supporting students through use of VLEs

Up to the period 2002 there were rapid national developments in the use of Web-templates and VLEs became commercially available to the UK higher education sector. Publishers, notably Pearson, Financial Times Management, and McGraw-Hill, had exploited these developments and as part of a strategic move incorporated the production of Web-supported programmes for Blackboard and WebCT (then a complementary commercial VLE) in order to offer bespoke modules or programmes to universities at commercial rates. In addition many publishers initiated e-book developments that could be accessed electronically and explicitly linked to VLEs. A facility was also made available to academic staff in Liverpool that enabled e-books to be tailored and constructed online to serve as module supports for students. The university adopted the McGraw-Hill model, primus, amongst others.

IN-HOUSE MODEL DEVELOPED AT LIVERPOOL BUSINESS SCHOOL (LBS)

In 2004 the LBS, within the university, developed an electronic and text-based version of the Masters in Business Studies (MBS). The authoring process differed slightly from the Hybrid model, in that here modules were written with strong reference to a focused textbook (referred to as a wraparound approach). The programme was offered by the school as a distance programme and marketed to a wider UK and overseas client base using various blended media. Twelve school academics contributed as authors of the module content on the project. The delivery of this programme (UK and overseas) occurred with the collaboration of a

non-university intermediary agent that marketed and provided tutor-supports for the programme in several countries.

The production process for this project required budgetary controls, monitoring, and planning with time constraints and targets, resulting in a 12-month development period. The materials produced were also to be used in the school's MBA programme. Issues surrounding the in-house aspects are outlined as: (1) the budget for production of electronic materials was just over £30,000; (2) the platform for delivery within participant universities was to be Blackboard. Local country agents had the option of offering text-based versions of the learning materials; (3) a distance model combined with an essentially Problem-based Learning model of delivery was to be used to complement learning materials. A series of aspects were observed. The positive aspects were collaboration between faculty academics using: faculty resources; peer reviewed learning materials; learning materials developed for part-time, full-time, distance and overseas students; resources complemented by web-links guides; supporting documents; e-books, and learning and teaching supports underpinned by a cross-faculty body of research for business students. The negative aspects were: the fact that the project was financed by the faculty; remote tutor arrangements; problems associated with distance study/students and lack of teaching supports. The blend of the modules, facilitated through the Blackboard VLE was the same as that outlined for the Hybrid model, only here wraparound texts and e-books were used more so.

EVALUATION OF DEVELOPMENTS

The LBS at the university has undertaken several studies involving students that have used a VLE template (designed by academics) for a range of modules see (McClelland 2001a, pp107-115;

Table 1. Research findings and conclusions from a range of university surveys (©2007, Robert James McClelland. Used with permission)

Research Findings	Conclusions
Academic designed Web-site supports enabled flexibility for both students and tutors, avoiding restrictions such as time, place, and accessibility of knowledge supports. Students at lower levels of a programme used sites more frequently. Observed in time period 2001.	Restrictions such as time, place, and accessibility of knowledge supports supported a continuous change model. Usage patterns indicate increasing usage of web-sites for less experienced learners.
Introduction of a commercial VLE, Blackboard, showed no major differences in student perceptions of quality, content, administration, and learning experience than those experiences of academic designed Web-sites. No differences in mean importance of all Blackboard site supports were observed when factored by the variable Student Learning Styles. Previous research on none Blackboard Web-sites in time period 2001 had found one variance from this with External Links (exploring the Web).	The no differences observation inferred continuous change from a simple to a more complex form. The Learning Styles observation inferred that Blackboard did not discriminate preferred learning styles of students and supports. This was a step improvement from observations on Web-sites designed by academics. This was viewed as continuous change.
At LJMU the principles of clarity; attention; integrity and strategic use of informal information have been used in it's strategic transformational change processes due to a combination of consistent information flows; a series of targeted internal studies; a focus of all communications supporting organisational objectives and through the transparency of the transformation process, and wide involvement of staff, strategic use has been made of informal information. Time periods 2000 & 2001	Action and communication was developmental rather than seen as major changes. The communication within LJMU was to effect change and influence action in the direction of the university's overall interest.
Almost 1000 LJMU students responded to a survey of Blackboard use (n = 900), 50% stated that all or most of their module leaders employed use of Blackboard. 71% indicated that they would like it used for more of their modules. There is evidence that Blackboard had a role to play in widening participation. Majority of staff and students viewed Blackboard as having great potential in enhancing and supporting learning but acknowledged that it needed to be exploited much more. Time period 2002	Uptake was gradual in the transition from LJMU supported and academic designed Web-provision, but greater than that previously experienced. There was a wider acceptance and greater perceived benefits. Awareness was widened and initiatives developed. The changes were developmental and not fundamental complete changes. Time periods 2001 & 2002
In a case study on Edith Cowan University's introduction of Blackboard (Australia) the lessons that were taken on board were 'establishing a clear relationship between institutional strategy for online learning and the platform selection process; mapping the necessary links between the platform and existing in-house information technology and the value of active engagement and support for one learning platform, whilst other systems were allowed where local markets dictated.' (The Observatory On borderless Higher Education, 2002).	Research supported LJMU experience of internal monitoring, evaluation and consultation processes, but focusing and supporting one VLE platform whilst allowing flexibility. Research endorsed incremental changes.

2001b, pp 2595-2600; 2002, pp154-159), they are summarised in Table 1.

As part of the overall studies of Web-based learning in the faculty a standard questionnaire (used within the university) has been developed and adapted by staff and used consistently as a vehicle to gauge student perceptions (complemented by qualitative information), in order to refine the design and content of subsequent sites. Figures 1 and 2 show additional examples of course evaluation for undergraduate and postgraduates using multiple correspondence analysis (MCA). An interpretation for both MCA plots is provided in Table 2.

The goal of MCA is to describe the relationships between two or more nominal variables in

Figure 1. Multiple correspondence analysis plot for postgraduate course resources (©2007, Robert James McClelland. Used with permission)

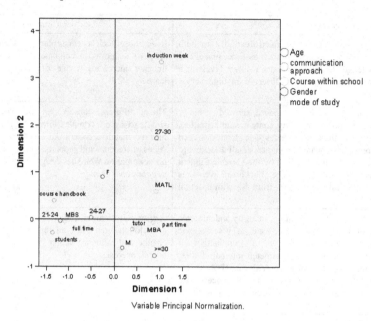

Figure 2. Multiple correspondence analysis plot for undergraduate course resources (©2007, Robert James McClelland. Used with permission)

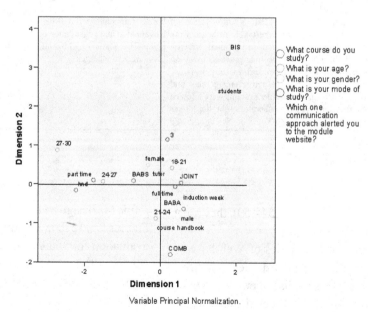

a low-dimensional space containing the variable categories as well as the objects in those categories. Objects within the same category are plotted close to each other, whereas objects in different categories are plotted far apart. Each object is as close as possible to the category points for categories that contain that object. MCA can also be viewed as a principal components analysis of nominal data. The nominal data characteristics such as age group, course, mode of study, gender, and communication approach concerning Web-sites for postgraduate and undergraduate modules examined can be presented on plots in four quadrants when analysed (see Table 2).

The course handbooks used in the MCA studies were both electronic as well as hardcopy, and it is interesting to note that male undergraduates initially rely on course handbooks as a communication approach whereas the trend is for females to have this approach on postgraduate courses (Figure 2). A contrasting trend is also observed for males and tutor communication on postgraduate courses, whereas the trend is for females and tutor communication on undergraduate courses. (Figure 1).

The positive and negative aspects of in-house production models and outsourced production models at University College London (UCL) have also been the subject of research by Secker & Plewes (2002). Generally, the costs attached to developments of resource-based learning materials vary from project to project and period to period, as do the technical specifications. The costs per credit for production for postgraduate and undergraduate resources in different time frames for developments in the LBS at Liverpool JMU have seen a reduction by almost fifty percent in eight years (Bachelors degrees costing on average £1,000 per credit to produce between 1992-96 and Masters Degrees costing on average £500 per credit to produce in 2004).

The term electronic study pack has been used in reference to a set of core readings in digital format that are specific to one particular course, however, in the examples discussed here, both models have built in flexibility, in that the electronic modules have been developed as units (in all cases each module consisted of ten units). This unit-based construction provides for flexibility as modules can be deconstructed into separate units and reconstructed to provide for different, or more tailored modules and subsequently variable business programmes. The number of units existing for modules developed in the school to

Table 2. Explanations of the four quadrants for multiple correspondence analysis (©2007, Robert James McClelland. Used with permission)

Type of Student	Top left quadrant	Bottom left quadrant	Top right quadrant	Bottom right quadrant
Postgraduate	Use of course handbook is closely related to females in the 24-27 age group	Full–time students on the Masters in Business Studies course and in the 21-24 age group are closely related	The induction week communication is closely related to the 27-30 age group and Masters in Leisure and Tourism course	Use of a tutor for communication on the Masters in Business Administration course is closely related to males in the above 30 age group
Undergraduate	The tutor ommunication approach was closely related to female students on the Business Studies course who are part-time and between the ages of 24-27 and 27-30.	The Business Diploma course (hnd) is closely related to the 21-24 age group	The student communication approach is closely related to students on the Business Information and Joint degree courses who are between the ages 18-21	Induction week and course handbook communication were closely related to male students who were full-time on the Business Administration Degree

date is 360 for Business Bachelor Degrees (36 modules) and 300 for Business Masters Degrees (30 modules).

The learning blend in both Hybrid and In-house models was innovative in the emphases placed on use of tailored media, e-learning materials as well as e-books, (McClelland & Hawkins, 2005, p. 156-157).

COMMERCIAL VLES AND STUDENT LEARNING APPROACHES

With the VLE Blackboard embedded as a university wide learning support at LJMU, and ongoing evaluations being undertaken that take on board architectural considerations, there existed opportunities to trial a range of learning approaches supported through e-learning. Since the early 1990's, the LBS had provided students with a range of blended learning approaches based on standard models, (Singh, 2003, p. 52; Osguthorpe & Graham, 2003, p. 228-229). This included adapted approaches to learning including problem-based learning and action learning.

PROBLEM-BASED LEARNING AND BLENDED SUPPORTS

Problem-based approaches have been used in LBS based on the premise of Boud (1985, p. 13) who has said: "The principal idea behind problem-based learning is that the starting point for learning should be a problem, a query or puzzle that the learner wishes to solve." The approach has found wide application in Engineering, Medicine, and Law undergraduate and graduate programmes, it has found growing application in Business and in LBS has leant itself to subjects such as Database Development, Marketing Research Methods, and Research Methods. In LBS two subject areas that

were consistently evaluated using this problem-based approach with e-learning supports in the blend were the undergraduate module Market Research Methods and the postgraduate module Research Methods. Evaluation outcomes of these modules, moving from supports in the blend, using academic designed e-learning templates, to supports using commercially designed e-learning templates, can be seen in Table 1.

ACTION LEARNING AND BLENDED SUPPORTS

The idea for evaluating action learning on a Masters in Enterprise at LBS came originally from the UK northwest university consortium e-learning project. Liverpool JMU was a member of this consortium. The aim of the Masters programme was to support and provide e-mediated postgraduate study through flexible action learning sets and delivery patterns, knowledge transfer supported by electronic module resources in order to specifically serve employees of Small to Medium Enterprises (SMEs) in the northwest of England. In 2004 the NWDA funded a further regional project group called NetworkingNorthwest to facilitate five action learning (AL) projects for delivery to Northwest enterprises. Five universities were successful in bidding for the project monies to deliver the action learning (Liverpool JMU was one of the successful bid teams) and an action learning research group from Leeds University was appointed to evaluate the resultant five pilot projects. Howell (1994, p. 20) had observed that "action learning and action research have become popular among managers and their sponsors from a variety of academic and business backgrounds because these programmes are work-related, results-based, group-focused, and appropriate to the preferred learning styles of these managers."

FRAMEWORK AND BACKGROUND TO AN ACTION LEARNING RESEARCH STUDY AT LIVERPOOL JMU

(McClelland, 2006, p. 58) reported that students on the pilot programme at Liverpool JMU studied three modules; they provided stage-one of a Masters programme. This is a free-standing qualification (postgraduate certificate in Enterprise).

The blend of the modules supported through a VLE was the same as that outlined for the Hybrid Model, only here action learning sets were used. The Masters in Enterprise Programme was launched in January 2004. This is the only Programme of its type in the UK, hailed as innovative by the UK government commissioned research (Lambert Review, 2003, p. 115). The programme was designed to offer an action learning approach in order to help small and medium sized businesses (SMEs) learn better for enterprise. A regional research award was received to study the action learning sets that supported modules of the programme for the first cohort of students enrolled. There was a prescribed framework suggested by the NetworkingNorthwest group who directed the generic approach to research projects. The projects constituted a one-year pilot study. The framework specified the following: (1) there must be one AL set per month for 12 months for each subject module studied; (2) each AL set must consist of seven members (and they must be managers or owners of their respective SMEs); (3) each set member must provide appropriate data concerning their organisations (in order to construct the measure Gross Value Added or GVA); (4) each set must have an academic facilitator and recorder for each session.

The pilot M.Ent cohort in Liverpool JMU consisted of 21 students studying three modules (stage one of the Masters), this was known as the group. The group was split into action learning sets that numbered seven in size. All 21 students in the group were female entrepreneurs that were nominated by a women's support agency Train 2000 based in Liverpool. Seventy-five percent of the group came from micro businesses (that is less than 10 employees). This was an important consideration for this first cohort as the funding streams for SME development in the region (especially for this pilot project) emphasised the need to engage micro businesses. The gender focus was also attractive to the funders. Notably Anderson (2004, p. 739) has reported: "some senior managers did not have a positive attitude to women managers and there was a sense that, being women only, the course did not have the kudos that a mixed course would have had." There are three subjects on the stage one of the Masters (postgraduate certificate stage), two of these are core and each being 20 M-Level credits in size (equivalent to 200 learning hours at Masters Level). The subject disciplines formed the focus for action learning sets and the three subjects studied were:

- Research for Enterprise, a core subject for the postgraduate certificate stage
- Creative Problem Solving, the second core module required
- Project Management, an option that was based on student selection

At the interview stage the Project Management module was elected most popular option to study by successful student candidates. Within the group of students (subsequently split to three AL sets of seven) the organisational profiles were as follows: two members from Social Enterprises (Health Area); a beautician/holistic therapist business; four members from HR consultancies; a management development consultancy; a Kennels/Stables business; a Photographic Agency; A Promotions and Marketing consulting agency; an acting agency; an Internet cafe, bistro, art business; a large city Chamber of Commerce (marketing); a training agency; a local building business; an interior design and furnishing manufacturer, two members of project groups (semi-charitable); a business and accounts advisory company and a Web-based restaurant/food consultancy.

All set members were senior managers that owned companies or were senior managers in the companies.

The three AL sets (A, B and C) were formed based upon company context in action, for example, set A consisted of a range of managers/owners that included: a training agency; promotions and marketing consulting agency; an Internet cafe, bistro, art business; the Liverpool Chamber of Commerce; a project group (semi-charitable); a management development consultancy and a HR consultancy.

Group members shared a context; typically:

- The set students came from similar types of organisation
- The material was always 'live' and highly relevant to all concerned
- There were excellent learning resources fully presented on Blackboard (an earlier £0.4million development of 21 subjects)
- Action learning was learning from experiences of set members
- The group agreed to meet over a period of time—on the framework this was once per month per subject
- Three group sessions occurred each month (one for each subject)
- The length of a session depended on the group size: on the M:Ent it is three hours
- Twelve sessions ran for each subject over a period of one year
- Assessments, if they were taken up, consisted of a 5000 word assignments (individual consultancy in the subject areas, for participants own organisations)
- Assessments were optional and each of the subject modules stood as a qualification in its own right (a Certificate in Professional Development or CPD).

The key aspects of the process model for modules on the M:Ent were that: each group member had a period of strictly bounded time to discuss and record their issues that they keep for reflection in their set (with six other students); the focus was on action—what she had done and intended to do—together with reflection on the action; the set members presented a set feedback for facilitators, when they were not completing their own and the group (consisting of the three sets) received a formal academic input based upon requests and feedback from previous sessions.

Each of the sets had a facilitator (subject specialist) whose role was to manage the time boundaries, negotiate and maintain the contract (timing, confidentiality, etc.). The role differed from that of a committee chair, seminar leader, supervisor, or mentor. Some groups (not this particular M:Ent. group) can be self-facilitating (members take turns at this role as they take turns to be presenter).

Each of the sets had an independent recorder (subject specific-developed and receiving training by the regional evaluators of the project) that recorded the set discussion and collected the set group feedback (there were three in total, one each for each of the sets A, B and C, that occurred once per month). The session activities were transcribed by recorders and formed the basis of qualitative data for evaluation, addressing action learning issues for each of the three subjects and feeding back into the delivery pattern. An inductive approach to key issue identification and collating quotes from voices was employed, facilitated by the use of NVivo (version 2) computer aided qualitative analysis software.

On the M.Ent project the team attempted to follow the model process of Revan's Classical Principles (RCP) (see Revans (1983)) whilst giving the model a new emphasis on management skills and inter-group relations the 'set,' whilst supporting the group and sets with e-learning materials, freeing up the sessions to allow members to focus on inquiry, reflection, review, and planning.

RESULTS OF THE ACTION LEARNING APPROACH AT LIVERPOOL JMU

What follows are accounts (triangulated) of the experience at points in and after 37 contact sessions and reflections on them (in true action learning style). The author hopes that the anonymous accounts will exemplify the approach and encourage others to attempt this action.

At induction students were asked what attracted to the programme, all voices from the cohort contributed to the list as follows: enterprise focused; women only (this cohort); supported on-line; flexible; new course; "bit of a buzz;" free of charge.

The cohort was also asked of their expectations of the university. The responses were what you would expect from most students with all voices concluding: "Support process, learning, access to resources, support for their businesses, better understanding of issues, motivation when feeling disheartened, to be kept informed." The drivers for taking up the subjects offered were not therefore to gain qualifications but its flexibility, use of technology, access to resources and a means by which they might obtain drive and improve their businesses.

A feedback session occurred at a point eight months into the one-year pilot programme with all students (excluding those who had withdrawn). The students (who were now experienced in action learning approaches) were asked to brainstorm what they felt about the programme. The presentation approach they took was to tell a story. The following is a recorded summary of a presentation from six voices in set A.

The story portrayed the group members as maidens, who were all working on their own, and were having problems. A fairy princess from Train 2000 (the agency originally forwarding students) pointed them in the direction of the M:Ent that could solve their problems, because it would allow them to share their worries with others who

were going through the same problems. The leader of the M.Ent project was portrayed in the tale as "Bob the Business Builder"—a wizard! The story describes the maiden's woes and how their interactions and shared views of problems, as well as the time taken out from their busy working lives, has helped them to see the light and to make a more informed judgement of their situation. The story ends with maidens not only living happily ever after, but being transformed into "professional business women who could now be confident. "

This story is self-interpreting and highlights how there had been growth and bonding into a cohesive group with common goals. At this stage there was a realisation of learning achieved and programme outcomes.

All students discussed some of the skills that they had acquired over the previous eight months, as a result of this project. Primarily the collective voices identified time management and information management skills.

Reflecting on their experiences over the previous eight months all voices reported: "we feel that the attendance at the M:Ent and interaction with other women in our positions has allowed us to take a different angle on our work, develop our own personal skills and highlight areas that need improvement."

The programme seemingly met a gap that the students' felt existed in their businesses. In addressing how the course had addressed changes to the individuals and their businesses the group analysed the three modules that had made up the M.Ent to the eight month point in the course, in order to reflect on the impact that individual aspects of each module had on their working lives. They plotted their analysis on a flip chart pad in order to map out the interaction of their learning from the three modules. Some observations on this and other general comments are identified in Table 4.

The recorder observation in Table 4 identified a rites of passage exercise that was timed to de-

Table 4. Some observations on the action learning process for different modules (©2007, Robert James McClelland. Used with permission)

Module	Collective Voices (Mapping)	Voices General
Creative Problem Solving	*"Targeted marketing; Intranet/internet Web design; Group problem solving; Stakeholder analysis; Rational decision making and Organisational learning"*	One voice (M) talked about trying to be *"all things to all people"* at the beginning of a company's life.
Project Management	*"Management of risk; Planning – realistic milestones; Microsoft Project; Critical path issues and Lifecycle issues."*	One voice (P) suggested: *"carrying out regular reviews, monitoring and evaluating projects effectively is an important lesson, although this is potentially difficult within small organisations."*
Research for Enterprise	*"Importance of research philosophy; Need for qualitative & quantitative data; Primary & secondary data needs; Online information resources; Data analysis using SPSS and Questionnaire design."*	Recorder observation (B) *"When faced with "real" problems the group approached them with confidence and professionalism. The M:Ent students surprised themselves as to how much they did know and how much useful advice they were able to give the undergraduates."*

velop consultancy skills within the group (many of whom practice as consultants in their own work environments). This enabled enhancement of that understanding, to become better able to act on the world.

RESULTS

Feedback from the students, recorders, facilitators, and evaluators attached to the LJMU pilot study students certainly endorsed the collaborative approach of action learning as well as the e-learning approach. Observations in McClelland (2006) from the facilitators and recorders on programme team include the following results concerning the framework used on the pilot programme:

• Feedback from students throughout the programme was positive. Eighteen students from the original cohort completed the programme (86%). As a cohort that attended in part-time study mode, attendance records were high at each session. It was interesting to note that all students applied the learning in their workplace environments and fed the

outcomes of the application into the action learning sets. The action, review, planning, action was therefore seen to be enhancing their understanding, to be better able to act on the world.

• Students gel in action learning sets—A series of post session meetings (formal and informal) were organised by the groups to extend networking and learning. Many collaborated and helped each other on real-life work projects (especially the consultants within sets).

• Networking occurs within and across sets—The structure of the programme was such that lunches were facilitated, buffets as well as a social event in a December review meeting. This created an excellent support for social networking across the sets. Formal sessions and electronic networking was also well developed within the sets.

• Students engage with the learning materials—Irrespective of the flexibility concerning their use the structure and operation of sets did stimulate students to engage with the learning materials provided (on a Blackboard Web site). This was evidenced in their continued questioning surrounding the content of the learning supports within sessions, (especially in Research for Enterprise and Project Management modules).

- Students own their own learning and its process—Although the framework of the modules dictated the academic disciplines to be followed and the learning supports provided, students did request specific inputs and emphases for the sets and workshops that supported skill development. In a true open learning approach students could also make decisions about whether or not to engage in an assessment process. This flexibility removed many barriers (such as meeting academic deadlines, academic writing and balancing workplace and academic pressures).

- Action learning components were manifested on this pilot programme, in that the problems/issue were identified; there was questioning and listening in every session; there was a focus throughout the programme on learning for business development; there was a series of commitments to take action for the range of businesses represented on the programme; there was action learning coaching presented throughout the programme by facilitators and there were established learning teams formed as part of the programme.

FUTURE TRENDS

Jennings (2005, p.166) has said something that is certainly the observation at Liverpool JMU "It is apparent that the majority of Blackboard users in University College Dublin (UCD) is only just beginning to tap into the potential on offer, and they are using the system as an effective means of delivering and managing an array of multimedia content. Our VLE has become a Course Management System (CMS). As time goes on users will become more familiar with the tools and attempt to blend them into the day-to-day process of teaching and learning. However, those that are already familiar have begun to look elsewhere to enhance the environment by including outside sources of interactivity in the guise of digital video or Flash files."

Roberts et al. (2005, p. 10) outline the challenges and opportunities for informal learning in ubiquitous computing environments can be thought of involving three interrelated aspects, namely: educational environment; personal environment; technical/computing environment

Formal to informal learning is a continuum: at the formal extreme all control over the learning process lies with the tutor and at the informal extreme the control over the learning process lies with learner.

Richardson and Watts (2005, p. 118) highlight that with widening internet access, life long learning and increasing numbers of mature, distance and disabled learners, electronic education has to grow. Use of Web-based learning and in particular the feedback obtainable from formative assessment, such as quizzes in WebCT, will help develop the confidence of the returning learner. WebCT is a good vehicle for the delivery of a course at a remote study centre, for example, to support a franchised network of colleges. With the increase of student numbers wishing to study at their local college, this provides better access to higher education.

Interestingly Huang and Luce (2004, pp. 533-534) showed that 50% of surveyed MBA students agreed they learned more from the MBA largely supported by a VLE than one only supported by a Traditional Learning Environment (TLE), whereas 12.5% disagreed 37.5% felt no difference between the two teaching modes. In summary they concluded that:

- Due to the key advantages of MBA program supported by VLE such as convenience and more interesting, there should be a good market potential for MBA program in VLE to grow in the future.

- Incorporating suitable teaching modes in VLE is the key for the success of online MBA programs. A combined teaching mode of VLE and TLE can be a good choice.

- Those online MBA programs or other programs that have had difficulties in keeping a high level of teaching quality and students' satisfaction may need to consider revising there teaching mode by combining both VLE and TLE teaching modes.

This blend, recommended through research at Ohio University, is mirrored in many of the postgraduate programmes at Liverpool JMU with similar student feedback. This can form the basis of a strong recommendation concerning a future trend for business postgraduate education supported by digital information technologies.

The development of quality resources is key to the future use of VLEs and Wise (2005, p. 113) outlines: "Academics are more likely to be recognized and rewarded for writing research articles and books than for creating imaginative e-learning materials. Many higher education institutions are, however, investing in authoring tools and so the university sector might be a net exporter of re-usable learning materials. There may be opportunities to change acquisition practices, and thus encourage more imaginative production of e-texts and other learning materials. This would also signal to university leaders that publishers are important partners in driving change and supporting the widening participation and other strategic agendas of importance to policy makers."

A proposed future look at VLE use was made by Totkov (2003, p.7) who outlined that: "The evolution in learning and training at distance can be characterised as a move from distance learning (d-learning) to e-learning to mobile learning (m-learning). These three stages correspond to the influence on society of the Industrial Revolu-

tion of the 18th to 19th centuries, the Electronics Revolution of the 1980s and the Wireless Revolution of the last years of the 20th century. The European project, from e-learning to m-learning, sets in place the first building block for the next generation of learning (the move from d-learning and e-learning to m-learning). The Leonardo da Vinci project sets out to design a Wireless VLE as harbinger of the future of learning."

This may be the immediate future direction for blend of e-learning to develop, however a more succinct future look may be found from the statement made by De Vries et al. (2006, p.10) who say: "The involvement of regular teachers and professional instructional designers is needed to further educational innovation through the development and sharing of Learning Designs. Ultimately, individual teachers are the carriers of educational innovation in their institutes. Opportunities for this are created by instructional designers who in explorative projects guide new directions of educational innovation."Conclusion

A comprehensive infrastructure, backed up by a robust Learning and Teaching Information strategy is essential for the support VLE mediated university courses. McDougall et al. (2003) endorses this by outlining that as institutions throughout the world clamber to offer courses via the Internet, many are blissfully ignorant of the support infrastructure that is required to deliver a high quality service to their new market. Within a globally competitive environment, the University of Southern Queensland's (USQs) strategically planned, systematically integrated, and institutionally comprehensive student support infrastructure provides a model for sustainable and quality distance education (p. 37-38). This is also the case for Liverpool JMU, for distance as well as on campus courses.

Blackboard is now embedded in the Learning and Teaching process of LJMU. From the period 2003 onwards feedback from students concerning Blackboard has diversified and been streamlined to address:

- Contributions to each of the university modules, as part of the student module feedback process students are asked to rate their satisfaction on the degree to which Blackboard supports their learning.
- Particular learning research questions concerning student approaches to various learning approaches or blended learning VLE resource supports. This has resulted in targeted research.
- The efficacy of communication or assessment tools supported by Blackboard.

In terms of the development of blended e-learning resources, costs of production, amongst others, have been a major barrier to resource developments in higher education. Generally the barriers fall into categories like: costs; project management (expertise); author expertise amongst academics; pedagogic issues related to the subject-matter; learning and teaching strategy emphases on resource provision for different HEI's; and the offer of complete programmes with full web-based supports from publishers (but at a cost).

More recently, in the complementary area of electronic book developments, there have been three evaluations of electronic textbooks on the Web through the Electronic Books ON-screen Interface (EBONI), which focused on assessing how appearance and design can affect users' sense of engagement and directness with the material (Wilson et al., 2003, p. 462) The EBONI Project's methodology for evaluating electronic textbooks is outlined and each experiment is described, together with an analysis of results. In recommending for future design, based on the main findings of the evaluations, users appear to want some features of paper books to be preserved in the electronic medium, while also preferring electronic text to be written in a scannable style.

Falk (2003, p. 258) has observed that university libraries are discovering that new digital resources are sometimes accompanied by new problems. For digital materials that originate on-campus, these libraries are able to retain primary responsibility, and to control content and access. But the bulk of electronic journals typically come to the libraries through licenses, and the ability to ensure long-term access to the journal files often remains in doubt. Observations have also been made that increased reliance on digital collections is leading to a decline in the importance of collections of printed materials (*ibid*, p. 261).

These observations are mirrored at Liverpool and the importance of the currency of the learning blend is paramount in the way students receive the VLE supports. There is an increased reliance on digital collections and linkages from VLEs are an essential component, as are the incorporation of e-books and structured, well-prepared e-learning resources.

To a large extent, on the VLE supported action learning programme at Liverpool JMU, the management of the learners and individuals was undertaken through adherence to the framework prescribed by funders, however the theory to overlay the concept of: action; review; planning; action was provided through comprehensive e-learning materials. It was not mandatory to follow these blended support materials, nor were they compulsory learning supports, students were studying three CPDs where assessment was optional.

It was proposed by the Liverpool action learning team that flexibility of delivery and assessment offered, was paramount in attracting busy SME manager/owners.

For this study it is also important that we should not lose sight of the single-gender nature of the cohort. This facilitated a whole range of benefits in terms of learning and discussions, not for reporting here. The programme team made strides towards a claim made by Anderson (2004) who stated: "Positive action training can help raise women's awareness and understanding of organizational attitudes but strongly implies that this initiative will have limited impact unless it is part of a wider portfolio of measures designed to induce change at organizational level."

The programme did not really suffer unmet expectations or needs from students. Corley and Thorne (2006, p. 43) have reported unmet needs with a postgraduate County Council development programme on management and change, where action learning is used. Their particular unmet needs centred on disillusionment with managers as a problem with implementing change. Students on this pilot programme did not mirror that feedback, this was probably due to the students being predominantly owner/managers they were in fact the drivers of change in their own companies.

Feedback received for this pilot praised the e-learning supports approach, and many voices felt that "it provided an excellent resource for students." The supports existed outside of the sessions (hosted on a Blackboard web site) and provided for self-paced learning, guidance and theory. Cox (2003, p. 354) has stated: "E-Learning represents a process to align people, knowledge and strategy to build agile organizations that adapt to create value for internal and external stakeholders in a global industry." This may be viewed as a panacea as Graham (2004, p.314) argues: "Now what this suggests is that they (the students) do not simply require useful information, but a composite educational experience, and it may be that this is not something that digital technology can supply because it crucially involves learning with others."

Learning with others (group work) is critical to the action learning process, however the team and philosophy of the M.Ent. Programme offers the blended approach to learning whereby provision of e-learning supports does not exclude group work, rather, it complements the group work and because use of the supports is not compulsory it allows for the sets to be used according to Revan's Classical Principles of action learning.

Many of these observations have been mirrored in action learning studies supported by VLE's. Orsini-Jones (2004, p. 207) has reported that their action-research cycle was directly informed by students' feedback. It was refreshing to have the students' direct input into the shaping of a new module and the analysis of the research data relating to it. It was also possible to act on some of the student feedback during the time-span of the academic year. The thrust of developments at Liverpool JMU has been to include academic staff and students at the heart of all developments concerning the learning blend. In turn a committed group of academic staffs and Learning and Teaching development practitioners have developed the VLE support infrastructure and resources over a number of years, cognisant of the needs of students, their learning styles and needs, in order to maximise effective learning in the digital age.

REFERENCES

Anderson, V. (2004). Women managers—does positive action training make a difference? A case study. *Journal of Management Development*, Vol. 23 No. 8, pp. 729-40.

Boud, D. (1985). Problem-based learning in perspective. In D. Bond (Ed.) *Problem–based learning in Education for the Professions*. Sydney: Higher Education and Development Society of Australia.

Corley, A., & Thorne, A., (2006). Action learning: avoiding conflict or enabling action. *Action Learning: Research and Practice*, Volume 3, No. 1 pp. 31-44.

Cox, M., (2003). The E-MBA action learning: lessons for hospitality leaders. *International Journal of Contemporary Hospitality Management*, Volume 15 Number 6 pp. 352-354.

De Vries, F., Tattersall, C. & Koper, R. (2006). Future developments of IMS Learning Design tooling. *Educational Technology & Society*, 9 (1), pp. 9-12.

Falk, H. (2003). Developing digital libraries. *The Electronic Library*, Vol. 21 No. 3, pp. 258-61.

Graham, G., (2004). E-Learning: A philosophical enquiry. *Education and Training* Volume 46 Number 6/7 pp. 308–314 Emerald Group Publishing Limited.

Hmelo-Silver, C. E., (2004). Problem-Based Learning: What and How do Students Learn? *Educational Psychology Review* vol. 16 No. 3 pp. 235-266.

Howell, F (1994). Action Learning and Action Research in Management Education and Development: A Case Study. *The Learning Organization*, Volume 1 No. 2, pp. 15-22 © MCB University Press.

Huang, W., & Luce, T., (2004). Proposing an effective teaching pedagogical mode for online MBA Education: An exploratory empirical investigation Iissues in information systems. Volume 5 No. 2 pp. 530-536.

Jennings, D. (2005). Virtually effective: the measure of a learning environment. *Emerging Issues in the Practice of University Learning and Teaching*, available at: (Retrieved on March 27, 2007 from http://www.aishe.org/readings/2005-1/jennings- Virtually_Effective.html

Kirkwood, A., & Price, L. (2006). Adaptation for a changing environment: developing learning and teaching with information and communication technologies. *The International Review of Research in Open and Distance Learning*, Vol. 7, No. 2, pp 1-14.

Koper, E.J.R. (2004). Learning technologies in e-learning: an integrated domain model. In W. Jochems, J. van Merriënboer, & E.J.R. Koper (Eds.) (2003). Integrated eLearning (London: Kogan Page), pp. 64-79.

Lambert Review of Business-University Collaboration, December 2003 HMSO pp 115.

McClelland, R.J., (2001a). Digital learning and teaching: evaluation of developments for students in higher education. *European Journal of Engineering Education* vol. 26 No. 2 pp 107-115.

McClelland, R.J., (2001b). Web-based delivery of a generic research methods module (for Social Sciences): The graduate and post-graduate experience, *Conference: Society for Information Technology and Teacher Education, Orlando, USA 5-10 March*, pp. 2595 – 2600. Association for the Advancement of Computing Education (AACE).

McClelland, R.J. (2002). Evolving web-based delivery: managing the transition from VLEs designed by academics to commercial VLEs, the postgraduate experience. In *Proceedings of the 28h EUROMICRO Conference (EUROMICRO 2002) on Multimedia and Telecommunications* (pp. 154-159). Dortmund, Germany.

McClelland, R.J., & Hawkins, N., (2005). Perspectives on the use of e-books in higher education when considering the emphases on development of e-learning materials by academics and the increased use of virtual learning environments. *International Journal of the Book*. Volume 2 pp. 153-162.

McClelland, R.J. (2006). Action-learning for postgraduate business enterprise education: A flexible e-learning approach, *The International Journal Of Learning*. Vol 13 No. 4 pp. 55-64.

McDougall, K., Young, F.R., Apan, A., (2003). Operational infrastructure for quality distance and online geospatial programs. *Cartography* 32 (1) pp. 25-38.

Mumford, A., (1995). Managers developing others through action learning. *ndustrial and Commercial Training.* Volume 27 Number 2 pp.19–27.

Norton, L., Richardson, J. T. E., Hartley, J., Newstead, S., & Mayes, J. (2005). Teachers' Beliefs and Practices Concerning Teaching in Higher Education. *Higher Education 50* (4), pp. 537-571.

Observatory On borderless Higher Education (2002). *Leading Learning Platforms: International Market presence* 2 March, International Strategic information Service.

Orsini-Jones, M., (2004). Supporting a course in new literacies and skills for linguists with a virtual learning environment. *ReCALL*. Volume 16 (1) pp.189–209.

Osguthorpe, R., & T. Graham, C., R. (2003). Blended learning environments: Definitions and directions. *Quarterly Review of Distance Education*, vol. 4 no. 3 pp. 227-33.

Prosser, M., Trigwell, K., and Taylor, P. (1994). A phenomenographic study of academics' conceptions of science learning and teaching. *Learning and Instruction. 4* (3), 217-232.

Revans, R. W., (1983). *The ABC of Action learning.* ,Chartwell-Bratt, Bromley, UK.

Richardson, D., & Watts, B. (2005). Re experiences of using a VLE with a concentrated class *Int. J. Cont. Engineering Education and Lifelong Learning,* Vol. 15, Nos. 1/2, pp. 108-120.

Roberts, G., Aalderink, W., Windesheim, W.H., Cook, J., Feijen, M., Harvey, J., Lee, S., Wade, P.V., (2005). Reflective learning, future thinking: digital repositories, e-portfolios, informal learning and ubiquitous computing *ALT/SURF/ILTA1 Spring Conference Research Seminar* Trinity College, Dublin 1 April pp. 1-13.

Schön, D. A. (1983). *The Reflective Practitioner: How professionals think in action.* New York: Basic Books.

Secker, J., & Plewes, L. (2002), Traditional and electronic study packs: a case study of the production process. *Program*, Vol. 36 No. 2, pp. 99-108.

Sept, J. (2004). The stone age in the information age. In W. E. Becker and M. L. Andrews (Eds.) *The scholarship of teaching and learning in higher education* (pp. 47-80). Bloomington, IN.: Indiana University Press.

Singh H (2003). Building effective blended learning programs. *Educational Technology*, Volume 43, Number 6, pp.51-54.

Totkov, G., (2003). Virtual learning environments: Towards new generation International Conference on Computer Systems and Technologies (pp. 1-9) *CompSysTech'2003.*

Wilson, R., Landoni, M., & Gibb, F. (2003). The WEB book experiments in electronic textbook design. *Journal of Documentation*, Vol. 59 No. 4, pp. 454-77. Retrieved on March 27, 2007 from

http://www.ebooks.strath.ac.uk/eboni

Wise, A., (2005). Virtual learning environments: setting the scene. *Serials* 18 (2) pp. 107-115.

KEY TERMS

Action Learning: A process of disciplined small group discussion where each group member gets a period of strictly bounded time to discuss and present their company issues; the focus is on action and group members act as consultants. Action learning is learning from experience. The subject material is preferably always live and highly relevant to all concerned. A group agrees to meet over a period of time; they may come from the same type of organisation. The length of a session depends on the group size (the ideal size denoted by researchers is seven).

Blackboard: A virtual learning environment that you can access on and off a campus.

Blended Learning: A set of learning supports provided by academics and their universities that provide for a strategic mix tailored to the subject of study. This mix may include core learning materials; software; event-based activities; tailored learning approaches (problem-based, action learning, distance learning, activity-based learning), on-line conferencing; classroom teaching; workplace learning.

Commercial VLE: A commercially produced Virtual Learning Environment that is sold to universities or organisations under license, to host Web-based learning materials. Access to the VLE materials is usually via passwords held by university employees/students or organizational employees.

Hybrid Model of Resource Provision: One based on traditional Web-based supports but where the core subject specific learning materials and blend is developed by a range of institutions, widely accepted (across institutions) and designed, written or reviewed with cross institutional peer reviewing.

In-House Model of Resource Provision: One based on traditional Web-based supports where the core subject specific learning materials and blend is accepted (within institutions) and designed, written or reviewed with peers inside the same institution or possibly external reviewers.

Problem-Based Learning: Centred around a problem, a query or puzzle that the learner wishes to solve. The approach uses stimulus material to prompt student discussion and problem solving. That is usually reflective of professional practice. Critical thinking is encouraged by providing students only limited resources to help them develop resolutions to the problem in question, having students work cooperatively in small groups, in and out of class. The approach enables students to identify their learning needs and the appropriate set of solution resources. The approach also encourages students to self-evaluate and self-validate their learning processes by reapplying the new technical knowledge and problem solving approaches to other problems in the field.

Virtual Learning Environment: A system that supports a range of learning contexts, ranging from conventional, classroom implementation to off-line, distance learning and online learning.

Chapter XXII
Education Research with Electronic Focus Groups

Kathryn Moyle
University of Canberra, Australia

Robert Fitzgerald
University of Canberra, Australia

ABSTRACT

An emerging trend in education research methods is to integrate digital technologies into the research process. Electronic focus groups represent one such innovation. Drawing on four examples of research and practice undertaken using a synchronous, digital system, this chapter reflects on how an innovative tool can assist in focus group research in the fields of school and higher education. The examples presented illustrate how some of the theoretical, practical, and ethical problems that have arisen with traditional approaches to focus groups research can be overcome. It is anticipated that reflecting on such experiences and building upon the findings of these research projects will enable an understandings about the potential for innovative practices in education research that are possible with digital technologies.

INTRODUCTION

The use of technologies to assist in undertaking research is not a new phenomenon. Technologies such as notepads and pencils, cameras and tape recorders have assisted qualitative researchers' recording of data for some time. Since the turn of the 21st century however, there has been an emerging interest in the incorporation of digital technologies into research methods including in focus group techniques. Electronic, synchronous focus groups and online, asynchronous focus groups have both emerged as research strategies. Choices about what digital technologies are used in research and how they are utilised through the syncronous digital system depend on the nature of the research to be undertaken, and have consequences for the nature and quality of the data collected. While early work (Fitzgerald & Findlay, 2004) with *Zing* has shown it has the capacity to scaffold complex thinking while fostering collective sense making, it is argued here that when brought together with focus group techniques, the *Zing* system enables the incorporation of group interview strategies and generative social processes that are highly suitable for robust qualitative research data collection.

This chapter examines innovative examples of how the *Zing* digital system has assisted in the generation of qualitative research data. But before investigating these examples of research, it is useful to contextualise the discussion. We do so by firstly providing an overview of what is *Zing* and secondly by conceptualising digital technologies in relation to research, and in particular focus group research methods. Clarifying what is understood by these products and concepts is important because it is at the intersections of these that the arguments in this chapter are positioned.

BACKGROUND

This chapter starts from the premise that the use of digital technologies in research requires a level of technical knowledge, socially and theoretically applied in order for the technologies to meet their purposes. Different people require different levels of technical knowledge depending upon what sorts of technology they are using and for what purposes they are being used. Technologies are social and cultural constructs. They are created by people to apply to or to solve particular problems; they do not miraculously appear from thin air for no purpose. In order to consider the role of *Zing* in education research a brief description of what is the *Zing* system is provided here and shortly an explanation of how it is used in qualitative research methods is outlined.

The *Zing* system is a tool that combines hardware with a software application to enable the connection of multiple keyboards to a single computer to create a shared working space. It therefore allows individuals and groups to work together in the same space and time. *Zing* can be used in face-to-face or online settings, with both versions enabling several cursors to work on the same screen at once. Each cursor is allocated its own self-contained space on the screen. The face-to-face version of the tool comprises a computer with up to 12 keyboards attached via a multiplexer to display the multiple monitors as a common image to all participants. As such *Zing* can be arranged with the 12 keyboards linked to a portable computer thereby allowing a total of 13 cursors (i.e., the 12 keyboards and the portable computer's cursor) to operate at once on the same screen. With the use of a datashow and large screen, research questions can be shown visually to all the participants simultaneously. The online version of *Zing* employs a similar interface to the face-to-face version, and enables a network of computers to be connected via a server over the Web for real-time online sessions.

Zing has its origins in Group Decision Support Systems (GDSS) as an electronic meeting system for business purposes. It was originally developed as a tool to help organizations work more effectively in teams. Over the past 10 years it has become widely used in Australia and the United Kingdom as a tool for team building, strategic planning, business process re-engineering and stakeholder facilitation (Fitzgerald & Findlay, 2008). More recently, the software has been used for data collection in education research projects. In order to demonstrate how the system can contribute to data collection in qualitative research, it is necessary to reflect on what we understand by research, digital technologies, and the emergent notion of electronic focus groups as "e-research."

RESEARCH, DIGITAL TECHNOLOGIES AND THE "E" IN RESEARCH METHODS

Research is a process of exploring and learning about phenomena in systematic and rigorous ways. Regardless of whether it is more scholarly academic research or less formal everyday investigations, creativity, curiosity, and uncertainty are core elements of the research process. As Albert Einstein is purported to have said: "if we knew what it was we were doing, it would not be called research, would it?"

In the academic setting definitions of research necessarily become more formalised but still acknowledge the role of creativity and the importance of broader views. As an example, Australian universities draw frequently on a definition of research promulgated by the Australian Government's, Department of Education, Science and Training (DEST, 2004, p. 2) as: "creative work undertaken on a systematic basis in order to increase the stock of knowledge, including knowledge of humanity, culture and society, and the use of this stock of knowledge to devise new applications." Applying this definition to the field of education, education research here is considered to be the conduct of planned, systematic, creative, and communal acts to investigate and understand questions and problems concerning the education of individuals, communities, and societies.

Research in the field of education has attributes that make it distinctive from other disciplines. Education research has consistently been characterised by its diversity, complexity, and multidisciplinary character (Johnson & Christensen, 2004; Keeves, 1987; Lingard & Blackmore, 1997). Education research is often complex, in part because of the dynamic and inherently social, political, and cultural nature of education.

Both quantitative and qualitative approaches to education research have their place and indeed the application of technology to data analysis; particularly, quantitative techniques like regression analysis have occurred since the early 1960's. Like most research areas however, in education research the choice of method is heavily dependent upon the problem or issue to be investigated. The complexity, diversity, and multidisciplinary nature of many education research problems often justifies qualitative approaches to the research, and it is indeed the complexity of education research that sees a place for the assistance of digital technologies to such enterprises. Furthermore, advances in software and hardware developments including the moves towards more networked systems, and developments in Internet communication technologies such as using electronic mail and the World Wide Web have opened up new possibilities for how researchers can work together and conceptualise their work. Indeed recent Internet developments, particularly the so-called Web 2.0 technologies are beginning to focus attention on the potential of the Internet as an interactive and generative research environment that may be able to engage participants in new and different ways.

As a result of these digital developments a recent linguistic phenomenon has been to add the letter 'e' representing electronic to a range of fields of human endeavour that previously have not been considered part of the digital world. The term *e-research* for example, is emerging to encompass the use of digital tools, technologies, and processes being applied to the research activities. While the notion of e-research is opening up new spaces for conceptualising research, we must be cognisant however, of Heidegger's (1977) warning that instrumental approaches to conceptualising technology and thereby instrumental definitions in themselves can hide the overall relationships that exist and are embodied in technologies. To this end the social constructivist definition of technologies proposed by Hakken (1999, p. 23) is adopted here and problematised. He argues that technologies are: "networks of interacting human, organizational, and artifactual entities and practices. Particular elements both constitute and are constituted by the networks in which they participate."

Developing an understanding of the potential ways in which different technologies can have structuring influences on the activities undertaken in research then is an important part of understanding the ethical and theoretical issues digital approaches in research can bring. It is the relationships between digital technologies, research, and people participating in the research that are presented here to highlight how research can hinge upon how humans exercise their power and control with technologies and how emancipatory approaches to research can be undertaken by incorporating technologies into the research processes. These approaches however, are not without theoretical and ethical issues.

FROM TRADITIONAL TO ELECTRONIC FOCUS GROUPS

To highlight some of the issues concerning the inclusion of digital technologies in the field of education research, and how technologies can contribute to addressing some of these methodological issues, an overview of the nature of traditional focus groups methods is provided. It is followed with some discussion about how electronic focus groups can address some methodological issues.

Traditional Focus Groups

One data collection method that can be used for qualitative education research is focus groups. Focus groups are traditionally conducted with a small number of participants working as a group, who volunteer their time and expertise to contribute to data production processes about a particular topic.

Focus groups can be characterised as either a group interview or a more generative activity like brainstorming. The traditional focus group interview approach involves a moderator taking participants though a set of semi-structured questions. Another variation of the focus group approach involves a facilitator employing open-ended questions and/or provocations to generate, test, and synthesise ideas. In practice the 'interview approach' tends to be found in academic research while the 'facilitation model' is most often used in market research. Neither approach however is mutually exclusive because both of them have strengths and weaknesses. The practicalities of conducting focus groups though, means that one approach often assumes greater significance, depending on the context.

The purpose of focus groups is to elicit participants' feelings, attitudes and perceptions about a particular topic through group conversations (Puchta & Potter, 2004). The facilitator or moderator of a focus group uses carefully constructed questions to encourage dialogue for the specific purpose of obtaining data about the research questions. The collection of the data usually occurs by one or more observers taking notes along with the use of audio or video recorders. The recorded dialogue is then transcribed and coded, and turned into texts. The written notes taken together with the transcripts of the focus group conversations become the data ready for analysis.

Traditionally, focus groups use people's voices as part of a research methodology. Such an approach affects the power relationships between the researcher and the participant; to listen to people is to empower them (Casey, 1995). Listening requires the researcher not to dominate and control the airspace but to share it, and to attend to the messages being told. This approach requires constructing the relationships between the researcher and the participants in the research so that the researcher moves away from a position of a neutral observer to that of being engaged in a relationship (albeit temporarily), with the people with whom the questions forming the research are being discussed (Casey, 1995; Herda, 1999).

To achieve this sort of relationship between the researcher and the participants however, requires consideration of where the power lies within the research method and how that is reflected in the structure of the group conversations (Casey, 1995). It requires the researcher to recognise that he or she is not accorded an elite or privileged external position from which to conduct the discussions, but requires the researcher to be conversant with the issues in order to hold meaningful and meaning making conversations with the participants in the research.

Focus groups then can be emancipatory in their approach. They can be seen as one way to change the social dynamics in qualitative data production. That is, the researcher can specifically empower the participants through the chosen research techniques. Theoretical issues concerning the use of focus groups for qualitative research arise however, where the approach is premised on the notion that by fostering conversations in groups means *ipso facto* the research is emancipatory.

Sometimes claims are made that focus groups can alleviate the emergence of the power relationships that arise in one-to-one interviews; or that focus groups can empower participants by encouraging them to collectively address problems and make these explicit in their collective consciousness of the group. To achieve such outcomes however, assumes that the facilitators of focus groups are aware of some of the practical and ethical problems that can arise with this approach to data collection. These problems can include that:

- Discussions can be dominated by a few vocal individuals and can thereby distort the data collected
- The recording of data through tape recorders and note takers can inhibit some participants' conversations
- Separating individual viewpoints from the collective views can be difficult

- Individuals may be unwilling to reveal sensitive information, thereby creating the potential for the data to lack depth
- Sometimes too few participants attend the focus groups sessions to make the discussions meaningful
- Maintaining participants' anonymity in traditional focus groups is hard and can be an impediment to attracting volunteers as participants and an impediment to attracting multiple points of view about the subject under question

E-Focus Groups

In comparison, electronic focus groups or e-focus groups can overcome some of the aforementioned theoretical, practical, and ethical issues that can arise when conducting traditional focus group research. The working definition here for electronic focus groups is the ability of group participants to communicate electronically with digital technologies while also contributing to focus groups in traditional face-to-face settings. Electronic focus groups can also refer to asynchronous, online focus groups; these are not discussed here. E-focus groups in this chapter refer to the face-to-face synchronous focus group settings that are conducted with the assistance of the digital systems. These e-focus groups leverage the quality of the interactions of face-to-face focus group research with electronic data collection mechanisms suitable for qualitative research.

The *Zing* system is based upon the facilitation of group processes to gain input information from the participants. The role of the facilitator is to foster how the groups' discussions are conducted in order that the best possible data can be collected. The role of the facilitator is according to Bacal (2003) to foster processes to generate content, manage the time and space available in a purposeful manner, provoke participation and creativity, honour and affirm the group's wisdom; remain outside of the group processes while at the same time be skilled in reading the dynamics of the group, demonstrate professionalism, self-confidence, and authenticity, and maintain personal integrity.

The *Zing* system incorporates tools and scaffolds that embed some of these key attributes of an experienced facilitator in the system allowing even a relatively inexperienced person to facilitate group conversations. The system is handled by one person who is designated as the facilitator, and his or her job is to use the software and hardware to guide the group processes by selecting research items and to facilitate the conversations around those items in order to collect the main ideas raised during a session.

Participants are encouraged to contribute and view their ideas simultaneously. The participants respond synchronously to a sequence of research questions that act as a guide for a thinking journey consisting of generally three to seven items in length. Since each participant has an allocated space on the display, everyone can see all the ideas as they are generated. The focus group sessions follow a format or etiquette so that when each question is presented, participants are encouraged to talk in small focus groups for a few minutes, then they are asked to type their ideas using the keyboards. The records of ideas are available for all to see and may be read aloud, in order for common themes or disparate ideas to be recorded by the facilitator within the system.

It is the unique combination of a graphical user interface that enables the shared visual space, combined with these group processes designed to facilitate discussion that allows participants to take part in focused activities. As such, using focus group data collection methods melded with the *Zing* technologies, data can be collected directly from participants in a digital format. These electronic approaches combined with focus group research methods then represent an innovation in qualitative research methods and data collection techniques. There are nonetheless some hazards about which researchers ought to be

aware when facilitating electronic focus groups. Some of these potential hazards include: the risk that the technologies have an alienating affect on the participants; the participants may feel they cannot type fast enough to record their thoughts and the necessity to incorporate techniques that extend member-checking processes beyond basic transcript verification stage.

In order to illustrate how electronic focus groups can assist in the data collection for education research, it is worthwhile outlining some examples of how *Zing* has been applied in research practices. The examples illustrate how some of the theoretical, practical, and ethical problems that have arisen with traditional approaches to focus groups have been overcome, and how some remain.

Examples of Conducting Electronic Focus Groups for Research

We have argued that digital technologies, in particular a system called *Zing*, enable a reflexive approach to data collection that builds on the notion that research is a specialised form of learning involving the creation of new knowledge (Fitzgerald & Findlay, 2004). It has also been argued here that the deployed system is effective in supporting various qualitative process management techniques such as those found in qualitative research and action research (Newman & Pollnitz, 2002; Whymark, Callan & Purnell, 2004; Willcox & Zuber-Skerritt, 2003). In light of these claims, the following examples of using the software for qualitative data collection are presented and examined. The following research projects undertaken by the authors employed electronic focus groups using the system to collect data:

- Leadership and Learning with information and communication technologies (ICT)
- Partnerships in ICT Learning (PICTL)
- Re-imagining and re-visioning Australian educational leadership

- Leadership performance review at Sekolah Global Jaya in Jakarta, Indonesia

The first three of these projects were Australian national research initiatives. The final project is an example of research and development undertaken as part of a performance review and planning activity within an Indonesian school.

LEADERSHIP AND LEARNING RESEARCH PROJECT

Zing was used to collect data through focus groups for the *Leadership and Learning with ICT* research project. This project was conducted in 2005 to investigate the question of how educational leadership supports learning with ICT in Australian schools. Through this project 40 electronic focus groups were conducted across Australia and involved over 400 educational leaders. The research was sponsored by the Australian Government-funded agency *Teaching Australia: the Australian Institute for Teaching and School Leadership*. The aim of the research was to develop deeper, more specific knowledge about the nature of educational leadership required in Australian schools to assist in the integration of ICT into teaching and learning (Moyle, 2006). The research was grounded in the world of lived experiences of school leaders (Denzin & Lincoln, 2000).

The inclusion of *Zing* was constructed as an integral part of the focus group processes for this research project. As the nature and content of the research was to study the relationships between school leadership and learning with ICT, the researcher wanted to model the integration of ICT into the research method. The *Zing* system provided the vehicle to achieve this goal.

Incorporating the *Zing* system as a seamless component of a research method for data collection however, required that the planning was both robust and detailed. Issues actively considered

in the planning processes included the time and place to conduct the conversations and the potential for unequal power relationships between the researcher and those participating in the focus group research conversations. Detailed planning of the questions, the processes to be used with the groups, the balances to be struck between talking and using technologies, and the roles the respective participants were to play in the research, were all requirements that were considered in the planning stages of the research. The questions and the research approach were trialled with critical friends before embarking on the national data collection processes.

In the focus groups themselves, each participant logged onto the system using a number to identify him or herself rather than using his or her real name. This number was cross-referenced back to the informed consent forms collected from the participants. During the focus groups, the participants were encouraged to discuss the research questions with each other to clarify their ideas, and then the participants were encouraged to record their views by directly entering them into the computer with the use of one of the keyboards, and without mediation from a third party. All the responses were anonymously presented.

A data projector was used to project onto a large screen the responses of the participants in each focus group. This projection enabled a sharing of responses across the group, while at the same time participants experienced a sense of distance from the responses. Once the participants had completed their responses to the focus group question, with the aid of the software, the responses were read through with the whole group, and participants were invited to make observations, identify themes, and add further comments. For example, several participants' comments at the end of the sessions indicated that they felt that the system had afforded them the opportunity to offer their thoughts anonymously and unencumbered by the social relations around them.

With a few key strokes the transcripts from each session can be seamlessly converted into a Microsoft Word document. At the conclusion of each electronic focus group session, the transcripts from the session were converted and emailed out to all the participants who indicated that they would like a copy of the transcript. As the transcript was a direct electronic translation of the session into a Word document, the necessity for member checking of the transcript was considerably reduced.

PARTNERSHIPS IN ICT LEARNING PROJECT

The *Partnerships in ICT Learning* project was an Australian national research project conducted in 2005-06 which aimed to generate and document examples of good-practice approaches to embedding ICTs throughout the educational experience of pre-service teachers, practising teachers, and teacher educators. It was funded by the Australian Government and comprised eight small-scale professional development projects with one project conducted in each state and territory across Australia. One of those small-scale projects, undertaken in the Australian Capital Territory (ACT) is used here to highlight innovative approaches and strategies to data collection and analysis.

The ACT PICTL project focussed on the use of blogs, wikis, and *Zing* with a small group of pre-service teachers and academics. The research addressed the question 'what are the pedagogical benefits, barriers and challenges to implementing collaborative ICT-based knowledge creation pedagogies in selected ACT secondary classrooms?' *Zing* was used with groups of university students (i.e., pre-service teachers) and practising teachers to encourage discussion about the possible applications of collaborative technologies to the classroom and about the role of ICT in education. The pre-service teachers were asked what skills,

capabilities and knowledge did they think current school students required to be successful in the future? In their focus group discussions they were encouraged to synthesise the group's responses and identify what they regarded as the key themes. Some of these themes included: competence with ICT; life long learning skills; ethical issues such as values, morals, confidence and self-belief.

As a way of triangulating these data the research took all the text generated by the participants and produced a weighted-frequency list or cloud tag of key words. Towards the end of the project the pre-service teachers were asked to reflect on their use of the *Zing* system using a Plus-Minus-Interesting (PMI) process. It was clear that they were very positive about the use of the system and saw its potential for supporting knowledge creation. Their comments about the use of *Zing* in electronic focus groups included the following participant comments from PICTL project collected in 2005:

Plus: "Fun, collaborative, fast and productive processes; Gets people to voice without verbal communication; Great for written collaboration and brainstorming; It changed to whole group dynamics for the better; Everyone seemed a lot more relaxed"

Minus: "Seems to be a lot of technology required; Can get out of hand without close monitoring; No graphic capability"

Interesting: "Has potential to be much better; Good interface for a collection of information"

To foster the collection of synthesized data and to identify key issues and conclusions emerging from across all eight states and territory PICTL projects, *Zing* was also used at a national meeting of all project managers. The research approach of qualitative data collection enabled substantial dialogue and rapid data collections about the issues under investigation at a national level. Like the *Leadership and Learning with ICT* project, the PICTL project benefitted from the inbuilt functionality of the system to enable the rapid collection of data using focus group research methods and to translate that data seamlessly into electronic formats that enabled digital data analysis and into Microsoft Word documents for immediate sharing with the research participants.

RE-IMAGINING AND RE-VISIONING EDUCATIONAL LEADERSHIP

In 2006, The Australian College of Educators, a national professional association representing Australian educators from across all education sectors (i.e., schools, training and higher education) invited Professor Brian Caldwell to work with leaders in education on the theme of re-imagining and re-visioning educational leadership. This work by Caldwell is based around a four dimensional model of governance that places students at its centre (Caldwell, 2006b). His work is derived from the work of Kaplan and Norton (2006) and is consistent with the work being undertaken by Sir Michael Barber, (Partner, McKinsey, et al.) in the UK on behalf of the Department for Education and Skills (Barber, 2006). Caldwell (2006a) argues that alignment of the elements of social capital, financial capital, intellectual capital, and spiritual capital is essential for transformation of schools to occur. He also argues that one of the biggest barriers to alignment is the failure of schools to abandon old practices.

To determine the state of Australian schools concerning their degree of alignment and capacity for abandonment, the Australian College of Educators invited school leaders to participate in electronic focus groups with Professor Caldwell to discuss these issues. The model for engaging school leaders that he used involved a one-day workshop based around nine core questions.

During June and July 2006, he conducted 19 of these sessions across Australia using *Zing* both as a tool for collaboration and a method for recording data.

Caldwell reports that "the result was thousands of ideas, ratings, concerns, predictions and recommendations" (Caldwell, 2006b, p. 2). He also indicates in his report of the research that the sorting, sifting, and synthesising processes of the data that were supported with *Zing*, allowed Caldwell (2006b, p. 30) to work with the school leaders to rapidly and confidently develop "a manifesto of policy and practice, implementation of which will help secure the preferred role for school leaders within five years." Caldwell then, was able to use *Zing* to foster meaningful discussion among school leaders and to generate considerable data in a short amount of time and to link that data with the theories of education he was researching.

LEADERSHIP PERFORMANCE AT SEKOLAH GLOBAL JAYA IN JAKARTA

In this final example, *Zing* was used as a part of a research and development project at Sekolah Global Jaya International School in Jakarta, Indonesia. Part of the overall processes included a 360 degree feedback and performance review process of the leadership team. Feedback was sought from people around each of the eight school principals and about the school leadership team as a whole. That is, school teaching staff, peers, administrative officers, parents, and students all participated in the review. As part of the review processes *Zing* was used for five group interviews comprising the following groups of participants in the school: the Executive Principal; three Expatriate School Principals; and four Indonesian School Principals; six Administrative Officers; sixteen students in two groups of eight, with four students drawn from years four, six, eight and 10 and eight parent members of the Parent Teacher Association

All the participants were bilingual although Indonesian was the first language of all but the expatriate, English speaking school principals. *Zing* works in English, and so to an extent the use of the system provided a mechanism for enabling all the participants to contribute on an equal footing. Prior to recording their views those participants who wished to could discuss the question in Indonesian before recording their views in English. Those using English as a second language were afforded the time and space to discuss their ideas in the first language and if required, to clarify with others how to record their views in English.

The use of keyboards was not an alienating factor for any of the participants. All participants including the eight and nine year old grade four students had sufficient keyboard skills to be able to quickly learn and use the system. Furthermore, although the groups were small and the participants knew each other, by being encouraged to use another identity for their logon names to work in the system, the participants did not know who was the author of what comments, thus providing a safe space in which to offer critical and constructive comments about the work of the school leadership team. Indeed, all groups indicated that they enjoyed the processes involved in taking part in the electronic focus groups with *Zing*.

POTENTIAL DIRECTIONS FOR FUTURE DIGITAL TECHNOLOGIES IN RESEARCH

The examples of research approaches in electronic focus groups presented here raise several scenarios for potential future directions and challenges concerning the integration of ICT into research methods. It would seem from the research methods we have outlined that an iterative relationship exists between using technologies for research and the constructions of those technologies. In the e-research environment it is not uncommon to use ICT to focus primarily on data collection and analysis (Anderson & Kanuka, 2003) and while these approaches are fundamental to any research activity, the examples presented here show that the *Zing* system goes beyond passive participant involvement in research activities to supporting participants' engagement in the research processes and through this engagement, encourages the participants to generate data and share ideas.

While collaborative tools such as the *Zing* system have the capacity to enhance focus group research, nonetheless, we are still in the very early stages of imagining how we can use ICT to do different and new work. It would seem then, that if emancipatory and participatory approaches are truly goals in focus group and electronic focus group research, then tools and techniques must continue to be developed that enable shifts in the 'conduct' of focus groups from academics and marketers to participant-groups generating new knowledge. Such shifts must enable groups to visualize and democratize their knowledge formation processes. The role and relationship of technologies in these shifts must similarly be conceptualised.

Integrating ICT into qualitative research methods is a newly emerging practice but it is likely to continue to grow. The necessity then to continue to reflect on our experiences and to build upon the findings of research projects where electronic focus groups have been used will also have to grow so that over time, deeper understandings about the innovative practices in data collection and analysis can be developed and extended. A recent Australian Government e-research discussion paper (DEST e-Research Coordinating Committee, 2005, p. 5) has argued that successful research is increasingly team-based. It is also increasingly necessary for research to be carried out across disciplines and across geographic boundaries, as researchers attempt to address more complex issues where boundaries are less relevant.

Capitalising on the new and emerging technologies available for undertaking education research is a challenge facing education researchers in the 21st century. Establishing multi-disciplinary relationships to undertake complex qualitative research will require the researchers and information technology (IT) developers to work closely together to build better paradigms and programs including better user interfaces and tools that shift the emphasis from data collection to data generation. Social technology tools such as those commonly referred to as Web 2.0 technologies are also emerging as holding potential benefits for conducting qualitative research. Monitoring these developments and trialling their use in low-risk research projects will enable the development of better understandings about the potential roles and purposes these technologies may offer to education research. Concurrently, reflection about how to build into research strategies, approaches that do foster emancipatory outcomes for the participants, remains important. Both reviewing traditional practices that are valued, and synthesising these with emerging practices that seem to hold merit, are spaces where future research are required.

REFERENCES

Anderson, T., & Kanuka, H. (2003). *E-research: Methods, strategies, and issues.* Boston: Allyn and Bacon.

Bacal, R. (2003). *The role of the facilitator. Understanding what facilitators really do.* International Association for Facilitators, USA. Retrieved on March 23, 2007 from http://www.iaf-world.org/i4a/pages/Index.cfm?pageid=3291

Barber, M. (2006). An obsession with delivery: public service reform in the UK, Core Seminar, Serco Institute, 11 January 2006, Ottawa Canada, Retrieved on March 27, 2007 from http://www.serco.co.uk/Images/Ottawa%20Presentation%20Core%202006_tcm3-11428.pdf

Caldwell, B. J. (2006a). *Re-imagining Educational Leadership.* Camberwell: ACER Press and London: Sage.

Caldwell, B. J. (2006b). *Alignment & Abandonment. Report of a National Series of Workshops on 'Re-imagining Educational Leadership'.* Canberra: Australian College of Education.

Casey, K. (1995). The new narrative research in education. M. Apple (ed.), *Review of research in education 21, 1995-1996.* Washington: American Educational Research Association.

Denzin, N., & Lincoln, Y. (2000). *Handbook of qualitative research,* (2nd ed), Thousand Oaks, California: SAGE Publications.

Department of Education, Science and Training (DEST) e-Research Coordinating Committee (2005). *An e-research strategic framework: A discussion paper.* DEST, Canberra, Retrieved on March 15, 2007 from http://www.dest.gov.au/NR/rdonlyres/F89601F7-6E10-4A2A-9E0A-E04C4AD17BB7/5864/20050602finaldiscussionpaper.pdf

Department of Education, Science and Training (2004). Research Expenditure 2002. Selected Higher Education Statistics, Commonwealth of Australia, Canberra, Retrieved on March 23, 2007 from http://www.dest.gov.au/NR/rdonlyres/9D59C09B-2322-422A-821E-3993C2FC19C2/2450/Research2002.pdf

Fitzgerald, R.N., & Findlay, J. (2008). Team learning systems as a collaborative technology for rapid knowledge creation. In F. Adams & P. Humphreys (Eds.), *Encyclopedia of Decision Making and Decision Support Technologies.* Hershey, PA: IGI Global.

Fitzgerald, R.N., & Findlay, J. (2004). A computer-based research tool for rapid knowledge-creation. In P. Kommers & G. Richards (Eds.), In *Proceed-*

ings of World Conference on Educational Multimedia, Hypermedia and Telecommunications 2004 (pp. 1979-1984). Chesapeake, Virginia.

Hakken, D. (1999). *Cyborgs @ cyberspace. An ethnographer looks to the future.* New York & London: Routledge.

Heidegger, M. (1977). The question concerning technology. In W. Lovitt (Ed.), *The question concerning technology and other essays.* New York: Harper.

Herda, E. (1999). *Research conversations and narrative. A critical hermeneutic orientation in participatory inquiry.* Westport, Connecticut & London: Praeger.

Johnson, B., & Christensen, L. (2004). *Educational research: quantitative, qualitative, and mixed approaches*, (2nd ed), Boston: Allyn and Bacon.

Kaplan, R.S., & Norton, D.P. (2006). *Alignment: Using the Balanced Scorecard to Create Corporate Synergies*, Boston MA: Harvard Business School Press.

Keeves, J. (Ed.). (1987). *Australian education: review of recent research.* Sydney: Allen and Unwin.

Lingard, B., & Blackmore, J. (1997). Editorial—The 'performative' state and the state of educational research. *Australian Educational Researcher, 24*(3), 1-20.

Moyle, K. (2006). *Leadership and learning with ICT: Voices from the profession.* Teaching Australia: Australian Institute for Teaching and School Leadership, Canberra, Australia.

Newman, L., & Pollnitz, L. (2002). *Ethics in action. Introducing the ethical response cycle.* Canberra: Australian Early Childhood Association.

Puchta, C., & Potter, J. (2004). Focus group practice, London: SAGE Publications.

Whymark, G., Callan, J., & Purnell, K. (2004). *Online learning predicates teamwork: Collaboration underscores student engagement.* Studies in Learning, Evaluation, Innovation and Development [Online], 1(2).

Willcox, J., & Zuber-Skerritt, O. (2003). Using the *Zing* team learning system (TLS) as an electronic method for the Nominal Group Technique (NGT). *ALAR Journal*, 8(1), 61-75.

KEY TERMS

Critical Friends: Peers, colleagues, or friends who challenge you by asking probing questions and offer helpful critiques and advice.

Education Research: The conduct of planned, systematic, and creative acts to investigate and understand questions and problems concerning the education of individuals, communities, and societies.

Electronic Focus Groups: The ability of focus group participants to communicate electronically with digital technologies while also contributing to focus groups in face-to-face settings.

Emancipatory Research: The processes of research which both in the data collection and in the analysis generate ways to change the social dynamics of given situations or circumstances.

E-Research: The use of digital tools, technologies and processes applied to the research activities.

Informed Consent: The process by which a person voluntarily confirms in writing, his or her willingness to participate in a particular research activity

Synchronous: Communications and associated processes occurring in real time and space.

Web 2.0 Technologies: Refers to second generation Web-based services which tend to have an emphasis on collaboration tools embedded into their interfaces.

Chapter XXIII
Learning and Meaning–Making in the Virtual Space

Staffan Selander
Stockholm Institute of Education, Sweden

Anna Åkerfeldt
Stockholm Institute of Education, Sweden

ABSTRACT

School pedagogy is being questioned. Increasing migration as well as increasing access to information and new patterns of communication are challenging traditional school work and school curricula. Teachers' and students' positions as didactic agents seem to be changing. The individualized curriculum puts new demands on schools. Teachers not only function as subject experts but also as individual "coaches" or "mentors." To a greater degree than ever before students are obliged to understand their own learning paths and to develop strategies for their school work. A new perspective on learning is needed to capture these changes in learning in institutional settings. Our aim is to outline a new perspective on designs for learning.

INTRODUCTION

The Swedish National Encyclopaedia ("Nationalencyklopedin") is, in its own estimation, the largest information base, constructed by 4,000 experts in different fields. Its data basis is continuously updated, and to be able to use it, one has to pay (Nationalencyklopedin, 2006). Wikipedia, on the other hand, is the "free encyclopaedia," whose content is constructed by the users themselves. Anyone with access to the Internet and a free Wikipedia account can create an entry or redefine an entry in this encyclopaedia. In Wikipedia it is possible to see who wrote the initial article and who has updated it. Added to each article is a forum for discussion and critical remarks. Wikipedia is an example of what today is called Web 2.0.

The "massive amounts of content" (Anderson & Whitelock, 2004) in digital space make traditional curriculum content and much of the teachers' subject knowledge obsolete. The development of local curricula and new demands on individualized content knowledge can be understood from this background (Alexandersson, 2003). The new emphasis placed on the students' capacity to communicate, collect, and judge information, as well as to present this information to others, involves a design perspective on learning (Kress & Selander, 2006). Interestingly enough, we also see developments towards stricter curricula, with international criteria for the assessment of knowledge acquisition. This development also calls for an institutional understanding of school activities.

FROM PREDEFINED LEARNING OBJECTS TO SHARING MATERIAL ON THE INTERNET

Koschmann (1996) argued that four different paradigms in the development of IT for learning could be identified. When computers were introduced into classrooms, the focus was on efficient learning; the CAI-paradigm (*computer assisted instruction*) was constructed on a behaviouristic perspective on learning. Each application was constructed in relation to a specific set of predefined goals. These goals were divided into small learning objects that the student worked through. The student became a passive receiver of predefined information. The role of the teacher was to check that the student had learned the different steps correctly. The feedback process was integrated in the program as a randomized feedback with phrases like "Well done!" or "Not so good, try again." Rapid e-learning applications can still be referred to this paradigm.

In the next paradigm, teachers as persons disappeared from the learning scene. The ITS-paradigm (*intelligent transportation systems,*

influenced by *artificial intelligence*) was based on the proposition that education could be globally improved by providing every student with a "personal" digital tutor. These applications were similar to those in the CAI-paradigm. The difference was mainly that it was the interaction between the computer and student, and not between the teacher and the student, that was in focus.

The third paradigm, *Logo-as-latin,* was built on a constructivist perspective of learning, inspired by Seymour Papert's (1995) use of the computer programming language *Logo* which he used for young children. The students could themselves play the role of the teacher. The program was also directed towards more general educational objectives. The fourth paradigm, CSCL (*computer supported collaborative learning*) was based on socio-cultural theories. The focus shifted towards the understanding of language, culture, and aspects regarding the social context. The applications were open, designed for the student's different aims and ways of using them. Interaction, communication, and assessment through portfolios now became the main strand of educational thinking (Dysthe, 2003). In this paradigm, the focus was on the learning process itself, not the outcome.

Today, yet another paradigm is emerging, focusing on the user as a producer of his or her own learning resources. The shift in interest from hardware to software, and from technological to pedagogical possibilities, indicated a shift in school work, although not all teachers have been trained for this change.

The educational Semantic Web highlight the role of the new tools in education, in relation to what is understood as learning in schools (Anderson & Whitelock, 2004). The concept "the educational Semantic Web" underlines a change in the understanding of communication, in line with semiotic tradition. Instead of seeing communication as a series of steps in the transportation of a message from a sender to a receiver through a medium that in different ways disturbs the message (adds "noise"), communication is seen as creation and exchange in meaning-making processes (the Latin word comunicare means " to share "). The learner is thus seen not as a passive receiver of a sign, but as an active person engaging in the world, searching for information. The reader/user interprets a message by way of experience, attitudes, interest, and feelings. This kind of thinking seems to be close to Deleuze's concept of rhizomatic structures with no clear centre. Learning can be understood as an ongoing process of transformation and meaning-making by means of different modes and media. The concept is also a kind of futuristic vision, is based on three affordances: (1) the capacity for information storage and retrieval; (2) agents; (3) and the possibilities of communication via Internet (Anderson & Whitelock, 2004).

THE USER IS THE KEY PERSON

Interactivity and hypertexts have long been part of the rhetoric concerning the digital media. However, what has often been called dynamic, non-linear, and open could in principle also be applied to printed texts like recipes for cooking and the Bible, which actually consists of many books from many centuries. Textual markers such as hyperlinks, or textual activities like reading bits and parts, also seemed to be a possibility when using printed texts (Anderhag et al., 2001). When the Internet had its great breakthrough in the 1990s, more emphasis was laid on the publication of information than the interactive use of information. Thus, in the beginning, digital media were often enough rather one-way and "stiff," just like printed texts.

A couple of years later, a new kind of Internet services started up on the Internet. These were called Web 2.0 and it was Tim O'Reilly who emphasized the concept: "Network effects from user contributions are the key to market dominance in the Web 2.0 era." (O'Reilly, 2005, p. 6). Examples of Web 2.0 are flickr.com (the possibility to load photos which could be shared by others) and youtube.com (for video clips). Users were now capable of creating and communicating their own content. The term IT (information technology) was now also extended to ICT (information and communication technology).

As a consequence of this development, the Swedish publisher Natur&Kultur started to use a Web-based "author's tool" to complement the resources for language acquisition in schools. They underline that this is the learning tool of new generations, in which the response from the users is of much greater relevance than earlier (Cleaverlearning, 2006). These new tools, like flickr.com and youtube.com, iMovie, iPhoto, Garageband and PowerPoint, and learning platforms like Guide&Tips and FirstClass and RSS-agents, which can give a hint when new information emerges in one's field of interest, allow students to become editors and producers of content. Here we see a change in resources that actually changes the way students may engage in their world in terms of both information sampling and information design (Jewitt, 2006).

RESOURCES FOR DESIGN

When communication is seen as meaning-making, the concept of design is close to it. Design is a way to configure communicative resources and thus also to design social interaction (Kress & van Leeuwen, 2001). From the students' point of view, they also learn to design learning facilities as well as learning processes. Central aspects of designs for communication are the *media* (newspapers, books, TV, computer, radio, etc.), the *modes* (letters, sounds, gestures, moving images, etc.) and the process of transformation and formation of knowledge and multimodal representations of knowledge.

In modern design theory, cooperation between the designer (e.g., of a software program) and the user is central and aspects such as structure, transparency, user-friendliness, possibility to take the initiative when using a program, control, autonomy, playability, personal connectedness, and social space are highlighted (Löwgren & Stolterman, 2004). Many of these aspects have been in focus in the making of computer games, a development that also addresses new aspects of learning compared to the development of learning in the compulsory schools, where the learners are all too often put in the position of passive receivers (Gee, 2004). However, new ways of working can be noticed when students, for example, make films, even if this is still only something extra beside the ordinary school work (Lindstrand, 2006). Institutional framing is preserved on many levels in school work, as well as traditional patterns of teaching. One example is the development of free music education in Sweden, where old patterns of music training and power relations prevailed in the classroom. There it is more important to play the notes correctly than to play the music in terms of rhythm or melodies (Rostvall & West, 2001). Strong traditions of schooling influence teaching and the conceptualization of what learning is about. These traditions also influence the way questions and tests are constructed, as open or closed, where closed questions lead to a kind of schoolwork that is characterized by searching for the right solution in a given text (Svärdemo-Åberg, 2004).

Concepts like 'education' and 'learning' are strongly linked to their institutionalized practices—formalized education learning in preschools, schools, universities or workplaces, or semi-formal learning spaces in museums and theatres. Will it at all be possible to combine the idea of institution with the idea of dynamic change, with "operative fictionality?" Post-modern institutions change the symbolic organization, combine registers and repertoires in new ways, and place the technological and social dimensions in "multiple cultural orders" (Knorr Cetina, 1992).[1]

DESIGNS FOR LEARNING

Design as a concept involves changed attitudes towards information and knowledge. It is not only, as in the new paradigm described above, a matter of using digital tools in a new way. It is overall a matter of how people engage with the world and with each other, and how representations are formed textually (in a wide sense, including pictures, three-dimensional objects, and other forms of multimodal constructions). What digital space offers is rather a change in time and space. The time aspect involves a change from synchronic to a-synchronic communication, and in terms of space, from natural to virtual space. The screen as a digital interface also changes our analytic, multimodal repertoire, adding aspects like depth and sequences by various (hyper-) links, comparable to what Kress & van Leeuwen developed in their analysis of printed pictorial illustration (Kress & van Leeuwen, 1996)

What emerges from the notion of design as an educational aim, and as a consequence of social, economic, political, semiotic, and technological changes? "Design" is a necessity both for teachers in terms of designing environments and processes of learning, and for the individual student in terms of designing his or her own learning path. The concept of "designs for learning" is one way of emphasizing the activities of forming and transforming knowledge, looking closely at both the modes and the media and the activities and processes of interpretation and design in meaning-making and learning. Designing the learning perspective gives another approach to communication and learning than has been prevalent in the constructivist notion of, for example, concept building (the Piagetian tradition) and in the social constructivist notions of the (rather general) role of the artefact for the collective memory and social interplay (the Vygotskyian tradition). The new perspective emphasizes the learner's meaning-making and sign production. Learning in this sense is a directed, carried out from an intention, but not directed as a predefined path of stepwise activities. It is rather a process of searching and changing, making decisions in small steps which will have consequences for the next possible step and so on. It is rather like an ongoing process of interpretation and sign-production. Learning could thus be defined as an "ongoing engagement to expand the repertoire of signs for meaning-making and an increased capacity to use signs in a meaningful way" (Selander, in press).

"DESIGNED INFORMATION AND TEACHING SEQUENCES" VERSUS "LEARNING DESIGN SEQUENCES"

"Designed information and teaching sequences" is a concept that encompasses the world of pre-fabricated learning resources, formalized work and strict timetables (lessons). The role of the teacher is to "bring" knowledge to the student, and the student's role is to remember by heart and to learn specific skills. For example, knowledge

about classificatory systems was once one of the most central aspects of education—to collect and classify flowers or animals from an evolutionary perspective, rather than understanding biological functions or how we can use natural resources in a careful way. To classify grammatical rules was in many instances seen as more important than the ability to communicate in a foreign language. To correctly prove a geometric theorem was more important than being able to think of different possible mathematical solutions to a problem and so on. Today, aspects like problem-solving, applications of knowledge and the protection of human environments are seen as more important and fruitful than classification as such. The ability to search, select, and critically evaluate information, as well as the ability to present information, is thus highlighted.

Learning design sequence (LDS) in Figures 1 and 2 is a theoretical map for the purpose of describing and analyzing critical incidents in (a creative) learning process, in a process of meaning-making.

Figure 1. Learning design sequence (i) (©2007, Staffan Selander and Anna Åkerfeldt . Used with permission)

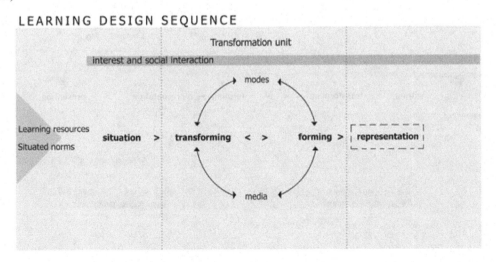

Central aspects are the situation and the resources, interest and social communication as starting points for the meaning-making process, by transforming and forming knowledge. Each cycle is linked to the next cycle, and these cycles could develop in many different directions. This basic, sequential learning process is, when we come to schools, formally framed by the institution, Figure 2, Formal—LDS . Now a new tension emerges between learning, teacher-led work and assessment structures, and between the first and the second transformation units, where the latter involves aspects like meta-reflections and discussions with the focus on both the process and the result.

The model helps us to describe and analyse the design of learning sequences, the formation and transformation of knowledge when students deal with their tasks in problem-solving, information-seeking, and sign-producing activities. The theoretical idea is based on a perspective of learning as a sign-making and meaning-making process.

A formal learning design sequence is framed by the curriculum, institutional norms and rules and the learning resources (media, instruments, etc.). A sequence starts when the teacher introduces a new task and *sets* the conditions for the work, which is also the beginning of the "primary transformation unit:" the interpretation of the task and the setting, and the process of transforming and forming knowledge—by means of various modes and media. The *setting* in the formal learning design sequence differs from the more open *situation* in the basic learning module. The setting as such is directed towards predefined goals.

The "secondary transformation unit" starts with students presenting their work. This is a meta-level, consisting of the mutual meta-reflections over the process and the product and includes, of course, the teacher's final assessment of the work. If the goals, as well as the expectations of

Figure 2. Formal-learning design sequence (©2007, Staffan Selander and Anna Åkerfeldt . Used with permission)

Formal - LEARNING DESIGN SEQUENCE

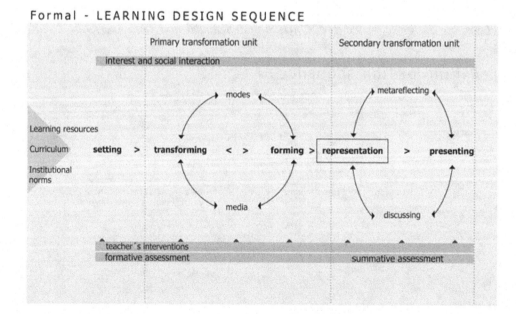

the process and product, are clearly defined and explained at the beginning, both students and teachers will have a powerful tool for reflection and evaluation. During the whole sequence, teachers make interventions and have the possibility to reflect over the signs and indications of learning that occur during the process.

THE MODEL IN ACTION

From Setting to Presenting

The beginning and end of a learning process in a school context can be described in terms of a narrative with a beginning and an ending, embracing certain crucial events. It is the teacher who is introducing the "skeleton of the story." During the setting, the teacher can inform the students about a large range of aspects—the idea of the process, the expected product, the criteria for assessment and so on. In our study (of Swedish schools), it seems to be the case that, first and foremost, it is at the upper secondary level that teachers give enough information to the students. If this is not the case, the teacher has already lost the opportunity to adequately support and judge the students' work and learning. At the end, the students present their work. The character of this presentation is dependent on the initial aim of the sequence. Sometimes it seems more like a show for friends and parents than a reflected process that focuses on the decisions during the process and on how the students have given a form to their understanding of the field of knowledge in question.

Transforming and Forming

Students seek and transform information, they cut and paste information from the Internet, but they also produce new information by way of interviews, making film, producing music or, for example, constructing three-dimensional objects.

Besides this, the students also test by means of mimesis different ways of working and behaving. This performative side of learning seems to be an underdeveloped field in the current understanding of meaning-making (Fischer-Lichte & Wulf, 2001). Students finally configure their representations in a form that reflects their understanding of the task. The whole process of sign-making is of importance for the teacher's work. The process of transforming and forming contains many choices and decisions that show choices and "signs" of learning.

Representations

The students' representations by way of various modes and media show what they perceive as central or peripheral. The representation itself indicates what students value as natural or divergent, important or unimportant, central or peripheral, necessary or unnecessary, and so on.

Social Interaction

Another aspect concerns both the socio-emotional group climate and the task-oriented interaction among the students. It entails issues like how members of a group develop (or do not develop) a common responsibility for the work, if someone is left out or if someone takes over, how students talk to each other while they are searching for information and forming their representations, and so on. Central question are: Who is active and who is passive? In what ways is the group supporting or hindering learning? How can the group handle tensions or insecurity?

Teachers' Interventions

During this process, the teachers may function as a support for the group. But is their interaction dominated by technical problems, problems of discipline, content-oriented questions, or do teachers simply interrupt group work by delivering last week's test results from another subject area? Interventions may also be carried out in terms of formative assessments to support the students' learning of a task.

Meta-Reflection and Discussions

The secondary transformation unit product, the representation, is presented, but also the product itself. Central questions are: How is the work carried out in relation to the student's earlier work? But also: How is the work in relation to the work of other students? The learning process is here oriented towards meta-learning and consciousness-raising reflections. To be able to make productive reflections, it is essential to relate these to the signs of learning during the process. The role of the teacher is to give a summative assessment of the work, the presentation and the product.

Indications of Learning

A crucial aspect of the LDS model is how sign-making can be documented as an indication or sign of learning. It not always easy to detect how and when learning occurs since learning is a term for many different and complex activities. Learning can be a change of behaviour and skills but also increased memory and a deeper understanding of new concepts. Learning can be an increased capacity to solve new problems or even old problems in a new way. Learning can be about new patterns of social communication. When activities are carried out without too much effort, we can see learning. When students start to discuss in new terminology, we can see learning. When students can suddenly solve a problem, learning has occurred. When students seek and talk about what they find on the Internet, the social aspect of learning is clear. When they use (digital) portfolios, learning steps can be observed.

Indications of learning in a formal setting are based on the students' sign-making activities, but made visible as a relation between an expected outcome (the institutional norms) and the activities themselves. Signs of learning may occur without anyone really noticing them, if the institutional rules and norms themselves do not especially take notice of these signs. Creative learning is not the same as learning by heart, learning certain movements (as in dance) is not the same as learning how to run a lab lesson and so on.

LEARNING DESIGN SEQUENCES IN VIRTUAL SPACE

In the research project *Digital learning resources and Learning Design Sequences in Swedish schools –a user perspective*[2], nine schools were selected to take part in a study that focuses on the design of the digital-learning resource, the use of this resource, the representation of knowledge and finally the users' reflection regarding their own learning process. These schools are in many senses in the forefront of using digital media; they have changed their pedagogy towards a more dynamic perspective of learning. But even if many dynamic aspects are emphasized, some obstacles, due to tradition or lack of experience, may also be noticed. In five of the nine schools, the pupils work with digital learning resources and the focus here is on creating their own presentation, film, radio program, or story-lines. In these schools, no CAI-applications were used. The pupils used for example programs like PowerPoint, iMovie, iPhoto, Garageband, and Word to create their presentations. In one of the schools, the pupils produced their own Web page on the school server, where they publish school work. They also produce their own blogs on this site. The following examples are from case studies, taken from the research project, of the digital-learning environment in some Swedish schools.

WORK AND LEARNING IN LEARNING DESIGN SEQUENCES RISKS...

What kind of learning takes place in different LDS's? Here we shall discuss a few examples to illustrate the gains but also some risks. When students work with digital films, make interviews and edit it all to create a film, many different activities take place. They invest interest, have to make many small decisions on the way (what to present, how to present it, etc.) and design the work, the content and the presentation. They have to film, copy it into the computer, edit the film, add music, and the like. In this process, many obstacles can occur and often enough students have to wait too long for help. They may become passive; this is not least a risk for younger students, when the medium itself absorb all their interest, not the content itself.

The following case may illustrate this problem. In a media class, six-year-old children are going to produce a slideshow about "What do I want to tell mum and dad about my school day?" The class starts with a short introduction, after which the children are divided into two groups and each group receives a digital camera. The first instruction is to take photos of something in the school environment that they find interesting. Before they spread out in the room, they discuss how many pictures they should take. After that they start work. The teacher follows the children around and gives them instructions. One child in particular is having problems with the button for starting taking pictures. He is not pushing it hard enough and is only adjusting the focus. He never gets to the next step of taking the picture. The teacher demonstrates how it works, and the child pushes the button harder. When the children have finished, they are going to download the pictures into the computer. The teacher explains what they should do in order to import them into iMovie. When this is done, the teacher tells them to select pictures that they want to show to their mum and dad and drag them down to the timeline. The children start work but soon need the teacher's attention because there are pictures missing. The teacher explains again that maybe it is because they have not pushed the camera button hard enough, so the picture has not been taken. This example shows that the children needed plenty of help while working with a digital-learning resource. They needed guidance and hands-on demonstrations. While the teacher here is focussing on content and the story-line, the children seem more focussed on the digital resource itself, how to operate and control it.

Another example is information-seeking on the net (Google, etc.) The children write a word in the search domain and a great deal of information may appear. It is then easy to lose focus and start doing something else. According to Wheeler et al. (2002), learning in digital space can be arbitrary and characterized by chance. There also seems to be a stress factor, when students try to complete their project before they have actually finished their investigation (Holm Sorensen, 2006; Wheeler et.al., 2002). Sometimes "cut-and-paste" activities dominate the information-seeking process, where information is not worked on but just copied into a PowerPoint presentation, for example.

In another example, there is a focus on medium and weak content orientation. In a theme project in grade seven in the compulsory school, the pupils work with the question of "the worst things that can happen." Four main themes are highlighted, and one of the groups chooses to work with "not being good enough." The members of the group work with a digital camera, external memory discs and (both stationary and mobile) PCs, and they use programs like iMovie, iPhoto, and Garageband. The students' questions to the teacher are more or less limited to the medium and the technology itself. Questions are raised about how to transfer filmed material from the camera to the computer, or how to create neat bridges between different film sequences, for example. The teacher answers these questions, but the content is not discussed, for example, "why" the students wanted a certain visual representation and "what" they wanted to tell with it. An example from a distance Swedish-language course (upper secondary level) shows the opposite. The students send their tasks to the shared, virtual classroom. The idea of the teacher is that the students should make comments on each other's texts, but this does not happen. The communication is highly teacher-oriented and the students do not use the medium to talk to each other. The course has the character of an older (letter-based) distance course. The potential of the medium is not utilised here. There is strong content orientation but a weak use of the medium. According to Loveless (2003), ICT is well used in education for the purpose of presenting and communicating information. Buhl (et al., 2005) highlights the use of digital portfolios for presentations and also as a source for teacher's judgements. Drenoyianni (2006) says that programmes for play and learning are rarely used and that writing and information searching are the most prevalent activities. In preschools, software is used rather than intelligent toys or small computers (Plowman & Stephen, 2003).

... AND OPPORTUNITIES

Also some of the great opportunities should be mentioned. Digital artefacts make it easier to visualize and explain complex structures (Säljö, 2005). The artefact itself carries resources which functions as affordances for students to engage in meaning-making (Kress et al., 2001). Their reading and writing can be helped by special programs for spelling, reading and the like (Mathiassen, 2003). The pupils' capacity to develop their own ideas and be inspired by others may increase (Sorensen et al., 2006). The medium also can inspire the students to have fun during their work (Alant et al., 2003). In terms of communication time and place are not any more limits.

IN CONCLUSION

Digital media, with its massive amount of content and communicative opportunities, will change the ways in which schools handle information and judge learning. This will also change our conceptualization of what learning is about. In this article we have outlined a new perspective on learning from a design perspective, which focuses on the learner's engagement and his or her sign-producing activities. Hereby we also pinpoint those instances in the learning process where critical incidents of interactivity and communication take place, both between humans and between humans and computers.

REFERENCES

Alant, L., Engan, B., Otnes, H., Sandvik, M. & Schwebs, T. (2003). *Samhandling med, foran og via skjermen. Småskoleeleven på vei mot digital kompetanse.* Oslo: Forsknings- og kompetansenettverk for it i utdanning Universitet i Oslo. ["Cooperation with, in front of and via the screen. Young kids and their way towards digital competence."]

Alexandersson, Mikael (2003). Att konstruera egna kunskaper via webben. In *Forskning av denna värld – praxisnära forskning inom utbildningsvetenskap.* Vetenskapsrådets rapportserie (pp. 17-22). ["Design own knowledge via Internet."]

Anderhag, P., Selander, S., & Svärdemo-Åberg, E. (2001). Interaktivitet och hypertextualitet? Om digital kommunikation och digitala läromedel. In Säljö, R. & Linderoth, J. (Eds.), *Utm@ningar och e-frestelser. IT och skolans lärkultur.* Stockholm: Prisma (pp. 166-189). ["Interactivity and hypertextuality? On digital communication and digital learning resources."].

Anderson, T., & Whitelock, D. (2004). The educational semantic web: Visioning and practicing the future of education. In T. Anderson & D. Whitelock (Eds.), *JIME Special issue*. The educational semantic web. (pp. 1-15)

Berners-Lee, T. (1999). *Weaving the web. The past, present andfFuture of the World Wide Web*. Butler & Tanner Ltd: Frome and London.

Bosco, A. (2004). ICT resources in the teaching of mathematics: between computer and school technologies. A case study. *The Curriculum Journal*, Vol. 15, No. 3, Autumn 2004.

Buhl, M., Holm Sorensen, B., & Meyer, B. (Eds.). *Medier og it – laringspotentialer*. Köpenhamn: Danmarks Pedagogiske Universitets Forlag. ["Media and IT - potentials for learning."]

Cleverlearnings pressrelease. (2006). Retrieved on September 19, 2006, from http://www.cleverlearning.se/Pressrelease_e-learning_i_skolan.pdf

Cetina, Karin D. Knorr (1994). Primitive classification and postmodernity: Towards a sociological notion of fiction. *Theory, Culture & Society*, 11. (3) (pp. 1-23).

Delegation for ICT in schools, it is (1999). Retrieved on April 27, 2006, from http://www.itis.gov.se/English

Drenoyianni, H. (2006). Reconsidering change and ICT: Perspectives of a human and democratic education. *Springer Science + Business Media*, LLC.

Deleuze, G. (2001). *Difference and Repetition*. London : Continuum. [*Différence et Répétition* , 1968. Paris : Presses Universitaires de France]

Dysthe, O. (2003). Dialogperspektiv på elektroniska diskussioner. In *Dialog, samspel och lärande*. Dysthe, O. (Ed.). Lund: Studentlitteratur. (pp. 295-320) ["A dialogical perspective on electronic discussions".]

Fischer-Lichte, E. & Wulf, C. (2001). Theorien des Performativen. *Paragrana*, Internationale Zeitschrift für Historische Anthropologie, Band

10, Heft 1. Berlin: Akademie Verlag. ["Theories of the Performative."].

Gadamer (1988). Truth and method. London: Sheed and Ward. [*Wahrheit und Methode*, 1960. Tübingen: J.P. Mohr (Paul Siebeck)].

Gee, J. P.(2004). *What videogames have to teach us about learning and literacy*. Palgrave MacMillan.

Holm Sorensen, B., Danielsen, O., & Nielsen, J. (2006). *Children's informal learning in the context of schools of the knowledge society*. Springer Science + Business Media, LLC.

Jewitt, C. (2006). *Technology, literacy and learning. A multimodal approach*. London: Routledge.

Koschmann, T. (1996). Paradigm shifts and instructional technology: An introduction. In Koschmann, T. (Eds.), *CSCL: Theory and practice of an emerging paradigm*. Mahwah, N.J.: Erlbaum. (pp. 1-23).

Kress, G., Jewitt, C., Ogborn, J., & Tsatsarelis, C. (2001). *Multimodal teaching and learning. The rhetorics of the science classroom*. London: Continuum.

Kress, G., & Selander, S. (in press). Designs for learning—individual and institutional formations of meaning. In Säljö, R. (Ed.).

Kress, G., & van Leeuwen, T. (1996). *Reading images. The grammar of visual design* London: Routledge.

Kress, G. & van Leeuwen, T. (2001). *Multimodal discourse. The modes and media of contemporary communication*. London: Arnold.

Lindstrand, F. (2006). *Att göra skillnad. Representation, identitet och lärande i ungdomars arbete och berättande med film*. Stockholm: HLS Förlag. [The making of differences. Representation, identity and learning in young students film narratives."]

Loveless, A. (2003). Creating spaces in the primary curriculum: ICT in creative subjects. *The Curriculum Journal*, Vol. 14, Spring 2003, 5-21.

Löwgren, J., & Stolterman, E. (2004). *Thoughtful Interaction Design. A design perspective on information technology.* Cambridge, MA: The MIT Press.

Mathiassen, H. red. (2003). *It og laringsperspektiver.* Copenhagen: Alinea A/S. [IT and perspectives on lerning"].

Nationalencyklopedin. (2006). Om företaget. Retrieved on October 14, 2006, from http://www.ne.se

O'Reilly, T. (2005). What Is Web 2.0. Design Patterns and Business Models for the Next Generation of Software: Retrieved on September 20, 2006, from http://www.oreillynet.com/pub/a/oreilly/tim/news/2005/09/30/what-is-web-20.html

Plowman, L., & Stephen, C. (2003). A 'benign addition?' Research on ICT and pre-school children, *Journal of Computer Assisted Learning*, 19, 149-164.

Papert, S. (1995) *Hur gör giraffen när den sover: skolan, datorn och kunskapsprocessen.* Göteborg : Daidalos. ["The children's machine"]

Rodrigo, M.M.T. (2003). Tradition or transformation? An evaluation of ICTs in Metro Manila schools. *Information Technology for Development.* 10, 95-122.

Rostvall, A-L., & West, T. (2001). *Interaktion och kunskapsutveckling. En studie av frivillig musikundervisning.* Stockholm: HLS Förlag. ["Interaction and Development of Knowledge."]

Selander, S. (in press). Designs for learning in Institutional Settings. In *Designs for Learning*, No. 1, 2008.

Sorensen, Holm, B., Danielsen, O., & Nielsen, J. (2006). Children's informal learning in the context of schools of the knowledge society. *Springer Science + Business Media*, LLC.

Svärdemo-Åberg, E. (2004). *Lärande genom möten: en studie av kommunikation mellan lärare och studerande i klassrumsmiljö och datorbaserad nätverksmiljö.* Stockholm: HLS förlag. ["Learning in meetings: a study of communication between teachers and students in class room environments and computer based networks".]

Säljö, R. (2005). *Lärande och kulturella redskap: om lärprocesser och det kollektiva minnet.* Stockholm: Norstedts Akademiska Förlag. ["Learning and Cultural Tools: on learning processes and collective memory."]

Vattimo, G. (1989). *Etica dell'interpretazione.* Torino: Rosenberg & Sellier. ["The ethics of interpretation"].

Wheeler, Steve., et al. (2002). Promoting creative thinking through the use of

ICT. *Journal of Computer Assisted Learning*, No. 18.

KEY TERMS

Design: Design as a concept involves changed attitudes towards information and knowledge. It is a necessity both for teachers in terms of designing environments and processes of learning, and for the individual student in terms of designing his or her own learning path.

Designs for Learning: The concept emphasizes the double aspect of learning, on the one hand resources and system created for learning, on the other hand the learners meaning-making as sign production.

Educational Semantic Web: Highlight the role of the new tools in education, in relation to what is understood as learning in schools. The concept is also a kind of futuristic vision, is based on three affordances; (1) the capacity for information storage and retrieval, (2) agents, (3) and the possibilities of communication via Internet (Anderson & Whitelock, 2004).

Learning Design Sequences: A theoretical map for the purpose of describing and analyzing critical incidents in (a creative) learning process, in a process of meaning-making. Central aspects are the situation and the resources, interest and social communication as starting points for the meaning-making process, by transforming and forming knowledge.

Representation: The final student work that the teacher assess. Show what the students' perceive as central or peripheral by way of various modes and media. The representation itself indicates what students value as natural or divergent, important or unimportant, central or peripheral, necessary or unnecessary and so on.

Transformation and Formation of Knowledge: Learning process that leads to the final representation. Students seek and transform information, they cut and paste information from the Internet, but they also produce new information by way of interviews, making film, producing music or, for example, constructing three-dimensional objects. The process of transforming and forming contains many choices and decisions that show choices and "signs" of learning.

User Control: User as a producer of his or her own learning resources. The shift in interest from technological to pedagogical possibilities, indicated a shift in school work, although not all teachers have been trained for this change.

ENDNOTE

[1] Gadamer (1988) claims that tradition is always recreated through practices. At the same time he sees tradition as 'given.' Vattimo (1997) discusses tradition as not given but as something 'handed over' (überlieferung), and thus as something open for negotiation and conceptual re-creation.

[2] The Knowledge Foundation research program Learn-IT financed the research project.

Section III
Ethical Issues

Chapter XXIV
Communication and Relation Building in Social Systems

Thomas Hansson
Blekinge Institute of Technology, Sweden

ABSTRACT

Research into human behaviour has produced much innovative modelling, some respectable instrumenta-tion, but little empirical theory-testing. This chapter follows suit, but rather than pursuing a traditional division between abstract conceptualisation and pragmatic procedures in the analysis of systemic human behaviour, focus is on social and psychological systems defined as information-processing entities in a context of verbal organisation, communication, and control.

INTRODUCTION

The ability in man to build holistic structures from miniature data is a creative and logical compe-tence. Although naturally occurring systems are only implicitly given in the physical world, they need to be explicitly identified before they can be studied. Checkland (1981) coined the concept *systems thinking* long after Wiener (1969, p. 31) had predicted the impact of modern technology in terms of human computer interaction (HCI): "in the future [...] messages between man and ma-chines, between machines and man, and between machine and machine, are destined to play an ever-increasing part." Wiener's prediction resulted in a strong belief in the ability in man to relate to others by means of verbal exchanges. In fact, this ability is a characterizing trait of humanity, mankind, fellowship, and togetherness. Further-more, the innate quality in man to conceptualize comprehensive structures rather than memoriz-ing isolated facts is a combined ontological and epistemological asset. A personal capacity to relate to sensations, perceptions, conceptions, and experiences in systemic terms, however, is different from the idea that any combination of items, things or situations make up an organized communicating structure. Such an understanding of wholeness makes the concept system void of meaning.

Communicative behaviour materializes in global networks shared by universal religions, faiths, and belief systems. For example, *The Golden Rule* epitomizes an idealistic idea of mutuality, collectiveness, and responsibility, implying that if you treat others in the way that you are willing to be treated in the exact same situation, you verify the essence of life. Implicit contextual influences embedded in the Golden Rule verifies to the Kantian maxim that experience without theory is blind and also that theory without experience is wasted intellectual play. In commenting on the theory-practice theme of the Golden Rule, Lewin (1947) says the most practical thing is a good theory. Consequently, the most rewarding input to theory building is a good practice. As a result, the (action) researcher's values, objectives, and priorities are united in efforts at understanding group dynamics by active participation in a communicating social system (Parsons, 1951) of shared experiences.

People participate in social systems like families, institutions, communities, and nations. They interact with family members at home, peers at school, workplace colleagues on their jobs, and even as virtual agents in Web-based communities of practice. Groupings of systematically organized people are identified by age, geography, professionalism, interest, or coincidence. However, interacting, interdependent, and interrelated virtual communities like chat sessions, focus groups, or pod casts differ from traditional systems because modern technology enables constellations of people to operate in time and place dislocated contexts. Today the channels for communication are more elaborate than primal screams, smoke signals, or the telegraph. But for a long time, interactions have been constituted by verbal exchanges materializing as situated speech.

According to Bruner (1999) traditional research on education is a politically and culturally infected practice—especially research on information and communication technology (ICT) highlights normative and technological pedagogy. For example, the introduction of software is sometimes seen as a vanguard for the elimination of educators. Still, educators try to adapt ICT interactions to teaching, studying, and learning, to combine motivational multiplayer software games with traditional curricular subjects like English, or general didactics like values. But an optimal design for studying the use of computers in education is hard to find. So rather than deploring the lack of measures for putting research on social systems right, we need to study the causal interdependencies, multiple influences, and evolving patterns of human communication.

SOCIAL SYSTEMS THEORY

The presumption of this chapter is that analysis of Web-based human systems may clarify the structure, functioning, and impact on human interactions. However, this is a difficult venture as the analyst is trapped in his own ways of thinking feeling and acting. More specifically, a Western tradition of linear Aristotelian or dualistic Cartesian thinking makes it hard for research to follow the epistemological logics of a more creative Eastern circular thinking tradition (Maruyama, 1963) with simultaneous interactions and non-sequential thinking.

Webster's Online Dictionary (2007) says that a *system* is a "regularly interacting or interdependent group of items forming a unified whole, which is in, or tends to be in, equilibrium." Likewise, the *Concise English Dictionary* cited in Dictionary. com (2007) says a system is a "coordinated arrangement or organized combination of things or parts, for working together, performing a particular function etc." Rowland (2004) says a system is whatever one chooses to label a system. However, such an understanding would open an unlimited space for the researcher to cultivate versus colonize human activities, processes, or situations. In modifying Rowland's stand, one might argue that the demarcation of a system has got more to do with the limits of human cognition than with the objective nature of the world. Besides tricky definitions, fuzzy terminology, and blurred demarcations, the characteristics of a social system include multiple and confounding variables like *agency, exchange, referentiality, correction, renewal, change,* and *expansion.* By *system* is implied a holistic understanding of the concept, acknowledging the impact of relations between individual units and an organising principle like, humanity, power or profit.

Is the systems approach superior to critical discourse analysis, hermeneutics, or participative inquiry? Herrscher (2006, p. 410) says: "the systemic approach is a sort of vaccine against the guru of the unique tool, against the consultant who applies only the methodology, against the board that leaps into the fast solution." By acknowledging the impact of human communications, this chapter recognises systemic thinking as a way of defining the functioning of social systems. So regardless if we choose a nation, a species or a chemical substance, the categorizations of systems theory provides an unexploited potential for identifying the organized arrangements and functioning of naturally occurring processes.

Over the years, researchers have studied groups, social classes, learning organizations, and communities of practice. The following quotations situate the philosophical and methodological positions related to systems thinking in the literature. Rohde (2006) defines the world by systemic equilibrium in which Linnæus, the biologist, explores the taxonomies of the birds and the bees. Smith, the national economist, studies the necessity of economic competition. Modern systems theory has been in vogue since the emergence of activity theory (Leontev, 1978). Eventually, Lewin (1969) set a framework for promoting action research and democracy, Wiener (1948) developed cybernetics for the army, Hutchinson (1948) investigated self correcting ecological systems, Maturana

and Varela (1980) defined autopoiesis in biology, Banathy (1996) studied participative inquiry, and Luhmann (2002) outlined communications in social systems. These inspirations for studying autonomous control mechanisms in a variety of contexts led to the development of models, understandings, and techniques that enabled for analysis of communicating internal relations. The purpose today is to find concepts and techniques that enable for research to develop social theory by classifying social systems. Here, a trajectory of theoretical development begins with social cybernetics; it leads through general activity theory and it finishes off with philosophy.

The idea of cybernetic control also characterizes an *open* systems theory where there is exchange and transformation of input-energy from the environment in which the organization is embedded. After the war, application to real life systems was a pre condition for studying social phenomena. In a detailed analysis, Katz and Kahn's (1966) goal directed deterministic theory builds on interactive feedback, essential to the survival of the system. The conditions are that exchange and transformation of the imported energy results in some kind of output which is in harmony with the system. The authors define systems theory as a discipline for dealing with organizational relationships, structures, and contingencies.

There are some prerequisites for development of a holistic systems thinking, other than suggested by dictionaries, history or conceptual definitions. The seemingly innocent term *information,* as in information and communication technology, is extensively defined (Wiener 1969, p. 32) as "a name for the content of what is exchanged with the outer world as we adjust to it, and make our adjustment felt upon it." Notice that, without any obvious indication, the components (agents) of such a system interact inside the system's boundaries as well as with the environment. To make matters more confusing, systems theory competes with similar theoretical constructs. Steffe & Gale

(1995) portray social systems theory as fundamentally different from social constructionist or constructivist contributions. Also, constructivist approaches employ black box variables hidden inside the individual subject. For example, Turner (1991) introduces *reflexive turn* and *ideology,* and Gergen (2006) employs *historical consciousness, moral identity,* and *narrative discourse.* At other times (Hwang, 2000) the social constructivist perspective is presented as a congenial approach to systems theory, suggesting (Berger & Luckman, 1967) that our knowledge of the world arises through individual representations of reality. But there is a difference because modern communication theory defines an arranged unit of interrelated or systematically interacting parts which exchange information within a set of delimiting or rather semi-permeable boundary markers.

There is another aspect of systems thinking to consider. Long before the emergence of a systems theory for learning organizations (Kim & Senge, 1994), people thought of a rainbow coalition of general systems theory, cybernetics, information theory, computation, and control. At the heart of such an approach lays a definition, suggesting a relational unit of analysis. In elaborating this crucial aspect, Rapoport (1969) says a system is a construct which by virtue of the interdependence of its parts functions as a whole. Methods in the context of justification which aim at discovering how this interdependence operates, seek to classify the studied system by the way its components are related. The patterns over relations, borders and operations of a system materialize as interactive dialogism (Bakhtin, 1993), typically expressing sender/receiver intensions categorized by process control and communicative loops for instruction, control, and learning. Stacey (1992) says that the ethical issues that arise in the management of teambuilding, working, and learning must be taken into account. Stacey's complexity theory appreciates the world as a whole, comprising interrelationships expressed in endless occurrences of spontaneous self organisation. As opposed to

systemically (re)constructed natural systems, social systems are different because human agents bend the rules and practices. Needless to say, the impact of self control applies for social systems of Internet users too.

RESEARCH QUESTIONS

In providing yet another aspect of the complexity of social systems, Geyer and van der Zouwen (1991) outline *cybernetics* as a theory for explaining the functioning of social control systems, for example how students react to the teachers' (virtual) didactics on the Web. Such a socio cybernetic perspective includes multi- and confounding variables like *subjects, actors, medium, planning, control, prognosis, credibility, and fulfilment.* Based on these concepts, and opposed to the rather vague problem statement in Flood (1999, p. 251-252) saying a critical issue is to clarify how *systemic appreciation is an apparently expanding activity* and to morally decide *who is to judge that any one bounded appreciation is most relevant or acceptable* (italics in original), the ambition for this chapter is to classify Web-based communications as systems, to explore what they consist of, and to outline their dynamics. This entails the pursuit of reflective and conceptual research questions (Hwang, 2000, p. 341). It is, however, beyond the purpose of this chapter to study how individual subjects develop their understanding of systems theory or how people communicate in an ethically correct manner. Focus is on the functioning of autonomous communicative systems. The approach covers an ambition to help people avoid quick fix problem solving solutions on, for example, lurking in Web 1.0 learning management systems (LMS). By employing a typology for social systems we can learn how collectives of people act together. But the question remains unsolved: Do the variables of those constructs provide unambiguous criteria for when targets have been reached? Do they account for the impact of the ethically relevant structures that in so many cases secure the survival of the system?

SUMMARIZING SOCIAL SYSTEMS

An open systems approach acknowledges the impact of environmental influences. A closed systems approach, on the other hand, allows most of the system's problems to be analyzed with reference to its internal functions. Furthermore, the latter approach fails to account for influences between the system and the environment.

As to the characteristics of social systems typologies, Banathy (1996, p. 80) says the agent should understand and act on the mission and the purpose of the system—the specifications that characterize the system, the functions of the system, the mission and the purpose of the functions, the components and their parts that are engaged in attending to functions, and the relational integration of the components into the structure of the system. Today we assume that the attributes of a social system are made up of interdependences and the interlinking of smaller subsystems within a comprehensive holistic system. But such a tendency toward attaining a sought balanced state through agreement rather than creative innovation brought about by differences between subsystems inspires the analyst to consider one dimensional—or single agent—causation rather than dynamic causation through multiple confounding variables.

In a straightforward definition, Flood (1999, p. 248) says systemic thinking defines "behaviour [...] as the result of loops where variables are interrelated. Behaviour results from feedback between variables." Furthermore, in a preferred open systems classification, the organization of a social system is influenced by and influences (through multi- and confounding variables) the external and internal contingency components of the environment.

And so, systems thinking about interlocutors committed to verbal exchanges—eventually forming a community of practice—purports to take The System as its prime unit of analysis. Such an approach gives the impression of being methodologically capable of including all relevant relations and also to handle any problem as it appears in real life. At this point, however, research needs to define completeness and closure, holism, and interbeing. Distinctions between correct perception and illusive deception seem to surface in situations where research is unable to cover everyday contradictory situations, so called wicked problems. This chapter argues they can only be researched by a soft systems methodology. The objective of describing social systems by their inherent quality of wickedness, identified by (lack of) completeness and closure is hard to meet because, as Berry (1988) puts it, the universe carries within itself a spiritual and a material dimension. Likewise, Rittel and Weber (1973) argue that wicked problems are best tackled as a social learning process in a co operative setting through a holistic approach enabled by good relations.

The old way of dividing systems theory into soft-open versus hard-closed systems needs to be substituted. I suggest a typology that builds on the balancing of epistemology, ontology, methodology, and different kinds of data, all of which make up a foundation for valid research. I also suggest a categorization of *natural-relational, interactive-typological, structural-transitional, dynamic-relational, value-focused,* and *operationally-constructive* systems. The first two systems cover morally questionable behaviourist (goal-directed) Web 1.0 mass media publication. The remaining systems describe ethically correct social constructivist (relational) Web 2.0 multimedia interactions.

In a context for classifying systems it is necessary to acknowledge the impact of ethics. The old way of categorizing communications rested on systemic thinking about agency, message, medium, and transport. The new way of categorizing communicating systems is all about dialogism, relations, and co-construction of meaning. To each of the suggested classifications is attached a major ethics operating from within the system (as reflection) and a complementary ethics operating from outside the system (as democratic control).

Natural-Typological Systems

As to the origin of systems thinking, it is hard to identify the genesis of an ongoing tradition. Regardless if we decide on the Bible, Greek mythology, or Central European Didactics (*Die Didaktik*), man seems always to have been prone to categorise small pieces of information as the building blocks of a bigger whole. From a European perspective, Comenius, (1999) marks the advent of systems thinking, especially for methodology and data. Comenius (1592-1670) advocated in his major publication *The Great Didactic,* a vision of the entirety of the world. Hence, as one of the fathers of intellectual, moral, and religious education he illustrated a divine world, expressing a moral mission and promoting a *religious ethics.* His intelligent design was a content system over a choice of classified objects. He mediated his missionary objectives through thematic illustrations of natural objects like trees or horses. In fact, Comenius supplied a moral ideal, much later referred to as Bildung. *Omnes, omnia, omnibus* suggests that everybody has the right to learn anything. Comenius' conception of an intelligent design of the world suggested a high level of cognitive progressing of natural perceptions organised into universal laws and general knowledge. This was for the students. For the natural systems that Comenius' illustrated, however, there is no room for a human ethics as living plants and animals are unable to value, evaluate, or judge environmental influences. Still, Comenius' understanding of the principle of life served a moral purpose insofar as it would enable for man to see the Grand objective

of a God given system. Today Comenius' didactical effort is merely a visualizing technique for illustrating the knowledge of man as perceived by the senses. The implication for digital information technologies is that of an instrumental tool typically materializing as a computer machine for transmission of data.

Interactive-Relational Systems

There are a number of *open systems* based on the complexity of the parts of the systems and the nature of the relations between them. Contrary to Comenius' systems thinking, Boulding's (1956, p. 200-207) typology of rather excluding systems reflects a mechanistic view of the world: "Frameworks like the anatomy of an animal; clockworks like the solar system; cybernetic systems like a thermostat in a radiator; open systems as in a living cell; blueprint-growth systems like pre programmed egg-chicken; internal-image systems such as detailed animalistic awareness; symbol-processing systems like human self-consciousness; social systems as with socially ordered actors." Today emphasis is on expansive, creative, philosophical symbol processing in transcendental soft systems. A *soft systems* categorization in Checkland (1971) specifies inclusive categories like natural systems (biology), designed systems (machinery), activity systems (industrial companies), and social systems (community). Even today, analyses into activity and social systems form the mainstream of behavioural research.

After the War, researchers felt the harmful effects of compartmentalization in science. Therefore, they introduced systems ideas, thinking, definitions and theory with relevance across a spectrum of disciplines. The initiative helped open narrow disciplines, introducing non religious and multivariable sciences. This was an effort at attaining a synthesis of scientific knowledge. According to von Bertalanffy (1969, p. 13) a general systems theory should "derive from a general definition of system as a complex of interacting components, concepts characteristic of organized wholes such as interaction, sum, mechanization, centralization, competition, finality and so forth,, and to apply them to concrete phenomena."

In complementing the list of open systems theory influences, Maruyama (1963) defines a *first* cybernetics as a deviation restraining/counteracting network of properties and relations for reaching static balance by means of restraining negative feedback flow between elements. For the researched context the approach applies for students who fail to discuss rules, constitutions or communicative principles of a web based community of practitioners. A *personal ethics* (to tell the truth, to tell everything, come to the point, have a genuine purpose etc) usually has a bearing on interactive social systems. And so, regulation by morally doubtful entropic feedback loops of text submissions in virtual learning environments brings status quo into place, a situation of little interest for an experimental design on the workings of an expanding communication system, for example in a Web 2.0 interactive environment.

However, a *second cybernetics* investigates the observer rather than the observed phenomenon. The issue is less what an object is and more how something is (re)constructed as a communication system. Focus shifts from the observed *it* to *s/he* observing individuals. Maruyama (1963) also defines such social (self control) cybernetics for amplifying mutual relationships by means of positive feedback loops with a flow of information between interlocutors who respond to an initial impetus that inspires creative deviation from an initial condition. In the lucky case the interactive features of a LMS is supported by reflective adaptation between the interlocutors. During such processes, some feedback loops amplify and others counteract generic change and cognitive development in the activity system. It seems as if in any socially organised collective of people, positive feedback loops inspire deviation from an intuitively agreed norm. As a result of the fact that socially informed heterogeneity increases in the communicative unit, new relations develop and the amount of shared information grows. There is a potential for synergy in such virtual communities. Knowledge of the functioning of communicating teams forms a basis for understanding verbal data as dialogical feedback regulation. The interlocutors' interactive control mechanisms on a LMS bring the expansive aspects of virtual and social games into play. The implication for digital information technologies in this categorization is however usually that of a system for non-productive *administrative control*, that is summative statistics, registering of chat logs, and tracking of interactions.

Structural-Transitional Systems

By definition, a system is classified by its contextual embeddedness within another (bigger) system. This fact is abundantly clear for a contextually situated system like education where the teacher is a language-using species, reaching for some pre-set learning objectives for the students.

An early generation of systems theory indicates the beginning of general activity theory (GAT), including mediation of human impressions, information and instrumentation by means of tools like sticks and stones, signs like speech and symbols like the Christian cross. GAT concepts like internalisation and externalisation of information build on Leontev's (1978) trajectory: activity, awareness, and personality. The concepts signify a prerequisite for development of higher mental functions. However, this exclusive ability in man to relate to Self, Other, and the world fails to separate between perceptions of objects and people. Figure 1 depicts a triangular model of causal impact by agency through one-directional relations, like for example salivation in Pavlov's dogs.

Modern software packages cover instrumental aspects of mediation between man and the world in/by signs, symbols, and letters. Operations of man, machine, and tools inspire computer efficacy, language processing and creative graphics. But

Figure 1. Mediation of meaning (©2007, Thomas Hansson . Used with permission)

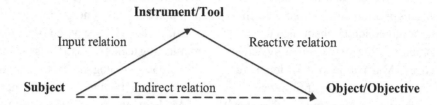

Figure 2. De-contextualised teaching and learning (Kansanen, 2003a, p. 229) (©2007, Thomas Hansson . Used with permission)

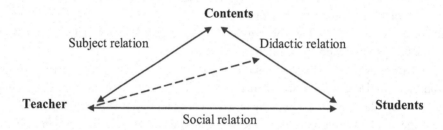

in order to investigate levels of systemic control, a prerequisite for dialogue, Kaptelinin and Cole (2004) highlight socio-cultural construction of the world. They interpret GAT as a way of understanding the human mind by means of individual subjects/agents (*Self*) exploring a world of virtual *and* physical objects/artefacts (*Other*) together. Even more important, Engeström's (1987) expansion of the original model of mediation in Figure 2 has enabled the study of socio-cultural activity systems through the inclusion of holistic contextual variables like Division of Labour, Rules and Regulations plus The Flock.

Interactive, praxis-oriented field study approaches to research and development in activity systems emphasise learning processes based on physically situated people who share identical time and place. Formal learning contexts like traditional schooling explore how people register, perceive of, reflect over and/or act on communicative and/or behavioural influencing, response, processing, and regulation. But in relating research to learning theory, we need to specify the researched subjects and the research objective which is to plan and implement a Web- based design for self-controlled learning. This specification contains inclusion of situated actors and relations.

Bildung, Bildsamkeit, and *Dannelse* approaches to education focus on de-contextualised teacher relations to contents, students, and learning. Such research explores the functioning of *professional* teacher-subject relations and *social* teacher-student relations. However, and in order to be able to develop the Didactic triangle, research (Figure 2) needs to focus on the teachers' ability to act on *the students' didactic relation* to some taught contents, be it learning objects or schoolbook chapters.

Still, the didactic model in Figure 2 fails to account for the difference between situated and holistic contexts. Therefore, we might admit to an ethical dilemma accompanied by a political mission in educational research. The communicating individuals of a social system seek to establish a relation with a receiving end—an interlocutor. But in vogue messy (Mellor, 2001) methods, discourses, and typologies do away with the impact of Didactic relations in the systemic design of situated teaching, studying and learning practices. Especially if the guiding rule is transfer of knowledge, there is a point in choosing a critical and participatory (= holistic) approach to learning, for example in Web-based courses. A positive implication for digital information technologies in this categorization is, however, usually that of a system for conversations, that is, e-mail, Web logs, chat, and conferences. It is essential that the teacher embodies a professional ethics in dealing with student groups defined as teaching and learning systems.

Dynamic-Dialogical Systems

As demonstrated in Figure 1 and 2 the didactical triangles are unable to account for the way we perceive differently of biological-psychological subjects and automat-animals. So it is time we introduced yet another categorization of systems theory. The researcher's spotlight on human relations appeared as a consequence of manipulation, propaganda, and atrocities during the Great War. Russell (1952) identifies social units, arguing that man is defined by actions within and between social systems. There are challenges of Man over Nature, Man over Man, plus Man over *Self*. The contemporary discourse covers all of these but in this chapter focus is on Man over Man relations. Buber (1988, p. 67) complements Russell nicely, suggesting an I-It /I-Thou account of internal double relations within *Self*, portraying how *I* wish to appear to *Thou* (or Thou wish to appear to I); *I* really appear to *Thou* or (Thou really appear to

I); *I* reflectively appear to *I* or (Thou reflectively appear to Thou).

In order to consider the ethical aspects of a systemic design for improved human behaviour, Hanh (2000, p. 172), introduces the term interbeing for describing a fundamental moral reality of life where "things do not exist separately and outside each other." Thus, a third generation systems theory, according to Buber (1988, p. 50), contains a twofold principle of human life for identifying in *Self* another human being by acknowledging a universal primal setting at a distance that enables for the establishing of an independent opposite; and for contact-making between *Self* and *Other*. Thus we acknowledge the necessity of entering a personal relation and make somebody present by imagining the *Other's* reality and his/her future potential.

The dynamic-dialogical approach reflects the mentioned *Bildung* tradition as it covers a relational understanding of the inter-human dimension of social systems. This approach lies at the heart of Buber's (1988, p. 61) programmatic statement of the functioning of human relationships: "the inmost growth of the self is [...] accomplished in the relation between one and the other, between men, that is pre-eminently in the mutuality of the making present, in the making present of another self and in the knowledge that one is made present in his own self by the other." Defined like this, a philosophical anthropology contains mutual acceptance, affirmation, and confirmation of perceptions and people equally. However, a *global ethics* defined by a philosophical anthropology is usually associated with systems of qualified adult interlocutors rather than school children.

Buber's original concept, inter-human (*Zwischenmenschliche*) identifies a narrowly defined scope of relations signifying the space between *I-Thou* and *I-It*. The former *I-Thou* relations, (Buber, 1988, p. 50) are future oriented mutual relations made up of acceptance, confirming speech, genuine meetings, and living processes. The latter *I-It* relations are one sided individual connections with the past, containing experiential and reflective access to knowledge. As a result, Buber's philosophy of knowledge supplies the underpinnings for understanding socially constructed meaning.

The impact of Buber's relation building theory is substantial. He argues that the world resides in man as an imagination, the same way as man lives in the physical world. But it would be a mistake to assume that the world is *in* man or that man is *in* the world. *I* and *It* are mutually and holistically encapsulated in each other. Also, there is no *I* by itself, but an *I* which belongs to the *I-Thou* relation and (the same) *I* that belongs to an *I-It* relation. In associating this line of I/man-It/machine thinking with digital information technologies, Buber (1988, p. 56) says: "Man has a great desire to enter into a personal relation with things and to imprint on them his relation to them. To use them, even to possess them, is not enough, they must become his in another way, by imparting to them in the picture-sign his relation to them." This quote is a description of how young people assess the motivational quality of, for example, computer games, Web sites or chat rooms.

Inter-human exchanges function optimally when people meet physically or when they orally, technically, or in writing mediate their thoughts/intentions. Web-based mediation by technical tools or symbolic communication through written text enables the interlocutors to enter interbeing relations with what is unique and important in *Other* and in the symbol-manipulative text medium or the personality enhancing graphical context. The assumption is that the positive effect of mediation on a virtual LMS platform helps integrate *I-Thou* and *I-It* relations. Man-man/man-machine mediation defined as instrumental psychological agency combined with available technology, didactics, instruction, support and so forth is fulfilled in/by/through the software. Unfortunately, instrumental mediation is often conceptualised as Vygotskian (1978) process of first perception and then internalisation within *I-Self*. But there is also

an externalisation process going on with *Thou-Other* identified by the interlocutors' positioning within an autonomous activity system. *Internal mediation,* here defined as appropriation, operates through conventional signs, letters or symbols. Engeström (1987) delineates a process of *external mediation,* or agency, operating through cybernetic (expansive and balance seeking) feedback loops with the environment and between people committed to social construction of meaning. This process equals the strengthening of *I-Self* and *Thou-Other* relations with/between systemically organised interlocutors.

As to the moral side of social interaction, Buber (1988, p. 49) says the only way to expose the ethical principle of becoming human runs through dialogue with the purpose "to contrast its (*the Subject's*, author's comment) reading with that of other beings." One would like to add so as to obtain the personally, privately and collectively unique. Buber's statement indicates the complexity of relations between *I, Thou* and the mediating tool, *It*. Some relations are counterproductive to learning. The reason is that relations that make a difference are ethically valid for the formation of activity, awareness, and personality.

By separating dialogism from education by instrumental agency, modern LMS software is designed as an integrating tool between internally produced sign meanings and socially influenced learning loops. But any exploration of a social system for developing an integrative tool needs to define a systems theory operating between the interlocutors' black box cognitions and their relation building communications. If properly introduced, controlled, and administered the software and the results of research enable the interlocutors to adjust their personified cognitions to input which influences a trajectory of human being and becoming. The implication for digital information technologies in this categorization is usually that of a *system for consultation*, that is, interactive knowledge systems or artificial intelligence.

Value-Focused Systems

Kansanen (2003b, p. 9-10), defines educational research as management of a bounded, non-holistic, and de-contextualised system, justifying his claim by pointing to the interrelatedness between a conventional understanding that education resembles human life and the undisputable fact that human life is moral. If we define educational research as informed by systems thinking, issues like integrity, honesty, empathy, and so forth, are bound to surface, especially so when academic theory meets professional practice. An applied ethics for dealing with learners as well as for conducting research poses a challenge, typically so in politically infected field studies like action research or participative inquiry. On the moral framing of pedagogical research, Howe and Moses (1999, p. 32-33) say "value laden descriptions and ends are always pertinent and always intertwined. [...] the researcher has no way to avoid moral and political commitments by placing ethics and politics in one compartment and scientific merit in another." The teachers' job of teaching factual pieces of information and normative democratic values equally involves a specific ability to combine descriptive schoolbook is-facts with moral should-values. Also, their professional planning, organising, instructing, supporting, managing, communicating, and evaluating competence is high but their status is comparatively low.

As we have seen value judgements are inextricably interconnected with systems theory and systemic practices. Therefore, values, technology, and communication form a systemic whole. The human ability to communicate is justified as an end in itself. Adhering to an is-factual approach to values and techniques, Dewey (1939) argues that value convictions persist only if attached to conceivable techniques for their manifestation, thus implying that intentions must be acted out as actionable knowledge rather than spoken as textual knowledge. Habermas' (1971) categorical imperative is an illustration of an unconditional requirement for human relation building through communications and textual knowledge. By following a should-normative approach to exploration of the relation between truth and values, he says that communicative competence is an indicator of levels of individual moral development. So is the individual communicator's ability to deal with the technology and other people. As suggested by these references, an individual *idealist ethics* is usually associated with morally influenced—influencing social systems.

People's values change as technologies develop. Something also remains the same, the fact that values are valuable only to the extent that they satisfy human needs. As to the communication process, Habermas (1971) further distinguishes between non-strategic and strategically controlled forms of interaction. As could be expected, the former are oriented towards honesty, openness, and truth. The latter are oriented towards lying, cheating, and deceiving. However, and more significant for understanding the purpose, subjects and setting of social systems, Habermas identifies non-strategic communication in an attempt to bring about a shared understanding of democracy, action oriented, reflective, or intercultural competence. In the good cases of digital information technology, the virtual context help the interlocutors agree that their communication is intelligible, the contents is true, the texts are adjusted to the context and the writer contributes to a positive group dynamics. Habermas' theory and value focused systems theory (VST) together, apply for Internet exchanges where administrative instructions stress the logic of discussion and social coordination at a level of descriptive and normative dialogue.

Modern system theory emphasises ontological and methodological aspects of research. So far, the battle between problem solving and system thinking has concentrated on the choice of technological or methodological means. But by being value focused, the technical and methodological rationalities become outdated. It would be naïve to argue (Hall & Fagen, 1956) that a system is merely a set of objects with relationships between them and between their attributes. After all, there is an intentional aspect of human behaviour to consider.

To the effect of rectifying the presumption that anything could be labelled *system*, Churchman (1968, p. 231-232) proposes compulsory rules for researching human systems. First there is the problem of completeness and closure of a system. In order to cope with these dimensions, the researcher must know how to observe and understand the world through the eyes of another person. Third, systems research is an ongoing inquiry and hence every investigator is an amateur, at least at the beginning of a study. Here Churchman outlines the criteria for some delimiting wilful options. Churchman argues that it is a common mistake to consider all things to be ontologically equal, be the researched objects inert, living, conscious, or rational subjects. The next illusion harbours the idea that the researcher fails to see that s/he is part and parcel of the studied system. Reason (1994, p. 13) says "Phenomena as wholes can never be fully known for the very reason that we are part of them." The third illusion springs from the fact that many systems are too complex and complicated to allow deconstruction. Flood (1999, p. 252) says "the human mind is not able to know the whole." But also, if there were a given blueprint of all conceivable (natural) systems, researchers' choice of observations would matter very little. The final illusion emerges from the fact that observations are inextricably dependent on the observer's value system. Wilbur (1998, p. 67) comments on the cue, saying: "Nowhere in this systems theory [*the scientific worldview*, comment by this author] can one find anything resembling value, moral, wisdom or compassion." This moral problem poses a threat to any kind of research into systems theory.

The concept of 'holism' is related to the concept of 'context.' Holism defines how the parts of a system relate to the overall quality of a comprehensive aggregate, a context. Holism and context define a synthesis, a conglomerate or a unit of analysis. In short, the whole is more than the sum of the parts (Gestalt). The whole is more than the whole in an organizationally dynamic context where the whole influences the parts that will eventually overturn the whole. But the whole is also less than the sum of the parts in phenomena where the whole loses some critical properties under the constraints of the organization of the whole. Modern people are usually ignorant of the totality of society, especially so if we are ignorant of our own objectives, aspirations, and dreams.

The concept of 'interbeing' leads to a way of acknowledging a fundamental reality of life where things are joined together within each other. Interconnectedness, interdependence, and inter-relatedness make up a comprehensive semantic field centring on the conception of a life world understood as a seamless whole. Low (2002, p. 59) says "it might be said that mind is the inside of matter and matter is the outside of mind." From an organizational perspective, closed and open systems reflect interbeing activities, predominantly with their members and the environment. Social systems theory links together the shifting coalitions of participants who are contingently dependent on continuing exchanges with the environments in which they operate. But seen from an ontological perspective, man has moved away from being fully connected to nature into a reductive kind of awareness based on Information Society characteristics like fragmentation, abstraction, and separation. Interbeing removes the deception in people of being individually alienated and separate. Thus one can begin to possess a sense of commonality, an essential attribute for the systems approach in digital information technology environments.

As a remedy to the illusion of contextual completeness and closure or *holism*, systems theory demonstrates why human beings are deceived by their view of the world, by their knowledge base, by their perceptions of activity systems, or by their information processing capacity. A word of wisdom suggests that to heal means making an injured body into a healthy whole. It seems as if a similar phenomenon applies for the human mind because people can only understand the world by becoming a part of it.

The motivation for elaborating systems theory is usually driven by an intention to understand how people move from fragmented partial thinking towards a cross-disciplinary understanding of themselves, their behaviour and their becoming. The implication for digital information technologies lies in a HRM system for *promotion of human capital*, that is, self control, freedom, initiative, and creativity in a personalized Blog or an interactive homepage.

Operationally Constructive Systems

The implication for digital information technologies contains a socio-psychological system for understandig Self by verbal interaction with Other. Neither of values, morals nor ethics, however, is associated with operationally constructive systems. The reason is that communication forms a different dimension as compared to the pre-set (systems inherent) functions of the categorisations in this chapter. Although it is a simplistic idea to assume that systems exist as real systems in a real world, Luhmann (1995) suggests that due to an increasing complexity of information, man must learn to understand the world by naïve thinking. Luhmann's (1995, p. 26) theory also implies that (transl. by this author): "Systems [...] constitute and sustain themselves by producing and upholding a difference to the world, and systems deploy those borders for regulation of that same difference. Without a difference to the world there would be no self reference, because difference is the functional condition for self referring operations." Thus conceptualised, individual borderline control mechanisms equal the meaning of how a system, defined in Luhmann's

terms, upholds its communicative functions and operational structure.

Luhmann's (1995) operational constructivism also contains a theory of natural contradictions, suggesting that social systems develop by way of a borderline phenomenon between internal and external operations of human being and becoming. Social communication systems are maintained by the self-generation of characteristics that people continuously (re)create without predefined scripts. Separation between differing systems indicates an emphasis on relations. Focus on relations implies a given contingency between the internal and the external system. Differentiation between the social and psychological systems is maintained in spite of fluent and comprehensive contact, communication, interaction, and dialogue. Contributors to modern situated or virtual communication systems make conscious choices. Thus the individual interlocutor chooses strategy, career and contents for him/herself and for others. It is reasonable to assume that a balanced complementary of internal and external influences makes up for human existence in virtual communication systems.

Furthermore, Luhmann's (1995) contribution to systems thinking lies in an outline of how human systems are closed-autopoietic and open-contingent at the same time. As opposed to biological (cells, organisms) systems, social (communications, society) systems, and psychological (awareness, motivation) systems are interrelated with the world through a structural connection. It enables for psychological and social systems to function as operationally closed entities in relation to surrounding systems. The psychological and social systems are able to register inputs and internally adapt to outside conditions. Thus they protect, maintain, and develop their closed self-referential processes for reproducing the vital elements that ensures continuity of the exchanges.

According to Luhmann's (1995; 2002) outline of social systems, verbal interactions provide an opportunity for research to approach communication defined as input to a shared virtual forum plus time and place dislocated feedback. Verbal data usually covers the interlocutors' selection of information, to some extent their selection of the form of their messages, and to a small extent their selection of understanding. Interpretations of Luhmann's (2002) communication theory have grown and today interactive communication in social systems is defined in socio cultural, economic, political, or educational terms.

FUTURE TRENDS

In order to expand pedagogical technology by means of systems thinking it is necessary to include a philosophical perspective on ethics in social systems. Professions and professional practices are established when relations between operations, actions, and activities become so complex and complicated that without the proper time and energy for theoretical reflection they become dysfunctional. Understanding ICT is a challenge for professional development because the analyst has got to account for the obvious fact that professional pedagogues should be able to separate between reflective theory and action oriented practice. The innate didactic ability in man to define and execute pedagogical acts, participate in pedagogical actions and shared pedagogical activities rests on a shared idea of relations among instrumental technology, natural language, and conscious intentions, all of which depend on how we balance reflection with action.

The background for this contention is that theories about ICT applications emerge the very minute when pedagogy is established in institutes of higher education, initially as an autonomous field of knowledge, eventually as an academic discipline and finally as an institutionalised (Scott, 1995) practice. By misdirected references to systems thinking, claims are made—even today—to establish a pedagogical technology, for example in attempts to justify so called evidence based research. The reason that such attempts are bound to fail is that the systems theoretical concept *pedagogical technology* harbours an implicit criticism against a misguided understanding of ICT-literacy. The concept is mistakenly understood as closed causality in the otherwise fruitful and practically exploitable relations between technology, language, and intentions. Therefore it is necessary to expand the systems theoretical perspective so as to avoid getting trapped in a situation where ICT-literacy equals functional technology.

Redefining the Pedagogical Paradox

Exploration of digital information technologies related to pedagogy form a problematic issue, sometimes even a taboo theme. The complicated nature of the combination between technology and pedagogy causes problems in several practically oriented and theoretically focused contexts, but especially in studies of pedagogical professions. Sadly, the literature rarely touches on professional pedagogy and technology as a shared theme. Exceptions would be the specific contexts and discourses described by for example Hargreaves (1996) and Jarvis (2002). Here pedagogy is separated from—or even better—described as a complementary force to the technology. Bearing in mind that pedagogical work is all about social, psychological, affective and cognitive relations, pedagogues should distance themselves from instrumental applications of the technology, this is clear. But it is equally reasonable that pedagogues should in fact influence the way learners think, feel, and act. Thus, professional pedagogues are bound to apply instrumentality, agency, and causality in order to do their job. Tools, initiative, and management form the essential components in the social systems that the pedagogues control and constitute. If we were to remove technology from didactics, contents, contexts, and discourses, the effect would be that pedagogical initiatives would fail to inform about the ways of the world. But any such removal would also suggest that the teachers' initiatives could change the transferred facts in the very process of offering it to the learners. Consequently, it is a reasonable claim that pedagogy is in fact closely coupled with technology. But still, there lies a pedagogical paradox in the given argumentation as teachers aspire to liberate students by means of disciplining/controlling/informing them about the ways of the world. And so, the question remains: What kind of technology suits descriptions and analyses of pedagogical professionalism, defined by the way that technology is applied in collective teaching and learning environments?

Collective-Social vs. Individual-Psychological Systems

Social and psychological systems exercise a strong impact on pedagogical professionalism. Relations between these systems emerge from an early understanding of the teacher's job as described in the didactic triangle. Figure 2 describes how the teacher establishes relations: subject-wise with the taught contents; socially with the learner; and consciously with the learner's relation to the taught contents. Before going into the characteristics of social and psychological systems, it is necessary to grasp a more comprehensive picture. Causal or technical systems like computer machines build on a linear-mechanistic relation between input, process, and output. Sometimes feedback for verification is included in such trivial but important systems. Some programmed algorithms within the system control the specific operations that enable the computer to produce pre-defined results. The machinelike cause-effect relation forms a one-dimensional operational entity. Therefore it is easy to predict, reproduce and/or repeat computer machine output.

On the other hand, social and psychological systems like people (Luhmann, 2002) differ from causal systems because people operate through a variety of orientations towards a multitude of outputs. People's thematic orientations reproduce

a width of options or differences, as Luhmann would put it. However, human operations are useful because they release output with a capacity for generative, expansive and productive actions in/by Self and Other. Put differently, operations in social and psychological systems are valuable as they (re)produce the complexity of the world.

And so, social and psychological systems operate from historically established pre-dispositions that materialize as continuous orientations, processes, and actions. A multitude of input generates a variety of outputs, effects, decisions, and dispositions. The reason is that the very process of transformation of inputs to outputs in, for example, ICT teaching and learning is non-transparent and hidden from within for the individual Self and from without for the analyst.

Pedagogy, Technology and Competence

A detailed account of mental operations during verbal ICT exchanges is hard to provide. As we have learnt from explorations into pedagogical technology, educators have a problem to deal with learner autonomy as the educators' instrumentality is so closely connected with classical conditioning objectives, methods, and expectations. The educators' professional approach is directed towards non-trivial systems, that is, complex and complicated human beings. But there is always a possibility that learners respond to input in another way than expected. And most of all, the very moment when teaching and learning is delivered offers a mix of influences emerging primarily from the social and the psychological system. This mix offers a special characterisation of teaching and learning as it promotes a double systemic reference. On the one hand the teacher establishes an open social-communicative relation with the learner. On the other hand both the teacher and the learner host their own communication systems. By their inherent qualities of self-organising, self-reference, and autopoietic influences the interlocutors' internal systems are closed for public scrutiny. They are also closed for the individual interlocutor by lack of transparency during reflection as well as during the actual exchanges.

Social and psychological systems produce infinities of complexity/differences. During operational phases of social-communicative exchanges a tripartite selection between information (data), messages (contents) and understanding (intention) is activated. Put differently, systemic operations of the human brain organises language input, that is, selections, into the tripartite data-contents-intention categories for ongoing processing. As a consequence of the differing selections, 100% consensual interpretation between teachers and learners of acts, utterances, signs and symbols becomes impossible. A communicative selection or a professional choice by the teacher in one system, focusing on for example, message-contents, implies that the learner makes an identical interpretation. Also, interpretations happen inside closed systems. Therefore Web-based system administrators are unable to control the flow of information, the delivery of messages or the meaning making of people.

Implications of the Technology

We have established that a system theoretical understanding of professional-pedagogical technologies allows research to define the social and psychological systems as a "paradox information and communications technology." But there are kinds and levels of systems thinking. An example clarifies the pedagogical paradox by means of relations between social and psychological systems. On the one hand professional pedagogues operate in a void of technological acknowledgement, and on the other hand they offer an actionable technological orientation. These circumstances materialize differently if we label pedagogical technology a quasi-technology by which educators act as if they knew although we are aware of

their impotence to prove so. Normative (what are we?), strategic (what do we do?), and operational (how do we do it?) influences control the actual selections that people make. Table 1 also suggests some key elements including actor, element, input, and output for understanding communication.

Table 1 suggests that because of predominant selections, structures, processes, and qualities, human communications determine the outcomes of an autonomous system for teaching and learning. However, this self-sufficient system is related to the world by a double contingency rather than by a single attachment between for example a main system for schooling and subsystem for learning. An implication of the double contingency of social and psychological communication systems is that the interlocutors always seem to have an option to choose responses and interpretations. The interlocutors are aware of their power to influence the Other by appropriating/imprinting personal selections of their verbal output before externalising it. Logical differences or natural contradictions (Engeström, 1987) rather than consensus (Habermas, 1971) between their selections provide the necessary impetus to keep the communication—schooling and learning—system going.

An example proves the point. The teacher knows that as a professional he could respond differently in a certain situation if he wanted to. His interlocutor, the learner, knows that the teacher knows that he, as a learner, could provide a different output too. So both interlocutors know that both of them could respond differently. The example illustrates the double contingency between representatives consciously operating in/on two significant socio-psychological systems.

Research needs to cover systemic influences of pedagogy, technology and dialogism on human interaction. It needs to do so in order to address the effect of time and place dislocated written interactions on the Internet. This need must be satisfied because interlocutors learn by practicing and experiencing mediated dialogism (Hansson,

Table 1. Conceptual structure (adapted from Kaplan & Norton 1996) (©2007, Thomas Hansson . Used with permission)

	Normative	**Strategic**	**Operational**
Actor	Teacher	Politician	Student
Element	Identity	Competence	Activity
Input	Values	Culture	Community
Output	Cultural cohesion	Problem solving	Responsiveness

2004). Thus they get a feel for the resources, opportunities, obstacles and threats in interactive social systems, be they Web-based or situated.

CONCLUSION

Analysis of the applicability of systems theory to digital information technologies suggests that the *strength* of a functioning application lies in providing the interlocutors with the proper inspiration to create cohesion among disparate facts. Systems theory offers a forum for informed decision making and negotiated problem solving, basically about how to conduct verbal interaction. Systems theory also increases the understanding of structural power relationships between sub systems. Development of a didactics for collaborative exploration of national value systems requires management of technical, social, psychological, and educational influences.

The suggested approach to systems theory demonstrates how control, instruction, and technology contribute to interaction, relation building, and learning. By practicing systems theory and modern technology, people become pro active learners, deliberately constructing and applying new knowledge. By deploying systems theory to teaching and learning, assignments, tasks and exercises are developed for analysis and for new practices. However, educational reformers must learn to analyze the flow of exchanges, information and ethics in Web-based systems. Interrelationships among the parts of a system have to be recognized or innovative designs in virtual networks will fail. Educators need to assume new roles and master virtually mediated negotiation, planning, communicating and decision making skills. Systems thinking about Web-based interactions requires regular and widespread evaluation, and feedback so as to ensure progress in viable social systems.

REFERENCES

Bakhtin, M. M. (1993). Toward a Philosophy of the Act. V. Liapunov & M. Holquist (Eds.). Austin TX: University of Texas Press.

Banathy, B. (1996). *Designing Social Systems in a Changing World*. New York: Plenum.

Berry, T. (1988). *The Dream of the Earth*. San Francisco. CA: Sierra Club.

von Bertalanffy, L. (1969). General systems theory—A critical review. In W. Buckley (Ed.), *Modern Systems Research for the Behavioural Scientist* (pp. 11-30). Chicago: Aldine Publishing Company.

Berger, P.L., & Luckman, T. (1967). *The Social Construction of Reality*. New York: Doubleday.

Boulding, K. (1956). General systems theory: the skeleton of science. *Management Science,* 2(3), 197-208.

Bruner, J. (1999). Postscript: Some reflections on education research. E.C. Lagerman & L.S. Shulman (Eds.), *Issues in Education Research* (pp.371-398). San Franscisco: Jossey-Bass Publishers.

Buber, M. (1988). *The knowledge of man. Selected essays*. Atlantic Highlands: Humanities Press International Inc.

Checkland, P. (1971). A systems map of the universe. *Journal of Systems Engineering*, 12, 107-114.

Checkland, P. (1981). *Systems thinking. Systems practice*. New York: Wiley.

Churchman, C.W. (1968). *The systems approach*. New York: Dell Publishing Co.

Comenius, J. A. (1999). *Didactica magna*. T. Kroksmark (Ed). Lund: Studentlitteratur.

Dewey, J. (1939). *Theory of valuation*. Chicago: Chicago University Press.

Dictionary .com. (2007). Retrieved on July 20, 2007, from http://www.dictionary.reference.com/browse/system

Engeström, Y. (1987). *Learning by expanding. An activity theoretical approach to developmental research*. Helsinki: Orienta-Konsultit.

Flood, R. (1999). Knowing the unknowable. *Systemic Practice and Action Research*, 12(3), 247-256.

Gergen, K. (2006). Narrative, moral identity and historical consciousness: A social constructionist approach. Retrieved on October 2, 2006, from http://www.swarthmore.edu/SocSci/kgergen1/web/page.phtml?id=manu3

Geyer, F., & van der Zouwen, J. (1991). Cybernetics and social science: Theories and research in sociocybernetics. *Kybernetes*, 20(6), 81-92.

Habermas, J. (1971). *Toward a rational society*. London: Heineman.

Hall, A., & Fagen, R. (1956). *Yearbook of the Society for the Advancement of Genera Systems Theory*, Vol. General Systems I, Ch. Definition of System. Ann Arbor.

Hanh, T.N. (2000). *The path of emancipation: Talks from the 21-day mindfulness retreat*. Berkeley: Parallax Press.

Hansson, T. (2004). Qualitative research on 'mediated dialogism' among nordic project educators. *The Qualitative Report*, 9(2), 280-300.

Herrscher, E. (2006). What is the systems approach good for? *Systemic Practice and Action Research*. 19. 409-413.

Howe, K.R., & Moses, M.S. (1999). Ethics in educational research. A. Iran-Nejad & P.D. Pearson (Eds.). *Review of Research in Education*, 24, 21-59. Washington: AERA.

Hutchinson, G.E. (1948). Circular causal systems in ecology. *Academic Science*, 50, 221-246.

Hwang, A.S. (2000). Toward fostering systems learning in organizational contexts. *Systemic Practice and Action Research*, 13(3), 329-343.

Kaplan, R., & Norton, D. (1996). *The balanced Scorecard: Translating strategy into action*. Boston: Harvard Business School Press.

Kansanen, P. (2003a). Studying—the realistic bridge between instruction and learning. An attempt to a conceptual whole of the teaching-studying-learning process. *Educational Studies*, 29(2/3), 222-232.

Kansanen, P. (2003b). Pedagogical ethics in educational research. *Educational Research and Evaluation*, 9(1), 9-25.

Kaptelinin, V., & Cole, M. (2004). *Individual and collective activities in educational computer game playing*. Retrieved on (10-02-2005) from http://www.129.171.53.1/blantonw/5dClhse/publications/tech/Kaptelinin-Cole.html

Katz, D., & Kahn, R. (1966). *The social psychology of organizations.* New York: Wiley.

Kim, D., & Senge, P. (1994). Putting systems thinking into practice. *System Dynamics Review,* 10(2), 277-290.

Leontev, A. N. (1978). *Activity, consciousness and personality.* Englewood Cliffs. New Jersey: Prentice-Hall.

Lewin, K. (1947). Frontiers in group dynamics. *Human Relations* ,1, 147-153.

Lewin, K. (1969). Feedback problems of social diagnosis and action. In W. Buckley (Ed.), *Modern systems research for the behavioural scientist* (pp. 441-444).Chicago: Aldine Publishing Company.

Low, A. (2002). *Creating consciousness: A study of consciousness, creativity, evolution and violence.* Scb Distributors.

Luhmann, N. (1995). *Social systems.* Stanford, California: Stanford University Press.

Luhmann, N. (2002). *Das Erziehungssystem der Gesellschaft.* Frankfurt a.M.: Suhrkamp Verlag.

Maruyama, M. (1963). The second cybernetics: deviation amplifying mutual casual processes. *American Scientist,* 51, 164-179.

Maturana, H., & Varela, F. (1980). *Autopoiesis and cognition: The realization of the living.* D. Reidel.

Mellor, N. (2001). Messy method: The unfolding story. *Educational Action Research,* 9(3), 465-484.

Rapoport, A. (1969). Foreword. W. Buckley (Ed.). *Modern systems research for the behavioural scientist.* Chicago: Aldine Publishing Company, xiii-xxii.

Reason, P. (1994). *Participation in human inquiry.* London: Sage Publications.

Rittel, H., & Weber, M. (1973). Dilemmas in the general theory of planning. *Policy Science,* 4, 155-169.

Rohde, K. (2006) *Nonequilibrium ecology.* Cambridge: Cambridge University Press.

Rowland, G. (2004). The concept of sustainability in the evolutionary guidance of an educational institution. *Systemic Practice and Action Research,* 17(4), 285-296.

Russell, B. (1952). *Menneskeheden paa skillevejen.* (New Hopes in a Changing World) København: Berlingske forlag.

Scott, R. (1995). *Institutions and organizations.* London: Sage Publications.

Stacey, R. (1992). *Managing the unknowable.* San Francisco: Jossey-Bass.

Steffe, L., & Gale, J. (Eds.), (1995). *Constructivism in education.* Hillsdale: Lawrence Erlbaum Publishers.

Turner, S. (1991). Social constructionism and social theory. *Sociological Theory,* 9(1), 22-33.

Webster's Online Dictionary. (2007). Retrieved on July 20, 2007, from http://www.websters-online-dictionary.org/definition/system

Wiener, N. (1948). *Cybernetics. Or control and communication in the animal and machine.* Cambridge: MIT Press.

Wiener, N. (1969). Cybernetics in history. In W. Buckley (Ed.), *Modern Systems Research for the Behavioural Scientist* (pp. 31-36). Chicago: Aldine Publishing Company.

Wilbur, K. (1998). *The marriage of sense and soul.* New York: Random House.

Vygotsky, L. (1978). *Mind in society. The development of higher psychological processes.* M. Cole et al. (Eds.). London: Harvard University Press.

KEY TERMS

Dialogism: All human thoughts are dialogic and everything ever spoken exists as a response to the things that have been said before and will be said in the future. All the ideas and relations that language contains and communicates are dynamic, relational, and engaged in a process of endless reconstructions of the world.

Interbeing: An element of the interhuman, a holistic principle of interconnectedness, interdependence and interrelatedness suggesting that everything is in everything else.

Learning Object: It is a mediating tool in learning activities, more specifically a digital or non-digital entity used for learning, education, or training.

Mediation: Human knowledge is embedded in artefacts which produce and transform human experience. It is a process in which tools are understood as objects or stimuli that bring about or enhance reflection, discussion or learning activities.

Soft System: A concept employed with a methodology for problem solving and management of change processes in complex situations where there are divergent views about the definition of the problem.

Social Cybernetics: An approach to describe how people create, maintain, and change social systems through language and ideas in an approach where knowledge is constructed to achieve human purposes.

Systems Thinking: A concept for describing a way of helping people view systems from a wide perspective, seeing overall structures, patterns and cycles in subsystems, rather than seeing only specific events in the main system.

Chapter XXV
Human Factors and Innovation with Mobile Devices

Agnes Kukulska-Hulme
The Open University, UK

ABSTRACT

Advancements in technology are a significant driving force in educational innovation, but a strong focus on technology means that human aspects and implications may not be given the attention they deserve. This chapter examines usability issues surrounding the use of mobile devices in learning. A key aim is to empower educators and learners to take control of personal devices and realise their potential in relation to teaching and learning. The background section reviews the development of usability studies and explores why mobile device usability presents specific new challenges. The impact of changing requirements in education, and new visions for ways of thinking and competences that learners should be acquiring, are also examined. Finally, the chapter provides a set of concepts that can inform conversations between educators and learners, mobile system engineers, developers, support staff, and others.

INTRODUCTION

Every new wave of technological innovation poses fresh challenges with regard to its compatibility with the people who are to make use of it and with existing social and cultural practices. The widespread, rising ownership of mobile devices is one key development that educators need to examine and reflect on as it starts to make its mark in all types of teaching and learning activity, both formal and informal. Advancements in technology are acknowledged as being a significant driving force in educational innovation and new technologies are often explored as a way to enhance teaching and learning, but a strong focus on technology inevitably means that human aspects and implications are often relegated to second place. It is only by raising levels of understanding and awareness of human factors that we can work towards achieving some kind of balance.

Mobile learning—using portable devices such as cell phones, personal digital assistants, personal media players, and ultra-portable PCs—is rapidly becoming a popular way of accessing and producing digital information on the move, and communicating and collaborating with others. The majority of mobile learning activity takes place on devices that were not designed with educational applications in mind, however, and furthermore, an assumption is frequently made that users know their personal device so well that it is not necessary to give them much support or training. This may contrast with experience of support and development that both instructors and learners receive in connection with the use of their desktop computer. As we start to experience 'the third wave of computing' (Dix et al., 2004, p. 184), in which devices far outnumber people, the device will become less personal again, although user interactions and content could become more personal.

Despite decades of usability research, problems with understanding the user interface and with performing essential tasks are still often reported by users, both on desktop and mobile systems. Arguably, the situation may be even getting worse, as open source software is not always tested for usability, and ever-changing interfaces put constant demands on users, who perceive that they have less and less time to keep up with the latest developments. What is more, in mobile scenarios users may have difficulties getting access to specialist technical support or to people with similar devices who can offer friendly help. They may also be relying on continuous online access to learning networks and resources, which in reality can be difficult to achieve. Therefore, new factors come into play that must be identified and analysed.

AIMS AND SCOPE

This chapter reflects critically on progress in usability and on recent developments in human-computer interaction, with particular reference to findings from studies of mobile learning. Usability cannot be considered in a vacuum: requirements specific to education have to be taken into account, but bearing in mind that educational goals and methods are constantly being redefined (e.g. Beetham & Sharpe, 2007; Laurillard, 2002). Accessibility and personalisation, which address the match between a user's individual (possibly special) needs and the device they are using, are also important. User skills and competences must be taken onto account. Increasingly, there is a need to paint a more detailed picture of the circumstances in which electronic tools are used, and the factors impacting on the quality of the experience for the human user.

The aims of this chapter are to present the issues in such a way as to empower educators and learners to take control of personal devices and to realise their potential in relation to teaching and learning, and second, to provide a set of concepts that can inform conversations with mobile system engineers, developers, and support staff. Over time, a holistic understanding of user experience can emerge from these conversations. An initial set of factors impacting on the usability of mobile devices in education has been documented by Kukulska-Hulme (2006). Placing human factors at the centre, the longer term ambition is to develop a set of concepts with reference to user skills and competences, giving greater clarity to discussions around the human needs of mobile technology users in activities connected to education, frequently undertaken whilst travelling and in other situations involving mobility.

BACKGROUND: USABILITY AND MOBILE DEVICES

Although much of the work in usability focuses on the evaluation of a user interface, over a decade ago Nielsen (1993) explained usability in terms of a system's overall acceptability, which included social aspects and practical aspects (such as reliability, cost, compatibility, and usefulness). Preece, Rogers, and Sharp (2002) have subsequently done a great deal to promote the concept of 'user experience,' with its focus on enhancing and extending the way people work, communicate, and interact. In recent years there has been a growing interest in motivational and affective aspects; for example, Porter et al. (2005) emphasise emotional and 'pleasure' needs, while Dix et al. (2004, p. 156) have stressed that "...it is not sufficient that people can use a system, they must *want* to use it." Usability research is also becoming more attuned to the requirements of different subjects or disciplines; Kukulska-Hulme and Shield's work (2004) on 'pedagogical usability' has included a focus on the requirements of different academic disciplines, as exemplified by the discipline of language learning. In Web sites that support language learning, usability might depend on whether the site uses the first or target language and on its ability to support multimodal and intercultural communication. The ways in which language experts conceptualise user interfaces may also be specific to the culture and sub-cultures of their discipline. These aspects can be hard to quantify and measure, but it does not mean that they are less important.

Usability continues to be reinterpreted in the light of new understandings and evolving contexts of technology use. Despite these advancements, however, Cooper (2004) and Nielsen (2005) have continued to point out the usability shortcomings of current computer software and technology. Schneiderman (2002, p. 26) identified users' attitudes as an important issue: "There is no magic bullet that will bring widespread use of low-cost devices that are easy to learn, rapid in performing common tasks, and low in error rates," predicting that change would only come about through users upgrading their expectations and demanding higher quality. Usability evaluator Baker (2006, p. 11) makes a similar point about user reticence to make demands on device manufacturers: "...the frustration felt by users is not always targeted

towards the device or product... many who have new mobile devices will often blame themselves for not reading the 300-page manual which came with it if they experience a problem." As yet, there is no real evidence of change in user attitudes in this respect. Device manufacturers, having "for years only pursued male wallets" (BBC, 2002, p. 7), have begun taking notice of the different needs and priorities of female customers, but this still largely translates into a focus on the style and fashion aspects of new gadgets—their outward appearance rather than the way they work.

There are many physical and psychological differences between people impacting on their learning and experiences with technology, but it is usage differences that are sometimes overlooked. Usage differences are particularly interesting in relation to mobile devices. As noted by Benyon et al. (2005, p. 33), novice and expert users have very different requirements, and then there are so-called 'discretionary users'—those who are quickly put off using a system if things are difficult to do. Mobile devices require a relatively long term personal commitment, on an ongoing basis, whilst accommodating different types of usage within one device.

The usability of mobile devices has generated its own literature (e.g., Weiss, 2002; Gilbert et al., 2005), which is set to expand over the next few years. The rate at which new devices and models come on the market means that usability is essentially a moving target. Each manufacturer has a different interface, and mobile devices are continually being replaced with new models, even before users have got to know them well. A review and synthesis of usability issues across a range of mobile learning projects (Kukulska-Hulme, 2006) found that the issues reported in the research literature could be summarised under four main headings: Physical attributes of mobile devices (e.g., size, weight, memory, battery life); Content and software applications; Network speed and reliability; The physical environment.

The research showed that the same usability issue can be perceived differently depending on the circumstances in which the technology is being used. In their theoretical work on mobile learning, Sharples et al. (2006, p.19) have remarked that "...the relative lack of usability in the technological domain inhibits developments in the semiotic." There is little evidence that usability problems might be fading away, in spite of some wishful thinking about increasingly intuitive interfaces and more sophisticated users.

There is another intriguing aspect of mobile technologies that makes it difficult to work on usability in relation to user requirements. Mobile devices are often used in real-world situations where unpredictable things can happen; people can respond constructively to such events (Suchman, 1987), but capturing what happened and feeding it back into technology designs is an enormous challenge. The highly personal and portable nature of mobile devices is also encouraging exploratory uses, and it is hard to predict what users will do. Those involved in designing mobile devices have been noticing that "new solutions are utilized in ways that never even occurred to their designers" (Keinonen, 2003, p. 2). Uses may also become more elaborate over time: Gilbert et al. (2005, p.207) have drawn attention to the period after initial use of a mobile service, "during which the scope of use expands to fulfil emergent needs." In their summary of key messages about learning with handheld technologies, Faux et al. (2006) point out that personal ownership of a device must go hand in hand with a more autonomous learner role, which means learners being encouraged to make choices about when and how they use their device to support learning.

There are many ways of acquiring a mobile device; it may be a personal purchase, a gift, a loan. Its subsequent use may evolve according to the duration of ownership, whether the device was wanted, emergent wants or needs. Users may never discover all the features of their device be-fore moving on to another one. How people get to know the features and possibilities of their mobile device over time has not been well researched to date, but social networks are sure to play a role, as well as the extent to which mobile services and content are 'pushed' in their direction by various providers. It has been observed that younger users may be quicker to master a new device; for example, based on their work with schoolchildren, Faux et al. (2006, p. 5) advise that "learners will develop a facility with the devices quite quickly, often led by class champions," but at the same time they add that learners should be encouraged to share their new knowledge with others. The next section examines requirements that are of particular concern to educators and learners engaged in mobile learning.

REQUIREMENTS IN EDUCATION

User-centred system design and evaluation have traditionally been driven by the concept of a 'task', task analysis being the process of analyzing the way people perform their jobs (Dix et al., 2004, p. 511). If learning were conceived of as performing a job, it might be straightforward to apply task analysis, but in reality this only works in quite circumscribed activities where everything about a learning task is very clearly defined and the focus is on observable behaviour. Rekkedal (2002) has suggested that mobile learners in distance education need to be able to perform tasks such as studying the course materials, making notes, writing assignments, accessing a forum, sending and receiving e-mail, and communicating with a tutor. These simple labels conceal great complexity in how materials might be studied and how communication might actually take place. Ryan and Finn (2005) have also commented on the difficulty of task analysis in relation to mobile learning 'in the field,' in the course of their attempts to define the generic requirements of users who typically operate out in the field, that is, geologists, archaeologists, journalists, technicians, police. There are multiple challenges are: representing what a learning task consists of; observing the task when it happens in faraway or variable locations; capturing how it is played out in practice.

Educational activity can sometimes be better understood by system designers when it is seen as an example of a 'rich context' involving different people, the spaces they meet in and the physical artefacts they use (Dix et al., 2004, p. 639-49). Current reference works on interactive system design certainly emphasize the importance of context, defined in terms of the "human, physical, organizational, historical and social environment in which a technology is used" (Benyon et al., 2005, p. 163), and recommend user participation in capturing requirements.

In relation to mobile learning, lessons from the MOBIlearn project (O'Malley et al., 2003, p.32) suggest observing "the usability requirements of all those involved in the use of the system in any way (learners, teachers, content creators) to assure system acceptability," considering the context of use and that the learner should be able to receive personalised information that is valuable in a given context. Pehkonen and Turunen (2003) have also argued that user-centred design means, not only planning learning goals and actions, but also specifying different contexts of use and the requirements of different 'actors', which might include teachers, students and even parents. Luckin et al. (2005) have defined a learning context as an 'ecology of resources' and have shown how technology can link different resource elements within and across learning contexts. Technology nowadays has to support collaboration, co-construction of knowledge, cooperative problem-solving, and distributed cognition (distributed between people and external artefacts or tools). This stretches human imagination in addition to testing the limits of existing tools.

If knowledge acquisition is becoming progressively less important, and ways of creating and synthesizing knowledge are seen as the way forward in education, technology will also need to evolve to support these developments. At Harvard Business School, Gardner (2007) has argued that the 21st century will belong to people who can think in certain ways, and to this end he identified five types of 'mind' that should be cultivated: the disciplined mind; the synthesizing mind; the creating mind; the respectful mind; and the ethical mind. This still assumes mastery of a discipline, that is, a particular profession, vocation or craft, but the selected ways of thinking are partly a reflection of how technology is forcing us to adapt. Disparate pieces of information must be synthesized, new questions must be asked, a respect for other cultures must be shown, and social conscience must drive our thinking on both a local and a global scale.

In a similar vein, Morgan (2007, p. 10) argues that in our changing world, the new economy needs "people who are innovative, flexible, creative, and who have high levels of emotional and social intelligence;" he cites the UK's New Curriculum initiative (2007) which posits that an information-driven curriculum is unlikely to equip young people adequately for adult life in the new century. The New Curriculum proposes five categories of competences that should be developed in young people—competences for learning, citizenship, relating to people, managing situations (time, change, emotions, etc.), and managing information. Although addressing different groups—adults and school students—there is a great deal of overlap between these attempts to map out the thinking and skills required in today's world and for the future. There is also a sense that education is in a state of flux, asking fundamental questions about its own aims and methods. The ways in which new technology is used in teaching and learning both reflects and drives forward these developments.

THE HUMAN BEING AT THE CENTRE OF INNOVATION AND CHANGE

If both technology and education are changing fast, it is not surprising if an individual caught up in these changes will find it hard to make sense of what is happening and what it might mean. It is useful to focus on some of the opportunities and challenges that present themselves to today's learners and how they relate to mobile technologies and their usability.

Mobility

Against a landscape of continual change we can discern some emerging patterns, such as greater learner mobility. This encompasses the sense of being able to spend time studying in another country, as well as the day-to-day mobility associated with new forms of work and evolving lifestyles that may sometimes merge with work. The daily mobility aspects may rely on mobile devices and services, and could be well-supported by them if issues of usability did not get in the way. In his guidelines for designers of handheld devices, Weiss (2002, p. 66) advises:

Whether in the back of a taxi or walking down the street, people are likely to need their handhelds to perform in distracting situations. ...designs must include context and forgiveness. .... Wireless users may be using their leisure time to gather information, but they typically have immediate goals.

Designing for mobile users should therefore begin with some exploration of how their mobility and the changing contexts they find themselves in impact on their thinking and their learning. A daily commute to work on the bus or by car might possibly present an opportunity to engage in mobile learning (Corbeil & Valdes-Corbeil, 2007), but it will probably be different from what can be done throughout the day, on a long train journey or on a plane.

New Thinking

A personal challenge for users of mobile devices is to get to know their device with a view to perhaps channelling their thinking through this device, in response to suggestions that what really matters is the ability to be flexible, innovate, create, synthesize, and develop one's social, ethical, and emotional intelligence. Could it be that mobile devices will help to focus attention on these valued ways of thinking, both on the part of their users and their designers? Knight (2006, p. 203) suggests that the ultimate goal of human-computer interaction (HCI) should be "to promote the benefit of well-being through a value-centred design approach" based on key ethical goals—autonomy, benefiance, non-malefiance, fidelity, and justice. This is in contrast with the functional and 'suprafunctional' (emotion and pleasure) goals of current interface design.

Any new technology can prompt users to question whether it is really helping them to learn and to think, but in reality people may not take the time to reflect on their experience, or even know how to do that. The New Curriculum mentioned earlier, draws attention on the ability to understand how to learn, take account of one's preferred learning style, and to learn to think. This assumes not only guidance on how to do these things but a great deal of personal reflection on progress. Perhaps the next step in the development of mobile applications should be tools that specifically support the development of some of the skills and competences that are being promoted by educationalists. With regard to competences in managing situations and managing information, relevant applications already exist but even those come from a different era and may need to be redesigned for the future.

Informal Learning

An important realisation is that mobile devices are proving themselves to be well suited to support informal learning. Scanlon et al. (2005) have been exploring what possibilities exist for science learners in informal settings, and in projects across many subject domains it is not unusual now to find a stated aim of developing systems or materials for informal learning. Fallahkhair et al. (2005) have developed a system to support informal mobile language learning, while Bradley et al. (2005) report on the development of materials for a mobile local history tour. In other situations, mobile devices are used more spontaneously for informal learning, using the device features and software that are available for general use. Some progress is also being made in understanding innovative practice at the level of the individual empowered by a personal mobile device and social networks that may amplify or modify its use (Kukulska-Hulme & Pettit, 2006; Pettit & Kukulska-Hulme, 2007).

In his book on informal learning, Cross (2007) claims that this type of learning deserves much more attention within organisations, as it can be credited with fuelling innovation and agility. Comparing most formal and informal types of learning across several dimensions including intentionality, timing, location, and so on, he concludes that most informal learning is incidental, unstructured, with unstated outcomes and fuzzy content. It can take place whenever needed and in any location. Although Cross does not say so, the alignment of mobile devices with informal learning is clearly an aim that needs to continue to be explored. To this end, learners themselves have to become more aware of when and how they learn informally, and whether their mobile device can assist them in this process.

KEY CONCEPTS FOR CONVERSATIONS

It has never been easy to communicate about human issues in relation to technology use – technical language typically presents a barrier that non-technical users find hard to overcome (Kukulska-Hulme, 1999). Even today, when familiarity with technology is often assumed, a set of concepts is needed to feed the conversations that educators and learners need to have with each other and with mobile system developers, IT support staff, and others who are immersed in the latest technologies and use them every day. A better understanding of user experience can emerge from these conversations and inform further developments.

In Kukulska-Hulme (2006), factors impacting on the usability of mobile devices in education have been mapped out, on the basis of a review of usability issues that emerged from across a range of mobile learning projects (Figure 1). This mapping can be extended to a set of questions that can be discussed. The key issues relate to six main aspects of mobile learning—the device being used, networks or connectivity, the user, other people, tasks engaged in, and the locations where learning happens. In conversations about desktop systems, the focus would typically be on the personal computer and the user, but in mobile learning there is a far greater need to discuss:

- **Locations of use:** Are they suitable for the type of learning envisaged, will quiet or privacy be available if required, will there be continuity of use across different locations, can location-based context be incorporated into the learning experience?

The questions that might be raised around the other five key aspects will also be different to previous conversations around older technologies. Here are some suggestions for what should be discussed:

- **The user:** How self-motivated is the learner, how familiar with all features of the device, what reward will come from mobile learning, can the device be adapted and personalised to suit specific needs, will it fit with lifestyle?

- **Other people:** Who can support the learner on the go, what spontaneous or pre-planned collaboration can take place, what communities can the learner be part of, what do others interacting with the mobile learner need?

- **Tasks engaged in:** Will there be tasks set by instructors or learner-generated tasks, will speed of network access impact on the task, is the task confined to the mobile device or does it connect with other environments and tools, do interruptions matter?

- **The device being used:** What input devices and other accessories are available, how long will the learner keep the device, is there compatibility or conflict with other tools being used?

- **Networks that might be used:** Are the wireless networks reliable, can learners manage to get connected, are they dependent on connectivity, what are the costs involved?

In addition, there is a cluster of questions to be asked about the less predictable and longer term requirements and outcomes of mobile learning, which can connect with any of the six aspects already mentioned:

- How are planned learning activities enhancing or extending current learning or current practices?

- What new habits and competences are learners expected to develop?

- What new kinds of social networks is mobile learning helping to develop?

- How are uses of a mobile device evolving over time?

- How can unpredictable or emergent needs and uses be captured so that learners, educators, and system designers can learn from this experience?

CONCLUSION

The present chapter is a contribution to the development of a human-centred perspective on the use of mobile technologies in education. We

Figure 1. Factors impacting on the usability of mobile devices in education (©2006, Agnes Kukulska-Hulme. Used with permission)

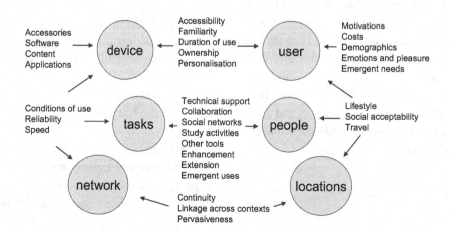

may be moving away from a world in which the use of any new technology was associated with going on formal training courses in to order to become proficient in its use, towards a world where more informal learning will happen among colleagues and friends, often in connection with travel and other forms of everyday mobility. This informal learning needs to be better understood, and its connections with formal learning need to be worked out. Mobile devices can play a role in developing that understanding as well as supporting both formal and informal learning as and when it takes place.

Technology-led developments are a fact of life even in education, but it is important to insist that human factors should be placed at the centre of innovation with mobile devices if their full potential is to be realised. A crucial aspect of this is encouraging and supporting jargon-free conversations around mobile learning, taking known usability issues as a starting point and extending them to take in the less predictable and evolving outcomes that are associated with mobile learning.

REFERENCES

Baker, F. (2006). Mobile technology and usability. nomensa—humanising technology. Retrieved on June 7, 2007, from http://www.nomensa.com/resources/articles/usability-articles/mobile-technology-and-usability.html

BBC (2002). Gadget makers target women. *Sci/Tech news*, 11 January 2002. Retrieved on June 7, 2007, from http://news.bbc.co.uk/1/hi/sci/tech/1754818.stm

Beetham, H., & Sharpe, R. (Eds.), (2007). *Rethinking pedagogy for a digital age: Designing and delivering elLearning*. London: Routledge.

Benyon, D., Turner, P., & Turner, S. (2005). *Design in interactive systems: People, activities, contexts, technologies*. Harlow: Addison-Wesley.

Bradley, C., Haynes, R., & Boyle, T. (2005, October 25-28). Adult multimedia learning with PDAs—the user experience. Paper presented at the Mlearn 2005 Conference, Cape Town.

Cooper, A. (2004). *The inmates are running the asylum: why high-tech products drive us crazy and how to restore the sanity*. Indianapolis: Sams Publishing.

Corbeil, J.R., & Valdes-Corbeil, M.E. (2007). Are you ready for mobile learning? *EDUCAUSE Quarterly*. No.2, 2007. Retrieved on June 7, 2007, from http://www.educause.edu/ir/library/pdf/EQM0726.pdf

Cross, J (2007). *Informal Learning*. San Francisco: Pfeiffer.

Dix, A., Finlay, J., Abowd, G.D., & Beale, R. (2004). *Human computer-interaction*. 3rd edition. Harlow: Prentice-Hall.

Fallahkhair, S., Pemberton, L., & Griffiths, R. (2005). Dual device user interface design for ubiquitous language learning: Mobile phone and interactive television (iTV). *IEEE International Conference on Wireless and Mobile Technology for Education (WMTE)*. Tokushima, Japan.

Faux, F., McFarlane, A., Roche, N., & Facer, K. (2006). *Handhelds: learning with handheld technologies*. Handbook for Futurelab. Retrieved on June 7, 2007, from http://www.futurelab.org.uk/research/handbooks/05_01.htm

Gardner, H. (2007). *Five minds for the future*. Harvard: Harvard Business School Press.

Gilbert, A.L., Sangwan, S., & Han Mei lan, H. (2005). Beyond usability: the OoBE dynamics of mobile data services markets. *Personal and Ubiquitous Computing*, 9 (4), 198-208.

Keinonen, T. (2003). Introduction: mobile distinctions. In: C. Lindholm, T. Keinonen & H. Kiljander (Eds.). *Mobile Usability: how Nokia changed the face of the mobile phone*. New York: McGraw-Hill.

Knight, J. (2006). Ethics and HCI. In: C. Ghaoui (Ed.). *Encyclopedia of human-computer interaction*. Idea Group.

Kukulska-Hulme, A. (1999). *Language and communication: Essential concepts for user interface and documentation design*. New York: Oxford University Press.

Kukulska-Hulme, A. (2006, October 22-25). *Mobile usability in educational contexts: What have we learnt?* Paper presented at the Mlearn 2006 Conference: Mobile Learning—Across Generations and Cultures, Banff, Canada.

Kukulska-Hulme, A., & Pettit, J. (2006, October 22-25). *Practitioners as innovators: emergent practice in personal mobile teaching, learning, work and leisure*. Paper presented at the Mlearn 2006 Conference: Mobile Learning - Across Generations and Cultures, Banff, Canada.

Kukulska-Hulme, A., & Shield, L. (2004, June 22-26). *Usability and Pedagogical Design: Are Language Learning Websites Special?*, Paper presented at the ED-MEDIA'04 - World Conference on Educational Multimedia, Hypermedia and Telecommunications, Lugano, Switzerland. Retrieved on June 7, 2007, from http://www.aace.org/DL/index.cfm?fuseaction=ViewPaper&id=16072

Laurillard, D. (2002). *Rethinking university teaching: A conversational framework for the effective use of learning technologies* (2nd ed.). London and New York: Routledge.

Luckin, R., du Boulay, B., Smith, H., Underwood, J., Fitzpatrick, G., Holmberg, J., Kerawalla, L., et al. (2005). Using mobile technology to create flexible learning contexts. *Journal of Interactive Media in Education*. Special Issue on Portable Learning, A. Jones, A., Kukulska-Hulme, & D. Mwanza) (Eds.).Retrieved on June 7, 2007, from http://www.jime.open.ac.uk/2005/22/

Morgan, J. (2007) The new basics. *Vision—looking at the future of learning*. Issue 4, 2007. Futurelab publication, Bristol. Retrieved on June 7, 2007, from http://www.futurelab.org.uk/resources/publications_reports_articles/vision_magazine

New Curriculum (2007). Opening Minds—curriculum network. Retrieved on June 7, 2007, from http://www.rsa.org.uk/newcurriculum/index.asp

Nielsen, J. (1993). *Usability engineering*. Boston MA: Academic Press.

Nielsen, J. (2005). Top ten web design mistakes of 2005. Jakob Nielsen's Alertbox October 3, 2005. Retrieved on June 7, 2007, from http://www.useit.com/alertbox/designmistakes.html

O'Malley, C., Vavoula, G., Glew, J.P., Taylor, J., Sharples, M., & Lefrere, P. (2003). MOBIlearn WP4—Guidelines for learning/teaching/tutoring in a mobile environment. Retrieved on June 7, 2007, from http://www.mobilearn.org/download/results/guidelines.pdf

Pehkonen, M., & Turunen, H. (2003). *Preliminary guidelines for the design of the mobile learning activities and materials*. Paper presented at the EUROPRIX Scholars Conference, Conference Papers and Presentations. Tampere: European Academy of Digital Media, MindTrek Association. Retrieved on June 7, 2007, from http://www.mindtrek.org/liitetiedostot/materiaalit_editori/75.doc

Pettit, J. & Kukulska-Hulme, A. (2007) Going with the grain: Mobile devices in practice. *Australasian Journal of Educational Technology (AJET)*, 23 (1), pp. 17-33. Retrieved on June 7, 2007, from http://www.ascilite.org.au/ajet/ajet23/ajet23.html

Porter, C.S., Chhibber, S., Porter, J.M., & Healey, L. (2005). RealPeople: making users' pleasure needs accessible to designers. *Accessible Design in the Digital World Conference 2005*. Retrieved on June 7, 2007, from http://www.bcs.org/server.php?show=ConWebDoc.3762

Preece, J., Rogers, Y., & Sharp, H. (2002). *Interaction design: Beyond human-computer interaction.* New York: John Wiley & Sons.

Rekkedal, T. (2002). *M-learning for PDAs: enhancing the flexibility of distance education.* Powerpoint presentation at Ericsson Education, November 2002. Powerpoint presentation. Retrieved on June 7, 2007, from http://learning.ericsson.net/mlearning2/project_one/presentation/torstein1911.ppt

Ryan, P., & Finn, E. (2005). Field-based mlearning: who wants what? In *Proceedings of the IADIS international Conference on Mobile Learning,* 28-30 June 2005, Qawra, Malta.

Scanlon, E., Jones, A., & Waycott, J. (2005). Mobile technologies: prospects for their use in learning in informal science settings. *Journal of Interactive Media in Education,* special issue on Portable Learning: Experiences with Mobile Devices, eds. Ann Jones, Agnes Kukulska-Hulme and Daisy Mwanza, 2005/25. Retrieved on June 7, 2007, from http://jime.open.ac.uk/2005/25/

Sharples, M., Taylor, J., & Vavoula, G. (2006). A Theory of Learning for the Mobile Age. In R. Andrews (Ed.). *The Sage Handbook of Elearning Research* (pp. 221-247)London: Sage. Pre-print retrieved on June 7, 2007, from http://www.lsri.nottingham.ac.uk/msh/Papers/Theory%20of%20Mobile%20Learning.pdf

Schneiderman, B. (2002). *Leonardo's laptop: Human needs and the new computing technologies.* Cambridge, M.A. and London: The MIT Press.

Suchman, L. (1987). *Plans and situated actions.* New York: Cambridge University Press.

Weiss, S. (2002). *Handheld usability.* Chichester: John Wiley & Sons.

KEY TERMS

Accessibility: A term interchangeably used with 'usability' or even 'availability,' but its core meaning is the extent to which a system can be used successfully and comfortably by users with disabilities or special needs.

Human-Computer Interaction: Within computer science and systems design, this area of concern involves the design, implementation and evaluation of interactive systems in the context of the user's task and work.

Informal Learning: Learning that is not organised and structured by an institution. It may take place in environments that already have some connections with learning, that is, museums and art galleries, or anywhere the learner chooses.

Mobile Learning: Learning with personal, portable devices; it enables learners to build knowledge and construct understandings in different contexts, and often changes how people learn and work.

Personal Digital Assistants (PDAs): Small, handheld computers, typically used for time management, simple applications and communication. PDA functionality is increasingly being integrated with mobile phones.

Pervasiveness: The aim of pervasive computing is to create a computing infrastructure that permeates the physical environment so that computers are invisible, that is, chips are embedded in everyday objects.

Usability: A computer system's usability is based on measurements of users' experience with the system, but the focus tends to be specifically on the user interface.

Chapter XXVI
Self–Construction in Computer Mediated Discourse

Irit Kupferberg
Levinsky College of Education, Israel

ABSTRACT

This chapter presents and illustrates the theoretical and methodological frameworks of a discourse-oriented approach to the study of self-construction in computer-mediated discourse (CMD). It is argued that this approach is suitable for the study of CMD, when the major traces of self are imprinted in discourse—language used in a specific context. Espousing functionalist approaches to discourse analysis which view language resources as the building blocks of human communication, the approach foregrounds the process of discursive positioning—a central theoretical construct and a methodological principle. It also shows how micro- and macro-levels of analysis can be integrated in the exploration of self-construction in CMD.

COMPUTER MEDIATED DISCOURSE—MICRO AND MACRO ANALYSES

Every second, myriad messages are dispatched across Planet Earth by netizens (Crystal, 2001) in synchronous and asynchronous computer-mediated communication. This digital undertaking is accomplished in the absence of "facial expressions, gestures, and conventions of body posture, and distance (the kinesics and proxemics) which are so critical in expressing personal opinions and attitudes and in moderating social relationships" (Crystal, 2001, p. 36).

How are selves constructed in these digital texts? This chapter will provide an answer to this question by presenting and illustrating the theoretical and methodological frameworks of a qualitative approach that focuses on the study of computer-mediated discourse (CMD). Before we embark on this undertaking, we will briefly provide broad definitions of the terms 'qualitative research', 'discourse analysis,' 'text,' and 'self-construction' which are inter-connected in this chapter. Qualitative research aims at understanding the meaning of human processes including self-construction by emphasizing interpretation, and contextualization of the study in situ and in vivo (Lincoln & Denzin, 2000; Schwandt, 2001).

What is discourse analysis? Brown and Yule's (1983, p.1) definition provides an answer in the following citation: "The analysis of discourse is necessarily the analysis of language in use. As such, it cannot be restricted to the description of linguistic forms independent of the purposes or functions which these forms are designed to serve in human affairs." This definition captures the transition from a focus on language as a closed system, to a focus on language as an open system (Schiffrin, 1994). Following Ricoeur (1981), we define text as spoken or digital discourse that is fixed by writing

We also espouse a narrative approach to self-construction (see overview in Bamberg, 2006a) which assumes that humans construct their selves in the stories that they unfold, and researchers can explore this process. Hence, the term self-construction is ambiguous since it refers to the narrated construction of self as well as to the researcher's interpretation of this process. In this chapter we propose discourse-oriented approach to self-construction that acknowledges this ambiguity.

To accomplish this objective, the chapter aligns itself with scholars who have applauded the advantages of the discursive turn in the study of CMD (Crystal, 2001; Herring, 1996, 2001; Markham, 2005; McIlvenny & Raudaskoski, 2005). These scholars share the tenet that meaning and self-construction can be explored by focusing on discourse.

We will examine two central discourse-oriented approaches to illustrate this tenet. These approaches are also pertinent to the process of discursive positioning that will be elaborated on

in the next section and will be directly related to self-construction. Proponents of conversation analysis (CA) (Sacks, 1992), the roots of which are anchored in ethnomethodology (Garfinkel, 1967), focus primarily on naturally occurring interactional discourse in order to explore how social order is unfolded in moment-by-moment conversational interaction. Espousing this view, the researcher micro-analyzes—describes and interprets explicit and implicit features of the interaction.

Critical discourse analysts (CDA) (Rogers, Malancharuvil-Berkes, Mosley, Hui, & O'Garro-Joseph, 2005), on the other hand, conceptualize discourse as a system of thought (Schwandt, 2001) and emphasize the impact of a priori non-discursive contextual conditions on the production of dominant constraining discursive practices. Accordingly, proponents of CDA often adopt a deductive stance which is guided by the idea that discourse analysis should move from "description and interpretation to explanation of how discourse systematically constructs versions of the social world" (Rogers et al., 2005, p.371). To this end, critical discourse analysts define a priori theoretical concepts such as 'hegemony,' 'asymmetry,' 'ideology,' 'control,' 'inequality,' and 'discrimination' (van Dijk, 2001) before they set out to explore how these concepts are expressed in the texts that they focus on.

We have seen that CA advocates a micro-analytic study of discourse in context that is by and large free from guiding theoretical principles, whereas CDA encourages the researcher to equip him/herself with explanatory macro principles. The two approaches seem incompatible at first glance. Current discourse-oriented studies advocate the construction of an interface between micro- and macro-perspectives on discourse analysis (see overview in Kupferberg & Green, 2005). These studies acknowledge the importance of micro text-analysis that is sensitive to changes in the participants' discursive positioning in relation to each other, but at the same time emphasize the need to relate the findings to theories and ideological concepts at a macro-level.

Holstein and Gubrium (2000, p. 96-97) guide the qualitative researcher on how to construct an interpretive interface. These researchers specifically relate to Foucault's top-down macro perspective on discourse analysis on one hand and micro-analytic ethnomethodology on the other:

If Foucault works in a historical register, and ethnomethodology in an interactional one, we tell the story of the self at the crossroads of narrative, social interaction, culture and institutional life. Working historically, Foucault had little access to the everyday operation of discourses, of discursive practice. We are more tuned to everyday interaction as it bears on self-construction. At the same time taking direction from Foucault, we are more deeply concerned with the resources and conditions of self-construction that is typical of ethnomethodology. While certainly appreciating the hows of self-construction, we are equally interested in the various whats—that extend to discourse and surrounding institutional environments of talk and social interaction.

These researchers emphasize that during the process of data analysis researchers may shift between micro-levels of analysis and the broader levels where pre-existing resources are used for interpretation. In this way, they can establish a connection with theory at a macro level after the completion of data analysis, instead of using it as an a priori framework that determines the entire course of the study.

To recapitulate, to explore self construction in CMD, the chapter espouses the theoretical and methodological framework of a discourse-oriented qualitative approach. The approach enables the researcher to micro-analyze digital discourse, and also relate this analysis to macro-levels of theory in an interpretive interface.

DISCURSIVE POSITIONING

Discursive positioning was defined by discursive psychologists (Davies & Harré, 1990) as locating oneself in ongoing discourse in relation to others by means of language resources as well as body language and facial expressions. This social activity constitutes "a dynamic alternative to the more static concept of role" (Langenhove & Harré, 1999, p. 14). Accordingly, this chapter puts forward a claim that in CMD studies, when the major traces of self are imprinted in language resources (e.g., lexical items, pronouns, figurative language, different syntactic structures, repetition, etc.), a close examination of these devices enhances self-construction of individuals as well as groups.

Our definition of discursive positioning is inspired by constructivism (Lincoln & Guba, 1998), and three functionalist approaches to discourse analysis (Schiffrin, 1994). Functionalist approaches emphasize that language resources constitute the building-blocks of self-construction in discourse that is related to the context in which it is produced. For example, pronouns show how interlocuters position, or locate, themselves in relation to others as individuals ('I') or groups ('we') when they talk, write or communicate digitally. Figurative language (e.g., metaphors and similes) enables interlocuters to conceptualize their positioning when they relate to complex topic domains such as 'life' by using source domains that are more familiar like, for example, a 'road') (Lakoff & Johnson, 1980) (e.g., Life is a road).

Following linguistic anthropology (Duranti, 1997)—the first functionalist approach—we assume that the locus of the quest for self-construction should be placed *in discourse that is locally produced, or constructed, in a specific context and is reflexively related to it* (Linell, 1998). The connection between discourse and context is succinctly defined by van Dijk (1997, p.11): "In the study of discourse as action and interaction contexts are crucial. Indeed, the main distinction between abstract discourse analysis and social discourse analysis is that the latter takes the context into account." The following excerpt shows how Linell (1998, p.264) further defines the symbiotic relations between discourse and context: "Any stretch of discourse, created in actors' interaction with other actors, is embedded in a matrix of contexts. However, it is not simply embedded or situated in contexts, but has a *reflexive* (emphasis in the original) relationship to the contexts. Discourses and contexts mutually constitute and select each other, and hence they form a basic, indivisible whole."

We see, then, that context is not an objective construct out there in the real world. Its cultural, social, psychological, and historical dimensions are constantly constructed by interlocutors. The definition of the symbiotic relations between discourse and context raises intriguing questions in the study of CMD. What is the meaning of contextual resources such as time, space, community, society, and history in cyber interaction where digital interlocutors do not always share "a common social space and history, and a common system of standards of perceiving, believing, evaluating and acting" (Kramsch, 1998, p.127)? How can global coherence (i.e., the central theme of the text) be accomplished interactionally in such circumstances? In the following section, we present an analysis of CMD and relate to these questions.

The second functionalist approach espoused in this chapter is micro-analytic CA that was presented in the previous section. Aligning ourselves with this approach, we can explore how selves are unfolded *in the sequential production of discourse in a local context.* The adaptation of this approach to CMD presents a methodological issue concerning the choice of an appropriate unit of analysis. This issue will be elaborated on in the next section.

Following narrative analysis (Bamberg, 2006a)—the third functionalist approach adopted in this chapter—we explore different 'small stories ' (Bamberg, 2006b; Georgakopoulou, 2006) such as past-tense, future, and hypothetical local stories produced when narrators attempt to make sense of their past experience, explore possible future worlds, and construct local versions of their selves in discursive practices that take place in the present.

What are small stories? A state of the art description of narrative inquiry (Bamberg, 2006a) argues that narrative analysts are often guided by one of the two following perspectives. The first, metaphorically entitled "life on holiday" (Freeman, 2006) highlights the importance of historical-cultural meta-narratives (i.e., collective stories narrated in spoken discourse or inscribed in written documents) in the study of meaning and self. The second perspective prioritizes the importance of small stories (Bamberg, 2006b; Georgakopoulou, 2006) that are locally produced. This rift presented at an important theoretical junction at which narrative analysts are located nowadays (Bamberg, 2004), is related to the discussion of micro- and macro-analyses presented in the previous section.

Bamberg's (2004, 2006b) definition of discursive positioning enables researchers to construct an interface between these perspectives. It also integrates Labov's (1972) traditional concept of narrative evaluation with the requirement to incorporate interactional dimensions of the narrative process into narrative analysis (Cortazzi & Jin, 2000).

At this point, we will make a short digression to define and criticize evaluation—a related concept preceding positioning. Then, we will present Bamberg's (2004, 2006b) and Kupferberg and Green's (2005) models of positioning. Labov's (1972) structural elements of past tense stories comprise the following elements. An abstract summarizes the gist of the story. Orientation provides the background. Complicating action is the sequence of events creating a problem or an unexpected situation. Evaluation provides the narrator's attitude. Resolution shows what happened finally, and coda shifts the perspective to the present.

Following Labov's (1972) traditional definition of evaluation, self-displaying evaluative language resources, or subjectivity markers (Georgakopoulou, 1997), such as repetition, pronouns, figurative language, and syntactic structures have been extensively explored. Georgakopoulou (1997) advises the discourse analyst exploring self-construction not to study evaluation as preconceived lists of evaluative devices defined a priori of discourse analysis, but relate this microanalytic investigation to the specific context in which evaluative devices are produced. Focusing on Labov's traditional definition of evaluation, Cortazzi and Jin (2000, p. 103-104) emphasize the need to relate to interactional dimensions of discourse in the analysis of evaluation:

We argue that the evaluation is not only in the narrative itself. Analytic considerations need to be broadened out to take into account how evaluation is negotiated between speaker and hearers. Evaluation is not always from the teller but can be from a story recipient. Relevant questions, therefore, concern who evaluates the narrative and how narrative responses affect the teller. Since these questions go beyond what happens in the narrative per se we need to consider evaluation of narrative in previous or subsequent talk. This can be further explored by looking at some consequences of narrative evaluation in wider contexts. Evaluation through narrative is a further important layer. Here tellers and their situations are evaluated through the narratives they tell

Cortazzi and Jin argue that the Labovian model (1972) focuses on evaluation *in* the narrative (i.e., narrators' use of self-displaying evaluative devices). This model does not relate to interactional dimensions of evaluation that are co-constructed by interlocuters (i.e., evaluation *of* the narrative), nor does it relate to the researcher's task (evaluation *through* the narrative).

Bamberg's model of discursive positioning (Bamberg, 2004, 2006b) highlights the interactional dimensions of narrative discourse and explains how an interpretive interface can be constructed between small and big stories. What are the characteristics of Bamberg's model of discursive positioning? Bamberg (2004, 2006b) focuses on self-construction at three inter-related levels. At level one, the texts are explored in quest for language resources used by narrators to position themselves *vis-à-vis significant others in the narrated past events.* At level two, the researcher looks for language resources that interlocutors use to position themselves *in relation to others in the present ongoing interaction.* Levels one and two relate to interactional dimensions in the narrated past in relation to others and in the online interaction in the present in relation to other participants, respectively. At level three, according to Bamberg, the researcher shows how narrators actually locate themselves *in relation to ideological positions*—big stories or master narratives that have been sculpted in the self by historical and social practices (Bamberg, 2006b).

In addition, at this level the researcher also distinguishes between the oppressive process of 'being positioned' (Bamberg, 2004) defined in the previous section in terms of critical discourse analysis, and the more liberating process of positioning (Bamberg, 2004) that was defined in terms of conversation analysis. Thus, Bamberg's level three constitutes an interpretive interface between micro- and macro-levels of analysis. The following excerpt shows how Bamberg (2004, p.366) distinguishes between positioning and being positioned:

We clearly distinguish between 'the being positioned orientation,' which is attributing a rather deterministic force to master narratives, and a more agentive notion of subject as 'positioning itself,' in which the discursive resources or repertoires are not a priori pre-established but rather are interactively accomplished. 'Being positioned' and 'positioning oneself' are two metaphoric constructs of two very different agent-world relationships: the former with a world-to-agent direction of fit, the latter with an agent-to-world direction of fit. One way to overcome this rift is to argue that both operate concurrently in a kind of dialectic as subjects engage in narratives-in-interaction and make sense of self and others in their stories.

Bamberg's model shows that the two opposing perspectives can be interfaced if one follows an approach that is tuned to small, local stories as well as to big, meta narratives. Following Husserl's definition of the past, present and future time continuum dominating Western cultures (see overview in Evans, 2005) and Bamberg's (2004, 2006b) level-analysis of positioning, we developed The Four World Model (FWM) for the study of positioning in face-to-face, telephone and CMD troubled communication (Ben Peretz & Kupferberg, 2007; Kupferberg & Ben Peretz, 2004; Kupferberg & Green, 1998, 2005; Kupferberg, Green, & Gilat, 2002). FWM is based on the tenet that narrative time enables humans to overcome the limitations of chronological time by constructing past and future temporal worlds in the present. According to this model, the researcher is supposed to extract meaning from these worlds via a micro-analytic procedure and then construct an interpretive interface in a fourth world.

Compared with Bamberg's level-analysis, FWM emphasizes the centrality of the present moment as the 'workshop' in which humans interactionally attempt to reach global coherence, or agreement on the meaning of their past, and future. It also emphasizes the researcher's construction of meaning—"evaluation through narrative" (Cortazzi & Jin, 2000, p.104)—foregrounded in FWM via the construction of an interpretive

interface in a fourth world of analysis. In the following excerpt, Kupferberg and Green (2005, p. 28) explain how traces of self are identified and interpreted via world-building:

World-making is a heuristic procedure that first calls for the breakdown of the complex discourse gestalt into self-revealing linguistic resources that display inter- and intrapersonal dimensions in the participants' worlds of the present, past, and future. Then, the linguistic resources identified in these worlds are examined closely, reassembled, and synthesized in the researchers' interpretive interfacing world.

To recapitulate, the researcher exploring self-construction in discourse can benefit from the models of discursive positioning presented in this section. Both models are tuned to micro- and macro-levels, or worlds, displayed in the text. In addition, these models provide the means for the construction of an interpretive interface between the micro- and macro-levels of analysis.

In the next section we will illustrate how self-construction can be constructed in CMD via discursive positioning—a domain that has not been sufficiently explored yet (Tirado & Galavez, 2007). We will also relate to the questions formulated in the previous sections with regard to CMD: How can self-construction be explored? What is the meaning of contextual resources? How can global coherence be accomplished interactionally?

ANALYSIS OF SELF-CONSTRUCTION

Methodological Issues

To illustrate self-construction via discursive positioning in CMD, we will analyze several excerpts taken from a corpus collected for the exploration of self-construction in a closed forum (Kupferberg & Ben-Peretz, 2004). The forum was inaugurated for the presentation and discussion of student teachers' professional problems in a teacher-education college. The corpus comprises 310 messages produced in 28 message-threads initiated by a problem-message sent by each participant during the first semester of the academic year 2002-2003.

Forum participants were 28 women, student teachers attending their final college year. Participants' ages ranged between 28-33 years. The forum-mates attended a face-to-face yearly course on the theoretical and practical dimensions of problem discourse in the educational setting. The study was guided by ethical concerns. Accordingly, the participants' permission to use the forum messages in the study was requested and granted. In addition, pseudonyms were used to protect the participants' anonymity.

Following FWM (Kupferberg & Green, 2005), the analysis presented in the following subsection focuses on the identification of positioning language resources in the participants' worlds. These self-displaying resources were allocated to three worlds: the world of the present interaction with forum-mates, the narrated world of past experience, and the future. The micro-analysis was also guided by 'the next turn validation' (Peräkylä, 1997), a conversation-analytic procedure aiming at the discovery of preceding or following co-text (i.e., text that precedes or follows) that provides confirming evidence that what one participant wrote has also been noticed and used by other participants.

The analysis proposed in this chapter differs from content analysis that often obscures the major features of the interaction because it does not study the sequentially organized turns, but rather requires that categories be set in advance or be developed during the analysis (Titscher, Meyer, Wodak, & Vetter, 2000). Following Crystal (2001), we define each digital message as a digital turn in synchronic and asynchronic CMD. This unit of analysis is based on the traditional definition of a conversational turn (i.e., the time when one

party speaks until a change takes place and another party takes over) (ten Have, 1999).

Data Analysis

The data analysis presented in this subsection is inspired by previous analyses of the corpus (Ben-Peretz & Kupferberg, 2007; Kupferberg & Ben-Peretz, 2004). The examples are taken from a message-thread initiated by Naomi, an experienced teacher. In examples 1 and 2, Naomi presents a professional problem and seeks her forum-mates' help. Examples 3 and 4 were produced in response to Example 1 by inexperienced and experienced forum-mates, respectively.

Hi girls. I'm sending you a problem I encountered during my work at the school. I'd be happy to hear what you think and what you'd have done in my place. In the school where I work, there's an English department consisting of eight teachers. We're very close-knit and supportive of each other. According to the subject coordinator's directive, every two teachers are responsible for a particular group level, with one setting the policy—for instance, I set the policy in the 7th-grade help group. In the 8th-grade group, my colleague sets the policy and I'm called her assistant. During the present semester, we managed to give two exams—the first was on the chapter I compiled, and the second was an unseen that she was responsible for devising. What she did was simply produce an exam from a previous year. She showed me the exam and said: "This is the exam we'll do." I told her that in my opinion, the exam was rather thin and there wasn't enough meat in it, and I suggested that we use another text. She refused and said: "No, don't worry, we've done this exam in past years and it isn't as easy as you think." I even offered to fatten the exam up a bit, perhaps add exercises to it, but she answered me in a kind of offended tone: "I don't know; if you like, come up with a different exam." I gave in. I didn't want to argue too much, and in the end, we did the exam she suggested. A few days later, a pupil from my colleague's class came to the teacher who teaches the A stream and told her she thought she'd done well on the exam and she was sure she'd get over 90 and she might move up a group. That A-stream teacher came to me and told me what that pupil had said, adding that we shouldn't have given that exam because it was too easy, and under no circumstances could the teacher in question be relied on blindly. You could say that I understood my mistake and I made a decision that I'd always get in first when it comes to exams.

Naomi presents both a problem and a solution via two small stories (Bamberg, 2006b). Using these narrative formats, she locates herself in relation to her forum-mates as an experienced, perhaps even an expert teacher (Berliner, 1986) who is able to identify problems and cope with them, and not as a troubled teacher who seeks immediate help. In the first story, Naomi positions herself in the world of the past in relation to another teacher who insisted on giving the class a test that was too easy in Naomi's opinion. The solution is unfolded in the second small story when Naomi narrates how a pupil who took the test and another teacher who was not involved in the first story said that the test was too easy. In the second story, Naomi positions herself vis-à-vis her colleagues at school in the past, as well as her digital forum-mates in the present. It seems that the second story aims at showing the forum-mates that Naomi was right. At the end of the message, Naomi generalizes what she has learnt from this experience and shifts her focus to the future where she will behave differently: "You could say that I understood my mistake and I made a decision that I'd always get in first when it comes to exams." In other words, during the reflective digital verbalization of the small stories (Example 1) in the workshop of the present, Naomi constructed knowledge (Shulman, 1987) that she may resort to in future classroom events. The learning experience is summarized via a formulaic phrase

produced at the end of Example 1: "I'd always get in first when it comes to exams." This phrase shifts the focus of the problem from pedagogy (i.e., What is a good exam?) to interpersonal relations with colleagues (Shulman, 1987).

Which language resources does Naomi use to construct her positioning? Naomi primarily resorts to constructed dialogue (i.e., reported speech) and figurative language. Using constructed dialogue, she produces several 'voices' via the same linguistic means (Bakhtin, 1981): the voice of the teacher who chose to give an easy test and the voices of the pupil and another teacher who thought that the test was easy. At the same time, she also expresses her own opinion protesting against the arbitrary decision of her colleague to give an easy test and aligns herself with the pupil and the teacher who claims it was too easy. Some of the voices are recycled in direct speech whereas others are reproduced via indirect speech. Example 2 shows that recycled speech is very salient in Naomi's small stories.

Direct speech: *She showed me the exam and said: "This is the exam we'll do"... She refused and said: "No, don't worry, we've done this exam in past years and it isn't as easy as you think" ... but she answered me in a kind of offended tone: "I don't know; if you like, come up with a different exam."*

Indirect speech: *I told her that in my opinion, the exam was rather thin and there wasn't enough meat in it, and I suggested that we use another text... I even offered to fatten the exam up a bit, perhaps add exercises to it... A few days later, a pupil from my colleague's class came to the teacher who teaches the A stream and told her she thought she'd done well on the exam and she was sure she'd get over 90 and she might move up a group. That A-stream teacher came to me and told me what that pupil had said, adding that we shouldn't have given that exam because it was too easy, and under no circumstances could the teacher in question be relied on blindly.*

The past voices mingle with the narrator's voice to display a professional self that was wronged. The narrator also uses formulaic language to summarize the meaning of her experience in "I even offered to 'fatten' the exam up a bit" and "I'd always get in first when it comes to exams." These positioning resources enable the narrator to locate herself in relation to her colleagues in the world of the past, as well as her peers in the world of the present, as an experienced pedagogue who knows what has to be done for the pupils. Examples 3 and 4 show how novice and experienced teachers related to Naomi's problem presented in Example 1, respectively.

Hi Naomi, I certainly understand you and your bitterness about the whole business. Because we are relatively new teachers, the more veteran teachers think they know better because they have experience from previous years. We are forced to be flexible about a lot of things and accept the decision of 'the more experienced ones' and as you saw, they aren't always right! I hope the pupils' exam results will make the teacher aware of her mistake and that she'll understand that she has to listen to you. Have you thought about presenting the problem to the English coordinator or consulting with another teacher? I don't know if it's acceptable to you people, but sometimes when there are differences of opinion it's a good idea to involve another party. Anyway, I understand that you're not about to rely on others concerning things you're sure about. Good luck in the future. Dana

In Example 3, Dana, a novice teacher, responds to Naomi's message by creating an "emotional supportive envelope" (Ben-Peretz & Kupferberg, 2007, p. 135) at the very beginning and at the end of the message. This support is constructed from the point of view of an individual: "I certainly understand you and your bitterness about the whole business." Then, Dana adopts a collective point of view: "Because we are relatively new teachers, the

more veteran teachers think they know better because they have experience from previous years." To construct this novice teachers' collective and position it vis-à-vis experienced teachers in the world of the past, Dana uses the pronouns 'we' and 'they.' Our analysis of Naomi's message shows that Naomi would have probably disagreed with the idea of being positioned as a member of the inexperienced teacher collective.

Dana also provides Naomi with a solution that attempts to shift the discussion to a future world. However, in the context of Naomi's previous detailed message that is deeply anchored in the classroom, Dana's ad-hoc and general advice does not seem to advance the digital interaction in any profitable direction. The message shows that at that point in her professional career, Dana is not able to tune herself to her forum- mates since she is absorbed in her own professional experiences as a novice teacher. In Example 4, we present an experienced teacher's message. Her goal is to find what is best for the pupils.

Naomi, from my brief acquaintance with you, I've discovered that you're a nice, easy-going and refined girl, and that's how you behaved with your colleague—you suggested that she fatten up the exam instead of replacing it with another one. I think you acted correctly by taking care not to spoil your relations with her since after all you have to work parallel to her the whole year and it's not nice to work with someone you aren't on good terms with. You also reached the correct conclusion—not to rely on her and to get in first when it comes to exams (it's a fact that the A-stream teacher thinks so too). If I were you, I would analyze the exam results with her and if they really are better than usual, I'd have a talk with her about the fact that perhaps the exam was too easy. I would share my feelings with her and make it clear that I have no intention of offending her when I offer alternatives. The goal is to find what's best for the pupils. Tali

In Example 4, Tali positions herself in relation to Naomi and supports her emotionally. Unlike Dana, Tali must have 'listened' to what Naomi wrote. This is also manifested in the future action that she advocates. This proposal shows that thanks to her experience, Tali must have learned to read and interpret the meaning of classroom experiences in a more profound way (Berliner, 1986). Naomi's final message, which is not presented in this chapter (see Ben Peretz & Kupferberg, 2007) emphasizes that she chose to accept Tali's advice. This message constitutes 'the next turn validation' (Peräkylä, 1997), showing that what Tali wrote has also been noticed and used by Naomi.

In conclusion, analysis of the forum messages shows that student teachers positioned themselves in different ways in relation to their forum-mates. Their tacit and explicit discursive positioning was shaped by their knowledge and classroom experience. Naomi, an experienced teacher, presented problems about which she had already reflected. Novice teachers sought any help and assistance they could get from their forum-mates. Experience also determined interactive patterns of response. Inexperienced teachers like Dana provided ad-hoc advice that did not contribute to the interaction. Experienced teachers like Tali were tuned to their forum-mates' needs and were able to propose relevant classroom-oriented solutions. The text-analysis also illustrates how positioning language resources used by narrators unfolding their present, past and future worlds, were identified and interpreted by the researchers. The latter constructed individual and group professional selves interactionally engaged in a closed digital forum.

Bearing this analysis in mind, we will now relate to the questions formulated at the end of the previous section. In response to the first question, the analysis shows that a close examination of the self-displaying language resources and interpretation of the functions that they accomplish in the world of the present, past and future enabled us to construct individual and collective selves.

The second question relates to the unique features of cyber talk where contextual resources are not as accessible as they are in face-to-face or telephone interactions. The data analyzed in this section is taken from an open forum in which participants' negotiation of meaning often leans on contextual resources constructed in face-to-face encounters. But what about open forums? How can global coherence be accomplished in online communities that sometimes become "sites of betrayal, violence and ultimately disintegration" (Reid, 1998, p. 40)?

A preliminary answer is provided by Kupferberg and Green (2005) in their analysis of a thread initiated by a suicidal message sent by an adolescent to an open forum. Using FWM, the researchers show that a virtual rescue team established online manages to reach global coherence and shift the adolescent's suicidal intentions (displayed in his positioning in relation to others in a tormented past world) to a future world where life is worth living. In other words, this study provides indication that the adolescent's self may have changed. It should also be emphasized that this analysis showed that "the hotline volunteers constitute professional anchors of empathy and emotional support who attempt to move the discussion to more practical grounds of coping… and mitigate the unleashed and careless criticism of careless digital writers" (Kupferberg & Green, 2005, p. 127).

FUTURE TRENDS

This chapter emphasizes that the study of positioning resources enhances the CMD analyst's work in a disembodied world where context is often fuzzy. Future studies should further explore open and closed forums, and chat rooms to understand how digital selves fare in CMD. A discussion of future trends, or future worlds that were defined in the previous sections, should also take into consideration technological developments that are likely to bring about a process of 'devirtualization' Such a process may change technology-assisted communication and make it more similar to face-to-face communication. Accordingly, in devirtualized computer-assisted communication, visual, audible and perhaps other sensory contextual resources will be available. Consequently, the task of interpreting the meaning of positioning language resources and achieving global coherence will probably become more feasible.

However, the fuzzy borders of cyber conversations often open new horizons where computer-assisted creative imagination can enhance the production of new meanings and new entities (Bell, 2001; Lister et al., 2003) and free humans "from the constraints of worldwide shackles like hierarchy, traditional social stereotypes, embodiment and even death" (Markham, 2005, p. 797). To what extent will the process of devirtaualization take place in CMD? Will digital interlocutors cherish this process? Will this process change the participants' positionings in relation to each other? Future research may use the theoretical and methodological frameworks presented in this chapter to address these questions.

CONCLUSION

This chapter presented theoretical and methodological frameworks of a discourse-analytic approach to the study of interactional self-construction in CMD. This approach shows how micro- and macro-levels, or worlds, of discourse analysis can be interfaced via models of analysis that are based on the concept of discursive positioning. It is argued that in CMD studies, when self-construction is mainly accomplished via language resources, a close examination of these 'tools' may enhance the study of self-construction. It is also argued that future technological developments may devirtualize internet communication by providing digital interlocutors with more contextual resources. Consequently, future

research will have to address novel questions and shed light on unexplored CMD processes.

REFERENCES

Bakhtin, M. M. (1981). Discourse in the novel. In M. Holoquist (Ed.), *The dialogic imagination.* (C. Emerson & M. Holoquist,Trans.) (pp. 259–422). Austin, TX: University of Texas Press.

Bamberg, M. (2004). Considering counter narratives. In M. Bamberg & M. Andrews (Eds.), *Considering counter-narratives: Narrating, resisting, making sense* (pp.351-371). Amsterdam: John Benjamins.

Bamberg, M. (Ed.). (2006a). Narrative: State of the art. *Narrative inquiry, 16,* (1).

Bamberg, M. (2006b). Stories big or small—Why do we care? In M. Bamberg, (Ed.), Narrative: State of the art. *Narrative inquiry, 16,* 139-147.

Bell, D. (2001). *An introduction to cybercultures.* London: Routledge.

Ben Peretz, M., & Kupferberg, I. (2007). Does teachers' negotiation of personal cases in an interactive cyber forum contribute to their professional learning? T*eachers and Teaching: Theory and Practice, 13,* 125-143.

Berliner, D. C. (1986). In pursuit of the expert pedagogue. *Educational Research, 15,* 5-13.

Brown, G., & Yule, G. (1983). *Discourse analysis.* Cambridge: Cambridge University Press.

Cortazzi, M., & Jin, L. (2000). Evaluating evaluation in narrative. In S. Hunston & G. Thompson (Eds.), *Evaluation in text* (pp.102-141). New York: Oxford University Press.

Crystal, D. (2001). *Language and the internet.* Cambridge, U.K.: Cambridge University Press.

Davies, B., & Harré, R. (1990). Positioning: The discursive production of selves. *Journal for the Theory of Social Behavior, 20,* 43–63.

Denzin, N., & Lincoln, Y. S.(Eds.). (2002). *The qualitative Inquiry reader.* Thousand Oaks, CA: Sage.

Duranti, A. (1997). *Linguistic anthropology.* New York: Cambridge University Press.

Evans, V. (2005). *The structure of time.* Amsterdam, The Netherlands: John Benjamins.

Freeman, M. (2006). Life "on holiday"? In defence of big stories. In M. Bamberg (Ed.). Narrative: State of the art. *Narrative inquiry, 16*, 131-136.

Garfinkel, H. (1967). *Studies in ethnomethodology.* Englewood Cliffs, NJ: Prentice Hall.

Georgakopoulou, A. (1997). *Narrative performance. A study of modern Greek story telling.* Amsterdam: John Benjamins.

Georgakopoulou, A. (2006).Thinking big with small stories in narrative and identity analysis. In M. Bamberg (Ed.). Narrative: State of the art. *Narrative inquiry, 16,* 122-130.

Herring, S. (1996). *Computer-mediated Communication: Linguistic, social and cross-cultural perspectives.* The Netherlands: John Benjamins Publishing Company.

Herring, S. C. (2001).Computer-mediated discourse. In D. Schiffrin, D. Tannen ,& H. E. Hamilton (Eds.), *The handbook of discourse analysis* (pp.250-264). Padstow, Cornwall: Blackwell.

Holstein, J. A., & Gubrium, J. F. (2000). *The self we live by: Narrative identity in a postmodern world.* New York: Oxford University Press.

Kramsch, C. (1998). *Language and culture.* Oxford, UK: Oxford University Press.

Kupferberg, I., & Ben-Peretz, M. (2004). Emerging and experienced professional selves in cyber discourse. In C. Vrasidas & G. V. Glass (Eds.), *Online professional development for teachers. Current perspectives on applied information technologies: Online professional development* (pp. 105-121). Connecticut, USA: IPA.

Kupferberg, I., & Green, D. (1998). Metaphors enhance radio problem discussions. *Metaphor and Symbol, 13*, 103-123.

Kupferberg, I., & Green, D. (2005). *Troubled talk: Metaphorical negotiation in problem discourse.* Berlin and New York: Mouton de Gruyter.

Kupferberg, I., Green, D., & Gilat, I. (2002). Figurative positioning in hotline stories. *Narrative Inquiry, 11*, 1-26.

Labov, W. (1972). *Language in the Inner City: Studies in the Black English vernacular.* Philadelphia: University of Pennsylvania Press.

Lakoff, G., & Johnson, M. (1980). *Metaphors we live by.* Chicago: University of Chicago Press.

Langenhove, L., van, & R. Harré. (1999). Introducing positioning theory. In R. Harré & L. van Langenhove (Eds.). *Positioning theory: Moral contexts of intentional action* (pp. 14-31). Oxford: Blackwell.

Lincoln, Y. S., & Guba, E. G. (1998). Paradigmatic controversies, contradictions and emerging confluences. In N. K. Denzin, & Y. S. Lincoln (Eds.), *Handbook of qualitative research* (pp. 163-188). Thousand Oaks, CA: Sage.

Linell, P. (1998). *Approaching dialogue: Talk, interaction and context in dialogical perspectives.* Amsterdam: John Benjamins.

Lister, M., Dovey, J., Giddings, S., Grant, I., & Kelly, K. (2003). *New media: A critical introduction.* London: Routledge.

Markham, A. N. (2005). The methods, politics, and ethics of representation in online ethnography. In N. K. Denzin & Y. S. Lincoln (Eds.). *The Sage handbook of qualitative research* (3rd edition) (pp.793-820). Beverly Hills, CA: Sage.

McIlvenny, P., & Raudaskoski, P. (2005). Meditating discourses of transnational adoption on the internet. In S. Norris & R. H. Jones (Eds.), *Discourse in action: Introducing mediated discourse analysis* (pp.62-72). London: Routledge.

Peräkylä, A. (1997). Reliability and validity in research based on tapes and transcripts. In D. Silverman (Ed.), *Qualitative research: Theory, method and practice* (pp.201- 220). London: Sage

Reid, E. (1998). The self and the Internet: Variations on the illusion of one self. In J. Gackenbach, (Ed.), *Psychology and the internet: Intrapersonal, interpersonal, and transpersonal implications* (pp. 29-42). San Diego, CA: Academic Press.

Ricœur , P. (1981). *Hermeneutics in the human sciences*. (Ed. and trans. by J. B. Thompson). Cambridge, UK: Cambridge University Press.

Rogers, R., Malancharuvil-Berkes, E., Mosley, M., Hui, D., & O'Garro-Joseph, G. (2005). Critical discourse analysis in education: A review of the literature. *Educational Research, 3*, 365-416.

Sacks, H. (1992). *Lectures on conversation* (1964–1972)(vols. I and II) (Ed. G. Jefferson). Oxford: Blackwell.

Schiffrin, D. (1994). *Approaches to discourse*. Cambridge, MA: Blackwell.

Schiffrin, D., Tannen, D., & Hamilton, H. E. (Eds.) (2001). *The handbook of discourse analysis*. Padstow, Cornwall: Blackwell.

Schwandt, T. A. (2001). *Dictinary of qualitaitve inquiry* (2nd ed.).Thousand Oaks, CA: Sage.

Shulman, L.S. (1987). Knowledge and teaching: Foundations of the new reform. *Harvard Educational Review, 52*, 1-22.

ten Have, P. (1999). *Doing conversation analysis: A practical guide*. London: Sage.

Tirado, F., & Gálvez, A. (2007). Positioning theory and discursive analysis: some tools for social interaction analysis. FQS, 8. Retrieved on June3, 2007, from http://www.qualitative-research. net/fqs/fqs-e/inhalt2- 07-e.htm

Titscher, S., Meyer, M., Wodak, R., & Vetter, E. (2000). *Methods of Text and Discourse analysis*. London: Sage.

van Dijk, T. A. (1997). The study of discourse. In T. A. van Dijk (Ed.), *Discourse studies: A multidisciplinary introduction. Discourse as structure and process* (pp.1-34). vol. 1. London: Sage.

van Dijk, T. A. (2001). Critical discourse analysis. In D. Schiffrin, D. Tannen, & H. E. Hamilton (Eds.). *The Handbook of Discourse Analysis* (pp.353-371). Padstow, U.K.:Blackwell.

KEY TERMS

Context: Non-linguistic resources such as time, location and prior knowledge that interlocutors use in the process of meaning-making.

Discourse Analysis: Discourse analysis can be micro-, or macro-analytic. Current scholarship calls for the construction of an interpretive interface between micro-and macro-levels of analysis.

Discourse and Text: Discourse is defined as language used in social, cultural, and historical contexts. Text is defined as any discourse that is fixed by writing.

Discursive Positioning: A theoretical construct and a heuristic procedure. Theoretically, it is defined as a process during which interlocurters locate themselves in relation to others in ongoing conversation. As a heuristic procedure, it enables the researcher to divide the text into several levels or worlds that are related to theory in an interpretive interface.

Functionalist Approaches: These approaches advocate micro-analytic study of language. They share the tenet that language resources constitute the building-blocks of interpersonal social communication, self-construction, and learning processes.

Global Coherence: The central theme of the text that is accomplished via the interlocutors' interactional process of interpretation.

Interpretive Interface: An integrative level of analysis in which the researcher interprets or clarifies the meaning of the text by relating to micro- and macro-discourse analyses.

Micro- and Macro Analyses: A close examination of discourse in order to highlight explicit and implicit features of the interaction. Macro-discourse analysis views discourse as an abstract entity that should be defined but which does not necessarily require a close examination of actual texts.

Positioning Resources: Self-displaying language devices such as repetition, use of syntactic structures, and figurative language that interlocutors use to locate themselves in discourse.

Self-Construction: Self-construction is often accomplished in the stories humans narrate. The term is ambiguous since it refers to narrators' construction of self in various settings via different positioning resources. It also refers to the researcher's interpretation of the narrators' production of self.

Chapter XXVII
Design and Implementation of Trust Enabling Functions

Jeanette Lemmergaard
University of Southern Denmark, Denmark

Damien Brigth
University of Southern Denmark, Denmark

Christopher Gersbo-Møeller
University of Southern Denmark, Denmark

Tim Hansson
University of Southern Denmark, Denmark

ABSTRACT

Through a case study based on a knowledge-sharing community of Danish plant growers, this chapter examines how an IT system can be designed to support strategic knowledge-sharing between firms participating in an industry-based virtual community. A suitable environment for trust is seen as an important part of making the community function effectively. Therefore, the system aims to support community members in making trust decisions related to knowledge-sharing. In the presented system decisions are based on digital evidence in the form of system-managed credentials. The chapter presents a model for trust, reputation, and performance management which supports the needs of the specific type of knowledge-sharing community. Further, the model is linked to an underlying public key infrastructure framework which supports the secure exchange of information and credentials between community members.

INTRODUCTION

Trust is a key requirement in a virtual knowledge-sharing community. Not only does trust play a key role in modeling interactional social concepts, trust also plays a key role in a macro-social context. This chapter presents a trust and security model which can support Web-based trust building from a socio-psychological and a technical perspective. The model demonstrates how community reputation can be linked to community-performance measures in a virtual community of practice (CoP). The presented model focuses on the basis of inter-personal and system-trust and looks at how trust can be related to the use of a form of digital context. More specifically, the model examines trust based on digital evidence in the form of credentials.

Trust in an IT-system perspective is often linked to reputation where a user builds a reputation and hence forms a basis for trust. Using reputation as a basis for trust-building raises the question of what reputation should be based on, particularly when entities do not have detailed knowledge of each other. In e-commerce systems, reputation is generally linked to ratings generated as feedback to transactions in the type of financial interactions. However, in the presented target community, the specific knowledge-sharing goals are not linked to financial transactions. Instead performance measurement for knowledge exchange is related to improving financial and process strategies. The value of the knowledge exchange depends on the quality, reliability, and level of detail of information provided. Consequently, the reputation system is linked to ratings of non-financial metrics which reflect how well a member participates in and contributes to the virtual community.

In this chapter, an appropriate performance-measurement framework using community-agreed metrics to support reputation building and management is examined. Both the socio-psychological and the technical aspects of trust in relation to the proposed model are discussed. The socio-psychological aspect of trust focuses on the operation of a community in relation to deciding on the value of information and metrics, sharing resources, and creating rules and policies. This includes community-based policy management (Feeney et al., 2004). And it is the basic assumption that a common set of rules can be applied to community members. The technical aspect of trust addresses the issues of designing an operational trust and security architecture. The trust and security model for information-sharing proposed here focuses on sub-groups within a specific CoP. The model is built on the assumption that knowledge acquisition evolves as members move from limited to full participation in the community, and is based on level of interaction. The model looks at group formation within the community and at the conditions through which community members can join groups. This supports a simple group hierarchy by which members can be compared.

WEB-BASED COLLABORATION

Companies increasingly look at how strategic alliances achieved through Web-based collaboration can benefit and add value to their businesses. Web-based collaborations are usually supported by networks (Brown & Carpenter, 2004) which extend beyond firm boundaries. The use of network technology to link participants and to support the formation of social networks, for example, underlies the concept of virtual communities (Malhotra, 2002). Recently, virtual communities have attracted interest from businesses as part of finding new ways to enable business-oriented knowledge exchange. This was done by leveraging the same form of virtual community model which has been successful in areas like e-market places, file-sharing networks, and online development communities.

One of the advantages of virtual business communities is that they foster collaboration within an industry without the costs of supporting specific partnership arrangements. Specialized communities limited to selected companies with common interests or goals facilitate knowledge-sharing. Hereby mutual gains are acquired without many of the drawbacks of more specific business partnerships. In this sense, knowledge-sharing between professionals, as well as collaborative knowledge building and transfer is similar to that of a CoP (Wenger, 1998). However, the knowledge-exchange takes place at an inter-organizational level instead of at an individual or team level, which is usually associated with a CoP (Wenger, 1998). This inter-organizational view of knowledge-transferring networks is in line with work from the theory on joint ventures and inter-firm alliances (Brown & Duguid, 2000).

For a virtual CoP to evolve, participation through contributions from its members is necessary. However, a number of limiting factors can prevent sufficient participation and hereby prevent a community from evolving. Competitive logic is often seen as an obstacle to a knowledge-sharing community composed of partners operating for example within a localized industry. Further, the reputation of the individual community members can influence the level of participation and commitment, which can further influence the basic level of trust exercised between the community members. As discussed in the theory of CoP, the social processes associated with acquiring knowledge and the status of the group members can determine the level of communal learning (Lave & Wenger, 1991), and hereby determine a community's capability of evolving.

Moreover, evolvement often requires some kind of participation from the outside. There has to be gateways for knowledge from non-members to enter the community as non-members bring new knowledge into the community. The tension which is often generated between the institutionalized community knowledge and the new knowledge is required for learning and for the progressive evolvement of the community (Wenger, 1998). This is particularly relevant in the presented model, where reaching the strategic goals of the virtual community depends on external knowledge, like international industry "best practice" knowledge.

In collaborations where participants have little shared experience, a more formal governance mechanism serves to mitigate initial concerns of distrust and potential misconduct on the part of an unknown participator. Prior history and duration of relations affect the degree of trust between participators and minimize opportunistic behavior. This is also the case in Web-based alliances and, therefore, models for trust and security need to be integrated into the system architecture. For firms to benefit from collaborative efforts and to affect success in garnering trust, sharing knowledge, and gaining mutual learning, an understanding of the technological processes and the underlying motives of participators is needed.

THE INDUSTRY CONTEXT

The model for trust and security and the system architecture presented here is developed to fulfill the requirements of the target industry, the Danish horticultural industry. The Danish grower-community is an example of a specific CoP: a system of relationships between people, activities, and the world, developing over time in the context of shared industry goals. There is a connection here to the concept of virtual firms in terms of sharing resources for mutual gain, although the focus is neither customer oriented, nor oriented towards integration of systems for process interoperability.

In order to facilitate the knowledge and resource-sharing needs, a service-oriented architecture (SOA) to support the Danish grower community was designed. The SOA supported information gathering through Web services and knowledge-sharing through an online benchmarking service. Hereby, it supports the growers in comparing operations and methods of production, as well as efficiency. The overall purpose of the SOA is to support and instigate a knowledge-sharing community, based on the network of collaborating services that are published and available for invocation.

The Danish horticultural industry already has a strong tradition of collaboration and unified development of systems, institutions, and infrastructures. Today, some of the more dominant service operators in the pot-plant trade are results of such collaborative initiatives. In addition to the tradition of unified commercial collaboration, there has been an even longer tradition for founding societies among growers producing specific crops. These societies have a tradition of sharing best practices and knowledge in general (Lemmergaard et al., 2005). However, competition is strong due to the internationalization of the markets, and consequently, the industry has experienced that knowledge-sharing and cooperative mechanisms are being mistrusted or even abandoned.

The intensified competition ought to force growers to find new ways of operating and necessitate more sharing of good practices amongst groupings or the entire industry. To meet this paradox Knowledge Lab at the University of Southern Denmark in collaboration with the Danish Association of Horticultural Producers has developed a virtual community for growers. Here knowledge concerning production methods and general business administration can be shared, leading to improvements in the competitive advantage of the entire industry.

THE CONCEPT OF TRUST

In the research literature, there appears to be a general consensus on the importance of trust, hence trust provides the foundation for a successful implementation and operation of a CoP.

Trust not only prevents opportunism, but also creates opportunities that would not be available otherwise. Although trust is the key coordinating mechanism in the community form, experience from existing communities show that many communities fail to meet the requirements upon which trust is established.

Trust is a complex, multifaceted phenomenon. Definitions of trust have become a confusing, and often conflicting, potpourri of definitions applied to a host of units and levels of analysis (Shapiro, 1987). Every author within the field of trust seems to provide his/her own definition, often aimed at being appropriate for the specific domain of interest. From social science research three types of trust are generally identified when dealing with generation of trust among unfamiliar actors.

First, interpersonal trust (Good, 1988), which is to be found at the personal level, is both an agent- and context-specific concept. Trust is a function of relatively rational decision-making processes, rather than personality characteristics. Trusting behavior appears when the long-term interests of the participants are stressed initially, where only small initial rewards are at stake, where there is no potential for threat, and where there is great potential for successful communication. This kind of trust is common to many business relationships and is important to the goals of strategic alliances. The strategic alliances are based on collaborative sharing of strategy amongst peers for shared competitive advantage against external rivals.

Second, system trust (Shapiro, 1987) is based on the perceived property or reliance on a system or institution within which trust exists. The belief that proper impersonal structures, such as for example regulations and guarantees, are in place, generates system trust. System trust also refers to the belief that the appropriate structure of roles has been defined. This is particularly relevant in the presented model where a community facilitator (CFac), who stores and enforces roles and policies within the community, needs to be a trusted third party. Members of the community need to trust the facilitator to act for the benefit of the community.

Third, dispositional trust describes the general attitude of the person seeking trustworthiness towards trust. This is also called basic trust and is independent of any other party or context. This type of trust is built on two basic assumptions. The first assumption is that others are generally trustworthy people. The second assumption is that irrespective of whether or not people are good, one will obtain better outcomes by trusting them. Dispositional trust is about how individuals develop their propensities to trust and how these predilections influence their thoughts and actions (Hardin, 1993).

When combining the three types of trust it is clear that trust is more than belief and knowledge. Trust is psychologically located and morally loaded, and it requires a platform that is regularly reinforced. As demonstrated in the proposed model, trust is built by a combination of technology, organizational procedures, and reputation of the community participants. Hereby, it is demonstrated that neither technology nor socio-psychology are a panacea as neither security measures nor interactivity and knowledgability are enough.

A NON-LINEAR RELATIONSHIP BETWEEN TRUST AND SECURITY

Trust from a computational perspective has been closely linked with research in security management, although the relationship between the two concepts is not linear (Abdul-Rahman & Hailes, 2000). A computer has to make trust-decisions based on available information. There is usually a trustee, an entity which needs to be trusted, and a trustor. The trustor is an entity that generally holds resources which the trustee wants to access (Grandison & Sloman, 2000). In a SOA perspective, both trustee and trustor need to believe in the competence of other entities to act dependably,

securely, and reliably. In such a context it can be useful also to represent distrust to help support the revoking of established trust (Grandison & Sloman, 2000). Moreover, trust in online systems is often linked to reputation-building where a reputation, which can be the basis of trust, has to be established over time starting from a initial state of non-existent or limited trust (Resnick et al., 2000). Reputation derives from expectations based on a history of past actions. Reputation ratings have the ability also to convey distrust through a negative rating.

The system presented here is oriented towards a phase/stage build-up of participation and commitment in the community. Participants are not expected to use or participate in all activities/functionalities in the community from day one. They are anticipated to follow a path where they start out by using the SOA only for self-referral on operational data. Once accustomed to the functionalities of this area, participants are expected to move on to self- and group-referrals on both operational and financial data. From here the path will go on to the layer of validated data in all three groupings, and finally the path of trust will arrive at the level of All. This level is used for both types of data, but without the necessity to validate everything through a system of institutions.

Trust and Security Management

Trust and security management in a computer-system perspective is not the same. Security is a prerequisite to trust. Security has to do with authentication such as verifying the claimed identity of a client or service (Saltzer, 1974), and authorization like allowing an authenticated client access to information or a particular service (Griffiths & Wade, 1976). In an online benchmarking application it is important to have a secure mechanism to exchange digital evidence which can support trust-decisions. The use of appropriate industry-standard security solutions can help generate system trust from users in the form of digital evidence being issued by the system.

Several existing trust management frameworks focus on decentralized, Peer-to-Peer (P2P) systems. xTrust (Branchaud & Flinn, 2004) and TrustMe (Xiong & Liu, 2003) are both examples of such frameworks. xTrust is aimed at making trust transitive across multiple domains, of which some may not be trusted. The framework supports mapping of domain specific semantics between domains and federated authentication. Both xTrust and TrustMe are reputation-based and concerned with requestor and provider anonymity for distributed management of trust. A number of problems concerning reputation in P2P electronic communities (i.e., eBay, Amazon, Slashdot) are identified and the TrustMe framework is presented as an improved solution (Xiong & Liu, 2003). The PolicyMaker (Li et al., 2002) framework approach trust at a more general level of abstraction. PolicyMaker is a X.509/PGP PKI-based query language for expressing trust rating and authorization requests. RT is a family of Role-Based trust management languages for representing policies and credentials in distributed authorization.

Most of the above mentioned reputation frameworks base reputation-ratings upon human feedback. Maximilien and Singh (2002) present an approach to evaluating the reputation of Web services. This approach is based on the interaction of software agents and is partly based upon the reputation-rating mechanism presented in Zacharia and Maes (2000). By expanding the concept of trust, reputation and reputation rating to Web services, Maximilien and Singh (2002) are closer to the approach presented in this chapter.

Performance Measurement

Member participation is critical to the support of the knowledge-sharing environment which the system presented here wishes to establish. Motivation for participation in the knowledge-sharing community is based on perceived mutual gain in terms of the value of contributed knowledge towards shared strategic goals. Therefore, it is important to have some form of performance management to evaluate individual participation as well as to score relative performance against shared goals. Performance management is often based on a number of different performance-measurement frameworks where different frameworks can give different perspectives and viewpoints.

Examples include scorecard approaches such as the balanced scorecard (BSC), benchmarking, and activity-based costing. Different measurement frameworks generally offer a specific perspective, like for example the external perspective. However, the BSC is an example that offers a number of perspectives, and modified versions even offer customized perspectives. The BSC (Kaplan & Norton, 1993) has been widely adopted and allows the inclusion of important non-financial measures in the measurement of organizational performance. In the system presented here, performance measurement is seen not only as a way of helping users check their relative performance against shared goals, but also as a way of trying to measure aspects of knowledge-sharing and management that are important to community building. It is proposed that performance measurement methodologies like BSC offer an effective tool for examining the performance of a virtual community using multiple key perspectives.

PROTOTYPE SYSTEM ARCHITECTURE

The presented prototype system uses a service oriented architecture (SOA) based on the use of the Web services model for service description, discovery, and integration. To support this, the CFac issues a plug-in application to members, which needs to be installed on their Web servers to allow them to participate in the SOA network. This plug-in application is needed to support secure data transmission and requires access to a read-only local directory on the Web server where members need to place data to be shared. This helps isolate the plug-in from access to sensitive member data, and is similar to the approach used by many file-sharing applications. A member can interact with the CFac server either by using a service interface, for access to standard services provided to members, or via a Web interface, for more complex interaction, as shown in Figure 1.

Initially, credentials need to be exchanged between a potential community member and the community server. Using public encryption keys a profile is established for the new member, after verification of credentials. The profile contains a private and public key pair. The private key is transferred to the new member for encoding data transmissions. The public key is stored on the server so that the server can read the member's data. A unique id code is assigned to the new member and associated with the member profile. The member is only identified using this id code to provide a level of anonymity. Data exchanges are based on the use of Web-based service interfaces or the Web-based user interface on the CFac-server, which is used for a member to manage credentials.

As part of a member profile, stored on the community server, the history of community interactions between the member and the community is tracked for one or more metrics. Initially, we are looking at metrics associated with the quality of the provided data; this is the sharing and participation perspective in Table 1. This allows members to dynamically build a reputation, which can be part of the basis of trust, in the context of community performance metrics. Managing

Figure 1. System architecture (©2007, Lemmergaard et al. Used with permission)

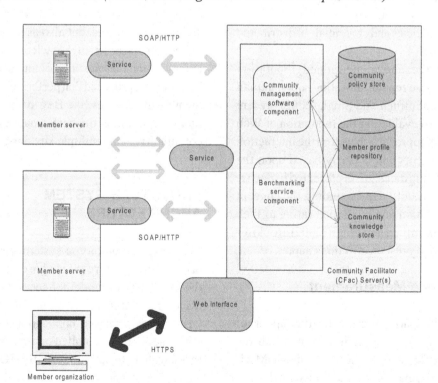

credentials and group memberships through the Web-based interface provides a mechanism that allows a firm in the wider community to become part of a particular trusted subgroup of the community.

Interaction with services is achieved by means of SOAP messages. The required security features include protection of message integrity, message confidentiality, and message authentication. Also, verification of the requester of data, the CFac-server, from a member-provided information service is needed. Likewise, it must be possible to verify member requests for access to services on the CFac-server. The SOA developed for the Danish grower community uses XML digital signature combined with SOAP messages to provide message integrity, confidentiality, and authentication. For the verification of a requester of service, the system uses Username Token Verification which allows username tokens to be sent as part of SOAP messages. The service owner can validate the sender identity by using digital signature technology based on PKI, where a security token refers to the key used, for example the X.509 Certificate Token. The prototype is experimenting with the use of the Java Web Services Developer Pack (WSDP) 1.5 XWS-Security Framework which supports XML Digital Signature, XML Encryption, and Username Token Verification. The WSDP XWS-security framework provides support for apache Web-servers and is based on the OASIS Web Services Security (WSS) core specification.

The system architecture is based on a number of Member servers connecting to a central CFac-server which is assumed trusted at the community level. Member servers and the CFac-server act as both client and server in the architecture. The CFac-server acts as server when it is the provider of community services. It also acts as client when harvesting knowledge from a service interface provided by members. A member server acts as a client when accessing community services and as a server when providing knowledge which can

be collected. The roles of the key parts of the system architecture can be described in detail as follows:

Member Server

The member server installs the plug-in component on the Web server which creates a Web service interface for supplying information to the CFac-server. When the service receives a request from the CFac-server, it creates an XML message, adds content, signs the message using XML signature, and then sends the message to the requester, the CFac.

Community Facilitator (CFac) Server

The community management software component handles credentials and can be uploaded to a member profile through the Web interface. A system-issued credential is automatically added to a member profile. Member issued credentials may be sent to another member through any electronic means, like emails. Moreover, the CFac-server provides a Web interface for members to connect to, and it performs more complicated management functions such as managing membership details and credentials. It supports secure connections using HTTPS over secure socket layer (SSL), but requires the member to have a certificate issued by the CFac-server.

Knowledge and Policy Storage

Storing of community polices in community policy store: Access control policies are stored using the XML Access Control Markup Language (XACML) (XACML RBAC, 2004) which provides an access control language based on XML syntax. The Ponder policy specification language (Damianou et al., 2001) has been chosen, which was designed with security management applications in mind, as the means to express group policies.

Storing of profiles in member profile repository presupposes that performance management information for members is stored using an XML-based format for defining BSC information such as perspectives, objectives, metrics etc.

COMMUNITY TRUST AND SECURITY MODEL

The prototype model is specific to the needs of an industry-based community where key requirements include: anonymity of members; a way for members to evolve trust and participation; a way for members to self-manage trusted groups formed within the community.

The model focuses on the context which can be the basis for trust-decisions between two parties. Context is related to digital evidence in the form of credentials asserted by the system about a user. The model represents our approach to trust management within the target community and is designed to work with an underlying security framework. This framework controls access to resources using role-based access control (RBAC) (Kuhn, 1997) and supports management of digital credentials within a public key infrastructure (PKI) environment (Thompson et al., 2003). In the target community there are interactions between members and the CFac and indirectly between members using the CFac-server as an intermediary. The model uses groups that fall into different levels of access rights to community-held resources.

Members of a group are assumed to trust each other. Within a level there may be many groups and trust between these different groups may be subjective. To support self-management of groups within the community, members need to make trust decisions about each other. A trust decision may be made by the system about a user or by a user about another user. Assuming there is a set of principals P which include all users of the system and the CFac system itself, or at least

the administrator of the system. Looking at trust between two members of such a community and following the approach of Mezzetti (2003), trust can formally be defined as a trust relation with a 3-ary (ternary) relation $\tau(\alpha, \beta, \mu)$ over P, μ which links two entities α, β (members of P) who wish to form a trust relationship to a context which can be the basis of that trust relationship μ. The proposed model, however, requires a context based on system-issued credentials and the status of a user linked to active roles inherited through group memberships, both of which may be time dependent. Within a trust-management system this allows us to define τ more generally for some set of principals P who are users of the system, as the set of 3-tuples satisfying the following relationship:

$$\tau \subseteq P \times P \times \mu \qquad (1)$$

We define μ as a subset of S ($\mu \subseteq S$) which is a set of system-held contexts about members of the set of principles P. For each user who is a member of P there is a system context $s \in S$ defined as:

$$s \leftarrow \{X, c\} \qquad (2)$$

X is a set of system-issued assertions held by the member, and c is the current member status. Member status is linked to a set of current group memberships and a set of current roles, inherited through group memberships. s is stored and managed by the system in a user's profile and is generally only accessible to the system and the user themselves. However, upon a request from the member who owns the system context the system can release a subset of s which can be used to form μ for another member who is not the owner of that context.

The model needs to include time dependence for a system-managed context to support the dynamic nature of trust. We wish to link part of the context to a member's reputation which can change over time. This requires that the system is able to make an assertion about a user which is valid for some period of time. To this end, we use an approach similar to that of Marchesini and Smith (2005) and define the lifespan of system-managed context μ, denoted l_μ as the time period Δt for which μ is valid as the basis for a trust decision. As Marchesini and Smith (2005) we define the time period Δt as an interval $\tau = [t_i, t_j]$ and we refer to the context μ as being active at time t if, and only if, $t \in \tau$.

A complex issue in a trust-management system is often how to deal with incomplete information. There is no easy answer to this problem. In our model, trust decisions are necessarily limited to the information that is permitted under various rules released by the system. This may still leave areas of uncertainty in terms of the basis of trust and, this is connected to the type of system trust the system-user has in this system's ability to support trust-decisions in the context of an information-sharing environment.

A credential is usually viewed in a security context (Barlow et al., 2001) as being some form of evidence issued by a trusted source and provided by the user for authentication of identity. Examples of such evidence are username/password pair, X.509 certificates (Houseley et al., 2001), Kerberos tickets (Kerberos, 2007), or digitally signed documents. However, we extend the usual notion of a credential to include evidence provided by the community system on the reputation of the user which is based on a history of interaction between the user and the system. There has been a lot of work in reputation systems (Resnick et al., 2000; Zacharia & Maes, 2000) and the use of credentials for trust has been studied in research on electronic markets (Barlow et al., 2001) and other areas of e-commerce where the focus generally has been on the relationship between a buyer and seller.

We denote a credential ξ in our model as $\xi(\alpha, \beta, A, \tau)$ which represents the situation that α (in this case always CFac) has been the issuer of the credential to the subject β and that the set of at-

tributes A has been bound to the public key of β during a time interval τ. The set of attributes can include system-issued assertions, in the form of name-value pairs, about the subject or about the credential itself (e.g., transferable=true). One of the attributes is always the type of the credential. Credentials are classified as being of different types depending on their intended usage. For example, a group-credential type might be used to assert membership to a particular group or it might contain assertions about the credential itself, which has been issued based on a policy linked to the group governing how group credentials may be used. This provides a way of controlling the use of credentials within the system.

Initially, there may be no evidence upon which to base a trust assessment and only basic entry-level credentials available to validate trustworthiness of an entity. The only approach, therefore, is to have a trust accumulation mechanism. Generally, trust accumulation mechanisms have been interaction based, which an examination of a history of interaction shows, or opinion based on for example trust validations or trust referrals from other community members. Using an interaction approach, we can create a measure of trustworthiness of an entity A based on an examination of the history of interactions that have taken place with A. This type of trustworthiness can be stored in a reputation indicator that evolves over time. There are many different approaches to what the reputation indicator can be based on, like different types of trust evidence, and how it can be calculated. When a member first joins/registers in the community he/she will receive one or more system-issued credentials from the CFac based on disclosure of identity information to the CFac. This establishes an initial basic entry-status for the new community member. Additional credentials can then be accumulated based on further interactions with either the CFac or with other members through community groups. These accumulated credentials will either result from some form of negotiation process or be linked to reputation rating, which is restricted to the CFac.

The model is centralized because the CFac is assumed to be a trusted third party who in a security context is the only entity who is authorized to issue credentials and revoke them. This means that the CFac can only issue credentials valid over our domain D which represents the information-sharing community. CFac handles all credential requests and tracks credentials held by each member. Consequently, members cannot issue credentials on behalf of each other, but they can exchange them in a system-approved credential transfer and request new credentials from the CFac-system. This is practical for the needs of our knowledge-sharing community, but may not be so for more general applications where it may limit possible interactions.

Assume that there is a set of groups g which have been set up by the CFac to support the current community requirements. A group can be defined in terms of P as $g \subseteq P$. The use of groups is partly motivated by the fact that community members are required to have a degree of anonymity, and groups therefore allow visible identity of a member within the community to be limited to the group level. Also, when using a role-based access control framework (Kuhn, 1997) to control access to community-held resources, the use of groups tied to roles instead of individuals tied to roles can reduce the complexity of the role hierarchy that needs to be maintained. We will assume that all community-level management is conducted by the CFac.

In the presented system, a knowledge-sharing virtual community is supported using community knowledge resources. These fall into different access categories depending on the status of a community member. All knowledge resources and details of community members are held on a third-party system operated by the CFac who is assumed trusted at the community level. The CFac system stores a series of community policies including group-policies and access-policies. Community policy management is an issue which includes the question of who is responsible for

proposing policies, setting policies, reviewing policies, and changing policies. There are many different approaches to how community policy management could be made a collaborative activity, like for example voting mechanisms and handling of multiple proposals. System trust would also be a key issue in any system supporting such collaborative activities.

In the proposed model, a group policy is used to define the membership requirements and entitlements which must be true for a community member to belong to a particular group. Group member entitlements are specified as rules about the rights of a member in regard to actions related to the use of system-issued credentials and roles. This includes delegation rules (e.g., under what conditions there might be a transfer of credentials and hence rights between members), refrain rules (e.g., what actions must not be performed using roles even if a member might qualify to perform the action), and rules governing the separation of duty (e.g., mutual exclusion of active roles) functionality (Kuhn, 1997). Community groups are linked to access rights through a set of roles mapped to a group. A subset of these roles may be inherited at some time by a group member if it is allowable under the restrictions of the group entitlements. We wish to support the ability of members to request new credential types based on their current group-membership rights. And also to support that members can transfer credentials to other members given certain conditions are met. A base entry-level group is automatically assigned to all new members of the system which has a number of default group policies. Members are then able to migrate upwards in terms of group memberships which exist at different trust levels in the system.

As part of group-membership requirements, a member must hold a valid group-membership credential or qualify for group-membership rights. Membership rights of a particular group g_i can be defined as a binary function $M(g_i)$ which depends on a negotiated group acceptance based on a set of held and valid, non-expired, credentials. Let ξ_i represent a particular credential ($\xi_i \in \xi$) and let f represent a boolean function which tests whether the credential is valid and also imposes a set of conditions $C_i \subseteq C$ based on assertions in a credential to test a set of assertions stored in the credential. f will be true if the credential is currently valid and all members of the set of test conditions are satisfied (i.e., strict and enforced). Then $M(g_i)$ for group g_i (evaluated the time of some request based on group membership rights) will depend on a combination of a number n of credentials of different types which must be currently valid and held by the potential member of the group:

$$M(g_i) \leftarrow \{f(\xi_1, C_1), .., f(\xi_n, C_n)\} \qquad (3)$$

Once group-membership rights are resolved at the time of a request a time limited group-membership credential could be issued as supported by security models such as SDSI (Rivest & Lampson, 1996). We propose that the input for a particular function M could be linked to an accumulator, a hash of a set of input into one value. The accumulator could be dynamically managed in combination with the group-membership credential (Camenisch & Lysyanskaya, 2001) and could form the basis for fast revocation by the system of group-membership if any of the necessary conditions C change, or credentials ξ_i are revoked within the time of validity of the group certificate.

In terms of knowledge-sharing and categorization of trust into different levels, the requirements of the grower community are as follows. There has to be a clear distinction between what is 'private' information, information shareable with a known group, and information available to everybody. We define three key categories: general group—limited access to resources; trusted sub-group—access to resources only through roles belonging to the sub-group; general reputable group—access to all community shared resources. These groups can exist at different levels of trust. The links between these groups and roles form a role hierarchy that map to a set of trust levels.

We are particularly interested in community reputation based on community performance metrics. The set of conditions C is general and can be used to support a number of purposes. One of the purposes of C, which is of key importance to our model, is when the credential is a system-issued credential linked to an ongoing assessment of a user's reputation rating. If the rating is a value in the range [0, 1] then we can specify a credential for example as $f(\xi_i, \text{type} = \text{rating}, \text{value} \geq 0.8)$. This requires the system-issued rating value contained in the credential to be greater than 0.8. Also, we would like the model to support inter-member referrals using credentials where a member can pass on credentials to another member under certain conditions. Hereby we allow groups within the community a degree of self-management. However, we do require that there are special community-level rating credentials which can only be modified by the CFac and which are linked to performance evaluation at the community level. The focus of the proposed model is a knowledge-sharing community where users need to be rated at the community level on transactions with collectively held resources. In contrast, online market-style communities often have users rate each other on their transactions with each other.

Another purpose of C is the evaluation of a credential under certain conditions of disclosure to protect privacy of information that may be part of a credential. An important community management issue is how to handle privacy for the community of competing growers who wish to share knowledge. The individual firms need to maintain a degree of anonymity, and it is therefore relevant to establish how a user may obtain credentials through a negotiation process. One approach to negotiation under such conditions is that of controlled disclosure where the key aim is protection of privacy while negotiating trust.

Controlled disclosure of knowledge has been studied by many researchers (Barlow et al., 2001) and can be supported through the use of conditions on credentials in our model. A condition can be linked to a required policy being satisfied before disclosure of a particular credential or parts of a credential is allowed. Here a member of a group might request from the system a transferable copy of one of their credentials, if such an action is allowed under any policy that applies, which he/she can then pass on, system mediated, to another user. We also wish to support the ability of the member requesting such a credential to request new assertions which can be added to the credential by the system and hereby restrict disclosure of information in the credential. For example under this scenario, a new attribute (visibility=value) might be assigned where value is a mask value that restricts visibility of fields in the credential to a user who is not the subject of the credential. The system will allow a member who is not the subject to receive the credential, but will enforce limited visibility on its content. Successful negotiations can be viewed as consisting of a number of agreements which have been reached where an agreement involves the exchange of credentials. As discussed in Hildreth et al. (2000), it can also often be important to use face-to-face contacts in conjunction with online activity as part of supporting community building. This could be true especially in terms of the negotiation process that may be connected with exchange of credentials.

As part of our system, we need to link the model of trust to an underlying security framework controlling access to community-held resources. We have chosen to use the RBAC-model, as it is widely used in service-based networks (e.g., Fuerst et al., 2002) and provides a mechanism for policy specification. Much architecture (e.g., Li et al., 2002) has been put forward linking RBAC with trust management. RBAC policies link access to information resources to a set of defined roles. In our model, the defined roles are linked to com-munity sub-groups which consist of community members. The policies can be expressed as rules of the following form:

$$\text{RuleX}: \text{can access}(e, r) \leftarrow f(c, r) \qquad (4)$$

'e' represents an entity (role), r a resource, and c a user status linked to current active roles inherited through group memberships. For this type of rule, a group g is linked to a set of RBAC entity roles, and the function f resolves the set of active roles linked to a member of some group or set of groups in terms of the required role to access r. This is to support separation of duty functionality as described by Kuhn (1997), which can enforce mutual exclusion of roles. The idea is that a member of a group or groups may qualify to hold a number of roles, but that some of these roles may be mutually exclusive and consequently cannot be held at the same time. This has significance in terms of fraud if inter-member transactions, such as trust referrals, are to be supported.

Community Performance Management

Important to our performance management requirements is how to score relative performance of participants in the context of shared strategic goals. This can be achieved by adopting a benchmarking process which can be defined as a form of group analysis using an external perspective to compare performance of individuals with agreed industry "best practices." As a part of process benchmarking, Danish growers would like to identify where (un)favorable gaps exist in their industry processes. They would also like to compare their financial performance. Since we also wish to analyze knowledge-sharing and participation in our community, the performance management requirements extend beyond only this type of external perspective and require a multi-perspective framework. This leads us to introduce a multi-perspective framework within which we include support for process and financial benchmarking. We introduce a separate perspective to look at the sharing and participation within the community. We have identified the following knowledge-sharing needs for performance management within our target industry community:

- **Information harvesting and analysis:**
  - Need to be able to collect information for metrics within a certain timeframe and without a high level of process change or cost incurred by information providers. To minimize disruption of employees of information providers the information collection and analysis should be automated.
- **Information formatting and quality:**
  - Community level agreements must be agreed upon and these agreements must define a set of information-formatting requirements and the requirements in terms of community information quality. These could be specified in community policies held by the CFac.
- **Performance measurement of information providers:**
  - It should be made clear to information providers under what perspectives and measures they will be subject to performance measurement in terms of supplied information. An agreed framework should be used which is appropriate for and meets the requirements of the community in terms of its shared goals. This framework should be transparent to information providers.

The Balanced Scorecard (BSC) style approach is being used as a performance management framework for the knowledge-sharing community of Danish growers. We adopt a dynamic BSC which makes use of multiple perspectives,

objectives, and measures. It is also dynamic in that we track instance data over time related to the measures in the BSC. A perspective is a particular viewpoint for the performance measurement. The standard BSC (Kaplan & Norton, 1993) uses four key perspectives: 1. financial; 2. customer; 3. process; and 4. learning and growth. We extend the BSC concept to allow for customized perspectives which are most appropriate for our specialized community. Objectives are defined for each perspective and represent a measurable goal. For our community this could for instance be a benchmarking target. An objective can be broken down into sub-objectives, with milestones on the track toward a goal. Once objectives are defined, measures need to be associated with objectives where a measure will define the metric details (e.g., type, purpose, and units) and be used to determine how performance will be evaluated in the context of achieving a particular objective. Using a dynamic BSC system, users can be rated at different points in time against a series of objectives to give a set of performance-rating values.

Within an industry-based knowledge-sharing community where the main commodity is the strategic value to individual firms, it is important to have different perspectives for performance measurement. We propose that a performance-measurement framework needs to have a way to rate or score community members in accordance with their contribution to the community. Such rating system requires a feedback mechanism to be supported as one of the perspectives in the performance management framework.

Table 1 presents a set of mappings ranging from the traditional BSC perspectives to a set that is appropriate for our target community (i.e., agreed at community level). This includes the re-mapping of the customer perspective to a community-member perspective, which allows feedback through predetermined metrics about the value of community-held knowledge (especially in terms of knowledge-sharing) to individual members. It also includes a mechanism for an individual member to rate the effectiveness of community process, like performance management, information provision, and policy selection. Benchmarking is supported through the use of the process perspective.

Performance management in a community environment requires appropriate knowledge to be provided by members of the community. In our proposed system this is achieved through knowledge harvesting from members via the services they provide. In this knowledge-sharing environment a key issue is the quality of knowledge provided, and this requires some kind of knowledge validation process.

In the proposed system, knowledge validation is initially to be done by the administrator of the CFac-server. However, as the community expands, this could result in a very large amount of data processing, which could easily become un-manageable. Therefore, it is necessary to look at the types of shared processes which are able to be performed collaboratively by members of the community. A possible solution is to randomly and anonymously assign newly gathered knowledge to a member, who has an appropriate reputation, for review in terms of data validation.

To discuss the functioning of our proposed rating system, we first need to define a rating value $\varphi = [0, 1]$, which corresponds to one of the selected metrics for performance management. The user starts with median value so as to allow for a negative change in the initial status. We need to define a rating scale and then a method to increase and decrease rating values:

$$\varphi \text{ increase: } \max(\varphi + \Delta\varphi, 1) \tag{5}$$

$$\varphi \text{ decrease: } \max(\varphi - \Delta\varphi, 0) \tag{6}$$

Here $\Delta\varphi$ represents the rating increment. Assume that a rating value r_{member} is changed a number n of discrete times forming a history for a user:

Table 1. Balanced scorecard perspective mappings on the Danish grower community (©2007, Lemmergaard et al. Used with permission)

BSC perspective	Customized perspective	Examples
Financial	Financial	Business administration data
		Accounting data
Customer	Community member	Feedback on knowledge value
		Feedback on community process
Process	Community process	Industry operations data
		Benchmarked production process
Learning and growth	Sharing and participation	Quality of knowledge-sharing
		Reliability of knowledge-sharing
		Level of knowledge-sharing

History : $\{r_{member} (t = 1), r_{member} (t = 2), ..., r_{member} (t = n)\}$ (7)

This results in a set of rating credentials ξ_φ (where $\xi_\varphi \subseteq \xi$) asserting each new value, which has been issued by the system. For our system it is appropriate to test the value of a rating credential, but there might also be an issue of time in terms of how the value has changed. This is important when considering the affect of the recent history of a user versus his/her longer term behavior. This would require an examination of a set of rating credentials. Assuming the use of conditions based on both value and time we can then link the rating value to a system issued credential $\xi_i \subseteq \xi_\varphi$ with conditions c_0 (type=rating), $c_1(t)$ and $c_2(r_{member})$ using the function f discussed above. For example, this would then allow a series of statements satisfying:

$f(\xi_i, type = rating, t > 5, r_{member} > 0.8) : \forall(\xi_i \in \xi_\varphi)$ (8)

This can be interpreted as matching any available credentials of type rating and testing both the rating value of a member and the time value asserted in each credential. The rating value for each credential must have been over 0.8 and the time greater than five, when looking at recent history for example. Different metrics may use different mechanisms to calculate the rating value.

FUTURE TRENDS

The quality of knowledge and knowledge validation processes are closely related to the issue of trust. Trust is a key requirement in a virtual knowledge-sharing community, and as described above trust plays a key role both in modeling interactional social concepts and in a macro-social context. It is, however, only possible to translate our physical interaction into an electronic interaction if sufficient trust in the system is established. In the presented model trust is both seen from a socio-psychological and a technical perspective, with the latter part focusing on digital evidence in the form of credentials.

With an increase in both strategic alliances between competitors based on Web-based collaboration and virtual communities in general, trust in an IT system perspective needs to expand beyond a reputation-building perspective. Using reputation as a basis for trust building underlies the question of what reputation should be based on. As demonstrated in the proposed model, reputation needs to be linked to more than the traditional ratings generated as feedback to financial interactions. Also, ratings of non-financial metrics, measuring how well a member participates in and contributes to the community, will have to be taken into consideration when determining the level of trust.

Moreover, as modern society is increasingly relying on the storage, processing, and transmission of knowledge and virtual communities are becoming larger and more diverse, the issue of trust will continue to increase, as lack of trust will be the preventing factor hindering virtual communities from growing. This development also presents major challenges in terms of privacy and integrity of firm-specific knowledge. With larger communities and hereby more diverse community-members there is also a likelihood of an increase in fake identities, violations of netiquettes, or even crime.

CONCLUSION

The main contribution of this chapter is the practical aspect of building trust for secure knowledge-exchange within a virtual community with shared strategic goals. The concepts presented are supported by empirical findings from a case study on an ongoing collaboration between academic researchers and industry partners. The aim of the collaboration is to facilitate a knowledge-sharing community for practitioners from the Danish horticultural industry, the pot-plant trade. The purpose of the community is to harvest and analyze information related to strategy, production processes, general business administration, and financial performance.

To support the knowledge-sharing community, a Web-based SOA, which utilized knowledge collection services and a benchmarking service, was designed. The key requirements of the system were anonymity of members, the possibility to evolve trust and participation over time, and the option for members to generate self-managed trusted subgroups. Participation and knowledge-sharing are used as key performance measures to rate system users, while feedback mechanisms are supported to examine the rating of performance of the system at the community level. Flexible group structures are used to manage members of the community and to provide a way for members to form their own social sub-groups as part of migrating to higher levels of participation and hence knowledge-sharing.

For the community to be able to evolve, participation through contributions to the SOA is vital. Participation is linked to the reputation of a community member, and is hereby part of the basis for trust. This is based on digital evidence in the form of credentials, which support feedback and reputation management. Finally, system-issued credentials and status of system users are dynamic of nature.

This chapter focuses on the applied trust and security model of the SOA. The trust and security model is discussed in a theoretical framework of a three-dimensional model of generic objects of trust. The objects of trust reflect both institutional phenomena (i.e., system trust) and personal and interpersonal forms of trust (i.e., interpersonal and dispositional trust). The objects of trust influence the security models applied to the benchmarking application. Long-term build-up of trusting relationships is complicated by little time to establish acquaintance, mutual understanding, remoteness, and lack of time. Instead infrastructure and process may be designed to support trustful interaction.

REFERENCES

Abdul-Rahman, A., & Hailes, S. (2000). Supporting trust in virtual communities. In *Proceedings of the 33rd Hawaii International Conference on System Sciences, Volume 6* (pp. 6007- 6015). Los Alamitos, CA: IEEE Computer Society.

Barlow, T., Hess, A., & Seamons, K. E. (2001). Trust negotiation in electronic markets. In Schoop, M. & Walczuch (Eds.), *Proceedings of the Eighth Research Symposium on Emerging Electronic Markets (RSEEM 01).* Maastricht, The Netherlands.

Branchaud, M., & Flinn, S. (2004). xTrust: A scalable trust management infrastructure. In *Proceedings of the Second Annual Conference on Privacy, Security and Trust (PST 2004)* (pp. 207–218), Fredericton, New Brunswick, Canada.

Brown, G., & Carpenter, R. (2004). Successful application of service-oriented architecture across the enterprise and beyond. *Intel Technology Journal, 8*(4), 345–359.

Brown, J. S., & Duguid, P. (2000). *The social life of information.* Boston, MA, USA: Harvard Business School Press.

Camenisch, J., & Lysyanskaya, A. (2001). Efficient revocation of anonymous group membership. *Cryptology ePrint Archive, Report 2001/113.* Retrieved on March 29, 2007, from http://eprint.iacr.org/2001/113

Damianou, N., Dulay, N., Lupu, E., & Sloman, M. (2001). The ponder policy specification language. In *Proceedings Policy 2001: Workshop on Policies for Distributed Systems and Networks* (pp. 17-28). Bristol, UK: Springer-Verlag LNCS 1995.

Feeney, K. C., Lewis, D., & Wade, V. P. (2004). Policy based management for internet communities. In *Proceedings of the 5th International Workshop on Policies for Distributed Systems and Networks* (pp. 23-32). New York, USA: POLICY.

Fuerst, K., Schmidt, T., & Wippel, G. (2002). Managing access in extended enterprise networks. *IEEE Internet Computing*, 6(5), 67–74.

Good, D. (1988). Individuals, interpersonal relations, and trust. In D. Gambetta (Ed.), *Trust: Making and Breaking Cooperative Relations* (pp. 31-48). New York: Basil Blackwell.

Grandison, T., & Sloman, M. (2000). A survey of trust in internet applications. IEEE Communications Surveys, *The Electronic Magazine of Original Peer-Reviewed Survey Articles*, Fourth Quarter, 2000. Retrieved on March 29, 2007, from http://citeseer.ist.psu.edu/cachedpage/458414/1

Griffiths, P., & Wade, B. (1976). An authorization mechanism for a relational database system. *ACM TODS*, 1(3), 242–255.

Hardin, R. (1993). The street-level epistemology of trust. *Politics and Society*, 21, 505–529.

Hildreth, P., Kimble, C., & Wright, P. (2000). Communities of practice in the distributed international environment. *Journal of Knowledge Management*, 4(1), 27–37.

Houseley, R., Polk, W., Ford, W., & Solo, D. (2001). Internet X.509 public key infrastructure, certificate and certificate revocation list (CRL) Profile. *RFC 3280 (RFC3280)*. Retrieved on March 29, 2007, from http://www.faqs/rfcs/rfc3280.html

Kaplan, R. S. & Norton, D. P. (1993). Putting the balanced scorecard to work. *Harvard Business Review*, 71(5), 134–141.

Kerberos (2007). Kerberos: The network authentication protocol. Retrieved on March 29, 2007, from http://web.mit.edu/kerberos

Kuhn, D. R. (1997). Mutual exclusion of roles as a means of implementing separation of duty in role-based access control systems. In *Proceedings of the second ACM Workshop on Role-based Access Control, ACM Workshop on Role-Based Access Control* (pp. 23-30). New York, NY, USA: ACM Press.

Lave, J., & Wenger, E. (1991). *Situated learning: Legitimate peripheral participation*. USA: Cambridge University Press.

Lemmergaard, J., C. Gersbo-Møller, D. Brigth, & T. Hansson (2005, April 21-22). *Trust and community management: Design and implementation of trust enabling technologie*. Paper presented at the First European Young Researchers Workshop on Service Oriented Computing, Leicester, UK.

Li, N., Mitchell, J. C., & Winsborough, W. H. (2002). Design of a role-based trust-management framework. In *Proceedings of the 2002 IEEE Symposium on Security and Privacy*, (pp. 114–130). Washington, DC, USA: IEEE Computer Society Press.

Malhotra, Y. (2002). Enabling knowledge exchanges for e-business communities. *information strategy: The Executives Journal*, 18(3), 26–31.

Marchesini, J., & Smith, S. W. (2005). Modeling public key infrastructure in the real world. In *Proceedings of the Public Key Infrastructure: EuroPKI 2005 Conference* (pp. 118-134), LNCS. Springer-Verlag.

Maximilien, E. M., & Singh, M. P. (2002). Reputation and endorsement for web services. *ACM SIGecom Exchanges*, (pp. 24–31). New York, NY, USA: ACM Press.

Mezzetti, N. (2003). Towards a model for trust relationships in virtual enterprises. In *Proceedings of the 14th International Workshop on Database and Expert Systems Applications (DEXA'03)*, (pp. 420- 424). Washington, DC, USA: IEEE Computer Society Press.

Resnick, P., Zeckhauser, R., Friedman, E., & Kuwabara, K. (2000). Reputation systems. *Communications of the ACM*, 43(12), 45-48.

Rivest, R. L., & Lampson, B. W. (1996). SDSI—A Simple Distributed Security Infrastructure. In *Proceedings of the 16th Annual International Cryptology Conference*. Retrieved on March 29, 2007, from http://theory.lcs.mit.edu/~rivest/sdsi10.html

Saltzer, J. (1974). Protection and the control of information sharing in multics. *Communications of the ACM (CACM)*, 17(7). 388–402.

Shapiro, S. P. (1987). The social control of impersonal trust. *American Journal of Sociology*, 93(3), 623–658.

Thompson, M. R., Essiari, A., & Mudumbai, S. (2003). Certificate-based authorization policy in a PKI environment. *ACM Press*, 6(4), 566–588.

Wenger, E. (1998). *Communities of practice. learning, meaning, and identity*. New York: Cambridge University Press.

Xiong, L., & Liu, L. (2003). A Reputation-Based Trust Model for Peer-to-Peer eCommerce Communities. In *Proceedings of the 2003 IEEE Conference on E-Commerce Technology (CEC'03)* (pp. 275-183). Washington, DC, USA: IEEE Computer Society Press.

Zacharia, G., & Maes, P. (2000). Trust management through reputation mechanisms. *Applied Artificial Intelligence*, 14(9), 881–907.

KEY TERMS

Community of Practice (CoP): Groups of people that emerge of their own accord with the purpose of sharing knowledge and learning from each other.

Credentials: Information used to verify the identity of a user of an information system.

Inter-Personal Trust: Existing or occurring reliance on the integrity and ability between community members.

Non-Financial Metrics: Versification of measurements not involving financial matters.

Reputation: The general estimation in which a person is held by the community members.

Service Oriented Architecture (SOA): A perspective of software architecture that defines the use of Web services to support the requirements of software users.

System Trust: Reliance on the integrity, ability, or character of a system.

Chapter XXVIII
Lost in the Funhouse, Is Anyone in Control?

Pat Jefferies
University of Bedfordshire, UK

Steve McRobb
De Montfort University, UK

Bernd Carsten Stahl
De Montfort University, UK

ABSTRACT

In this chapter, a framework which models at a high level the interactions between technology, pedagogy, and ethics is applied to the interpretation of a case study. The case study describes a student excluded from his course as a result of administrative error. Since his studies are, in part, mediated through a Virtual Learning Environment, the exclusion takes on additional impacts not anticipated by the human actors, and proves surprisingly difficult to undo even once the error is acknowledged. This reveals problematic aspects of the interaction between the domains. Conflicts between the aims and interests of the various stakeholders, combined with misunderstandings of the way that the technology operates, provide obvious surface causes of the problem. However, analysis reveals that the deeper cause lies in the fact that the life world of education has been colonised by a system that replaces human communication, and thus inevitably presents ethical problems.

INTRODUCTION

This chapter uses a case study to explore some aspects of the intersections between pedagogy, ethics, and technology, in the context of a Virtual Learning Environment (VLE). Nowadays it is clear that VLEs are gaining increased popularity as the favoured platform for e-learning in most universities and many Further Education (FE) Colleges. For example "the MLE landscape report survey in 2003, which received returns from 358 institutions across both HE and FE, reports a very high prevalence of VLE usage in all types of institutions surveyed. 85% of FE colleges, 84% of pre-1992 universities and 97% of post-1992 universities report using one or more VLEs in their institution" (Britain & Liber, 2003). However, despite the undisputable importance of ICT in education (see Lehtinen, et al., 1999 for a review), there clearly remain a number of issues that are not understood sufficiently (e.g., Lipponen, 2002; Phipps & Merisotis, 1999). These include the relationships between technological tools available for learning delivery and their links with ethics and pedagogy. One view of the connections and overlaps between each of these concepts has previously been illustrated as the Venn diagram shown in Figure 1 (Jefferies et al., 2006).

This diagram was originally produced to highlight the perceived **relationships** between pedagogy, ethics, and technology, as three impor-

tant constructs in the development of an ethically aware e-learning strategy. In developing this framework it was subsequently realised that a number of external influences in the form of such things as government/public expectations, institutional/stakeholder constraints and professional bodies would all, to varying degrees, impact implementation of such a strategy. It should, however, be noted that consideration of these "external" influences has largely been adjudged to be outside the scope of this particular paper, although the impact of institutional/stakeholder constraints will be highlighted within the case study to be described. However, the particular significance of the three central constructs (pedagogy, ethics, and technology) was first proposed by Jefferies (2004), who then used this framework to provide a pedagogically sound foundation for designing a "mixed mode" or "blended" context for supporting learning (Jefferies, 2004). Such foundation was based on the social constructivist model of learning (Vygotsky, 1978) and was illustrated within the Pedagogy, Ethics and Technology

Figure 1. The links between pedagogy, ethics, and technology (2007 © by ITTE Used with permission)

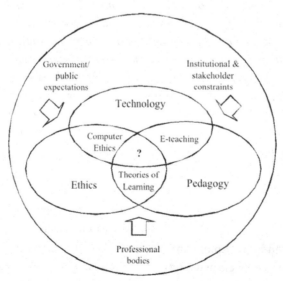

(PET) framework devised by Jefferies (2004) for developing modules of study where integration of asynchronous computer conferencing (ACC) within face-to-face (F2F) delivery is perceived as desirable to support specific, technology enabled learning objectives. It is true, however, that each of these three constructs separately—pedagogy, ethics, and technology—has already developed an extensive literature of its own, and some authors have considered some of the relationships between them. Pedagogy and e-teaching, for example have frequently been debated and there is some understanding that they refer to each other (e.g., Gifford & Enyedy, 1999; Harasim, 2000; Jefferies, 2003). Much has also been written about the relationship between technology and ethics. For example, it has been argued that technology can be shown to be "value-laden" rather than being "value-neutral" which means that its use necessarily has ethical implications (e.g., Littlewood & Stringy, 1995; Mason, 1986; Jefferies & Rogerson, 2003). Similarly in education, theories of learning and pedagogy can be clearly linked to the variety of philosophical approaches that underpin ethics. Scrimshaw (1983) for example, identifies several different educational ideologies—progressivism (meeting individuals needs and aspirations), instrumentalism (meeting requirements of the socio-economic order), reconstructionism (moving society in desired ways), classical humanism (transmission of cultural heritage), and liberal humanism (creation of a vision of common educational experience). Independent of which school of thought one feels appropriate for educators to adopt one can easily make a strong claim about a link between ethics and the particular theories of learning and pedagogical approaches that have been developed. Nevertheless, in reviewing the literature, what has been largely missing is an attempt to fuse these different strands of debate (pedagogy, ethics, and technology) and to come to a coherent understanding of their mutual influences. In previous publications (Jefferies et al.,

2007; Jefferies & Stahl, 2005; Stahl, 2005, 2004, 2002a/b), the present authors have sought to establish a conceptual framework for analysing the inter-relationships among these issues, and this chapter is an attempt to apply this framework to a case study that illustrates some potential consequences of ignoring these relationships.

The case study is drawn from life about a year ago at the institution where one of the authors was teaching. It concerns the experiences of a student who fell into an unintended black hole. For a period of time, through no fault of his own, he lost access to elements of his course that were being delivered through the VLE. Effectively this meant that his connection to a significant part of the overall learning experience was severed, and there was, during this period of time, a real risk of harm both to his learning and to the assessment on which tutors' measurement of his learning would be based. In addition, as is usually the case with technology malfunctions, the student's attention together with that of several staff, was distracted by the urgent need to fix the problem. The reasons why the problem happened in the first place turn out to be complex, and these will be discussed later. The impact turned out to be relatively light, but only because access to the VLE was restored before serious damage had occurred.

The analysis of the case study uses the presented theoretical framework. This concentrates on highlighting the interactions and intersections between the different fields of pedagogy, technology, and ethics. The aim in doing this is twofold. Firstly, we seek to identify and illuminate the ways that pedagogy and technology can interact and thereby have unintended effects that arouse serious ethical concerns. Secondly, we hope to develop the theoretical framework further through examining its application to a real-world case. Both aims, when fulfilled, offer the promise of identifying useful guidance to teachers striving to find the best ways to integrate e-learning into their pedagogic portfolio.

BACKGROUND

E-learning, defined as the use of information and communication technology in education, has a pervasive influence on the way modern societies organise their educational institutions and practices. Implicit in much of the debate on e-teaching is that it is morally desirable and therefore a worthwhile aim. As the Department for Education and Skills outlined in its 2003 Consultation Document "Towards a Unified E-learning Strategy" and subsequent related publications, e-learning holds considerable promise (Dfes, 2003). It can empower learners as well as teachers. It can support creativity and innovation. It can reach new students, thereby widening access to education and improving retention. E-learning has the potential to revolutionise assessment and long-term involvement in education. It thus helps create a better educated and more highly skilled workforce. It can equally uphold the value of education as an end in itself. At the same time, e-learning has become a substantial industry with specialist providers of e-learning software and hardware, service delivery, consultancy, and so forth. The e-learning segment of the ICT industry seems set to grow faster than most other sectors, probably outpacing even the ICT games and entertainment industry.

In light of the importance of e-learning, it is surprising that little attention is being paid to ethical risks that have the potential to damage the success of e-learning. For example, much research is undertaken on the technical side and implementation of e-learning as well as on the question as to how e-learning can support the pedagogical objectives of education. Much less emphasis is placed on ethical risks that may arise from the context of e-learning.

Before we get further into the discussion, however, we should first say a little about what we mean by 'ethical' issues in this context. There seems little point in attempting to give too precise a definition of ethics in such a book as this, when our purpose is not to argue for or against particular ethical theories. But as a working definition, we understand ethics to be the philosophical underpinnings for our morality, for what helps us to understand how we can choose those actions that are good, while avoiding those that are bad. As examples of things that result from human actions and that can be associated with good or bad moral value, we have previously observed (following Mason, 1986) that "among the most important issues of computer ethics one can find questions of data quality, access to data and systems, intellectual property, privacy and data protection, change of social structures through technology, and the impact of ICT on our view of human beings" (Jefferies et al., 2006). The case that we will present in this chapter impinges more or less directly on several of these issues. In particular, data quality, access to data and systems, change of social structures, and the impact of ICT on our view of human beings will all feature to some extent as the story unfolds. We believe it is this broad set of impacts that argues for the treatment of the case as a complex ethical issue, and not just as a system problem that could be addressed satisfactorily through a modification of administrative procedures, or through an exercise of organisational due process. We believe it can only be properly understood in all its ramifications by viewing it through an appropriately constructed framework that takes account of its ethical dimensions and their intersections with other aspects of the situation. Yet, as we shall see later, the case itself seems deceptively simple, an almost trivial series of events that probably resembles everyday occurrences in many organisations with which readers will be familiar.

Having said all that, we should still at this point identify the main philosophical foundation on which our ethical perspective is based. For several reasons, which are discussed more fully later in the paper, we have chosen to draw mainly on the work of Habermas, in particular his 1981 Theory of Communicative Action. By doing so, we have turned away from a number of other possible philosophical foundations. However, we do not see this as invalidating the insights offered by those other perspectives. Simply, it is not possible in a paper of this length to consider every possible theory.

Ethical issues will inevitably arise due to the introduction and use of e-learning. These can appear on many different levels from the individual to the institution and society (Stahl, 2002a). E-learning can change the delivery of education, giving advantages to some but disadvantaging others. It can change the roles of people involved in education. Electronic access to content can be used to increase control over learners and teachers. E-learning leads to the production of new information that can change power structures and interpersonal relationships. Due to the electronic capture of student information, it has the potential to raise completely new issues in data protection. E-learning databases may be linked to other databases, hence facilitating data misuse. The use of technology in education requires substantial resources, which can no longer be spent on other educational aims. The economically poorer may find access to education more difficult. E-learning can also affect debates on intellectual property: Who owns the data and content of e-learning and who gets to use it for which purposes? The design of e-learning technology is built on assumptions and beliefs that may go against the beliefs of the actual users of the technology. This list of potential ethical problems of e-learning cannot claim completeness. Its purpose is to show that e-learning will raise ethical questions. If these are perceived as serious problems then they can render users reluctant to use the technology or even to resist it. This can lead to the failure of individual e-learning projects or, if the perception spreads, to problems with the acceptance of e-learning in general.

Apart from such intuitive links between ethics and e-learning, one can establish more basic overlaps. A complete discussion of either ethics or education is impossible as both are old and well established fields that have bodies of knowledge associated with them that defy discussion in a short chapter. However, most ethical theories and traditions view education as a value. Education is supposed to lead to knowledge, which is meant to increase happiness. It can do so by allowing a deeper understanding of an agent's place in the world but also because it facilitates meaningful engagement in society. Education forms the student's character thus allowing him/her to be virtuous. Overall, moral development requires social interaction, and a considerable part of such development takes place in educational institutions. Individuals and society aim for the good life and being educated is often seen as part of this. Briefly, one can summarise that education is a requirement for leading a morally good life and it is thus a moral good that is worth defending. E-teaching and e-learning are an aspect of education. If, as we have indicated, the use of ICT in education has the potential to be morally of relevance, then it seems likely that a link between e-learning and philosophical ethics can be established.

For example, it is relatively simple to observe or imagine relationships between computer ethics and e-teaching tools. If we take the use of VLEs then we can identify aspects of these that are related to ethics. For example, privacy and data protection may be affected when data on students or staff is collected that previously was not available—data relating to specific times of access to and usage of the site by students. This can affect the teacher's evaluation of the student, which, in turn, may have grave consequences for the student. Similarly, a VLE may raise issues of intellectual property. If teaching material is put online and students are able to download it, then they may use and modify it electronically, thus allowing them an easy route to infringement of copyright. Interestingly, VLEs can also be used for the opposite where a lecturer may feel freer to post copyright material online because the closed nature of the system makes it less likely that the copyright holder will notice the transgression. Data quality is also important because the quality of the learning experience will be affected by the quality of the data provided. This was certainly true before VLEs but it becomes more salient due to the increasing reliance on quantitative data in an ICT environment. Another ethical issue regarding ICT is its impact on social relations, be they between nations, within societies or organizations. One part of this is the question of digital divides but it also extends to political and organizational power relationships. These tend to produce social consequences that in turn have ethical importance. For example, some tools, such as multiple choice tests, are very reliable, easy to use, and therefore favoured by teachers. What is noticed less often is that they also imply a certain relationship between teachers and learners, namely that of the 'sage on the stage' who tells students the truth rather than 'guide on the side' who encourages students to fulfil their own goals. In effect, this translates into a very strong centralised position of the teacher whereas other teaching tools, such as online chats, voting tools, and so forth, imply different power relationships. Such organisational relationships are central to the way we perceive humans and the resulting ethical questions. Are students machines of data digestion that need to reproduce the truth as taught and then function in their economic role or are they autonomous persons whose purpose in life is to flourish? Such questions of course go beyond the use of technology in teaching, but they are affected by our use of technology.

Similarly, particular pedagogical theories correspond to certain ethical approaches because they are based on similar ontological and general philosophical worldviews. For example, an educational positivist / realist who believes that true statements can be transmitted for the purpose of learning may be tempted to use VLEs as a simple repository of knowledge or as a surveillance mechanism to assess students' efforts from which

they will draw conclusions about their educational attainment. A constructivist who wishes to use the same features of technology might look at the students' use of communicative features of the technology such as blogs or discussion forums.

A further example may be the power relationship created by the technology, because an instructor can not only carry out surveillance upon their students, but they can also limit or open access to learning material in a much more focused way than before. This can be linked in with issues of intellectual property where VLEs can be used to enforce IP rules and regulations. The control features of teaching technology can also link directly to pedagogical views. A directly controllable environment with a corresponding increase in power for the instructor may be appealing to a positivist, who will find it easier to disseminate their knowledge whereas it is likely to be less appealing to the constructivist whose view of the process and purpose of instruction is somewhat different. The consequences for methods of assessment also correspond to these distinctions.

This chapter aims to address what we see as a neglect of the links between pedagogy, ethics, and technology. An otherwise successful implementation of technology in teaching risked its own undoing, since it was designed without due consideration to its ethical implications. The case study describes the experiences of a part-time postgraduate student who was incorrectly held to be in arrears with his payment of tuition fees. As a direct and immediate result, the student was un-enrolled from the course and automatically excluded from all access to the VLE. At the time that this happened, many aspects of the student's learning environment relied heavily on access to the VLE system, including his participation in an ongoing assessment. It took only a matter of a few days for the accounting error to be identified and acknowledged, and for the student's legal enrolment to be restored. However, converting this into a technical and practical reality took significantly longer. The student's exclusion from the VLE continued while various academic, administrative, and technical staff wrangled over what needed to be done to restore access, and whose responsibility it was to do it. This technologically enabled un-enrolment thus caused considerable disruption and worry to the student. It also, to a greater or lesser extent, distracted a number of staff from their primary function while the ripple-through effects were identified, disentangled and corrected.

Of course, there is nothing new in bureaucratic error, and scenarios that are (at least to some extent) comparable to this one have been enacted throughout the history of fee-paying education. However, in an e-learning context, the consequences for the student can be more drastic, and it can be much more difficult to discover who is actually responsible or in control.

THE CASE STUDY

In this section, we present the case study in more detail. This is necessary for an understanding of the analysis that will follow. While the essential story is true and all the events related were observed at first hand by one of the authors, all names (and some genders) have been changed to preserve anonymity.

First, we need to introduce some of the main characters. The most important character of all is Karl, a postgraduate student who works full-time and attends part-time classes each Tuesday afternoon and evening. Rosa is his course leader, Hector and Andrea are the module tutors who teach him, and Ambrose is a senior administrator in charge of the central department that deals with income from student fees. Some other participants will be introduced as they appear in the unfolding story.

At the beginning of the story, Karl is about half way through the second semester of the year, and studying two modules. Both make substantial

use of the university's VLE. Both Hector and Andrea are using the VLE as a way to disseminate course materials, such as lecture notes, tutorial exercises, Web links and so on. Andrea's module also requires regular participation in a series of online discussions. Student contributions to these discussions form part of the module assessment, and it is thus important that Karl has more-or-less continuous access. If he is not able to read other students' posts, then he cannot participate in the discussion in a meaningful way.

On a certain Tuesday shortly before the Easter vacation, when the discussions have been running for about 3 weeks, Karl suddenly finds his VLE access has been blocked. On Thursday he receives a letter from Ambrose (sent on Tuesday) which says his enrolment has been terminated because he is in arrears with his fee payments. Karl disagrees and on Friday sends by post a copy of his receipt for a payment made some months earlier, as evidence that his account is clear. He also tells Hector about the problem, and Hector emails Andrea and Rosa. Hector is worried, because Karl needs access to revision materials so that he can use the Easter break to prepare for the examination. He also knows about Karl's online assessment for Andrea's module and is concerned that this may be affected. On the following Monday, Ambrose (or perhaps his assistant Peter) receives Karl's evidence, agrees there has been an error, reinstates Karl's enrolment, and writes to Karl to let him know this has happened. Karl, however, does not know about this letter until almost a week later.

In the meantime, Karl explains his predicament to Andrea: "I was sent a letter by Ambrose on the March 28, 2006 from Income with regard to termination of my studies. I sent him my evidence on Friday March 31, 2006, I have also tried getting in touch with him to find out about my status on Tues April 4,,2006, he wasn't in the office so I left a message but he hasn't got back to me." Andrea replies: "Hector and Rosa both copied me in on emails about your situation earlier today. I am currently thinking about the impact this will have on your work for my module. If necessary, it is straightforward for me to provide access outside the VLE to the main teaching materials—lectures, tutorial worksheets, and so on. What will be harder to mirror is access to the online discussions. I'll talk to you this evening, and we can try to sort out a work-round. But in the meantime, the best I can suggest is that you email me your contributions till your VLE access is fixed. This is not ideal, but maybe the best we can do in the short term."

On the same Wednesday that this exchange takes place, Rosa phones the Income section and speaks to Peter, who tells him that Karl's termination has already been reversed. Peter also tells Rosa that Karl's access to the VLE will be automatically reinstated within 2 to 3 days of the restoration of his enrolment. Rosa emails Karl: "I have just spoken to Peter from Income and he checked your status. You were un-excluded this Monday (I can't remember the exact term) and Peter said that it takes 2 to 3 days for this to filter through to the VLE. He assured me that this is an automatic process and won't be held up if someone were ill and were not able to update your status." If this is so, Karl's access should be back to normal by Thursday at the latest, but this does not happen. Karl has now lost over a week of access, and there is now uncertainty about when the situation will end.

Meanwhile, in an attempt to increase the pressure for a solution to the problem, Andrea raises the issue with various other people, including Christine (the faculty's e-learning co-ordinator), Willy (director of the VLE project), and the faculty office manager. Christine responds immediately. She writes: "If the student can't access the VLE tomorrow let me know - I am not convinced that the process is automatic. I have known students in these circumstances to need a manual update." The following day, Christine checks and finds that Karl is still not enrolled on the VLE. She emails Andrea: "the statement that

his re-enrolment will be automatic... is factually incorrect... I spent a lot of time last year tracking down an inconsistency in the database where the enrolment system info and the VLE info diverged and the source of the error turned out to be the incorrect manual re-enabling of the student onto the enrolment system."

On Friday, Andrea checks again; Karl is still barred from the VLE. Over the weekend, Karl keeps trying too, but still on Monday has no access. However, on Monday he receives Peter's letter (sent and dated the previous Tuesday) confirming his re-enrolment and advising that he should continue with his studies. Rosa emails everyone she can think of connected either with managing student enrolments or with the VLE, in the hope that someone can find a solution. Andrea again offers to make course materials available to Karl outside of the VLE site, but there is no obvious way she can provide alternative access to the assessed discussions. Karl has now lost two weeks of access.

That Wednesday, Karl and his tutors explore possible explanations. Has his password been reset? It seems not. More emails are sent on Thursday. Andrea has already copied some earlier emails to Willy but has received no response, so this time she copies one also to Ramona, a technician in Willy's VLE project team. Ramona replies: "This student's enrolment record quite clearly states that he has been 'terminated' as a student. This means that his access to [the] VLE [has] been disabled via the systems. Once his status has been changed to 'enrolled' the systems will grant access the next morning." The same day, Rosa goes to see Thomas, an administrator in the faculty office. Together they spend some time searching through Karl's enrolment record, and eventually they find the obscure flag in his data record that has continued to block his re-enrolment for two weeks. Rosa phones Karl and emails Andrea: "I think that I've sorted Karl out. The system had him as not excluded but still as terminated. I've had that corrected and been assured that the 'overnight run' will pick it up and he'll be able to gain access tomorrow." That Friday, almost 3 weeks after the problem began, Karl emails to announce that his access to the VLE is finally restored.

DISCUSSION AND ANALYSIS

So what actually happened? First, we deal with the technical explanation. The VLE in question maintains its own internal file of student and staff enrolments on modules. For the university, however, VLE access is dependent on the student enrolment system. This dependency is enforced by a nightly run batch program, which synchronises VLE enrolments with the master enrolment database. The university also has a long-established policy for dealing with student debtors. Students who have not paid a set proportion of their fees by a certain point in the academic year are routinely excluded. Such exclusions are not seen as punitive, rather as motivational, and they are usually short-term. Once a student shows a tangible commitment to clearing their debt, their enrolment is quickly reinstated. In this case, an administrative error occurred in the financial record keeping, and as a result the normal procedure for dealing with a student in arrears was invoked. The official who did this had the clear power and also an explicit duty to do so, but in this case it was based on erroneous information. When Karl provided evidence of payment, his enrolment was immediately restored, in line with policy. There is no reason to doubt that the officer who did this honestly believed that VLE access would automatically follow after an unavoidable, but short, delay. During the next phase, things became a little more muddled. It seems clear that everyone acted in good faith, but also that control of the technology was not effective. Yet almost up to the moment of resolution, no one directly involved has a clear idea of what is happening,

what can be done, or even who is responsible for doing it.

Next, we consider how the course of this technologically mediated episode differs from what might have occurred had a VLE not played a central role in the landscape. One clear issue relates to a lack of alternatives when system malfunctions occur. Andrea set her students an assessed task that could only reasonably be completed with regular, although not necessarily continuous, access to the VLE. This was seen as pedagogically desirable, since it encouraged student interaction and the formative development of ideas and understanding. It was also seen as an attractive opportunity to exploit the potential of the technology, and to learn from the experience. Without VLE support for online discussions, Andrea would not (could not) have used this activity as part of the module assessment. Another issue is to do with the different timescales involved with different communication channels. Associated with this is the (presumably unintended) asynchronicity that has intruded into (what was almost certainly conceived as) an essentially synchronous procedure. Consider the timeline: Karl's termination happens on a Monday. The letter to inform him is posted on Tuesday; by then, the effect has already rippled through to the VLE. Thus Karl experiences the effects several days before receiving the letter that advises him what 'will' happen. Karl responds as soon as he can, and the officer who receives his letter also acts and responds as soon as he (or she) can. Yet a further week elapses before Karl receives this letter. In the meantime, Rosa has made independent enquiries, and as a result caught up with the status quo two days earlier. Rosa is given the honest (but incorrect) assurance that Karl's VLE access is already in the course of restoration and delayed only by the normal lag in system synchronisation. As a result, no one takes any action for a further couple of days. Prior to use of the VLE, the communication might have occurred by post, by phone, or perhaps by email.

Whatever the communication medium, there is the key difference that messages would have been synchronous. At each point, a triggering message must be received before the next step can occur. The VLE automates this process, hastens it, and also removes academic staff from any effective engagement in the process. This links to the third issue, which is about control of the technology. Previously, for any exclusion to take effect, academic staff would need to have been informed. Many of the people involved in this story are experienced officers with detailed knowledge of the operation of the enrolment system and/or the VLE, but also direct contact with students and an ethos of striving to do what is best for the student. Now there are no longer opportunities for academics to negotiate the timing, the rigour or the terms of exclusion. Moreover, until Ramona pinpoints the source of the malfunction, no-one really knows what to do. Prior to the intervention of the VLE into this process, academic staff and administrative staff in the faculty would have had much greater control over the process. In contrast, the technologically mediated procedure is invoked by a remote official in a central department who proves difficult to contact, not only for the student, but also for faculty staff. It also turns out that the way the technology works is only understood by a small number of experts. While the situation is not one that is frequently encountered, it is still fairly routine. Nevertheless, it is beyond the training and experience of most of the staff who have to deal with it.

THE APPLIED THEORETICAL FRAMEWORK

Overall, this story illustrates some clear overlaps between pedagogy, ethics, and technology in developing e-learning approaches. Andrea was using the VLE to support a social constructivist approach to learning and teaching through setting a piece of assessment that encouraged student par-

ticipation in online discussions. However, when deciding upon this course of action Andrea had not taken into account the ethical consequences of her decision in relation to accessibility—or rather, to the potential loss of access in the case of technology or system failure. As a result Andrea had not developed a course of action to mitigate the consequences in the event of its withdrawal. Neglecting to take into account such potential consequences clearly then had significant ethical impacts on a number of staff as well as the student. The case study also illustrates the overlap between ethics and technology and supports Feenberg's (1999) argument that control of technology is tantamount to a form of legislation. Those in charge of the technology, and the technology itself, were legislating against the student's right to access their learning, rather than faculty staff. That technology should be able to exert such power and have such ethical consequences needs, therefore, careful consideration in developing e-learning approaches.

Some other points are worth noting. First, there is the significance of both government and public expectations in creating an impression of desirability around the movement towards e-learning. Second, there is the role of institutional constraints, rather than Andrea the lecturer, in shaping the outcomes for Karl. Third, we can consider the various impacts of the story from several perspectives. In the central foreground is Karl, the student. He is a paying customer of the university and also a client of the staff, who teach, manage, and administer his course of study. For Karl, the impacts are direct and potentially injurious. Through loss of access to the VLE, he has almost certainly suffered some harm to his learning, the very service for which he was paying, and also increased his risk of failure in the assessment for two modules. At the same time, he is a participant in a community of learning, and other students were deprived of his input for a significant period of time. They also risked harm to their learning and to their prospect of success

440

in the assessments. Next to Karl in prominence are the various staff of the faculty who became directly involved with the story as it developed. In particular, Andrea, Rosa, and later also Thomas, spent a lot of time trying to resolve the problem. Especially for Andrea and Rosa, this was a significant distraction from their academic responsibilities, and used time that could have been spent on other students, or on a more productive interaction with Karl. On the other hand, we must acknowledge some potential benefits to staff. First, a greater understanding within the university—at least within this department—of how to fix such a problem and also of how to mitigate its effects, should a comparable situation occur again. Second, through the opportunity to analyse this case for publication, there may be a contribution to knowledge in the wider academic community.

Less visible in the story, but of great importance to it, are the various functionaries involved. Most of these have encountered changes in their work, or in its effects, as a result of the introduction of the VLE. For instance, Ambrose has the task of excluding students in certain defined circumstances. The VLE has made this task easier and much more dramatic in its impact. As a result, this sanction is probably both more effective and also quicker to take effect than was formerly the case. However, the VLE has also seriously disrupted the sequence of events and messages connected with this procedure, and the procedure does not yet seem to have been redesigned to take account of this. This may be expected to lead to higher levels of conflict with students, and also amongst staff. It may also prove at some future time to be a legal flashpoint, giving rise to litigation, although this has not happened yet.

For staff members who deal directly with student enrolments, there is some loss of control over aspects of their work. These may now, for example, be determined 'by the system' itself—although in fact this means by algorithmic assumptions of the system's designers and programmers which

have been reified in its operations. Or they may be imposed by other staff members with remote access to the system, who did not formerly have such immediate, detailed control over the process. For example, it would certainly once have been necessary for a central official to ask a faculty administrator to update a student's enrolment record by hand. The corresponding update can now be applied by that central official at a distance without reference to the faculty administrator, or indeed anyone else who knows, or has face-to-face contact with, the student.

IMPLICATIONS FOR THEORY

To some degree this case is so ordinary that many of the readers of this chapter will have encountered something similar. At the same time, readers will now realise that even such an everyday use of technology can have unintended consequences which, in turn, have ethical implications. The most obvious of these refer to Karl's inability to pursue his studies and his resulting loss of motivation and maybe even marks. There are issues of lost resources and opportunity cost where students', lecturers', and administrators' time could have been used better. True, one could make the argument that such issues are normal and occur in any organisation and we should thus not worry about them.

However, a closer look at the case reveals that there are underlying structures and assumptions of ethical relevance. An important aspect of this has to do with power relationships. Much literature on computer and information ethics as well as critical research in information systems deals with the question of how the use of technology affects power structures. This also links in with pedagogical considerations of the relationship between student and teacher. We have seen that the pedagogical approach in Karl's case was constructivist which broke down when the social construction of knowledge was no longer possible, due to the lack of availability of the construction tools. There are, however, further issues of power involved in this case, which are arguably typical for the type of technology use we are referring to here.

A central problem that pervaded the case was the issue of power relationships and attributions of responsibility. The VLE at this institution was configured in such a way that a centralised system, linked to the accounting system, had the power to allow or withdraw pedagogically necessary access to information. In practice that means that financial considerations overrode academic ones. In pre-technical times the university might still have un-enrolled students but there would have been the opportunity for the student to negotiate with lecturers about practical consequences. Such negotiations are no longer possible as the lecturers themselves have been disempowered and have lost control over who can use their teaching provisions. Such a redistribution of power structures may be desirable, but the interesting issue here is that they were never consciously decided, much less publicised. This means that the introduction of the technology and its configuration set social realities that other stakeholders were hardly aware of, even less in a position to discuss, and not at all able to challenge.

A different way of looking at these problems is the question of responsibility. Responsibility is a social construct of ascription. It is based on the idea that a subject is ascribed an object with the aim of leading to socially desirable outcomes, usually by attributing sanctions (rewards or punishments) (Stahl, 2004b). There is much literature that voices the hope that the use of ICT will lead to clearer ascription of responsibility by creating transparency and providing models of causality. At the same time, we all know examples of situations where ICT is blamed in order to avoid responsibility ascriptions ("I cannot do X, the system is down..."). In our case, there are clear examples of responsibility diffusion caused by the use of ICT. Some systems are in place where

responsibilities are clearly assigned. However, when these systems malfunction, responsibilities are no longer clear. Who is responsible for reinstating Karl, who is responsible for his regaining access, who is responsible for his loss of learning opportunities? Most importantly, there are no sanctions for malfunctions. If a lecturer does not provide necessary material for several weeks, then there are ways of addressing this. In this case, due to the involvement of ICT, this does not seem to be the case.

There are many ways in which this case can be rendered useful for the understanding and development of theory. As the case revolves around issues of data collection for the purpose of social control, albeit in an educational environment, one could apply a Foucauldian lens and discuss issues of the shaping of discourses and bodily discipline, culminating in a comparison with the Panopticon (Foucault, 1971; 1975). One could similarly take the lens of current surveillance studies and use their thoughts to understand how technology is not only used for imposing discipline but also for social sorting, which, according to Lyon (Lyon, 2002; 2003), is a more serious issue than privacy invasions. This might open new avenues of exploration, which may then shed a light on the relationship between the socio-economic and ethnic background of students and their treatment in a technically mediated way. A further fruitful theoretical approach to interpret the case would then be one that allows for sensitivity to culture and the impact it can have on computer-mediated communication, as suggested by Ess (2002; 2006). There is no space in this chapter to follow these different avenues in any depth. Instead, we will briefly explore one particular interpretation based on Habermas's work.

Habermas, a German philosopher and representative of the Frankfurt School of critical thought, is helpful for our purposes because he has developed a comprehensive theoretical framework that has strongly influenced critical work in the area of IT. It is furthermore of high interest because an integral part of his approach is ethics, more specifically discourse ethics. In his 1981 Theory of Communicative Action (TCA) Habermas establishes the most important building blocks of his theory. A central concept for him is that of a "discourse." A discourse is a type of communicative interaction that is characterised by the agent's willingness to take the other seriously and consider their argument. They are necessary because humans are fundamentally social beings who need to interact in order to act successfully. We cannot go into detail on Habermas's TCA here, but it suffices to say that discourses always have an ethical aspect to them. All speech acts carry normative validity claims and, by the very act of engaging in communication, we implicitly accept ethical conditions, such as our duty to recognise our interlocutor as an equal and dignified being. One aspect of this theory that is valuable for interpreting our case study has to do with Habermas's distinction between life-world and systems. The life-world (a term that Habermas has taken from phenomenology) is the horizon in which we all inevitably live. It is constituted by communication and it changes through discourses. For Habermas, the life-world has an ethical connotation because it stands for the willingness to engage in communication with others on the basis that they are equal and their views are valuable. The alternative way of coordinating action is constituted by systems. Systems facilitate cooperation without regards to individual views and communicative action. A prime example of systems is the market where decisions are made not on the basis of arguments but on the basis of price mechanisms. One can use our case study of Karl as an example of what Habermas has called the colonisation of the life-world by systems. The VLE is an example of a system that coordinates action but also crowds out communication. The ethical and pedagogical issues mostly come to pass because channels of communication are not foreseen in the system. From this perspective, the use of ICT in education is a fundamental ethical problem because it replaces the ethically necessary communication between individuals.

IMPLICATIONS FOR FUTURE RESEARCH

The case study analysis presented in this chapter makes it clear that there can be no taken-for-granted alignment of the pedagogic, technical, and ethical concerns in an e-learning situation. In fact, it seems likely that these will often prove to be in conflict. This picture gains in complexity when other environmental factors come into play, such as the institutional constraints and procedures that came to dominate in this case. The insights derived from this suggest some themes for future research. One of these is clearly to examine in more detail the attitudes, expectations and ethical consequences of each of the different stakeholders in a comparable situation. There may, for example, be some utilitarian trade-offs between the benefits to some students of participating in a constructivist learning opportunity like the one described here, and the clear risk of harm to those who, like Karl, find themselves summarily excluded from the discourse. It would be interesting to conduct further research and analysis to investigate how far the benefits outweigh the costs, if indeed they do. It is very unlikely that in every case they will do so. As mentioned earlier, both government and institutional policies assume at present that there is really no alternative to the rapid deployment of e-learning technologies. Academics have a responsibility for steering the development in positive directions, and, if necessary even resisting it. It is important to select applications that are both pedagogically and ethically appropriate, and it is not yet clear how we can identify these in advance. Another possible theme is to seek out and document further case studies where overlaps between regions of the Venn diagram in Figure 1 come into play. These are likely to be particularly interesting in cases where there are conflicts between the concerns of actors whose responsibilities position them in different regions of the diagram.

E-learning and e-teaching can be expected to develop apace right across the educational sector. Such burgeoning development is currently being encouraged by the increasing technological "pull." One example is the use of open source VLEs such as Moodle, which is freely available to schools and colleges. In addition, the political push for using technology to support the Government's "personalised learning" agenda (e.g., Dfes, 2004) is clearly having an impact. Based on the assumption that e-teaching and e-learning are ethically relevant uses of technology in education, the aim of this paper was, therefore, to use a framework that illustrates the overlaps of pedagogy, ethics, and technology, and to then apply this to a case study in order to test its relevance for developing e-learning approaches. Whilst there seems to be little interest in the exploration of the intersection of these areas within the extant e-learning literature, we feel that these are timely issues that need to be addressed now if we are to facilitate better use of ICT in education.

CONCLUSION

This chapter should now give a clear insight into some of the very important ethical issues raised by the introduction of ICT to the learning and teaching environment that are often overlooked. When we speak of ethics and technology, we often have big issues in mind, such as global poverty and digital divides. Either that or we are looking at technology that seems made for ethically problematic activities, such as surveillance. In this chapter we have discussed a use of technology that is generally accepted as beneficial and constructive, namely ICT for teaching. By looking at a case study that is probably quite ordinary, we have shown that ICT use can have unintended consequences that are of ethical relevance. With

regard to this handbook, this leads to questions about how such issues can be identified and addressed. These are large questions that go beyond what this chapter, and probably this book, can achieve. It is nevertheless an important one that we need to return to if we want to have technologies that lead to socially desirable outcomes rather than using technologies for their own sake.

As an overall conclusion, the model presented in Figure 1 has demonstrated its usefulness. It has helped to highlight some issues of concern and has served to show how ethical, pedagogic, technical, and procedural factors that originate from the concerns of different institutional stakeholders, represented in different regions of the model, have all combined to produce a novel ethical problem. It is our view, however, that such problems are not unique and that the role of research into e-teaching and e-learning should now take the model developed within this paper, and apply it to additional case studies in order to further illuminate the issues raised by the overlap between pedagogy, ethics, and technology. Such research would then not only help practitioners and administrators in their implementation of the technology but would also mitigate against some of the potential harmful consequences that might well be visited upon their students.

REFERENCES

Britain, S., & Liber, O. (2003). A framework for the pedagogical evaluation of virtual learning environments, JISC. Retrieved on October 16, 2006, from http://www.jisc.ac.uk/uploaded_documents/VLE%20Full%20Report%2006.doc

Dfes (2003). Towards a unified e-learning strategy. Retrieved on March 22, 2007, from http://www.dfes.gov.uk/consultations/conResults.cfm?consultationId=774

Dfes (2004). A national conversation about personalised learning. Retrieved on March 19, 2007, from http://www.standards.dfes.gov.uk/person-alisedlearning/downloads/personalisedlearning.pdf

Ess, C. (2002). Computer-mediated colonization, the renaissance, and educational imperatives for an intercultural global village. *Ethics and Information Technology,* 4(1), 11 – 22.

Ess, C. (2006). Ethical Pluralism and Global Information Ethics. *Ethics and Information Technology,* 8(4), 215 – 226.

Feenberg, A. (1999). *Questioning technology.* London: Routledge.

Foucault, M. (1975). *Surveiller et punir: Naissance de la prison.* Paris: Gallimard.

Foucault, M. (1971). *L'ordre du discours.* Paris: Gallimard.

Gifford, B.R.. & Enyedy, N.D. (1999). Activity centred design: Towards a theoretical framework for CSCL. In C. Hoadley. and J. Roschelle J. (Eds.), In *Proceedings of the Computer Support for Collaborative Learning* (CSCL) 1999 Conference, Stanford University, Palo Alto, CA. Mahwah, NJ: Lawrence Erlbaum Associates. Retrieved on March 5, 2001, from http://www.ciltkn.org/cscl99/A22/A22.HTM

Habermas, J. (1981). *Theorie des kommunikativen Handelns*—Band I/II. Frankfurt a. M: Suhrkamp.

Harasim, L. (2000). Shift happens: Online collaborative learning as a new paradigm in education. Paper presented at Fusion 2000. Glasgow: Scotland.

Jefferies, P. (2003). ICT in supporting collaborative learning: Pedagogy and practice. *Journal of Educational Media,* 28(1).

Jefferies, P. & Rogerson, S., (2003). Using asynchronous computer conferencing to support the teaching of computing and ethics: A case study.

Annals of Cases on Information Technology (ACIT), Vol 5. USA: Idea Group.

Jefferies, P. (2004). Aspects of technology mediated interaction and its impact on higher education, Unpublished doctoral dissertation, De Montfort University.

Jefferies, P., & Stahl, B.C. (2005) Some ethical considerations regarding the relationship of e-learning and pedagogy. Paper presented at ETHICOMP 2005: Looking Back to the Future. Linköping, Sweden.

Jefferies, P., Stahl B.C., & McRobb, S. (2006). A framework for exploring the relationships among pedagogy, ethics and technology. In Sobh, T. (Ed.), *Advances in Systems, Computing Sciences and Software Engineering.* Heidelberg: Springer.

Jefferies, P., Stahl, B.C., & McRobb, S. (2007). Exploring the relationships between pedagogy, ethics & technology: Building a framework for strategy development. *Technology, Pedagogy and Education,* 16(1), 111 – 126.

Lehtinen, E., Hakkarainen, K., Lipponen, L., Rahikainen, M., & Muukkonen, H. (1999). *Computer supported collaborative learning: A review of research and development.* The J.H.G.I. Giesderbs Reports on Education, 10. Netherlands: University of Nijmegen, Department of Educational Sciences.

Lipponen, L. (2002). Exploring foundations for computer-supported collaborative learning. In Koschmann, T. Hall, R. and Miyake, N. (Eds.), *CSCL2: Carrying forward the conversation.* Mahwah, NJ: Lawrence Erlbaum Associates. Retrieved on May 2, 2002, from http://newmedia.colorado.edu/cscl/31.html

Littlewood, B., & Stringy, L. (1995). The risks of software. In Johnson, D. G. and Nissenbaum, H. (Eds.), *Computers, Ethics & Social Values.* Upper Saddle River: Prentice Hall.

Lyon, D. (2002). Surveillance studies: Understanding visibility, mobility and the phenetic fix. *Surveillance & Society* 1(1), 1 – 7.

Lyon, D. (2003). *Surveillance after September 11.* Cambridge: Polity Press.

Mason, R. O. (1986). Four Ethical Issues of the Information Age. *MIS Quarterly* 10, 5 – 12.

Phipps, R., & Merisotis, J. (1999). *What's the difference? A review of contemporary research on the effectiveness of distance learning in higher education.* Washington, DC: The Institute for Higher Education Policy. Retrieved on October 28, 2003, from http://www.ihep.com/Pubs/PDF/Difference.pdf

Scrimshaw, P. (1983). *Educational Ideologies*, Unit 2, E204, Purpose and Planning in the Curriculum, Milton Keynes, Open University Press.

Stahl, B. C. (2002a). Ethics and e-teaching: The students' perspective. *Communications of the IIMA*, 2(3), 51 – 62.

Stahl, B. C. (2002b). Ethical issues in e-teaching—a theoretical framework. In King, G. (Ed.). In *Proceedings of INSPIRE VII, Quality in Learning and Delivery Techniques* (pp.135-148). Limerick, Ireland: The British Computer Society.

Stahl, B. C. (2004a). E-teaching—the economic threat to the ethical legitimacy of education? *Journal of Information Systems Education*, 15(2), 155 – 162.

Stahl, B. C. (2004b). *Responsible management of information systems*. Hershey: Idea Group Publishing.

Stahl, B. C. (2005). E-voting: An example of collaborative e-teaching and e-learning. *Journal of Interactive Technology & Smart Education*, 2 (1), 19 – 30.

KEY TERMS

The Effects of ICT on Power in Relationships: As with other technologies, those who control the deployment or operation of ICT can act as hidden legislators in determining what actions are permitted or denied to others.

Normative Issues Arising from the Use of ICT: An attempt to discover rules for 'good' behaviour in the design, development or operation of ICT systems.

Pedagogy for E-Learning: We advocate a social constructivist pedagogy and see e-learning as ideally embedded together with face-to-face delivery in a mixed-mode framework.

Philosophical Ethics: A form of meta-ethics that investigates the normative grounds of ethical behaviour

Privacy in Online Environments: Privacy is a complex concept related to control over and ownership of information about one's self; interaction in online environments brings new challenges to our perceptions of privacy.

Questions of Responsibility: Responsibility is a social construct that ascribes to a person (or other agent) the duty to answer to someone for something.

The Role of ICT in Learning: ICT offers the promise to empower learners, to support creativity, to widen access, to revolutionise assessment, but it can also damage the process and the outcomes when applied without due sensitivity to the risks.

Chapter XXIX
Ethical Issues in Digital Information Technology

Konrad Morgan
Northern Alberta Institute of Technology, Canada

Madeleine Morgan
Northern Alberta Institute of Technology, Canada

ABSTRACT

Since the inception of the Internet in the late 1960's, technological advances in the field of information communications technology (ICT) have created an ever-expanding digital arena for the development of human innovation, education, expression, communication, and interaction. However, the creation and use of this vast network of knowledge, whether it is for educational, commercial, entertainment, or creative purposes, has also produced its own set of ethical challenges. This chapter discusses the ethical implications associated with the topics of veracity, identity and ownership and the impact of these fundamental ethical issues on human behaviour in emerging digital technologies.

INTRODUCTION

Privacy and security, in relation to either the digital or the more traditional physical worlds, are fundamental issues for physical and mental well being. In the digital arena these issues have always been of great importance to government organizations, financial and commercial institutions. The topic of trust has become the focus of renewed attention in organizational theory and research (Knights et al., 2001). But with increasing reports of identity theft, internet banking fraud, illegal pirating, and a multitude of money making schemes, the questions of exactly who or what organization we are interacting with (identity), the truth, and reliability of the information that is being provided (veracity) and who has the right to the ownership of that information are questions that each individual user has the right to have answered.

In this chapter, the terms digital environment or digital arena are used to cover those technologies that include all aspects of Information Communications Technology for example, networked computers, hypertext and hypermedia and the Internet or World Wide Web, which in turn embody many different applications.

IDENTITY

Establishing an Internet Identity

Many philosophers and authors have long argued that the advances in digital technology can be an opportunity for mankind to avoid the inequalities and problems of the more traditional material world. A report by the United Nations (2000) supports the view that any group or society exposed to the digital environment undergoes a leveling of the existing hierarchies of authority. But research has also shown that typically the traits and characteristics of human nature can be reflected in the behaviour patterns which we see and experience in the digital environment (Morgan & Morgan, 2000). This is further supported by a recent survey examining the accuracy of personality impressions based on personal websites, a medium for self expression where identity claims are predominant (Vazire & Gosling, 2004). The observers in this study surveyed a number of websites and rated the Web site authors personality based on the information contained there and these ratings were then compared with both an accuracy criterion and the authors' ideal-self rating. The findings suggest that the identity claims were used to convey valid information about personality. This leads naturally to the question is cyberspace therefore simply a powerful means of reaffirming pre-established Physical-Reality identities or a medium that encourages the creation of Virtual–Reality personae (Romero, 2003)?

Research has also been carried out into the social implications created by the Internet and how it has affected contemporary culture and identity (Wood & Smith, 2001). Chat rooms provide an ideal environment for research into online identity and are a focus of activity for a huge cross section of society who use ICT's. For instance, they can be perceived by teens as a safer environment for exploring emerging sexuality than the real world, where they can develop creative strategies to exchange identity information with their peers, enabling them to pair off with partners of their choice despite the disembodied nature of the interaction (Subrahmanyam, et al., 2004). Other studies show that such anonymous interaction can act as a foundation for establishing real world relationships rather than the creation of fantasy personalities (Hardey, 2002) and that it is possible to develop trust from mutual self-disclosure in online friendships (Henderson & Gilding, 2004).

The internet also represents a huge new step in interpersonal communications for people with disabilities, providing a level ground where all can be equal as we have referred to previously. But if this leveling is occurring because impairment is invisible online, how will disabled people manage disability disclosure within this social context? (Bowker & Tuffin, 2002). Are they using the digital arena to develop friendships, enhance their self-identity, and social being, or are they simply using the Internet as they would use a telephone or a letter (Seymour & Lupton, 2004)? For people suffering from psychiatric disturbances, the private chat rooms and virtual communities of the Internet provide a degree of patient autonomy and operate outside the scope of medical, sociological, or psychiatric practitioners. But the interactions within these domains may themselves be the breeding ground for a new kind of identity disturbance, a powerful new force in the 'manufacture of madness' (Charland, 2004). When a user is unclear about what is real and what is manufactured or when they have created multiple personas there is enormous scope for psychological disturbance.

Ethical issues regarding identity are also raised within the scope of many online services, for example psychotherapy or counseling on-line. Once again with such disembodied interaction it may be difficult for the psychotherapist to verify the identity of the other party with whom they are interacting, or if conversations are private, which in turn could lead to a violation of patient confidentiality (Sanchez, 2002). Also there may be additional problems with assessing the validity of disorders in a disembodied client and more importantly evaluating the effectiveness of the counseling intervention.

Corporate Issues

The issue of identity within the digital environment is of course not only limited to individuals. The terms 'company identity' or 'company image' are usually taken to mean the visual marks, logos, and other systems used to portray the organization. Corporate Web sites could be very powerful tools for promoting such identities, but a recent study shows that surprisingly little progress has been made in this area from the pre-Internet era (Topalian, 2003). Research has also been carried out into how online negotiations differ from face-to-face situations, focusing on interpersonal factors and social identity factors and outlining four theories of interaction (rapport building, social contagion, coordination, and information exchange) that give an insight into social behaviour in the digital environment (Thompson & Nadler, 2002).

One of the major issues raised by the creation of the new digital medium is that an Internet user can assume the identity of any other entity. This leads to some interesting insights into human behaviour and also some problems for businesses trying to keep their workforce productive and legally oc-

cupied. One of the great paradoxes of the Internet is that it could have been dedicated to the pursuit of truth and the dissemination of knowledge for the benefit of all. Some parts of the system do aspire to such goals but a surprisingly high proportion of the total resources of the internet are devoted to activities and interests which are, if not illegal, then highly personal in nature. The very freedom and open access of the World Wide Web makes it subject to misuse. Recent surveys of how people use the facilities of the internet reveal that nearly 40% of workplace Internet use is not related to the core business of the company supplying the Internet facilities (IDC Consulting, 2000). Again nearly 37% of office workers say they surf the Internet constantly while they are at work (Emarketer, 2000) and nearly 70% of Internet pornography occurs between the normal office working hours of 9am to 5pm local time (SexTracker, 2004). It should not be a surprise therefore to learn that 77% of major US companies routinely monitor their employees' email, Internet usage, and computer files (American Management Association, 2001), but such action in turn gives rise to ethical concerns with respect to privacy and security of the individual.

Digital Predation

Identity deception has been a subject of much discussion and recent research, particularly with regard to differentiating between the different types of deception and the motivational issues behind them (Utz, 2005). An individual's reaction to identity deception on the internet may provide a valuable insight into online group processes, as investigated by Joinson and Dietz-Uhler (2002) in their study of the invention of a fantasy character by one member of an online community and the reaction of the other members on discovering the deception.

Given the ease with which any individual can assume any identity in the digital environment it is inevitable that many Internet users will fall victim to digital predators. There are many studies into children's use of the Internet, which suggest areas for further research into the opportunities and dangers that the interaction presents to children and young people (Livingstone, 2003). What is alarming is that recent surveys estimate that over 24 million children regularly use the Internet (U.S. Congress, 2000) and one child in five using the Internet has been solicited for sex within any 12 month period. One on four have been sent sexually explicit pictures and in the year 2000 in the US alone an estimated 725,000 child Internet users had been aggressively pressured by an adult online to meet physically for sex (U.S. Congress, 2000).

Children are not the only victims however and women have also been the subject of research in this area. A study into the problems and dangers prevalent when female Internet users accessed health and human service sites on the Internet showed that there were a number of reasons why such uncontrolled Internet use could prove harmful (Finn & Banach, 2000). Seven criteria were established from this study, including the possibility that users might encounter cyberstalkers, that they may receive misinformation from other group members, that communication might become disinhibited online leading to personal attacks and threats and also regarding the lack of information regarding the identity of members in self-help groups dealing with issues of violence and abuse which could create problems.

Digital Privacy

The question of stripping away a users online anonymity is becoming much more of a legal issue and some courts are now establishing guidelines as to when that anonymity should be surrendered, which is of course of particular importance to Internet Service Providers (ISPs). The current position would seem to be similar to that of a journalist keeping his sources confidential, in that

free speech on the internet is worthy of protection. But should the plaintiff be shown to have a valid case and be acting in good faith and there is sufficient justification the ISP may be forced to relinquish their subscribers' anonymity (Ekstrand, 2003). But methods are also being developed at a governmental level to try and protect users and society at large from the threat of digital predators particularly after the events of September 11th 2001, which changed the world's perspective on global terrorism.

In a reaction to Al Qaeda's use of digital communications technology, US Congress began discussing granting law enforcement agencies access to private encryption keys or secret backdoors to all digital security systems. This has sparked a huge debate with arguments against the proposals from civil liberty groups and also from e-commerce groups who believe such laws would damage consumer confidence in e commerce. In early 2002, the Bush Administration formed the National Strategy to Secure Cyberspace. This document describes actions that companies, individuals, and schools can take to improve cyber security. The NCSD also created the Cyber Interagency Incident Management Group (Cyber IIMG), an organization dedicated to finding ways to pre-empt cyber attacks and to help the government prepare for future attacks. In 2004 the Bush Administration also established a critical infrastructure information network—a private version of the Internet that is not accessible through the public Internet. It is thought that this network is intended to function as a resource in case the Internet and other forms of computer-based communications become inoperable. However its isolation from the public Internet also makes it less vulnerable to threats of privacy and security.

At the commercial level VeriSign, one of the Internet's major controllers of .com and .net registries, indicated in their February 2004 report (VeriSign, 2004) that site hacks, online fraud, and identity theft were rising dramatically. Verisign also reported that those countries which ranked highest in percentage of fraud per transaction were predominantly third world nations although it is believed that this may be just a reflection of poorly maintained software and systems. But this issue does serve to raise some important questions regarding the effectiveness and use of digital technology to level out the inequalities in wealth in the real world.

Extremist Recruitment

Increasingly the internet has become an effective tool for collective action. Its powers of mass communication boosted by an antiauthoritarian ideology, makes online action an effective alternative to offline action although it may also slightly alter the motives underlying such action (Postmes & Brunsting, 2002). The more sinister aspect of this online activity can be seen where extremist groups are using the Internet as an effective method for recruiting new members who are then used either as a free workforce to achieve the organizations goals or in extreme cases the new recruits are encouraged to sacrifice their possessions and even their lives.

Conversion and indoctrination are present in most human societies so it is natural that we should find them in the new digital society using the digital medium to achieve their ends. Cialdini´s six principles that direct human behaviour (Cialdini, 1998), consistency (justification of earlier behaviour), reciprocity (repayment in kind), social proof, authority, liking, and scarcity (not wishing to miss opportunity) can easily be adapted to be used on the Internet.

The very characteristics of the digital medium that make it share information quickly and cheaply also make it a near perfect mechanism for mass recruitment. Indeed the new digital medium begins to assume an air of authority and divinity to many users who report finding the Internet infinite and ethereal, almost a deity in itself (Davis, 2002). For this reason the Internet has become the new location of choice for recruit-

ers of both new religions and extremist terrorist groups. The Internet is very economical for cults, e-mail is cheap, and it keeps cult members hooked, wherever they are, with messages of support and propaganda. The groups do not have to rent land or buildings as the Internet itself becomes their virtual commune.

Identity Theft

Ownership is a fundamental aspect of our established society structures and is one of the most powerful anchors in our mental understanding of self and our relation to the world around us. It is no surprise then that one of the most disturbing and popular crimes within the digital world is that of identity theft. Whether simply using a stolen credit card number or the more complex theft of an individuals total online identity, the problems associated with this crime are not just financial, the victims of identity theft also suffering damage to their reputations and emotional stress (Kreuter, 2004). Research is also being undertaken to determine and examine those behaviours which may increase or limit the risk of online identity theft and to provide suggestions regarding online privacy protection to public policy makers, managers and consumers (Milne et al., 2004).

VERACITY

Truth or Misinformation?

The World Wide Web is a rapidly evolving decentralized set of relationships or links with no established mechanism to establish the worth or authority for any idea or fact. A search for a set word or item on two different occasions is likely to produce different results and even a return visit to the same website can produce different information. So although internet users have access to enormous numbers of potential sources for their inspiration or entertainment there is no accepted method to tell the valuable from the disposable, the true from the false.

Various studies have been undertaken to investigate this problem of misinformation on the internet, particularly with regard to health information, both for physical illnesses like cancer or HIV/AIDS (Benotsch et al., 2004; Matthews et al., 2003) and also for mental illness (Morahan-Martin & Anderson, 2000). The information provided to parents by child development websites has also been the subject of such evaluation (Martland, 2001) and Internet resources relating to the financial marketplace have also come under scrutiny (Kimmel, 2004).

Scams, Web Spoofing, and Phishing

However, the problem of veracity or adherence to the truth goes much further as to whether the information on a website is reliable and accurate. In some instances it is the Web site itself which is not what it would appear to seem. Many users rely purely on the address information given in their Web browser tool bar to authenticate the site they are using. But it is possible for both this and other information to be faked and the user directed to a copy of the web page they are seeking (Web spoofing). Similarly, a new tide of phishing attacks on the internet, in which a user receives an email purportedly from a reliable source and is deceived into giving out personal information such as passwords or banking details is also proving a cause for concern. Both Web spoofing (Felten, 1997; Herzberg & Gbara, 2004; Yuan et al, 2001 & 2002;) and phishing (Adida et al., 2005; Jakobsson, 2005) have provoked substantial research interest.

For individual users wishing to find out about the current internet scams and schemes operating or to report on fraudulent activity a number of websites can be found on the internet, ranging from Web sites operated by the U.S. government, for example the Internet Fraud Complaint Center, a partnership between the FBI and the National

White Collar Crime Center (http://www.ifccfbi.gov/index.asp), the UK governments Home Office Internet Crime site http://www.homeoffice.gov.uk/crime/internetcrime/ and various other scam-busting consumer oriented sites http://www.scambusters.org.

OWNERSHIP

Many authors have noted how the new digital technologies have revolutionized knowledge representation and dissemination (United Nations, 2000). However there is a less well recognized secondary effect to these rapid advances, in that it is now much more complex to establish and maintain the ownership of these intellectual ideas within the digital environment. This is especially important in the setting of education where ideas or work is assessed.

Whenever a person uses the internet for actions of creativity or learning, for example students accessing Web sites for educational materials or designers looking for inspiration, problems are increasingly emerging with regard to recognising and defining intellectual ownership. But when the medium and tools of creation within the digital world implicitly use the creations of others and there is no way to know the truth, value or ownership of any item this raises some interesting questions about the future of the digital society.

Any casual observer of the music industry will be aware of the problem of music piracy but this is not the only issue to be considered. Often the very tools that are used in the creative process have the contributions from others built into them and no longer even consciously involve making a decision about whether or not to use the contribution of another. Similarly problems of ownership often occur within the increasing use of sampling other artists work to produce a new work. Clip art, search engines and sound libraries have all helped to automate this new type of plagiarism.

An in-depth analysis of the complex issues involved with regard to Intellectual Property ownership within the digital environment is beyond the scope of this paper. But there are many online organizations devoted to this topic which provide a plethora of information about this constantly evolving, convoluted area, for example the World Intellectual Property Organization (WIPO) and the Electronic Frontier Foundation (EFF).

CONCLUSIONS AND FUTURE CHALLENGES

The highlighted problems and challenges are merely an overview of the issues relating to identity, veracity, and ownership in the digital age. In this ever fluctuating and technologically advancing society, these areas will continue to be exhaustive topics for research, discussion and possibly future legislation. But of the three, the most fundamental of these aspects is that of identity, our own and the identity of those we interact with in the digital arena. Without identity, we cannot build trust, we cannot develop meaningful online relationships that are essential for learning, and we become vulnerable and open to abuse by digital predators. Without identity, we cannot prove ownership of an intellectual idea, or without knowing the identity of its source, trust that a Web site or electronic work is all that it seems. But these problems should not be unsolvable and if a system of online identity checks, of establishing an identity management framework as suggested in recent studies (Cassassa-Mont et al., 2002) can be introduced then this will also impact positively in the other areas we have discussed. But future researcher must ask themselves at what cost could we introduce such strict controls? What effect will this have on free speech on the internet, on being able to lift ourselves above our physical constraints, to interact freely with others online without limitation, throwing off the moral and ethical constraints imposed by society in the real world?

REFERENCES

Adida, B. Hohenberger, S., & Rivest, R. (2005). Separable identity based ring-signatures: theoretical foundations for fighting phishing attacks. Technical report, Computer Science and Artificial Intelligence laboratory, Massachusetts Institute of Technology, U.S.

American Management Association, Survey of Business Monitoring of Employee Internet Use, June 2001, AMA

Benotsch, Eric G., Kalichman, Seth, & Weinhardt, Lance S. (2004). HIV-AIDS Patients evaluation of health information on the Internet: the digital divide and vulnerability to fraudulent claims. *Journal of Consulting and clinical Psychology*, 72(6), 1004-1011.

Bowker, Natilene & Tuffin, Keith (2002). Disability discourses for online identities. *Disability and Society*, 17(3), 327-344.

Cassassa-Mont, M., Bramhall, P., Gittler, M., Pato, J., & Owen, R. (2002). Identity Management: a key e-business enabler. Technical report HPL-2002-164. HP Laboratories, Bristol, U.K.

Charland, L.C. (2004). A Madness for Identity: Psychiatric labels, consumer autonomy and the perils of the Internet. Philosophy, Psychiatry and Psychology, 11(4) 335-349.

Cialdini, R. (revised 1998). Influence: The psychology of persuasion. U.S: Collins.

Davis, E. (2002). Experience Design (And the Design of Experience). Paper presented at Subtle Technologies, University of Toronto, Canada.

EFF (Electronic Frontier Foundation) http://www.eff.org

Ekstrand, Victoria Smith (2003). Unmasking Jane and John Doe: Online anonymity and the First Amendment. Communication Law and Policy, 8(4), 405-427.

Emarketer, (2000). Bosses disapprove employees still surf. http://www.emarketer.com/estats/daily-estats/demographics/20001030_work.html:

Felten, E. W., Balfanz, D., Drew, D., & Wallach, D. (revised 1997). Web spoofing: an Internet Con game. Technical report 540-96. Department of Computer Science, Princeton University, U.S.

Finn, J., & Banach, M. (2000). Victimization online: the downside of seeking human services for women on the Internet. *Cyber Psychology and Behaviour*, 3(5), 785-796.

Greenfield, D. (1999) Virtual Addiction: Help for Netheads, Cyberfreaks, and Those Who Love Them. New Harbinger.

Hardey, M. (2002). Life beyond the Screen: Embodiment and identity through the internet. *Sociological Review* 50(4), 570-585.

Henderson, S. & Gilding, M. (2004). 'I've never clicked with anyone this much in my life': Trust and hyperpersonal communication in online friendships. *New Media and Society*, 6(4), 487-506.

Herzberg, A., & Gbara, A. (2004). *Trustbar: protecting (even naïve) web users from spoofing and phishing attacks*. Cryptology: Eprint Archive Report 2004/155.

Jakobsson, M. (2005). *Modeling and Preventing Phishing Attacks*. Presentation to Phishing Panel of Financial Cyptography, Indiana University, U.S.

Joinson, A. N., & Dietz-Uhler, B. (2002). Explanations for the perpetration and reactions to deception on a virtual community. *Social Science Computer Review*, 20(3), 275-289.

Kimmel, A. J. (2004). Rumours and the financial marketplace. *Journal of Behavioral Finance*, 5(3), 134-141.

Knights, D., Noble, F., Vurdubakis, T., & Willmott, H. (2001). Chasing shadows: Control, virtuality and the production of trust. *Organization Studies*, 22(2), 311-336.

Kreuter, E. A. (2004). The impact of identity theft through cyberspace. *Forensic Examiner*, 12(5-6), 30-35.

Livingstone, S. (2003). Childrens use of the internet: Reflections on the emerging research agenda. *New Media and Society*, 5(2), 147-166.

Martland, N. E.F. (2001). *Expert criteria for evaluating the quality of web based child development information*. Dissertation Abstracts International: Section B: The Sciences and Engineering, 62(2-B), 1116.

Matthews, S. C., Camacho, A., Mills, P. J. & Dimsdale, J. E. (2003). The internet for medical information about cancer: Help or hindrance? Psychosomatics: *Journal of Consultation Liaison Psychiatry*, 44(2), 100-103.

Milne, G.R., Rohm A. J., & Bahl, S. (2004). Consumers Protection of Online Privacy and Identity. *Journal of Consumer Affairs*, 38(2), 217-232.

Morahan-Martin, J., & Anderson, C. D. (2000). Information and misinformation online: Recommendations for facilitating accurate mental health information retrieval and evaluation. *CyperPsycology and Behavior,* 3(5), 731-746.

Morgan, K. & Morgan, M. (2000). *The Role of Classical Jungian Personality Factors in CSCL Environments*, Norwegian Research Council Publications Series 2000, 183-191.

Postnes, T., & Brunsting, S. (2002). Collective action in the age of the Internet: Mass communication and online mobilization. *Social Science Computer Review*, 20(3), 290-301.

Romero, A.A., (2003). WHOIS? Identity: Collectivity and the Self in IRC, *PsychNology Journal*, 1(2), 87-130.

Sanchez, Carmen del Rio (2002). On-line psychotherapy: Ethical, deontological and practical considerations. *Revista de Psicologia Universitas Tarraconensis*, 24(1-2), 111-131.

Seager, P. B. & Wiseman, R., (1999) Fooling All of the People Half of the Time? *Science Spectra*, 15, 32-37.

SexTracker (2004). Survey of Internet use in the workplace, Retrieved on http://www.vault.com/vstore/SurveyResults/InternetUse/index.cfm:

Stewart, W., & Barling, J. (1996) Daily work stress, mood and interpersonal job performance. *Work and Stress*, 10(4), 336-351.

Subrahmanyam, K., Greenfield, P., & Tynes, B. (2004). Constructing sexuality and identity in an online teen chat room. *Journal of Applied Developmental Psychology*, 25(6), 651-666.

Thompson, L., & Nadler, J. (2002). Negotiating via information technology: Theory and application. *Journal of Social Issues*, 58(1), 109-124.

Topalian, A. (2003). Experienced reality: the development of corporate identity in the digital era. *European Journal of Marketing*, 37(7-8), 1119-1132.

United Nations. (2000). *The role of information technology in the context of a knowledge-based global economy*. Report of the UN Secretary-General, New York, 5 July-1 August 2000.

US Congress. (2000). Children's Internet Protection Act: Study on threats to minors from the Internet, submitted June 8, 2000, US Congress.

Vazire, S., & Gosling, S.D. (2004). E-perceptions: Personality impressions based on personal websites. *Journal of Personality and Social Psychology*, 87(1), 123-132.

VeriSign (2004). Internet Security Intelligence Briefing Reporting Year-End Trends in Internet Usage, Security, and Fraud, February 9, 2004.

WIPO (World Intellectual Property Organisation) at http://www.wipo.int

Wood, A.F. & Smith, M.J. (2001). *Online communication: Linking technology, identity and culture*. Mahwah, NJ, US: Lawrence Erlbaum Associates.

Yuan, Y., Ye, E., & Smith, S. (2001). *Web spoofing 2001*. Technical report TR2001-409. Department of Computer Science, Dartmouth College, U.S.

Yuan, Y., Ye, E., & Smith, S. (2002). *Web spoofing revisited: SSL and beyond*. Technical report TR2002-417 Department of Computer Science Dartmouth College, U.S.

KEY TERMS

Digital Identity: The persona, name or identity which some person or organization creates and uses in a digital environment.

Digital Predator: A person or group of persons who actively seek to abuse other people with a weaker status within digital environments. This can be for financial or sexual purposes.

Intellectual Property: The production of some original work or thought which by legal right is recognized as having been produced by or owned by some individual or organization.

Misinformation: The process of adding, editing or creating incorrect or misleading information on to a digital information source in a digital environment. This can be a Web site, an email, a podcast or a streaming video.

Musical Piracy: A specific form of ripping where copy protected music files are copied without financial or intellectual attribution of the ownership.

Phising: The use of misinformation and deception to lure an individual to give private or privileged information. The most common application of this phrase is to pretend to be a bank or other trusted organization and seek to obtain financial details.

Ripping: The process of taking a sound or movie file and removing the protection against copying so it can be freely used in a digital environment.

Chapter XXX
Philosophy of Web–Based Mediation

Olli Mäkinen
University of Vaasa, Finland

ABSTRACT

This chapter deals with the influence of mediation in different kinds of virtual environments such as virtual conferences, e-learning platforms, distance learning environments and surroundings, Internet Relay Chat (IRC), and various other user interfaces. Mediation is a means in which messages, discussion, and behaviour are becoming more and more conceptual and abstract and have an effect on our social being. As a result of mediation there is no first-hand experience of reality; everything is constructed, and in virtual reality we have receded a long way off from real life. Mediation affects our capability to make independent ethical decisions. The same process is discerned in all the social and commercial practices where it is rationalized by processing techniques or when it is made virtual. Here mediation is studied from a phenomenological perspective. Quantification, modelling, and regulation also describe aspects of mediation. This chapter is a review article and an opening in mediational ethics based on classical philosophy.

INTRODUCTION

In this chapter the concept or the problem of mediation is approached at different levels. To begin with, the etymology and metaphysical meaning of the concept of mediation is studied. Secondly, some of the different aspects of mediation are illustrated. And thirdly, mediational practice is presented in new and modern environments, such as distance learning environments, different virtual environments, and in user interfaces for the customers of libraries and social services.

The aim of this research is—in accordance with Critical Theory—to take a stand. The goal is, as the Frankfurt School (Horkheimer, 1982, p. 244) emphasized, human emancipation "to liberate human beings from the circumstances that enslave them." As Horkheimer pointed out the normative task of Critical Theory cannot be accomplished apart from the interplay between philosophy and social science through interdisciplinary empirical social research (Bohman, 2005; Horkheimer, 1993, p. 19-21). Horkheimer's thesis emphasized that Critical Theory is adequate only if it meets three criteria—it must be explanatory, practical, and normative, all at the same time. This declaration is followed also in this study, so the point of departure is both normative and ethical. The study is, however, also descriptive; the aim is to find the different variations of mediation. Partly because of the aims of Critical Theory the phenomenon of digital divide is also treated in this chapter.

Mediation is a means in which messages, discussion, discourse, and behaviour are becoming more and more conceptual and abstract and have an effect on our social being. Methodologically this research is phenomenological. In addition, an empirical study and some cases dealing with mediation are presented (e-learning platforms, distance learning environments and surroundings, two user interfaces, namely the web 2.0 of Stockholm City Library, and the interface between customers and social services in the City of Helsinki). Phenomenological bracketing has been chosen as a research method particularly because of its "being behindhand" (Mays, 2002, p. 177-186). In phenomenology central concepts or phenomena are taken into consideration from different perspectives. It is quite obvious that for example the concept mediation has a number of meanings depending on chosen discipline, or viewpoint. In phenomenological reduction, the attempt to define significance and discipline becomes a systematic attempt on controlling chaos (Ricoeur, 1984; Zahavi, 2003).

The background materials for this research are retrieved from classical philosophy but mostly from Jean Baudrillard, renowned for his analyses of modes of mediation and of technological communication and mediation. Baudrillard (1993) claimed that mediation accelerated because of the fast transfer to virtuality or hyperreality. He describes pessimistically the effect of mediation technologies on the human experience of reality. We do not meet our fellow men face to face any more but in different kinds of virtual environments. This has certainly both alienated us from traditional ethical decisions and at the same time brought about new ways how to make a choice. (Baudrillard, 1994, p. 20-21; Chandler; 1995, p. 89) Baudrillard's most important works dealing with mediation are *Symbolic Exchange and Death* (1976) and *Simulacra and Simulation* (1981).

However, mediation is an ongoing process. Our life is changing into more and more abstract direction. Mediation is an obligatory way that controls our lives and ever-increasing complexity in society (the world), and transforms and changes our life-world.

Existentialism dealt with practical philosophy, for example, ethics, and therefore mediation is studied for instance in the light of the thoughts by Søren Kierkegaard.

Mediation has an influence on different everyday social and commercial practices and virtual environments. Distance learning is used to respond to the challenges of life-long learning. In distance learning, virtual learning environments are used to rationalize and standardize education. Virtual learning may cause alienation and estrangement, when the traditional social contacts are missing. But it has its advantages, too. Virtual education is dealt with in the light of a case study made in the Tritonia Academic Library in 2005-2006.

The research area of the topic "mediational ethics," which has been taken into account in this study, is difficult to define. It certainly has to deal with virtuality. The main focus is to try to understand how mediation influences our life-world where the ethical decisions are made. When connecting the concept of mediation with philosophy the researcher will meet many contradictory, paradoxical elements and challenges.

The research examines critically the scientific and technical worldview, the environment, where an individual cannot affect his life the same way as before. As the area of mediation opens up, which is the main goal of the research, the individual variations of mediation become also clear. In this research some topical and typical cases are brought up. Some of them are negative variations of mediation that describe individuals who are becoming more and more frustrated and estranged. This is because they feel that the decisions relating to them are made in non- transparent systems. A recent case dealing with negative mediation—this will be presented later in this chapter—is the vigorous criticism against the social services of the City of Helsinki due to the fact that the social welfare officers almost entirely finished meeting their customers face-to-face. However, mediation is not always negative. If the customers can take an active part in planning the virtual environments concerning them, they can feel the solutions meaningful. This democratic process of participation was applied in Stockholm City Library, when the new beta version of Web 2.0 application was tested.

The structure of this chapter is: The concept of mediation; The relationship between mediation and virtuality; Mediation and the ethics of virtuality; Case 1: mediation in distance learning; Case 2: mediation in information retrieval; Cases 3 and 4: mediation in different kinds of user interfaces; Conclusion.

BACKGROUND

The history of mediation begins with Greek Philosophy. Although Aristotle thought that there is a strict connection between the language and the particular things in the world, and that we pick out these things by our words and we say things about those things that are picked out as the subjects of our discourse, not even he thought there was an immediate relation between nature and language (Hamlyn, 1987, p. 44).

Language has a major role in mediating experience. Romantics supported the naive epistemology according to which the experience of the world is immediate. We would attempt to stay as close as possible to that experience which they called authenticity or immediacy. There are according to (Chandler, 1995 p. 193, 224) realist, relativist, and idealist standpoints describing the mediational relation between the things of the world and the language. First, the physical world has an objective existence, which has no dependence on our use of language. Language may come between us and the world but at the same time it is distorting the reality, the world and the things. If we use language in an effective way it can mirror the reality and have a correspondence to the things in the world. Second, language plays an important role in constructing the social world but it is not all. It also constructs the physical world for us. We have no possibility to avoid imposing different kinds of frames and categories in the world when we use language. This distorts the reality all the time and distances us from it. Third, the world is only subjective and constructed by our use of language. Idealists deny or are disinterested in the independent objective existence of the world.

We are constantly determined to operate in the middle of very complicated frame-systems, says (Chandler, 1995, p. 197-198). It is possible to get rid of a particular frame, but we are not able to step outside this framing. Phenomena and things are framed by language and the ways it is used (conventions), by "the concepts of thought" (cognitive style, mood, and purposes), by the social situation and so forth. As human beings we exist in the middle of a life flow. We are often unaware of all the determinant factors, for example, the frames that influence our thought and sense perceptions.

There is, of course, an economy principle in the language. It means that the words are defined only once and that we are constantly economic. It would not be economical if we used only particulars in our language. We would be lost between the words. That is why we are formalizing, categorizing and generalizing—making the language more economic (Ricoeur, 1978, p. 115). The generalization means that we are able to build and examine ideas. On the other hand, we can never include the totality of our experience into the language. "The words fail me" and "There are no words to describe how I feel" are quite common sayings. Many Romantics experienced a sense of inadequacy of language as a medium for expressing what they meant (Chandler, 1995, p. 38). Derrida (1976) and Sartre (1966) have both said that writers do not have any possibilities to say exactly what they have in mind.

Lakoff and Johnsson (1980) have emphasized that when we extend our ability to categorize, the selectivity of language reduces the particularity of experience. Categorization as one form of mediation means that certain properties are highlighted, some downplayed and still others hidden (Chandler, 1995, p. 38, 40).

Mediation alienates human beings from real and typical human experiences, such as experiences of introjection, decision, anxiety, insight, self-awareness, and self-identity (Ballard, 1978). The same applies to our moral life and ethical decisions; they are strictly tied to our existential life. The more we grow apart from it, the less able we are to make moral decisions.

It is obvious that mediation has a close relation to and a strong effect on all kinds of activities in virtual realities. Virtual environments have grown apart from real life experiences, they have been conceptualized and standardized, otherwise they would not work. The virtual environments and philosophy of mediation are discussed in the next section.

PHILOSOPHY OF MEDIATION AND VIRTUAL ENVIRONMENTS

According to Deleuze (1990) philosophy is necessary especially in situations where new phenomena already exist, and where both undefined concepts and words are trying to find exact meanings. It is the philosophers' duty to clarify the unclear situation. The main task in philosophy is to invite and define new concepts (Deleuze, 2004, p. 73-98; Mäkinen & Naarmala, 2006). Mediation as a concept has multitudinous meanings:

In business and jurisdiction the term mediation covers any activity in which an impartial third party (often a professional) facilitates an agreement on any matter in the common interest of the parties involved.

In postmodernism, both in post-modern philosophy and mass communication theory, hyper-reality is the result of technological mediation, where what passes for reality is a network of images and signs without an external referent. What is represented is representation itself (Aylesworth, 2005). According to Baudrillard (1994, p. 6) the signs and images take over the reality. He says that the real has become an operational effect of symbolic processes, just as images are technologically generated and coded before we actually perceive them. This means that technological mediation has usurped the productive role of the Kantian (2003) subject, the locus of an original synthesis of concepts and intuitions, as well as the Marxian worker, the producer of capital through labour, and the Freudian unconscious, the mechanism of repression and desire. From now on signs are exchanged against each other rather than against the real, so production now means signs producing other signs. The system of symbolic exchange is therefore no longer real but "hyperreal" (Aylesworth, 2005).

In Hegel's (1770 -1831) philosophy, mediation (Vermittlung) is a process according to which dialectic process functions: two opposing positions are mediated into a synthesis. Hegel means that all movement occurs in the form of mediation. All the progress we perceive of is really a process of mediation. Because mediation occurs at the level of ideas, it also takes place at the level of the universal. Thus, mediation is firmly bound up with the ethical, idealistic, and universal sphere.

Kierkegaard (1813 - 1855) strictly opposed Hegel's interpretation, saying for instance, that there is no mediation between different existential stages (Mäkinen, 2004, p. 31-33). Kierkegaard (2001, p. 32-33) regarded Hegel's understanding of mediation (Vermittlung) as a false impression of the nature of reality. Kierkegaard suggested the concept 'repetition' instead of 'mediation' (Mäkinen, 2001, p. 33-34). In the dialectical movement, which is play of ideas and concepts, life itself vanishes and becomes an empty shell. A great deal of Kierkegaard's philosophy came into existence as a protest against the Hegelian influence (Mäkinen, 1998). In *The Sickness onto Death*, Kierkegaard (1929) mocks and describes those huge constructions and systems that consist of nothing but ideas. The philosopher creates a perfect system that explains and includes everything, both the world history and everything that exists, a brilliant palace, but he is himself compelled to live outside this creation—in a kennel. Kierkegaard (1987) wrote an exemplary book as a parody of mediation. In *The Seducer's Diary* the protagonist is practicing the art of seduction so far that he is transformed into a concept. Conceptualisation destroys emotions and all burning sensations in love and other strong feelings.

Kant (2003) explained in *Transcendental Logic* that we have central concepts that we employ when we are thinking about the world. According to Kant our most fundamental convictions about the natural world derive from these concepts. The most general principles of natural science are not empirical generalizations from our experiences, but synthetic a priori judgments about what we could experience, in which these concepts provide the crucial connectives. (Table 1)

In this way we produce mediation, concepts, and standardization all the time. Traditionally this has been the main task of sciences and bureaucracy. It is interesting that the founder of the Phenomenology, Husserl (1859-1938), thought that philosophy had to save the sciences from the natural attitude and careless theorizing (Moran, 2000). But at the same time we are in the middle of the life flow (Baudrillard, 1994, p. 7). When an individual is interpreting his own life, he is actually moving in the same way as is life itself. Husserl calls life-world the ultimate horizon of all human achievement. Individuals as conscious beings always inhabit life-world. It is given in advance and experienced as a unity. It is the general structure that allows objectivity. In Husserl's later studies an observer or scientist (philosopher) is then situated in the middle of the life flow, bound to historicity and life-worlds, and somehow he is able to outline the ethical condition of the culture. (Husserl, 1976; Moran, 2000, p. 11-12; Rauhala, 2006, p. 126) The final condemnation to mediation came from existentialism or life philosophy, from Heidegger (1889-1976), Sartre (1905 – 1980), and Merleau-Ponty (1908-1961).

Table I. The central concepts of thought (©2007, Olli Mäkinen. Used with permission)

Quantity	Quality	Relation	Modality
Unity	Reality	Substance	Possibility
Plurality	Negation	Cause	Existence
Totality	Limitation	Community	Necessity
Axioms of Intuition	Anticipations of Perception	Analogies of Experience	Postulates of Empirical Thought

The conclusion is a rather pessimistic one. It seems that we have no possibilities to avoid mediation and conceptualization. What effects does this have on our everyday life? Getting on in the world is becoming more and more abstract-difficult all the time. We are producing new language games or are obliged to follow the rules of numerous games others have developed. Life also becomes more complicated and it lacks the personal relations and strong feelings. At the same time we are fleeing, voluntarily or not, all ethical decisions, the language games have taken over this kind of activities.

ETHICS OF MEDIATION

Ethics has also become different owing to mediation. Via the Internet many traditionally located bound problems like pornography, sex, and business have become closer to everyone by means of an Internet connection. At the same time we do not make any important ethical decisions—they have vanished or have been mediated. There is an ethical void in the hyper-real world of the Internet.

What is cyberethics? Defining the cyberethics is a cross-disciplinary project. The topic is related to such concepts as Internet ethics, self regulation, game theory, plagiarism, trust and privacy, digital divide, professional ethics, surveillance, and regulations related to freedom of speech, to name a few. These are common topics in publications related to Internet ethics (Edgar, 2003; Spinello 1997, Spinello 2002, Lessing, 1999; Wall 2001)

According to pragmatism, values are being tested all the time with reality (Rosenthal, 1999). This is to say that pragmatism does not accept any permanent values. Therefore the tradition is suited for describing virtual ethics and reality. Usually development in value hierarchies is slow, but sometimes it is surprisingly fast too. Pragmatism is also based on scientific optimism (Pihlström,

1997, p. 11), where for example pragmatic ethics reflects advances in IT.

There is a common principle that applies to both the Internet specifically and information technology in general. As soon as a new technology is being introduced, everyone is eager to utilize it. There are, however, no significant attempts in creating standards to follow. Instead solutions are created by the vendor. They will quite soon become de facto standards. Applications are accepted by the general public without being defined and accepted officially, because this would take too much time.

Similar de facto practice appears to exist in moral issues related to the Internet. Moral codes are being molded and introduced by taking only pragmatic issues into account. Actors are everything but professionals. A new moral is being created in the Internet constantly; new virtual communities are being born all the time, and these form their own rules and practices, which depart greatly from commonly accepted ethical codes in society. From an ethical viewpoint this phenomenon is interesting—it appears that everything is happening so fast on the Internet (Mäkinen & Naarmala, 2006). Pragmatism is a suitable way for describing the development of the Internet, all de facto practices, which are being measured based on their suitability alone. Likewise, the concept of self regulation is more than applicable with pragmatic ethics.

Baudrillard (2006) deals thoroughly with the process of mediation in his essay *The Precession of Simulacra*. In images and through concepts the different phases are presented: reflection of profound reality; the masking and denaturing of profound reality, the masking of the absence of profound reality, and the total lack of any relation to reality. The mediation is seen as a natural and ongoing process.

Not only have nature and animals but also our fellow-men, or faces as Introna (2002, p. 71) says, become representations, images through electronic mediation. If there are less real experiences, there is more interpretation. Facelessness makes it easier to handle and organize sums, groups and people at the expense of existential good. Baudrillard (1993) talks about theoretical violation and speculates about death.

Internet and IT are foundations to virtual life. They should not be mixed up with virtual life itself. IT-applications are not ethical subjects but they can be useful, effective, fast and cheap. These qualities would not gain the upper hand as a de facto ethical point of view suggests. Usability is one of the main qualities when virtual environments are evaluated. The Internet has also introduced some important immaterial values. Everything is not material, technical, and measurable. It may be that all the high hopes of the information age have not been fulfilled. However, with regard to democracy, the Internet has improved the citizens' possibilities to participate. Some researchers like Salter (2003, p. 117-118), however, say that the Internet grows apart from the ideals of free communication which were so typical of it in the beginning.

Communication is the most important barometer of democracy, as stated by Habermas (1989, p. 136-142). According to his theory of discourse ethics, the more the people and institutions communicate in a society, the more efficiently democracy works. The Internet represents pluralism, competition between different opinions and genuine free public debate, says Salter (2003, p. 117-118). And most important of all, the Internet offers a foundation to interactivity. This may be the most important democratic value of the Internet.

Digitalization has improved the possibilities of mass communication and entertainment. On the one hand virtual entertainment alienates people from real feelings. On the other hand it is time-saving. Virtual entertainment is either spatially bound or bound to some place. Electronic mediation adds yet another layer of mediation to the already saturated layers of mediation, according

to Introna (2002, p. 71-84). War games are good examples. In Play Station games, the players never meet in a face to face situation. Instead, the games treat people as categories. It is easy to be violent against a human role category (thieves), rather than against the whole race (humans).

MEDIATION IN DISTANCE LEARNING

Distance learning environments in schools and universities are good examples of free activities that are solved in a very standardized and regulated manner when moved into virtual reality. Almost all the indirect speech acts and possibilities to convey through mime and different kinds of behaviour are lacking in virtual environments, or they have very small possibilities to get through. In real classroom situations it is easy to feel anger, dullness, admiration, acceptance, exhaustion, and to show these feelings. On the contrary, in virtual environments it is easy to hide these feelings. In virtuality it is also possible to hide—to be anonymous, which can not be done in ordinary classroom surroundings. For example irony and parody are literary and stylistic effects, but they also have a performative and contextual character.

Anonymity has been a standard that the users take for granted when connecting to the Internet. Anonymity has been so valuable that it is regarded as a basic right in the Internet. It is also used in some applications in distance learning environments. Anonymity protects privacy, but it has also some disadvantages. It is very likely that the possibility to operate anonymously has a negative effect on the individual's behaviour in the Internet. Many sociological and psychological studies show we behave differently depending on the type of relationship we have to the opponent. The physical presence and familiarity apparently reduce the undesired behaviour—the physical distance and anonymity, on the other hand, increases it. This most certainly affects the development of the rules which are generally used in the Internet. We like to operate in the net anonymously or behind pseudonyms. Wallace (1999, p. 239-242), for instance, shows, referring to numerous classical studies, that our behaviour differs a great deal in that kind of situations. (Naarmala & Mäkinen, 2005)

An example of mediation in distance learning is the course in information literacy that has been developed in the Tritonia Academic Library at University of Vaasa (Mäkinen & Mäntymäki, 2006). Information literacy as such is a very standardized phenomenon. The concept of information literacy is new and it has been defined at the same time it has come into existence. The association of College and Research Libraries created a standard for information literary (Information Literacy Competency Standards for Higher Education) already in 2000 (ILCS, 2000).

Information Literacy (IL) is a set of abilities requiring individuals to "recognize when information is needed and have the ability to locate, evaluate and use effectively the needed information." IL is also increasingly important in the contemporary environment of rapid technological change and proliferating information resources. Because of the escalating complexity of this environment, individuals are faced with diverse, abundant information choices in their academic studies, in the workplace, and in their personal lives. "Information is available through libraries, community resources, special interest organizations, media, and the Internet—and increasingly, information comes to individuals in unfiltered formats, raising questions about its authenticity, validity, and reliability [...] IL enablers learners [...] to determine the extent of information needed, access the needed information effectively and efficiently, evaluate information and its sources critically, incorporate selected information into one's knowledge base, use information effectively to accomplish a specific purpose and to understand the economic, legal and social issues surrounding the use of information, and access the use of in-

formation ethically and legally." (ILCS, 2000).

In the Tritonia Academic Library the plans to fulfil Vaasa University's requirements in the education of information literacy started already 2002, when a member of the staff began to plan a course in that subject. The administration of the university came to understand gradually how useful it would be to introduce an obligatory course in information literacy. This new opening included fresh methods of learning through self motivated-studies. Earlier, the studies in information search and information retrieval (IL studies) had been voluntary but now they become compulsory (Mäkinen & Mäntymäki, 2006).

In the autumn 2004 the course had been completed and it was experimented with a group of students. The Tritonia Academic Library arranged a pilot course in Information retrieval and information literacy for a group of new students in the autumn 2004. This course was a part of Vaasa University's virtual orientation studies. Tritonia's part consisted of both traditional lectures, work-shops in information retrieval, and self-motivated studies with material in the Internet. The Information Literacy Competency Standards for Higher Education were used in the planning of the course. (ILCS, 2000; Mäkinen & Kuoppala & Rintamäki, 2006, p. 65-73).Very good results in learning were achieved.

In 2005 this course became compulsory to all new students. After the evaluation the course was developing into a more and more virtual packet. The main reason for this was the large number of the students; the resources of the Tritonia Academic Library were not sufficient. So in autumn 2005 the lectures held in lecture rooms were "moved to the Internet," the test that had earlier been an essay was performed by means of questionnaire and all the material was available in the Internet. The open, critical discussion and all face-to-face performance were moved into virtual discussion forums.

Progress in the course certainly had many administrative advantages. First of all, the governance of the course was now easier. The students registered for the course in the Internet, the quiz counted the results automatically, it was easy for the teachers to see how the course went on, how many students had dropped out, which modules they had performed. The teachers could evaluate the degree of difficulty in the test and regulate it and so on. The students were also able to test the standard of their information literacy skills and pass the course by taking the test. The test was based on The Information Literacy Competency Standards for Higher Education and it was developed in cooperation with different Finnish universities. (ILCS, 2000; Mäkinen & Mäntymäki, 2006)

There were 90 questions in the quiz and the system generated (drew) 30 of them to each student. In the autumn 2006, when 140 students (out of 550) had taken the test, the teachers noticed that only 40 per cent had passed it. So the teachers lowered the standards/requirements.

With the help of the Moodle-based virtual environment it was easier to govern the course. At present it is impossible to say if the goals in the learning have been achieved—the evaluation is going on. The same concerns the educational standards of the course. In the pilot project the students' information retrieval skills (Boolean logic, truncation, use of keywords, etc.) developed notably after two workshops. The real benefit of the course can be evaluated and shown up in few years when the new students are doing their diploma works. But according an interview the students were satisfied with this virtual course; they said that virtual studies spared their time and made it possible to make home works in the evenings and on weekends.

But the course in information literacy had other objectives, too. The librarians and information specialists wanted to come nearer the students, meet all the beginners, to make the library a pleasant place, a kind of extension to the living room. The library is worried about how the use of digitalized material changes the way the students use the library.

Because of the virtual course the teachers and the librarians seldom meet the students and vice versa. All the personal and existential have been eliminated. Discussions are going on virtually in discussion forums, students and tutors do not meet each other face-to-face any more. In the quiz-test there are only the true or false answers, no intermediate forms as in modality logic (possible, occasional, random, probable, for example.). Reality is not as simple as the course, the concepts and mediation let you understand. It may be easy to govern the course but the reality and the contents of the course do not encounter. In the future the teachers would try to play the game on the same ground with the students, this means that virtual environments would be improved and developed.

MEDIATION AND INFORMATION RETRIEVAL

As mentioned, in the pilot project the students' information retrieval skills like Boolean logic, truncation, use of keywords, and so forth developed notably after two workshops. The information is stored in library databases and it can be characterized as structured, controlled and as a whole a good example of meta-language.

When searching information in databases it is very important that in the retrieval both the meta-language in the database and the needs of the client (searcher) encounter. That is why in information literacy education the learning of formal skills is important. In the Tritonia Academic Library the development of students' information retrieval skills were estimated during the course in information retrieval (Mäkinen, Kuoppala, & Rintamäki, 2006, p. 83-84). The group consisted of 80 students. Their information retrieval skills (Boolean logic, truncation, use of keywords, etc.) developed notably after two workshops (Table 2).

It was not very surprising that the students learned without any difficulty to use the right terms in information search. And it was natural that they first used the wrong way in searching, that is, the natural language of free text, because it is the way you search in Google. The same development was seen when the students were asked to make a search for information on immigration/emigration in Finland (Table 3).

The students' behaviour was developing towards a more abstract direction. They had learned to meet the demands of the database very practically and usefully. Google, on the contrary, is constantly trying to develop its search engine towards a Semantic Web. To conclude, these processes, mediation, and the progress of semantic utilities, are very contradictory.

MEDIATION IN ANOTHER VIRTUAL ENVIRONMENT

Many virtual environments try to control and direct the behaviour of the end users. As good examples we have all the different user interfaces

to databases, virtual libraries, and electronic journals (ScienceDirect, EBSCO, ABI Inform, Voyager Databases). Everything has been standardized in these databases. The documents have been described with standardized words, so called subjects or keywords (in Thesaurus). It is possible to make models or describe different processes in these databases with terms of modal logic (the database itself as construction; the one who updates the database, processes; the designer (or the analyst) of the database, processes; the end user, processes. So, all the processes are predictable. Here too, the databases do not meet reality, mediation has cast the different actors in the same mould.

People do not necessarily accept the fact that mediation simplifies and conceptualizes reality. Of course it is in people's interests that there is a limited amount of possibilities because life becomes less complicated that way. The problem is that people are unable to give expressions to their feelings, describe the complexity and the "biodiversity" of the world in the strict limits of the mediated and standardized virtual environments. They want more, they want to know this: how to express exhaustion, sorrow, anger, love, hope and joy, all the colours of the world—and this is not possible within these limits.

Table 2. How would you truncate "immigrants" for the best possible search result? (©2007, Olli Mäkinen. Used with permission)

	Right	Wrong	No reply
Before the workshops	32	68	0
After the workshops	66	30	4

Table 3. "How would you search immigration to or emigration from Finland.?" (©2007, Olli Mäkinen. Used with permission)

	Right	Wrong	No reply
Before the workshops	43	43	14
After the workshops	68	25	7

Google tries to make the search engine work interactively and to develop Semantic Web. As far as the popularity of Google's search engine is concerned, they have succeeded in their efforts. People want the user interface to comment or answer even though they have placed the comma in a wrong place or asked a silly question.

Web 2.0 may be a possibility to solve these mediational problems. It is a philosophy based on interactivity between the end-users and the software producers. When Stockholm City Library was planning and developing its new user interface, all the voluntary users were welcomed to participate in the development work (www. biblioteket.se). Is this the beginning for a new creative period in the Internet development—a new Habermasian communicative era? The ideal of Internet communication was interactivity, whereas communication has recently become more and more one-sided and none-communicative. Johnson (2000, p. 196) claims that commercial interests have increased their influence on the development of the Internet. This is based on the fact that the free market forces have realized that the Internet is an important and efficient tool and media and have taken over it.

Public libraries have the same dilemma as the teachers in academic libraries; they find it difficult to meet the customers who have moved into the virtual environments. That is why Stockholm City Library is developing a virtual meeting place, a marketplace and a Hyde Park Corner for the customers. Stockholm City Library summed up the mission of the new user interface like this (Mäkinen, 2007).

- The goal is to present the whole Stockholm City Library, both the collections and the services, so that more attention is paid to the display of the materials. This requires detailed linking to the documents describing the contents of different materials. Stockholm City Library is also going to make the huge reserves of metainformation or metadata (information about information) available to the general public. The great variety of different kinds of cultural and social happenings, that the libraries are arranging, is advertised on the Web site.

- It is the end users who are actively participating in the production of the contents (the wikies, the blogs, literary and art criticism, etc.). It is possible to write and express your opinion on whatever subjects you want—after you have logged in with your own password. The library is seeking and recruiting new moderators all the time. (Ibid.)

- The skills and know-how of the staff of all the 44 branch libraries are presented on a common interface, where the specialists and the customers (audience) meet each other. The web site includes also the intranet of the staff. (Ibid.)

- The aim is to create an open meeting place and forum, where the customers and citizens have a possibility to talk, discuss, take a stand, change information and solve problems—regardless of place, nationality, education, race, date or time. The role model of the Swedish library activities has traditionally been the so called Agora model (Agora was a market place in Ancient Greece, a Hyde Park). Now this same idea has been implemented also virtually. (Ibid.)

It seems that at Stockholm City Library, the Habermasian principles of free communication have been understood properly.

MEDIATION AND COMMITMENT IN SOCIAL SERVICES

The operations, both successes and failures, of the social services of the City of Helsinki have been evaluated annually by impartial ombudsmen, that is, people appointed to investigate complaints against maladministration by a particular category of organization or in a particular area of public life, such as local authorities, hospitals, or pensions. The report from the year 2006 contains strong criticism against the social services of the City of Helsinki. Two ombudsmen (Autti & Soppela, 2006) interviewed the staff and the customers in the social services. Hundreds of decisions, which have an influence on the lives and livelihood of the citizens, are every day made by the social welfare boards and officials.

The citizens contact the ombudsman if they think they have been treated unfairly. There were 1,370 contacts in the City of Helsinki in 2005 and 1,252 in 2006. 46 official complaints were made in the year 2005. The customers of the social services find it difficult that they have to make the income support applications by letter; the application forms may also be found on the Internet. The applicants do not meet the officials face-to-face at all, and this has been quite problematic for some groups of people, especially elderly people and immigrants have complained that it is almost impossible to fill in the application without guidance. The representatives want to pay attention to one case in 2006, where a customer was totally left outside the social security system, because of problems making the application for the income support. This customer was physically disabled so he could not visit the social security office. The only way was to make income support application by letter. Although the social service had known the difficulty of the situation of this customer for years, he was left outside the social service and the main benefits. The information about his problems had not been transmitted from one official to another.

Oksanen (2007) says that the customers do not meet personally with the officials when they fill in the income support applications but they write a letter or meet via the Internet. This has resulted in a situation where the customers have to give complementary information. They feel they will be drowned in administrative procedures and at the end they become depressed, give up and drop out of the system.

The Internet is increasingly becoming the channel or medium for people to get information about the society and social services. It does not matter if the services are available virtually on the Internet or if they are real customer-official services in the social office. The customers are either well-educated or people with high standard of living, as the students in the Case Tritonia Academic Library. (Mäkinen, Kuoppala, & Rintamäki, 2006). For the young people, Internet means additional value. They are able to look after things regardless of time and place. Young people use social services quite rarely, mostly when applying for study grants. The elderly, the immigrants and the sick as well as the unemployed are more likely to be regular customers of the social services; they often depend on social security. But they do not always know how to use computers and the Internet. It is also possible that they do not even have an Internet connection at home.

Mediation, virtuality and information society are creating digital divides, which is not necessarily due to a person's economical situation, but to his know-how or inability to take care of his business or to work with bureaucracy or to navigate on the surface of different user interfaces. Excellent Web architecture does not always guarantee that the use of the Internet is successful (Brennan & Johnsson 2004; Mäkinen 2006; Norris, 2001; Rooksby & Weckert, 2004).

Educational background is directly related to the flexible use of the Internet and also to the ability to use different social services. According to a Swedish study (Findahl, 2004; Mäkinen, 2006) education-related differences become more and more distinct after the age of 25. Other international studies support also this assumption.

According to the study by Autti and Soppela (2006) it was first and foremost personal guidance and face-to-face contacts the customers of the social services want. The officials in the social service may be the only human contacts they have. If this is left out, they feel they are left alone. To move the services to the Internet may be economically justified, but at the same time it means that the service standards of the marginal groups of society are weakening.

CONCLUSION

What are the dangers in all mediation and standardization? The benefits have to do with predictability, simplifying of complicated phenomena through modelling, evaluation and process engineering. It is, however, difficult to calculate the winnings in time and other. It seems that the processing of great amounts of information requires both standardized contents like data, information, messages, knowledge and designed IT-applications.

We have discussed the existential loss of ICT mediation. When people have economic surplus they begin to look for the experiences that are reduced in virtual environments. That is why the producers of such virtual environments and the providers of virtual services are trying to bring back life to these environments. They develop new user friendly languages, smileys, videos, and so forth. So, development is contradictory; it is based on rationality and on a desire for real and original experiences. Web 2.0 solutions seem to be able to solve these problems. It is paradoxical that we are back at the beginning of the Internet era. People are talking about democracy and freedom, social communication and participation. It is possible that the new interactive ways to communicate and provide contents are growing now that the IT infrastructure is in place.

As seen in the given examples, mediation makes it possible to develop new kinds of learning environments. The lack of traditional class room circumstances reduces conventional ways to experience interactions. Virtual applications form a serious challenge for university teachers

and library users. Wikipedia is a good example of interactivity that destroys old structures. The brief review of the history of the concept of mediation showed that the same problems have existed in the philosophy since the Ancient times.

When new virtual environments are planned, it is of vital importance that the users are able to influence the form, functioning and content—in other words usability of the system. Without the test runs made by the end users, the great ideas are realized only partially, or virtually. The end users have no use of the virtual environments and the whole system becomes an empty bureaucratic application.

When virtual environments are planned for the marginal groups of the society, the digital divide should be taken into account. As the case "The social service in the City of Helsinki" showed, the digital divide has a clear connection with the education and technical IT-skills of the citizens, it is not so much a question if people can afford IT-equipment. People with a good command of the use of IT get the greatest advantage of the improvements of the information technology together with the developers of the technology. The marginal groups of society who should be the target groups of these programs, but they become the losers.

When technological-instrumental extremes of mediation take over, there is always a risk that the matters of form dominate at the expense of contents. It is important to make everything in the only possible way, as in rites or services. There is a risk that a scholar composes a paper according to the rules and formalities and knows that this is enough to get it accepted.

There is an acute risk is that hyper-reality is making our ethical sensibility indefinite when we encounter serious ethical situations. Where do the ethical contents disappear? I think this is the core question when uncoiling the problems relating to the concept and phenomena of mediation. Maybe it is more important to meet face to face than to get a chance to meet as many persons as possible regardless of the location?

It is obvious that real and virtual mediation is an ongoing process or a trend that will continue to grow. It is part of the development trends typical of information society. But if we think about conceptualization and mediation, the rise of different expert groups as a historical phenomenon, there have always been protest movements that have tried to turn the direction of the development. Kuhn (1962, p. 68-85) has described this trend in his work *The Structure of Scientific Revolutions*. In the world of art progress is going according to the same dialectics as in the world of science. Existentialism was a philosophical and literary protest movement against conceptualization and mediation. What is going to be the next?

REFERENCES

Autti, L., & Soppela, M.-T. (2006). Asiakkaan asialla: Mitä asiakkaat kertovat yhteydenotoillaan? Selvitys Helsingin sosiaaliasiamiesten toiminnasta vuonna 2005. Helsinki: Helsingin kaupunki. Retrieved on May 24, 2007, from http://www.hel.fi/wps/wcm/resources/file/ebb5dc4ccdbe64e/Sosiaaliasiamiehen_raportti_2005.rtf

Aylesworth, G. (2005). *Postmodernism*. In The Stanford Encyclopedia of Philosophy. Stanford University, 2005. Retrieved on March 28, 2007, from http://plato.stanford.edu/entries/postmodernism/

Ballard, E. G. (1978). *Man and technology*. Pittsburgh, PA: Duquesne University Press.

Baudrillard, J. (1993). *Symbolic exchange and death*. London: Sage.

Baudrillard, J. (1994). *Simulacra and Simulation*. Trans. S. Glaser, Ann Arbor: University of Michigan Press.

Bohman, J. (2005). *Critical theory*. In The Stanford Encyclopedia of Philosophy (Spring 2005 Edition), Edward N. Zalta (Ed.). Retrieved on May 25, 2007, from http://plato.stanford.edu/archives/spr2005/entries/critical-theory/

Brennan, L. & Johnsson, V. (2004). *Social, ethical, and policy implications of Information Technology*. Hershey: Information Science Publishing.

Chandler, D. (1995). *The act of writing. A media theory approach*. Aberystwyth: University of Wales.

Deleuze, G. (2004). *Difference and repetition*. Trans. by Paul Patton. London: Continuum.

Deleuze, G. (2005) *Filosofiasta, (Sur de philosophie*, Pourparlers, 1990). In Gilles Deleuze: *Haastatteluja*. Trans. by Anna Helle et. al., Helsinki: Tutkijaliitto, 73-98.

Derrida, J. (1976): *Of grammatology* (trans. G. C. Spivak). Baltimore, MD: Johns Hopkins University Press.

Edgar, S. L. (2003). *Morality and machines: Perspectives on computer ethics*. Boston: Jones and Barlett.

Findahl, O. (2004). *Svenskarna och Internet 2003*. Stockholm: WII.

Habermas, J. (1989). The public sphere: An encyclopaedia article. In Stephen Eric Bronner and Douglass Kellner (Eds.), *Critical Theory and Society: A Reader*. (pp. 136-142) New York: Routledge, pp. 136-142).

Hamlyn, D.W. (1987). *Metaphysics*. Cambridge: Cambridge University Press.

Horkheimer, M. (1982). *Critical theory*. New York: Seabury Press.

Horkheimer, M. (1993). *Between philosophy and social science*. Cambridge: MIT Press.

Husserl, E. (1976). *Die Krisis der europäischen Menschentum und der Philosophie*. In W. Biemel (Ed.), Die Krisis der europäischen Wissenschaften und die transzendentale Phänomenologie. Eine Einleitung in die phänomenologische Philosophie (Husserliana Gesammelte Werke, Band VI. The Hague: Martinus Nijhoff).

Information Literacy Competency Standards for Higher Education = ILCS (2000). Retrieved on March 28, 2007, from http://www.ala.org/ala/acrl/acrlstandards/standards.pdf, Jan. 2000

Introna, L. (2002).The (im)possible of ethics in information age. *Information and Organization*, 12, 71-84.

Johnson, D. (2002). Democratic values and the Internet. In. D. Langford (Ed.), *Internet Ethics* (pp. 1810199) London: MacMillan Press.

Kant, I. (2003). *Critique of pure reason*. Trans. by Norman Kemp Smith ; with a new introduction by Howard Caygill. Houndmills, Basingstoke, Hampshire: Palgrave Macmillan New York.

Kierkegaard, S. (1929). *Sygdommen til Døden: En christelig psychologisk Udvikling til Opbyggelse og Opvækkelse*. In Søren Kierkegaards Samlede Værker XI, 129-272, Kjøbenhavn: Gyldendlske Boghandel, Nordisk Forlag.

Kierkegaard, S. (1987).*Either-Or*. Ed. and trans. by Howard V. Hong and Edna H. Hong. Princeton, NJ : Princeton University Press.

Kierkegaard, S. (2001). *Toisto. (Gjentagelsen)*. Tras. by O. Mäkinen. Jyväskylä: Atena.

Kuhn, T. (1962). *The structure of scientific revolutions*. Chicago: University of Chicago Press.

Lakoff, G., & Johnson, M. (1980). *Metaphors we live By*. Chicago, IL: University of Chicago Press.

Lessing, L. (1999). *Code and other laws of cyberspace*. New York: Basic Books.

Mays, W. (2002). Piaget and Husserl: Theory and Praxis in Science. (In B. E. Babich (Ed.), *Hermeneutic Philosophy of Science, van Gogh's Eyes, and God* (pp. 177-186). Dordrecht: Kluwer Academic Publishers.

Moran, D. (2000). *Introduction to phenomenology*. London and New York: Routledge.

Mäkinen, O. (1998) *Yossarianin hyppy esteettisestä uskonnolliseen. Kierkegaard, Joseph Heller ja Catch-22*. Oulu: Oulun yliopisto.

Mäkinen, O. (2004). *Moderni, toisto ja ironia. Søren Kierkegaardin estetiikan aspekteja ja Joseph Hellerin Catch-22*. Oulu: Oulun yliopisto.

Mäkinen, O. (2006). *Internet ja etiikka*. Helsinki: BTJ.

Mäkinen, O. (2007). *Tukholman kaupunginkirjasto on web 2.0:ssa*. Kirjastolehti 2/2007, 19.

Mäkinen, O., & Naarmala, J. (2006, November 28December 2)). *Defining Cyberethics*. Paper presented at the meeting of the ICEB + eBRF, Tampere Hall - Tampere, Finland; in press.

Mäkinen, O. & T. Mäntymäki. (2006, August 16-18). *Living interaction and flexible solutions in the changing world of academic studies*. Paper presented at the meeting of the Creating Knowledge, International conference at The Royal Library and University of Copenhagen, Copenhagen.

Mäkinen, O., Kuoppala, H., & Rintamäki, K. (2006). *Informaation luonne ja plagiointi: empiirinen tutkimus opiskelijoiden käsityksestä tiedosta, sen käytöstä ja heidän suhtautumisestaan virtuaaliopetukseen*. (In O. Mäkinen (Ed), *Akate emisia opiskelutaitoja oppimassa. Opiskelijoiden kokemuksia verkkokursseilta ja tiedonhakutaitojen kehitys lähiopetuksessa* (pp. 59-118). Selvityksiä ja raportteja. Vaasa: Vaasan yliopisto.

Naarmala, J., & Mäkinen, O. (2005, May 4-7). *Ethical and privacy Issues in Information Society. Comparative study of privacy and trust in state of emergency*. Paper presented at the meeting of the EURAM, Münich, Germany.

Norris, P. (2001). *Digital divide: Civic engagement, information poverty, and the Internet worldwide*. New York: Cambridge University Press.

Oksanen, K. (2007). *Sosiaalitoimi jättänyt asiakkaansa yhä useammin yksin Helsingissä.* Helsinki: Helsingin Sanomat, May 23, p. A11.

Pihlström, S. (1997). *Tutkiiko tiede todellisuutta? Realismi ja pragmatismi nykyisessä tieteenfilosofiassa.* Helsinki: Helsingin yliopiston filosofian laitos.

Ricoeur, P. (1978). *The rule of metaphor: Multidisciplinary studies of the creation of meaning in language.* London: Routledge & Kegan Paul.

Ricoeur, P. (1984). *Time and narrative.* Chicago: The University of Chicago Press.

Rooksby, E., & Weckert, J. (2004). *Digital divides: Their social and ethical implications.* In L. Brennan & V. Johnsson (Eds.), *Social, Ethical, and Policy implications of Information Technology* (pp. 29047). Hershey: Information Science Publishing.

Rauhala, L (2006). *Hermeneuttisen tieteenfilosofian analyyseja ja sovelluksia.* Helsinki: Helsinki University Press.

Rosenthal, S. B. (1999). *Rethinking business ethics. A pragmatic approach.* Cary: Oxford University Press.

Salter, L. (2003). Democracy, New Social Movements, and the Internet: A Habermasian Analysis. In L. L. Brennan & V. E. Johnsson (Eds.), *Cyberactivism: Online Activism in Theory and Practice* (pp. 117-144). New York: Routledge.

Sartre, J.-P. ([1956] 1966). *Being and nothingness: A phenomenological essay on ontology.* New York: Washington Square Press.

Spinello, R. (1997). *Case studies in information and computer ethics.* New Jersey: Prentice Hall.

Spinello, R. (2000). *Morality and law in cyberspace.* Boston: Jones and Barlett.

Wallace, P. (1999). *The psychology of the Internet.* Cambridge: Cambridge University Press.

Wall, D. (2001). *Crime & the Internet.* Florence: Routledge.

Zahavi, D. (2003). *Husserl's Phenomenology.* Palo Alto, Stanford University Press.

KEY TERMS

Cyberethics: The term refers to a code of safe and responsible behaviour for the Internet community. Practicing good cyberethics involves understanding the risks of harmful and illegal behaviour online and learning how to protect ourselves, and other Internet users, from such behaviour.

Digital Divide: The term refers to the gap between those with regular, effective access to Digital and information technology, and those without this access. It encompasses both physical access to technology hardware and, more broadly, skills and resources which allow for its use.

Distance Learning: Education in which contact between students and teacher is principally by correspondence or broadcast programmes, rather than face to face.

E-Learning: Learning conducted via electronic media, especially on the Internet.

E-Society: Virtual environments in the Internet: for example, e-commerce, e-business, and e-government.

Ethics: The science of morals; the department of study concerned with the principles of human duty.

Frame: A set of standards, beliefs, or assumptions governing perceptual or logical evaluation or social behaviour.

Mediation: A means in which messages, discussion and behaviour are becoming more and more conceptual and abstract and have an effect on our social being.

Phenomenology: A method or procedure, originally developed by the German philosopher Edmund Husserl (1859-1938), which involves the setting aside of presuppositions about a phenomenon as an empirical object and about the mental acts concerned with experiencing it, in order to achieve an intuition of its pure essence.

Virtual: Something made by software to appear to be real from the point of view of the program or the user.

Virtual Reality: A notional image or environment generated by computer software, with which a user can interact realistically.

Chapter XXXI
Unstructured Information as a Socio-Technical Dilemma

Lars-Erik Nilsson
Kristianstad University College, Sweden

Anders Eklöf
Kristianstad University College, Sweden

Torgny Ottosson
Kristianstad University College, Sweden

ABSTRACT

The purpose of this chapter is to illustrate how access to information through the implementation of digital information and communication technology challenges traditional school practices and introduces dilemmas about democracy, school development, ethics, information management, and learning. Video data together with screen captures are used to present three cases where students try: to match questions to search expressions; to make decisions about whether sites can be visited; and how they make decisions about relevance and credibility. Data illustrate that information always appears to be unstructured to the students and that restructuring poses a socio-technical dilemma involving appreciation of ideological and ethical nature.

UNSTRUCTURED INFORMATION AS A SOCIO-TECHNICAL DILEMMA

The aim of this chapter is to illustrate how access to information through the implementation of digital information and communication technology challenges traditional school practices and introduces dilemmas about democracy, school development, ethics, information management, and learning.

Structuring, categorizing, and sorting can be considered to be a fundamental part of human cultural activity (Bowker & Starr, 1999). Structuring information in terms of theorizing and building models, organizing disciplinary and professional knowledge, sorting data about citizens, organizing items in a data base or for that matter for a student report are activities that permeate modern society bringing about order. Still there are certain ambiguities in the discussion of students' work with information illustrating a socio-technical dilemma. Apprehending structure is considered to be an important aspect of learning. In course books and other educational media, structure appears to be considered to be there waiting to be apprehended. Internet is considered to introduce *"unstructured information,"* thus lacking a structure to apprehend. Structure instead needs to be constructed. Embracing a modern technology that introduces "unstructured information" into education thus appears as somewhat of a paradox ultimately challenging the way we learn. We will approach the paradox first through a presentation of the ambiguous appreciation of its introduction, then we will continue by discussing implications of conceptualizing Internet based information as unstructured, anchoring the presentation in research on literacy. We will introduce a plug-in aimed at supporting students' efforts to structure information for reports. We will then introduce information management in education as a socio technical dilemma and present excerpts from three cases to illustrate how this dilemma may be studied. Finally we will relate it to issues of democracy and ethics.

THE AMBIGUOUS APPRECIATION OF INFORMATION AND COMMUNICATION TECHNOLOGY

Policies in many countries emphasize the importance of technology in education, presenting implementation as a national urgency tied to such goods as the welfare state, democracy, and the ability to compete in the global market place

(Cuban, 2001; Postman, 1996; Riis, 1999; Robertson, 2002). Consequently many governments have decided on policies designed to facilitate implementation of technology in education. A generic feature of these policies is an understanding of future students and workers as citizens in an information society/economy. As such they have a democratic right to become information literate and be able to use technology to find, retrieve and manage information.

The centrality of "unstructured information" in making sense of information and communication technology is reflected in the foreword to the English edition of the Swedish Government Communication *Tools for Learning* (1997/98:176, p. 12). There the Swedish Minister of Education asks how education is "affected by the constant availability of unstructured information?" The communication presents the challenge as follows, indicating that education is undergoing change:

Traditionally, teaching has been based on a textbook in which the various sections of the subject are usually presented in an instructive and orderly way. A different arrangement, using the Internet or teaching media, is for pupils to collect data from various sources; thereafter making presentations or reports based on the material they have collected.

A particular view on what it means to learn in the age of the Internet is presented. Students need to prepare for a society where "information management and processing make up an ever larger share of many people's occupational roles" (ibid., p. 8). Consequently it has become a democratic right to have access to and learn how to use modern technology to support this mode of working. At the same time order is traded for chaos as information structured by the text book is replaced by the unstructured information on the Internet represented by "various sources;" placing demands on the education system to teach students how to manage information and students to collect data and impose their own structure in order to make presentations and produce reports.

The ambiguity is also reflected in research. In some perspectives, notably cognitivist, constructivist, and socio-cultural perspectives on learning, there is the understanding that new artefacts will change what we can learn and the way we learn. Databases and other storage media facilitate externalization (Säljö, 2005), network tools facilitate the construction of learning communities (Barab, Kling & Gray, 2004; Land & Jonassen, 2001) and distributed cognition, mind tools enhance problem solving capabilities (Jonassen, 2000), and word processors and presentation software enhance our ability to utilize different media forms for presentation and re-presentation (Kress, 2003). At a socio-genetic level this development is considered to represent advances in human learning (Säljö, 2005). With specific reference to information Breivik (1998) argues that the proliferation of pre-packaged information in schools and higher education makes it impossible to prepare students for lifelong learning. Problem solving based on such material provides artificial and limited environments and bear "little resemblance to problem solving in the real world" (p. 128), thus failing to take into account that in that world information needs be collected and pieced together or in the parlance of this chapter to be restructured. Schools that use such material to scaffold learning could in such a perspective be considered to fail their students by not preparing them for a life outside the classroom.

With the event of training, word processing, and presentation software and the Internet we have also witnessed a growing concern from educational institutions that student use of technology can be detrimental to the kind of learning required by policies. Research implies that the effects may not be as conducive to learning as has been expected (Alexandersson & Limberg, 2005; Ivarsson, 2000), or that different ideas about using technology may contribute to sorting students into different futures (Warshauer, 2000).

THE STRUCTURE OF UNSTRUCTURED INFORMATION

"Information wants to be free" has been a battle cry from those who want to keep Internet from being controlled by authorities or other powers. Worries about free information are multiplied in studies discussing the impact of net based information. Student users may be: confronted with inappropriate information (Fox, 2005); unable to find appropriate information (Bilal, 2002; Joint, 2005; Karchmer, 2001); unable to value information; encouraged to transport and transform information (Alexandersson & Limberg, 2004); prone to plagiarize information (Mallon, 1989/2002) and so forth. At worst easy access to information may lure students to buy, borrow or steal the work of others, putting them in danger of being "cheated out of skills" (Cowen, 2001). Easy access to information and features that allow students to copy and paste prevent students from becoming skilled, critical, and creative users and producers of scholarly work (Auer & Krupar, 2001; Burke, 2004; Mallon, 1989, 2002). In such dystopian presentations information mediated by the Internet poses a threat to student learning and when all is said and done modern technology may introduce information in forms that are deskilling. Questions may be raised about the ethical ramifications of introducing such a technology.

The notion that free information also implies unstructured information is debated. An alternative view can be found in informatics, systems design, and computer engineering. In these perspectives structure is generally considered to have been imposed on information and once imposed structure is treated as a property. From that vantage point a Web-page, even if it is freely available is: a highly structured type of information; marked up by standard protocols; and searchable by search engines like Google. The intention behind Berners-Lee's (1989) report *Information management: A proposal,* and later Berners-Lee and Cailliaus' (1990) *The World Wide*

Web, was to provide structure making it easier for scientists to find and retrieve information. Such descriptions make the notion that information on the Internet is "unstructured" appear strange. Structure however is not always easy to impose. Simon (1973) claims that ill-structured problems make programming, searching for, retrieving and similar actions difficult. In his perspective structure is not just something humans impose or apprehend. Problems have affordances making it more or less difficult to structure information to deal with them.

INFORMATION TECHNOLOGY AND THE QUEST FOR LITERACY

Information technology has brought a deepened interest in skills and competencies needed to deal with information. Discourses about these skills and competencies often appear under the label information literacy. Such studies and reports commonly use the concept for the individual's ability to interact with information tools to seek for, find and manage information, in other words to search for and impose structure. Generic lists of skills and competencies required to solve these tasks abound (cf. ACRL, 2000; CAUL, 2001; SCONUL, 1999).

Research on students' information literacy has foremost targeted searching for information. Students have been asserted to have trouble locating the information they need to complete their assignments, especially in the allotted time frame (Alskans & Jusufovic, 2005; Marchionini, 1997, 2003). This is often formulated as an inability to construct searches that yield an appropriate result due to a focus on procedures and techniques instead of content, but also due to an endless access to unstructured information.

Lately a number of studies have covered issues in a wider area of managing information. Knowing what kind of information counts as an answer to a certain question provides resources for structuring. Students need to structure information according to credibility and quality aims (Boström, 2005; Leth & Thurén, 2000; Limberg & Sundin, 2006; Rieh 2002; Rieh & Belkin, 2000; Thurén, 2003) that are emphasized in curriculum. Valuing information has been argued to be something students are unable to master and that should therefore not be considered an object of teaching. Knowing how to assign credibility to information provides another kind of resource for structuring.

STRUCTURE AS A SOCIAL COLLECTIVE ACCOMPLISHMENT

Widening this scope outside the area of searching for information, a number of issues emerge that can be viewed as research accounts about structuring as a social accomplishment. Limberg and Sundin (2006, A wider repertoire ... para 2) claim that: "evaluation of information sources through negotiating relevance in different contexts, assessing the credibility and authority of sources and coping with information overload might be observed as aspects of the object of learning in the teaching of information seeking."

Structure is considered to be imposed through negotiation of contextual relevance and it is emphasized that context is a resource that students need to draw on in order to evaluate the results of their searches. The assumption that information literacy is primarily individual is however questioned in perspectives with a social and collaborative view on learning. Bruce (2000), Kapitzke (2003a, 2003b), and Marcum (2002) argue a socially distributed, dialogically driven view on information literacy. In such a perspective all forms of information management, including apprehending and imposing structure, are situated in particular contexts and take place in shared social practices. Such an extension of information literacy allows us to approach structure as an affordance of information as well as of social practices. Studies have for example emphasized the lack of consistency between the intended knowledge content and what is made explicit in the assignments, causing a failure for students to establish such a connection (Limberg & Sundin, 2006). Such a failure is considered to have a negative impact on student motivation. Kulthau, Aringer and Auby (2006) argue that more structured assignments increase the students' motivation. A perspective that emphasizes social distribution and dialogicity would not reduce this issue to the information literacy of a teacher and his or her attempts to pre-structure information or the information literacy of a student and that students' ability to apprehend that structure. Focus would instead be placed on work on assignments that include collaborative management of information in a particular social context.

STRUCTURING AS A SOCIO-TECHNICAL PRACTISE

Tuominen, Savolainen and Talja (2005) argue that studies on information literacy also need to include technology. Understanding something as socio-technical implies seeing the social and technical as elements constantly interacting, contributing to the shaping of each other. This relationship between social practices and technology has been widely discussed through the centuries including such aspects as alienation (Marx, 1864, 1974), technology and power (Marx, 1864, 1974; Ure 1861, 1967), division of labour (Babbage, 1835; Taylor, 1947), industrial organization (Woodward, 1965), technology and design (Ehn & Sandberg, 1979; Checkland, 1981) and today in discussions on science and technological systems (Bijker, 1995; Hughes, Pinch, & Bijker, 1987; Schot and Rip, 1997), technology assessment (Smits, Leyten & Harthog, 1995) and for that matter technology and learning (Säljö, 2005).

Discussion of information literacy tends to emphasize the individual users' mastery of tech-

nology. Focus is placed on mastery of particular technical devices and applications such as computers, the language used to search databases, and the knowledge of particular information services to take a few examples. Tuominen, Savolainen and Talja (2005, p. 341) argue that information literacy "is embedded in particular groups and communities" and that these groups and communities practice literacy through the use of appropriate technologies. Knowledge of these technologies and their use is socially distributed, shared and maintained within these communities. As a consequence a socio-technical approach to information literacy must focus research efforts on "the social, ideological and physical context and environment in which information and technical artifacts are used" (ibid., p. 340).

A RHETORICAL APPROACH TO THE STRUCTURING OF INFORMATION

We argue that structuring should be seen as a rhetorical accomplishment. Duffy (2003, p. 42) defines rhetoric as "the ways that institutions and individuals use symbols to structure their thought and shape their conception of the world." This perspective makes it possible to unite more recent takes on rhetoric also including the importance of ideology in forming a new literacy. A rhetorical approach invites us to treat structuring of information as a socio-technical dilemma. Billig (1988, 1996) claims that when encountering dilemmas actors often draw on opposing themes as part of their sense making. Thus, presenting the issue of unstructured information as a dilemma serves to accentuate that what appears as structured or unstructured needs to be made sense of in social practices involving technology.

A rhetorical approach directs us to the way students make sense of information together, working with technology. Burbules (2001) claim that the standard criteria for judging credibility of information are frustrated by the special characteristics of the web may be taken as recognition that not only individual abilities count when students structure information. Socio-technical aspects such as the scope of available information, the self-referencing character, and the rate of change also get included. The Web does not only appear in the guise of an archive, but as a technology mediating communication in social networks where people interact with information and ideas.

Consequently the type of analysis we attempt is one that takes an interest in how students interact in a particular context with other students, teachers, and technology in order to manage information on subject matter. The collection as well as analysis of data has been inspired by interaction analysis (Jordan & Henderson, 1995) taking as a point of departure studies of interaction at work (e.g., Goodwin, 1994; Heath & Luff, 2000; Luff, Hindmarsh, & Heath, 2000). Learning has been approached as a situated activity (e.g., Brown, Collins, & Duguid, 1989; Greeno, 1997; Lave, 1988) through students' ability to take part

in what Goodwin (1994, p. 606) refers to as "a socially situated, historically constituted body of practices through which the objects of knowledge which animate the discourse" are constructed and shaped. The context is seen as a particular socio-technical environment and the analyses focus on how students turn information in the form of theories, instructions, software design, rules for valuing information, and putting together written products into objects of knowledge that constitute a domain for learning.

DATA COLLECTION

Cole and Engeström (1993, p. 43) assert that the availability of different media for recording and managing data has allowed us to interact with "phenomena of the mind in more sophisticated ways." In the type of rich audio and video material collected here there is a wide range of aspects that can be analysed and it is important to find and keep a focus (Duranti & Goodwin, 1992). This has been an increasingly pressing demand

Image 1. The video setting (©2007, Anders Eklöf. Used with permission)

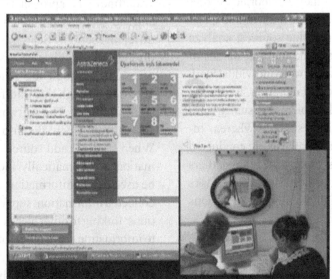

given that data appear in many guises in our empirical material. Performing their work students interact with each other (ee Image 1). They also interact with as well as use a variety of artefacts to accomplish interaction and they are often on the move. Thus, data streams that represent talk, movement, and screen activity to mention a few have constantly been generated.

Data collection has been conducted in typical Swedish gymnasiums. The word typically indicates that students have access to broad band connections, the open Internet, and a very limited set of information sources particularly designed for education, office type applications for managing and compiling information and communication through e-mail. Special applications that support scholarly work such as tools for data collection, transcription, quantitative or qualitative analysis or collaboration about data, are not part of the environment.

The students reported in the first two cases had entered the last grade, whereas the students in the last case were in the second grade. Observations were made during scheduled periods when the students were active in different stages of larger projects on cross disciplinary themes going about their everyday activities. In the cases reported here students work in groups of 4-6 with a range of issues. Among others they collaborate in order to: formulate a purpose; break it down into questions; find information; value sources; analyze and synthesize information; and find modes of presentation. They move between individual work and different modes of collaboration. Formulating purpose and initial problems is usually work performed in whole group sessions whereas information gathering and synthesis are conducted by one or two students. Finally the team gathers and puts their work together. Most of the tasks they undertake both individually and in various forms of groups.

THE SOFTWARE

An application called the Researcher has been introduced for the students by the researchers. The Researcher is a plug-in that was originally a part of Microsoft Encarta. It installs itself as an add-on to the browser visible through a special button in the toolbar that can be used to activate the application. When activated an additional frame appears in the left corner of the browser window. The Researcher is designed to support collection and structuring of information during the collection phase, making it possible to add information found on different Web sites either by menu options or by drag-and-drop. It is presented by the vendor as an application that helps students collect and organize text and pictures as resources from Encarta and the Web, so they can construct exceptional reports and projects in less time. Encarta automatically creates relevant footnotes and bibliographies, and then includes them in the finished reports (Microsoft Web page).

The suggestion from the vendor is that organizing is what it takes to construct exceptional reports and in the process also save time. The Researcher has some features aimed at supporting structure. Students set up a project. Information can be added to this project at different levels. They can create an outline of their project through adding sections and sub-sections and add information as notes to different sections. Searches may be run directly through the application interface. Any source accessible through the school network can be accessed through this interface and added to the student project. The software keeps track of the source from where the information is collected. When students add sources bibliographic information is automatically included. Editing can be used to add information about or comment on collected information, supporting: general reflections; linking to other electronic sources; aligning to information about other sources than electronic; making inclusion of quotes from books or aligning with other types of data. The Researcher can be

Image 2. The program view (©2007, Anders Eklöf. Used with permission)

used to build a report containing all information collected, including the students' own notes, comments, and questions. At the end of the report a reference list of all the sources used during the collection phase is generated. This can be a "raw report" the students intend to continue to work on or a finished report exported to several different formats, like HTML or Word.

RESULTS

Apprehending a structure behind questions guiding student work surfaces as a problem in the first case reported here. M and K, two third grade gymnasium (upper secondary school) students conduct several searches but have problems locating information that they find helpful. M comments on his difficulties silently almost as if talking to himself asking "vad menar vi egentligen med innebar?" The problem is further complicated by the fact that the students conduct searches both in Swedish and English. Their question does not easily lend itself to translation into English. The Wordfinder dictionary suggests that "innebar" means the implication of, the consequences of, the meaning of or the signification of, here translated "what do we actually mean by significance?".

Revolution 1:
(©2007, Anders Eklöf. Used with permission)

53. K: But check it out eh uhm

Biting his lip

Thoughtful gesture

53. M: Presstext Yeah It remains there to [unhearable] (7,1)
54. M: What do we actually mean by significance?

56. K: Oh, well they are a bit vague these questions

53. K: But check it out eh uhm
54. M: Presstext Yeah it remains there to [un-hearable] (7.1)
55. What do we actually mean by signifi-cance?
56. K: Oh, well they are a bit vague these ques-tions.
57. M: Bra Böckers encyclopaedia
58. K: They only account for. The most impor-tant is this one actually.
59. M: Yes.
60. K: What impact has it made on the Swedish society that is what kind of
61. memories have been found what kind of memories have been found that is
62. what kind of things that stem from.
63. M: This is Bra Böckers encyclopaedia too shit.
64. K: But just take that one then
65. M: But the question is whether this is not just
66. K: But that's where it originated from then we have these
67. there are booklets and that kind of to
68. M: What was that? Was it Bra Böckers lexicon?
69. K: No take Presstext check Sweden.
70. M: Should I search for Sweden?
71. K: Sweden
72. M: I still don't think we will get something different. Then I think
73. we will only get the same thing.

The students attend a school where students should be active, projects cross disciplinary, where focus on what students perceive as authentic problems is argued to make questions their own. As owners the students ought to be aware of the underlying structure of a question and able to use it to guide searches for information. Instead M finds this hard. When he tries to search using the full phrase there are no hits. When he tries to search using "significance" and "the industrial revolution" he gets plenty of information but he remains unsure about its relevance.

K coordinates with M stating that the questions are "a bit vague" but supposed to guide towards what is important in their assignment. He tries to structure the question, making an interpretation of "the significance of the industrial revolution." He indicates that significance may have something to do: with the impact on society; with what remains as a memory from that time; or with artefacts reminding us, making relevant that you need to know what you want to find in order to search. Their activity seems to corroborate the assertion that students' prior knowledge about content influences their success at formulating searches (Bruce, 1997), but at the same time it raises some doubts as to whether pre-structuring of questions to match content provides a solution.

The continued activity reveals something about the complexities of finding a matching structure and the skill with which the students collaboratively approach finding what can be considered a useful structure in their enterprise. They approach the significance of the industrial revolution through what Billig (1988) refers to as particularisation, trying to find out what applies to their special case. Their dilemma can be illustrated through their attempts at particularizing "significance." From the start the students have been trying to locate information about the industrial revolution including Sweden in their search phrase. This has not been a successful strategy. When, however, they leave out Sweden in their search expressions, they get little that is particularly about Sweden and much about England/Great Britain. What counts as relevant information surfaces as a dilemma when K comments on an entry and recommends M to add it to the Researcher project. M objects pointing to the word England, indicating that the content of the entry does not match what they are looking for. They should be looking for information about the impact "on the Swedish society." K retorts that "that's where it originated from." M particularises content whereas K seems to be looking for com-monality. Their approach illustrates that searching involves more than knowledge of the subject and the tools for conducting searches; factors usually suggested in research on information literacy (Limberg & Sundin, 2006). It indicates that you need to know what a good search expression is in this school context, given this mode of working and with this type of thematic orientation.

The issue of what counts as an answer to what the significance of the industrial revolution in Sweden was in the context of their school project remains a topic through the whole session and also influences how they construct their searches. Further down M talks about it as "that Great Britain kind of significance" particularising search results as possibly typical only for Great Britain. Later he suggests that for most parts the only difference may be "that Sweden was a little bit later than England" and K argues that this may explain the dominance of information about the industrial revolution in England. That examples appear in texts about Great Britain should not rule out that they can also be used in a description of Sweden. The suggestion to save a text about Great Britain indicates that K sees this as a lesser problem and that the significance of the industrial revolution may be more of industrial revolution significance than England significance. K argues that texts about Great Britain may work well when you sketch something "backgroundish" about industrialisation. M aligns with him in stating that it may be typical "on the whole." Through a consorted effort they arrive at a structure where general information about the Industrial revolution is considered to be if not sufficient so at least helpful in the construction of a case about the industrial revolution in Sweden.

Apprehending rules for using information tools in a school context surfaces as a second dilemma as two third graders, J male and F female, work on an assignment to investigate which Web sites that are most commonly used by youths. The objective of their study has been handed to them by a company that does market research.

Webcontent 1:
(©2007, Anders Eklöf. Used with permission)

J: Well, I don't know what it is.
[J glances quickly towards the camera]
F: So shall we?

J: We were just looking at what it's about.
C: OK
K: Yes but what is it.
J: Well it's a site [Laughs

84. J: Yes Handelsbanken we know, Blocket we know Dagens industri, and do we dare enter that one?
85. F: *[Laughs]*
86. J: Well, I don't know what it is.
87. *[J glances quickly towards the camera]*
88. F: So shall we?
89. J: *[writes www.virgins.se]*
90. J: HE HE HE
91. C: What is it?
92. F: Laughing loudly.
93. J: We were just looking at what it's about.
94. C: OK
95. K: Yes but what is it.
96. J: Well it's a site *[Laughs]*
97. *[J: Looks towards the screen]*
98. F: Free porn it says
99. C: What?
100. F: Find sex on the web
101. *[F:Turns towards the girls at the table]*

Working down a list they have compiled they follow a routine not opening sites they collectively claim they know. Encountering a site they are unsure about J asks whether they need to "check what it is." The students have their attention directed towards the site that comes after "Dagens Industri" (newspaper) on their list. F hesitates. J asks "do we dare enter that one?" J points with his finger to the address www.virgins.se. The students express hesitation about what it is (laughs indicating that both may have a pretty good idea) before they enter the site. At first their hesitation seems to have to do with that they guess what will come. A graphic display of nude men and women appears on the screen, some showing streaming videos of varied forms of intercourse. As they enter the site their continued laughs draw two female group members into their activities. The two girls show disapproval when they see what is displayed on the screen and questions their right to visit that particular site. A discussion about pornography takes place among the students and K asks whether that really was "one of the most popular sites." When this is confirmed she says "that's scary." This also seems to settle the issue about whether J and F had a right to visit that particular link.

J and F decide rather quickly to leave the site. F writes the address of the next site on the list. It is www.kth.se, the address of the Royal Institute of Technology in Stockholm. When they press "enter" the browser automatically goes to a site were it is possible to download porn movies. It appears that there was a jumper tagged to the virgin site. J claims that now they have "been hit by a virus or something" and when F says "oh shit" he goes on to say that "now we are being redirected." They are out of control trying to shut down browser windows more rapidly than they open. Their attempts to gain control and impose their own structure on what is displayed indicate that this is not okay.

Their activities show that they need to manage different sets of rules. Hesitation about whether they are permitted to enter the site or not illustrates the institutional nature of structuring. Visiting pornographic sites is not allowed in school. Their visit at www.virgins.se can be contrasted to their visit at www.playahead.se. J is in control of the mouse and keyboard and suggests that they should check out Play Ahead. He orients to the keyboard and as he writes he simultaneously reads out "we we we play" coordinating F with his actions. Visiting a youth site like PlayAhead is not considered

okay in many schools and sites like the particularly popular Lunarstorm are often filtered out. However, J enters PlayAhead playfully humming. Looking at the display of a young boy in front of a wall with graffiti he invites F to confirm that they have found the correct site. They engage in a discussion about cute boys and how the site is financed, and they collect data they find relevant. The playful tone and casual talk about features at the site indicate that visiting a youth community with pictures of cute boys does not constitute a problem. In research the worry about what kind of content students will encounter appears as a regular concern (Davis, 2003; Fox 2005). The issue is discussed more from a moral perspective than from the perspective of learning. In the related sequence these perspectives collide as the students face the dilemma of deciding whether they should be guided by rules guiding the use of technology or rules guiding their assignment. They settle this question pursuing the objective of their assignment to find the most frequented youth sites. Their reaction to being redirected can be taken to indicate that visiting pornographic sites is not allowed in school unless it is a result of the focused activity, whereas any other such visit is considered to be a breach of proper conduct.

How to value sources appears as a dilemma to a group of second grade students who have conducted literature searches on the net and are collectively working up a report. Their interaction and inter-thinking reveal negotiation of a structure built on the value of information. One of the girls (F1) sits in front of the computer in control of mouse and keyboard appearing to be most active. We enter early in their session. They finished listing the different kind of sources they have used in their project.

Anorexia 1:

520. (F1): Ok now you are talking about the wrong things. Listen to me, to what I have written. We thought that it was good with

articles and interviews to get an insight into real events. Does that sound strange?

521. (F1): Cut it out now! We found articles and interviews good enough to give an insight into real events?

522. (F2): Now we have to shape up! We have 4 hours. Printed sources

523. (F1): Books, yes, printed sources. Oh, printed sources are good for getting pure facts

524. (F2): Yea to get absolutely secure facts

525. (M1: Sources

526. (F1): To receive absolutely pure facts, can you say it so, do you get it that

we get only pure facts.

_____

546. (F1): What did you say about the electronic sources? Why is it so good with electronic sources? Why is it so good with the Internet? Because there is such a large supply?

547. (F2): Yes

548. (M1): Supply

549. (F1): The sources are good, because on Internet you get a big

550. (F2): Big choice of selection

551. (F1): Selection

552. (F2): You also have to be observant on what is

553. (F1): You must not forget, or what did you say?

554. (F2): You also have to be observant on

555. (M1): Pay attention to sounds better

556. (F1): Yeah but that comes later

557. (F2): Yes that's true, good that's good

558. (F1): But you must not forget to be observant when you

559. (M1): Seek

560. (F1): Surf

561. (M1): Surf

_____

623. (F1): Ok you must not forget to be observant so you don't use a false source

624. (F2): Yes or on all false sources that

625. (M1): Unreliable sources

626. (M2): Mm

627. (F1): But do you get it, you must not forget to be observant so you don't use

628. (M2): Stay away from the unreliable sources

629. (F1): So you don't take

630. (F2): Information from an unreliable source

In this storyline we can hear how the students try to categorise and thereby structure sources by working through different criteria for how to make judgements about what sources can be used for. Articles and interviews are connected to "real events" whereas books are considered to contain "pure facts." Articles and interviews are found good enough to support descriptions of real events. They are not described as accurate. They are just good enough. Books and printed sources are considered to provide another kind of information. The value judgement connecting books to pure facts reflects an understanding of books as a homogenous medium that can be relied on not only to provide pure but, as F1 rephrases it, to "get absolutely secure facts." The students appear to be in agreement. Their interest in facts reflects research reporting that students' search behaviour reveals a strong fact orientation (Alexandersson & Limberg, 2004; Limberg, 2001) and an additive approach to information seeking (Todd, 2006), but their acceptance of other sources of information indicates that their judgement is made relative to what information should be used for.

Later the students turn their attention to electronic sources. They agree that there are benefits from using electronic sources because they offer a big variety of information to choose from. "A big variety" seems to indicate that one must approach this information with special caution, not only because there is so much but because there is such a variety. Electronic sources are particularized by F2 claiming that you need to "be observant" and by M1 claiming that you need to "pay attention." Observant is something you need to be when you surf for information but pay attention "comes later" according to F1. What does that imply? Should they be observant about what places they surf to and later pay attention to the content?

The notion of "false sources" brought up by F1 and F2 echoes the first concern. False sources can be thought of as sources that appear to be something they are not, say a site appearing to be a research institute when in reality it hosts a lobby group. M1 utters what may be an attempt to correct or perhaps an attempt to challenge their understanding claiming that it is not a question of false sources but about "unreliable sources" suggesting that it is what they contain that should be approached with caution. The girls go along with his suggestion reformulating it as a warning not to "take information from an unreliable source. Their exchange illustrates a problem concerning valuing information, namely whether valuing should build on an assessment of the cognitive authority of the source or the credibility of the information (Eklöf & Nilsson, 2004; Rieh, 2005).

The excerpt illustrates the importance of contextualization. Policies on ICT in education often stress the importance of source criticism (Eklöf & Nilsson, 2004). There are explicit instructions to their assignment stating that their report should include a passage on source criticisms and evaluation. The passage highlights how they turn these instructions into an object of knowledge drawing on codified schemes for how to value information. This is a kind of talk that is necessary to engage in if they are to structure their report according to the requirements of the template for their assignment. Later on a discussion emerges among them concerning what a reliable source is.

GOVERNANCE IN KNOWLEDGE (INFORMATION) SOCIETY

In the introduction we presented the metaphor unstructured information to highlight a particular view on Internet based information often appearing in policy texts. What is produced in these texts can be glossed as governance in the name of a knowledge (information) society. In that society knowledge plays an increasingly important role in all aspects of social endeavours. A central problem in a knowledge society is how to deal with information and turn information into individual or organisational knowledge (Brown & Duguid, 2000), particularly making use of information that has not been pre-packaged for the purpose it is later used for.

A corollary to this problem is how to reproduce a society with individuals that make use of different forms of information and turn it into knowledge. Seen this way unstructured information presents a dilemma of governance. Education may be seen as a technology to deal with the problem turning students into objects of governance in the name of the knowledge society. To become citizens students need to learn how to deal with information, thus mastery of information tools becomes a basic of education.

Discourses on the societal transfer from an industrial to a knowledge society are as we see it replicated in the political discourse on education. These produce particular subjects such as for example the competent user, the global learner or the digital learner. The first educational policies mentioning computer technology turned students into objects of a discourse aimed at educating for citizenship. The future citizens should be subjects with knowledge of and an interest in computer technology. More importantly perhaps, this future citizen should have learnt social civic engagement in order to be able to take an interest in and dare influence the development of technology (National Board, 1986, p. 10-11). Thus there was a strong emphasis on citizenship education.

In the 1990's the same citizen needs to have learnt how to deal with unstructured information. The socio-genesis of learning is presented as one where students move from access to and dealing with information structured in and restricted to school-books to open access and dealing with unstructured information on the net. Willingness to approach and deal with such information is presented as vital to society, to industry, as well as to the individual and can be said to provide for part of an ideal for the future citizen. Consequently the normative political stance in many countries has been to produce students that become subjects that are information literate or digitally competent. The suggested technologies aimed at producing such a student require them to work in forms where they learn how to manage unstructured information.

LEARNING AND UNSTRUCTURED INFORMATION

A particular identity is built for students in a knowledge society. Not only do these students work with unstructured information, they also take a personal responsibility for learning, formulate their own problems, take a cross-disciplinary approach, value their sources, build their own knowledge networks, navigate epistemic communities, join communities of practice, and above all use networked technology. To reproduce such an identity education must give students access to information tools and provide opportunities for them to learn how to deal with unstructured information.

We find that students in our study work in forms that resemble those used to describe the modern learner in a knowledge society. Concerns have however been raised about what this might mean in terms of learning. In a socio-cultural perspective learning is a result of human activity. What we learn, however, is not necessarily for good (Säljö, 1999, 2006). When it comes to

technology Kenway (2001, p. 165) argues that "little attention is being paid to the manner in which we produce and consume such technologies and to associated issues of politics and justice." We would argue that there are a number of studies that raise questions about how technology is consumed in education and what this means for: learning (Alexandersson & Limberg, 2005); exposure to inappropriate information (Fox, 2005); and ability to value sources (Bruce, 2000; Rieh, 2002) to mention a few. The worries echoed in these studies concern possibly negative effects on learning and what is learned as effect of students' exposure to unstructured information.

In a socio-cultural as well as a constructivist perspective dealing with structure is inseparable from learning. The issue is not whether information is unstructured or structured but instead the conditions and results of structuring for student learning. A number of studies indicate that students find structuring information difficult and it is argued that they fail to master the required skills and that the potential for disciplinary learning become negligent (Alexandersson & Limberg, 2004, 2006). To the contrary our data illustrate the complexity of finding structure in the type of information our students have been working with, but also the skill with which they go about solving some of the problems.

In contrast to the view that the Internet introduces unstructured information our data suggest that all sources can count as unstructured. They are perceived of as unstructured by our students for a number of reasons that require them to impose their own structure on available information. This can be seen in M's and K's explorative talk on how to find a fit between the type of assignment they work on, the questions they need to answer and the sources of information they can access. It can bee seen in J's and F's hesitation about what has priority, the task set for them, or the rules set for their use of computers at school. It can also be seen in the way the group of students navigates their particular epistemic culture with its requirements on using a wide variety of sources, valuing sources, and following rules about citation, to take some examples. We would argue that these were issues to students long before the particular political and educational discourse on unstructured information present today.

STRUCTURING AND THE LITERACY DISCOURSE

Returning to Säljö (1999), there is still the pressing issue about whether students' learning is for good or bad. In information literacy studies, where according to Tuominen, Savolainen, and Talja (2005) focus is on the literacy skills of the individual students, studies reporting on student mastery of such skills often provide insights into what seems to be problematic to the individual. Our study suggests that these skills are always tested in particular contexts and rarely by individuals in isolation.

But students work together, in particular schools, governed by particular rules, representing ideologies, religious beliefs, beliefs about learning and what counts as knowledge. The inherently social nature of information structure is present in our students' orientation to each other both in speech and movement. More so, however, the inherently social nature is present in the way they discuss how to value information, interpret assignments and how to set up search expressions. Their talk is seldom just aimed at collecting and producing lists. Instead they discuss solutions and argue their points engaging in what Dawes, Fisher and Mercer (1992) have called explorative and disputational talk. What is done is done in a shared social space with an infinite number of rules for re-structuring information. These may be said to be part of disciplinary discourse as in the case when M and K discuss if facts about the industrial revolution in England/Great-Britain can be used to illustrate the significance of the industrial revolution in Sweden. They can be said

to be part of a local institutional discourse requiring them to turn local school rules for using the Internet and rules for working on assignments into objects of knowledge that guide structuring.

TECHNOLOGY AND INFORMATION STRUCTURE AS A DILEMMA

How do students deal with technology? A number of studies assert that it is technology and the way technology makes information accessible to students that cause problems. Technology is treated as a natural source with fixed effects on student learning. Because of the way technology works students cannot find the information they need, and select among the various sources they find. In our study students do not talk of technology as a problem in itself, rather their talk reflects a view that construction of school assignments does not take technology into account. Students need to put a lot of work into making sense of their assignments to be able to use tools they are expected to use. They orient to: the need to match questions to search expressions; evaluate information; make judgments about relevance; what is required by the assignment, afforded by technology and forbidden in local rules; and make sense of what it means to be critical students when appreciating sources. Their comments concern the difference in accessibility, reliability and appropriateness between information they locate through their own efforts and information that has been provided for them.

There are several references in the transcripts to texts that are hard to read, hard to extract good information from and alike. In the included transcripts, M and K agree that a text they find is hard. M still seems intent on using both the software and on searching the Internet whereas K indicates that "there are booklets." Only J and K can be said to be forced to use the Internet because of the assignment. So why insist on using sources that are hard to find, navigate, restructure, and value? Knowing how can be considered to be an important aspect of being successful. The suggestion here is that M sees the Internet as a primary source of information whereas K sees the booklet that way. These are concerns impeding on structure present in all transcripts.

Technical discourse becomes part of defining what is unstructured and what is structured. The Researcher was introduced by the research team to support structuring and editing of information. J and F used it to add their sites as a list but did not use it to edit their collected material and not to print out a report. M and K, however, provide an interesting insight into how unstructured information is treated as a socio-technical dilemma. For most parts technology integrates almost seamlessly into the students work. On several occasions, however, students highlight what they see as affordances and account for how these influence the way they work. At the end of the first session M and K get into a discussion about the impact editing with the Researcher may have on their end-product. K expresses the concern that there might be a "risk with a thing like this" and M fills in that "you copy." K is however not talking about copying. He is concerned that if you order texts in a system that automatically adds a reference and then go in and edit them you might accidentally cause a misrepresentation. Your statements appear as part of statements from an author you make a reference to. M objects claiming that the text they generate should not be the final text, but should contain referenced material and their comments too, and reflections about how to work on them. His line of reasoning reveals that he is unsure about what a text structured like that should be called, stating that it is "more like a summary no not a summary like a reference to."

K accepts this way of categorizing the genre. The students' efforts to make sense can serve as a commentary of the heated debate in research (e.g., Austin & Brown, 1999; Mallon, 1989, 2001; Swearingen, 1999) about the effect of the Internet on writing. It may be premature to write students'

unclear presentation of authorship off as attempts to plagiarize or misrepresent on their part. How to paraphrase, make summaries, and keep track of insertions appear as dilemmas our students need to deal with and technology sometimes as opaque. Our assertion is further strengthened as the students comment on the 15 page long generated text. K laughs and says "You can turn it all in later. Doesn't look at all suspicious" and M joins him in his laughter. The students structure their expectations about the text making relevant particular rules for text production in their context and the possible impact from technology.

INFORMATION STRUCTURE AS AN ETHICAL DILEMMA

Student talk points to a particular aspect of what unstructured information might mean. This can be seen in M's and K's attempt to find suitable information. It can be seen in J's and F's visit to a porn site. It can bee seen in the other students' attempts to value information. Student talk indicates a sense of agency. Information they find is never ready to consume. Contrary to what is reported in many studies on student plagiarism (Austin & Brown, 1999; Mallon, 1989, 2001; Swearingen, 1999) writing is not just a cut-and-paste job. How information can be used is something they orient to in talk, including issues about how to value information and what can pass as appropriate information. They also show an awareness of rules for proper use of sources. These rules may be hard to interpret, but the students turn these issues into objects of knowledge, trying to come to terms with what they might mean to their particular projects.

There are other considerations that may appear to be pressing from an ethical perspective. In this text we have included students' deliberate entry into a porn site. The schools we collected data at do not use filters to block out particular Web services. None of them use any other means to pre-structure Internet information. Students are considered to be responsible users and to make sense of whatever rules for computer use that the local school has set up. Consequently students visit sites that present information concerning politics and religious beliefs. Covering different aspects of their course plan most students are likely to visit sites that contain information their parents might react to (though we might add, the reported section shows the only incident we saw where students visited a porn site). Visits to sites that contain what is often called inappropriate material are not only accidental. At many occasions they are the result of exploratory and disputational talk between the students about how to reconcile their needs for information with local rules. Rather than constituting these rules as moral absolutes they constitute them as guidelines applying what Norris and Dodder (1979) call situational ethics.

Other ethical implications arise outside the concern about how students turn local rules into knowledge objects. On the one hand Swedish national curriculum aims at reproducing subjects of a knowledge society. On the other hand it requires school to respect that parents have the ultimate responsibility for fostering their children. Can students become ethical subjects of a knowledge society and learn to respect fundamental values if they so not enter into situations where ethical judgements need to be made? And if they are left free to take on the responsibility for using information can we guarantee that they will exercise discretion that matches curricular standards for ethical conduct?

In this perspective free access to information subject only to local rules may be considered to introduce an ethical dilemma. This dilemma we feel is well illustrated and may be discussed in relation to the skill displayed by students as they value information. Burbules (2002) argues for a distributed view and claims that issues like credibility, relevance, interest, and worth cannot be assessed outside the places where production and legitimization takes place. This is precisely

what we see in our third case. The students face a dilemma requiring them to turn these aspects into objects of knowledge. It is obvious that they do not really evaluate the content of their sources, or at least they consider everything that they have used as reliable. Their primary argument draws on feelings. They ask whether they can write, in the section about source criticism, "that all the articles and interviews are not reliable but we felt that we could take those from Sydsvenskan" (newspaper) and that "we felt that it was interviews that seemed to be reliable, it's another thing if we use articles that feel unreliable." They also make relevant that they have to write the passage and that it should contain some worries concerning the articles and electronic sources. There are no real discussions on any of the concepts concerning how to evaluate different sources. Internet is unreliable and printed sources are reliable. Morning papers are reliable and tabloids to be doubted. Interviews are really beyond control since they are merely a window into reality and not containing facts. Such discourse illustrates the technical nature of their dilemma. Free access to information does seem to present an ethical problem. Critical thinking, ability to value information and a number of related skills are supposed to render students immune to inappropriate information.

UNSTRUCTURED INFORMATION AS A SOCIO-TECHNICAL DILEMMA

Information structure surfaces in student talk in a way that illustrates that student encounters with information have deep democratic and ethical implications. They encounter information pre-packaged by publishers and authorities, but also, as we have seen, by anti-democratic forces and porn distributors. They are thrown into a sea of information and expected to swim, with the help of their teachers, peers and knowledge about their context and its requirements. They can be said to work in ways that represent ideals about student identity such as: the global learner who works in epistemic communities (Tuominen, Savolainen, & Talja 2005) or communities of practice (Wenger, 1998); the networked learner who finds his or her own contacts on the Internet (Postman, 1996); the responsible learner who plans and scaffolds his or her own learning (Harrison, 2000; Masschelein & Simons, 2002); the critical learner who structures information according to trust, credibility, cognitive authority, bias, dialectical reading and other aspects (Bruce, 2000; Burbules, 2002; Leth & Thurén, 2000); students approaching information as critical citizens; or entrepreneurs who run their own projects finding their own solutions to problems.

It is when all these things come together—institutions with their rules and ways of framing activities, technology with its affordances, the structure of information—and students turn them into objects of knowledge that we discern socio-technical dilemmas. In discourse about societal development, the development of technology and the development of learning, these are often painted with the same palette. In policies change is seen as unavoidable, but more to the point change is good not only for society at large but also for education. Our stance, based on data used for this study, is that change is not always beneficiary and the learning it brings for students is not always good.

Be that as it may, in national as well as international policies students are governed by a rhetoric that presents them as self governing entrepreneurs. Our data show students that deal skilfully with their assignments. We fear however that the implementation of these policies might create a second kind of digital divide. The kind of skills necessary to handle the different kind of dilemmas that we have described in this paper is often considered to be footed in special class and habitus. Dovemark (2004) claims that the winners are the children who enter with certain prerequisites. They come out even stronger, leaving the others behind. Warschauer (2000) shows

that this is not only a matter of student habitus. Whole schools may have different approaches to how to implement technology. In his example the rural school teaches students to use technology only for production (writing, Web-publishing), whereas the upper middle class school teaches students to use technology to deal with disciplinary content. These apprehensions were one major theme in the OECD conference *The new millennium learner* in March 2007:

Since differences in use seem to be extremely correlated with socio-economic status and, at the same time, those differences can be expected to have an impact on such status, there is ground for political and educational concern: the lack of political action in this domain, using education as a change agent, can contribute to amplify not only the second digital divide but, what is even worse, the socio-economic differences which such a divide is already reflecting. (OECD, 2007)

If students need to be mindful of unstructured information, among other things in order to become citizens of a knowledge society, they may need to be where they meet unstructured information. One thing seems clear in our transcripts, if they go there they will be challenged, and forced to make decisions concerning learning as well as democracy and ethics.

CONCLUDING REMARKS

Information is always in some sense unstructured. Just as it has been structured in order to display on a Web page, fit into a database, or the ideological interests of a party, our data illustrate that it appears unstructured when someone approaches it for other purposes. Access to information through the implementation of digital information and communication technology challenges traditional school practices, and introduces dilemmas about democracy, school development, ethics, information management, and learning. Where does this put us if we compare to Bruce's (2000) suggestion that students need a better match between assignments and proposed result and to Breivik's (1998) suggestion that pre-packaged assignments are detrimental and do not prepare students for future work with information? There appear to be consequences for school-development tied to these assertions with democratic and ethical underpinnings. What Bruce and Breivik argue from what appear to be diametrically opposing positions is that failing to introduce information "the correct way" may cause students to learn with less quality. Our data instead indicate that structuring of information is a ubiquitous practice present whether students have access to pre-structured assignments and information or not and that it always presents them with socio-technical dilemmas. That we know so little about the impact of working with net-based information is unsatisfying. Especially in view of what seems to be the only certainty, that the proliferation of Internet based information will put increasing demands on teachers' and students' ability to structure information.

REFERENCES

Alexandersson, M., & Limberg, L. (2004). *Textflytt och sökslump: informationssökning via skolbibliotek*. Stockholm: Myndigheten för skolutveckling / Liber distribution.

Alexandersson, M., & Limberg, L. (2005, August 23-27) *In the shade of the knowledge society. The importance of information literacy.* Paper presented at the 11th biennal EARLI conference, University of Cyprus, Nicosia.

Alskans, J., & Jusufovic, F. (2005). Wandering around in the darkness: Students information seeking and relevance judgements during school assignment. Unpublished Masters Thesis. Bibliotek och informationsvetenskap / Bibliotekshögskolan.

Association of College and Research Libraries (2000) Information competency standards for higher education. Standards approved by the Board of Directors of the Association of College and Research Libraries (ACRL), January 18, 2000, at the Midwinter Meeting of the American Library Association, San Antonio, Texas. Retrieved on October 12, 2000, from http://www.ala.org/acrl/ilcomstan.html

Auer, N. J., & Krupar, E. M. (2001). Mouse click plagiarism: The role of technology in plagiarism and the librarian's role in combating it. *Library Trends, 49*, 415-433.

Austin, J. M., & Brown, L. D. (1999). Internet plagiarism: Developing strategies to curb student academic dishonesty. *The Internet and Higher Education, 2*(1), 21-33.

Babbage, C. (1835/1971). *On the economy of machinery and manufactures* (Repr. ed.). New York: Kelley.

Barab, S. A., Kling, R., & Gray, J. H. (2004). *Designing for virtual communities in the service of learning.* Cambridge: Cambridge University Press.

Berners-Lee, T. Information management: A proposal. Retrieved on March 5, 2004, from http://www.w3.org/History/1989/proposal.html

Berners-Lees, T., & Cailliaus, R. (1990). The World Wide Web. Retrieved on March 5, 2004, from http://www.w3.org/Proposal.html

Bijker, W. E. (1995). *Of bicycles, bakelites, and bulbs: Toward a theory of sociotechnical change.* Cambridge, MA.: MIT Press.

Billig, M. (1988). *Ideological dilemmas : a social psychology of everyday thinking.* London: Sage.

Billig, M. (1996). *Arguing and thinking : a rhetorical approach to social psychology* (New ed.). Cambridge: Cambridge University Press.

Boström, E. (2005). Källkritik, kognitiv auktoritet och domänanalys: Värdering av trovärdighet vid informationssökning. Unpublished Masters Thesis. Högskolan i Borås.

Bowker, G. C., & Star, S. L. (1999). Sorting things out: classification and its consequences. Cambridge, Mass.: MIT Press.

Breivik, P. S. (1999). Take II-information literacy: revolution in education. *Reference Services Review, 27*(3), 271-275.

Brown, J. S., Collins, A., & Duguid, P. (1989). Situated cognition and the culture of learning. *Educational Researcher, 18*(1), 32.

Brown, J. S., & Duguid, P. (2000). *The social life of information.* Boston, MA: Harvard Business School.

Bruce, B. C. (2000). 6. Credibility of the web: why we need dialectical reading. *Journal of Philosophy of Education, 34*(1).

Bruce, C. (1997). *The seven faces of information literacy.* Adelaide: Auslib Press.

Burbules, N. C. (2001). Paradoxes of the web: the ethical dimensions of credibility. *Library Trends, 49*(3), 441-453.

Burke, M. (2004). Deterring plagiarism: A new role for librarians [Electronic Version]. *Library, Philosophy and Practice, 6*, 1-11. Retrieved on January 31, 2006, from libr.unl.edu:2000/LPP/lp-pv6n2.htm

Checkland, P. (1981). *Systems thinking, systems practice.* Chichester: Wiley.

Cole, M., & Engeström, Y. (1993). A cultural-historical approach to distributed cognition in Salomon G (ed) *Distributed cognitions. Psychological and educational considerations*: Cambridge University Press, Cambridge, NY.

Council of Australian University Librarians. (2001). Information Literacy Standards. 1st ed.

Underdale, South Australia: Library Publications, University of South Australia, 2001. Retrieved on May 18, 2001, from http://www.caul.edu.au/cauldoc/InfoLitStandards2001.doc

Cowen, T. (2001, June 3). Your work, or the web's? *Christian Science Monitor,* p. 17.

Cuban, L. (2001). *Oversold and underused : computers in the classroom.* Cambridge, MA: Harvard University Press.

Dawes, L., Fisher, E., & Mercer, N. (1992). The quality of talk at the computer. *Language and Learning, 10,* 22-25.

Davis, P. M. (2003) Effect on the web on undergraduate citation behaviour: Guiding students scholarship in a networked age. [Electronic version] portal:Libraries and the academy, 3, 41-51.

Dovemark, M.. (2004). *Ansvar - flexibilitet - valfrihet : en etnografisk studie om en skola i förändring.* Göteborg: Acta Universitatis Gothoburgensis.

Duffy, J. (2003) Other gods and countries. The rhetorics of literacy. In Nystrand, M., & Duffy, J. *Towards a rhetoric of everyday life: new directions in research on writing, text, and discourse*: University of Wisconsin Press.

Duranti, A., & Goodwin, C. (1992). *Rethinking context: language as an interactive phenomenon*: Cambridge University Press.

Ehn, P., & Sandberg, Å. (1979). *Teknik och arbetsorganisation.* Stockholm: Arbetslivscentrum.

Eklöf, A., & (2004), N. L.-E. (2004). *Critical students: how and by whose definition.* Paper presented at the 32st congress of the Nordic Educational Research Association (NERA).

Fox, L. H. (2005). The use of web resources by elementary school library media specialists. School of Information and Library Science.

Goodwin, C. (1994). Professional vision. *American Anthropologist, 96*(3), 606-633.

Government Communication. (1997/98:176). *Tools for learning : a national programme for ICT in schools*. Stockholm: Ministry of Education and Science (Utbildningsdepartementet).

Greeno, J. G. (1997). On claims that answer the wrong questions. *Educational Researcher, 26*(1), 5.

Harrison, R. (2000). Learner managed learning: managing to learn or learning to manage? *International Journal of Lifelong Education, 19*(4), 312-321.

Heath, C., & Luff, P. (2000). *Technology in action*. Cambridge: Cambridge University Press.

Hughes, T. P., Pinch, T. J., & Bijker, W. E. (1987). *The social construction of technological systems : new directions in the sociology and history of technology*. Cambridge, Mass.: MIT Press.

Ivarsson, J. (2003). Kids in zen: computer supported learning environments and illusory intersubjectivity *Education, Communication and Information, 3*(3), 383-402.

Jordan, B., & Henderson, A. (1995). Interaction analysis: foundations and practice. *The Journal of the Learning Sciences, 4*(1), 39-103.

Joint, N. (2005). Traditional bibliographic instruction and today's information users. *Library review, 54*(7), 397-402.

Jonassen, D. H. (2000). *Computers as mindtools for schools: engaging critical thinking*: Merrill.

Kapitzke, C. (2003a). Information literacy: A positivist epistemology and a politics of outformation. *Educational Theory, 53*(1), 37-53.

Kapitzke, C. (2003b). Information literacy: A review and poststructural critique. *Australian Journal of Language and Literacy, 26*, 53–66.

Karchmer, R. (2001). The journey ahead: thirteen teachers report how the Internet influences literacy and literacy instruction in their K–12 classrooms. *Reading Research Quarterly, 36*(4), 442-466.

Kenway, J. (2001). The information superhighway and postmodernity: The social promise and the social price. In C. Paechter, M. Preedy, D. Scott & J. Soler (Eds.), *Knowledge, power and learning. Learning matters: Challenges of the information age* (pp. 186) London: Paul Chapman.

Knorr-Cetina, K. K. (1999). *Epistemic cultures: how the sciences make knowledge*. Cambridge, MA: Harvard University Press.

Kress, G. R. (2003). *Literacy in the new media age*: Routledge.

Kuhlthau, C. C. (1993). *Seeking meaning : a process approach to library and information services*. Norwood, N.J: Ablex.

Kuhlthau, C. C., Aringer, A., & Auby, M. (2006). *Informationssökningsprocessen : en lärande process med lärare och bibliotekarie i samverkan med elevens informationskompetens i fokus*. Lund: Bibliotekstjänst.

Land, S. M., & Jonassen, D. H. (2000). *Theoretical foundations of learning environments*. Mahwah, NJ: L. Erlbaum Associates.

Lave, J. (1988). *Cognition in practice* Cambridge University Press, Cambridge.

Leth, G., & Thurén, T. (2000). *Källkritik för Internet*. Stockholm: Styrelsen för psykologiskt försvar.

Limberg, L. (2001). *Att söka information för att lära : en studie av samspel mellan informationssökning och lärande* (2 ed.). Borås: Valfrid.

Limberg, L., & Sundin, O. (2006). Teaching information seeking: relating information literacy education to theories of information behaviour paper 280 from [Electronic Version]. *Information Research, 12* Retrieved on December 12, 2006, from http://InformationR.net/ir/12-1/paper280.html

Luff, P., Hindmarsh, J., & Heath, C. (2000). *Workplace studies : recovering work practice and informing system design.* Cambridge: Cambridge University Press.

Mallon, T. (1989/2001). *Stolen words: The classic book on plagiarism*: Harvest/HBJ Book.

Marchionini, G. (1995). *Information seeking in electronic environments.* . Cambridge: Cambridge University Press.

Marcum, J. W. (2002). Rethinking information literacy. *Library Quarterly, 72*(1), 1-26.

Marx, K. (1974). *Kapitalet: kritik av den politiska ekonomin. Bok 1, Kapitalets produktionsprocess* (3rd. ed.). Lund: A-Z.

Masschelein, J., & Simons, M. (2002). An adequate education in a globalised world? A note on immunisation against being-together. *Journal of the Philosophy of Education, 36*(4), 589-608.

Mayo, E. (1945). *The social problems of an industrial civilization.* Boston: Harvard University

National Board of Education. (1986). *Utbildning inför datasamhället: information om fortbildning inom dataområdet för skolpersonal.* Stockholm: Skolöverstyrelsen.

Norris, T. D. and Dodder. R., A. (1979). A behavioral continuum synthesizing neutralization theory, Situational ethics and juvenile delinquency " *Adolescence XIV(55),* 545-555

OECD. (2007, march 5-6). Summary: Emerging issues from the first expert meeting. Paper presented at the *The new millenium learners,* Florence.

Postman, N. (1996). *The end of education: Redefining the value of school* ([New ed.). New York: Vintage.

Rieh, S. Y., & Belkin, N. J. (2000). Interaction on the Web: Scholars' judgment of information quality and cognitive authority. *Proceedings of the 63rd ASIS Annual Meeting, 37,* 25–36.

Rieh, S. Y. (2002). Judgment of information quality and cognitive authority in the Web. *Journal of the American Society for Information Science and Technology, 53*(2), 145-161.

Rieh, S. Y. (2005). Cognitive authority. In K. E. Fisher, S. Erdelez & L. McKechnie (Eds.), *Theories of information behavior* (pp. xxii, 431 s.). Medford, N.J.: Information Today.

Riis, U. (1999). *"-utvecklingen beror då inte på användningen av datorer." : IT-användningen i den svenska skolan våren 1998.* Stockholm: Skolverket : Liber distribution.

Robertson, J. (2002). The ambiguous embrace: twenty years of IT (ICT) in UK primary schools. *British Journal of Educational Technology, 33*(4), 403-409.

Schot, J., & Rip, A. (1997). The past and future of constructive technology assessment. *Technological Forecasting & Social Change, 54*(2&3), 251-268.

Society of College, National, and University Libraries (1999). Information Skills in Higher Education: A SCONUL Position Paper. Retrieved on October 12, 2005, from http://www.sconul. ac.uk/pubs/stats/pubs/99104Rev1.doc

Simon, H. A. (1973). The structure of ill structured problems. *Artificial Intelligence, 4,* 181-201.

Smits, R., Leyten, J., & Den Hertog, P. (1995). Technology assessment and technology policy in Europe: New concepts, new goals, new infrastructures. *Policy Sciences, 28*(3), 271-299.

Swearingen, J. C. (1999). Originality, authenticity, imitation, and plagiarism: Augustin's Chinese cousins. In L. Buranen & A. M. Roy (Eds.), *Perspectives on plagiarism and intellectual property in a postmodern world* (pp. xxii, 302 p.). Albany: State University of New York Press.

Säljö, R. (2005). *Lärande och kulturella redskap: om lärprocesser och det kollektiva minnet*: Norstedts akademiska förlag.

Taylor, F. W. (1947/1972). *Scientific management : comprising Shop management, The principles of scientific management, Testimony before the special House committee.* Westport, Conn,.

Thurén, T. (2003). *Sant eller falskt? metoder i källkritik.* Stockholm: Krisberedskapsmyndigheten.

Todd, R. J. (2006). From information to knowledge: Charting and measuring changes in students' knowledge of a curriculum topic. *Information Research, 11*(4) paper 264. Retrieved on January 21, 2007, from http://Information R.net/ir/11-4/paper264.html]

Tuominen, K., Savolainen, R., & Talja, S. (2005). Information literacy as a sociotechnical practice *Library Quarterly, 75*(3), 329-345.

Ure, A. (1835). *The Philosophy of manufactures: or, an exposition of the scientific, moral and commercial economy of the factory system of Great Britain.* London: Knight.

Warschauer, M. (2000). Technology and School Reform: A View from Both Sides of the Tracks. *Education Policy Analysis Archive, 8*(4).

Wenger, E. (1998). *Communities of practice : learning, meaning, and identity.* Cambridge: Cambridge University Press.

Woodward, J. (1965). *Industrial organisation : theory and practice.* London: Oxford University Press.

KEY TERMS

Affordance: The term refers to the fit between an animal's capabilities and the environmental supports and opportunities. An affordance is a potentiality for action; in other words, an action that can potentially be performed by a specific organism in a specific environment.

Categorization: The term has been frequently used in etnomethodology, conversation analysis and other methods for analysing discourse and refers to the practice of sorting into collections and naming these collections common to human discourse.

Dilemma: A social dilemma would imply a situation where a person decides between promoting his personal interest or according to collective interest. Some people use dilemma to describe a rhetorical construction where participants' accounts frequently draw on opposing themes as part of there sense making process, in their construction of claims and in justifying and corroborating these. Categorization and particularisation are such opposing themes.

Information Literacy: The concept is usually seen as the generic ability to make well informed choices based on the critical evaluation of a wide range of information sources. There is a substantial commonality in identifying it as an individual generic skill both in science and political texts. Some say the concept includes an ability to find, control and evaluate information sources in order to create personal knowledge and use these wisely. Others argue that literacy cannot be separated from the domain specific socio-technical practices that give rise to them that is, information skills evolve in disciplinary and other contexts, and they are practiced by communities using appropriate technologies.

Particularization: The term has been used to point to a need to reverse categorization. If categories can be built they can also be taken apart. Claims are constructed to support making sense of something as an exception to what is generally seen to be the case, such as for instance when an omission of a reference is described as an example of common knowledge rather then an example of plagiarism.

Project Management Software: Project management software generally include provision of tools that support collaborative work on projects. Elaborated software of this kind would include features that allow users to plan, schedule, prioritize, and divide tasks, as well as communicating and storing information. Slim versions may include only support for storing, collecting and editing information in order to generate a report as in the case of Microsoft Encarta Researcher.

Socio-Technical: Focus is on the influence of the technical on the social and vice versa yielding such perspectives as socio-technical mapping and actor network theory. The social and technical is seen as constantly interacting, shaping each other such as when social and technical elements are interwoven in discourse and used to support accounts.

Source Criticism: The term was developed in the late 19th and the early 20th century as a method to separate sources that gave well founded knowledge from those that did not. Through critical examinations, by means of a set of criteria's, you examine if the information is true or false, usable or useless in connection with the question you seek answer to. The set of criteria's has changed and evolved as a result of new media forms and the growth of digitally distributed information.

Chapter XXXII
An Ethical Perspective on ICT in the Context of the Other

J. Ola Lindberg
Mid Sweden University, Sweden

Anders D. Olofsson
Umeå University, Sweden

ABSTRACT

The importance of incorporating an ethical perspective in the development of digital competence is discussed. It is argued that an ethical perspective that emphasises mutual understanding as a possible conception of democracy is of importance in the light of the current global e-learning trend, especially when it comes to designing e-learning ventures as online learning communities.

INTRODUCTION

During the last decade, one of the most significant changes for the way we educate, teach and learn has been the Internet. Today, this is a development that is probably the most expansive in tertiary education. In the formation of a global education system, the building of virtual learning environments and the deployment of e-learning has become a substantial part of the educational practice. Having access to education is then also about having access to the technological skills

that otherwise leaves the practitioner behind. In the recommendations from the European Union (EU) about future goals for the educational system, the importance of having competence in using Information and Communication Technologies (ICT) is stressed. For future European citizens, having key competencies in this field is crucial, according to the EU (ET 2010 WP, p. 3), for at least three aspects of life:

for personal fulfilment and development throughout life (cultural capital): key competences must enable people to pursue individual objectives in life, driven by personal interests, aspirations and the desire to continue learning throughout life; b. active citizenship and inclusion (social capital): key competences should allow everybody to participate as an active citizen in society; c. employability (human capital): the capacity of each and every person to obtain a decent job in the labour market.

Formulated this way, these aspects of key competencies point towards several important areas where the use of ICT for education, learning and for promoting democracy seems vital. Nevertheless, they are all aspects that seem to be articulated without any deeper concern for what neither an ethical perspective on education nor the use of ICT within education might imply, nor what an ethical perspective might imply in terms of democracy.

Democracy and education have been closely aligned for a long time. Having a well-educated and skilled population was a driving force behind the Swedish compulsory school-system. It was an attempt at creating a stable society. This base for a democratic component in education has had several proponents over time. In the early 20th century, Dewey (1916) gave voice to a need for a democratic view of education. In the later parts of the century, education was put forth by Freire (1972) as an emancipatory issue. In these two views the link between education and democracy is obvious. But this aspect of education has not been un-challenged. In the educational system there have been several examples of a contradictory view (Bernstein, 2000), that education as such conforms and disciplines its subjects. Education then becomes an ideological formation of the human being, a transformation into a certain pre-determined ways of understanding the world. These are issues with an interesting touch of ambiguity; access to education could be a democratic issue as well as an ideological for-

mation into something already given, issues that easily lend themselves to further thought as they become contextualised in the knowledge society. Will for example the democratizing affordances of the Internet win out, or will the result be new forms of control?

What could it mean, then, to be a democratic person engaged in democratic processes? A part of the answer lies in conceptualising democracy. According to Held (1996, p. 297), democracy entails "a form of politics and life in which there are fair and just ways of negotiating values and value disputes." Democracy, as Held views it, tries to re-conceptualise and reconcile a concern with individual and collective self-determination in which 'autonomy' or 'independence' are central. Self-consciousness, self-reflection, and self-determination, with opportunities for deliberation, choice, judgement, and action, are all aspects of autonomy.

If one accepts autonomy as a principle related to democracy, a democratic person is someone who is preoccupied with making choices, with the freedom to determine and justify actions of their own. It would also include the skills and resources they need to take advantage of opportunities before them. This view of the democratic person places the individual at the core of democracy. Democracy based on the ideal of autonomy becomes that quality which serves to regulate the behaviour of the individual in relation to others.

But then there is also a need in this chapter to provide for a discussion concerning the possibility to understand humans and their dispositions in relation to others, a discussion that will have to focus on the human condition of being human as well as on the ethical aspects that it might imply. Ethics, Lévinas (1969) tells us, is the first philosophy and as such it precedes ontology and epistemology. Thereby an ethical perspective is needed to understand humans and their disposition, whether they are gender, cultural, ethnical, or social, in a situation, in which they are given a meaning, not decided in advance, where these dispositions instead are being a part of a system of norms and values and constructed in a process of always considering the Other, in the specific circumstances of online education and a developing digital competence.

In this chapter we discuss the importance of developing a digital competence in the light of the current global e-learning trend, and in that discussion incorporate an ethical perspective emphasising mutual understanding as a possible conception of democracy, a conception which can embrace in autonomy also a sense of responsibility for the Other.

TRANSFORMATION IN VIEWS OF LEARNING

The theoretical framework for this chapter is anchored in theories of learning, in particular, the way learning and human participation in communities of various kinds can, and have been, understood. Over the years there have been considerable changes in the way learning and participation have been conceptualised within an educational context. For a long period of time behaviourism (Skinner, 1974; Watson, 1925) was the most common theory used when there was a need to explain how people learned, and in particular how people participate in educational activities. For behaviourism, building primarily on understanding humans as biological beings, learning and participation was a question of conditioning. And as such it could be viewed only in terms of behaviour. In other words, learning and participation was viewed as a result of a repeatedly reinforced and thereby trained human behaviour that was controlled by the provision of different stimuli. In the late era of this somewhat simplified view of human behaviour, focussing only on the externalised aspects of the processes occurring in humans when encountering the world, a reaction

to behaviourism evolved. These were the theories in the cognitive paradigm (Bransford, 1979; Piaget & Inhelder, 1969). In the cognitive view, learning and participation is a matter of how the human being, by means of her cognitive capacity and skills, uses and processes the information confronting her. Learning and participation will be possible due to a process of adjustment, to new information or to new situations, where the human has to adapt and develop new skills and strategies. In the succeeding cognitive theories, there is an increased interest in the social dimension of learning and participation, highlighted for example in the social learning theories emphasising culture (Bruner, 1996). One perspective of those that pays attention to this dimension, and that could be seen to further develop the cognitive perspective, is the theory of social constructivism (Barlebo Wenneberg, 2001; Jonassen, 2007; Searle, 1995). The social context is together with the knowledge-constructing individual, given special attention, within the social constructivist perspective. By sharing other's views of different phenomena's and by participating in different settings, the individual human being is constructing a new understanding of the phenomena's in question. Another perspective highlighting the social dimension is the sociocultural theories, though they pay less attention to the individual human being (Säljö, 1999; Wenger, 1998). Within the sociocultural perspective, learning is understood in terms of activity and participation is understood through the assumption of the human being as a social being. The human being is learning when participating in different kinds of activities and settings and the learning process is dependent on cultural, historical and social conditions (Bonk & Cunningham, 1998; Vygotsky, 1978). When describing learning and participation, these theories are often used. And as theoretical perspectives for analysing and understanding different educational settings, they are still all frequently consulted.

TRANSFORMATIONS AND THE EXTENDED USE OF ICT IN EDUCATION

One of the most prominent and important aspects of human development is the interactive use of technology (Mitcham, 1994). Technology can be understood in different ways, but it is in one sense enough to consider it merely as a tool, an artefact, to realise its importance. At the same time it might be enough to merely consider the development of technology as a tool in education to realise how the transformed use of technology has had an impact on education. Although some critical voices of the technological development (Borgmann, 1984; Mitcham, 1994; Westera, 2005), the increased use of technology have paved the way for humans to communicate, socialise, and build relations across distances and borders in many ways. For example, behind the increased use and extended scope of distance education seems to be the development of ICT. Within this movement, the rapid improvement of the Internet and its possibilities to provide for communication has made distance education possible to understand as an interactive learning experience supported by the use of ICT (Vrasidas & Glass, 2002). But the development of technology, and in particular ICT, has also had an effect on the kind of education carried out in person. To some people (Tait & Mills, 1999) the development of ICT causes distance education and campus education to converge into a new practice in which ICT is integrated in all aspects, at least in tertiary education.

An early description on how ICT and technology affect education is found in Koschmann (1996), who outlines how certain theoretical assumptions have influenced the ways technology has been used in education. He also shows how the meanings of these have changed along with the technology and its possibilities. Koschmann claims that this has emerged through four phases, called paradigms, with the purpose of showing how different understandings of learning have influenced the way technology has been converted into educational technology. Beginning in how a behaviouristic understanding for learning provided an early framework for educational technology, Koschmann thereafter turns to two new paradigms, which he claims are influenced by cognitive theories, and which have increasingly come to influence the ways that technology has been used. In the fourth and final paradigm, Koschmann claims that the social dimension in learning has come to play a crucial part in relation to how technology is used for educational purposes. This forth paradigm, the Computer Supported Collaborative Learning (CSCL) paradigm, he suggests, implies a shift towards aspects such as active participation, collaboration and dialogue between learners.

COMMUNICATING AND PROVIDING A SOCIAL LEARNING ENVIRONMENT

As mentioned, over the last decade several theories of learning have emerged with an increased focus upon social dimensions in learning. Learning is claimed to occur together with others in all kinds of social situations or contexts (Bliss, Light, & Säljö, 1997; Bruner, 1996). Gibson (1977) provided early assumptions of learning in a specific social environment. He proposed that it was the relationship between the learner and properties of specific environments that decided the affordances or constraints of action. Thereafter this idea was developed into a perspective of ecological psychology that allows an understanding of the learner (or more exact, the agent) as an information detector. The agent has, depending upon the environment, different opportunities to act or participate. In short, importance is placed on the dynamic interactions between the agents and their environments (Young, Barab, & Garrett, 2000).

The social dimension is also palpable in Wenger's (1998) social theory of learning. Wenger stresses that the opportunity to participate in a community in order to create meaning and understanding is utterly important for a learner. According to Wenger, learning is connected to a process of meaning-making, always dependent on social, relational and temporal aspects and is always the product of a process of negotiation. Living in the world, in terms of membership of communities and active involvement in social enterprises, is to participate in a primarily social experience.

Anderson and Garrison (1998) argue that those involved in distance education, mainly built around the use of technology participate through interaction, collaboration, and communication in a social context provided by the technology. They claim that learning in such distance education includes a complex interplay between teacher, student and content. Similarly, Paulsen (2003) focus on different kinds of online teaching. In line with Paulsen, communication or dialogue that enables participation in a distance education could be carried out in the following ways and include the following aspects: one-alone (online databases, online publications); one-to-one (learning contracts, apprenticeships, correspondence); one-to-many (lectures, symposiums); many-to-many (debates, role plays, case studies).

In education different technical solutions may be used in order to allow for participation in all four modes discussed by Paulsen (see also Renninger & Shumar, 2002). For example, functions enabling both asynchronous and synchronous participation could be used (Jaldemark, Lindberg, & Olofsson, 2005; Kowch & Schwier, 1997;). This provides the students with immediate (synchronous) and continuous (asynchronous) access to an educational program. Examples of functions within these technological systems are blogs, chats, computer conferences, e-mail, threaded discussions, and video conferences. These func-

tions offer flexible opportunities to participate independently of place and time.

Also implied in this line of reasoning, is that a concept such as the learning environment, could be taken into a virtual dimension in education and be used for understanding such educational settings as Web-based learning environments, Web-based conference systems, and Web portals (Harasim, 1989; Paulsen, 2003). Thus, learning environments that are created by means of technology have gone from being places only for downloading ready-made educational material to be places which make learning with others in a social context possible (Bonk & Cunningham, 1998; Haythornthwaite, 2002; Koschmann, 1996; Stephenson, 2001).

GLOBAL PERSPECTIVES ON ACCESS, DEMOCRACY AND E-LEARNING

Using technology the way we have suggested opens up for a learning experience in an educational context that could be both rich in its communication and quality, as dependent upon social aspect and authentic as any learning experience. This would in a sense imply that the use of technology, the overcoming of educational constraints such as space and time would inevitably lead to a democratic process in education. In short, education is always reachable for those who need it. A global movement towards e-learning would then be a democratic movement perhaps as great as the tearing down of the Berlin wall. But who will benefit and who will suffer from the global e-learning movement? This question is difficult to answer concisely; it can be problematized in different ways. It can be a question of access, a question of democracy, a question of ethics, and even a question of colonization, Carr-Chellman (2005, p. 2) says.

For most of us, the idea of open access—the elimination of elitism as a function of place and prestige—holds the promise of equity. The basic premise of the rhetoric of democracy in online education is that if we can make education available to those who currently must work to earn a living and cannot attend residential programs because of geography or family obligations, then we are making these opportunities available more equitably.

This quotation argues the idea that a viable democracy is one in which diversity is accepted and promoted as something good. At the same time it refers to what is understood as the fundamental problem in the global e-learning movement—to convert political rhetoric into practice that works, in broad meaning, in reality without being thwarted by human greed, power, money-making, good willing.

Global economy and globalization are thus two important concepts related to e-learning. The commercialization of the concept, or idea, of e-learning and the effects such development will promote are not yet researched. A likely possibility is that this process could result in a rather negative form of development for many people around the world. One question of globalization and, for example, internationalization, worth stressing is whether this is merely expressions of a new Western way of colonizing what we call the developing countries? Can a global e-learning movement and open access to education everywhere imply that everyone is educated with the same basic notions of, for example, democracy. Is it possible to include all the different cultural differences that exist in the world in an e-learning venture, and not only the perspective of the Western countries? How will developing countries deal with the fact that within one country you might have two or more different cultural rationales guiding the everyday life of its people? Can a need to be culturally sensitive be combined with a recognizing of intra- as well as intercultural

understandings in a movement of e-learning into a global venture? Latchem (2005, p.185) chose to articulate this by posing the following question: "Who will write these rules and to whom will the providers of international distance education be accountable?" Similar thoughts of Zembylas and Vrasidas (2005a) sharpen this point—is this movement towards globalization, in a world of e-learning, a process of inclusion or a new electronic version of colonization?

These questions seem at the moment hard to answer, more research is needed. What one may say, though, is that questions such as these call for an ethical stance. Not only in relation to technology as such, but in relation to the question of human involvement in the ways of world. We ask ourselves what the future community will be.

GLOBAL E-LEARNING AND THE BUILDING OF A FUTURE COMMUNITY

A fair starting point to a discussion of building future communities could be a question posed by Sergiovanni (1999, p.9): "What is the story of community?" According to Selznick (1996) community is not to be associated with a fixed and objective definition with a clear and central meaning open to only one understanding. Rather community is a concept open to different kinds of meanings and understandings, depending upon social, cultural and societal frameworks in which a community as such is to be understood. Bauman (2001), for example, argues that the story of community is related to a tension between safety and freedom. In his view, this gives a two-fold understanding of community. On the one hand community is associated with a feeling of being part of, and sharing, something positive with others, for example a society. On the other hand, community threatens us as humans in our autonomy, beckoning us to give up our sense of individuality.

A further understanding of the in-built tensions in the concept of community can be found in Tönnies (1963). Making a distinction between Gesellschaft and Gemeinschaft, Tönnies finds in the latter a coherent community in which culture and social practice are infused with moral unity and intimacy, also described as a kind of norm-based enterprise. In the former Tönnies describes how social contracts connect individual human beings. In a community coloured by Gesellschaft, each member's autonomy and mobility is favoured. Instead of negotiating a system of norms to live by in the community, the members have to live by certain rules that ensure that each member gets what he or she wants. In the words of Tönnies (1963), in Gemeinschaft, human beings remain essentially united in spite of all separating factors, whereas in the Gesellschaft they are essentially separated in spite of all uniting factors. This accentuates one possible built-in paradox or tensions in the concept of community: what unites and what holds the community together?

From a communitarian understanding of community, Etzioni (1993, p.31, italics in original) claims that an essential property of a community is a shared morality, saying "*Communities speaks to us in moral voices. They lay claims on their members.*" Members of a community adjust their behaviour through a process of negotiation of what is right and what is wrong. In this process the individual members still have some degree of freedom, but in case of repeated misbehaviour, the community will respond powerfully in order to end behaviours not included in, and sanctioned by, the negotiated ways. This functioning provides another possible basis for community, morality, ethics and values.

Thus, in one sense, community could concern the prospect of creating an identity, developing individually held values and norms and complying to the values held by others, and the tension between individual identity and assimilation within a group (Hand, 1989). However, in another sense, community seems to be illusive, letting itself be defined and used in multiple ways (Delanty,

2003; Keller, 2003; Paccagnella, 2001; Söderström et al., 2006). Holding aspects such as these in mind, educating the world through the means of e-learning could be even more a question of building future communities in which humans share notions, values and beliefs, which accentuate the need for an ethical position.

ICT AND COMMUNITIES IN EDUCATION

The idea of using community as an aspect closely related to learning builds on studies of cultures with major influences from first Lave and Wenger (1991), and later also Wenger (1998). In Lave and Wenger's focus of different practices, the successive or gradual inculcation into the habits and ways of a practice was formulated as an apprenticeship, as a learning process. In describing the situated aspect of learning, learning the practice, they identified the achievement of becoming a full member of a community as a movement along a specific trajectory of participation. Members are being fostered into the ways of the practice, and move from being only peripherally involved towards the centre, and in this movement the members are said to embrace not only the common ways of doing things, but also the ideas, values, beliefs, and assumptions underlying the practice.

Wenger (1998) refined the idea of the situated character of learning, focusing even more on the community. The use he made of community underlined aspects of learning, meaning, and identity that are connected to a specific practice. In the learning community, members are considered to be bound by their joint participation in the negotiation of meaning and the development of a shared history. The negotiation of meaning is considered to be bound by two reciprocal processes—participation and reification. These processes become the foundation for a shared practice, which is seen as a source of coherence of a community. Wenger formulated three dimensions of a practice that form the properties of a community—mutual engagement, shared repertoire, and joint enterprise. The concept of community, then, is understood in terms of a way of talking about the social configurations in which our enterprises are defined as worth pursuing and our participation is recognizable as competence. Wenger use of the learning community becomes more of a metaphor for creating a common ground in the service of a specific learning.

THE LEARNING COMMUNITY IN EDUCATION

Many arguments have been given for applying the metaphor of the learning community in educational settings. It seems that several different interests use the metaphor for somewhat different purposes. For example, it could be the democratic joint venture of schools and universities (Grundy, 1999), or a perspective for school improvement (Holden, 2002), a view where school leadership primarily leads to community forming (Bredeson, 2003), or a way of organising education (Barab & Duffy, 2000). Often students are said to form a learning community (Ó Murchú & Sorensen, 2003; Palloff & Pratt, 1999; Wenger, 1998). The learning community should enable students both to support each other as well as collaboratively learn with and from each other.

Furthermore, when associated with education it seems possible to design communities with the specific purpose of learning, and the learning community is thereby re-conceptualised as an educational issue. It seems no longer to be only the practice and the situated aspects of certain practices that are focussed upon, but also the intended or expected outcomes of certain educational designs. The possibilities of fostering learning communities appear to be central. This trend can also be traced in the fields of educational research and instructional design, in studies that aim to find ways of transferring and implementing the concept of the learning community (Reigeluth, 1999).

Technology can be regarded as part of building communities in a virtual sense; communities that acknowledge no borders, that are present only in information systems inhabited by their users, and belonging to communities of their own choice (Lewis & Allan, 2005). The online community can be divided into several sub-groups (Carlén & Jobring, 2005), depending upon its focus. Carlén and Jobring describe a typology building on a rationale in which each online community is examined in relation to its main focus. Transferring the learning community to the Internet and building Online Learning Communities (OLC) (Carlén & Jobring, 2005; Lindberg & Olofsson, 2006; Olofsson & Lindberg, 2005; Seufert, Lechner, & Stanoevska, 2002) could be seen as one of the most recent developments among researchers and practitioners that use the community as a metaphor for their activities.

E-OLC AND NET-BASED EDUCATION

Within an educational framework, net based education is probably the educational mode, in which the use of the community concept has expanded the most (Olofsson & Lindberg, 2006a; Olofsson & Lindberg, 2006b). The inherent barrier in earlier distance education provided by time and space constraints seems, during the last years to have been continuously reduced in education provided through the Internet. In net-based education, the educational online learning communities (E-OLC) can be a way of understanding the learning processes of those attending courses and belonging to classes, taking degrees, or just educating themselves in the virtual company of others. E-OLC could be seen as a way of allowing learning in online classrooms to involve an understanding in ways that move beyond the factual content or informational aspects of education. In the perspective of belonging to an E-OLC, members can be regarded as being part of a practice, and the sum of all aspects of that education becomes part of the understanding of their learning. This seems to embody possibilities to include both aspects of being together with others as well as possible value-based outcomes. This understanding opens for the idea that the E-OLC is a question of belonging and being with others (Lindberg & Olofsson, 2006).

BENEATH ICT—BEYOND THE INTERFACE—TOWARDS THE OTHER

Online learning is claimed to be time and space independent (Paulsen, 2003). But the conception of timelessness is then dependent upon a conception of time as being present merely in the now. If time is considered through the lens of Gadamer (1976), online education, net-based education, distance education, and an OLC is not timeless. As will be developed here, time in the sense of a tradition, prejudice and effective history gives humans a timely context to relate to. This is not only unavoidable but a necessary condition for being, and as such permeated by time. Likewise, the conception of spacelessness is dependent upon a conception of space built on a metaphysical conception in which the world is merely understood as a world of things. Building a conception of the world as an inevitable human condition (Heidegger, 1962), provides a lens to consider space in which online education, net-based education, distance education and OLC is not spaceless. A human being is inevitable a being-in-the-world, and being present always means a presence in the world (Zahorik & Jenison, 1998).

In accordance with Heidegger (1962), human and world is one. This unavoidable participation and presence in the world is understood as conditioned by relational and socially defined aspects of human and world. As Arendt (1998) puts it, humans are born into an already existing world of humans, and all individual actions and speech are thereby preceded by a web of human relations.

Humans become humans through a process of always being in the world (Bourdieu, 1995) and in accordance the world is understood as social, built on relations and in which the human, through language, embrace joint understandings, and conceptual constructions that decides the world (Gadamer, 1976). This togetherness, or Mit-dasein if speaking with Heidegger (1962), is the world as it is shared with others. It lays the ground for humans to understand both world and others. The understanding humans make of the world is not to be understood as static or un-flexible, a world inherited rather than constructed. It is more a question of a dynamic and reciprocal co-construction allowing the world and thereby the humans to be in an always changing and evolving mode. Due to the relational and social conditions that frame the togetherness, change is an open possibility. As these conditions evolve, they leap ahead of things, making the understanding humans may have of themselves and the world dependent upon a being-in-the-world always ahead of itself in an instable way, always potentially becoming something else, something unpredicted.

This idea of a continuously changing understanding of the world is further developed by Gadamer (1976). Especially three central concepts seem more important to discuss—prejudice, tradition, and effective history. Prejudices are to be regarded as judgements, executed before encountering the thing, any thing, in question. Prejudice decides both what and how humans may understand. They are in that way literally 'pre-judices,' and as such they lead the thoughts to conservation and indifference. But prejudices are not in this context to be regarded as negative judgements. Instead they form the premises for constituting something, anything, and as such they are impossible to avoid. Bernstein (1991), for example, claims that there is no knowledge without prejudices. Gadamer (1976, p. 9) expresses the necessity with prejudices as "They are simply conditions whereby we experience something—whereby what we encounter says something to us." Tradition, in turn, refers to the sum of all prejudices making up the influence of the past and thereby the repetition of the history we bring about. History repeats itself, it is often said, and prejudices can be said to fill tradition with meaning. As part of an existing tradition the human is seen as already being part of not only what have been and is, but also what seems possible to be—that is the force and guiding principle of what Gadamer call the effective history. History that determines and decides at the same time as it lends itself to be open for new possibilities.

The human is always directed towards what is becoming, towards new possibilities. At the same time, though, placed in a situation in which the human is under influence of what have already happened. All human understanding then, is a consequence of the tradition and can as such be seen as already, once and for all, decided. An understanding can, though, be detailed and conceptually separated from another understanding. Due to specific dimensions of the tradition and to specific situations humans together with other humans are part of, human understanding is reciprocally dependent on being decided by tradition and prejudice and constituting tradition and prejudice. This implies that humans at the same time create and re-create interpretations and understandings in a never ending process, in a dynamic repetition of the past, the present and the future (Risser, 1997). Humans are, in one sense, continuously de-contextualising, contextualising, and re-contextualising their position as beings, as a being-in-the-world. Time- and spacelessness becomes obsolete concepts.

AN ETHICAL PERSPECTIVE: THE QUESTION OF THE OTHER

But if technology does not release us from the space and timeless constraints of being in the world, can we be released from the human condition of being in the world with others? In the sense that time and space becomes the socially and relationally given what happens to the Other?

If the use of technology for educational purposes, and if the context of e-learning and the building of E-OCC's is to be further developed, our suggestion is to include a conception of the Other based on an ethical position. If the use of technology is to move beyond the technical skills sought for by the EU (ET 2010 WP), to include and embrace not only a singular human, it would seem that the condition of the being-in-the-world has to be provided with an elaboration of the even more fundamental condition of being together, an elaboration of the implications of being-with-the-other that is conditioned in the realisation of the Other. This condition, it is proposed by Lévinas (1981), is to be found in philosophy and ethics (Zembylas & Vrasidas, 2005a). Ethics, Lévinas tells us, is the first philosophy. Ethics precedes ontology in that the ethical responsibility for the Other is not a question of free will or choice (Zembylas & Vrasidas, 2005b). For Lévinas the togetherness of being is a being-for-the-other. But the Other is to Lévinas (1969) not knowable in her or himself. The Other is knowable only as an obligation to learn from the Other, to know the Other as her or him summons me, calls upon me to meet her or him in a meeting face-to-face that gives meaning to this otherness that the Other implies. The face of the Other signifies that which is otherwise, that which I am not and thereby the Other invokes in me that which is me in a non-reciprocal relation of responsibility for the Other (Lévinas, 1981). A face, then, can signify both that which is close and known and that which is distant and abstract, both that which can be found in community and in difference. As such it goes beyond that which is present in the representation of the face; it includes an already given trace of the Other (Lévinas, 1986). A trace that is not a sign, but signifies, a sign that denotes but never appear, a given that will not be known, at the same time as its being is irreversible. The Other in her- or himself invokes the obligation, the responsibility, to know oneself through the face and the trace of the Other. The being as a human is understood as being-for-the-other.

In the use of technology, in the E-OCC, in the e-learning experience, the development of shared repertoires and shared goals will be directly dependent on the conceptions that the Other will invoke through the always present trace of the Other. The Other then, will be present in the technology before the humans enter. Not because the designers have built in affordances that may come into play as the participants gradually learn to navigate a given system, but through the presence that the Other will have left, as a marking upon each possible action they will take. Each spaceless virtual room created will have the Other as guide. The Other will give face to its Intelligent Tutoring System (ITS), and the Other will provide the trace that is it manual. The context will first and foremost be space and time dependent, anchored in the human condition of always sharing the world with others. In the trace, that also gives view of the face of the Other, says Lévinas (1981).

No virtual space and place can be regarded as empty until it has some marking or reified human action manifested within it. Considering the possible trace of the always present but never visible Other proposed by Lévinas (1986), the space will always be inhabited by the Other, and the Other will always be dwelling in the binary code as the possibility to be enacted as the difference between each participant when each human enter into online communication with other humans and thereby signify themselves and others.

Through Lévinas (1986) and the metaphorical sense of knowing the Other only through a face and a trace, it is possible to provide an understanding of the use of technology to overcome time and space constraints, an understanding of the humans participating at the inter-face of computer screens involved in giving meaning to educational experiences together with others. It is possible to give an additional understanding of how the Other summons the participants to reveal for, rely on,

and relate to each other as they in different ways perceive the trace of the Other in the differences and the saying and the said, in the signified and the signifier. This, in turn, reveals and relies on the ethical challenge of education (Zembylas & Vrasidas, 2005a).

FUTURE TRENDS

At this stage, it is possible to sketch at least two kinds of future trends. The first trend, in a way placed in a non-academic context, mirrors a development of a tremendous growth in the belief in the power of e-learning. This trend is present both in the context of the so-called market and in the context of governmental instances like the EU. What these two contexts seems to share is an idea of ICT in education, embodied in the concept of e-learning, as the saviour that will pave the way for a democratic and tolerant world inhabited by humans with high digital competence ready to lead the world into the future. Within such a development a possible scenario could also be that the ethical issues of e-learning becomes a question of instrumentalism and a design issue, in the respect that several, and general, principles are constructed with the aim of steering how people should be together in for example E-OLCs. Once again with a risk that the Western world sets the agenda with little or no understanding of the importance of being-for-the-other in a way that goes beyond the interface towards the face of the Other.

The second trend is positioned in an academic context. Here we have in mind both the educational and the research practice located inside the walls of the universities and on the Internet. The trend is that the ethical aspects will become important to include for educating students online and for conducting research of such activities. Exactly what this means seems difficult to tell. But it seems to be crucial that both practices are characterized by an idea that being a human always also is a being-for-the-other. Such an idea can never be reduced to be a question of providing the "right" guidelines rather it is a question of democracy and the rights for everyone to participate in educational activities on for all included equal terms.

CONCLUSION

The idea of using learning theory and designing for community forming in education is presented as a question concerning democracy, and the development of e-learning is therefore argued to benefit from including an ethical perspective. The importance of such a perspective on education online (or e-learning) is exemplified with the ideas of Lévinas and his concept of the Other. If it seems important to avoid a development leading towards a less democratic citizenship in the world, then the Other might be a person always there as a projection but not always physically at hand to take into account. With the ethical perspective and the responsibility for the Other, democracy is extended in its scope towards a view in which the Other becomes a part in the just way of negotiating values and value disputes that Held (1996) includes in a possible conception of democracy. Democracy and ICT becomes less of a question of access and skills, and more of a move beneath the surface, appearing as a time and spaceless face, a trace, of the Other.

REFERENCES

Arendt, H. (1998). *The human condition* (2nd Ed.). Chicago, Ill: University of Chicago Press.

Barab, S.A., & Duffy, T.M. (2000). From practice fields to communities of practice. In D.H. Jonassen & S.M. Land (Eds.), *Theoretical foundations of learning environments* (pp. 25-56). Mahwah, NJ: Lawrence Erlbaum Associates.

Barlebo Wenneberg, S. (2001). Socialkonstruktivism: positioner, problem och perspektiv [Socialconstructivism: positions, problems and perspectives, in Swedish]. Malmö: Liber.

Bernstein, B. (2000). *Pedagogy, Symbolic Control and Identity. Theory, Research, Critique. Revised Edition.* New York: Rowman & Littlefield.

Bernstein, R. J. (1983). *Beyond objectivism and relativism: Science, hermeneutics, and praxis.* Oxford: Basil Blackwell.

Bliss. J., Light. P., & Säljö, R. (Eds.). (1999). *Learning Sites: Social and Technological Resources for Learning.* Oxford: Pergamon.

Bonk, J.C., & Cunningham, D.J. (1998). Searching for learner-centered, constructivist, and sociocultural components of collaborative educational learning Tools. In C.J. Bonk (Ed.), *Electronic collaborators. Learner-centered technologies for literacy, apprenticeship, and discourse* (pp. 25-50). Mahwah, NJ: Lawrence Erlbaum.

Borgmann, A. (1984). *Technology and the character of contemporary life.* The University of Chicago Press: Chicago.

Bransford, J. D. (1979). *Human cognition: Learning, understanding and remembering.* Belmont, CA: Wadsworth.

Bredeson, P. (2003). *Designs for Learning: A new architecture for professional development in schools.* Thousand Oaks, CA: Corwin Press.

Bruner, J. (1996). *The culture of education.* Cambridge, MA: Harvard University Press.

Carlén, U., & Jobring, O. (2005). The rationale of online learning communities. *International Journal of Web Based Communities, 1*(3), 272-295.

Carr-Chellman, A.A. (Ed.). (2005). *Global perspectives on e-learning. Rhetoric and reality.* Thousand Oaks, CA: SAGE.

Delanty, G. (2003). *Community*. Routledge: London.

Dewey, J. (1916). *Democracy and education: an introduction to the philosophy of education*. New York: Macmillan.

Etzioni, A. (1993). *The spirit of community. Rights, responsibilities and the communitarian agenda*. London: Fontana Press.

European Commission. (2004). *Implementation of "Education and Training 2010" Work Programme*, European Commission, Directorate General for Education and Culture. Brussels.

Freire, P. (1972). *Pedagogy of the oppressed*. Harmondsworth: Penguin Books.

Gadamer, H-G. (1976). *Truth and method*. London: Sheed and Ward.

Gibson, J.J. (1977). The theory of affordances, In R. Shaw & J. Brandsford (Eds.), *Perceiving, acting, and knowing: Toward an ecological psychology* (pp. 67-82). New Jersey: Lawrence Erlbaum Associate.

Grundy, S. (1999). Partners in learning. School-based and university-based communities of learning. In J. Retallick, B. Cocklin, & K. Coombe (Eds.), *Learning communities in education* (pp. 44-59). London: Routledge.

Hand, S. (Ed.). (1989). Introduction. In E. Lévinas, *The Lévinas Reader*. (pp. 1-8). Basil Blackwell: Oxford.

Harasim, L. M. (1989). On-line education: A new domain. In R. Mason & A. Kaye (Eds.), *Mindweave: communication, computers and distance education* (pp. 50-62). Pergamon, Oxford.

Haythornwaite, C. (2002). Building social networks via computer networks—Creating and sustaining distributed learning communities. In K.A. Renninger & W. Shumar (Eds.), *Building virtual communities—learning and change in cyberspace* (pp. 159-190). Cambridge, Cambridge University Press.

Heidegger, M. (1962). *Being and time*. Oxford: Blackwell.

Held, D. (1996). *Models of Democracy*. Cambridge, UK: Polity Press.

Holden, G. (2002). Towards a learning community: the role of mentoring in teacher-led school improvement. *Journal of In-Service Education, 28*(1), 9-21.

Jaldemark, J., Lindberg, J.O., & Olofsson, A.D. (2005). Att förstå hur man deltar via redskap i en lärgemenskap. In O. Jobring & U Carlén (Eds.), *Att förstå lärgemenskaper och mötesplatser på nätet* [To understand learning communities and places to meet on the net, in Swedish]. Lund: Studentlitteratur, 109-147.

Jonassen, D. H. (2007). *Design of constructivist learning environments*. Retrieved on March, 27, 2007, from http://tiger.coe.missouri.edu/~jonassen/courses/CLE/

Keller, S. (2003). *Community. Pursuing the dream, living the reality*. Princeton, New Jersey: Princeton University Press.

Koschmann, T. D. (1996). Paradigm shifts and instructional technology. In T. D. Koschmann (Ed.), *CSCL: Theory and practice of an emerging paradigm* (pp. 1-23). Mahwah, NJ: Lawrence Erlbaum Associates.

Kowch, E., & Schwier, R. A. (1997). Considerations in the construction of technology based virtual learning communities. *Canadian Journal of Educational Communication, 26*(1), 1-12.

Latchem, C. (2005). Towards borderless virtual learning in higher education. In A.A. Carr-Chellman (Ed.), *Global perspectives on e-learning. Rhetoric and reality* (pp. 179-197). Thousand Oaks, CA: SAGE.

Lave, J., & Wenger, E. (1991). *Situated learning: Legitimate peripheral participation.* Cambridge: Cambridge University Press.

Lévinas, E. (1969). *Totality and infinity.* Pittsburgh: Duquesne University Press.

Lévinas, E. (1981). *Otherwise than being or beyond essence.* Pittsburgh: Duquesne University Press.

Lévinas, E. (1986). The trace of the Other. In M. Taylor (Ed.), *Deconstruction in Context* (pp. 345-359). Chicago: University of Chicago Press.

Lewis, D., & Allan, B. (2005). *Virtual learning communities. A guide for practitioners.* Berkshire: Open University Press.

Lindberg, J.O., & Olofsson, A.D. (2006). Distancing democracy: organising on-line teacher training to promote community values., *UCFV Research Review,* Vol. 1, pp.1-10, Published on the Web, available at http://journals.ucfv.ca/ojs/rr/

Mitcham, C. (1994). *Thinking through technology: the path between engineering and philosophy.* The University of Chicago Press: Chicago.

Ó Murchú, D., & Sorensen, E.K. (2003). "Mastering" communities of practice across cultures and national borders. In A. Gaskell & A. Tait (Eds.), *Collected Conference Papers.* Cambridge, UK: The Open University in the East of England Cintra House.

Olofsson, A.D., & Lindberg, J.O. (2005). Assumptions about participating in teacher education through the use of ICT. *Campus Wide Information Systems, 22*(3), 154-161.

Olofsson, A.D., & Lindberg, J.O. (2006a). Enhancing phronesis. Bridging communities through technology. In E.K. Sorensen & D.Ó. Murchú (Eds.), *Enhancing learning through technology* (pp. 29-55.). Information Science Publishing: London.

Olofsson, A.D., & Lindberg, J.O. (2006b). Whatever happened to the social dimension? Aspects of learning in a distance-based teacher education programme. *Education and Information Technologies, 11*(1), 7-20.

Paccagnella, L. (2001). Online community action: perils and possibilities. In C. Werry & M. Mowbray (Eds.), *Online communities. Commerce, community action, and the virtual university* (pp. 365-404). Upper Sadle River, NJ: Prentice Hall PTR.

Palloff, R. M., & Pratt, K. (1999). *Building learning communities in cyberspace: effective strategies for the online classrooms.* San Francisco, CA: Jossey-Bass.

Paulsen, M. F. (2003). *Online education: Learning management system: Global e-learning in a Scandinavian perspective.* Bekkestua, Norway: NKI Forlaget.

Piaget, J., & Inhelder, B. (1969). *The psychology of the child.* London: Basic Books.

Reigeluth, C.M. (Ed.). (1999). *Instructional-design theories and models, volume II. A new paradigm of instructional theory.* Mahwah, NJ: Lawrence Erlbaum.

Renninger, K. A., & Shumar, W. (2002). *Building virtual communities: Learning and change in cyberspace.* Cambridge: Cambridge University Press.

Risser, J. (1997). *Hermeneutics and the voice of the Other. Re-reading Gadamer's philosophical hermeneutics.* New York: SUNY Press.

Searle, J. R. (1995). *The construction of social reality.* London: Allen Lane.

Selznik, P. (1996). In search of community. In W. Vitek & W. Jackson (Eds.), *Rooted in the land: essays on community and place* (pp. 195-203). New Haven: Yale University Press.

Sergiovanni, T. (1999). The story of community. In J. Retallick, B. Cocklin, & K. Coombe (Eds.), *Learning communities in education* (pp. 9-25). London: Routledge.

Seufert, S., Lechner, U., & Stanoevska, U. (2002). A reference model for online learning communities. *International Journal on E-learning*, January - March, 2002, 43-55.

Skinner, B. F. (1974). *About behaviorism*. New York: Vintage.

Stephenson, J. (Ed.). (2001). *Teaching & learning online. Pedagogies for new technologies.* London: Kogan Page.

Säljö, R. (1999). Learning as the use of tools: A sociocultural perspective on the human-technology link. In K. Littleton & P. Light (Eds.), *Learning with computers: Analysing productive interaction* (pp. 144-161). London: Routledge.

Söderström, T., Hamilton, D., Dahlgren, E., & Hult, A. (2006). Premises, promises: connection, community and communion in online education. *Discourse*, 27(4), 533-549.

Tait, A., & Mills, R. (Eds.). (1999). *The Convergence of Distance and Conventional Education: Patterns of Flexibility for the Individual Learner.* New York: Routledge.

Tönnies, F. (1963). *Community and Society* (Charles P. Loomis, Trans.). New York: Harper.

Vrasidas, C., & Glass, V.S (Eds.). (2002). *Current Perspectives on Applied Information Technologies: Distance Education and Distributed Learning.* Greenwich, CT: Information Age Publishing.

Vygotsky, L. S. (1978). *Mind in society: The development of higher psychological processes.* Cambridge, MA: Harvard University Press.

Watson, J. (1925). *Behaviorism*. London: Kegan Paul.

Wenger, E. (1998). *Communities of practice. Learning, meaning and identity.* Cambridge: Cambridge University Press.

Westera, W. (2005). Beyond functionality and technocracy: creating human involvement with educational technology. *Educational Technology & Society, 8*(1), 28-37.

Young, M.F., Barab, S.A., & Garrett, S. (2000). Agent as detector: An ecological psychology perspective on learning by perceiving-acting systems. In D.H. Jonassen & S.M. Land (Eds.), *Theoretical foundations of learning environments* (pp. 147-172). Mahwah, NJ: Lawrence Erlbaum Associates.

Zahorik, P., & Jenison, R.L. (1998). Presence as being-in-the-world. *Presence, 7*(1), 78-89.

Zembylas, M., & Vrasidas, C. (2005a). Lévinas and the "inter-face": The ethical challenge of online education. *Educational Theory, 55*(1), 61-78.

Zembylas, M., & Vrasidas, C. (2005b). Globalization, information and communication technologies, and the prospect of a 'global village': promises of inclusion or electronic colonization? *Journal of Curriculum Studies, 37*(1), 65-83.

KEY TERMS

Community: A social group linked by common interests through residence in a specific locality, or, whether or not in physical proximity, whose members perceive themselves as sharing a common ideology, interest, or other characteristic

Computer Uses in Education: The use of computers for instruction, testing, student/pupil personnel services, school administrative support services, and other educational purposes

Digital Competence: Digital competence involves the confident and critical use of Information Society Technology (IST) for work, leisure and communication. It is underpinned by basic skills in ICT: the use of computers to retrieve, assess, store, produce, present and exchange. information, and to communicate and participate in collaborative networks via the Internet.

Education: Process of imparting or obtaining knowledge, attitudes, skills, or socially valued qualities of character or behaviour, including the philosophy, purposes, programs, methods, organizational patterns, and so forth, of the entire educational process as most broadly conceived

Globalization: A global cultural system within education, business, medicine, and so forth, made possible by the availability of modern technology and communications

Learning: A process for acquiring knowledge, attitudes, or skills from study, instruction, or experience

Technology Uses in Education: A broad concept for the use of emerging technologies for educational purposes

Chapter XXXIII
Mobile Learning in a Social, Ethical, and Legal Environment

John Traxler
University of Wolverhampton, UK

ABSTRACT

The increasing diversity, availability, and functionality of mobile and wireless technologies over the last 4 or 5 years has accelerated the proliferation of pilots and trials in mobile learning. But the evaluation of these has been methodologically and ethically flawed, and consequently substantial and sustained mobile learning has not happened. These technologies are also transforming many aspects of society including ideas of communication, discourse, community, culture, and ethics. Mobile learning is uniquely aligned to contribute to this transformed society but only once evaluators understand the ethical challenges. This chapter is important because it addresses the issue of the ethical evaluation of mobile learning.

INTRODUCTION

The *m-learning* project was one of the earliest large-scale mobile learning projects. It was a 3 year pan-European project, which began in October 2001 and finished in September 2004. The project was funded by the European Commission under the Education Area of the Information Society (IST) Programme. It was led by the UK's Learning and Skills Development Agency (LSDA). The Consortium was composed of the Consorzio Centro di Recerca in Matematica Pura

ed Applicata (CRMPA) in Italy and Lecando AB in Sweden. Project partners in the UK were Cambridge Training and Development Limited (CTAD), a Learning Technology Research Centre based at Anglia Ruskin University. The project addressed three social/educational issues relating to many young adults aged 16-24 in the EU: Poor literacy/numeracy; non-participation in conventional education; lack of access creating ICT haves and have-nots.

The project was large and some 200 learners were involved in the final trials. There were several different software deliverables, including a range of educational games, a micro-portal, and a learner management system. The impact of the project on its target group was positive and rewarding, and provided grounds for exploring the potential of mobile learning across a variety of socially disadvantaged groups including travellers and the homeless (Attewell & Savill-Smith, 2004). In the course of this project it became apparent that mobile learning presented unique ethical challenges if it was to be evaluated effectively and appropriately. A series of internal guidelines was developed that attempted to define and address these challenges before they were published to a wider audience (Traxler & Bridges, 2004). It has however subsequently become obvious that these issues are embedded in a wider and more profound social context, that mobile learning has moved on considerably in since the early days of *m-learning* and that the ethics of mobile learning evaluation can no longer be considered in isolation from wider social change driven by the increasing availability, functionality, and acceptance of mobile and wireless technologies.

A BACKGROUND TO MOBILE LEARNING

Mobile learning is a concept that is becoming increasingly familiar to researchers and practitioners in higher education. Over the last 4 or 5 years there have been a variety of pilots and projects that have explored the educational possibilities of using handheld computers, mobile phones, personal media players, and games consoles to deliver, support, and enhance learning, assessment, guidance and administration. It is now sufficiently mature and varied to have a major textbook (Kukulska-Hulme & Traxler, 2005) and a number of prestigious international conferences. MLEARN in Birmingham 2003 was followed by MLEARN 2003 in London, attracting

more than 200 delegates from 13 countries. The series continued with Bracciano, Rome in July 2004, Cape Town in October 2005, Athabasca in November 2006, Melbourne in November 2007, and Wolverhampton in October 2008.

Mobile learning now has a wide-ranging literature (see for example reviews by Cobcroft, 2006, and Naismith et al., 2004—but no dedicated journal—and a greater clarity about the significant issues (Sharples, 2006), defining the big issues, and a more sharply defined research agenda (Arnedillo-Sánchez et al., 2007). The mobile learning community is now theorising in its own right (Sharples et al., 2005) and challenging established theories of technology enhanced learning (Laurillard, 2002).

At the same time, recent publications (Kukulska-Hulme et al,, 2005; JISC, 2005), and conference proceedings (Attewell & Savill-Smith, 2004) have put a large number of case studies documenting trials, pilots, and their evaluations into the public domain. In looking at these, Kukulska-Hulme and Traxler (2007) found some emergent categories that characterise the current state of mobile learning:

- Technology-driven mobile learning in which some specific technological innovation is deployed to demonstrate technical feasibility and pedagogic possibility;
- Miniature but portable e-learning in which mobile, wireless and handheld technologies are used to re-enact approaches and solutions found in conventional e-learning;
- Connected classroom learning covers the same technologies as those used in classroom settings to support static collaborative learning;
- Informal, personalised, situated mobile learning contains the same core technologies that are enhanced with additional functionality, for example location-awareness or video-capture;

- Mobile training/performance support are the technologies used for improving the productivity and efficiency of mobile workers by delivering information and support just-in-time and in context for their immediate priorities;
- Remote/rural/development mobile learning are the technologies used for addressing environmental and infrastructural challenges to delivering and supporting education where 'conventional' e-learning technologies would fail;
- Large-Scale Implementation meaning the deployment of mobile technologies at an institutional or departmental level to learn about cultural and organisational issues;
- Inclusion, Assistivity & Diversity covers the use of assorted mobile and wireless technologies to enhance wider educational access and participation.

This taxonomy has implications for evaluation, both methodological and ethical, since each category must have different implied or tacit aims and objectives to be evaluated against. Each category also implies different settings and types of learners to work with. These accounts derived from an analysis of Kukulska-Hulme and Traxler (2005) also provide a range of reasons for adopting mobile learning techniques.

- Access to assessment, learning materials, and learning resources or increasing flexibility of learning for students
- Changes in teaching and learning, for example, guiding students to see a subject differently than they would have done without the use of mobile devices. The time and task management facilities of mobile devices can help students to manage their studies.
- Alignment with institutional or business aims or example making wireless, mobile, interactive learning available to all students

without incurring the expense of costly hardware
- Ways of delivering communications, information and training to large numbers of people regardless of their location or harnessing the existing proliferation of mobile phone services and their many users

Other more general motivations addressing the future of mobile learning were identified: find out in which arenas handhelds are used, how and why they are used, and what role they can play; the future take-up of new services and facilities on mobile phones and other technology devices might be; find out whether young adults would be willing to use their phones for literacy and numeracy learning; understand the range of actions and opportunities open to mobile learners, and seek ways of extending this range to support what learners want to do.

These reasons and motivations also have methodological and ethical implications for evaluation since they imply different stakeholders. Evaluation is crucial for the embedding and sustaining of mobile learning in whatever category or setting and so the methodology and ethics of evaluation are also crucial.

EVALUATION OF MOBILE LEARNING

In an earlier work (Traxler, 2002) some attributes of a good evaluation were outlined alongside the reasons why such an evaluation is unusually challenging. Some of these attributes were:

- Rigorous, meaning that conclusions must be trustworthy and transferable
- Efficient, in terms of cost, effort, time
- Ethical, specifically in relation to the nuances of evolving and untried forms of provision

- Proportionate, that is, not more ponderous, onerous or time-consuming than the learning experience or the delivery and implementation of the pilots themselves
- Appropriate to the specific learning technologies, to the learners and to the ethos of the project concerned—ideally *built in*, not *bolted on*
- Consistent with the teaching and learning philosophy and conceptions of teaching and learning of all the participants
- Authentic, in accessing what learners (and perhaps teachers and other stakeholders) *really* mean, *really* feel, and sensitive to the learners' personalities within those media
- Aligned to the chosen medium and technology of learning
- Consistent across different groups or cohorts of learners in order to provide generality; time, that is, reliably repeatable; whatever varied devices and technologies are used

In addition to the explicit mention of ethics, many of the other attributes has ethical implications. Evaluation, good or otherwise, is however not straightforward. It exists in a context. One respected evaluator (Somekh, 2001, p. 101) sums up the challenges and hints at the wider context, saying: "Evaluation is a fascinating, socially useful, morally demanding and highly politicised activity. Its future depends on the uses we put it to, and the role it is given by sponsors and politicians."

Evaluation will inevitably precede and accompany any sustained and substantial deployment of mobile learning involving public, institutional or organisation funds, resources or commitment. In much of Western Europe and North America, part of this wider context, the public or political part is the movement for evidence—perhaps evidence in the interests of openness and transparency and perhaps evidence as opposed to expertise. However, evidence-based policy formulation is,

in the words of Ian Gibson's MP Chair of the Committee Science and Technology Committee remark (Hansard, 2004) in the UK Parliament increasingly derided as policy-based evidence formulation. Some in the social research community (Sanderson, 2004) have asked: "Has evidence-based policy any evidence base?" In looking at the local ethical issues around evaluation we must recognise that the wider issues could be problematic.

At a practical level, significant ethical issues and ethical differences may not be raised, discussed or resolved because they are taken-for-granted or conversely considered not-worth-mentioning (Rugg & McGeorge, 1999). Similarly, ethical frameworks are often assumed and therefore obscure (Warner, 2004). In terms of epistemology, ethics can be based on divergent philosophical foundations that take, for example, different positions on reality, knowing and the self. A simple division can be made between modernism with its confidence in the ability of scientific method to give access to a pre-existing reality and postmodernism which is far more sceptical about such truth claims believing instead that reality is continuously and collaboratively constructed. Within a modernist framework the researcher—or evaluator—strives for objectivity. Engaging in postmodern research involves the researcher—or evaluator—reflexively asking why they are doing this research in this way, what is it silent about, what gives it authority, and who is privileged by it? These apparently highly philosophical issues make a profound difference to practical ethics, as we shall see when we look at informed consent.

THE ETHICAL DIMENSION OF MOBILE LEARNING

Mobile learning is now increasingly a focus of attention in parts of the developing world (Traxler, 2007). Pilot studies of the ethical aspects of non-Europeanised cultures, perhaps subsistence farmers or street children, is still relatively rudimentary. In order to consider the impact of mobile learning on the ethics of evaluating educational provision, it is easy to start with models of pure mobile learning. In this sense, pure mobile learning means learning delivered solely by mobile technologies. This thought experiment is an extreme example allowing us to elucidate the issues The major ethical issues in relation to the evaluation of pure mobile learning include informed consent and participant withdrawal, anonymity and confidentiality, participant risk, payment to participants and cultural differences (Anderson & Kanuka, 2003; Hewson et al., 2003).

Informed Consent

Informed consent is a core ethical issue for evaluation. It refers to participants' or learners' understanding of the nature, extent, duration, and significance of their involvement with the evaluation. In terms of the issues of underlying philosophy, where truth is problematised then informed consent cannot be straightforward, and so for postmodernists it can never be total. The evaluation process is complex and dynamic and as such it cannot be simply represented to participants. Data can take us in unexpected directions to which the participants have not given prior consent (Weatherall et al., 2002). The binary division between evaluator and evaluatee is seen as problematic too, especially with regard to privilege and power. Consequently, there is more likely to be an ongoing process of negotiating issues of informed consent. However, from a realist position, giving information required for informed consent may influence the responses given and so 'contaminate' the data. The recent analysis (Traxler & Kukulska-Hulme, 2005) indicates little evidence of this kind of methodological or ethical awareness in mobile learning to date.

In face-to-face learning, informed consent might be achieved by a briefing or a written out-

line with the opportunity for follow-up questions. This might cover the aims and objectives of the evaluation and then issues such as anonymity and confidentiality, data protection, parental permission, participant risk, withdrawal and remuneration. Participants have the chance to ask questions and then to express their consent by signing a consent form. But for pure mobile learning or a purely mobile community this is problematic.

The *m-learning* project, for example, worked with travellers, gypsies, and circus-folk, this is potentially problematic because it may be difficult to explain fully the scope of mobile learning in a succinct and appropriate fashion in a way that is consistent with mobile learning itself. Another reason is that participants may only engage in mobile learning via text messaging, picture messaging or text-to-speech/speech-to-text technologies, where there are very few precedents for gaining and signifying informed consent. Much mobile learning is inherently noisy or contextual, taking place in short informal opportunistic bursts and informed consent under these conditions may be questionable. A mobile learning system may not preserve persistent learner identities across sessions or across devices thereby possibly confusing the source of consent and the data to which it relates. Furthermore, in any remote research, it is easy to deceive researchers and evaluators. Hence, mobile, internet-based or online researchers may have no reliable face-to-face cues. Another problem is that there may be insufficient means for would-be participants to check their understanding of the research and their part in it. Consent can only legally be granted by participants who understand the nature of their participation. In mobile learning, it may be difficult to establish whether this is the case without face-to-face contact. Expressing consent, especially in a legally meaningful fashion, usually requires a conventional written signature. Finally, informed consent assumes that any information or explanation upon which the consent rests is expressed in a fashion that is inclusive of varied literacy, linguistic and physical abilities (and accords with the provisions and spirit of accessibility legislation).

Existing practice in relation to obtaining informed consent comes from a variety of internet-based evaluation and research formats. None of these is satisfactory for mobile learning, and accepted and appropriate forms still have to evolve. It is necessary to obtain consent for:

- Email interviewing where the explanatory briefing is mailed or emailed to participants, or they are directed to the project Web site. Here consent is emailed back or printed, signed and faxed or posted back.
- Conferencing involves an explanatory statement posted in the conference; participants then post or email queries and signal consent.
- Chat is in real-time and so informed consent is problematic. An asynchronous area may be used in parallel to engage in the consenting process.
- Participant observation includes mail lists, news-groups, and so forth present possibilities for undisclosed but problematic participant observation. The so-called "virtual ethnography" (Hine, 2000) contains a consent issue.
- Collecting personal electronic documents is a consent issue, also associated with harvesting system data on users' behaviour.

The issue of informed consent is however apparently less legally problematic than it might appear since mobile learning trials only run the risk of participant withdrawal rather than litigation and could easily put itself in a position where participation implied consent. The involvement of minors in evaluation does not require parental consent as long as the participants are sufficiently mature to understand the nature of their participation. So-called minors give their *de facto* consent to all sorts of transactions in everyday life without needing to refer to their parents. In each case, the issue is whether they comprehend the implications of the specific transaction in question.

Participant Risk

Mobile learning trials pose risks to participants insofar as they may inadvertently expose participants to unsafe or unsavoury behaviour or material via various media, from external Web-based sources and from other participants. Participants should be aware of the nature and extent of this risk, and so especially should the parents or guardians of any under-age participants. Risks might include access or exposure to harassment, abuse, spam, hate mail or unsafe Internet sites, or indeed to user-generated content. It is clearly the duty of evaluators to shield participants from harm and to minimise its consequences. In many countries, monitoring traffic can imply or confer liability. For both learning and for evaluation, monitoring or moderating is however an essential feature of online learning and of evaluation. Although this will imply liability, moderators have merely to act promptly, appropriately and reasonably in anticipation of potential harm and similarly once actual harm has taken place in order to mitigate substantially the severity of the offence.

The *m-learning* project had its own portal and mobile chat facilities, for example. This form of mobile learning encouraged or allowed peer-to-peer collaboration - essentially invisible to any moderation. This raises the possibility that participants may be exposed to risks, for example obscene picture messaging, over which the evaluators cannot possibility have any control.

Participant Withdrawal

From an ethical point of view, evaluation procedures should make withdrawal easy at any point. Evaluators are clearly interested in keeping participants live within the trials and there is some tension between these two considerations.

Payment or Compensation

In much evaluation work, it is understandable that participants are recompensed for the time or effort of their involvement. This establishes some kind of contract between them and the evaluators and thus raises two kinds of issues. The first issue is methodological and in essence is the question of whether payment or compensation has skewed or contaminated any results or conclusions. The second issue is ethical and concerned with whether the compensation can be viewed as fair or equitable for the time or effort involved. Issues related to differentials in culture, status, and power may obscure easy access to answers about whether the contract is actually perceived as fair by participants, especially the learners themselves. Where benefits are tangible, the relationship is legally contractual but if participants are merely being recompensed or reimbursed or the benefits are intangible, this is probably not the case in law.

Confidentiality and Anonymity

Evaluators are expected to guard the anonymity of participants in any published accounts. There are routine practices for this in conventional evaluation. In purely mobile, virtual or online learning, this may not be an ethical problem since participants' identities and attributes could be wholly fictional. Such an eventuality would however be a considerable methodological problem. Researchers must also guarantee the confidentiality of any data from or about participants. In large and complex mobile learning consortium projects with many people, partners, intermediaries, components and devices this is potentially quite challenging legally. Some researchers (Buchanan, 2004) have pointed out the inherent contradiction, when quoting respondents verbatim, with acknowledging their copyright whilst preserving

their anonymity. The widespread availability of camera-phones and picture messaging is a specific aspect of this problem.

A different issue involving privacy is the extent to which some mobile learning technologies reveal data about individuals that they might not know was accessible. Some devices are location-aware and disclose the participant's movements. There are few references to ethics in the literature of mobile learning but one of them relates to privacy and context-awareness (Lonsdale et al., 2004). Benford (2005, p. 12) raises a similar issue: "Privacy is perhaps the most significant long-term challenge facing the successful roll-out of location-based experiences." Other authors from the wider community are starting to consider privacy and location (Junglas, 2005; Junglas and Spitzmuller, 2005; Minch, 2004). Recent projects that exemplify the potential for violations of privacy, or indeed for surveillance, include Savannah, (Facer et al., 2005) a mobile game was designed for use by groups of children moving around in the school playing field, aimed at encouraging the development of children's conceptual understanding of animal behaviour in the wild, CAERUS, the Context Aware Educational Resource System, is deployed in Birmingham's Botanic Garden (Naismith et al., 2005) to support visitors with location-based information that reflects their interests and needs and the project *Mudlarking in Deptford*. Schoolchildren have used PDAs to take part in, and to co-produce, a guided tour of the riverbed at Deptford Creek (Sutch, 2005). All these forms of location-awareness are relatively short-term and impersonal examples of context-awareness. Work at the University of Wolverhampton is currently looking to extend the context to include social and pedagogic contents to associate with a persistent identity. This work clearly has enormous implications for enhancing and supporting learning, inclusion and diversity in higher education but also has enormous implications for privacy.

Distinctions Between Private and Public

There is an increased need in online interaction to distinguish whether the participants regard online exchanges and interactions as public or private. This is relevant to email, mailbases, newsgroups, chat, forums, and so forth since the distinction can become blurred or forgotten or the interaction can quickly move from the public to the private or vice versa. These interactions are normally in specific physical spaces, for example internet cafes or computer labs, that act as a reminder of the context, but mobile learning is more likely to place away from such designated spaces. Many people will have observed that one can be in a public space listening to people having the most intimate conversations on their mobile phones or gesticulating on the mobile; one can hear people using their mobile phones, ostensibly the tools to demolish physical distance and physical space, opening the conversation by saying exactly where they are! These everyday examples illustrate that pervasive mobile technologies blur the boundaries of private and public spaces and private and private discourses. Furthermore, Gergen's challenge of absent presence (2002) underlines the relationship between these phenomena and the shifting roles of public and virtual presence, all of which make mobile learning evaluation problematic as the various boundaries become blurred.

Traxler (2002) and Traxler and Kukulska-Hulme (2005) have argued, as an axiom of evaluation, for the alignment of the evaluation techniques with project technologies, that is specific mobile and wireless technologies, walking the talk perhaps, and conducting evaluation in the spirit of the project itself. There is a practical ethical aspect of this, in that it preserves whatever identities learners have assumed rather than transgressing them. If learners have opted to learn with mobile technologies because they have high-functioning autism or agoraphobia, then an evaluation using the same technology exposes them to least harm.

The Roles of the Researcher, Teacher, Organiser, and Manager

Mobile learning projects seldom have external or dedicated evaluators (Traxler & Kukulska-Hulme, 2005). Similarly, there is a need to maintain distinctions about roles. A mobile learning project worker will probably have more than one role in relation to participants, most likely developer, teacher/lecturer with pastoral and academic responsibilities, evaluator and researcher. These roles have different and possibly conflicting ethical requirements and responsibilities and hence it is important for participants to understand the context for any given interaction.

Status and Power

Researchers and research organisations, employers, trainers, universities, or colleges, must recognise that any interactions with participants, including gaining and maintaining informed consent, take place across myriad differentials in status and empowerment, for example learner/teacher, participant/researcher, and so forth. These differentials are related to positions within organisations, within social structures, within society itself and within the education system. They pose ethical and methodological problems, which may be at odds with each other. Feminist research in particular has been at pains to tease out the consequences of these issues for participant research and to develop appropriate methodologies. Some of this thinking has informed research and evaluation within online communities.

Cultural Differences

Many evaluations take place across cultural or sub-cultural divides where various parties may be dissimilar in terms of language, expectations and values. This will be true in mobile learning, especially where mobile phones are the technology of choice. It is used in order to maximise inclusion although the participants might be culturally and ethnically diverse, usually young, and often economically exposed and possibly close to street culture. The mobile learning evaluators are usually university lecturers or highly paid consultants. They will be party to rather different types of discourse and expectations.

Developing Effective Debriefing

Evaluators are obliged to ensure that participants are unharmed at the conclusion of their involvement with evaluation. To this end, debriefing procedures should be established. These procedures might provide debriefing text with contact details and invite comments and queries. This may be relatively lightweight but mobile learning evaluators should nevertheless consider some mechanism to conclude participants' involvement and give closure. Evaluators should consider making their interpretations available to participants (often called member checks) and this might be part of the informed consent process. For modernists it is likely to be seen as increasing accuracy, whereas for postmodernists it may be to allow a more collaborative or co-constructed process, to give greater credence to previously excluded voices and to respond to challenges regarding responsibility in representing the other.

Netiquette and Norms

Each new communications technology evolves its own specific expectations governing language, interactions and exchanges, originally termed netiquette. The earliest of these govern email, chat, and conferencing. First, email netiquette includes emoticons and smileys, and a relaxed attitude to grammar and spelling and the expectation of brevity. Second, instant messaging

and chat netiquette includes expectations about inappropriate ringing, and even greater brevity; communicating near-synchronously. Third, forums and conferencing often have published codes of behaviour precluding, for example, spam and flaming; communicating asynchronously.

New technologies, for example e-portfolios intended for educational reflection and self-evaluation, soon to be joined by m-portfolios and blogging now joined by moblogging have their distinctive forms of expression, protocols and norms, and texting had conventions and 'txt-speak' from its very beginnings. These are all usually informal, fluid and permeable to each other. But nevertheless each serves to define a community or a sub-culture, rather than just\being a rational reaction to the constraints of the technology in question.

An early use of educational messaging (Traxler & Riordan, 2003) produced feedback from students that was basically ethical in that it described what they thought was acceptable, for example: Messages only sent out within one part of the day, for example between 12-1; The times that sms were sent out eg between 9 am and 9 pm some were being sent early and very late; Don't txt to [sic] early in the morning!!

The current large-scale messaging project at the University of Wolverhampton (www.wlv.ac.uk/celt/MELaS) aims to explore these ethical issues further, in particular homing in on students' attitudes to the type, frequency, volume, and timing of messages.

Netiquette, in all its forms, is an instance of ethics, which is an instance of norms and expectations about behaviour. Mobile and wireless technologies have however far wider effects on society and on the ethics of its various cultures and sub-cultures. These technologies underpin new forms of behaviour and misbehaviour, new forms of misdemeanour and crime, not to mention new forms of commerce, artistic expression, employment, and economic asset. Obvious examples are blue-jacking, smart-mobbing, and happy-slapping plus identity theft. Katz and Aakhus (2002) vividly describe the different patterns of use involved in mobile communications across a variety of countries and communities, and their accounts bring out the extent to which communities, cultures, and sub-cultures are defined in terms of language and behaviour, in this case mediated by mobile communications technologies. The relations between mobility including personal mobile technologies and culture, hence discourse, community and identity, is now a growing research area (Sheller, 2004; Sheller & Urry, 2003; Sheller & Urry, 2006; Souza e Silva, 2006; Tamminien et al., 2003; Urry, 2000). Outside the specialised domain of evaluating mobile learning, these are the reasons why the relations between ethics and mobile technologies are significant.

CONCLUSION

Imaginative and exciting mobile learning in a society increasingly transformed by mobile devices is a significant challenge to evaluate rigorously, effectively, and appropriately and this brings the challenges to recognise ethical issues in novel situations and to devise procedures and protocols that are ethically acceptable. Many of the issues involved are embedded in the wider cultural, social and consequently, ethical changes in society increasingly permeated by personal mobile and wireless technologies. The evaluators of mobile learning must meet these methodological and ethical challenges if mobile learning is realise its potential to deliver sustained and substantial learning in the spirit of this transformed society. This chapter has brought together the practical aspects of those ethical challenges and sought to identify practical problems and practical solutions to the ethics of evaluating mobile learning but at the time link these to these wider social changes.

REFERENCES

Anderson, T., & Kanuka, H. (2003). *e-Research - methods, strategies and issues*. A. E. Burvikov, (Ed.). Boston, MA: Allyn and Bacon.

Arnedillo-Sánchez, I., Sharples, M., & Vavoula, G. (Eds.). (2007). *Beyond mobile learning workshop*. Dublin: Trinity College Dublin Press.

Attewell, J., & Savill-Smith, C. (2003). Mobile learning and social inclusion: focusing on learners and learning, In *Proceedings of MLEARN: 2nd World Conference on mLearning*. London: LSDA.

Attewell, J., & Savill-Smith, C. (2004). Mobile learning and social inclusion: focus on learners and learning. In *Proceedings of MLEARN2003 Conference*. London: LSDA.

Benford, S. (2005). *Future Location-Based Experiences*. JISC: Technology & Standards Watch. Bristol: Joint Information Services Committee. Available online at: http://www.jisc.ac.uk/uploaded_documents/jisctsw_05_01.pdf

Buchanan, E. (Ed.). (2004). *Readings in virtual research ethics-issues and controversies*. London: Information Science Publishing.

Cobcroft, R. (2006). *Literature review into mobile learning in a university context*, Queeensland University of Technology. Online available: http://eprints.qut.edu.au/archive/00004805

Facer, K., Stanton, D., Joiner, R., Reid, J., Hull, R., & Kirk, D. (2005). Savannah: Mobile gaming and learning? *Journal of Computer Assisted Learning*, Vol. 20, 399-409.

Gergen, K. (2002). The challenge of absent presence. In J.E. Katz & M. Aakhus (Eds.), *Perpetual contact—mobile communications, private talk, public performance*. Cambridge, UK: Cambridge University Press.

Hansard (2004). Science And Technology Committee, Committee Office, House of Commons, No. 81 of Session 2003-04, Retrieved on November 8, 2004, from http://www.parliament.uk/parliamentary_committees/science_and_technology_committee/scitech081104.cfm

Hewson, C., Yule, P., Laurent, D., & Vogel, C. (2003). *Internet research methods.* N. G. Fielding & R. M. Lee (Eds.). London: SAGE Publications.

Hine, C. (2000). *Virtual ethnography.* London: SAGE Publications.

JISC. (2005). *Innovative practice with e-Learning: A good practice guide to embedding mobile and wireless technologies into everyday practice,* Bristol: Joint Information Services Committee.

Junglas, I., & Spitzmuller, C., (2005). A research model for studying privacy concerns pertaining to location-based services. *HICSS '05: In Proceedings of the 38th Hawaii International Conference on System Sciences,* 2005, track 7 vol. 7. Washington: IEEE, p. 180.2.

Katz, J. E., & Aakhus, M. (Eds.). (2002). *Perpetual Contact—Mobile Communications, Private Talk, Public Performance.* Cambridge, UK: Cambridge University Press.

Kukulska-Hulme, A., & Traxler, J. (Eds.). (2005). *MobilelLearning: A handbook for educators and trainers.* London: Routledge

Kukulska-Hulme, A., Evans, D., & Traxler, J. (2005). *Landscape study in wireless and mobile learning in the post-16sSector, Technical Report,* Bristol: Joint Information Services Committee.

Laurillard, D. (2002). *Rethinking university teaching—A conversational framework for the effective use of learning technology,* 2nd ed, London: Routledge.

Lonsdale, P., Baber, C., Sharples, M., & Arvanitis, T. N. (2004). A context-awareness architecture for facilitating mobile learning. In J. Attewell and C. Savill-Smith (Eds.). *Learning with mobile devices: Research and development,* London: LSDA.

Minch, R. (2004). Privacy issues in location-aware mobile devices. In *Proceedings of the 37th Hawaii International Conference on System Sciences,* 2004, track 5, vol. 5. Washington: IEEE, 50127.2 Also available online at: http://csdl.computer.org/comp/proceedings/hicss/2004/2056/05/205650127b.pdf

Naismith, L., Sharples, M., & Ting, J. (2005, October 25-28). Evaluation of CAERUS: A context aware mobile guide. In *Proceedings of MLEARN 2005: 4th World Conference on mLearning,* Cape Town, South Africa. Available online at: http://www.mlearn.org.za/CD/papers/Naismith.pdf

Naismith, L., Lonsdale, P., Vavoula, G., & Sharples, M. (2004). *Literature review in mobile technologies and learning.* Bristol: NESTA FutureLab.

Palen, L., & Dourish, P. (2003). Unpacking "privacy" for a networked world. CHI '03: In *Proceedings of the SIGCHI conference on human factors in computing systems.* (pp. 129-136) New York, NY: ACM Press.

Rugg, G., & McGeorge, P. (1999). *Questioning methodology.* Northampton: University College Northampton Faculty of Management and Business.

Sanderson, I. (2004). *Is it 'What Works' that Matters? Evaluation and evidence-based policy making,.*Economic Research Institute of Northern Ireland Ltd: Belfast. Available online at http://216.239.59.104/search?q=cache:FTLz6DYzdlgJ:www.qub.ac.uk/nierc/documents/SandersonPaper.pdf+policy-based+evidence+formulation&hl=en

Sharples, M., Taylor, J., & Vavoula, G. (2005, October 25-28). Towards a theory of mobile-learning, In *Proceedings of MLEARN 2005: 4th*

World Conference on mLearning, Cape Town, South Africa.

Sharples, M. (Ed.). (2006). *Big issues in mobile learning*. Nottingham: Kaleidoscope Network of Excellence, Mobile Learning Initiative.

Sheller, M. (2004). Mobile publics: Beyond the network perspective, *Environment and Planning D: Society and Space*, vol. 22, 39-52.

Sheller, M., & Urry, J. (2003). Mobile transformations of public and private life, *Theory, Culture & Society*, Vol. 20, 107-125.

Sheller, M.. & Urry, J. (2006). The new mobilities paradigm, *Environment and Planning A,* Vol. 38, 207-226.

Somekh, B. (2001). The role of evaluation in ensuring excellence in communications and information technology initiatives. *Education, Communications and Information*, *1*, 75-101.

Souza e Silva, A. (2006). From cyber to hybrid: Mobile technologies as interfaces of hybrid spaces, *Space and Culture*, Vol. 9, 261-278.

Sutch, D. (2005, October 25-28). Bossing adults and finding spotty bras: Learners as producers within mobile learning contexts. In *Proceedings of MLEARN 2005: 4th World Conference on mLearning*, Cape Town, South Africa. Available online at: http://www.mlearn.org.za/CD/BOA_p.63.pdt

Tamminien, S., Oulasvirta, A., Toiskallio, K., & Kankainen, A. (2003). *Understanding mobile contexts*. Udine, Italy: Springer.

Traxler, J. (2002, June 20-21). Evaluating m-learning. In *Proceedings of MLEARN 2002, European Workshop on Mobile and Contextual Learning,*(pp. 63-64). University of Birmingham.

Traxler, J., & Bridges, N. (2004). Mobile learning—The ethical and legal challenges, *Mobile Learning Anytime Everywhere,* In *Proceedings of MLEARN2004*, Bracciano, Italy.

Traxler, J., & Riordan, B. (2003). Supporting computing students at risk using blended technologies. In *Proceedings of ICS Annual Conference,* Galway, Ireland: ICS-LTSN.

Traxler, J., & Kukulska-Hulme, A. (2005, October 25-28). Evaluating mobile learning: Reflections on current practice, In *Proceedings of MLEARN2005: 4th World Conference on mLearning*, Cape Town, South Africa. Available online at: http://www.mlearn.org.za/CD/BOA_p.65.pdf

Kukulska-Hulme, A., & Traxler, J. (2007). Design for mobile and wireless technologies. In H. Beetham & R. Sharpe (2006). *Rethinking Pedagogy for the Digital Age* London: Routledge.

Traxler, J. (2007). Managed mobile messaging and information for education In *Proceedings of IST-Africa, Maputo*, Mozambique.

Urry, J. (2000). *Sociology beyond societies: Mobilities for the 21stt Century*, London: Routledge.

Warner, S. (2004). Contingent morality and psychotherapy research: Developing applicable frameworks for ethical processes of enquiry. *Journal of Critical Psychology, Counselling and Psychotherapy*, 4(2), 106-114.

Weatherall, A., Gavey, N., & Potts, A. (2002). So whose words are they anyway? *Feminism and Psychology*, 12(4), 531-539.

KEY TERMS

Ethics: Any prescription by a culture of how things ought to be or ought to be done, expressed on a spectrum from legal and regulatory frameworks to social disapproval.

Evaluation: The activities intended to assess the value, worth or benefits of a pilot, trial or intervention in the light of the values and aims, perhaps only tacit or vague, of stakeholders such as policy-makers, funders, managers, developers, teachers ..... and hopefully learners and their communities.

Evidence-Based Policy Formulation: The notion that policy should be based on evidence rather than for example professional expertise, political ideology, public opinion or religious faith.

Mobile Learning: Originally any learning delivered, supported or enhanced by mobile and wireless technologies and now the learning associated with societies where these technologies are increasingly conspicuous.

Information & Communications Technologies (ICT): Narrowly, computers, their networks and peripherals; broadly and in a developmental context, includes also phones, videos, radio, and so forth.

VLE: Virtual learning environment, aka LMS, learner management system, a system such as Moodle or SAKAI that supports the delivery of educational materials, discussion and assessment.

About the Contributors

Thomas Hansson, holds a PhD in teaching and learning at Luleå University of Technology, working as associate professor in pedagogy at University of Southern Denmark and Blekinge Institute of Technology. Thomas is registered educational consultant and assessment expert for Socrates/Erasmus European Commission, Directorate-General for Education and Culture, and Comenius European Commission. Lifelong Learning: Comenius, Grundtvig, ICT and Languages. Project management covers Socrates-Comenius Heart of Learning Organizations. Nordic Council 890/2002-2004, Teaching and Learning of English as a Foreign Language. Nordplus/Nordic Council 1022/2005-2007, Values in Education.

*   *   *

Mikael Alexandersson is professor of education at Göteborg University, Sweden. He has two main research interests: teaching and learning processes as they occur in ICT environments (e.g., via artefacts such as CD-ROM, the Internet, e-mail, and multimedia)—knowledge formation and information seeking; the effect of school reforms on teachers' daily work and teachers' learning through their own practice (professional development through learning). Professor Alexandersson is co-director of The Linnaeus Centre for Research on Learning, Interaction and Mediated Communication in Contemporary Society (LinCS), funded by the Swedish Research Council, and is Dean at the Faculty of Education, Göteborg University.

Abdul Azad is an associate professor of engineering technology with the Technology Department of Northern Illinois University. He obtained PhD (control engineering) from the University of Sheffield (UK) in 1994. He has worked at various academic and industrial establishments since graduation in 1987. His research interests include mechatronics, vibration control, real-time computer control of engineering systems, adaptive/intelligent control, and mobile robotics. Dr. Azad has over 75 papers and one edited book in these areas. He is actively involved with in several learned societies including the IEEE, ASEE, IET, and ISA, and also is an IEEE-nominated program evaluator for the Accreditation Board for Engineering and Technology (ABET), USA.

Eun-Ok Baek is an associate professor in the Educational Technology Program, California State University San Bernardino. Her research interests include exploring what technology can do for the support of learning and performance, and specifically, the designing of online learning communities, technology integration in education, and the exploration of social-cultural understandings of the adoption of technology.

Carl Bagley, PhD, is professor of educational sociology at the University of Durham in the United Kingdom. He is interested in exploring the (re) presentational embrace between educational policy research and the arts and the ways in which this is able to evoke meaning with feeling and engender new ways of knowing. On this theme he co-edited (with M.B.Cancienne) the book, *Dancing the Data*, and an interrelated CD-ROM, *Dancing the Data Too*.

Anne Bartlett-Bragg, PhD candidate (UTS), MEd Ad Ed (UTS), BEd Ad Ed (UTS), Dip e-Learning (UTS), Dip HRM (Monash), currently lectures at the University of Technology, Sydney and is involved with the design, development, and delivery of e-learning qualifications and subjects in the Faculty of Education. She is currently completing her PhD that is investigating the adult learners' experiences of developing learning networks through the use of Web logs or self-publishing technologies.

Josianne Basque holds a PhD in psychology and a Master in Educational Technology. A professor in educational technology at *Télé-Université* (TÉLUQ), the distance education university of the *Université du Québec à Montréal*, she has designed numerous Web-based courses in the fields of instructional design, cognitive science and learning as well as computer-based learning. As a researcher at the LICEF Research Center (Laboratory on Cognitive Informatics and Training Environments) at Télé-Université, her research interests span distance education, computer-supported co-construction of knowledge, self-regulation of learning as well as knowledge modeling techniques for learning, knowledge management and instructional design.

Mads Bo-Kristensen holds a PhD in multimedia didactics in Danish as a second language for adults from the Danish University of Education, an MA in French as a second language from the Université de Franche-Compte, France, and a BS in education from the Ålborg University (Denmark). Since 1985, has been involved in teaching of Danish as a second language for adults—both as teacher and as developer of media- and multimedia-based teaching materials. At present, he works for the Resource Centre for Integration as a teacher and as a consultant (second language pedagogy and IT-based training courses for teachers).

Albino Claudio Bosio is professor of consumer and marketing psychology, applied social research and qualitative methods at the Faculty of Psychology, Università Cattolica, Milan, Italy. He is also scientific director of the Master in Qualitative Methods Applied to Social and Marketing Research. He has published more than 100 scientific publications on the subject of healthcare, prevention, public opinion and methodological issues in quantitative and qualitative research. Besides his academicals achievements, he has been researcher at GfK-Eurisko (Milan) since 1975, where now he covers the role of vice-president. Since 2006 he has directed the Centre for Training and Research in ASSIRM.

Marc Bria is a computer scientist from the UAB, expert in the construction of Web learning systems and virtual communities. He has been working with psychologists and education professionals during the last 7 years and as a way of obtaining synergy he coordinates the technical development of an EU project called "5thD: Local Learning Communities in a Global World."

Damien Bright is a researcher and consultant in the IT industry. He graduated with a BSc (Hons) in applied mathematics from Sydney University in 1994, and received his PhD from the Australian

National University. He then worked as an IT consultant before joining the Department of Computer and Information Sciences at the University of South Australia. In 2005 he joined Knowledge Lab at the University of Southern Denmark and worked in the areas of knowledge management, information retrieval, and distributed systems.

Holder of a PhD in education, **Kim Chi Dao** is an educational technologist at *Télé-université* (TÉ-LUQ) and an associate professor at the LICEF Research Center (Laboratory on Cognitive Informatics and Training Environments). She has led or participated in over 50 multimedia training and distance training design and development projects. Her research interests include the cognitive aspects of instructional design as well as learning styles and models.

Betty Collis, Prof, Dr, is a specialist in the application of technology for strategy, learning and change in educational organizations and corporate training. She is an *emeritus* professor at the University of Twente after taking early retirement at the end of 2005. She currently works as a consultant in the Moonen and Collis Learning Technology Consultants B.V. She is a prolific author with more than 660 scientific publications, a frequently-invited conference speaker with close to 700 presentations including 52 keynotes in more than 35 countries, and currently works with a number of universities as an advisor.

Julien Contamines is a PhD student in cognitive informatics at *Télé-université* (TÉLUQ). Since 2002, he has supervised students enrolled in online distance courses in the fields of instructional design, cognitive science and learning, computer-based learning and knowledge management. His PhD research, which he started in 2004, addresses the management of competencies in online learning environments. He is frequently involved in the design of Web-based courses at Télé-université and in research projects at the LICEF Research Center.

Isabel Crespo is lecturer in the UAB, specialized in child at risk development. A member of DEHISI, her research is focused in intercultural education and minority development. She has developed a method for supporting gypsy communities in the use of ICT.

Roberta Devlin-Scherer teaches advanced teaching strategies and contemporary assessment to graduate and undergraduate students at Seton Hall University. Her research interests include reflection, uses of ePortfolios, and teacher and school effectiveness. Her recently published book, *Teaching for Real Learning*, features a section on contents and competitions.

Kathryn Dixon, Dr, (BEd, Post Grad Dip Ed Admin, MEd and PhD), is a senior lecturer who coordinates the postgraduate program in the School of Education at Curtin University of Technology in Western Australia. She teaches at both undergraduate and postgraduate level in the areas of adult education, teaching strategies, training and development, reflective and professional practice and organisational change. Kathryn's research focuses upon organisational development and online and blended learning. Supporting the adult learner is at the forefront of her teaching and postgraduate supervision and research.

Robert Dixon (BEd, MEd) is a lecturer and coordinator of the Training and Development Program, School of Education at Curtin University of Technology in Western Australia. He teaches in the area of adult education, teaching strategies, training and development, reflective practice and organisational change as well as being responsible for facilitating teaching qualifications for academic staff. Robert is at the submission stage of his PhD which relates to educational leadership and reflective practice through the use of electronic portfolios.

Anders Eklöf is a lecturer in educational science at Kristianstad University. He has been working in different K-12 projects as well as in teacher education and for several years in teacher in-service training, with aspects on the connection between digital technologies and education, such as distance education, problem based learning, information literacy, presentation technique and so forth. His main research interest is students' sense making, critical thinking and source criticisms in connection with project work.

Robert Fitzgerald, Dr, is a research fellow at the University of Canberra. His research and consultancy work explores the role of information and communication technologies in learning, particularly as it relates to information literacy and building online communities. His current work involves the application of social software and Web 2.0 technologies to the development of collaborative systems for research and learning. "Developing Digital Learning Communities with Social Software" and "Using SMS to Develop an Electronic Marketing Communication System in Cambodia" are leading-edge projects attracting international interest and involvement.

Christopher Gersbo-Moeller is a PhD student in strategic organization design at University of Southern Denmark. He graduated with an MSc in computer system engineering after performing part of his thesis work at the Distributed Systems Technology Centre (DSTC), University of Queensland in Brisbane, Australia. He then worked as a software developer for three years mainly building online e-commerce and business intelligence applications. His research interests focus on the impact of software systems on the social organizations that use them; especially alignment of software system design with organization designs.

Guendalina Graffigna received a PhD in social psychology at Università Cattolica of Milan (Italy), where she is sectional lecturer in qualitative methods and applied social research and didactic coordinator of the Master in Qualitative Methods Applied to Social and Marketing Research. She is currently CIHR strategic training postdoctoral fellow at the International Institute for Qualitative Methods, University of Alberta, Edmonton, CA. Guendalina works as qualitative researcher at GfK-Eurisko (Department of Health Care) in Milan and she is coordinator of the Centre for Training and Research in ASSIRM where she coordinates several training events on Qualitative Methods. Guendalina's main areas of interest are online focus groups, discourse and conversational analysis, cross-cultural qualitative research, and health communication.

Tim Jasper Mario Hansson CEO at MercIT, graduated with an MSc in international management from University of Southern Denmark in 2003. In the period 2003-2004 he worked as research assistant at Knowledge Lab, University of Southern Denmark, and from 2004-2006 he worked as project manager at Knowledge Lab, affiliated to the Institute of Marketing & Management.

Leah M. Herner-Patnode, EdD, is an assistant professor in special education in the College of Education and Human Ecology at The Ohio State University at Lima, Ohio, USA. Her scholarly interests include technology use to encourage reflection in teacher candidates, teacher training in working with diverse student populations, and professional development school models for developing reflective practitioners.

Leena Hiltunen graduated as Master of Science in computer science and qualified as a computer science teacher in 2001 at the University of Jyväskylä. She got a degree of Licentiate in philosophy in computer science for teacher education in 2005. She is currently finalizing a dissertation on Web course design methodology. Hiltunen started as a researcher in 1994 at the Department of Mathematics with a research project related to hypermedia in education. She has worked as computer science teacher at the Jyväskylä Polytechnic, School of Engineering and Technology. She has been a postgraduate student since 2001 and lectured master courses about virtual learning environments and Web course design in Computer Science Teacher Education at the Department of Mathematical Information Technology. Hiltunen has co-authored a book titled *Multimedia: Toward hypermedia* in 1994 and published articles and reports related to hypermedia and Web course design.

Hamish Holewa is the program manager of the International Program of Psycho Social Health Research (IPP-SHR). His research interests include the development and implementation of new technologies to improve research accessibility and dissemination, as well as the health economics associated with patient care in non-acute settings. He has an ongoing interest in open access publishing methods and has implemented an open access community based model of publication for the *Austral-Asian Journal of Cancer*.

Jonas Ivarsson has a background in cognitive science and communication studies. He has a PhD in educational science, and his general research interests concern the role of representational technologies in the preservation, transmission and development of knowledge and competence. His current research explores the creative and envisioning possibilities offered by representational technologies through the study of design and problem solving activities in architectural education. Also within the domain of architectural education, there is an ongoing investigation into the learning and instruction of visual, discursive and practical competence by targeting so-called design reviews.

Pat Jefferies, Dr, (awarded a National Teacher Fellowship, 2007) is a principal lecturer and university teacher fellow within the School of Education at the University of Bedfordshire. In addition to her role as course leader for the PGCE 14-19 provision, she has recently been appointed as director of the Institute for Research in Education. Pat's primary research interests are in "blended" learning approaches and she is currently leading a research project funded by Becta. Pat has been an invited guest speaker at several universities as well as having gained an extensive range of refereed international conference and journal publications.

Göran Karlsson is a science teacher with master's degrees in biology and pedagogy. He has a wide experience from teaching science in compulsory school, secondary school, and adult education. His research interest lies in designing and evaluating digital learning environments that support the formation of scientific concepts. Currently he is engaged in the Bio-HOPE project which is a bilateral co-operation between Stanford University and Gothenburg University. The purpose is to provide free and on-line biology teaching resources for high school and university students.

Andrew Kitchenham's research interests include educational technology, e-learning, adult education, teaching and learning, transformative learning, special needs, second language acquisition, reading, and gender differences. Dr. Kitchenham has published in refereed journals and books, has presented at numerous international and national conferences, and has taught over 50 courses at eight universities. He is the principal investigator for a Social Sciences and Humanities Research Council (SSHRC) national research study and a co-investigator for another SSHRC study on multi-modal literacy which partially funded the research described in this chapter (Grant Number: 410-2004-1647). He is currently writing a technology integration handbook for classroom teachers.

Agnes Kukulska-Hulme is a senior lecturer in educational technology and deputy director of The Open University's Institute of Educational Technology, where she also convenes the Telelearning Research Group and has chaired the production of the postgraduate course *Innovations in eLearning*. Agnes has been working in mobile learning since 2001 and is co-editor of *Mobile Learning: A Handbook for Educators and Trainers*. Agnes' background is in foreign language learning and from this perspective she has a long standing research interest in user interface design for effective communication.

Gennadiy G. Kuleshov is a professor of physics and computer science at Touro University International (TUI), Cypress, CA, and at Touro College, New York, USA. He graduated from Moscow Technical University for Power Engineering and obtained (1972) his PhD in molecular physics at A.V. Lykov Institute of Heat and Mass Transfer. Since 1987, he holds a DSc in physical chemistry obtained from N.I. Lobachevsky State University, Russia. Dr. G. Kuleshov has over 100 papers in the fields of molecular physics, physical chemistry, power engineering and distance education published in refereed journals and conference proceedings. He has been awarded a number of local, national, and international medals and prizes for his contributions in science and education.

Irit Kupferberg is an associate professor in discourse analysis at Levinsky College of Education, Tel Aviv, Israel, where she founded the Shahak Institute for Language, Society and Communication, chaired the MEd program Language Education in a Multi-cultural Society and the English department. Her current research focus is on interpersonal communication and the discursive construction of self in institutional talk in different cultural settings and metaphorical communication. Her books comprise *Troubled Talk: Metaphorical Negotiation in Problem Discourse*, co-authored with David Green, *Discourse in Education: Researching Educational Events*, co-edited with Elite Olshtain, *Metaphorical-Narrative Bridges in Interpersonal Communication*, co-authored with Izhak Gilat, *Drinking it All: Poems* and *The Babayaga's Curse: Poems*.

Tommi Kärkkäinen earned a PhD in computer science in 1995. He qualified as a computer science teacher in 1996. Since 2002 he is a full professor in software engineering at the University of Jyväskylä, Department of Mathematical Information Technology (Finland). Kärkkäinen has written 25 journal articles in computer science and authored tens of book chapters, articles in conference proceedings, posters, reports, etc. He has taught multiple graduate courses of computer science, software engineering, and teacher education. He is a leader of multiple research and development projects. He has been the head of Software and Computational Engineering Study Line in COMAS. He is a principle professor of software engineering and teacher education MSc at University of Jyväskylä, Department of Mathematical Information Technology, leader of COSSE, and member of multiple academic, areal, and national development groups for research and education.

José Luis Lalueza is associated professor of developmental psychology in the UAB and director of Research Group on Human Development, Social Intervention, Interculturality and Technology (DEHISI). He is coordinating the development of a set of learning communities based on 5D model of computer supported collaborative learning.

Annika Lantz-Andersson is a PhD student in pedagogy at the Department of Education, Goteborg University. Her overall research interest concerns the introduction of new technology and its implications for learning and education. One of the research projects that she has participated in concerns students' information seeking for learning assignments where the general interest is to describe the relation between differences in the quality of students' information seeking and the quality of their learning outcomes. A further research project together with the PhD thesis aims at developing knowledge of educational software and learning.

Hea-Jin Lee has a PhD in mathematics education from the Ohio State University. She is currently an assistant professor at the Ohio State University, Lima. Her research interests include improved reflective thinking and practice, professional growth, and the teaching of mathematics to children. With training and research grants, she has provided professional development that supported improving teachers' knowledge and skills of teaching mathematics. Through these grants, she developed professional development program models that are teacher needs-based and enhance reflective practice.

Jeanette Lemmergaard is assistant professor and project manager of Strategic Human Resource Management at University of Southern Denmark. She graduated with an MSc in international business and modern languages in 1997, and received her PhD in business economics from University of Southern Denmark in 2003. She is best known professionally for her work on the influence of organizational norms and values on the decision-making processes. Her current research includes knowledge management and psychological climate.

Louise Limberg, Dr, is professor of library and information science, specialising in information seeking and use, at the Swedish School of Library and Information Science, University College of Borås (UCB), Sweden. Her research interests concern the interaction between information seeking and learning. Currently, she is the co-ordinating leader of two major research projects focusing on libraries, ICT and learning. She is a co-director of the Linnaeus Centre for Research on Learning, Interaction and Mediated Communication in Contemporary Society (LinCS) and a member of the permanent committee of the international research conference Information Seeking in Context (ISIC).

Ola Lindberg, Dr, earned his PhD in education at Umeå University, Sweden. Dr. Lindberg's main research interest lies in distance education supported by ICT. His research follows a philosophical hermeneutical approach with an overall aim at understanding social and ethical processes of teaching and fostering. In distance education his focus is on how the participants negotiate meaning in educational online learning communities (E-OLCs). Dr. Lindberg has contributed with book-chapters, conference-papers and journal articles on this specific topic. He is member of the international network 'The Research Network on Online Learning Communities.'

Heather Lotherington is associate professor of multilingual education at York University where she has taught in the Faculty of Education and in the graduate program in theoretical and applied linguistics since 1999. Dr Lotherington is currently involved in several studies on digital literacies, including the collaborative research project on developing emergent multiliteracies in the elementary school featured in this chapter, where children are constructing postmodern, digital narratives that involve their cultural and language worlds. Her collaborating teachers at Joyce Public School in Toronto have recently won a national technology award for innovative work that includes this research project.

John Paul Loucky has taught all areas of EFL in Japan for over 20 years. His dissertation compared the use of an extensive text-based sustained silent reading approach to both intensive audio-lingual and CALL-based methods of vocabulary development. Research interests include exploring L2 vocabulary acquisition, use of various glossing and translation programs and devices, electronic and Web dictionaries; designing depth of lexical processing and vocabulary knowledge scales and taxonomies of reading comprehension and vocabulary learning strategies. His homepage provides a clearinghouse of CALL organizations and a virtual encyclopedia of language education sites worldwide.

Edoardo Lozza, psychologist, received his PhD in social psychology. He is currently assistant professor at the Faculty of Psychology at Catholic University of Milan where he teaches methods and techniques of interviews and questionnaires and consumer research methods. His research interests range over the field of consumer behaviour, economic psychology and applied research methods. He has published numerous peer-reviewed articles and chapters in these fields. Beside his academic achievements, Dr. Lozza has also worked as a professional in the social and market research since the 2001 and he is currently project research manager at GfK-Eurisko in Milan.

Olli Mäkinen has a PhD in literature research and philosophy. He is a publisher at the University of Vassa in Finland as well as an information specialist at the Tritonia Academic Library in Finland. He is a Quest Researcher at the Kierkegaard Research Center at the University of Copenhagen, Denmark. His research areas include the internet, internet ethics, anonymity, pseudonyms, mediation, information retrieval, Scandinavian Literature, stories about pauperism, and sports ethics.

Anoush Margaryan, Dr, is a lecturer in learning technology at Glasgow Caledonian University. Anoush has over 10 years of experience in research, development and teaching in technology-enhanced learning (TEL), in the higher education and corporate learning sectors. Her research is focused on work-related learning and sociocultural aspects of TEL. Anoush is currently principal co-investigator of the "Learning from digital natives: Integration of formal and informal learning" project (UK HEA). Anoush has held research and visiting lectureship positions at Universities in the UK, The Netherlands and Germany; she has worked as a research analyst at Shell EP Netherlands and was a consultant to the World Bank.

Robert McClelland is a reader in educational technology, fellow of the Higher Education Academy and fellow of the Royal Statistical Society. He leads Enterprise and two Masters programmes at Liverpool Business School. He has held two teaching Fellowships. Other achievements include research into the introduction, use and effectiveness of virtual learning environments (VLEs), and blends of learning offered to students in higher education. Holding the largest worldwide collection of Web-based learning supports for business, he has designed web-sites for student learning and was first to use e-learning resources and VLEs to support action learning for postgraduate students.

Steve McRobb is a principal lecturer in information systems at De Montfort University, UK and course leader for the newly validated BA (Hons) Society and Information. He is an associate researcher with the Centre for Computing and Social Responsibility and is also co-author of a highly successful textbook on Object-Oriented Systems Analysis and Design. His current research interests are in privacy online and the effects of ICT on power and trust. Steve was formerly principal administrative officer at the Yorkshire Dales National Park.

Bente Meyer is an associate professor at the Department of Educational Anthropology at the Danish University of Education and a member of the research programme media, ICT and learning. Her research interests are foreign language education, intercultural and citizenship education as well as technology based language teaching and learning. She has edited several books on media, ICT and learning, the most recent one being *Digital Media and Educational Design* at The Danish University of Education Press.

Konrad Morgan, PhD (Edin.), MBCS, MBPsS, CITP, is dean of the School of Applied Media and Information Technology (SAMIT) at the Northern Alberta Institute of Technology (NAIT). Prior to coming to NAIT from the University of Bergen in Norway he was professor of human computer interaction and head of the Information Science School. He also served as research director at the InterMedia Lab in Norway, attracting funding for applied research projects from industry, as well as national and international organizations. Morgan has written extensively on computers, technology, information and society and has been involved in a United Nations program to implement the distance delivery of IT degrees to remote, impoverished areas of the South Pacific.

With a background in law and information science **Madeleine Morgan** coordinated the intellectual property division within a leading blue chip technology multinational before becoming interested in addressing ethical issues within ICT. Now living and working in her apartment overlooking the city skyline of downtown Edmonton she works on her current research interests, including the impact of ICT on gender, personality and cross cultural issues. She has been involved with national and European funded research projects including the IDEELS and MASSIVE EU projects. She is the author of numerous peer reviewed scientific articles and an invited contributor to numerous edited books.

Kathryn Moyle, Dr, is one of Australia's leading researchers about ICT issues in education. Kathryn lives in Australia's national capital city: Canberra, where she is an associate professor at the University of Canberra in the School of Education and Community Studies. She is also the director of the Learning Communities Research Area. Kathryn researches and publishes on a diversity of topics that focus on both the practical and theoretical educational issues about ICT in education. Politicians through to educational practitioners refer to Kathryn's work.

Lars-Erik Nilsson is a lecturer in educational science at Kristianstad University and PhD student at Göteborg Univerity. He has been active in several K-12 projects such as ThinkQuest where he was a national partner. He has presented at international conferences on education, technology and K-12 education, instructional design and collaborative learning. His research interests include implementation of technology and socio-cultural aspects of information and communication technology. He completed his BA at Lund University and special teacher education at Malmö School of Teacher Education. He is in the final stages of completing his PhD with a thesis on cheating in education, plagiarism and technology.

Monica E. Nilsson is an assistant professor of education at the Blekinge Institute of Technology, in Ronneby, Sweden. She received a PhD in education from the University of Helsinki, Finland in 2003. Dr. Nilsson's research focuses on school development and alternative forms of learning. She is interested in digital storytelling, particularly the way narrative and multimodality mediate creative forms of learning. Dr. Nilsson is affiliated with the Laboratory of Human Cognition at the University of California, San Diego. Dr. Nilsson has a background as a pre-school teacher.

Anders Olofsson earned his PhD in education at Umeå University in Sweden. From a philosophical hermeneutical approach his research is aimed at understanding the meaning of social processes of teaching and fostering, establishing the meaning of ethics, democracy, learning and teaching, in educational online learning communities (E-OLCs). Dr. Olofsson has contributed with book-chapters, journal articles and papers to conference proceedings on this specific topic. Dr. Olofsson is member of the international network 'The Research Network on Online Learning Communities.'

Torgny Ottosson is since 2001 professor of education at Kristianstad University and at University College of Borås. He was licensed as a teacher in 1976. After taking up further academic studies in 1978 he took his PhD in 1987 at Göteborg University where he was promoted to associate professor in 1995. His main research interests focus on the variation in how different phenomena may be experienced or understood, and how understanding may be developed. Earlier research has had a certain focus on studies of people's understanding of graphic representations like maps, graphs, and charts.

Nancy Sardone teaches instructional design systems and production of instructional resources to graduate and undergraduate students in the College of Education and Human Services at Seton Hall University. Her research interests include student learning, learning environments, and active learning strategies using instructional technology to support and enrich learning.

Staffan Selander, PhD, is professor at Stockholm Institute of Education and head of the research group DidaktikDesign. Also the leader for the research project "Digital learning resources and Learning Design Sequences in the Swedish school: User perspective" and "Museet, utställaren, besökaren," Selander has published *Pedagogiske tekster for kommunikasjon og laering* together with D Skjelbred, *Text & Existens, Hermenutik möter samhällsvetenskap,* edited with Per-Johan Ödman and *Design för lärande. Ett nytt perspektiv på hur kunskap formas och transformeras* edited together with A-L Rostvall.

Bernd Carsten Stahl is a reader in critical research in technology in the Centre for Computing and Social Responsibility at De Montfort University, Leicester, UK. His interests cover philosophical issues arising from the intersections of business, technology, and information. This includes the ethics of computing and critical approaches to information systems. He is the editor-in-chief of the *International Journal of Technology and Human Interaction*.

John Traxler is reader in mobile technology for e-learning at the University of Wolverhampton. He works with its Centre of Excellence in Learning and Teaching looking at innovative technologies for diverse communities and Centre for International Development and Training, exploring appropriate technologies in developing countries. John co-wrote a guide to mobile learning in developing countries and is co-editor of a book on mobile learning. He is jointly responsible for workshops on mobile learning for UK universities, has delivered similar workshops to university staff in several African and Indian universities and advises UK universities on mobile learning projects.

Anna Åkerfeldt has, among other things, a background as a producer of custom made digital learning resouces. Work as a coordinator within the project "Digital learning resources and Learning Design Sequences in the Swedish school: User perspective" at the Stockholm Institute of Education. She is also the editor of the journal *Designs for Learning*.

Index